Richard L. Holm has had a ri[...]
career as a distinguished offic[...]
in retirement near CIA headq[...]

THE
AMERICAN
AGENT

My Life in the CIA

Richard L. Holm

ST ERMIN'S
PRESS

A *St Ermin's Press* Book

First published in Great Britain in 2003 by St Ermin's Press
in association with Time Warner Book Group UK

Reprinted 2005

A CIP catalogue record for this book
is available from the British Library.

ISBN 1 903608 14 7

Printed and bound in Great Britain by Bookmarque Ltd, Croydon

St Ermin's Press
in association with
Time Warner Book Group UK
Brettenham House
Lancaster Place
London WC2E 7EN

www.twbg.co.uk

To Judy, my inspiration

CONTENTS

ILLUSTRATIONS
AND MAPS

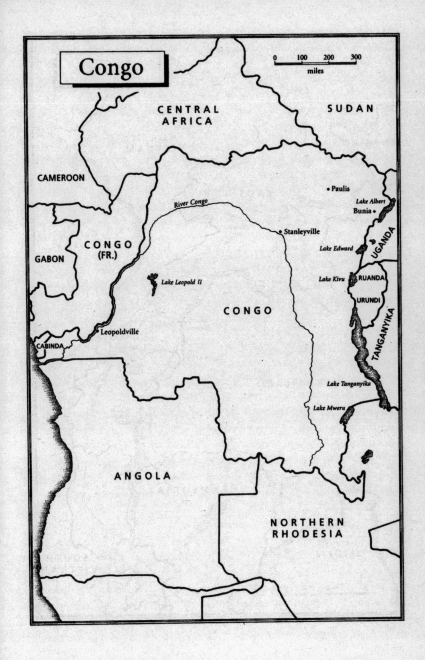

FOREWORD

If this book were fiction, it would justify superlative descriptions. The plot (in this instance there are many) would surely justify 'unbelievably imaginative'. However, this is not fiction. Everything is true and even more remarkable, this is the autobiography of one man who has served his country, mostly in secret, and now offers an inside view of that life and of the Central Intelligence Agency.

The overwhelming number of events Dick Holm was involved in were not those we ever knew about. Most of us know little about the Congo in 1964, with its leftist uprising that threatened the stability of that country, or the vital war that was fought in Laos – an American victory, obligating two North Vietnamese Divisions to cover it. That success was due to the dangerous and heroic work of men like Dick Holm.

This book is filled with unexpected information. One begins to understand the time and attention to detail required to develop and run an agent in another country to be sure that the information ultimately provided is meaningful and reliable. The descriptions of deception and intrigue in uncovering a double agent are offered next to the cumbersome roadblocks of bureaucracy and the difficulty in making the case for appropriate prosecution.

Most autobiographies expose lives that have none of the excitement and intrigue experienced by Dick Holm. Real risk defined a large part of his life. And, I can personally attest to the fact that such risk came extremely close to taking it.

This book offers not just a window into a life of secrets, but a wide open door. But most important, by his descriptions and frankly spoken opinions, one comes away with an in-depth view of a dedicated and ultimately honest man. Not only has the United States realized great benefit from Dick Holm's hard work, but the reader is offered an extraordinary view of the CIA. His disarming honesty gives a unique, but not always favourable, view of the personalities he has encountered from politicians to diplomats and CIA Directors (he worked under thirteen different Directors).

Dick Holm does not write with a broad brush.

Names are named: Philip Agee, a former CIA agent, who was not prosecuted for divulging names of agents who were subsequently murdered; and Directors whose lack of qualifications and misdirection compromised the effectiveness of the Agency, usually at the expense of the Clandestine Service – a mistake that our very recent history emphasizes was indeed error.

Of great interest, not to mention some reassurance, is the fact that Dick Holm is still at work. He offers unusual and compelling parallels between events in Vietnam and Laos and current policy decisions. And by raising important questions, he offers not only a geopolitical opinion formed by years in foreign service literally the world over, but a tour for the reader from Laos to France with stops in between in Lebanon, Kuala Lumpur, Hong Kong and Belgium.

He was Chief of offices in France, Belgium and Hong Kong and was responsible for the development and expansion of the Agency's Counter Terrorism Center. He was awarded the Donovan Award. These accomplishments, it is important to keep in mind, were achieved after a life-threatening burn injury that took much of the function of his hands and one eye. This is no average man. He deserves the term 'hero' at a time when that honour can be accurately ascribed to only a few.

There is humour in everything and this book is no exception. Ever purchase a piano only to worry there is a listening device placed inside by your tennis buddy? Or know that the Simbas in the Congo considered magic a defence against bullets, or learn first hand that tiger urine (as some natives told you) does *not* put North Vietnamese-trained attack dogs off your trail?

There has been, to be sure, a great deal of criticism of the CIA. For those who agree with this often biased view spoken by the media, Dick Holm's disarmingly blunt description of his career, which spanned over three decades, should provide good reason for re-examination. While the author is unquestionably special in his accomplishments, temperament and experience, it is difficult to come away after reading this account with anything but three conclusions: first, that the CIA is subject to political pressure and significant alterations in manpower and even direction (summary: this Agency was very recently weakened by a change in direction during the Clinton administration); second, reassurance that there are many others like Dick Holm in that Agency who are dedicated to the protection of the United States and are willing to assume danger as part of their job; and third, as recent history affirms, that human intelligence has no substitute.

Mr Holm offers a view of mistakes and puts forward solutions: for example, there was a method to bring the North Vietnamese to us rather than the other way around; it was possible that a road from the coast, coursing directly inland, could have defeated the effectiveness of the Ho Chi Minh Trail. He cautions about reliance on sophisticated air power and the incremental, gradual escalation of a war a long way from home, particularly when there are powerful negative emotions directed towards a war effort.

The author has witnessed the fall of the Berlin Wall and the end of the Cold War, the dramatic changes in China and the war in Afghanistan. He has lived all over the world and, as an essential part of his job, studied varying cultures. It is this reality about CIA agents that is not often understood. Their mission, and their lives, are dependent upon their appreciation of the culture and people where they are stationed and their fluency of language. The fact is, they cannot be effective unless they are knowledgeable. Dick Holm speaks Mandarin, French and Thai with consummate ease.

By intensive training and broad experience, Holm is an advocate of clandestine intelligence and operations – a unique arm of the United States Government. There were critics of that approach. However, those opposing such 'secret' operations, even with congressional oversight, wished those efforts had been intensified after 11 September. The more polite now refer to such points of view, and in particular the embarrassing changes in direction by the Clinton administration, as 'misguided'. How can an agency be taken over by those with no experience and still prosper?

The world is not an entirely friendly place. Not only do we consider the consequences of travelling today, but of simply living in our own country. There can be no doubt we need protection. It is that sober responsibility the Central Intelligence Agency, in very large part, assumes. It must be strong and it must be directed by people like Dick Holm. We all owe a great debt to men and women like him.

A final point: the reader should know that there is more to the conclusion of this outstanding book than exists on the last few pages. I suspect, but do not know, that Dick Holm is, for reasons of security, not disclosing many of the elements that led to his withdrawal as Chief in Paris. The facts are as reported by many, but particularly by Vernon Loeb of the *Washington Post*: when Mr Holm assumed command, he inherited an operation already under way that was compromised by French counter-intelligence. It was reported in many newspapers and magazines in 1995–96 that at the root of his dismissal was politics – both in the United States and in France.

In France, there were political problems. To bring the focus away from the issues of a heated election, attention was directed towards an American CIA officer. It was, in the short run, effective. The media in both countries played a role.

In this country, articles in the *New York Times* suggested there was great criticism within the Agency by those who knew the facts. Experienced officers attempted to point out that a career CIA officer with an unblemished record of more than thirty years of superlative service to his country was being considered for dismissal by individuals who had just assumed (without the most basic qualifications) leadership roles in the Agency. One of those individuals went on to visibly demonstrate his ignorance of such matters by violating the most basic principles of the handling of sensitive material when he took an Agency computer to his home. He was saved from prosecution by one of Mr Clinton's pardons. That such an individual would have influence on a man such as Dick Holm is very difficult to accept.

Perhaps the best summation of the author's maturity and composure under the most serious and unwarranted character assassination was one of his statements: 'You just take your lumps.' Lesser men would have come out swinging, but not necessarily with so much dignity.

The reader should know that Richard L. Holm was, after his retirement, awarded the Distinguished Intelligence Award, the highest award given by the Central Intelligence Agency.

Timothy Miller M.D.
Professor of Surgery, Chief, Plastic Surgery
UCLA School of Medicine
Los Angeles, California
November 2002

AUTHOR'S NOTE

This book is about a career – mine – in the Central Intelligence Agency. For three and a half decades, under thirteen Directors, I worked in the Agency's Directorate of Operations – America's Clandestine Service. From the lowest to the highest level, I laboured as an operations officer. I have tried to describe not only what I did in the various postings of my career, but also why and how I did it. To add perspective, I have included a chapter about the early years of my life and how I came to join the CIA. Since they were a joy and an inspiration throughout, I have also written about my wife, Judy, and our platoon of wonderful daughters.

Most authors of non-fiction works, and I am no exception, profess to be as objective as possible. I made that effort while realizing that to be truly objective is far easier said than done. The process of selecting issues and subjects to discuss is itself subjective. But I did try. I also attempted not to gloss over problem areas and failures, but readily confess that I found it easier to recall and write about the good times than the bad.

During my career (the vast majority of which occurred during the Cold War years), I, and most of my colleagues, were opposed to the idea of an operations officer writing a book or anything else for overt publication. The end of the Cold War, however, and the uncertainties the United States now faces changed my mind. We won the Cold War, and I think it is fair to say that the Agency played a key role in that victory. In many ways, the twenty-first century began in 1989, when the Berlin Wall came down and communism collapsed. In the ensuing decade many new threats have emerged, not the least of which is the violent and intolerant interpretation of Islam promoted by Osama bin Laden and his followers. As we meet the threats they pose, the Clandestine

Service will again play a vital role. That role must be understood and supported. Put bluntly, the Agency needs a constituency, and the more the public understands about the Clandestine Service and its role, the stronger that constituency will be.

It is my hope that readers will acquire a greater understanding of what the CIA, tasked by the President, will be doing for the country. While targets and priorities for collection have shifted, the craft (art) practised by the Clandestine Service remains much the same as it was during the Cold War years. Technology has been introduced in various ways, but the human side is the same. Regrettably, the public has been ill-served by journalists and academics who have written about the CIA, in general, and the Clandestine Service in particular. Most, not all, of what has been written is skewed and inaccurate. Critics, sometimes in ignorance, have been overly harsh in their criticisms. This description of my career is for anyone seeking a better understanding of what CIA officers do. It is 'unvarnished' and as balanced as I could make it. It is one man's account and is presented to the best of my recollection. I kept no diary.

Some of the names in the text have been changed for reasons of privacy or security. In some cases, for the same reasons, surnames of colleagues use only an initial. In other cases I have used true names.

The final draft of this book was reviewed by the Agency's Publication Review Board. This is a requirement by the Agency, which I accept. The Board's review is accomplished with the sole goal of finding and identifying for deletion any pieces of information that might currently be classified. The Board has no charge to censor or alter the text of my manuscript in any way. The contents of the book are mine.

Richard L. Holm
Virginia
November 2002

PREFACE TO THE PAPERBACK EDITION

Since the hardback edition of this book was published in February 2003, reaction to it has been abundant and positive. I am tempted to believe that the book actually has, via this account of a CIA career, given readers a greater understanding of what America's Clandestine Service is doing and what its role is for the United States government. Most of the questions I have received relate to the situation in the United States, especially within the intelligence community, in the wake of the attack suffered on 11 September 2001, and what lies ahead for the Clandestine Service. To address those questions, I offer the following paragraphs.

The world stage has dramatically altered since 11 September 2001 and a return to 'normalcy' lies far in the future. Regaining that coveted status will be dependent upon significant changes in the Islamic world, where nothing short of a civil war is underway. The war is between radicals, such as Osama bin Laden, who want to return Islam to the norms of the ninth and tenth centuries, and reformers/moderates, who seek grounds upon which Islam can cohabit with democracy and secularism in government. The winners will dictate how the twenty-first century unfolds for Muslims everywhere.

As that struggle continues, the highest priority for the United States should be to defend itself against the terrorism inspired by the radical elements of Islam. A second important action will be to encourage and, where possible, support the moderates and reformers. Given the depth of anger and distrust towards the United States that exists in the Muslim world, this will not be easy. Yet we really have no choice but to persevere. Unfortunately, military force was imperative in Afghanistan and Iraq. Hopefully, the use of that option can be limited as we move ahead, and progress can be recorded with the use of diplomacy, compromise and reason.

There have also been major changes within the United States that affect the intelligence community and the Clandestine Service (CS). The changes include a new Department of Homeland Security, several commissions formed to investigate issues related to 9/11, a possible new domestic intelligence agency, and the Patriot Act passed in late 2001.

The Department of Homeland Security is up and (mostly) running but with much yet to be accomplished. Given its size and its mission, it is not surprising that there have been bumps in the road. Despite these bumps and some intermittent controversy, structure and organization were introduced in an area never before addressed as a whole – homeland security. Many potential terrorist targets have been strengthened and the country is safer, despite the continuing threat. However, this effort has not been without enormous cost. Indeed, Osama bin Laden, wherever he is, must be smiling at the thought of the vast treasure he has caused us to expend.

It is in this unsettled climate that the CIA's Clandestine Service must regroup, rebuild and take stock of the enormous challenge it faces. As the War on Terrorism continues, the nation will count on the CS as a first line of defence. To understand what the capabilities of the CS will be in that effort, a look at how the CS fared during the 1990s is necessary. What were its strengths and weaknesses as we suffered the horrors of 9/11? Regrettably, the Service's traditional strengths had been dissipated, partly by resource constraints and partly by the multitude of problems it experienced during the 1990s, and weaknesses were abundant. I have alluded to them in the final chapter of this book, but for emphasis and clarity let me expand upon them now.

The political climate at the end of the Cold War brought about a strong desire for what was called a 'peace dividend'. The result was cuts in the intelligence community's budget and reductions in personnel strength. The Aldrich Ames betrayal that came to light in 1994 and the scapegoat-seeking investigation that followed threw the CS off balance. In the mid-1990s, a weak and inexperienced Deputy Director for Operations, who emphasized process over operational activity, promoted people into positions for which they were unqualified, and the Service's tradition of meritocracy seemed to be suspended. Morale sank and, as prospects for the future dimmed, many junior officers opted to leave the Service. In the period from 1990 to 1997 the Agency was headed by five different directors, each with his own road map and none with effective influence over a White House that was inattentive to intelligence community needs. In addition, an edict in 1995 proscribed the recruitment of individuals with tainted human rights records, which meant, in effect, that only boy scouts and choir boys could be recruited, who had no access to information the Service was tasked to collect. As a result, morale sank even lower and risk aversion – a death knell for an intelligence service – reared its ugly head. Faced with personnel cuts and inadequate funding, the CS was unable to pursue language training at normal levels, which resulted in a lack of language-qualified operations officers. Similarly, the reduced budgets coupled with personnel cuts meant that the Service could not bring on board new officers, and an experience gap was the result. The CS had no bench strength. Excessive legal constraints inhibited operational initiatives and co-operation with law-enforcement organizations like the FBI. Throughout the 1990s there were poor relations with a White House that seemed disinterested in the Agency's product or the potential of the CS.

Set forth as a mathematical equation the status of the CS on 9/11 would have resembled the following:

The quest for a 'peace dividend'
+ the budget cuts
+ the personnel cuts
+ the aftermath of the Ames betrayal
+ the inconsistency and instability at leadership level
+ the suspension of the tradition of meritocracy
+ the exodus of promising young officers
+ the restrictions placed on the Service's ability to recruit agents
+ the advent of risk aversion
+ the shortage of language-qualified case officers
+ the lack of new blood and the experience gap

+ the excessive legal constraints
+ the strained relations with the White House
= a less eager and less agile CS with fewer capabilities.

The bold and effective organization that served the country so well during the Cold War was a mere shell of its former self. Perhaps most serious was the adverse impact of all those issues on the men and women who served in the CS.

The fact remains, however, that despite its best efforts, the CS had not penetrated the al Qaeda network at a level that would have permitted it to forecast the attack we suffered on 9/11. That constituted an intelligence failure – a fact that is not debatable. But it is fair to ask, I think, how much better prepared and more effective the CS would have been had it not just suffered the worst decade in its history.

In attempting to come to terms with the intelligence failure, the government, in typical fashion following an unsettling event, established a gaggle of commissions. Some have completed their work and made recommendations, but at least one is still working to formulate its recommendations for changes in the intelligence community. For more than two years there has been intense scrutiny of what we knew about al Qaeda in the period prior to the attack. Unfortunately each of the commissions has succumbed to partisan politics and the process has become one of finger-pointing and efforts to deflect or ascribe 'blame' for the attack. Results of the investigations have been published and/or filtered into the public domain. Little has been revealed that wasn't known publicly within a few months after 9/11. No critical piece of intelligence that might have thwarted the attack has been found, and we know by now that none will be found. But the political furor continues.

The commission mandated to investigate the intelligence community's role during the period before 9/11 published its final report on 10 December 2002. It was a joint Congressional body composed of members of the House Permanent Select Committee on Intelligence (HPSCI) and the Senate Select Committee on Intelligence (SSCI) and was headed by Representative Eleanor Hill. Its findings and conclusions, which range from the general to the specific, are interesting and indicate that their effort was wide-ranging and thorough. Neither the findings nor the conclusions came as a surprise to intelligence community professionals. The bulk of both the findings and the conclusions involved issues that had been of concern and under discussion within the intelligence community for years prior to 9/11. Still, it was an effort that had to be undertaken, and the recommendations, coming with a Congressional stamp of approval, carried great weight and were, therefore, much more likely to be implemented than was the case previously. Many have already been implemented, and most will likely be folded into existing intelligence community regulations and procedures.

Inevitably, politics and partisanship surfaced in the commission's efforts. Subjects that were probably discussed and debated failed to appear when the final draft was written. For example, no mention is made of the Congressionally mandated budget cuts the CS suffered during the decade prior to 9/11. With oversight committee(s) blessings (they drafted the legislation), intelligence community budgets were cut every year from 1990 until 1996 and then remained flat until 2001. The committees also knew but did not mention that Agency personnel strength had been cut by over 25 per cent and that some overseas stations had been closed due to resource constraints. Nor is any mention made of the politically inspired legal and regulatory restraints placed on the CS during the 1990s. Those factors had a major effect on the Service's readiness to act and should have been included in any balanced discussion of the failure that was investigated.

There is irony in the composition of the various commissions. Many of the members are the very people who oversaw and countenanced what happened to the CS during the 1990s. They heard the regular briefings from the Director of Central Intelligence and the DDO with pleas for additional resources and routinely turned a deaf ear. The oversight committees had been in a position to question Agency officials about any concerns they might have had. They didn't. From at least 1997 onwards, they heard the DCI tell them that al Qaeda and bin Laden were great threats to national security. There was little reaction and no recognition of the fact that the CS needed additional resources to combat the threat. One member of the 9/11 commission was the Assistant

Attorney General in 1995, who had actually drafted regulations that reinforced the separation that inhibited co-operation between law enforcement officers and the intelligence community. She has not been questioned under oath and one must ask why. Those regulations, coupled with the recruiting constraints, represented a serious impediment to aggressive operations against the terrorist threat. Only recently have a few oversight committee members acknowledged that the committees presided over damaging cuts to the Agency's budget and that their actions were ill-advised and short-sighted. They were simply too busy, is the essence of their excuse. Yet these people now sit in judgement on the intelligence community, which awaits the wisdom they will impart.

As post 9/11 steps were taken by the government, debate began regarding several subjects. One concerned a proposal made by some in the government to create an entirely new intelligence agency/department modelled on Britain's MI5, which would be responsible for collecting domestic intelligence. This was, of course, a slap in the face for the FBI, which figured prominently in many of the Hill Commission's findings and conclusions. The FBI had failed us, proponents of an MI5 type agency insisted, and there was no reason to believe that the FBI would ever be able to change its 'culture and mentality'. Many, including me, disagreed. Opponents of the proposal put forward several arguments, which included: the expense and effort required to create an entirely new organization and open offices nationwide would exacerbate budget problems while offering only the 'hope' that it might perform better than the FBI; efforts to staff the new agency would mean dipping into the same or the prospective pool of people now work-ing in the intelligence community, notably the CIA or the FBI – in effect robbing Peter to pay Paul; and that the FBI could change and become an effective collector of domestic intelligence. Regarding the latter point, I think it is eminently feasible that FBI officers will be capable of changing their understanding of a national need and, over time, developing new skills to enable them to cope with a new mission. It will not be easy, and it will take time, but progress has already been recorded. At senior levels in the FBI, major change has been mandated and at mid- and lower levels those changes are taking hold. Joint CIA/FBI terrorist task forces already exist nationwide and by working together officers from both organizations are learning new skills. Happily, the idea of a new, MI5 type agency seems to have fallen from favour, but there is no guarantee that it won't resurface in one form or another.

Another area of concern is the USA Patriot Act passed on 25 October 2001, just weeks after the attack. Although it was passed with overwhelming bipartisan support, 97 for and 2 opposed in the Senate, various parts of the Act, including changes and modifications made to existing laws, have ignited furious debate. It was designed to empower primarily the FBI, but also other domestic collectors of intelligence, and to enhance their ability to monitor and collect intelligence on suspected terrorists. Officially it was described as the 'Uniting and Strengthening of America Act by Providing Appropriate Tools to Intercept and Obstruct Terrorism' and was intended to 'loosen the shackles' that inhibited the FBI prior to 9/11. It went too far, critics now argue, and threatens citizens' privacy. It also raises concerns about civil liberties and human rights violations. Complaints have been raised about an alleged abandonment of basic principles of our legal system including our courts; more limited access to government information; abuses in the treatment of immigrants and refugees; and the profoundly negative effect the Act has had on our human rights image in the world.

Critics of the Patriot Act have been particularly upset about changes in the Foreign Intelligence Surveillance Act (FISA) brought about by the Act. 'FISA orders' (akin to a search warrant) can now be obtained, following court review and approval, with fewer procedural checks than prior to 9/11. (Accordingly, and not surprisingly in view of the FBI's far greater focus on terrorist activity, the number of FISA orders issued since passage of the Patriot Act is noticeably higher.)

Concern about and criticism of the Patriot Act has come mostly from organizations such as the American Civil Liberties Union (ACLU), less well-known groups such as the Lawyers Committee on Human Rights and the Humanitarian Law Project, and various other human rights and civil liberties groups and activists. Their complaints, which are to be expected given these organizations' *raison d'être*, are substantive, sensible and sincere. They find these issues to be troubling, as do many Americans. I believe the majority of Americans, however, understand and accept the need for the enhanced powers given to our domestic investigative and law enforcement agencies by the Patriot Act. I think most Americans support the Act, but debate will continue because much of what is being argued about is unprecedented. The terrorists are not a uniformed military. The battlefield has no geographic limits. While some of the terrorists are supported by specific countries, there is no clear target – Afghanistan was an exception and some would argue that Iraq was as well. The distinction between a criminal, enemy combatant and prisoner of war is still unclear.

I mentioned these differences of opinion two years ago and concluded that we would find middle ground, i.e., to what extent should constraints on privacy and civil liberties be sacrificed in the name of national defence and our ability to protect ourselves against terrorist attack. That middle ground continues to elude us, but unless there is a hue and cry from the majority the Patriot Act is likely to be renewed when current legislation expires.

The sampling of controversy outlined above reflects the difficulties the United States faces as it tries to answer numerous questions. Why were we attacked? How could people hate us so much that they would come here to commit such an atrocity? The questions have no ready answers. There is also another question: how much is too much? How many lives lost demands the declaration of war? It is the same question we asked in the Counter Terrorism Group in 1962. At the time, we were dealing with tens of lives lost. After the bombings of our Embassy and the Marine barracks in Lebanon, it was hundreds. But tens of thousands of lives are lost on the nation's roads each year and thousands more are murdered in our cities and towns. Is that too many? We can 'tolerate' those deaths which we understand. However, we can neither understand nor tolerate having foreign terrorists attack and slaughter our citizens. Three thousand is too many and to that number you must add the hundreds of others killed by al Qaeda attacks since the first Twin Towers bombing in 1993. Although few Americans realize it, the War on Terrorism has been underway since the early 1990s. Would that our government had taken the opportunity to apprehend Osama bin Laden on the three occasions when it would have been possible. Leaderless, the group might well have fallen into disarray.

What are the best paths for US policy? Most importantly, we must not be fooled into thinking that the enormous expenditure of money and manpower that we have made since 9/11 will somehow render us invulnerable. More attacks are possible, even likely. Those who argue that we should seal our borders, or check every container that enters the country, or guarantee the security of every flight that enters or leaves the country, or whatever else they dream up, are simply not looking at the world the way it actually is. In a society as open as ours, it is not realistic to believe that we can anticipate and thwart every possible terrorist attack against us. Indeed it is a tribute to the effective work of the intelligence community and the military that we have suffered no other attacks since 9/11. One can only assume that planning and efforts to execute attacks are severely hindered when communications are blocked, logistics lines have been cut, training camps have been destroyed, financial links have been severed and you are 'hiding in a hole'. But the threat is still there.

What to do is a question that can be divided into two parts: domestic efforts and efforts abroad. In the US, we know that our defences will never be perfect. We can only continue to take steps that will 'harden' prospective terrorist targets. As we already know, this will involve large expenditures of money and manpower. For the time being, there is no alternative. Our efforts abroad, on the other hand, allow us the possibility of taking the offence. I still believe that in this situation, the best defence is a good offence. We should pursue efforts aimed at dealing with this problem where it originates, where radical Islam provides the fighters who attack us. It is in that arena that the CS will make its greatest contribution.

There is much to be done, however, to rebuild the CS before that contribution will be as successful as it must be. Much has already been done. Within weeks of 9/11 the unrealistic restraint levied in 1995 on the CS's ability to recruit agents was rescinded. This was seen as a vindication of widely held concerns within the CS. The Bush administration, demonstrating a far more positive view of the intelligence community, increased the community's budget soon after taking office, providing the CS with the monies it needed to start rebuilding its capabilities. Efforts to increase the personnel strength of the CS are underway, and it is rewarding to see that thousands of highly qualified young Americans are vying to join the CS. Leadership of the Agency has become stable and effective again. Morale is high and risk aversion is no longer a concern. The Service's capability to recruit and train incoming officers has been rebuilt. Language training is a high priority again. The CS is closing the experience gap and starting to build bench strength. Changes brought about by the Patriot Act have lessened legal constraints and fostered greater co-operation and sharing within the intelligence community. Relations with the White House and Congress are vastly improved and the CS is a player again. Indeed, a mathematical equation today would show a totally changed picture of the CS and its ability to meet the challenges it is being given.

The rebuilding cannot be accomplished overnight and much remains to be done. The DCI recently said that attaining the capabilities the Agency and CS needs would take five years. Although optimistic, that's a fair and honest assessment. After joining the Service, a minimum of five years is necessary before an officer is trained, learns a language if necessary and has tours in the field to hone tradecraft skills, before he/she is really 'pulling weight'. We must also bear in mind that today's officers are facing a much more difficult challenge than I and my colleagues faced during the Cold War. Given the fact that religion, often fanatical, is a part of the 'enemy' makeup, what we used to think of as rational or reasonable is no longer valid. The challenge is greater as are the risks. The CS must now operate in the most turbulent parts of the world against zealots whose values we do not understand. But I continue to believe that today's CS will devise and implement whatever means are necessary to accomplish its mission.

June 2004

PROLOGUE

1965

It was spring in Washington, a pleasant time of year in the capital, but the changing season didn't seep into the Walter Reed Hospital where I was a new patient. I was a deeply unhappy man. It had been over three months since the plane crash and I still couldn't see or use my hands. I was dependent upon other people for everything. It was the complete opposite of my life before the accident. As I lay there thinking about the future and trying to take stock, I realized I was frightened. Blindness generates great fear. The doctors had assured me that a corneal transplant would restore my sight and I believed them – I desperately wanted to believe them. But doubts were creeping into my mind. What if the operation was not a success?

It would be two more years before I completed the necessary reconstruction surgery and got back to work. I had no idea, of course, in the spring of 1965 that it could take that long.

The Walter Reed, the Army's showcase hospital with superbly qualified staff at all levels and state-of-the art care in virtually any field of medicine, was, and still is, highly regarded. Situated near the Maryland border in the far northern part of the District of Columbia, it includes a large research centre, a nursing school, and various support buildings. (The hospital, built before the Second World War, was named after an Army doctor who had carried out early research on malaria in what was to become the Canal Zone.)

The day after my arrival, I was visited by the man who was to be my doctor for the rest of my stay, a young lieutenant colonel named

Michael Duffy. I would soon discover that he was reputed to be the best plastic surgeon at Walter Reed. As things turned out, we became close personal friends, and I had great respect and admiration for his competence and dedication. He was particularly adept at hand surgery – one of my greatest needs.

'So you crashed a plane in the Congo,' Duffy said, examining each of my hands carefully.

'That's right. I don't recommend it,' I responded.

'I can't imagine that you would. How much can you see?'

'Not much. Just light versus dark.'

'That's got to be a bitch, but it won't slow us down,' he said bullishly. 'We need to get your hands in shape and a few other things need fixing too.'

'Will I ever have a jump shot again?' I was halfway serious.

'That I don't know, but I doubt you'll be a concert pianist when we get finished,' he remarked, catching just the right tone. He knew what I was trying to ask him, albeit obliquely: What were the prospects?

'I am going to do a series of operations, I don't know now just how many,' he continued. 'We'll start on Monday morning and schedule subsequent operations as often as seems feasible.'

'What makes them feasible?' I asked. 'No sense in dragging this out.'

'We need to have skin donor sites heal and you feeling OK,' he replied.

'The faster we go, the better I'll feel,' I told him in all seriousness.

'I understand,' he said quietly. And he did.

The plane crash that had brought me to this point occurred in the north-east part of the Congo in central Africa in mid-February 1965. I was twenty-nine years old and working as a CIA Chief in Stanleyville, now called Kisangani. It took ten days for me to be rescued.

It was what could be called a 'harrowing' experience. Leaving aside any particular label, I can say with conviction that it was a major event in my life and it began at Agency Headquarters, Langley, Virginia, in September 1964.

ONE

THE CONGO CRASH

1964–65

'You just got back from Laos?' asked the female admin clerk at Headquarters who was checking me in.

'That's right,' I replied.

'How long were you there?'

'I went out there in July 1962,' I explained, 'and I was initially on TDY [Temporary Duty Station], but I was extended twice so it ended up being a two-year tour.'

It was now mid-September 1964, and, after a couple of weeks' leave with my parents, I was checking into the Africa Division, my original choice for an assignment before I had volunteered for paramilitary work in Laos.

It seemed there was an inordinate amount of paperwork, but the clerk assured me that all of it was necessary. We finally finished and I prepared to leave. Having noted, however, that she was pretty and not wearing a wedding ring, I was trying to think of something to keep our conversation going. (This may have been one of the results of having lived upcountry in Laos and Thailand for two years.) Although I didn't really think she'd know anything, I asked about my assignment in Africa Division.

'You should act surprised when you find out,' she said. 'They are going to put you in the North Africa Section.'

I was delighted. Some years previously, I had spent time in France with the US Army Counter Intelligence Corps (CIC), which had enabled me to learn something about Algeria, Tunisia and Morocco.

The clerk told me to report to Glen Fields, the Division Chief. In fact, it was John Waller, the Deputy, who welcomed me. Waller was a nice man and I was pleased to see that he actually knew who I was and something about me. However, it soon became clear that, for him, I was brand spanking new at Headquarters and would need some breaking in. That was, of course, true, although I preferred to think of myself as an experienced officer with a field tour under my belt. But I didn't labour the point. Waller said all the right things and then told me that I was going to work on North African matters. I feigned surprise, but didn't have to pretend delight. His secretary called the Branch Chief, who dutifully appeared in a couple of minutes. We were introduced and then we walked over to the Branch area, where I met everyone. I was pleased to see that one of my junior officer trainee classmates was also assigned to the Branch.

I didn't find Headquarters intimidating exactly, but it sure was different from Laos. My Headquarters tour was officially under way. My friend from training days was a big help in getting me settled into the Branch. There were two of us on my desk and, as the new kid, I naturally got the least exciting operations and activities to work on. Ours was the mundane, but important, task of supporting the Algiers office, from the Washington and Headquarters end. 'Compartmentation' kept me unaware of the more sensitive operations, but this was, to me, a great job for starters.

At my low level, any Headquarters job was, by definition, less interesting and less rewarding than a field assignment. But it had to be learned and it offered the opportunity to get a field assignment lined up for the summer of 1965. Little did I know that it would be at Walter Reed Hospital.

Things went well and, in addition to the work I had to do in support of our field office in Algiers, I started working and preparing for what I hoped would be a field assignment to the Magreb the following summer. I picked up several books about the history, culture and politics of the Magreb countries and read them whenever I had some spare time. (This was to be a common practice throughout my career and it was greatly facilitated by the fact that one could obtain, in our Headquarters Divisions, literally dozens of good books about each country supported by that Division. Our Russian and Chinese components, in particular, offered a great array of good books.) I read mostly about Algeria, but also about Morocco. And, as I had hoped, portions of what I knew from my CIC days came in handy in my deskwork. By early October, I felt that things were right on track.

I thought about opting for Arabic language training, a two-year programme, but finally decided against it. I figured that two years' training was just too long, and that, given the differences between classical and Magrebian Arabic, it just wouldn't be that useful for an Africa Division officer. My French could certainly use some work though and that seemed a good thing to do at this point. My grammar, weak in France and weaker still in Laos, cried out for study and drills – not the most enticing prospect for what little spare time a young bachelor in Washington had, but important from a career perspective. So I signed up for part-time French language training.

My teacher, Colette, was a former French citizen married to Larry Devlin, one of the Division's most senior officers. He was Chief of another Africa Branch and a former Chief in Leopoldville in the Congo. They had met in Algiers during the Second World War when both were engaged in intelligence work. She was, of course, a native French speaker. She was also pleasant and a good teacher. Two nights a week, I would stop by their house for an hour's lesson with Colette. Often, we would be finishing our lesson about the same time that Larry would be arriving home. A couple of times, the three of us would have a drink together before I left. I got to know Larry (who was subsequently to head our office again in the Congo) and we talked about the Congo, which was then in the midst of a Simba rebellion, and also about Laos and what I had done there. I was fascinated by his anecdotes about central Africa. We also discussed, of course, the fact that our Chief in Stanleyville, David G., and his two communications officers were, at that moment, being held captive by the Simba rebels.

One morning in mid-October, I arrived at work and found a note saying that I should call Glen Fields. This was highly unusual. I supposed that he knew who I was since I was in his Division, but what did he want to talk to me about? I called right away and was instructed to come to the front office at 10 a.m. I talked with my Branch Chief, but he had no clue. And it hadn't been cleared with him, which put his nose a bit out of joint, I noticed. I made a mental note to be more careful in the future. If a Division Chief wants to see you, just go. When I arrived at the front office, Larry Devlin was there, chatting to the Chief's secretary. He greeted me and, promptly, we were shown into Glen Fields's office. Why was Larry here? I wondered. What was going on?

It didn't take long to find out. Following some perfunctory small talk welcoming me into the Africa Division and congratulating me on the medal I had recently been given for my work in Laos, they got down to the point of the meeting.

Glen Fields led the conversation and moved smoothly on to the subject of the Congo, which was then the highest priority issue for the Division. He briefly reviewed the situation: David G., our Chief in Stanleyville, was being held hostage by the Simbas, who were now in control of the city. Several other Americans, including the Consul General, two of our communications officers and a number of missionaries, as well as several hundred Belgians and other Europeans who had been residents of the city, were also being held and threatened by the Simbas.

'The Simba rebellion poses a grave threat to the government in Leopoldville,' Glen went on, 'and our policy makers are extremely concerned.'

'We are in dire need of current intelligence about what is going on in the north-east Congo,' Larry interjected.

I listened carefully, still wondering what the point was going to be.

Glen continued. 'A military operation to liberate Stanleyville and free the hostages is being planned. US planes are going to transport Belgian paratroopers to Stanleyville probably sometime next month, November. The first wave will parachute onto the airport and secure it. Then planeloads of troopers will land and assault the city. We are hoping, of course, that the element of surprise will cause the Simbas to panic and will keep casualties to a minimum. We haven't got a lot of choice.'

'And after the operation is concluded, we are going to need someone on the ground in Stanleyville to provide intelligence,' Larry pointed out.

Then Glen dropped the bombshell: 'I'd like you to replace David G. as Chief in Stanleyville, on a temporary basis.'

He was looking me directly in the eyes and I am sure he could see how surprised I was. Being offered a Chief's job in such a high profile and important place for the Division was the furthest thing from my mind. I assume he got the reaction he had expected – or hoped for at least.

'I'm pleased to accept,' was my prompt response. I couldn't have imagined saying no.

'You're my best candidate,' Glen went on. 'You're young, you aren't married, you speak decent French [better than decent I was thinking, but without justification since he clearly had an assessment from Colette via Larry], and you've had paramilitary experience.'

Doubtless it was Larry who had suggested me for the job – he later confirmed it – and he nodded sagely in concurrence with Glen.

'But this won't be a walk in the park,' Glen warned. 'This is going to be a tough job and it may well be dangerous at times. You never know what to expect out there. But I don't think it will be any worse than Laos was,' he added, 'and you handled that.'

Within months, I would discover that he had been right to warn me of tough times in the Congo.

'When will I be leaving?' I asked.

'Take it easy,' Glen responded. 'I'm not going to send you out there until Belgian paratroopers have secured Stanleyville. Think in terms of December. For now, get yourself transferred to the Central African Branch because you've got a lot to learn in the next few weeks.' And with that comment, he stood to signal that the meeting was over. 'I'll see you before you go,' he said. Larry shook my hand and stayed to talk with Glen.

My mission in Stanleyville was straightforward. Before the Simba takeover, David G. had built and managed a network of agents who were reporting to us about the general and specific situation in the city and the region. After the Simbas arrived, there was a total disruption and our network was now in a shambles. I was being sent out to reassemble it and establish a flow of intelligence reporting. It sounded simpler than it was. I would need to steep myself in knowledge of both the general situation and the network's members.

The ensuing weeks were busy. The North African Branch Chief, who had had my services for all of about five weeks, was none too happy, but that didn't change anything. I had learned that my assignment was to be TDY for 'about eight weeks, just to get things going again' so I told him I'd be back before he knew it. Given my experience on 'TDY' in Laos, however, I wasn't taking any bets on how long I'd be gone. Even upon reflection, I was pleased with the assignment. I liked the fact that Division management knew me and apparently had confidence in me. I was mildly concerned about the security (my own physical security that is) problems that were so evident, but I didn't dwell on that and just figured that I could handle whatever came up. A little cocky? A little naive? You bet.

Reaction in the Division was mixed, as it was among my friends. You must be crazy, some said. The place has been over-run, what can you do? Knowledge of the operation to liberate Stanleyville was strictly compartmented so I just responded that I wouldn't be going until it was safe. Like never, was a common response.

Others, case officer colleagues mostly, viewed it, as did I, as a good assignment that ought to be damned interesting. Word got around. The support staff people were mostly in the 'you must be crazy' group. When I went to get my booster injections, the nurses couldn't believe that I was going to Stanleyville.

'Do you read the papers?' one of them asked.

'Of course I do,' I said. 'I won't be going until it is safe.'

'Yeah, and you'll be going with a shot of everything we have,' said the other nurse who was consulting her global chart.

Both nurses laughed knowingly. Stanleyville, almost directly on the equator and with practically no medical facilities, was in the middle of a red zone, which meant that anyone going there needed injections for just about every disease known to man. It took me three visits to get everything up to required standards.

By the middle of November, I had accomplished a lot. All the relevant files had been carefully read, sometimes reread, and I had finished a couple of interesting books about tribal conflicts in central Africa, which was essentially what was going on in the Congo. The Simbas didn't give a hoot about communism, and the central government, headed by Moise Tshombe, was certainly not democratic, but the global politics of the time, a very cold Cold War, dictated superpower involvement, thus we were involved trying to prop up the 'good guys'.

I had continued working with Colette on some vocabulary with Belgian and African nuances. All the admin matters were settled. I even had my plane ticket in hand – with an open travel date. I was ready. I was following closely the plans for the Belgian paratrooper drop onto Stanleyville. I noted, as did many others, the added urgency caused by the sporadic, but ominous reporting we were able to get out of the beleaguered city. The hostages were increasingly maltreated and concerns were voiced about the possibility of executions intended as an example of Simba resolve. The policy makers consulted more and more urgently and the paratroopers were positioned on Ascension Island – poised to act at a moment's notice. It couldn't come soon enough, we all thought. As the day neared, all on the desk became tense. Our workload increased with the heavy flow of cable traffic related to our planning, and anxieties also rose noticeably.

This wasn't to be a classic SWAT team assault with every precaution taken to minimize casualties. That concept didn't exist in 1965. We were looking at a risky effort. An airdrop at dawn would secure the airport. The rest of the paratrooper battalion would then land. Travelling in US C-130 planes, they would have with them a limited number of armoured vehicles and heavy machineguns. As quickly as possible, they would then move into the city to liberate hostages and rid the area of Simba forces. None doubted that the Simba occupying force would break and run, but what would they do before fleeing? It would take at least an hour, we calculated, for the Belgians to actually get into the areas where the hostages were being held. A savage and bloody slaughter was a possibility that could not be discounted. Reports of Simba violence in the provinces of the eastern Congo, including wanton murder and rape, lurked in the back of our minds. By this time, since there was little actual work any of us could do, most of our time was spent worrying

Despite all the doubts and concerns that had been voiced for several days, if not weeks, the operation, code-named Red Dragon, was finally launched at dawn on 24 November 1964. It went just as planned. Within a few hours, the entire city of

Stanleyville was liberated from Simba control. Over twenty hostages were killed by the Simbas as they lashed out violently while fleeing the city, but our Chief, David G., the Consul General, and our two communications officers all escaped harm. In fact, losses had been minimal and central government control over the city had been re-established. The operation had been a success and we all celebrated that fact.

Inwardly, I saw the success as another step towards my departure and the start of my efforts to re-establish a reporting capability out of Stanleyville. Within hours, the Belgians had been withdrawn in favour of a Tshombe government-sponsored mercenary force that arrived in the ransacked city the same day. Congolese army troops were also ferried into the still surrounded city to help secure the area.

Within days (it was now the first week of December), David G. reported in at Headquarters. A bachelor, and an absolute bear for work, he was so intensely involved with the situation in the eastern Congo, and with the assets he had been handling, that he couldn't stay away. He desperately wanted to know what was going on and therefore spent only a few days with his parents before reporting back to work. It was clear that the 111 days in Simba captivity, during which he was threatened with death on several occasions, hadn't slowed him down at all.

I met David G., remarkably composed considering his harrowing experience, for the first time a couple of hours after he arrived at Headquarters. He had, of course, been welcomed back by Glen Fields, who took him up to meet the Director, John McCone. After that meeting, he came back to the Division and met with friends and well-wishers of all sorts. Then, I think to his relief, he came to the Congo desk, where we met. I was introduced as the man who was going out to Stanleyville to pick up the pieces.

'Good. When are you leaving?' he asked.

'As soon as Glen gives the OK,' I replied.

There followed a barrage of questions about the whereabouts and status of assets and acquaintances of his in Stanleyville and the eastern Congo. This guy must be running on fumes and adrenaline, I thought. Very intense, he looked so thin as to almost seem frail, but the force of his personality and the strength of his desire to know what was going on at 'his' office made it clear that this man was not frail at all.

From my background reading, my review of his reporting on individual assets, and my time on the desk, I was able to fire back answers to most of his questions. Many of my responses were, 'We don't know,' but I could see that he was pleased to know that someone was standing in the wings ready to go out to Stanleyville, and pleased to see that that officer seemed to be well-prepared. And I was glad to meet him. We grew to be close friends. I liked his strong work ethic, his great loyalty, and the willingness and patience he demonstrated while fielding my questions. I learned a great deal from him over the next several weeks.

Together, we launched a not too subtle campaign to get me out to Stanleyville. The operation had been successful and the city was, although still surrounded by the Simbas, more or less secure with a safe and steady air link to Leopoldville. Glen was unmoved. I soon discovered that David would be going with me. I wasn't sure why and questioned the wisdom of that decision, but didn't raise any of my concerns. I later found out that it had been David's idea. So be it, I thought, a personal introduction is always better than a cold turnover. And maybe it would end up being therapeutic for David. Certainly it would make things a lot easier for me since David knew volumes about the Congo and central Africa. By the middle of December, we had our travel date.

'Have Christmas at home,' Glen had insisted, 'and then go see what you can do.' We made arrangements to meet at Newark airport the day after Christmas.

Before my departure, things at home were delicate. I had only recently arrived back in the States from Laos, where I had been doing work my mother knew little about, but instinctively sensed was dangerous. In my letters I talked only about mundane matters, never mentioning things that would, in my mind, have worried her. But her stress level was high anyway and got higher when one of my brothers, a Marine Corps lieutenant at the time, was shipped to Vietnam in 1963. Two sons in South-East Asia fighting an enemy she didn't understand at all was pretty tough on my mother. To tell her now that I was going, TDY again, to Stanleyville, was something I just couldn't do, so I told her I was going to Morocco. I told my father where I was going and that if he really thought Mom should know, he could tell her. I only wanted to keep her from worrying – again. Being untruthful to my mother was difficult and it would come back to haunt me sooner than I thought.

On 26 December 1964, David G. and I took a helicopter from Newark to Idlewild airport (now JFK) and departed for Brussels, which was cold, damp, and grey. It was a considerable change from the only other time I had been there in 1959. I had visited with my dad one beautiful clear night, rare in Belgium. In the city's central square, the Grande Place, spotlights gleamed off the gold leaf on all the fifteenth-and sixteenth-century buildings that lined the square, and wonderful classical music was played from loudspeakers placed all around. It happened to be 4 July, and the US Marine Corps band marched for Independence Day. Resplendent in their dress uniforms, they boomed out a medley of John Philip Sousa marches ending with 'Stars and Stripes Forever'.

Those memories were distant indeed as our airport taxi cruised across a deserted and rainy Grande Place and deposited us at the Amigo Hotel, less than fifty metres off the square. It was early morning and I hadn't slept much on the plane so I was looking forward to some rest. It was not to be. David suggested that we grab a quick shower and a cup of coffee and then walk over to the office to check cable traffic from Leopoldville. 'Sounds fine,' was about all I could say.

There was no traffic of interest to us, but it was useful to talk with some of the officers about the Belgian reaction to the Stanleyville operation the month before. Not surprisingly, the Belgians were delighted with what had happened and relations between their government and ours were great. Many questioned the wisdom of David's return to the Congo. And that I was going to try to reopen in Stanleyville. All were cordial and supportive, however, and they wished us good luck, as we left to return to our hotel. Our Sabena flight to the Congo was leaving late the next afternoon. I was getting pretty anxious to get there and get started.

I was alert as we made our landing at Leopoldville's Ndjili airport the next day. It reminded me of Vientiane airport in Laos and had definitely seen better days. The first, and overall, impression left me with little doubt about the fact that I had just entered the Third World. One of the support officers, with a car and driver, was there to meet us and we moved through customs without delay. We were carrying diplomatic passports, of course, which helped. There was a long line of others not so fortunate.

The support officer took us to a Belgian guesthouse (almost like a motel) located near the Embassy. We were due at the office at about 4 p.m., so we had several hours to kill. Surprisingly, I didn't feel tired at all and I asked David if he wanted to take a walk around the city. 'Nope,' he said, 'I think I'll grab a shower and get some rest.' Our roles reversed from the previous day, I took a quick shower, felt even better, and set off to explore central Leopoldville.

All cities have sounds and smells of their own. Leopoldville's were quite different from those I had known in European and Asian cities. That shouldn't have surprised me I guess, but it did. Even on a sunny day, the air seemed heavy and humid. It reminded me of Hong Kong in July. Sounds seemed muffled. The pace of things struck me as very slow.

The smells were pungent, strong, and very new to me. I couldn't distinguish anything in particular, or indeed anything that I recognized. Nothing was neat or clean and nobody seemed to care. Neither streets nor buildings seemed well maintained, or, in some cases, maintained at all. I passed stalls and shops as well as office buildings and restaurants. It was only a first impression, I was telling myself, but it certainly wasn't a good one. The city lacked both charm and personality and seemed like a dirty and rundown southern European city.

We visited the office that afternoon and I was disappointed there too. Our Chief, Ben Cushing, whom I had never met or heard of, was a New Englander and a man of few words. He had served mostly in Eastern European posts before coming to Leopoldville. His office featured models of old ships and pictures of the Maine coast. It seemed to indicate where his heart was. In preparation for this assignment, Cushing had learned Lingala, the native tongue. However, when he first used Lingala with President Mobutu after the latter secured power following the Simba rebellion, Mobutu chastised him.

'Do you think I'm some uneducated native?' Mobutu said. 'I speak French.'

Cushing had problems with local officials as well. Insensitive, was the rap. He just asked questions from his list, said goodbye, and left. I'm now told that, although bright and experienced, he was inflexible and didn't really like paramilitary operations. I may have caught him on a busy day and got a false impression. But since there was negligible follow-up with me after my trips to Stanleyville with precious little guidance, I never had reason to change my initial impression.

Cushing gave us only a brief meeting at which he demonstrated no real interest in what I was going to try to do. After only enough conversation to be polite, he showed us out and turned us over to his Deputy. The latter was more interested and questioned me about what I would be doing in Stanleyville. To this day, I can't figure out what the problem was with Cushing or why I got the impression that he was not very pleased about me being there or me going up to Stanleyville. Maybe he was prescient. Or felt that it was too dangerous and too soon to restart our activities in Stanleyville. Maybe he was opposed to the idea of sending anyone at all up to Stanleyville at that time, but neither he nor his Deputy made that clear. If they were arguing with Headquarters' decision, it never got down to my level. I was bound and determined to pursue Glen Fields's tasking. Even if support was grudgingly given, I thought, I had a job to do. Ever enthusiastic, David ignored the coolness with which we were received and started efforts to get us up to Stanleyville.

Control of all flights to Stanleyville, which delivered supplies to the mercenaries and Congolese army units holding the still besieged city, was in the hands of the military attaché's office and our air proprietary in the Congo. Given the close contacts maintained with those offices, it was not difficult to get appropriate arrangements made. A problem had developed, however.

Word came from Headquarters that David would not be permitted to go back up to Stanleyville. David was not at all pleased, but there was nothing he could do unless Headquarters could be convinced to change their minds. For the moment, we got my name added to the (very short) passenger list for the next flight to Stanleyville in two days. I would be arriving with a shipment of hops for the brewery.

The brewery was the only business really functioning in Stanleyville as the Congolese soldiers absolutely refused to stay if they didn't get beer. Hops were therefore considered to be a strategic matériel for the war effort. I was happy to see that ammunition was also on the manifest. Whatever the Congolese soldiers might be doing, I wanted to be sure that the mercenaries were well supplied with weapons and ammo.

Those first few days we spent in Leopoldville left me a little perplexed. Nothing was as I had expected it to be. Certainly not our reception in the station, nor the city itself.

Leopoldville, the capital of a vast country rich in resources, which had only been independent since 1960, gave no hint of the fact that the country's north-east quadrant was in the throes of a bloody and destructive civil war. Even at the American Embassy, there had been no outward sign of much interest in or concern about what was happening in Stanleyville or elsewhere in the area. This was a stark contrast to Washington and my past three months' preparation. For week upon week, I had been steeped in matters concerning the conflict under way in the north-east. And yet here, at the scene, nobody seemed to care.

It was true that I was a young man who knew precious little about politics in Africa, only what I had recently read. Perhaps I just didn't understand what was really going on. It was also true that Leopoldville, the government, and the Congolese in general, had witnessed similar turmoil in the few short years since independence in 1960. Political intrigue and sharp debate had begun almost immediately afterwards. Rebellion and conflict followed and had become all too familiar. Maybe everyone here was inured to the Congo's seemingly endless problems. Some might even have thought that the lions had been tamed ('Simba' is the Swahili word for lion) and that life in the north-east would return to a state approaching normality.

The Congo was nothing more than a square on the global chessboard of the Cold War – albeit an important one if you happened to be there, playing the game. Given its abundant resources and its 'strategic location' (where have I heard that before), both superpowers and their camps had been watching carefully as the Congo tried to set its course as an independent nation. Both sides attempted to influence events to strengthen their interests.

Neither side seemed to realize that there was a dynamic to this particular tribal conflict that was resistant to influence from outside sources.

The Simbas, a ragtag bunch of illiterate dissidents, certainly weren't communists. But they posed a threat to the pro-Western Tshombe government in Leopoldville. Thus they gained the support of the Soviet Union, China, and their minions. And that prompted determination from the United States and its allies to provide all support possible to Tshombe and his government. It was that simple and was a scenario played out elsewhere in the world many times over during the first decades of the Cold War.

I took off for Stanleyville very early one morning in a C-130. The military, for reasons of its own I guess, always starts the day early. The ride to the airport was quick and easy since there was almost no traffic on the roads at that time of day. As it turned out, I was the only passenger that day so it was just the crew and me – and the hops and ammo.

Partly sunny or partly cloudy, take your pick, but clear enough so that when there were openings in the clouds it was possible to see the terrain. Our north-easterly route took us over the heart of the Congo basin, and its great tropical rain forest – one of only two that size in the world, the other being the Amazon basin. Except for an occasional glimpse of a dirt road or a collection of crude huts, there was just lots of jungle; dense double and triple canopy, I was told. I was happy to be well above it.

The flight to Stanleyville from Leopoldville took forever. It's a long way. With about equal doses of apprehension and expectation, I mulled things over as the hours passed. I think I spotted the Congo River first and then saw the city, which, from the air, looked pretty normal. I was soon to discover that it wasn't normal at all.

There were no formalities when we landed. A crew of Congolese appeared to unload the plane and a couple of trucks arrived, but not much else. I planned to stay at the Immoquator, an eight-storey, modern (relatively speaking) apartment block with two wings, and I bummed a ride over there from one of the plane's crew. It was almost the only place in Stanleyville where one could stay at the time. Before the rebellion, several members of the Consulate staff lived in apartments in the Immoquator and, as things turned out, I was assigned to one of those apartments.

The ride into the city revealed how misleading the view from the air had been. For starters, there were few people and little activity or traffic. After the Red Dragon operation by the Belgian paratroopers, virtually every European had been evacuated and almost none had returned. The vast majority of them were still in either Leopoldville or Europe. Moreover, many of the Congolese population, especially the rich and the educated, had fled to the bush during the Simba occupation and were not yet convinced it was safe enough to return. The population, which before the Simba occupation had been estimated to be as high as 150,000, was nowhere near that now.

It was a strange feeling to be in a city with so few people around. There was garbage and debris everywhere. Broken doors and windows on virtually every house attested to the fact that all had been looted and vandalized. Vehicles, mostly cars that had been stolen or 'appropriated' by the Simbas, littered the streets. Many were smashed against trees or walls. The vast majority of the Simbas had no idea how to drive. They simply pushed pedals until disaster struck. Or they tried to drive after smoking hashish with similar, predictable results.

My overall impression was one of sadness. It was apparent that the city had been an attractive and well-tended place before the occupation. But now it looked as if Attila the Hun and his pillaging horde had just passed through. How was I going to get anything accomplished in a place as devastated as this?

The Immoquator had been spared the destruction so evident elsewhere in Stanleyville although one block had been heavily damaged by gunfire during one strange incident. In a confused night battle, as the Simbas were consolidating their control, communications between some of their forces broke down. As a result, believing that there were opposition forces within, the Simbas fired on the building from across the river for most of the night. The other block was mostly intact and seemed, at that point, to be part guesthouse and part apartment building. I was assigned a small apartment by a surly Greek and went up to leave my bag. It was close to noon by this time and I was thinking about something to eat. I asked at the lobby desk and was directed to the dining room. I still hadn't seen many people.

The 'dining room' had probably been a cocktail lounge or bar in better times and had a view of the Congo River. Now it seemed to be an all-purpose place where the few occupants of the Immoquator could gather to eat, drink, talk – and probably fight from the look of the clientele. The furnishings had been nice in their day. They weren't any more. The tiled floor needed sweeping and there were no lights on although the natural light was adequate. There were a few tables and chairs, and, seated at most of the tables or standing at the bar, was the roughest, toughest, nastiest bunch of men I had ever seen. No women at all. In Vientiane, Laos, I had seen some bad guys, but nothing like this crew.

They wore an assortment of military and civilian apparel with no hesitation to mix the two. Few were clean-shaven. A variety of weapons was strewn over the tables or lying on the floor. There was a low murmur of conversation that seemed to stop as all noticed my arrival. Not the most comforting feeling I've ever had – standing in the doorway looking at what I now knew was a group of mercenaries.

I was wearing slacks, a short-sleeved white shirt and a tie. And loafers – not combat boots as the others were wearing. Clean-shaven with crew-cut hair. I was also carrying my briefcase, which I hadn't wanted to leave in my room. I couldn't have stood out more and the attention was unwelcome indeed.

I walked over to the nearest empty table, put my briefcase on the table and opened it. I had the feeling that many were watching me, but I ignored them all. I took off my tie and put it in my briefcase. Then I took out the Walther 9 mm pistol I had been issued in Leopoldville and stuffed it into my waistband. This was uncomfortable since I wasn't used to it, but I was doing it more for effect than anything else. Then I looked at the waiter next to the bar, ordered a beer, and sat down. I was relieved to sense that this play-acting seemed to do it. The murmur of conversation started up again. Any that had thought about it (it's likely that few did) would probably have guessed that I was an American. And that I might have something to do with the regular flights coming in from Leopoldville. I posed no threat. The waiter brought my beer – horrible stuff as it turned out, probably brewed the day before – and I asked him what there was to eat.

'Rice and beans with chicken,' he said.

'I'll take it,' was my quick response.

The meal was as bad as the beer, but eating it did give me time to get a better look at this motley group of mercenaries with whom I was lunching.

They were actually worse than my first impression. From my preparatory reading I knew that there were former French Foreign Legionnaires, ex German SS troopers, various soldier-of-fortune types and criminals on the run, amongst the mercenary ranks, as well as former (or current without admitting it) South African military personnel. I heard snatches of conversation in English, French, German, and, I guessed, Afrikaans, and I tried to sort out in my mind who was who. I don't know why. None seemed the slightest bit approachable, nor would I have had any reason to try to start a conversation. Conversations seemed to be about recent firefights they had been in and how many blacks had been killed. Not necessarily Simbas, just blacks. Some wore strange (to me) medals and many carried knives. They really were the dregs.

While I was drinking coffee after my meal, I was relieved to see a familiar face approach my table, a man called Koenraad, whom I'd met two days earlier in Leopoldville.

I had had a meeting in a hotel room with Mike Hoare, a South African who was the leader of the mercenary group hired to support Moise Tshombe. David G. did not accompany me to the meeting. 'Mad Mike', as he was affectionately known, had been part of a column of mercenaries that had raced to Stanleyville starting in mid-November 1964, with the goal of liberating the city. They planned to arrive in time to support the Belgian paratroopers. There were those who doubted that they would make it, but to almost everyone's great surprise Mike's troop covered over 100 kilometres on some days and very nearly got to Stanleyville before the Belgian paratroopers landed and freed the city. They arrived a few hours after the Belgians. 'Periodic skirmishes with Simba groups slowed us down a bit,' Hoare had said. Following the Belgian withdrawal, an element of Hoare's mercenaries, supported by Congolese army troops, had remained in Stanleyville to hold the city while the Belgians and the rest of the mercenaries moved to cities elsewhere in the eastern Congo in an effort to end the Simba reign of terror.

My meeting with Hoare had been a liaison contact. Since I was going to be working in the north-east, it had seemed prudent to have me make contact with him. The goal was to let each other know what we were up to. He wasn't a particularly likeable guy, but he briefed me in some detail on the grim situation in and around Stanleyville. At the end of our meeting, he called in Koenraad, his number two, who would be in Stanleyville when I arrived. Hoare would remain in Leopoldville to work on personnel and logistics matters. Koenraad, also South African, was polite and reserved at that first meeting.

Today he smiled as he sat down and said, 'Well, what do you think of Stanleyville?'

'Looks a mess and there aren't many people,' I replied.

'Every city and town we came through looked like this,' Koenraad told me. 'It's really pretty sad.'

I was surprised at this comment from a mercenary. Later I came to understand that Koenraad was a military man (on extended leave, he claimed) and that he was in the Congo to gain experience. South Africa anticipated similar rebellions in the future and he was here to learn.

'We need to get you some clothes,' he commented. 'You really stand out.'

'Don't forget that I'm supposed to be a diplomat,' I responded, 'but I know what you mean. I'm going back to Leopoldville the day after tomorrow and I'll pick up some field clothes and boots.'

Koenraad was making an effort to be friendly and I appreciated that. We talked about the current situation, which seemed to be getting better. Simba control in rural areas was weaker than it had been just a week ago and Congolese who had fled seemed to be returning to the city. The Congolese soldiers were hopeless, but the mercenaries had developed ways to work around that problem. The food was awful – I already knew that – and there was no hard liquor and no women.

'Sounds like a wonderful place,' I joked, and Koenraad laughed.

In Leopoldville, I had been careful to meet contacts discreetly, if not clandestinely, to avoid curious eyes and the journalists who were always in quest of a story. Here in Stanleyville, there was no reason for that since we were practically the only Europeans in town.

Walking around a deserted and devastated Stanleyville that afternoon was an eerie experience. I heard an occasional car or truck pass by and saw a few people standing off to the side of the street, but, for the most part, I was alone. I thought about trade-craft – the mechanics of running intelligence operations – but given the situation that seemed silly and I just moved ahead. I was happy to have the Walther 9 mm. I found the US Consulate. It was empty and it had been ransacked. There was almost nothing left in it. I also found David's house and went inside. No problem getting in as the doors were either gone or hanging open on their hinges. I had promised David I would look around but there wasn't much to see and I didn't stay there for long. As I continued my walk, I felt increasingly uneasy and couldn't decide why. Finally, I concluded that it probably wasn't very smart for me to be walking around this recently liberated, but still semi-deserted, city alone. As I headed back toward the Immoquator, I wondered again what the hell I was going to be able to do in this violated place.

I was up bright and early the next morning. Somewhere there must have been a bakery functioning because I remember having rolls and coffee for breakfast. Afterwards, I was scheduled to accompany a small mercenary patrol out to the city's defence perimeter. The mercenaries had vehicles so we drove out to the edge of the city in a three jeep and one truck convoy. Our desti-nation was a main road approaching the city from the south-west. A Congolese army platoon and a couple of mercenaries were standing around when we got there. This was the defence perime-ter?

Within a short while after our arrival, one of the mercenaries said, 'Here they come.'

I looked down the road and saw a line of men, Simbas I was told, moving in single file towards the city. The Congolese soldiers were clearly agitated and started taking cover, but the mercenaries didn't seem very concerned. The Simbas were still a couple of hundred yards away but walking steadily, if slowly, towards us. As they got closer I could see that the guy in the lead was wearing something on his head, an animal skin of some sort I guessed, and was muttering and waving a palm branch.

'He's the head medicine man,' Koenraad informed me. 'They still do this most days.'

Then, the Congolese soldiers started shooting.

'But they aren't aiming at the Simbas,' I pointed out as calmly as I could, although it must have been clear that I was alarmed.

'Don't worry about it,' Koenraad muttered and gave a couple of mercenaries a signal.

At his sign, two mercenaries stepped into the road and levelled a couple of bursts of machine gun fire at the approaching group of Simbas. Several were hit and fell. Behind them, the column, if you could call it a column, stopped, and the guy with the skin on his head waved his arms. Then the whole bunch turned around and started retracing their steps. It was quite bizarre.

The Congolese soldiers stopped shooting and looked down the road with happy smiles.

'What the hell is going on?' I asked Koenraad.

'Our magic is stronger than theirs,' he explained.

Apparently, the Simbas often approached the defence perimeter in this way and were always led by the sorcerer with the skin on his head. It never took much to discourage them for the day.

Magic for the Simbas originated with 'Mama Bangala', the head sorceress, who was reputed to have only one breast in the middle of her chest. Apparently, she convinced somebody high up in the Simba command (if such a structure ever existed) that her magic would turn bullets to water. Simbas who believed and practised this magic could not be hurt by bullets. Obviously, those who were killed or wounded had not been practising believers. All Simbas were indoctrinated and all knew Mama Bangala.

So this is Africa, I was thinking.

On the ride back to the Immoquator, I saw Africans on the street – many more than the previous day.

'Some of the locals stayed through the occupation,' Koenraad said. 'And of those that fled some have returned. But they all keep a pretty low profile. You wouldn't have seen many at all on the airport road or in the area where you walked. That's the European quarter and really is deserted. That's what I think is sad,' he added. 'All the people that make this city work are gone.'

I could see how my initial impression had been a false one. In fact, there were people around. Things were far from normal, but the city was starting to revive. Clearly the Simba threat, at least in Stanleyville, was low and getting lower all the time. The more familiar I became with the current situation, I thought, the easier it would be to assess my chances of re-contacting our agents, our 'assets'. I could then go over my findings with David G. and our other officers and we could start to develop a plan of action. This was our first on-the-ground look since the occupation and I was the one doing the looking. I felt a combination of pride and excitement, but also a sense of great responsibility.

As Koenraad had said, I found more people in the mixed neighbourhoods or in areas where only Africans lived. I didn't talk to anyone. No one was friendly. I won't say that I was discouraged, but I wasn't happy with what I was finding. I spent the rest of the morning and all afternoon moving around the city.

Surprisingly, the phone system had worked throughout the Simba occupation and was available if I needed it, but mail was still unreliable. I found no way to make discreet, let alone clandestine, contact with anyone. My effort to re-contact our agents was going to be a lot harder than I had initially anticipated. I returned to Leopoldville the next day.

I met David right away, of course. We talked well into the night after having dined together and I filled him in on what I had seen and heard in Stanleyville. David listened carefully, posing questions from time to time. It didn't take us long to agree that, given the current situation in Stanleyville, we might have to alter our approach. We had to conclude that most of our agents were either dead or had left Stanleyville and not yet returned. We certainly didn't want to endanger any of them. As it became known in Stanleyville that I was there and had replaced David, we hoped that our agents would find ways to get word to me securely. In the meantime, I would assess the evolving situation and make my moves when it seemed prudent to do so. It was not what any of us had hoped for, but there wasn't much choice.

So it was back to Stanleyville again. Back at the Immoquator, nothing had changed except maybe that the increasingly bored mercenaries were more sullen and hostile than ever. I wasn't going to have much contact with them though, so I didn't worry about that. Staying away from them seemed the best idea. I started trying to find and meet some of David's social friends and contacts just to get the word around that I was there. We had been able to scrounge up a car so things were easier. I did meet a few people, but those contacts yielded no positive results. There was still no word from any of our agents.

There was no change in the situation during the rest of January and early February despite my best efforts. Security was better and confidence on the part of the populace seemed to be increasing, but that wasn't helping us make the contacts we were after. By early February, Headquarters shifted its position and sent approval for David to go up to Stanleyville. Our hope was that he would be recognized and that might prompt some positive results.

Thinking that he would be the source of much current information about activities in the city, we went first to the home of Alexander Barlovatz, an expatriate Yugoslav doctor who had become a Belgian citizen. With his former concert pianist wife, Barlovatz had lived in Stanleyville since just after the Second World War. Barlovatz had established a clinic for the local population as well as a private practice that served Europeans, but the majority of his patients were Africans. Most could pay him no money and many offered food and services instead.

An intelligent and engaging man, Barlovatz had devoted his life to helping the African community of Stanleyville. It had not made him rich, but he and his wife enjoyed a comfortable living. Both had stayed in the city during the Simba occupation. Like hundreds of other Europeans, they had had no choice. But they were virtually the only Europeans in the city during that period who were not held hostage. Barlovatz's devotion to his patients, and the fact that the entire local population loved and respected him, saved him from the imprisonment and mistreatment suffered by the other Europeans. As I discovered after we met, however, neither he nor his wife escaped periodic harassment and threats from the unpredictable Simba occupiers.

In addition to his status in the town, Barlovatz was a leftist thinker sympathetic to the nationalist dreams of some of the Simba leadership. Those sympathies were part of the reason he was allowed freedom of movement during the occupation. And with that freedom, he brought food to David and the other American hostages almost every day during their 111 days of captivity. When David got sick at one point, Barlovatz gave him medicine and a shot. He was little short of being a lifesaver for the Americans. Our visit was an opportunity for David to thank the Barlovatzes again for all they had done for the hostages during the ugly period of the Simba occupation.

Lacking reliable means to announce our arrival, we simply showed up at their house and knocked on the door. David introduced me and we were immediately welcomed into their home. It was late afternoon and they asked if we could stay for dinner. Our social schedule was completely clear, we told them and they both laughed. Barlovatz was about to do his afternoon rounds and asked me if I wanted to accompany him.

His clinic was long and narrow with rows of beds. A corrugated tin roof and some type of thatch walls hung on a frame made of wooden posts. Electric light bulbs, bare, hung from the ceiling every twenty feet or so. There were sinks with running water at both ends of the building. Toilets must have been in the back. I didn't see them. There were few windows and no doors. Open at both ends. It was a no frills medical facility. There were patients in almost every bed – about thirty of them. Family members surrounded the beds and they provided much basic care, including feeding I was told.

It became immediately clear that Dr Barlovatz was held in great esteem by all in the clinic. I watched him go about his work and to say that he was genuinely concerned about each patient would have been an understatement. He cared about every one and they felt it.

Dinner at the Barlovatzes' home was a great joy in all respects. That the alternative was bad food and rotten company at the Immoquator had no effect on that judgement. It would have been a great pleasure to dine with these two delightful and sophisticated people under any circumstances. Their home was like an island of calm and order in the middle of a sea of tension and turmoil.

The living room, where we had drinks, was simply but tastefully appointed with appropriate attention given to the fact that Stanleyville, being almost on the equator, was routinely hot and humid. A fan whirled slowly above us. The rattan furniture was cool to sit in. It was a large room and in one corner there was a beautiful grand piano that seemed strangely out of place.

Barlovatz said that once, during the Simba period, they had had guests for dinner and, as was her habit, Mme Barlovatz was playing the piano after dinner. Suddenly, several armed Simba soldiers literally burst into the room, despite the efforts of two servants to keep them out. They started shouting at Mme. Although both the Barlovatzes understood the local dialect, neither could make out what the soldiers were so excited about. They were brandishing their weapons. Following a determined effort to make sense out of the increasingly dangerous-looking situation, they discovered that the Simba patrol had heard the piano and was convinced that Mme Barlovatz was using it to communicate, illegally, with government forces in Leopoldville. Barlovatz was stunned when he realized what they were saying and was initially at a loss for words. 'How could you respond to something so absurd?' he said. He attempted to reason with them explaining that a piano could not transmit messages. His efforts were to no avail. The Simbas threatened to arrest Mme and take away the piano. Barlovatz protested and demanded that they bring their commanding officer. Otherwise he would immediately report them to Gbenye, their political leader. The threat seemed to get their attention. Two more Simbas arrived at that point. The Simbas talked. One of the new arrivals said he wished to inspect the piano. Barlovatz, sensing a compromise, agreed. The new arrival, by now clearly identifiable as the patrol leader, then made a great show of carefully looking under and inside the piano.

'No transmitter,' he declared. 'And no antenna.' The Simbas left as abruptly as they had arrived.

Fresh meat and vegetables were in short supply. Dinner was not a gourmet delight, but it tasted good and it was tastefully presented. The conversation was free flowing and wide ranging with us providing news from abroad and the Barlovatzes commenting about life in Stanleyville both before and during the Simba occupation. I quickly took note of the fact that both had great respect and affection for David. After dinner, Mme Barlovatz played classical music, beautifully, while the three of us listened and sipped cognac, which had appeared as if for a special occasion. We were honoured and very appreciative. It would have been a splendid evening in Paris or Washington. In Stanleyville in February 1965, it was incredible.

It was just too soon, we discovered, to expect to meet with either our former agents or with many of David's other contacts in Stanleyville. Time after time we had come up empty trying to locate someone. Usually the house or apartment was unoccupied. Sometimes someone was there, but not the individual we were looking for. Our north-eastern Congo network was still in a shambles. Our goal remained to collect whatever intelligence we could, hopefully from our agents, about the presence, activities and supply lines of the Simba units.

After this trip to Stanleyville in early February, we discussed the possibility of expanding my area of operations. Specifically, I proposed a short visit (a couple of weeks) to Bunia, located on a high plateau on the Congo's far north-eastern border with Uganda. I had two reasons. First, we had a couple of agents who were originally from Bunia and had family still there. One of them had been one of our best assets. When fear drove them from Stanleyville, I reasoned, perhaps they had retreated to either Bunia or Uganda. And second, I might be able to collect, from people in the area, information that might satisfy some of the requirements levied upon us by our political level customers. I left Leopoldville for Bunia on 12 February 1965. David, having concluded that there was little more he could do in the Congo, made preparations to return to Washington.

A mercenary column had liberated Bunia on 30 November 1964 – just six days after the Belgian paratroopers carried out the Red Dragon operation that had freed Stanleyville. About a dozen whites in Bunia had been slain by the Simbas as well as an undetermined number of Congolese. Over thirty whites and forty-seven ANC soldiers had been rescued by the mercenaries. This had been a familiar story all over the north-eastern Congo during December 1964 and January 1965. Now, in February, clean-up efforts were continuing. Mercenary columns were systematically moving from town to town, securing central government control and sending the Simba forces fleeing into the countryside. There were frequent reprisals carried out by the Simbas and over three hundred whites were killed, often viciously, during that violent period. Although the exact number is unknown, thousands of Congolese were killed by the Simbas. Many others, some innocent bystanders, died at the hands of either mercenary or ANC forces.

By the time of my arrival in Bunia, most towns in the north-east were in government hands and (relatively speaking) safe, but there was an unknown number of armed Simbas still roaming the countryside wreaking havoc. The mercenaries simply didn't have the manpower or resources to chase down the Simba units. The highest priority was given to rescuing whites being held hostage by the Simbas. Another high priority for the mercenary columns was 'liberating' (looting) all banks they came across in the towns they secured. The north-east Congo, an area the size of France, was in great turmoil in early 1965.

I landed at Bunia airport, a few kilometres south-east of the town, in a C-46, which was also carrying supplies for our small group stationed in Bunia, comprising a chief of the unit, a couple of Cuban pilots, two mechanics, a radio operator and a logistics officer. There were a couple of these flights per week.

We drove into town in a Land Rover. Bunia was deserted. And this was not just an initial impression. There was almost no traffic and very few people. Bad feelings surfaced again as we approached the one small hotel that was open. Bunia had not been sacked as badly as Stanleyville. But the fear and uncertainty had been such that the population simply fled into the bush and back to rural villages. The Simbas had indiscriminately committed rape, murder and looting to such an extent in this area that the people were in a state of real terror.

The Belgian couple who owned the hotel had never left. Bunia had not been permanently occupied by the Simba forces and they had stayed out of sight when any Simba units were in town or passed through. Had they left, they said, they would have lost everything, so why not stay and take their chances? Not the soundest reasoning in the world, I thought. I felt they had been lucky.

Despite many problems (food shortages, no workers, power cuts), the place was tolerable. It was certainly better than the thatch huts in Laos. The couple did what they could to ease the hardships and were a congenial pair for the most part. She was a good cook and made the most of what was available, including fresh fish from time to time. The men at the hotel told me that dinner was best the day after a C-46 visit. She ran everything. Her frail husband simply followed orders and seemed happy to do so. There were a few Africans who cleaned and did the laundry, poorly. One of them substituted water for the gin in a bottle in my room so my martini hour stopped. As things turned out, it didn't matter much. Our small contingent, all men, worked, ate and slept in the hotel compound. Work wasn't hard, but there was stress. We all felt the strangeness of being in a ghost town. We knew, or felt at least, that the Simbas were out there, but knew nothing about their real strength or intentions. I had to find out where they were and what they were going to do. They must have known we were there but had done nothing. Was this a sign of weakness? No one knew. The T-28 air activity in the region, which was staged from Bunia, would have been reason for them to be most unfriendly, but nothing happened. There were neither mercenary nor Congolese army elements actually in Bunia, but some were nearby. We only talked about the situation jokingly, but none of us was comfortable. We were armed, but only with handguns and a few UZI automatics. Had a Simba group attacked us, things would certainly have been difficult.

I set to work trying to find my agents. There were no city maps of Bunia, but the Belgian couple pointed me to the right area of town. I had what passed for addresses, house numbers of four houses on ill-defined streets, and I was determined to check them out. Walking, alone, through Bunia at that time was, as Glen Fields had put it, no walk in the park. I didn't see anyone or hear anything except for the echo of my footsteps. I walked quickly. Was this trip necessary? There was no response at the first house. As I approached the second house, I thought I saw movement inside but couldn't be sure. I knocked. A woman appeared. I think we were both surprised. She spoke passable French, funny accent, and told me she was the wife of the man I was seeking. This was the first piece of luck I had had. 'Where is he?' I asked. She was wary and said he wasn't there, but would be the following evening. 'Tell him I'll be back tomorrow at five p.m.,' I told her. She nodded and I left. The other two houses were empty and still.

After dinner, several of us gathered on the hotel terrace to have coffee, beer, or whatever was available. There was nothing else to do. Apparently this was routine. I noticed two Cuban pilots who flew the T-28s. Quiet conversation for an hour or so and then we all retired. That night I felt, for the first time in my life, earth tremors brought about by a mild earthquake. Although I hadn't remembered it at the time, Bunia is located on the Rift Valley fault line.

I met the next night with the agent, who was educated, fairly well to do and happy to see me. His wife had been frightened, but had passed on the message. I was gratified to have finally had some success. We had been right. Fearful for his life, he had fled Stanleyville as the Simba forces arrived. He was originally from this area and his relatives owned this house in Bunia. He and many others were more confident about their safety now because the Simba influence was clearly on the wane. Mercenary 'magic' was much stronger and everyone knew it. In fact, he was planning to return to Stanleyville within the week. Accordingly, we arranged to meet there later in the month.

I debriefed him. What did he know about the fate of Congolese government officials and prominent citizens in Stanleyville? I had lists of names in my head – including some who had been agents. Several had been executed. Most he knew nothing about. I was reassured to hear him say that the area around Bunia was safe and that Simba control in general was falling apart. We talked for over an hour. The next morning, I wrote three reports and sent them to Leopoldville. A special flight was coming in that afternoon and I was pleased to have them out of the way.

We went out to the airport after lunch to meet the flight, an incoming C-130. 'We' included Wes, my communications officer who had just been transferred to the Congo from Ethiopia, 'Big' Bill Wyrozemski, the chief of the air unit in Bunia, and me. We didn't know who or what would be arriving and it turned out to be Russ Lefevre, a colleague.

Russ was about my age or a little younger. He had been a Navy officer and had lots of experience with small boats. He had recently arrived in the Congo and was charged with establishing a programme aimed at patrolling the lakes on the eastern border of the Congo and stopping what we believed to be a channel being used to bring in arms for the Simbas. We had much in common and hit it off right away. We have been friends ever since. The Headquarters approved plan was that Russ would use this opportunity to test one of his boats on Lake Albert and the C-130 crew off-loaded a twenty-foot boat Russ had brought with him. It was sleek and powerful looking and Russ called it a 'V-20', so named because it had a V-shaped hull that enhanced speed and manoeuvrability. It boasted twin inboard/outboard engines (350 horsepower) and looked like it would really move in the water. It would run down anything on Lake Albert, that's for sure. There were 30 calibre machine-guns mounted fore and aft that said 'don't mess with me'.

After dinner, Russ and I discussed in more detail what he would be doing over the next several days. In Leopoldville, he and another officer had met with Mike Hoare to discuss mercenary operations in the north-east Congo. Lots had been accomplished, but there was still plenty to do. They agreed to more or less combine forces in an effort to rid an area just west of Lake Albert of Simba presence. The mercenaries would launch their sweep from Bunia and move along the lake forcing the Simbas east. Russ would be on the lake in the V-20 and 'take appropriate action' if Simbas tried to flee by boat. It wasn't all that firm, but the outline fitted with the tests Russ wanted to accomplish so it seemed reasonable. Hoare was due in Bunia the next day for discussions about which areas the mercenaries would attack before starting the operation.

However, unforeseen events were to cut short Russ's efforts on the lake. My next meeting with him would be under most unpleasant circumstances. Hoare led his column of mercenaries out of Bunia shortly after Russ had left.

The day after Russ's departure to Lake Albert, Wes drove me out to the airport after lunch. He had never seen a T-28 fighter and he wanted to get a look at one. I had seen them in Laos, but had never flown in one. In discussions with Big Bill the day before, we had agreed that this would be a good time for me to get a look at the terrain, road network, and level of activity visible from the air in the area north of Bunia along the border with the Sudan. It was via this border that we suspected arms and ammo for the Simbas were being infiltrated; a portion of them at least. The two T-28s made daily flights out of Bunia, in effect on search and destroy missions. They were looking for 'military targets', which, it seemed, was almost anything that moved on the roads. That day, they had been scheduled to cover the area that interested me.

The T-28 had a range of several hundred miles. Given that the north-east quarter of the Congo is so huge, that limited range was restricting. But they were able to cover areas north, west and south of Bunia. They did not fly in Uganda, east of Bunia.

I had done a lot of this type of flying in Laos and was confident I'd get a good idea of what, if anything, was going on along the Sudanese border. If it were me, I would bring the arms and ammo in at night. Security was an issue too, but as far as we knew, the Simbas didn't have weaponry to bring down a plane. I felt good about that. That had not been the case in Laos where we did lose aircraft to ground fire. The weather was good and it looked as if an easy and, hopefully, productive afternoon awaited me.

I met the Cuban pilots just before we were due to take off. I had seen them, of course, at the hotel. Juan Peron and Juan Tunon were young, but experienced, and both were good pilots, Big Bill told me. I went over some maps with them and explained what areas I wanted to cover, if possible. My tasking was second priority. Military targets, if we found any, would take first priority. I could always go again if necessary. The T-28 has two seats, one behind the other, under the same canopy, and I was to fly behind Juan Peron.

Born in Havana in 1940, Peron had an interesting background. In his teens, he learned to fly light planes and became a crop duster for a small rice growing company in Cuba. In 1960, about a year after Castro overthrew Batista, Peron was sent to Miami, Florida, to pick up a new plane. He had a three-day visa. Foreseeing what Castro's rule would mean for Cuba, Peron's father instructed him to stay in the United States and Peron did so. Thus at the age of twenty he found himself in a new and strange country. Under programmes established by President Kennedy, Peron served first in the United States Air Force (he did not fly) and then the United States Army. In 1963, he accepted employment with the air propriety company organized by the Agency and was sent to the Congo. Beforehand, he received training in the Second World War vintage T-6 fighter. After arriving in the Congo, he was trained in the T-28 and the C-46. At the age of twenty-five he was already a talented and experienced pilot.

Close up, the T-28 was bigger and, in a way, more menacing than I remembered. I climbed onto the wing and then into the back seat of the narrow cockpit. Wes had taken some photos and was standing about fifty yards away waiting for us to take off. I had been given a flight helmet, with a push-to-talk intercom, and put it on as Peron was climbing in. We both wore parachutes. As I strapped on the harness, I was thinking that this was different from anything I'd ever flown in Laos. Peron closed the canopy, I waved to Wes and the others, and we taxied out to the runway. Our take-off confirmed the difference. This thing was hot. It needed speed to fly, lots of speed. This was especially noticeable since Bunia is about 4,000 feet above sea level and we needed lots of runway to get airborne. After our take-off, in tandem with Juan Tunon, we circled and came back for a fly-by right down the runway at about ten feet off the deck. The Cuban pilots were showing off. I didn't mind. The fly-by ended with a sharp ascent. My stomach noticed.

As planned, we headed north, more or less, along the Sudanese border. It was unremarkable high plateau terrain – plains and what Peron called rivers of trees, although not dense jungle at this point. I saw nothing of any interest. Then, after less than half an hour, Peron spotted some trucks. They were near a road junction of two unpaved roads. There were three trucks and they had evidently heard the planes as they were pulling in under some trees. Peron, as flight commander, decided to attack and destroy the trucks. It wasn't clear to me that these were military targets but it didn't matter. I had no vote and accepted his decision.

We circled around and, with us in the lead, started a strafing run. We only had machine guns. The dive was steep and again my stomach took immediate notice. Coming out we were 'pulling g's' as they say. It was no big deal for Peron, but I had never felt it before so it was for me. I had trouble seeing and couldn't tell what, if anything, we were hitting. Nothing on the ground moved.

Tunon had been right behind us, but I didn't see him either. Two more runs. Still nothing moved. No fire either. Peron said we were done. Fine, let's get out of here, I thought.

I don't know how long our attack took, but after we levelled off and resumed cruising, it was clear right away that the weather had changed. A front had appeared behind us and heavy clouds and rain were moving towards us. Peron and Tunon talked in Spanish, so I couldn't pick up anything. Peron said we had best return and that he'd try to get around the storm. But it wasn't going to be that easy.

I should point out that flying in the middle of Africa in the 1960s presented many challenges. Weather forecasting help was almost nonexistent. You knew there was a storm coming when you saw one. Navigational aids were few and far between. There were no beacons to speak of. And great distances with nothing in them except an occasional plantation or small village. There were few roads or large rivers to key on. Everything was 'visual flight rules'. You had to see it and know what it was. To the south of where we were flying, the lakes were a big help. But we couldn't see them. In addition, only Bunia and Paulis (now called Isiro) had airports that could handle a T-28.

We tried to skirt the storm. It was nasty and threw us around, but we managed to stay together and took the path of least resistance. When we got out of it, Peron and Tunon talked again. Peron told me we had been knocked off course. I wasn't surprised. He wasn't sure where we were, but thought it best if we headed for Paulis and spent the night there. If we got more altitude, could we see the lakes? I asked Peron. He didn't think so nor did Tunon. I couldn't press the point and had to rely on their experience. I had confidence in them both. We flew on hoping to find Paulis. But we saw nothing familiar to either of them and soon Peron gave me the rotten news.

'We are going to have to go down,' he said. 'The storm screwed us up bad. We don't know where we are and fuel is getting low. I'd rather take it in while I can choose a clearing. And it will be dark soon.'

Shit, I thought. 'Let's jump,' I said into the intercom. 'We all have 'chutes.'

'No way,' he responded. 'We're better off to crash land.'

Shit, I thought again, a pilot's mentality! Unless the plane is on fire or the wings fall off, they won't jump. (Years later Peron confirmed that mentality by telling me that he 'never had any confidence in parachutes'.) I was not at all happy at the prospect of crash landing in a T-28. It needs way too much space, I was thinking, and I could see no clearings down there that looked big enough. Again, however, I had no real choice. I couldn't open the canopy and I couldn't just leap out of the plane. It was all happening so fast.

Tunon decided to stay up a while longer. They wished each other luck. Bloody hell, I thought, I'm wishing us all good luck.

Peron picked out a clearing. It didn't look long enough, but choices didn't abound. Shit, I was thinking, yet again. He made his last turn and we started losing altitude. We wanted a long approach with time to cut off switches, after full flaps and slowest speed possible.

'You have a weapon?' Peron asked, as we more or less glided in, just short of stalling out.

I reached down and felt the Walther 9 mm. 'Yeah,' I responded, 'and I'll keep it with me.'

His question highlighted the fact that we were going down in unknown territory likely to be controlled by the Simbas. Oddly perhaps, I felt no fear, just frustration and irritation at our predicament. I was confident that we would make our landing somehow. Then we would lose ourselves in the bush and make our way out to safety, however long that might take. I had run similar risks in Laos, but had never had to walk out. I worried that I didn't have an escape and evasion kit with a radio. Peron opened the canopy and there was a rush of air. The approach seemed endless as he tried to manoeuvre the plane for the longest possible slide before we hit trees. In order to get a better look at the clearing, I reached up and raised the sun visor on my flight helmet. I would live to regret it.

We were going awfully fast. Too fast really, but there was nothing Peron could do about it. Our first touch caused us to bounce. We touched again and started skidding along the rough clearing, which had looked better from 3,000 feet. Peron saw flames under the left wing. I was hunched over, seat belt and harness as tight as they would go, bracing myself for the end of our slide. Although it all happened quickly, the slide, probably several hundred yards, seemed to last a long time. Suddenly we came to an abrupt stop. The force caused me to lurch forward and then back and my head jerked up. At the same instant, a splash of flaming aviation fuel was thrown across the rear cockpit from the left wing. I caught it in the face, left front mostly, left shoulder, and both hands as well as a bit on the tops of both legs. The splash missed the front cockpit and Peron was unhurt. Not immediately realizing what had happened to me and, eager to get the hell out of the T-28 now burning on the left side, he leapt out of the cockpit, jumped off the wing and ran.

I was stunned and in considerable pain. This would certainly screw things up, I remember thinking, although I had no idea how seriously I had been burned. I couldn't see. That was the worst and most immediate problem. My eyelids had been singed shut and I couldn't open them. I could hear and smell fire and I knew I had to get out of the plane. I heard Peron shouting at me to get out. I'm sure trying, I was thinking. My seat harness remained snugly fastened. My hands hurt a lot and I couldn't use either one. Somehow, I managed to push open the release with one of my elbows and, with considerable effort, I started to climb out – hindered severely by my hands and the bloody parachute hanging behind me. The fire was a great motivator. I half climbed, half stumbled out of the cockpit, and fell off the wing on the right rear side. Instinctively I had moved away from the fire. Peron was there. He helped me away from the burning plane. It exploded into higher intensity flames as we moved away. I could feel the intensity and felt thankful and lucky to have got out.

Peron felt, and I agreed, that we needed to get as far away from the plane as possible before impending nightfall. Had any Simbas seen the plane come down, we reasoned, they would surely be coming to check things out. The problem was that I could barely walk, even after we got the parachute off me. There was lots of pain and I seemed to have almost no strength. Peron couldn't carry me very far either. I outweighed him by twenty pounds or so. We stopped and I tried to think. Flashes from earlier training (army, jungle warfare school when I got my initial Agency training, and even Boy Scout training) came back to me. Burns mean infection and dehydration. Also, bad burns mean swelling. I pulled off a college ring I was wearing on my left hand. This hurt like hell and skin came with it, but I knew I had to get it off or suffer worse consequences. I was wearing contact lenses and knew they should come out. I asked Peron to help since my hands wouldn't work. It was impossible. I couldn't get my eyes open. They would simply have to stay where they were until we could find help. Peron was very upset. Who wouldn't be? Clearly me being hurt had shifted the playing field, and certainly not to our advantage. 'We'll make it out of here,' I told him. 'I don't know how, but we will.' Of that I was certain and determined.

It started raining. I don't know how far away from the plane we made it. Not far. Peron says we walked for only thirty minutes or so. We stopped under some trees next to a small stream. It rained most of the night. We just sat there. Peron made me move periodically, fearing an adverse impact on my circulation. The pain got worse and I must have passed out for short intervals. We neither saw nor heard any sign of patrols moving in the area. We had absolutely no idea where we were. The night seemed to last forever, but finally daylight came. I could at least discern that much. Peron used his knife to cut charred skin hanging from several of my fingers. There were already bugs on some of my burns. We talked. We decided that since I was in no condition to walk – I could barely move by this point – Peron should leave me by the small stream (so I could drink water regularly) and try to find help. Although unstated, we both knew that our chances were far greater if Peron, moving alone, could find help and then get back to me. He left me and by that time I was in left field – great pain that took me into and out of consciousness. He took my Walther with him.

We hadn't covered much ground after our crash landing and as Peron partially retraced our steps, he passed near the wreckage. There was no sign of anyone in the area. He was relieved. At the same time, he was concerned about not knowing where we were. He could see that nothing, not his flight maps and not the light submachine gun that had been behind his seat, would be salvageable from the plane. He had his pistol and mine. In ever increasing circles, Peron started to explore the area around the crash site, looking for anything – a village, a road – that would help us start to locate ourselves. He was cautious for fear of running into an armed Simba group. Sometime around midday, he saw some natives and tried to approach them. They fled. He walked in the direction they had gone and came upon a small cluster of huts,. For the north-eastern Congo, that qualified as a village. There were people there, mostly women and children. Peron approached them. He could see an old man talking excitedly to a group of women.

None spoke French, English or Spanish, and Juan was having trouble making himself understood. The women were very hesitant and wary. While Peron was trying to somehow communicate, a group of men suddenly appeared. Wondering whether or not he should attempt to flee, Peron saw that they were unarmed and were likely the male residents of this village returning from their fields. Also looking wary, the men came towards him cautiously. Peron addressed them, in English, and was greatly relieved to receive a response also in English. Many questions and answers later, he had learned that the village chief, Faustino, had been educated by British missionaries who had taught him English. These people were Azande, a tribal group scattered across central Africa in the Congo, the Sudan and the Central African Republic. They had little use for governments or borders. They knew little and probably cared less about Moise Tshombe and his Congolese central government. Of great importance to them, however, and of paramount importance to us as it turned out, was the fact that the Simbas, for reasons never made clear, had killed Faustino's brother, a leader of the Azande tribe. Faustino hated the Simbas. Thank God and what a stroke of good luck for us.

Peron explained our situation and told Faustino that we were hunting elephants. From a T-28? Peron doesn't think Faustino believed him. I don't think so either. I have no idea what prompted Peron to come up with such an implausible story. I had been planning to pose as a French journalist. Whatever he may have thought of Peron's tale, Faustino agreed to help us get to safety.

'Where is that?' Peron asked.

'We are near the Sudan border,' Faustino replied, 'and the nearest government post is Paulis. That's about 280 kilometres.'

'*Dios mio*,' Peron murmured. 'We will walk?'

Faustino didn't reply. In his mid-thirties, he had a strong build and a ruggedly handsome look about him. He looked like a warrior and had the aura of a leader. Peron sensed right away that the people in the village respected him and would obey him. While his authority stemmed mostly from his family ties, which was traditional among the Azandes, it also seemed as if Faustino was genuinely liked and had somehow earned the village's respect. The Azande were a strong and proud people who had been powerful and independent in their lands even through the slave trader raiding periods.

Lying waiting for Peron, I can remember stumbling into and out of the stream several times. I have to drink lots of water, I kept thinking. The water also gave some relief from the bees that seemed to be all over me. Peron says he was shocked when they found me. I was lying about twenty metres from the stream. 'You were covered with bees and you looked like a monster,' he said. In pain and barely conscious, I didn't realize at first that he had come back. It had been almost twenty-four hours since we had crash-landed. Seeing that I would be unable to walk, the villagers and Peron fashioned a crude stretcher from branches and began the walk back to the village. It was a painful journey. Each movement of the stretcher was agony, as whatever scabbing had begun, broke open again.

A villager had reported another plane down nearby – Tunon's no doubt – and Peron and Faustino had checked out the site on the way to get me. Tunon was nowhere to be found. Based on its location and the condition of the plane, and the fact that there had been no fire, Peron believed that Tunon had stalled out on his final approach. Lacking sufficient air speed, the plane dropped like a rock. The trees, some over 100 feet tall, served to cushion its drop to the ground. Tunon, who had received jungle warfare and escape and evasion training before coming to the Congo, had taken his weapon but left his maps, which Peron was able to retrieve. Without knowing our present location, however, they weren't of much use. Faustino couldn't read a map.

Tunon was never seen again. Several months later, missionary reports confirmed that while trying to make his way out to safety, he had been captured by a Simba patrol. The Simbas killed him and subsequently, believing that if you eat the flesh and vital organs of your enemy you gain strength, devoured him. God rest his soul.

We had crashed late afternoon on 17 February. Peron made contact with Faustino's village twenty-four hours later and it was almost evening on that day when I was carried into the village. This was an unusual event, to say the least, for the inhabitants. There was great excitement as the women and children clustered around the stretcher to look at me.

I was in bad shape. It was plain to see that I would need help, but the village had absolutely none to offer. There was no doctor and no medicines, but they would do their best, Faustino promised Peron. The village men had a meeting and Faustino, as chief, proposed the plan that was ultimately adopted. While they would help, they had to protect themselves as well. Accordingly, I would be hidden in the bush outside the village and someone from the village would stay with me at all times. Faustino and two others would guide Peron to Paulis to seek help and return for me. By this time, I was in such poor shape that I was not thinking clearly at all, but I seem to remember trying to make clear that if they helped us, my government would help and protect them. I have no idea whether or not I ever got that across. In my mind, I remember giving Faustino my Walther (Peron says he did) and giving his son my Omega wristwatch. I guess that, at the time, I would have offered the Brooklyn Bridge if I could have. I strained to understand and participate in the planning. I could not do it. I remember only snatches of the meeting. Peron made the decisions for us and he was right on all counts. Trying to take me along, to carry me for almost 300 kilometres, would have been folly. It was unlikely I would have survived such an ordeal.

They carried me into the bush away from the village. I don't know how far. I was laid on the ground in a crude lean-to. It wasn't much, but it really didn't need to be. I wasn't a particularly demanding patient. It would protect me from rain and a small fire seemed to keep out bugs. Moreover it had been selected not for its patient comfort features, but because it was in an out-of-the-way location. No one wanted a Simba patrol to discover me anywhere near, much less in, the village. All would suffer if that happened. Someone came to care for me although I have only fleeting memories of it as my periods of consciousness became fewer and fewer.

I vaguely remember being washed off with warm water, and someone cleaning my burns – with a knife. The bees were gone, but smaller worm-like bugs had got into my burns while I lay on the ground in the bush before Peron and the villagers got back to me. Except for my hands, the bugs were easily dealt with. Just scratch them off, or out of, the wounds. My hands were much more painful. Whoever it was systematically dug out every bug he or she could see. The effort had predictable, to American hand surgeons, results on the extensor tendons of my fingers. Many were cut and no longer function. Lest that sound like a criticism, it most definitely is not. I survived and I do still have fingers that work. Yes, it played hell with my jump shot, but I still play tennis. I will always be grateful to that individual.

When it was judged that my wounds had been thoroughly cleaned (Lord knows what else might have been used), the village 'doctor', or 'medicine man', applied a grease or salve-like substance onto all of my burns. I am vague in describing it because, to this day, I don't really know what it was. It turned bluish-black, hardened and became a sort of protective coating over my burns. Essentially, it prevented loss of fluids or infection that are the greatest dangers for someone who has suffered severe burns. In due course, doctors at the National Burn Center in San Antonio, Texas, would discover how effective this 'primitive' tribal treatment had been. There is little question that it saved my life. But time was the key question. Was I strong enough, physically and mentally, to hang on till Peron got to Paulis and returned with help? Some, looking at my condition, may have had doubts. I had none. I simply would not die in this rotten Congo, I decided. I was determined to hold on against any odds. But I was to be tested – severely and soon.

They took off the morning of 19 February, two days after we had crashed. Peron left my parachute with the villagers with instructions for them to spread it out on the ground when a helicopter came for me. He was optimistic. Faustino had requisitioned three bicycles. Two other villagers, Balde and Christie, would be making the trip with them. It could be dangerous, they all knew. They would, at all costs, avoid any encounter with a Simba patrol or outpost. Great care would have to be taken when anywhere near towns or villages. They would move at night through areas they thought suspect. Water would come from streams and wells that they passed and food would be from the bush or purchased from villagers they could trust – other Azandes. Although lacking in formal education, Faustino was intelligent and resourceful. Peron, of course, knew nothing about the area so he deferred to his judgement. In the end, we would both owe our lives to Faustino.

They started and finished the trip using the same tactic. Balde, sharp-eyed and alert, rode ahead. He was responsible for spotting any danger, avoiding it, and warning those behind to take care. He periodically left 'safety' signals on the trail or road for the others to follow. Peron was amazed that the signals could ever be seen. A rock, a broken twig or branch, leaves arranged just so, or some other indication were regularly placed along the road or trail. Peron almost never saw one, but Faustino always did – according to Faustino. Faustino had my Walther 9 mm and Peron was carrying a .45 automatic. Neither Balde nor Christie was armed. Peron and Faustino didn't talk much, but there was good rapport between them – despite the fact that there was an almost constant high level of stress. When a given situation required a decision, Faustino made it. No one questioned his authority and leadership. Christie followed behind making sure that nothing could come upon them from the rear that would present a problem. Nothing ever did, but they never changed their tactic and Christie always followed behind.

Big Bill, in Bunia, sounded the alert when we did not return on 17 February. No one knew, of course, what had happened. Some feared the worst. Early on 18 February, planes were out looking for us. Peron remembers seeing search planes. But without a survival kit or radio he was unable to make any contact or signal his position.

Russ had no radio, but a message was dropped to him on the shore of Lake Albert and he immediately broke off his lake patrols and drove back to Bunia to help organize search efforts. Runners were sent into the bush to visit distant villages to see if anyone had word. None was forthcoming. Big Bill knew the areas we had hoped to look at, but knew nothing about the storm that had blown us off course. Moreover, portions of the area were fairly mountainous and therefore hard to search. That both planes were missing was odd and even more worrying. The search continued for several days. Needle in a haystack. Hope dimmed.

As far as Peron could understand, our crash site and the village were not far at all from the Sudanese border – fifteen or twenty miles. As they made their way west and south towards Paulis, the terrain along the border gave way to more openness and even plains. The rain forest became grassland. The reason being that the lower river basin to the west has steadily changed as the altitude above sea level increases. They covered as much distance as they could, riding as much as possible and carrying or pushing the bicycles whenever the way was impassable. Peron doesn't know how they found their way. They carried only Tunon's maps and they were of no use. Had they, or one of them, made the trip to Paulis before? Were they questioning villagers along the way when they, infrequently, purchased food? Were there road signs that he didn't see? He never knew.

But they never hesitated. They moved for as long each day as they could. Some days, of course, were better than others. Twice they were able to use canoes to cover substantial distances with minimal physical effort. Bicycles loaded on the back, they floated or paddled easily for hours at a time. While physically it allowed them rest, it seemed to increase the stress. Peron said he felt more vulnerable on the rivers, because they would have little warning of possible danger. Still, it was a welcome respite for his body – his legs in particular. Peron was young and strong, but not used to constant physical exertion. He never lagged though and maintained the pace set by Faustino.

A few times, they rode through enormous plantations. They were beautiful but almost deserted. Here it was easy to find food and water without much fear for their safety. The few natives who were there hated and feared the Simbas and were willing to help them. Peron was struck by the amount of effort that must have been required to clear and plant the plantations.

They usually slept in the bush, although occasionally they found empty huts that they were able to use. Fatigue caused sleep to come easily despite constant concerns for their safety. It was well known that the Simbas did nothing at night or in the rain because they thought their magic wouldn't work. The four of them reminded themselves of that and all felt reassured.

Their few contacts with local villagers along their way were limited almost exclusively to other Azande. Faustino would speak with elders or chiefs and let them know who he was – brother of a Simba-slain chieftain. Help was always forthcoming. Food was made available and safe areas for sleep were indicated to them. It was a smart move on their part.

The days passed and they continued their trip; for Peron, it was an escape to safety. Three, four, then five days of good progress covering chunks of territory without incident. Only a few times did Balde warn them of traffic that they wished to avoid. If possible, they didn't even want to be seen on the road. On those occasions, they would simply melt into the bush alongside the road or trail and wait for the traffic to pass. Peron felt that they had been covering 35 to 40 kilometres each day, but still had no feeling for how far they were from Paulis. Faustino's response to his questions was always, 'Not too far.' They had not yet seen any sign of the Simbas. So much the better. A few times they had been worried and twice they rode for a few hours at night to move beyond an area of concern. By the end of the fifth day, Peron was feeling hopeful.

Late in the afternoon on 24 February, the sixth day of travel, they came upon an outpost about twenty miles east of Paulis. It was manned by whites – Belgians and mercenaries. Balde spotted it first and actually rode back to meet Juan and Faustino so he could tell them the good news. All three were very happy and greatly relieved. They had made it. They rode together towards the outpost and, to be safe, Faustino approached it first. Soon he waved joyfully and all four entered the compound.

As soon as they understood who these four men were, the men manning the outpost were also excited. By then, hope of our survival was dim. Peron immediately began to explain that I was still in the bush. They knew of our crash and would certainly help, but could do nothing until morning. It was almost that time of day when darkness falls very abruptly, as it does year round near the equator. Peron was disappointed, but confident now that he would be coming back to get me. Although there were no comforts to speak of, knowing that they were safe, all four travellers slept well that night.

Morning brought lots of activity. Immediately after breakfast, including hot coffee, Peron, Faustino and their two companions were driven into Paulis by truck. The truck ride took about an hour. Word of their arrival preceded them via a single sideband set. They went directly to the airfield where there was a small contingent similar to the one at Bunia. Several planes were positioned there and the support crews and pilots were living in Paulis. There were a couple of Agency air operations officers there. They had direct communications by radio with Leopoldville. The Cuban pilots greeted Peron, warmly expressing their delight that he had survived the ordeal. They asked about Juan Tunon and Peron told them what he knew. By this time, the air operations officers had joined in and began firing questions at Peron about my condition and whereabouts. Peron carefully explained everything that had happened. He included high praise for Faustino, Balde and Christie, who were at that point standing off to one side. One of the air officers went over to thank all three villagers personally. We will be helping you as well, he told them. Peron emphasized that my condition was poor and urged that a helicopter take off immediately to return to the village to pick me up. The only choppers there were Belgian and the rescue needed to be authorized. There followed a flurry of cables back and forth to Leopoldville. And in Leopoldville there were phone calls to the Belgian air command. 'Yes, of course, immediately,' was the Belgian response. And the station flashed cables to Washington saying that my whereabouts were known, but that I had been badly hurt. No one knew how badly. Paulis had the necessary approvals within two hours. Preparations for the chopper rescue mission were already under way. Peron and Faustino were crouched over maps with the Belgian pilots and Agency air operations officers trying to locate the area of Faustino's village. This was not an easy task but they were able to narrow it down and felt confident they would find it. They decided that Faustino, Balde and Christie would fly in the helicopter (their first flight) and Peron would fly in the back of an accompanying T-28. The original plan had Peron in the chopper as well, but the Cuban pilots persuaded him to fly overhead in a T-28. None of them had any confidence in the 'banana' that the Belgians were flying.

Peron's description of my condition so concerned the air operations chief in Paulis that he requested a C-130 be dispatched immediately from Leopoldville to be standing by when I was brought into Paulis. With all preparations made and approvals from Leopoldville in hand, the two aircraft took off just before noon on 25 February – eight days after we had crashed.

Heading east and north, the two aircraft flew for forty-five minutes with both Peron and Faustino straining to pick up some landmark that would put them on course. They flew over small towns they had passed while riding their bicycles and knew they were headed in the right direction. It was Faustino who finally saw a village, an intersection of two roads, a river bridge, and familiar sights, even from the air, which led him to his village. Overhead, Peron was cheering and shouting into his headset. They could see a parachute being spread out on the ground by villagers who had seen the chopper and T-28, but the clearing it was in looked small and the chopper pilot was hesitant. There was no way to signal the villagers to change it and nothing that much better in sight. What to do? He decided to land. Peron, watching intently, sensed the hesitation and was pleased to see the chopper start its final descent.

Moments later he was shocked to witness the helicopter crash on landing. One of the rotor blades had struck a heavy tree limb and the craft rolled over. No one was hurt, but it was clear that the chopper was too badly damaged to fly again. Cursing himself for not following his instinct not to land, the pilot used his emergency radio to communicate with the T-28 flying overhead. He reported the accident and asked that a second chopper be sent in to pick us all up. All were frustrated and disappointed. Above, Peron and the pilot of his T-28 had no choice but to return to Paulis to await the replacement helicopter.

Meanwhile, my condition had been steadily deteriorating. Someone might well have been with me all the time in the lean-to, but I wouldn't have known it. I had only fleeting moments of consciousness and each seemed more painful than the last. There was no relief. I had learned the Swahili word for water, 'mai', and that was all I could think of. They tried to feed me – eggs and pineapple, I think. I couldn't eat and what I did manage to get down I retched up almost immediately. I was indeed being tested and my body wasn't liking the test at all. I had strange, even bizarre, delusions. I imagined myself on a giant roller-coaster careering up and down its track. Going down was awful because there were intense flames and the pain would be excruciating until the roller-coaster came back out of the flames and up again. A tall, menacing African stood by the tracks and jabbed at me with his spear each time I passed. More pain. This would go on and on and on. I must have thrashed around because hands would come to restrain and calm me. I had no idea of the passage of time. I felt myself slipping away and was determined to hang on. My body was down to its last cells and I clung to them as to life itself. Gradually, at some point, I don't know when, it was as if cells I had lost floated by and I grabbed them. I was fighting to make myself whole again, to save my life, although I didn't really know it at the time. Periods of any sort of consciousness were diminishing. It all depended now on whether or not Peron made it out and when he got back. Days were passing in a fog. I had no knowledge of the arrival and crash of the Belgian helicopter.

The chopper crash prompted concern, frustration and disappointment in Paulis, and after it was reported, in Leopoldville and Washington. Peron, who had been so close, in his mind, to getting me out, was truly saddened by this unexpected turn of events. I can only imagine that Faustino, Balde and Christie must have thought it a rather unbecoming way to return to their village – rolling and scrambling out of an overturned helicopter. Belgian air command immediately authorized a second flight to pick up their pilots and me. It was too late that day to return so the flight was readied for early the next day. A C-130 had arrived from Leopoldville with a doctor. It would be standing by. With the location of the village now known and with an experienced and unhurt Belgian pilot on the ground, all were confident that the second effort would be a success.

And it was. Early on 26 February, a Belgian helicopter, also with armed personnel aboard and also accompanied by a T-28 fighter, landed at the village to pick up the crew of the first chopper and me. I was in terrible shape, according to a colleague who was on the chopper. Whatever it was that the village 'doctor' had put on my burns had hardened enough to form a coating over my burns. That was good although no one there at the time realized it. The bluish-black colour looked ominous indeed. My face was a mess as were my hands. I don't know what clothes I still had on or what covered me. But I was definitely alive.

I was put into the chopper and we left for the return trip to Paulis. I fear that the rushed departure, over concern for my precarious state, precluded adequate thanks to Faustino and the villagers for what they had done. I was unable to express anything. And despite what I owe them, I have never had the chance to meet or thank those who did so much to save my life.

I was immediately transferred from the helicopter into the C-130 for the long flight to Leopoldville and a hospital. How he managed to be there at that time, I don't know, but Russ was there and he was helping to carry the stretcher. He later told me that while they were carrying me from the helicopter to the C-130, a Belgian priest, with the kindest of intentions I'm sure, approached the stretcher. They stopped briefly. The priest looked at me and concluded that the blue-black paste was likely gangrene. And considering how I looked, it was very doubtful that I would make it to Leopoldville alive. Without further ado, he proceeded, right there on the tarmac, to give me the last rites. Russ told me that I raised my head and said, 'I am not one of your guys, and I'm not ready to say any last words.'

I have no recollection of that incident, which would have passed unnoticed but for a crucifix on a silver chain that the priest put around my neck. About two weeks later, at the National Burn Center in Texas, I was being moved to a ward from intensive care. The nurse wondered what she should do with my crucifix that had been hanging on the foot of my bed. I was puzzled. 'I'm not Catholic', I replied, 'and I don't have a crucifix.' 'That's strange,' she said, 'it's the only thing you had on you when you got here.' It was a mystery to us all and it was only when, weeks later, Russ visited from Washington and I happened to mention the crucifix, that the mystery was solved. There remained the question of what to do with the crucifix. It was in fact quite beautiful. I spoke with the same nurse, who had told me that one of her daughters was in a convent. I asked if I could give it to her. She was touched and said yes. It was done. I have since regretted parting with that crucifix, which was given to me in such a sensitive and kind gesture.

I now know that Faustino gained much stature from his adventure. He returned several times to Paulis, where he was given weapons and ammunition with which to defend himself and his village. Had the Simbas become aware of what had happened? I still don't know. But Faustino was taking no chances. He soon joined a group of Spanish mercenaries operating in the area of the village and received training, a weapon and a uniform. Juan has a picture of Faustino in his uniform and he looks every inch a fighter one would not want to mess with.

The Agency arranged to air-drop a planeload of medicines, tools and clothing for the village. It was well received and understood to be, as intended, a gesture of our thanks for what they did to save my life. And I add my thanks to all you taxpayers who funded the effort.

Peron rested for a while in Leopoldville and then resumed flying until the operation was terminated several months later. Many thought he would hang it up after his narrow escape, but he never considered stopping. With a lust for flying, he was later to fly for companies in the Canary Islands, Puerto Rico, Aruba and Miami over the next three decades.

Several months after the February accident, Big Bill Wyrozemski was transferred to Albertville, still on the Congo eastern border but south of Bunia. Shortly after his arrival in Albertville, and concerned about a possible rebel force moving towards Albertville from the west, Bill called Leopoldville on the single sideband and was given approval to make a short reconnaissance of the area. He had been instructed not to go alone but no one was readily available and he ignored the instruction. Returning, alone, to Albertville in his Land Rover, Bill rounded a turn and was hit head on by a Congolese army truck speeding, on the wrong side of the road, in the opposite direction. The impact killed him. It was an ironic ending for a man, an ex-Polish army officer, who had sought out, and survived, many dangerous situations during his life, including flying a Spitfire in the Battle of Britain and, it was rumoured, a B-26 at the Bay of Pigs. Peron piloted the transport plane that brought Bill's body back to Leopoldville.

At Louvainium Hospital in Leopoldville, doctors took stock of my condition. Very poor indeed was the conclusion. Apparently, an American doctor took one look, saw no hope and left the room. He reported his conclusion to a senior Embassy officer who was standing outside my room. Russ, who had accompanied me all the way to the hospital, was also standing in the hall outside my room and overheard the American doctor's comments. Russ refused to accept that conclusion and was approaching the American doctor to voice strong opinions to the contrary when a second doctor approached. An older Belgian doctor with much experience in the Congo, he realized that after nine days in the bush without care my body needed help. That was an understatement. Russ was delighted. The Belgian doctor proceeded to put IVs into both my ankles. He then gave me everything he could think of. Antibiotics and nutrients literally flowed into my body. It welcomed them with open arms. It was a boost I sorely needed and it no doubt helped prepare me for the long flight to the National Burn Center at Texas that awaited me – although I didn't know it. Thanks to the Department of Defense, an Air Force 707 was en route with a 'burn team' of a doctor, nurses, and corpsmen, to pick me up.

The pilot of the 707 later told my father that, mid-way across the Atlantic, as we were heading for the north-east tip of Brazil, my condition and vital signs improved slightly. No one knew why. It was probably, I think, the result of all that the Belgian doctor had pumped into me during my short stay in Leopoldville. The changes caused the prognosis to shift from 'really lousy' to 'he might just make it'. The doctor reported the changes to the pilot, who decided to fly straight through to Texas. The odds for me were not good but my condition was improved and stable. We arrived in Texas late on a Saturday evening. It was 27 February 1965.

TWO

REHABILITATION

1965–67

Tim Miller had just finished a can of beer and was relaxing with some team mates after a basketball game one late Saturday afternoon in 1965. He was a young Army doctor putting in his military service and, as a plastic surgeon, had been assigned to the United States Army's Surgical Research Unit (SRU) at Brooke Army Hospital on Fort Sam Houston, in San Antonio, Texas. SRU was the heart of the National Burn Center that, at the time, was considered the best in the United States, if not the world, and patients were not solely from the military.

Although he was a captain in the Army, Tim was not a military man. As a doctor, however, and a plastic surgeon, it was already clear that he was going to be one of the best and he later served a tour with Special Forces in Vietnam. He was soft-spoken, but tough, and willing to put his principles on the line.

That afternoon Tim was on call. Normally he wouldn't have had even one beer, but he knew the routine for weekend calls. If you were needed, they would call and schedule your flight time – usually two to four hours ahead. Then the flight would take several more hours. Thus there was a minimum of four, most likely eight, hours before he would get to a patient. It wasn't going to be that way this time.

Just after the game, Tim got a call. Routinely, it would be the Fort Sam Houston duty officer, who would tell him when and where he was going. Instead, a colonel identified himself and said crisply that Tim would be 'flying somewhere'. He was vague.

That was not usual. In every other instance, he had known where he was headed, when he was leaving, and what sort of aircraft he would be flying in. The type of aircraft was determined by the distance between the Burn Center and the patient. The colonel did make it quite clear that the helicopter, which would take him to Lackland Air Force base to catch a larger plane, would be landing on the pad in front of Brooke Hospital in twenty minutes. Then, abruptly, he hung up.

'Something's going on and I don't know what,' Tim told his friends as he grabbed his stuff and headed for his car.

Fortunately, the hospital was nearby and he was there within the twenty minutes. Normally, the helicopter was late and he would arrive and then wait for it – sometimes for a long period. On this occasion, while Tim was parking, he could see that a chopper was already on the pad with rotors turning. This time they were waiting for him.

The colonel he had talked to minutes before was there and motioned Tim into the chopper. Sergeant Hawkins, who would accompany Tim as corpsman, arrived at almost the same time. Things moved fast. Tim and Hawk jumped on board and the chopper took off.

'What the hell's going on?' Tim shouted over the noise of the ascending chopper.

'Sure don't know, sir,' was the response. 'But I have a medical kit for you and some hospital clothes as well.'

Tim changed in the helicopter. He asked the pilot where they were going, thinking perhaps that it was somewhere outside of San Antonio. The only information they had was that they were headed for Lackland. Hawk looked at Tim and shrugged his shoulders.

Moments after they landed, an Air Force major came up to Tim and, taking him to one side, told him that they were about to receive a patient, a 'missionary' who had been injured in Africa.

Within four or five minutes, a grey 707 landed. It had no markings of any kind and taxied up to the ramp next to the helicopter. Tim immediately boarded the plane, which was gutted. There were maybe eight seats, and two stretchers were attached to the wall. I was lying on one of them. The doctor on the plane, very fatigued from the long flight, started briefing Tim on my condition. Tim listened intently.

Then he introduced himself to me. According to him, my first words were, 'I made it out of there.' Tim, of course, had no idea where 'there' was, but could see that I was in poor shape. Wondering just how coherent I was, he identified himself again. Apparently, my briefcase had accompanied me and I was concerned about it. Lord knows why because I'm sure there was nothing important inside – maybe my passport and some personal letters. I never carried classified material in the Congo.

The interior of the plane was dark and when Tim first looked at me, he thought I was black because of the paste on my burns. Maybe he half expected a missionary from Africa to be a black man. Soon he realized that this was not the case. The briefing went on. Tim knew immediately that my condition was very serious. He wondered what had been put on my burns and by whom. The odds were about 30–70 that I'd make it, the briefing doctor concluded.

'But he seems strong,' he said.

'Bloody right,' I would have said if I had really been strong. In fact, I don't remember saying anything at all. I remember nothing of my first encounter with Tim. But it was the start of a relationship that would still be alive and well more than three decades later.

I was transported to the helicopter where Tim recalls trying to reassure me and let me know what was happening. He didn't get much response.

When we landed on the helipad in front of the main entrance to Brooke Army Hospital, there were quite a few lights. That was unusual for a Saturday night. Major General Snyder, Commander of the hospital, was waiting for us. Tim remembers there was lots of brass.

Immediately after the helicopter had landed, General Snyder, Colonel Jack Moncrief (Chief of the SRU) and another man in civilian clothes (who was not introduced) talked to Tim. They disclosed that I was not really a missionary. They didn't provide Tim with any further explanation, but made it clear to him that for the moment I would continue to be a missionary for identification purposes. Someone told Tim that the 707 flight had been authorized by the Secretary of Defense. There was no further explanation. That explained all the brass, Tim thought.

Within a few hours, several other people arrived on the scene. Among them was Phil DeCaro, an officer I knew from my tour in Laos. Phil had crashed and been burned while serving in Laos, although not as seriously. He was there to see how I was doing. It seemed to Tim that Phil and the others were all dressed by the same fashion consultant: bland suits, ties (an occasional paisley) and shined shoes, usually wingtips. Smiles, but not sincere. Analytical. Sizing him up. Who is this guy? Has he ever taken care of a burn patient before?

The message was clear, according to Tim. 'Fuck up and you are in it, boy, well above your knees.'

When news of my rescue reached Headquarters, Dick Helms, the Deputy Director for Plans (now called Operations), went straight to John McCone, the Director of the Agency.

'The officer missing in the Congo has been found,' he told the Director, 'but his condition is very poor. The only real hope', Helms went on, 'is to get him to the National Burn Center in Texas as soon as possible. We need an Air Force plane to pick him up as soon as possible in Leopoldville.'

McCone decided to call Robert MacNamara, the then Secretary of Defense. MacNamara asked only one question.

'Is he still alive?'

'He is,' McCone replied, 'and he'll make it if we can get him to Texas.'

'Then we go,' said MacNamara.

News of the crash had reached my parents in New Jersey the day after it had happened. An Agency officer went to my parents' home. It was about seven in the evening. He knocked and my mother opened the door. He introduced himself, showed his credentials, and asked to speak with my father. Mom sensed right away that something was wrong. 'Mr Holm has gone bowling,' she told him. 'May I help?' He wanted to speak to Mr Holm, he repeated. Could my mother please explain where the bowling alley was? She did and he left.

Half an hour later, having been unable to find the bowling alley, he returned. 'May I wait here until Mr Holm returns?' he asked my mother. My mother said yes and the visitor sat down in our living room. Mom went back to the family room. My younger sister and younger brother were, by this time, also worried that something was wrong. My father came home soon after and the officer gave them the news of their eldest son.

'Dick is missing in the Congo as of yesterday,' he told them. 'His plane did not return from a routine mission and we do not know where he is. We are making every effort to find him and the two pilots he was with.'

The news hit hard. My mother's first reaction was that there must be some mistake because she thought I was in Morocco. Dad then explained to her that this wasn't true and we hadn't wanted her to worry. This didn't help. My decision to mislead (lie to) her had backfired. It had been a foolish decision because, if anything, things now were worse because of the shock she suffered. She cried, as did the others. The officer assured my father that he would receive periodic reports on the progress of the search.

The days passed slowly for them. Every two or three days, someone would call to report no success. My family suffered but kept their hopes alive. Finally the call came with news that I had been found, but that I was seriously injured and was en route to a hospital in Texas. The Agency flew my parents there the next day, a truly sensitive and generous gesture. Yes, I had been asked to take on a tough job. But when the chips were on the table, the Agency left no stone unturned in their efforts to support and help in any way possible. I have never forgotten.

My parents were met in San Antonio by an Agency representative and driven directly to Brooke Hospital, where I had arrived the night before. It was a Sunday afternoon. They were ushered into the office of Colonel Moncrief, Chief of the SRU. He briefed them carefully about my condition, trying to prepare them for seeing me. He made a special point of mentioning the black substance on my burns. 'We don't know what it is,' he said, 'but I'm starting to think it helped him a lot.'

He brought them to my bed in the intensive care ward. I really did look pretty bad. So bad, in fact, that my mother was overcome with emotion. Dad spoke to me and the effect on me was both mentally and physically noticeable. The nurse and the doctor were pleased to see that I was mentally alert enough to recognize his voice. I knew I was talking to my dad. It was as if he had jerked me back into consciousness. According to him, I asked a couple of questions: Where am I? How did I get here? What day is it? They reassured me and said everything was going to be all right. My mother spoke to me as well, but I do not remember her being there. That was the good part. The bad part was to come soon.

In my mind, I suddenly felt safe. I had made it. My father was talking so I was somewhere with help at hand. I could relax, rest and sleep. I was exhausted from fighting and had been straining both mentally and physically to hang on. Now that struggle was over, I gave in to the fatigue that hung so heavily on my whole body and almost had a relapse. My vital signs wavered dangerously and my condition weakened ominously shortly after my parents' visit. The hospital reacted immediately, but from that point on it was to be all uphill. It would be a very long hill.

Tim still didn't know who I was or anything about me except that I had crashed in the Congo about ten days ago and had had minimal medical treatment. His first priority was to change those 30–70 odds. I was taken straight to intensive care, where he supervised a variety of steps designed to strengthen my condition, and IVs again to fight possible infection as well as to give my body nourishment. My reserves were, by that time, almost drained. It's hard to say how much longer I could have lasted in the Congo village until Peron's return – probably not very many more days. I was young and strong. I had been in good physical condition. Given the assignment I had accepted, I felt I had to be. Still, I was lucky. There are limits. I wouldn't have wanted to push them much further.

Tim stayed with me almost continuously for more than twenty-four hours. He did everything he could and, gradually, the odds shifted in my favour. Even the near disaster when I had talked to my father didn't change a steady trend of improvement in my condition. I was going to make it. Tim had done it. He is yet another individual to whom I owe very much. The list gets longer and longer.

As the days passed and I was moved out of intensive care, Tim and I developed a strong relationship for reasons not entirely clear to either of us. We had much in common having both been active in sports our whole lives, but there was more to it than that. For me, of course, there was the fact that he had saved my life. Still, there is something else. I cannot really articulate what it is, but it has lasted. To this day, I know I could count on him and I'm sure he feels the same way. As he lives in California and I live in Virginia (or elsewhere in the world before I retired), our contacts have been infrequent, but that hasn't changed the chemistry. It's still there.

After that first visit, my father was taken by the arm by one of the doctors in the room and led out into the hallway. The doctor introduced himself as an eye surgeon. There was no small talk.

'My colleagues and I have concluded', he said simply, 'that it will be necessary to remove your son's left eye.'

It was another terrible shock for my poor father.

'Why?' he countered. 'How could you know so soon? Can't they treat it?'

'That won't be possible,' the surgeon said. 'Either the trauma or the lack of treatment for such a long time has caused a perforation and an infection of the eyeball. There is a danger that the other eye could be affected if we don't act now.'

The doctors had, of course, found the contact lens when they surgically opened my singed eyelids. They realized right away what had happened. A debate followed over whether the lens had been the cause of my loss of the left eye or if the reason my right eye had survived the splash of burning gasoline had been the other lens. I understand that some research papers were written on the case. It is, of course, academic to me.

The doctor emphasized that every minute counted. They strongly recommended immediate surgery to remove any risk to my right eye. In the end, my father had no choice. He signed the papers, but with great regret. He knew what a loss I would suffer. He told my mother and she cried – again. I have always regretted the pain my crash caused them.

My left eye was removed. I didn't know it. The next morning the eye doctor and my father told me about the operation and why it had been necessary. Outwardly, my reaction was one of resignation. How could I question the eye surgeon's decision? Especially after the fact. Inwardly, it hurt. I thought of the contact lens that I had been unable to remove. And I thought of the sun visor on my flight helmet that I had raised during our final approach. Lifting that visor gave me the last clear look at something that I've ever had.

My dad felt awful, I could tell. My mother emphasized that there had been no choice. I agreed with her. I questioned the doctor about my remaining eye. I tried to brace myself for his response.

'It's in good shape', he said, 'except for the cornea that has been scarred. Once the trauma has subsided, we will be able to do a corneal transplant and you'll regain your vision.' It wasn't going to be that easy, but it was awfully good news.

My condition improved and stabilized and Tim had to clean my wounds in order to start treatment. That meant removing the blue-black paste the Congo 'doctor' had put on my burns. That proved to be a difficult and extremely painful task. Burn patients at that time (still do for all I know) routinely faced a process called 'debriding', which involved the removal of all burned and damaged skin from the areas that had been burned. This was done to completely cleanse the affected areas and thereby reduce (hopefully eliminate) the possibility of infection. It was also the required first step in preparation for skin transplants. In my case, because of the paste, debriding was an exceedingly tough and most unpleasant process. Although still sedated to some extent I'm sure, I was by this time mentally alert. My mother, bless her for the love she demonstrated, had elected to stay with me during my early period of recovery. My father had to return to New Jersey. Mom stayed in a base guest house and visited me for most of every day. She came to dread the debriding sessions as much as I did. Actually, there couldn't have been more than five or six, but it seemed as if they lasted for weeks.

The first debriding sessions prompted another mini-crisis. A corpsman had rolled a gurney next to my bed and said it was time to go to the tub. My debriding was all done in a large tub of warm water, which made it easier, I guess, to do the cleaning. All serious cases were done in the tubs and since I had suffered burns over about 35 per cent of my body, I qualified as a serious case. Lucky me. The corpsman picked me up and put me on the gurney.

As I could not see him, I said, 'You must be a pretty big man.'

'What makes you say that?' he asked.

'You picked me up like I was a little doll,' I responded.

'Well, fella, you only weigh ninety-eight pounds,' he said.

I was dumbfounded. Absolutely shocked. I had weighed 165 pounds when we crashed a couple of weeks earlier. How could that be?

'Is that true, Mom?' I asked my mother, who was sitting by my bed.

'Yes, it is, and now that you are better we just have to get you to eat a lot.'

'Don't worry about that,' I told her. I could hardly believe I had lost so much weight. No wonder my parents had been shocked. I resolved there and then to regain my weight and strength as fast as possible.

When the corpsman wheeled me off and put me into the debriding tub, the warm water actually felt pretty good.

Tim arrived after I had been soaking for about ten minutes. He explained what had to be done and why. Then he started debriding, which means that he took a pair of tweezers and picked off dead or charred skin. The paste on my burns just wouldn't come off, even after having been soaked for fifteen minutes. It seemed to have a quality that made it stick tenaciously. Instead of picking, Tim had to pull it off. It hurt. And I told Tim that it hurt. Tim was torn. He knew I was suffering, but he also knew it was imperative that he get the burns cleaned. He ordered a pain shot for me. I was raised up out of the tub enough to get a shot in my butt as my arms had burns and were very thin. It helped, but only until he started pulling off dead skin again. Nasty pain.

'It isn't working, it still hurts,' I told him.

'But I gave you a painkiller,' he said.

'What I'm telling you, Doctor, is that it still hurts.'

'I'm sorry,' Tim said. 'I'll try to be careful.' He knew it was causing me a lot of pain and he was frustrated, but he had to continue. We laboured through several debriding sessions and Tim finally announced that he had finished. It goes without saying that I was pleased. Tim was too. First because I could relax a bit, but also because the burns looked so clean. There was no infection at all. Whatever the paste was, it had done wonders for me. The next step was to be skin transplants.

As the premiere burn treatment facility in the world, Brooke Hospital welcomed, on any given day, a steady stream of visiting medical personnel and doctors interested in learning about the treatments employed there. Many of the visitors were from abroad. One afternoon, before I was debrided, I was resting in my bed and chatting with my mother, and a couple of foreign doctors were being escorted through my ward. When they got to me, Tim briefly summarized my situation: recently arrived; plane crash in Africa; serious burns.

One of the visiting doctors, an Ethiopian, said, 'Oh, I see you use the same thing for bad burns that is sometimes used in Africa.'

'Pardon me?' Tim queried.

'I mean the black substance on his burns,' the Ethiopian said.

'Do you know what it is?' Tim and his colleagues asked.

'Not really,' he responded. 'It's used mainly in rural areas. It's a tribal remedy that has been handed down for years and years, maybe centuries.'

'Do you know what's in it?' Tim asked.

'No idea,' the Ethiopian said. 'I've heard that part of it comes from a boiled snake,' he added.

At least this was a lead. Tim told the Ethiopian that doctors at the Burn Center credited it with having saved my life by preventing infection and dehydration and thanked him for the piece of the puzzle he had provided. Still they wanted very much to know more about the makeup of the substance. Several months later, two Air Force doctors were dispatched to Africa to investigate what it was. They were able to obtain samples and, apparently, a breakdown included snake oil, tree bark and herbs. Some of the herbs could not be specifically identified. Whatever it was, I love it!

My first skin transplant wasn't all that much fun either. Nobody really explained to me what the procedure was going to involve. Probably just as well. They rolled my gurney into the operating room at about 7 a.m., and I just lay there, waiting for whatever was next. I was apprehensive and couldn't see, but I was listening carefully and I could sense activity in the room.

Several people were chatting. I was appalled to hear that they were talking about a picnic the previous day. What the hell is this? I was thinking. Who cares about the bloody picnic? A delicate operation is about to start. Who's in charge here anyway? They must have thought that I had already had a sedative and was in la la land. Finally, I could not refrain from speaking.

'If the picnic talk is finished,' I said, 'are we gonna get serious about this operation?'

There was no response to my question, but someone put a rubber mask over my mouth and nose. Ether flowed in – awful stuff – but after a couple of breaths I was out. It was later explained to me that tension in an operating room is often relieved by seemingly inane chatter. Apparently what I had heard was not all that unusual. Tim appeared on the scene some time after I had been put out.

I woke to find myself in intensive care again. My chest felt constrained. I was still groggy, but I tried to assess what had happened. I couldn't figure it out. I started to sit, but was gently restrained. A nurse asked me to just relax. So I did, until my head cleared and I could pee. Then I was taken back to the ward. Mom was waiting. She tried to conceal it, but I could tell that she was shocked when she saw me. Three corpsmen very carefully moved me from the gurney into my bed. They kept me flat and the reason soon became obvious. My entire upper torso, untouched by the flaming gasoline and therefore 'virgin' skin, had been stripped of skin that had then been used as grafts on my burns. The grafts were bandaged. The 'donor sites', as they are called, had simply been covered with a gauze-like material. Blood was seeping through everywhere and I truly was a bloody mess. No wonder she was shocked. Tim came and explained what he had done. It had all worked out well, he said, and I would be experiencing some discomfort. He was right on both counts, most especially the second. For 'discomfort' he meant real pain. As the anaesthetic wore off, I discovered that my chest hurt a lot. As the bleeding stopped and the drying started, it was painful to move. Deep breaths, sneezes, coughs, or laughter were to be avoided. Happily, the situation was shortlived. Within several days, the donor site had dried up and the gauze fell off. After about a year, one could hardly tell what had happened. It had all been for a good cause.

Not long after my arrival at Brooke Hospital, a psychiatrist came to see me. I immediately knew why he was there. The delusions that I had experienced in the Congo village had continued. Frequently, every night and sometimes two or three times a night, I was being chased by the same spear-carrying black man who had stabbed at me while I passed in the roller-coaster. Now, however,

I was able to run – but only fast enough to avoid being killed. He was able to stab me, often repeatedly, and I just couldn't get away. He always came when I was unconscious. I would groan (awful sounds I'm told), shout and thrash around in my bed. A nurse, or a corpsman, sometimes both and sometimes my mother, would calm me. My sleeping was fitful at best and the nurses dutifully recorded these incidents. A couple of times, I even dreaded going to sleep.

I knew perfectly well that this was all in my head. I knew that these were simply ugly nightmares that were the result of my experience in the Congo. Still, they were very real and they were causing me much distress. And they weren't helping my healing process at all. My mother, who had witnessed a couple of these scenes, was very concerned.

The psychiatrist was, in fact, very good. We talked over the whole episode and I tried to explain, as best I could, what had happened: roller-coaster ride and all. He listened carefully, as did my mother, who got frightened all over again. I had been close to death, we agreed.

Then it was his turn. He explained that I had no doubt been feeling quite insecure. No shit, I thought, but didn't say. He went on. These were just dreams and their frequency would gradually lessen. One day they would stop. The sooner the better, I hoped.

He was right. As I got stronger and the interval between operations lengthened, the nightmares grew less and less frequent.

The end of the black man with the spear was definitive. It came more than three years later. I was married and living in Hong Kong. My wife had experienced a couple of the nightmares, during which I would shout and roll around until she awakened me. I explained and she understood, but it bothered her nonetheless. Then one night, in my dream, he came again. But this time I had a pistol. I saw him in the bush and I fired. He was far away, but I saw him fall. It was all over. I have never had another dream about him. I don't know if I killed him or just wounded him, but he hasn't messed with me again.

For the two months I was at Brooke, I had lots of visitors. The Agency, wanting to help me work through the ordeal, gave at least one person per week round trip air tickets to San Antonio to visit me. It provided a link to reality. I enjoyed all of the visits immensely. They took my mind off of the crash.

David G., a real hero to be sure considering all that he went through while a hostage of the Simbas, visited and brought me up to date on events in the Congo. The Simba revolt was all but crushed by the spring of 1965. Like all the others, David was distressed at my condition.

I remember that my brother Bob, eleven months younger, came too. We used to have arm-wrestling contests. He suggested we continue the practice and challenged me. Mom protested. We laughed and I begged off saying I wasn't ready yet. In fact, I couldn't even hold a pencil at the time and was still being fed. My hands were incredibly weak. But I was about to start trying to walk again.

After weeks of being horizontal I had been taken to a pool to start using my legs again. Now I was ready. The corpsman carefully wrapped my legs, to protect against ruptures in my veins, and I got up. Bob was there to help me. He guided me around obstacles and corners, and we marched up and down the halls for as long as I could handle it. That became a daily ritual as I strove to regain strength. Having Bob there for the first effort was good. Dad came back to visit, as did an aunt and uncle from Houston and my Swedish grandmother. After she had listened to the whole story she said, 'I've always known that Vikings are tough, but this proves it.' My saintly mother spent from early March until early May at Brooke with me. She became well known and very popular in the Burn Center. Whenever I was asleep, being treated, or in the operating room, she would help others. Kind and sensitive, she was a godsend to many – as of course she was to me. I worried about home and my siblings, but she wouldn't leave. 'When you get better,' was always her response. When would that be? I wondered. I knew it had been a close call, but I just couldn't believe or accept that I'd be in the hospital more than a couple of months. I was anxious to be done with this problem, but had decided it was probably best to take things a day at a time. I was to discover that that had been a good decision.

One morning, my mother, who was sitting next to my bed as usual, gasped. That was not like her.

'What's wrong, Mom?' I asked.

'We got a bill,' she replied.

'What for?' I said.

'$23,400.'

'What's the bill for?

'We'll be in debt for the rest of our lives.' She could hardly speak.

For our family $23,400 was a lot of money. Calmly, I asked her to explain to me what she was talking about. She did. In our mail that day was an envelope from the United States Air Force. It was a bill – to me – for the cost of transporting me from the Congo to Texas. Actually, it was for the whole trip made by the 707 jetliner. From McGuire Air Base in New Jersey to Leopoldville, to Texas, and back to McGuire. At several hundred dollars per hour (I can't remember the exact figure), I owed the Air Force the grand total of $23,400. I couldn't help laughing. My mother didn't think it was funny at all.

It all stemmed from the fact that my voyage had been so unusual. All the Air Force knew was that the Secretary of Defense had sent them to Africa to get me. Very few people knew that the CIA was involved or that I was a CIA officer. My arrival had been shrouded in secrecy and unanswered questions. 'James Bond has been hurt,' was the rumour at Brooke. Bottom line was that when the Air Force's administrative people started processing everything, the only name they had for the bill was mine. So, I got the bill for costs incurred. In its own way, it was perfectly logical.

What to do? Call the Agency's representative in San Antonio, I told my mother. He will just send it to Headquarters. That's what she did and I never heard anything more about it. It was paid. One could easily ask how many countries in the world had, or would so willingly expend, the resources needed to make such a flight to rescue one wounded junior officer. The answer is one.

Two months at the Burn Center served to stabilize my condition and get the initial grafting of my burns accomplished. Regrettably, much remained to be done. We talked it over and decided that I ought to be transferred to Walter Reed Hospital in Washington. That decision taken, my mother, reluctantly, left me and returned to New Jersey. Walter Reed was only four hours' drive.

Oddly, I remain ambivalent towards the Burn Center. On the one hand, it clearly saved my life and started me on the road back. On the other hand, I could never see it in my mind once I had left and was unable to develop any real feelings towards the place. My ward, the debriding tubs, the hallways I trudged up and down are vague memories. There is no sharpness to them. I have never been back there.

The trip to Walter Reed was tedious. I said a few goodbyes at Brooke Hospital. Tim was on TDY somewhere so I didn't get to thank him or say goodbye. The flight was uneventful.

At Walter Reed in Washington, they wheeled me into Ward 9. The corpsman stopped at the nurses' desk to announce our arrival.

'Patient from Brooke in Texas,' he said.

'Yep, we've been expecting him,' the nurse replied. 'Just follow me.'

I noticed that, unlike the ward in Texas, it was quiet. They shifted me into the bed. The nurse explained how things would be in Walter Reed. I was surprised to learn that my ward, Ward 9, was the VIP ward normally reserved for senior military officers. She showed me my call button and instructed me not to get out of bed alone, even to use the bathroom.

This was to be the beginning of what, in medical terms, is called the 'reconstruction period'.

On my first weekend at Walter Reed my parents, my younger sister, Diann, and my youngest brother, Greg, came from New Jersey to visit me. Both were shocked. Greg, in particular, I could sense, was distressed at what he saw. It was a nice day and we got permission for me to take a walk in the small park just across the street from the hospital. I had to be led and Mom and Dad asked Greg to help me. He held my arm and tried to guide me, but since neither of us had any experience in this sort of thing, it wasn't long before I fell. It wasn't serious and I didn't get hurt, just a couple of scratches, but Greg was upset, thinking somehow that it had been his fault. I remember feeling bad for him, but there wasn't much I could do or say.

My biggest frustration then was time itself. I felt sidetracked and I wanted very much to get my recovery accomplished in as short a period as possible. I was still in denial about how seriously

I had been injured. In fact, I never did accept that I had been seriously hurt and would need time to get through it. I continually believed that in 'a few more months' I'd be out of the hospital and back to work. No one ever disabused me of that thought. I worked on blocks of time and added new blocks only because there was no other choice. I had never had any physical limitations and that made this situation all the worse. Still, I was hurt and was in hospital, and I had to deal with those two realities. I tried to use each day to make some little bit of progress so that I'd be that much nearer getting back to work. That approach got me through some tough periods.

As promised by Dr Duffy in that first conversation, my initial operation, one to remove scar tissue from the webs of my fingers, was on the Monday morning after I had arrived at the hospital. There would, unfortunately, be many more. (Counting big and small, local anaesthesia and general, I have had over thirty-five operations.) I was first on the day's list – I always liked that because I didn't have to lie around all morning waiting. It was the same routine as in Texas. I got a shot of something to start putting me into la la land. They wheeled me up to the hallway near the operating room that we would use. The anaesthetist stopped by and asked a few questions, routine ones. Then they wheeled me into the operating room. Sometimes, like that day, I would hear Dr Duffy – sometimes not. Early on, they put me out with a mask and gas. In later operations, they used an IV and at the appointed time just put in sodium pentathol, which knocks you (me anyway) out in the middle of a word – instantaneously. On this occasion it was the gas, which I never did like.

I woke up, as usual, in the post-op room. Vital signs are checked every quarter hour or so and you remain there until everything seems normal and you can urinate. I was always anxious, I don't really know why, to get out of the recovery room and back to Ward 9. As soon as I figured out the system, I would concentrate hard on getting lucid again and ask for the bottle (in the later stages) or a corpsman so I could pee. After you have done it enough times it becomes automatic. On this day, I quickly realized that something was unusual. It took me a moment to figure out why – my right hand, encased in a great ball of bandage was hanging from a mobile post next to the bed. Nothing hurt yet because

I was still groggy from the general anaesthetic. The pain would come soon enough. It was awkward to lie in bed with one arm suspended from a pole, but there was no choice. I had to keep my hand raised at all times so that blood pressure on the surgery just accomplished wouldn't mess anything up. It was hard to judge how long I stayed in post-op that day. Finally, the nurse announced that I was going back to Ward 9.

It was just about time for lunch so I had been in either the operating room or post-op for most of the morning. I didn't feel like eating anything so I passed on lunch. The nurse tried to arrange some pillows to make me comfortable, but with my hand hanging from the pole that wasn't easy to do. Gradually at first, but then in a rush, my hand started to hurt. It hurt a lot. Despite my wife's insistence to the contrary, I have always had a pretty high threshold for pain. This pain exceeded that threshold. So much so that I found and rang the buzzer for the nurse. She arrived promptly.

'Problem, Mr Holm?' she asked.

'My hand hurts like hell,' I blurted.

'Yeah, hand surgery is rough,' she said. 'I can give you a shot for the pain if you like.'

'Sooner the better,' I responded immediately. 'It's actually throbbing.'

'Sure,' she said as she left the room. She was back in just a couple of minutes. 'OK, it'll be in the left hip,' she instructed. I rolled onto my side and she stuck me with the painkiller.

'Many thanks,' I said. 'How long does it take?'

'You'll feel better real soon,' she replied. And I did. I was, by then, focused on the pain and the throbbing and within five or ten minutes, I could feel myself drifting off to sleep. There was no more pain.

If this is repetitive, it's purely to make a point. Hand surgery hurts a great deal. It's the pits, in today's jargon. Because of the density of nerves in your hands, the sensation of pain is amplified and intense. Unfortunately, this scenario was to be oft repeated: one hand after the other for the next two years.

Within a couple of hours, the pain was back. I tried to ignore it for a while after I was fully awake, but that didn't work for long. I pressed the nurse's button again.

'Are you OK?' the nurse asked.

'No, my hand is hurting again,' I responded.

'I'm sorry,' she told me. 'The pain shots are prescribed for every four hours and it's only been three and half hours since your last shot.'

I was perplexed and I didn't understand. 'But my hand hurts now,' I said.

'I'm sorry, that's what the doctor ordered,' she said. 'I'll be back in half an hour, promise,' she said as she walked out of my room.

It was hospital policy – silly, but unchangeable. This was to be a continuing problem for me, especially in the first couple of days after surgery. But there was no option at all. I waited for what seemed a very long time and pushed the buzzer again. There was an intercom system, so sometimes the nurses, rather than come to the room, would just ask what the patient wanted.

'My hand is still hurting. Is it time yet?' I asked.

'Fifteen more minutes, Mr Holm,' she responded. 'I'll be in as soon as I can.'

It was enormously frustrating, but there was no give, so I lived with it.

During the day, there were three or four nurses on Ward 9, and several corpsmen. In the evening and at night, however, there was only one nurse on duty. Inevitably, I got to know those two much better. From four to midnight, Mrs Lee, a delightful petite Chinese woman from Georgia, was on duty and, over my extended stay, I got to know her quite well. Midnight to eight was handled by Mrs Moore, an older, very experienced woman who was always cheerful and sympathetic at the same time. Both were civilians and highly competent, which was another stroke of good luck.

The night of that first hand operation, the same intense pain before my four hours was up, repeated itself a couple of times. And I waited until the four hours had elapsed. Despite the friendly relationship that developed with both nurses during my stay at Walter Reed, the four-hour policy for pain shots was never breached.

And there was the ever-present 'donor site', the spot on my body (the left thigh in this case) from which Dr Duffy had elected to take a piece of my skin to use in making the repairs that were the object of that operation. The donor site was raw and bloody, as if someone had just ripped off a chunk of skin. Actually that is what they did, but in a sophisticated way using a device that looked something like an electric razor. There must have been a plan for why they took skin from a particular place, but I never figured it out. It always seemed to be in an awkward spot – the spot that all visitors would invariably hit the moment they walked into my room. It was always unwitting, of course, but that made it hurt no less.

To help the site heal, an electric lamp with an extendible flexible neck was set up next to my bed. It was trained on the donor site twenty-four hours a day to dry it up so that the gauze covering it would dry up and fall off. That usually took about four days unless it was a particularly large site.

I spent about forty-eight hours getting shots for the pain every four hours. It took that long for the pain to subside. By that time as well, my butt was getting sore too, but I never complained about it. Then I would go five or six hours and gradually that period would lengthen until I could stop taking any painkiller – no pain. I had a lingering fear of addiction and erred on the side of stopping the pain shots as soon as I could handle it. Usually that would be sometime in the third or fourth day. During this three or four day period, sleep was difficult. I always dozed off after a shot, but only for a couple of hours. More pain would awaken me and it would start over again. Almost as tedious was the hand hanging on a pole bit. There are only so many positions you can lie in with one arm suspended off the side of your bed. Not to mention the lamp trained on the drying donor site. I tried them all I'm sure and never did find one that was comfortable.

During the post-operation periods, just getting out of bed to go to the bathroom was a problem. But I always did it because I stubbornly refused any alternative – like a bedpan. Getting me to the bathroom required at least a corpsman and sometimes a nurse as well who would change the bed while I was in the bathroom. The nurses and corpsmen were terribly sympathetic and helpful, but it was always a relief when they could take down my bundle of bandage and just lay it on a pillow next to me.

After I 'recovered' from that first operation, which meant

about four or five days lying in bed, I got my first session at the physical therapy facility at Walter Reed. It was impressive indeed. I couldn't actually see it, but I sensed that it was big and there was much activity so I concluded that there must be a pretty large staff. Dr Duffy had prescribed work for me every day. Push and pull on my fingers, and work on straightening out my left elbow that had ended up in a bent position. The therapists were great and they carefully explained what they were doing and why. I learned a lot about hands during my time with them.

Boiled down, it wasn't all that complex – get more mobility in all finger joints, my wrists to include rotation, and the stiff left elbow. Early on, they just did the best they could, considering the restrictions caused by scarring. My hands really were a mess and I still have major limitations in my manual dexterity. But I do have hands and for that I have an unknown African 'doctor' to thank.

Work by the therapists on my left elbow was basic. No operation was required at first although one was ultimately done to release heavy scars. Much of the problem was caused by me spending all of the time in Texas trying, in essence, to protect my hands because of the pain bumping them against something would cause. I had kept my left arm that hurt more lying across my chest almost constantly, even when I started to walk. Calcium, they told me, had developed on the elbow joint. To treat the problem, a therapist would simply grab my left arm at the wrist and pull to straighten the arm. Little by little, I was told, the calcium would break up and in time I would regain full use of the elbow joint. All well and good. Problem was that this was an exceedingly unpleasant activity. It took about six months of pulling, and ultimately the operation on scar tissue, to give me the flexibility I have today – almost 100 per cent.

Soon I concluded that one session a day wasn't enough. My reasoning was that two a day would speed up the whole process and get me out faster. Accordingly, I convinced Dr Duffy to prescribe two sessions a day with the physical therapists. Despite the pain that was always a part of a session, I looked forward to them for the progress I felt I was making. And I never failed to thank the therapists for what they had done that day. I developed close relationships with several of them and felt that they were truly dedicated individuals. They readily agreed to work with me twice a day and they acceded to my requests for additional work on general strength building. To get back into shape, I started, and pursued for as long as I got physical therapy, doing sit-ups, leg exercises and stretching. Within less than a year, my weight and general strength were as they had been when we crashed.

With the first hand operation behind me, I asked Dr Duffy for an update on my eye. He fully understood my concerns and responded that I was already scheduled for an appointment with the head of Walter Reed's eye clinic. I was later to discover that one of the reasons Walter Reed had been selected for me was the strength and reputation of the eye clinic there. Dr Raines, an ophthalmologist who was the chief of the section, was well prepared to see me. I liked him right away. He assured me that he had been following my case ever since I had been assigned to Walter Reed. He understood my concern, he said, and was confident that an operation would restore my sight. He and a colleague carefully examined my eye using a variety of machines and instruments, all of which were new to me.

'There is less trauma,' he told me, 'but it is certainly too soon to consider the transplant.'

'How long might it be?' I persisted.

'I don't really know,' he replied. 'It is not something we will want to rush. You'll just have to be patient and trust me. I know it's difficult.'

I returned to my room – was led back to be more accurate – resigned to the fact that there was no way to mess with the healing process. When the trauma in my eye was gone, we could go ahead – not before.

Immensely gratifying was the response of friends and colleagues to my situation. As soon as word got around that I had been transferred to Walter Reed, a parade of visitors started. It never stopped. Nurses and staff on Ward 9 could hardly believe it. Rarely did an evening, and virtually never a weekend, go by when I didn't have a visitor and often several. It continued for the entire two years I spent there. It would be impossible to overstate how much it did for my morale.

Dede, whom I had been dating before I went to the Congo, visited me several times a week. Pretty, sensitive and shy, she was very supportive and faithful. She lived in Georgetown and worked at the Agency so she had to ride a bus for an hour to get to Walter Reed to visit me. In the first four or five months, several other girls had come to visit me, sometimes when Dede was there. She was never deterred. Nor were they, and Mrs Lee, the evening nurse, used to tease me after my female visitors had left. I told her that they were just being nice and I appreciated it.

An Agency colleague, Peter Connell, who later became a lawyer, and his wife, Ann, were wonderful. Ann is charming, cheerful and understanding, a very special person, and I will not forget how kind she was to me. Regularly, during the year that I was blind, 1965 to 1966, she would visit and read to me from either news magazines or newspapers for an hour or so. I was always grateful to her for the sense of 'inclusion' I felt in being able to follow current events. Her generous gift of time meant a lot.

Starting with the first month I was at Walter Reed, I could also regularly count on a visit on Sunday morning from Ray Barkley, whom I had first met in Laos where he worked as a case officer in the station in Vientiane. I didn't get to see that much of him because he worked in the capital city and I worked upcountry. But I liked him and we were friends. Still, I didn't expect the thoughtfulness he displayed for the whole of the year I was blind. Barring an out-of-town trip, he showed up after breakfast on Sunday mornings with a copy of both the *Sunday New York Times* and the *Sunday Washington Post* under his arm. Over the next hour, sometimes, two, he would read me articles from the various sections of the paper. We had similar tastes so he always spotted and asked me about articles of particular interest. And he also passed on bits of information from the office about what was going on in South-East Asia. Again, his visits served to keep me abreast of things so that I felt, albeit from a distance, involved. How could someone be that nice? I really don't know. I do know that I still feel terribly grateful to him for the many hours he spent with me.

Because of my close friendship with Mike Deuel, another previous colleague and classmate in my training year with the CIA (1961), I had also met and enjoyed time with his parents, Wally, also of the CIA, and Mary. As articulate and entertaining as Wally was in his lectures during our training, he was even more so in an informal social setting. Along with a couple of the other single members of our class, I had had dinner with the Deuels a couple of times during that training year. It was always most enjoyable. Wally would relate stories about their life in Beirut, Rome, Berlin, or elsewhere and Mary, who had doubtless heard some of the stories countless times, would interject with pertinent comments designed, I think, to keep Wally on track.

When Wally heard that I was at Walter Reed, he promptly called and asked if he could come out to see me. He was a wonderful visitor because he made me forget all about my problems. Full of enthusiasm, he related tale after tale and spoke glowingly of what we would do after I healed. He also brought news about Mike, who had returned to Laos. Before we both left Laos in the summer of 1964, Mike had been dating (to the extent that was possible given our jobs upcountry) a young woman, Judy Dougherty, who worked in Bangkok and was pretty, talented and vivacious. They had got married in late October 1964 and were now living in Pakse, Laos, and Mike was running a major project aimed at stopping traffic on the Ho Chi Minh trail.

By the fall of 1965, Dr Duffy and I had developed a very friendly relationship. Of Irish descent (obviously with a name like Duffy), he had been born in Boston during the Great Depression. He made it to medical school but his youth was tough. He would tell me how the family would eat lobster night after night and he would crave a hamburger. (During the Depression, lobster in Boston was plentiful and cheap. Indeed it was standard fare for servants, who complained about getting too much of it. How times change.)

One day, just before another operation, he asked, 'Really, over-all, Dick, how are things going?' I could sense that it was a sincere question.

'I'm hanging in there, Mike,' I told him. 'I don't need a shrink, if that's what you mean.'

'I know that for sure,' he said. 'Just wanted to give you a chance to voice your thoughts.'

I thought for a moment. 'Well, I wouldn't mind having a martini once in a while,' I said half-jokingly.

He was quiet for a minute.

'Why not?' he asked rhetorically. 'Why not indeed. I think it would be good for you psychologically.' He was speaking in a mock professional tone now and said, 'I'll prescribe it so that the nurses won't rebel. But you have to get the booze.'

'It's a deal,' I responded, pleased that I'd raised the idea in the first place. 'Mrs Lee will be no problem, but Major Axeman will probably be appalled.'

'Not to worry,' Mike told me. 'I'll take care of everything.'

At that time, the head nurse on Ward 9 was Major Axeman, I never knew her first name. Nor did I ever see her as she transferred out of Walter Reed before my eye operation. But I had a mental image of her that was vivid: career army nurse who had served in combat zones. A strong woman both mentally and physically, she probably had hair pulled back tight into a bun. Not many smiles. An expression as if she had just eaten something sour. Actually, she was a nice enough person, just hopelessly uptight, very rule-bound and fastidious. However, my unusual status, as a civilian (and a junior one although she didn't know that) on the VIP senior officers ward caused her to treat me with care. Hence we got along OK. Still, I can only imagine how perplexed she was to find out that there was liquor on her ward – and that it was legal.

'And just what is that in your closet, Mr Holm?' she asked accusingly one day.

'I can't really see, Major,' I answered, 'But you must be talking about the half gallon bottles of gin, vermouth, scotch and bourbon that are on the shelf.'

She knew, of course, that the bottles were there. She just wanted to make it clear to me that she wasn't pleased about it.

'Yes, I am talking about those bottles,' she muttered. 'I certainly hope you are happy.'

'Well, it does help me relax after a stressful day lying here in bed,' I replied.

No response. I don't know if she glared at me or not, but she left.

The germ of the martini idea had come from another visitor, Charlie Whitehurst, who had been the Chief while I served in Laos. He was now posted at Headquarters and was the Chief of China Operations, within the Far East Division. He was responsible for our worldwide effort aimed at collecting intelligence about China. Charlie came to visit me one evening in late summer. I couldn't see that he was carrying a sack. We chatted for a while about what had happened in Laos after I left and about mutual friends. Then he asked if I would like to have a martini.

'Sure would,' I responded, 'but this place doesn't have a bar.'

'I was afraid of that,' he said, 'so I brought my own.' He reached into his sack, brought out a thermos and poured us each a martini. It tasted great.

I remember Whitey asked what I planned to do when I got back to work. I told him I didn't really know except that it would be as far away from Africa as I could get.

'Come to Far East Division,' he urged me. 'You have a lot of friends there. Think about China Operations. It's a first-class effort.'

I was pleased that he had made the offer and I promised that I would think about it seriously. Later, in spring 1967, I did join China Operations and, when I returned to Headquarters, Whitey welcomed me back by taking me to lunch with several senior officers, including the Director. Still later, in early 1969, I went to Hong Kong, where Whitey was the Chief and had approved the assignment. He was a colleague and a friend, and I had great respect for him.

Over a few weeks, other friends brought in bottles (people were always asking me if I wanted anything) and I was, of course, pleased to share. Major Axeman was nowhere to be seen in the evenings and Mrs Lee was most understanding.

'What do you want, ice?' she would say over the intercom when I rang the call button and she knew I had some visitors. It became a regular routine.

It just developed. In the privacy of my room, we would, in effect, have cocktail parties almost every evening: a martini (on the rocks, thanks to Mrs Lee), bourbon and water, or scotch and water. It was a small thing, but it helped dim the fact that we were in a hospital and I was badly hurt – but recovering. I looked forward to those evening visits and they were a great boost to my morale.

Patterns developed during those first months at Walter Reed. Although other work would eventually have to be done, Dr Duffy had decided to give first priority to my hands. Early on he told me, 'The more they look like hands the better they will function, so that's our goal.' So the programme was set. Hand operation, painful recovery period, physical therapy, a brief respite (as brief as possible as I continually urged him to get on with it), and then another hand operation. That routine persisted for much of the first year I spent at Walter Reed. It was not fun. Luckily, the visitors kept coming and coming. My parents visited at least monthly and Dad even more often if he had a business trip to Washington. There seemed to be no end in sight, but I didn't dwell on that thought.

My hands presented the physical therapists with a real challenge. How best to strengthen each tendon and gain flexibility in each joint was the question. And to take care with newly grafted skin that was the result of each operation. There were added complications. Whoever had cleaned the bugs out of my hands in Africa after I'd been found had, as I've said, inadvertently cut or damaged many tendons. And that damage, mostly on the tops of my hands, coupled with the heavier scarring, impaired the ability of extensor tendons to lift my fingers. My ability to pull my fingers down and grip something (albeit weakly) was far greater than my ability to lift them up and spread them out.

Working closely with Dr Duffy, who recognized the problem and wanted to solve it, the physical therapists fashioned a device, literally from a coat hanger, that would strengthen my extensor tendons. A partial cast was formed on my arm between the wrist and elbow. Built into it was the bent coat hanger that loomed out over my hand. Attached by strong rubber bands were five leather loops that were hooked onto each finger. The idea was to strengthen my tendons by pulling against the leather loops. When I had it on, my hand looked almost normal and I was pleased with the whole idea. Sounds good, and it was, but there is always the other side of the coin. After about half an hour, it hurt like hell. Judging, however, that the gain outweighed the pain, I wore it religiously for much of my time at Walter Reed. I did get encouragement, orders maybe, from Dr Duffy and the physical therapists and I'm confident they were right. The infernal machine did my hands a lot of good. I never got to the point where I could handle a diaper pin, but I can hold a tennis racket.

One evening in mid-October, Dede arrived, and I could sense right away that something was wrong. After a few amenities, she said she had to tell me something.

'What's wrong, Dede?' I asked her.

'Mike Deuel crashed in a helicopter,' she blurted. She knew that Mike and I were close friends.

'Was he hurt?' I asked. I couldn't see her face, but I knew she was very upset.

'He died in the crash,' she said softly. 'Oh Dick, I'm so sorry.'

I couldn't believe it. I was shocked and couldn't speak. Lots of thoughts flooded my mind. It's not fair. Why him? Why Mike? We lose our best men. I had memories of our time together in training and in Laos. It hit me very hard.

'Are you sure?' I was finally able to say.

'Yes, it's confirmed,' she answered. 'I don't know any details,' she added.

'What about his wife?' I asked.

'She's on her way home,' Dede replied.

Judy, three months pregnant, left Pakse immediately and, via Bangkok, returned to her home in Bulpitt, central Illinois. The tragedy, for her, was compounded because her father was terminally ill. He died in January 1966, just three months after she got home. It took great inner strength for her to cope.

I wanted to call Wally and Mary, but I didn't know what to say so I decided to call the next day. I tried to talk for a while to Dede, but I couldn't concentrate on anything except the awful news she had just brought me. She understood and left. I lay there for a long time. Ultimately I fell asleep.

I talked with Wally and it was hard. He put on a brave face, but I knew he was deeply wounded. Mary wouldn't, or couldn't, talk to anyone. Judy, accompanied by her two sisters and brother, came to Washington for the funeral and showed much courage in the face of what must have been a terrible ordeal. Mike was buried at Arlington National Cemetery with full military honours in accordance with his status as a Marine Corps officer. I attended the burial ceremony, as did many of our Agency colleagues.

In late fall, fearful of what was still an unknown future, and worried that Dede was too committed while I could make no commitment at all, I told her to stop coming to see me and get on with her life. It was a very difficult conversation. She cried, but ultimately agreed that it would be best to break off our relationship.

The routine went on at Walter Reed. In December 1965, I was asked if I would talk to some patients about their injuries. By that time, I was pretty well known in the hospital because of my long tenure and because of my attitude – deal with the problem and get on with the healing process. Someone, I don't know who, suggested that I be asked to try to help patients who were coping much less well. I said I would help if I could, but I wasn't sure what I was supposed to do. 'Just talk to them,' they responded.

The first time, I was led into a lounge attached to an enlisted man's ward and sat down near a young soldier just back from Vietnam. I had met some soldiers returned from Vietnam while I was in Texas, and I was familiar with the war in South-East Asia, so there was an initial rapport. As we talked though, it became clear that this young man was despondent and lacked any will to fight for his recovery. We talked further and I asked him what wounds he had suffered.

'I lost my left foot on a land mine,' he replied.

'And?' I asked him.

'That's all,' he answered.

'That's all,' I echoed, 'so what the hell is your problem?'

My question took him by surprise and set the scene for the rest of our conversation. I was blunt. And coming from me (he could see that I was blind and one of my hands was encased in a giant bandage, the other was a mess), he sat there and took it. Things could be worse, fella, was the message.

'You just gonna give up on life?' I asked him. 'Don't be stupid. This hospital can fix you up in short order and you'll hardly know the difference. Enough with the self-pity stuff, just get on with life, which means get the hell out of here.' I believed what I was telling him, which no doubt added to its impact.

It truly was foolish for this young man to lay around whining and feeling sorry for himself when he should be healing. I made that as clear as I could. I did that, at hospital request, about a dozen times over the next few months. Often there were close family or friends sitting with us. I knew they agreed with me and loved the direct message I was sending. Often I heard 'Right on' or 'Amen, brother,' while I spoke my piece. I was told that it helped. I hope it did.

I visited Dr Raines at the eye clinic monthly so that he could monitor progress in my right eye. He scheduled my visits to coincide with a monthly seminar of Washington area eye surgeons. They met monthly at Walter Reed to discuss eye-related issues. My case always generated lots of interest. Not only because of the story about the crash in darkest Africa, but because of the circumstances surrounding my eye injuries. Did the contact lenses save an eye or cause the loss of it? It was, still, an academic question for me, but doctors seeing my eye for the first time were always very intrigued with the history. The seminars became a little tedious because I got tired of being the subject of their debate, but I viewed it as an opportunity to have my eye checked by the best doctors around. Also, I sensed that the trauma was lessening because my vision was marginally better.

'That's because the windshield is muddy, so to speak, but the eye is healing well,' Dr Raines told me in late fall.

'So where do we go from here?' I asked.

'We're ready,' he replied. 'We're going to do a partial thickness corneal graft, It's called a Lemaller graft. What we need now is the right donor cornea.'

I had, of course, been waiting for that day. I was both elated and fearful. From then until after the operation, doubts and hopes were almost constantly on my mind. I have to see again, I told myself, or I don't know what I'll do.

Christmas 1965 came and went. The operations kept coming and so did my visitors. Dr Duffy scheduled his work so that I had some respite over the holidays, but my vision and hand problems were ever-present limitations. My family visited me and we enjoyed the time together. It had been very tough on my mother to see me still immobile, but she bore up well. They stayed in my apartment in the District on MacArthur Boulevard. I had rented the apartment after I returned to Washington from Laos in late August 1964. I kept it when I went to the Congo, reasoning that I would only be gone for a couple of months. After the crash, various friends had lived there, subletting from me. That went on for the entire time I was in the hospital and I lived there again when the ordeal was over. In fact, after the eye operation and as my condition continued to improve, I was able, periodically, to spend weekends or evenings at the apartment.

One afternoon, earlier in December, Dick Helms, the Deputy Director of the Agency at the time, visited me. There had been several changes at the senior levels of the Agency while I had been lounging in hospital beds. In April 1965, just weeks after my February crash and while I was still at Brooke Hospital, John McCone resigned as Director. He was deeply frustrated at President Johnson's reluctance to accept the thrust of the Agency's negative and pessimistic reporting and analysis about Vietnam. Also, he was resistant to the Johnson administration's efforts to get the Agency more deeply involved in the war effort. McCone had simply had enough and decided to return to the private sector. Inside the Agency, I was told, there was also frustration and deep concern about the Johnson administration's conduct of the war. McCone, an outsider who had not been particularly beloved by Agency people, nonetheless commanded great respect for his intellect and for the way he had handled himself as our Director. He wasn't Allen Dulles, friends said, but he was a 'good guy'. Recalling his decision to call MacNamara and get a plane sent to drag me out of the Congo, I certainly concurred with that assessment.

The loss of John McCone, a dedicated standard bearer for the Agency, was exacerbated when Johnson named retired Admiral William Raborn to replace him as Director. All of this was, of course, beyond my ken at the time, but from comments made by visiting friends, I quickly sensed that Raborn wasn't up to the job. A nice, but simple man, he lacked the intellectual capabilities and the 'presence', especially during such a stressful period, to cope with the demands of the Directorship. Dick Helms, who had been the Deputy Director for Plans (Operations), was promoted to the Agency's number two spot as Deputy Director of the Agency. Helms's promotion helped because of the great respect he enjoyed, but it didn't save the day.

After just over a year, it became painfully clear to all involved that Raborn had to go and in June 1966, he (in the most polite terms I can put it) re-retired – to no one's great surprise because of the manner in which the White House was relying on him. To the Agency's considerable delight at this difficult stage in its history, Johnson named Dick Helms to replace Raborn as Director. Helms had to face the same problems McCone had dealt with – indeed they were worse because Raborn had acceded to every request from the administration and the Agency had, by then, become much more involved in the Vietnam War effort. He was, however, able to walk a fine line until Johnson's departure in 1968. At my junior level of the Directorate of Plans (well below the level at which the elephants were dancing), the promotion of Helms, one of us, to Director was welcome news.

When Helms showed up at the hospital in December 1965, security detail in tow of course, we chatted for about fifteen minutes. He inquired about my condition and about what I planned to do when I got back to work. I did not offer him a drink – it seemed inappropriate and, at 5 p.m., too early. He gave me the impression, and I believe it was an accurate one, that he cared. His sincerity was apparent. I was impressed, even touched, by that visit. That someone at his level would come to visit a junior officer like me spoke volumes about the kind of organization I was working for, I thought.

I had many other senior officers visit me at Walter Reed and when I mentioned Dick Helms had been there, few expressed surprise. 'That's the kind of man he is' seemed to be the general reaction. And it was a widespread feeling within the Agency. I felt then, and still feel today, that the Agency in general, and the Clandestine Service, which I know best, in particular, is populated by bright, sensitive and wonderful people.

Dick Helms's visit more or less did away with any bit of cover I still had. The Deputy Director of the Central Intelligence Agency doesn't visit just anybody. Explaining it to the nurses, doctors and staff wasn't easy, but it was a small price to pay and it added to the mystique. Certainly I was a version of James Bond, they all concluded.

It was a Monday morning in early February 1966 when I was called up to the eye clinic for an unscheduled meeting with Dr Raines. I was expectant, hopeful. There were brief amenities and then he gave me the news.

'We've got the right donor cornea,' he told me. 'We want to operate late this week. Does that give you any problem?'

Even half expecting it, I was taken aback. The day had come, I thought to myself.

'No problem at all,' I responded. 'I'm more than ready.'

'We should talk about Dr King,' he said, 'and I'll want you to meet him before the operation.'

I was puzzled. 'Who is Dr King?'

'He is the nation's leading surgeon for corneal transplants,' he replied. 'Since they realized how important this operation is,' he went on, 'your Agency insisted that we get the best surgeon to do it. Happily, Dr King practises here in Washington and he agreed to do this operation. I am pleased that I will be his assistant for the operation, but he will be in charge.'

I tried to digest what he had just told me. As it sunk in, I was elated that, again, the Agency had left no stone unturned in their efforts to help get me through these tough times.

'Do you know Dr King?' was all I could think to say.

'I certainly do,' Dr Raines responded. 'He's tops in our field. I'll be delighted to work with him.'

'So all I have to do is show up,' I joked. My mind was a jumble of emotions and I couldn't put a serious thought together. Dr Raines understood, I think.

'That's right, Dick,' he said. 'Dr King and I will take care of the rest.'

The operation was scheduled for a Thursday morning. I had called my parents, of course, and the Deuels, but not many other people. I didn't want to deal with well-wishers or questions. I was nervous and apprehensive. Scared to death, but trying as hard as I could to be optimistic. And it got worse as the week wore on. Dr Duffy knew it was coming and he stopped by to wish me luck. 'Now you'll be able to see what I've been doing,' he laughed. The nurses on the ward knew too because I was moved to an eye-patient ward specially fitted for post eye-operation situations. Mrs Lee and Mrs Moore in particular were kind and optimistic.

I was moved to the eye ward on Wednesday afternoon. I spent several hours just lying in bed thinking about my whole life until that time – nothing in particular and everything in general: family, sports, girlfriends, training in the Agency, Laos, the Congo, the day we crashed.

After dinner, about 8 p.m., Dr Raines visited me and Dr King was with him. After introductions, Dr King took a look at my eye and made positive comments. He had read my file carefully, he assured me, and had studied pictures of my eye. Then he asked a few general questions and tried to put me at ease. Apparently, everyone sensed that I was nervous. I liked Dr King – Harry was his first name – and did feel reassured by what he was telling me.

'This is a two-step effort,' he said. 'I'll take off half your cornea, the scarred part.'

'The muddy windshield,' Dr Raines interjected.

'That's right,' Dr King continued, 'and then replace it with the clear donor cornea. Dr Raines confirms what I've just seen. The trauma is completely gone and your eye is in good condition for this procedure. I'm very optimistic. We're gonna do just fine.' I was taking it all in and I must say that he made me feel better.

'What's the second step?' I asked.

'We can never be sure how your eye will react,' he answered. 'Often the grafted cornea clears up nicely so that, looking through your clear bottom half and clear grafted half, your vision will be fine. In that case, no need for step two. Sometimes though, the grafted portion doesn't clear up enough to make us happy with the results. In that case, this step will have served to prepare your cornea for a full thickness graft. That would be somewhere down the road.'

I listened carefully, trying to absorb and understand what he was saying.

'So, in fact, we have two shots to put your vision back to normal,' he concluded.

'Does a bad first graft result compromise anything for the second step?' I asked.

'Not at all,' he assured me. 'It just gets the cornea ready. We wouldn't want to do a full thickness now with all that scarring.'

'We agree completely,' Dr Raines added as if speaking for the whole of Walter Reed's eye clinic, which, of course, he was.

That seemed to be the end of our conversation and I could sense that they were getting ready to leave. I was scheduled first in the operating room the next morning. They were both standing now. Dr King came over to the bedside.

'We can do this with a local anaesthesia,' he said.

I didn't understand at first. 'What do you mean?' I asked.

'You can be awake the whole time,' he answered. 'We will have your eye anaesthetized and will immobilize your head so you can't move it. No problem for us.'

I couldn't believe what he was saying. Stay awake? I'd be afraid to breathe for fear of messing something up. No way!

'Absolutely not,' I blurted out. 'I want a general anaesthesia and I want to be totally out. I'll wake up back here and I want to hear you say the graft looks great.' They both laughed.

'As you wish, Mr Holm,' Dr Raines said soothingly. Then he patted my arm. 'I know you are concerned and I have ordered a sleeping pill for you. Don't argue with the nurse, just take it.'

I woke up after the operation back on the eye-patient ward. I woke up slowly, sensing that I was in a different place. I was afraid to open my eyes. I didn't know what I would see – if anything. Finally I did and what I saw was less muddy, but not clear. I wasn't sure what to do. I did nothing. Soon, as if on cue, Dr King and Dr Raines came in. I could distinguish their forms, I noted, although the room was only dimly lit with the curtains having been drawn.

'Everything went just great,' Dr King told me. 'I'm really pleased with how the graft fitted in and your eye is fine.'

It was exactly what I had wanted to hear and I was greatly relieved. 'It's not clear,' I said.

'Don't worry about that,' he replied. 'It will take time. The graft will get clearer and clearer for about eight weeks. It will be hard for you, but progress will be steady. You'll just have to be patient.'

'You'll be on this ward for a few days', Dr Raines said, 'and we will keep the light level down. You just lie quietly – no quick movements with your head. Soon we will send you back to Ward 9.'

It all went according to plan. While examining my eye later, after Dr King had departed, Dr Raines exclaimed about how impressed he had been with Dr King's skill and knowledge. Part of it may have been intended to reassure me, but I had the sense that he was sincere and I was gratified all over again that the Agency had arranged to have Dr King do this, for me, terribly important operation.

I tried to be as patient as I could and the results were as Dr King had predicted. Almost day by day my vision got better. When I woke up and could see the ceiling, I was elated. I stared at it for a while, thinking, perhaps, that it might go away. Then I could make out things in my room, people and, if they were close enough, features on people's faces and my elation grew. It was a wonderful time, and everyone around me helped in my celebration and, in many ways, my liberation. I simply don't have the words adequately to convey my feelings as my sight slowly returned. It was just wonderful.

Over the next several months, my vision improved to the point where, with a contact lens (glasses wouldn't work well enough for me because the contour of my cornea isn't smooth), I could see at 20/40 plus. That is I could see a couple of the letters on the 20/40 line of an eye chart. I couldn't make it back to 20/20, but with the restored vision, I can drive, play tennis (lousy overhead), ski and read. Pretty normal vision in other words. Depth perception gave me fits at first and still gives me trouble when I'm playing tennis or skiing, but, for the most part, I've adjusted.

Not surprisingly, things got a lot better for me in the weeks after my sight was restored. I really did feel liberated in that I could now do many of the day-to-day things that had been so difficult before the operation. I could eat, dress, go to the bathroom, walk around the hospital, go outside for walks and, after some months, even watch television. There were some down sides. I could see how I looked. My face and hands were (are) pretty scarred and it was a jolt. Nothing had prepared me for what I saw. Mike Duffy said the redness and scars would blend over time and that he could do a lot more to help in the reconstruction. That was, as they say, a downer, but I had to take his word for it and there was nothing I could do about it anyway, so I decided that I just wasn't going to worry about how I looked. Good thing too, because it would have been a heavy burden to carry for all these years.

And soon it was spring 1966, over a year after the crash, and I was still at Walter Reed. The hand operations continued, but with a new twist. Now we had progressed to work on individual fingers and to make sure the grafts healed correctly, the fingers had to be immobilized for a period after the operation. To do that, Dr Duffy inserted a metal pin down through the centre of the finger, three was the most he ever did at one time. That didn't really hurt too much (I was knocked out when he put them in) and a bonus of sorts was that I couldn't wear the 'coat-hanger monster' while I had pins in a finger. Taking them out, however, was a different story. The technique was rather unsophisticated. Dr Duffy would simply take a pair of pliers (medical looking but still a pair of pliers) and pull each pin out of my finger. That hurt – a lot. It was a shock wave of great pain just as he pulled it out. Initially, I took shots for pain before he pulled out a pin, but that always made me feel drowsy or queasy for up to a couple of hours. Before long, I just took a couple of aspirin after he pulled one out. My hands were getting better and better and the pain seemed to be lessening.

There were other operations as well. My nose needed some repair work and, with the kind assistance of some cartilage from my left little toe, Dr Duffy did the job. My ears got messed up too and for the work that was needed, which was pretty extensive and required two different operations, Dr Duffy took cartilage from my rib cage and rebuilt my ears. I also needed eyebrows and that required a chunk of my scalp. He did that operation under a local anaesthetic. I was awake and alert and I could hear him and his assistant talking as they worked. By that time, we all were good friends and they had decided to pull my chain a bit.

'Is he out?' Dr Jerry Quinn asked Dr Duffy. He knew full well that I only had a local.

'Nah, Jerry, it's only a local,' Dr Duffy replied. 'You OK, Dick?'

'I'm fine,' I answered.

'OK, Jerry, let's get to work,' Dr Duffy said. 'Give me that big knife.'

'You gonna use the big one, Mike?' Dr Quinn asked.

'Well, we need a lot of scalp,' Dr Duffy replied.

It was quiet for a while.

'Wipe away all that blood, Jerry, I can't see what I'm cutting.'

'I am, I am. Sure is a lot of blood up here.'

'Oops, damn.'

'What happened?'

'No problem. It'll make a nice eyebrow.'

'Yeah, but we want it to look like the other one, don't we?' Dr Quinn could barely conceal his amusement.

'It'll be close,' Dr Duffy said, 'but with all that blood it's hard to see. You just keep wiping.'

I was smiling and I knew their banter was all for my consumption.

'You guys having a good time?' I asked.

'Don't you worry, Dick, we are,' Mike said. 'And we'll be finished in just a while, right, Jerry?'

'I can't tell,' Jerry replied, 'too much blood.'

In the end, I had two narrow slits in my scalp. One was stitched over each eye, and, *voilà*, I had eyebrows again. Mrs Lee said she hadn't even noticed that I had none before the operation. They grow just like the hair on my head and I have to keep them trimmed regularly.

In all the operations I had, there was only one serious mishap. After about six months of work on my hands, Dr Duffy concluded that the little finger on my left hand just wasn't going to make it. The scarring was such that he couldn't release it enough to get the flexibility I needed. It was actually hindering his efforts with the rest of my left hand. So it must come off, he concluded, and he explained very carefully why. The little finger would be surgically removed and a graft would close the wound; nothing particularly unusual. I agreed and the operation was scheduled. Everything was as usual until I awoke in the recovery room. There were three problems, only one of which was normal – the big bundle of bandage around my left hand. It wasn't hurting yet, but I knew that the pain would come. A second problem was that my left side was heavily bandaged and felt strange. Never before had a donor site been bandaged. And thirdly, my left little finger hurt, which caused me to wonder if something had gone wrong. Had they been unable to take it off? I wondered. It didn't take long for each problem to be resolved.

Soon, my left hand started hurting, more than usual in fact and the nurse claimed that was because of the amputation. Problem one resolved. In late afternoon of the same day, Dr Quinn came in to see me. He had screwed up, he said, and he wanted to explain and apologize. Must have something to do with my left side, I thought.

'Here's the story, Dick,' Dr Quinn said. 'I was assisting Dr Duffy, as you know. He wanted me to get the experience so he had me do much of the work. The amputation went just fine.'

'I was going to ask about that,' I told him. 'My left little finger hurts.'

'I'll get to that,' he said. And then he went on. 'When I was taking skin from the donor site on your left side, my hand slipped. The device I was using, like an electric shaver, operates at very high speed and there is not much margin for error. My slip took a large gouge out of your side for which I am very sorry. Mike understood, he wasn't happy, but he understood. I hope you do too. We got the skin we needed and we repaired your side, but it will hurt for a while and you'll have a scar.' I listened carefully. And I knew he was sincere in his apology. I was pleased that he had apologized personally.

'So I'm gonna have a scar?' I asked him.

'Yeah, I'm afraid so,' he replied.

'Will it blend with all my other ones?'

'Yeah, it sure will,' he said, 'and thanks for understanding. And I did get that little finger off. You are experiencing what is called "ghost pain". It lasts for several months. But believe me, the little finger is gone.'

After I could see again and was obviously doing much better, I got transferred out of my room to another on Ward 9 that had two beds in it. For the rest of my stay at Walter Reed, I usually had a roommate. It didn't change much. Two of the roommates were of some note.

One was an old Navy officer who came to Walter Reed to have an aneurysm repaired. I cannot recall his name, but I do remember his background. I don't know when he joined the US Navy, but he was a young ensign when, in the early 1900s, he went ashore near Vera Cruz, Mexico, in search of the Mexican bandit, Pancho Villa. He related the story and I was spellbound. Unfortunately, his memory was failing and he didn't get the details straight – like exactly when, where, how, and did they get him – but I enjoyed the story and admired the courage.

He also told me about an experience he had in England shortly after the end of the First World War. I assume he had been serving somewhere in Europe and had either been assigned or volunteered (probably the latter) to an experimental project somewhere south of London. The project involved some of the first parachute jumps ever made and he told me that he jumped from the basket of a balloon with his parachute over his arm! (You can't be serious, I was thinking, recalling my own first jumps with a static line.) When he got clear of the basket, he went on, he simply threw the parachute above him like it was a large fishing net. It caught the wind and he landed, roughly but safely. He did it several times and got better and better at it. I couldn't believe what I was hearing. I was in awe of the courage it must have taken to do such a thing. He was a pleasant, friendly guy and I enjoyed his company. He was accepting of the need for his operation, but fearful of the possible outcome. It went just fine and we said our goodbyes about a week later.

The other unusual roommate was a young Lao army officer. There were side benefits for the ward. He couldn't speak English and they knew I spoke French. In fact my Thai, which is very close to Lao, was still pretty good too, so with one language or the other, I became his buddy and his translator. As we talked, I developed a picture of this young man. It wasn't a very nice one. His father, I found out, was a very senior officer in the Lao army. That explained a lot. My initial impressions of him were that he whined a lot and had a weak character. I knew the Lao pretty well and I had wondered how this man had become an officer. His father's position explained it. I then learned that he was at Walter Reed to have cosmetic plastic surgery on a large scar on his neck. It started low on his cheek and ended on his neck. It didn't look that bad actually, but he was very upset about it.

It wasn't a bayonet wound gained in combat with the Viet Minh. He got it, he said, in a fight in a nightclub over a girl. He was a bit ashamed to admit it and I don't know how many people at the hospital knew. A US Army military attaché, who knew his father, offered, for greater influence I'm sure, to have the scar 'fixed' at the US Army's finest hospital, Walter Reed. So the US Army flew this young man to Washington for an operation. As I got the whole story straight, I had less and less respect for him. I was sure that he had never seen combat and probably never would. He was a Vientiane-based non-combatant who had been injured 'out' of the line of duty; a bar crawler who got a knife wound fighting over a hooker. Despite my feelings, I tried to be nice.

Before the operation, he confided to me that he was worried about bad '*Pi*' – the Lao word for spirits and ghosts. I told him Walter Reed had no *Pi* at all. He didn't look convinced. He went up for his operation early one morning right on schedule. He was back a few hours later, unconscious and looking awful. There were no bandages and his scar was untouched. Something had gone wrong.

I was briefed so that I could explain to him when he came to again. I didn't get the full story because I know they were very embarrassed, but I got a version thereof. After the Lao officer had been put under with ether, there was an interlude before the surgeon showed up. Somehow tubes and valves had been mixed up and he was getting only gas, no oxygen. He was turning blue or green when the surgeon took his first look and they initiated emergency steps to stabilize his condition. They had to abort the operation. It would be rescheduled as soon as he felt better, they said. And he would feel bad for a couple of days.

'I'll bet he will,' I said, laughing now that the danger was passed.

Explaining to him in French and Thai was more than I could handle and I was never able to convince him that it had just been an unfortunate accident. Bad *Pi* was all he could think of. Accompanied by a couple of officers from the Laotian Embassy, he left the next afternoon, still looking green and wobbly. The US military attaché's plan for increased influence had clearly backfired.

Wally Deuel came much less often after Mike's crash. When I could see again, I visited the Deuels from time to time, despite the fact that I was torn because I knew I would remind them of Mike. I phoned them periodically as well and Wally kept me apprised of Judy's situation in Illinois. We were all concerned about Judy and in April 1966 her baby, Suzanne Michelle, was born.

I can't remember who first had the idea of a trust fund, but we all embraced it immediately. Ralph McLean and I were the initial organizers and we received cheques from many of Mike's college and Agency friends. The fund was to be for Suzanne's college education and, after due deliberation, we invested the several thousand dollars that had been amassed into a growth mutual fund and told Judy and the Deuels.

In the months after the birth of Suzanne, Judy became more and more restless in rural central Illinois. She did not want to spend the rest of her life there. We all encouraged her to come to Washington. The Agency guaranteed that, whenever she wanted, she would immediately be re-employed. Moreover, it would not be difficult to find her an apartment. In the fall of 1966, Judy and Suzanne moved to Washington. She was welcomed warmly by everyone (Wally and Mary Deuel were particularly pleased) and felt good about her decision, a difficult one for a young widow to make.

The only drawback after she actually did start working again, from her point of view, was the fact that she had to put Suzanne in day care when she went to work. She didn't like that at all and eventually she decided to stop working and get married again – to me.

I'll try to explain.

Judy moved to Washington, got settled into an apartment, also on MacArthur Boulevard, which made the commute to Headquarters quite easy, and started her new life. Initially, she enrolled at American University to finish her BA degree. She had previously attended the University of Illinois, but stopped after two years to join the Agency and go overseas. At American, she decided to major in music – she was and still is an excellent piano player. Because of Suzanne, she decided against enrolling full time and just took a few courses. She attended American University for two semesters before deciding, in mid-1967, to start working again at the Agency.

Soon after coming back to Washington, Judy came to visit me at Walter Reed. A variety of reasons were probably involved. She knew that I was a good friend of Mike's and of the Deuels. We had known each other in Bangkok and we had many friends in common both in South-East Asia and in Washington. And she was just a nice person. I wondered what to say, but she made it easy. I told her how sorry I was about Mike's crash. It wasn't easy to express my feelings, but she understood. We didn't talk much about Mike after that. There simply wasn't much either of us could say.

I was pleased that she had come and I enjoyed her company. She felt the same way, she said. Later she told me that somehow I seemed nicer at Walter Reed than I had been in Thailand. Initially, in Bangkok, she had found me to be a bit (and I use the word because she did) 'cocky'. I have no idea how she got such an impression, and I was shocked to hear it. At Walter Reed, she said, I seemed more patient, subdued, and overall just nicer. I hadn't noticed any change. Maybe that's what an airplane crash in the jungle does to you. She came again and I invited her to come often. By that time, I was able to leave the hospital evenings and weekends and I visited her and Suzanne at her apartment, where she would have several friends to dinner.

After operations, while I was confined full-time to the hospital, Judy would come to visit me often. I looked for ways to extend the length of her visits and gradually I found that I liked being with her more and more. No great surprise there. She was all she had been when we first met in Thailand – pretty, charming, thoughtful, and intelligent. It was not difficult to spend time, lots of it, with a young woman like that. But I still looked terrible and I wondered how she felt about that. I was pleased to see that it didn't seem to faze her at all.

The Deuels, possibly sensing something that had not yet occurred to me, invited us both to dinner at their house; not once, but often. Those were very pleasant evenings where Wally seemed more like his old self. He and Mary adored Suzanne and she responded with great affection towards them. Judy and I saw each other more and more frequently for the first half of 1967 and by fall we were dating as steadily as my situation would permit. Clearly, I had fallen deeply in love with her. Still, I didn't know how she felt. We went to dinner, to movies and plays, and on picnics with Suzanne and friends. I took Judy and Suzanne to New Jersey to meet my parents. This was getting serious. In January 1968, with our relationship blooming and my prospects on all fronts looking brighter and brighter (I had by that time returned to work), she invited me to dinner one night. It was a great evening as usual although she seemed a bit pensive. She gave me a ride home and we were standing in front of my apartment building when she made the announcement.

'I've been offered a position in Taiwan this summer.'

I was shocked at the news. My mind was racing as I tried to think of something to say. That's a rotten idea, I was thinking. I don't want you to go.

'That's a terrible idea and I don't want you to go,' I told her.

'Why?' she asked calmly. I was upset. It had been so sudden. There had been no warning at all, just awful news. I was hesitant, but finally figured that it was now or never.

'Because I want you to marry me,' I blurted out in a rush. 'Soon!'

'I'm not sure,' she said hesitatingly. 'Do you think you're ready?'

I'm not going to bore readers with the next ten minutes' worth of conversation during which I finally convinced her that I was indeed ready to marry. I can't remember what I said or what arguments I used. Nor can she. Suffice to say that to my great delight and joy she said yes, she would marry me. I couldn't have been happier and we promptly called her mother and my parents to announce the glad tidings.

When I told the Deuels that Judy and I were going to get married, they were absolutely delighted. Wally couldn't stop saying how pleased he was, and that made us both even happier about our plans. I still wonder if Wally and Mary had seen that day coming long before we did (or maybe hoped for it) and tried to encourage it.

Judy's arrival on the scene changed a lot of things, but it didn't get me out of the hospital. The routine went on for the rest of 1966 and into 1967. With my vision restored and my hands getting better and more functional with each operation, I was getting more and more anxious to be done with Walter Reed and get on with my life. I had decided to return to Far East Division and join China Operations when I returned to work. I made my thoughts known to Charlie Whitehurst and he asked if I wanted to start learning Mandarin Chinese. At first I thought he was kidding. He wasn't. Well, yes I would, I told him, and he promptly made arrangements to have a Chinese instructor visit me twice a week at the hospital. As Whitey must have known, it did wonders for my spirits, as I felt like I was that much nearer to being back to work. It was yet another step taken by the Agency to support and encourage a wounded junior officer. I should note here that I was promoted while at Walter Reed. I was amazed to receive word of this. The Agency didn't want me to fall behind my peers, I was told. Seemed like pure charity to me, but I was grateful.

I grew more and more friendly with Mike Duffy. He knew about Judy and how I felt and invited us to his home for dinner many times, where we met his wife, Caroline, and his four children. At another evening at their home, my brother, Bob, and his new wife, Carol, were also invited. Bob, who was married in September 1967, had been assigned to Washington by the Marine Corps for one year to study the Thai language. We all got along well.

One evening, after dinner at the Duffys, the men, Mike and Bob and I, went onto the porch at the rear of the house to fire a 22 calibre rifle. Mike apparently fired from there out into the woods behind his house for target practice. There were acres of privately owned woodland behind his house so there was no danger he told us. It was dark and Mike had set up a lighted candle about 50 or 60 yards into the woods on the fence marking the end of his property.

'Just put out the candle,' he said, handing me the rifle.

I took three shots and missed, likely by a large margin. Mike shot next and on one shot we thought we saw the flame waver a bit. But the candle kept burning.

'Let's see what the Marines can do,' Mike said to Bob. From a kneeling position, Bob took one shot and the flame disappeared. We strained to see. There was no flame. I don't know if he just knocked down the candle or actually snuffed the flame, but the candle was definitely out. I also don't know if it was just a lucky shot. But I was duly impressed, as was Mike.

'Nobody's ever done that,' he said.

Finally, in April 1967, the day came.

'This one will be just about it, Dick,' Mike told me.

'You mean I'm out of here?' I asked, almost not believing what I'd heard.

'There's a couple more small things I'll want to do,' Mike responded, 'but they can be handled on an out-patient basis. Yeah, get the hell out of here.'

I knew it had to come, of course, but after this long a time, it almost shocked me that it was now a reality. I would be leaving Walter Reed and going back to work.

Lots of questions and doubts filled my mind. How would I do? Would people react badly to how I looked? Could I just pick up where I left off? Psychologically, I experienced a sudden and unexpected crisis of confidence. I had never lacked for confidence before and this was difficult to cope with. Why would it be so difficult to *leave* the hospital? I asked myself. I had grown accustomed to and comfortable with the 'protected' life I had there, I concluded. I had to break that link and get on with things.

To start off, I had to prove to myself that I could function independently in the world 'outside' the hospital. So I planned a trip to Casablanca, Morocco, to visit Andre LeGallo, another CIA training classmate and ex-colleague, and his wife, Cathy. I had known Andre since I first joined the Agency. We had developed a friendship as we trained and had shared a house on MacArthur Boulevard. Andre, Mike Deuel and I had also gone to Laos together.

I decided I would travel alone via Madrid, Spain, where I would see a few of the local sights. It seemed a good plan to me. Nobody else thought so, however. Too much too fast, my parents chided me. Judy didn't like it either nor did many of my friends. I was determined though and flew out of Dulles in early May. Results of my effort to 'start off right' were mixed at best. Possibly it was a lousy idea.

On the plane, a hostess saw me wrestling with my steak and volunteered to cut it for me. I was embarrassed, but I let her cut it. Frustrating. In Madrid, I checked into a hotel and took a brief nap during the siesta period. In late afternoon, I took a walk. The city was bustling with shoppers and traffic. While crossing a narrow side street, I got knocked down by a passing taxi. He didn't even stop. An old woman cursed him and came over to help me up. Again, I felt embarrassed. I still had not adapted to my reduced peripheral vision and I hadn't seen the taxi that hit me. I thanked the lady for her concern and headed back towards my hotel. Nothing was broken, I knew, but I had some scratches and would probably be sore the next day. I needed to wash off. Back at the hotel, I cleaned up as best I could and lay down on the bed.

I didn't get up again for two days. Inexplicably, I had grown terribly weak and tired. I had no dinner and just stayed in bed. During the night, I developed a fever and started sweating heavily. I sent the maid away in the morning when she came to change the bed and clean the room. I lay in bed all day. I ate no food and took no medicine, and was predictably sore from my bout with the taxi. By evening, the fever broke and I felt much better. Still weak, I decided to stay in bed until morning. I slept badly, but woke in the morning feeling better and very hungry.

I left Madrid that afternoon for Casablanca, where the LeGallos met me and drove me to their apartment in the middle of the city. I spent several pleasant days with them. Andre took some time off and we drove around Morocco a bit. We went up to Tangiers and took a ferry to Gibraltar, where we spent a day shopping. I bought a Rolex watch there (replacing the Omega given to Faustino, the chief of the Congo village), which I have had for thirty years.

The one bad episode was the result of another bad idea of mine. A couple of days before I was to leave, I suggested that Andre and I hit some tennis balls. Andre and Cathy were hesitant.

'Just so I can see what I can do,' I told them.

I borrowed Cathy's racket and we went over to their club. It was a nice club, but the experience was terrible. First, I couldn't even meet the ball with the racket. My depth perception was totally lacking. It was just awful and very frustrating. Worse yet, when the ball did happen to hit the racket, my hand was so weak that the racket would fly out of my hand. It only took about ten minutes to convince me that I wasn't ready yet to play tennis. I was depressed. Cathy and Andre tried to put a positive light on it, but it was a bad experience.

I returned to Washington via Madrid again. Things went better on the return trip. I did some sight-seeing and bought several pieces of Spanish furniture made of oak – nice pieces that we still have.

On balance, the trip had positive results. I did get away on my own and managed travel abroad without serious mishap. On the other hand, I couldn't deny that there were low points caused by limitations that I would be dealing with for the rest of my life. While I didn't like that at all, I consoled myself by thinking that, at least I wasn't lying somewhere in the north-east Congo, and I did, after all, have the rest of my life to live.

THREE

ROOTS

1935–58

There were about fifteen Boy Scouts lined up in sleeping bags on the hardwood floor. Four fathers were in bunk beds in the corner.

After an active day in the woods around the cabin, situated on the shore of Lake Herrick near Chicago, we had dined on hot dogs and baked beans that had tasted far better than they were because we were so hungry. Then, as was the norm on these camping trips, we sat in front of the fireplace and horsed around. Depending upon the mood, we sometimes sang. Although tired from a day of outside activities, everyone felt good. It was late fall and cold outside, but the fire was blazing brightly and the heat it radiated made the whole cabin cosy.

Soon, with encouragement from the fathers, the process of getting everyone into their sleeping bags for the night began. That took a while. You had to go outside to an outhouse to pee and that produced lots of milling around. Other needs, real or imagined, produced further delays. Still keyed up and excited, most of us were reluctant to call it a day. One by one though, each boy got himself into his sleeping bag. But after the lights were turned off, talking and laughing persisted. Despite fatigue, no one was ready to sleep.

The fathers knew the game. After about ten minutes, the lights came on again and we were sternly admonished to 'knock it off' and go to sleep. Otherwise, it was implied, something awful would happen. We never knew what that might be and it never did happen. After the lights were turned out again it was quiet – for a while.

'Ping!' The sound of something hitting the wooden walls echoed around the cabin. There was no other sound.

'Ping! Ping! Ping!' The same sound on the other side of the cabin. Then some giggles.

Then, clearly in response, several 'pings' back the other way and some shouts of glee. That opened the floodgates and there was an immediate deluge back and forth with accompanying shouts and laughter. Bedlam.

The fathers hadn't seen this particular game. The lights came on and all four leaped out of their bunks to take charge of the now raucous cabin.

'What's going on?' one father shouted over the din of the battle. With the lights now on, he saw right away that we were busily flinging acorns back and forth across the room at each other's group. We had been doing it in the woods that afternoon and, in anticipation of this battle, each of us had returned to the cabin with pockets stuffed with acorns that had been stowed in, or near, our sleeping bags in readiness.

One of the fathers moved in between the warring groups and ordered a cease-fire. The pinging stopped.

A second father, picking up a large bucket, said, 'OK, troops. Let's have every acorn in the cabin stored in this bucket, now!'

Amidst lots of laughing and shouting about how clever we had been, all complied and soon he had a brimming bucket of acorns.

With the battle unceremoniously stopped, calm returned and, once again, the lights were turned off. Fatigued from the day's outings and the just concluded ruckus, no one resisted and soon all were asleep.

This scout trip was typical of experiences I had in my youth. We lived, during that period, in Elmhurst, Illinois, a small, quiet, middle-class town about twenty-five miles west of Chicago. It was a great place to spend a childhood and I have fond memories of my life there.

I grew up with a group of friends with whom I attended grade school, junior high school and high school. All were boys. From about second grade at Lincoln Elementary on the south-west side of Elmhurst, through high school at York Community, we spent much of our spare time together. We all joined Cub Scouts and in due course moved on to Boy Scouts. Both held their weekly meetings in the gym at Lincoln Elementary. I freely admit, and I'm sure Dad suspected as much, that a strong motivation in the beginning and a reason for regular attendance at the weekly meetings was that we got to play basketball in the gym both before and after the meetings. I paid attention though and, over time, garnered enough merit badges to become a 'Life' Scout, which is just below 'Eagle', the highest rank a scout can attain. And, an honour I cherished at the time, I was elected to the 'Order of the Arrow'. My friends all lived in the same neighbourhood and, with bicycles providing a consistent means of transportation (even in the winter), we saw each other almost daily. Among the group were Chuck Price, one of my closest and oldest friends, John Fredericksen, with whom I later attended college, the Baldwin twins John and Jerry, Ron Bosenberg, Jimmy Backoff, Bill Shineflug, Alan Hill and Gordon Kirchoff.

School was just something we had to do every day. We didn't think or talk much about it. We all did what we were told and, at my house at least, homework was always done and checked. I usually had a 'B' average and most of my friends were the same. In later years, I realized that there was little doubt that I could have done better academically. I did enough to get by and not much more. I simply wasn't motivated to study.

Sport was my passion. We played football in the fall – tackle until we got big enough to hurt each other and then flag. Basketball was an almost year-round sport, especially when we could get access to the gym at Lincoln School; we even shovelled snow off the outside court to play on warmer winter days and played ice hockey whenever the pond at the nearby water treatment plant was frozen. As soon as it was warm enough to hold a bat without gloves on, we played baseball. The baseball games went on all summer and, as we got older, we played games against teams in other parts of Elmhurst. It all seemed perfectly normal to me and I never gave much thought to the fact that I was spending a lot of time 'playing games'. My mother and father were supportive, thinking perhaps that it wouldn't hurt me and might keep me out of trouble. In the process, I learned about winning and losing (I was better at winning) and about how to play on a team. Certainly, those are good things to have experienced and I now tell myself the time I spent on sports was justified.

Those years, between second grade at Lincoln School and graduation from York High School, were easy and good years for me. I did all the things that boys did at that time and passed without problems into my teenage years.

Elmhurst was an old town featuring many elm trees that arched over the streets creating a kind of tunnel. There was no crime, no drugs – no dangers of any kind in fact. The worst thing I can remember was that a few boys smoked cigarettes in the high school bathroom and drank beer on Saturday nights. I never have smoked (a junior high coach convinced me I wouldn't be able to run if I did) and I didn't start drinking beer until I was in college. And, scandal of scandals, a girl in our senior class got pregnant! It sounds tame, but the atmosphere was positive and warm.

I was born in Chicago in the middle of the Depression. My parents had both grown up in Chicago and Dad was also born there, the eldest of three sons born to an immigrant Swedish family. His father was originally from Ljungby in central Sweden, where life, in the late nineteenth century, was tough. He had left for the United States in June 1898 and, in Chicago, he met his wife-to-be, another young Swedish immigrant. They were married in 1910.

Grandfather had been an apprentice tailor in Stockholm before deciding to emigrate and that led him to start a small tailoring business in Chicago. His shop overlooked the corner of Belmont and Sheffield Streets, a few blocks from Wrigley Field where the Cubs play baseball. Dad took me to a World Series game in 1945 where the Cubs lost to the Detroit Tigers. Undeterred, I have been a life-long Cub fan. I know, therefore, how to handle disappointment.

I remember many Swedish aspects of my early life. My grandparents spoke Swedish to each other, and sometimes to my father. They attended a Swedish Lutheran church (I did too). Foods, cultural events and celebrations (especially at Christmas) were of Swedish origin. My grandfather once made it clear to me that it was the Vikings, not Columbus, who had discovered our country, and I said as much to my fourth-grade teacher, who was gracious and understanding when I explained that she'd got it all wrong.

My mother, one of eleven children, was born in northern Michigan not far from the Upper Peninsula, where her father was a copper miner. Her grandfather had been born in Prussia and emigrated before the turn of the century. The family name, Laux, had both French and German pronunciations depending, I guess, upon who controlled Alsace and Lorraine at the time; Germany after the Prussian War of 1870 and France again after the First World War. Problems associated with the unionization of the mines in northern Michigan caused the family to move to Chicago, where Grandfather Laux took a job as a supervisor in the construction of the city's water-pipe system. Grandmother Laux was of Irish heritage and I know nothing about how they met. They died when I was still very young.

Both families were of modest means and my parents' wedding in 1934 was accomplished with minimal fanfare. Dad had graduated from high school in January 1930, just months after the October 1929 stock market crash that signalled the start of the Depression. It was fortunate indeed that Dad had graduated at the top of his class at Lane Tech High School (one of Chicago's best). As a result, he was offered (and happily accepted) a job with Illinois Bell telephone company. When the Second World War began, Dad (at the age of twenty-nine) had been married for six years and had two children. In addition, he was working in a 'strategic' industry. He was not drafted and never served in the military. Both of his younger brothers served, however, one in the Army and one in the Navy.

I was about seven years old when, in what was considered to be a bold move, Dad signed a mortgage and bought our house, a modest brick bungalow, in Elmhurst. No one else, on either side of the family, had ever left Chicago. Elmhurst certainly wasn't far, but in the early 1940s, it seemed far. Dad commuted into the city on a small railroad and life was idyllic.

My father never left the telephone industry. He soon shifted to AT&T and spent a total of forty-three years working in increasingly senior positions on teams that developed area code programmes to revolutionize long-distance telephone service. The company sent him to college and he earned the equivalent of a college degree in electrical engineering. He was a splendid father and role model for me, my two brothers, Bob and Greg, and sister,

Diann. My mother, ever loving and caring, worked hard to be a wife and a mother. She was wonderfully successful.

When I was about eleven and my oldest brother, Bob, was ten, Mom decided that we should learn how to play the piano. Neither she nor my Dad played, but she wanted us to have the opportunity and lined up Mrs Lapino, a neighbour, to be our teacher. It was tough. Mrs Lapino was demanding and so was Mom. She insisted that we practise at least a half an hour a day – even on weekends. And that wasn't all. Mrs Lapino's house was right next to the open field where all the neighbourhood kids played pickup football and baseball. We could hear them out there having fun while we hammered the keys. I doubt either one of us had (or has) much musical talent and certainly neither of us wanted to practise the piano, but it made Mom happy and we were dutiful boys. We thought of it as one of the chores we were expected to perform around the house.

At the start of our second year as pianists, Mrs Lapino decided it would be nice to have the Holm boys play a duet at the year-end recital. We were appalled at the prospect, but had little choice. Mom thought it a splendid idea. So we laboured through several months of work; first learning our respective parts, then, even harder, putting them together while sitting on the bench with each other. Mrs Lapino was patient and persistent, and eventually we could bang out the piece with only a few mistakes.

Recital day dawned. It would be memorable. For reasons never clear to me (perhaps to get it over with as soon as possible), Mrs Lapino put us first on the programme. A Lutheran church was being used for the recital, and we joined the rest of the pupils who were seated in the front, where the choir usually sat. We could see people coming in as well as Mrs Lapino in the back. She would signal the beginning. We waited. Finally Mrs Lapino gave the signal. A débâcle ensued.

We got up and moved towards the piano. We'd seen our listing. We were first, weren't we?

Another kid, Ronald Coons (I'll never forget his name), got up too and since he was closer, he was seated at the piano when we got there. Although a little shy, he was a nice kid.

Ronald has screwed things up, we thought. Without hesitation, we shoved Ronald from the bench so we could sit down. He retreated to his seat.

We started our little duet and some people started to stand up. What is going on? I thought. It had all happened rather quickly and suddenly there was commotion and confusion.

Unbeknownst to us, Mrs Lapino had scheduled Ronald to play 'The Star Spangled Banner' as an introductory piece *before* we were to play ours. Ronald was now crying softly in his seat. Some people were standing and some were not. Those standing knew they weren't hearing 'The Star Spangled Banner'. Dad was bemused. Mom was dismayed. Mrs Lapino came to the rescue!

She hurried down the aisle to usher us back to our seat. 'We'll start over again,' she announced.

Ronald played the national anthem and all dutifully calmed down and stood while he played. We followed and actually did a pretty good job.

It had been an innocent mistake, but it cut short our musical careers.

Mrs Lapino forgave us, but Mom decided we weren't old enough yet to take the whole thing seriously. I think she harboured a suspicion that we had somehow stage-managed the chaos that started the recital. 'There won't be any more lessons', she told us, 'until you are more mature.' We regretted having embarrassed her more than we regretted ending the piano lessons.

As I began my last semester at York Community High School, I decided, abruptly I now realize, that I wanted to go to college. We didn't have much spare money and my parents, while supportive, greeted my decision with caution. 'I won't be able to help much,' Dad told me, but that hurdle was cleared when, at my friend John Fredericksen's suggestion, I applied to and was accepted at Blackburn College, a small private school in Carlinville, Illinois. Blackburn had (still has although it's certainly easier on students now) a work programme that kept costs to an absolute minimum. I started at Blackburn in September 1953.

Again I must confess that my motivation was as much to try to play college basketball as it was to obtain a college degree. Half in jest, I have told people that I decided to major in economics only after I realized that I couldn't major in basketball. The truth is that, while I did play four years of basketball at Blackburn, I soon figured out that a college degree would indeed be good to have. In fact, with strong encouragement and a letter of recommendation from Dr Plotnik, my economics professor, I almost attended Washington University in St Louis, Missouri, to get a Masters.

I have never had much trouble making friends and that was the case at Blackburn. In such a small school, that meant that I soon knew virtually everyone on campus, including the girls, and there soon developed a second, in addition to sports, drain on my free time. I had dated girls in my last two years of high school; now I was much more interested. In my second year, I was so enamoured with a young girl from Wisconsin that I invited her to our home. She left Blackburn after only one year, however, and our romance didn't withstand the separation. In the end, I left Blackburn in June 1957, still single.

After a summer working as a labourer for a pipeline construction company to pay off lingering debts, I went to Kansas City, where my father had been transferred the summer after I had graduated from high school, and accepted a job with Hallmark Cards as a junior executive. I felt that life was beginning at last. Instead, a sharp change of direction was on the horizon.

Once I had graduated from Blackburn, my draft status changed from II-S (student deferment) to I-A (ripe for the draft). I had been quite open with Hallmark. Problematically, I was particularly ripe for the draft because of my age and four years of II-S deferment, but Hallmark took me anyway. But my future with the company was blocked by the draft axe hanging over my head. Training and choice assignments were, quite naturally, pushed towards those who had completed their 'military obligation'. There was no malice in this practice and I took no offence. It was simple common sense.

And so, in the late fall of 1957, I decided to get my military obligation behind me. Blackburn had not offered a Reserve Officer Training Course (ROTC), so I had only one option – to join the army. I wasn't overjoyed at the prospect, but felt it had to be done.

As luck would have it, my college roommate, Herb Gibbs, who was in a similar situation, called at about that time and suggested that we join the Army together on the 'buddy' system. I promptly agreed. We naively thought that all would go as planned and that it would be 'fun' to get our military obligation out of the way together while 'seeing the world'. So, in early January 1958, in Chicago, we joined the Army. It was a big step and I can recall thinking, at the ceremony to swear all of us in, that three years was going to be a long time. Had I waited to be drafted, it would have been just two years. Nonetheless, I was determined to make of it what I could.

With 150 other new recruits, Herb Gibbs and I travelled by train from Chicago to St Louis and then by military bus to Fort Leonard Wood, Missouri, for our basic training. On the way, Herb suggested that we play some bridge to pass the time. I agreed, but noted that we lacked two other players. 'No problem,' says Herb, 'I'll find two bridge players.'

The Army had apparently made special arrangements for its new recruits because there were three or four cars of the train filled with young draftees and volunteers in a mixed group. All were young men from the Chicago area and northern Illinois, and included inner city blacks, ethnic (Polish, Italian, German) pockets of Chicago, Latinos, and kids from small towns or farms. By contrast, Herb and I had both grown up in suburbs and then gone to college.

Herb started off down the aisle asking if anyone wanted to play bridge. He had no luck in our car and so moved into the next car of the train. While he was gone, I heard a guy several rows in front of me say, loudly, 'Can you believe that jerk is looking for someone to play London bridge with him?' The comment spoke volumes and I had to grin when I heard it. I also doubted that Herb was going to be successful. He was not. There weren't a lot of bridge players in our group.

Fort Leonard Wood was experiencing one of its coldest winters in decades and it was indeed bitterly cold. Thankfully, our military clothing issue was up to the task, and we bundled up every morning to tackle that day's training. But, after just a few days, Herb got pneumonia and was admitted to hospital. His illness signalled the end of the 'buddy' system that we had, naively to be sure, counted on. After a couple of weeks in hospital, which put him behind the training schedule of our company, Herb was stuck into another company just starting their cycle of training. We tried to fight the system, but with no success. Herb went to his new platoon sergeant, a tall black man, and complained that he had been separated from his buddy. The sergeant's response seemed to settle the issue. He said, 'Youngblood, I'z your buddy now.' Herb's illness put us on separate tracks that would ultimately lead him to Korea and me to France.

The first few weeks at Fort Leonard Wood included a couple of days of testing designed to give the Army hints about where we might best be assigned after basic training. Both aptitude and basic intelligence were tested. My results prompted an interview at which I was offered either Officers Candidate School (OCS) or Army intelligence. I took a couple of days before responding and, during that time, I tried to weigh the pros and cons of both options. OCS was certainly attractive, especially after having experienced military life from the bottom rung for a couple of weeks, but I had two lingering concerns. First, it would mean adding yet another year to my military time and I already had serious doubts about the wisdom of my decision to sign up for three years instead of waiting to be drafted for two. Second, I knew that the majority of second lieutenants were assigned to places like Fort Leonard Wood, where they spent their military time getting up at 5 a.m. to train new recruits.

In the end, I could resolve neither concern and opted for military intelligence. Without knowing it at the time, I was making an important life decision. In fact, I was simply shying away from a fourth year in the Army and hoping that Army intelligence, which I then knew nothing about, would offer up some interesting and tolerable possibilities. Considering the 'buddy' system outcome, this was probably an equally naive hope.

The remainder of my eight weeks of basic training was unremarkable. I learned how to march and half-chant half-sing along the way. I learned how to shoot an M-1 rifle. I did forced marches and daily physical training. I washed pots and pans at the mess hall one morning. And I melded in with my platoon members. This was a good experience, I think, for us all. City kids, farm kids, white kids, black kids, Jews, Catholics, it didn't matter. What mattered was to make your squad, platoon and company function well and work as a team. It was made clear to us that concerns about race, religion, or economic status had no place at all in our military life. I was named platoon leader and I value what I learned during those eight weeks. To this day I regret that the draft was ended because I believe that service in the military is beneficial in many different ways. Even in today's world, I would be a strong supporter of universal military (or some equivalent) service. Giving something to your country, for perhaps two years of your life, is not a bad thing.

I did get a break during the last two weeks of basic training. Knowing that I had played basketball in college, I was asked if I would play for the battalion basketball team. So the deal was either play basketball in the afternoon for two weeks, or go to the firing range in twenty-degree weather and practise with my M-1. This was a decision that today is called a 'no-brainer' and our team made it to the finals of the Fort Leonard Wood annual tournament.

After finishing basic training, I was transferred to Fort Holabird, Baltimore, the headquarters area for military intelligence training at that time. During the flight, my first, I got sick during the landing and was terribly embarrassed when one of the attractive young stewardesses brought me a paper bag – which I did use. Fort Holabird was to be my residence for a six-month intelligence training-course.

When I reported in, I discovered that, inexplicably, I had been assigned to photo-interpreter training instead of counter intelligence. Photo interpreters are trained to scrutinize photos (mostly taken from the air – now from satellites) and to write reports about what they find – for example, troops, vehicles, weapons, planes, trains. I was ill-suited to it and protested, but the sergeant wasn't listening. Persisting, I went higher and ultimately got approval to apply for the CIC – the Counter Intelligence Corps. I wasn't sure then what that meant, but I agreed. I was sent to a CIC office in downtown Baltimore for an interview. After much discussion, they determined that I was indeed well qualified to join the CIC. The glitch meant that I would have to sit in a holding company for several weeks until the next class started, but I was more than willing to accept the wait.

Life in the holding company for three weeks was boring but tolerable. My duties were to read and declassify, or purge, old intelligence files. Nothing very exciting that's for sure, but it did give those of us doing it a look at the CIC style of writing, which

I found to be uninspired and pedantic. I found a couple of guys I could play tennis with and played almost every day after work. I had a few beers in several of the bars near the post and found them to be just what you'd expect around a military installation – drinking, women, and periodic fights caused by mixing the afore-mentioned. They were not places where you'd enjoy spending much time. But the hours passed very slowly at that point so I spent two or three evenings a week wandering around with some of my fellow holding company colleagues. Needless to say, I was pleased when the CIC training course began.

My CIC training group numbered about 100. We were divided into classes of about twenty-five or thirty and we had classes six hours a day, five days a week. The material presented, by experi-enced CIC officers, was not at all difficult to grasp and it was hard to keep focused during class. How to write a report, ques-tioning and debriefing techniques, and source evaluation stick out in my mind, as well as witnessing, and then describing in writing, an incident. The bottom line was that a lot more time was allotted to this training than would really have been necessary. Thus, with no homework and no papers to write, we had plenty of time on our hands after work and on the weekends. We even put together a company softball team and entered the post league for the summer of 1958.

My time at Fort Holabird was unremarkable and the friend-ships I made during that period were not lasting ones. My training experiences were certainly enjoyable since they were certainly new ones for a young man who grew up in a Midwestern suburb that was, in many ways, isolated from what was happening in the rest of America. Then again, the 1950s were not a period of great tur-moil in the United States. To the contrary, many have argued that my generation was not 'activist' enough, but there just weren't any causes that would stir activism of the sort seen in the 1960s and later. After the Korean War (I call it a war, not a 'police action'), a simmering Cold War to contain communism was really the only issue on our plate. Domestically, life in the United States after the Second World War was comfortable for most people. Gay rights, the glass ceiling, multiculturalism and civil rights were issues of the future. Digesting all the effects, on our society, of the Second World War, understanding (and learning to accept) our role in the world as a superpower, and starting the baby boom took up a lot of our time.

At home, politics was always a rare subject of conversation. Nor was it discussed when we visited relatives. The earliest memory I have of a political subject (and at the time I didn't realize it was political) was when Dad complained about just-introduced farm subsidies. 'I never got paid for *not* working,' he said. He was a Republican and that, of course, influenced me. I can remember being confused when, contrary to the incorrect *Chicago Tribune* headline ('Dewey Wins!'), Harry Truman was elected President in 1948.

In our final weeks at Holabird, we were given the opportunity to make choices concerning our place of assignment as a CIC agent. I was astonished, during the barracks chatter on the subject, to hear that the vast majority of my classmates were asking for assignments in, or as near as possible to, their home towns. What a waste, I thought. It was our first opportunity to see other places. I remember being one of a small number who opted for foreign assignments. Given my experience with the buddy system and the photo interpreter screw-up, I made my choices without much optimism, but I certainly wasn't going to ask for Kansas City or Chicago; even if the latter would have offered regular access to Cubs games. Assignment day finally came and to my great surprise, and delight, I was assigned to the 66th CIC in Orléans, France. And I was perplexed to see most of my colleagues similarly pleased to be assigned back to or near their home towns.

After several days' leave with my family in Kansas City, I reported to a transportation base in New York City and left the States by ship destined for Bremerhaven, Germany. Our ship, the *General Patch*, a Second World War (perhaps even First World War) troop ship, departed in mid-December for a stormy and singularly unpleasant crossing of the North Atlantic. I suppose I shouldn't have been all that surprised since the North Atlantic in December is not known for pleasure cruises. Literally hundreds of soldiers were packed, and I do mean packed, into the *General Patch*. Each man, lugging one large duffel bag, was assigned to a bunk. That was to be our only private space for the crossing.

The bunk was, in reality, a piece of canvas stretched between iron pipes. They were stacked so that three, maybe four, men slept one atop the other. Space between you and the man above or below was about enough to slip in sideways. The bunks were designed more for space economy than comfort, one could say. Duffel bags, all locked per instruction, were stowed under or next to the stacked bunks. Bathroom facilities failed to meet even minimal expectations: a row of shower heads on the wall, a row of sinks and a row of stools. That was it. These conditions were the same for all of us, however, and there was very little grumbling. We all worked to make it through each day.

Not long after our departure, we left harbour (read protected) waters and entered the sea. It was a pleasant day and many were standing around on deck or lolling about in what passed for a lounge on a troopship. Soon after entering the sea, we all perceived a distinct difference in the motion of the ship. The primarily forward motion we had been used to in the harbour waters had been augmented to include up, down and sideways motion; lots of motion. All were faced with the problem of dealing with this. It wasn't pleasant. With memories of the airplane landing at Baltimore lurking in my mind, I feared the worst. I heard a member of the ship's crew tell a small group of sick and getting sicker soldiers to watch the horizon. I had no idea what that could do to help, but I was more than willing to give just about anything a try.

I stood outside in the chilly December air and fastened my gaze onto the horizon. To my great relief, I did not get seasick. In fact, I never again suffered any kind of motion sickness. I don't know if watching the horizon helped or not, but I was thankful to the seaman who offered the suggestion. Perhaps my Viking genes saved the day. The vast majority of the other soldiers on board were not so lucky. Soon most containers (trash and other) and toilet stools on the ship were filled with vomit. As I said, it was not pleasant. The closest I came to getting sick myself was when I had to go indoors and I saw others, many others, vomiting. Ugh! And the weather was not at all co-operative. The further we steamed north and east, the worse the sea conditions became. More motion. Lots more motion. It seemed to me that about three-quarters of those on board suffered at least mild and frequently very severe seasickness.

By the end of the second day, most on board had recovered, but some were queasy throughout the crossing and others never did hold down anything but crackers. We ran into a bad storm on the third day and that didn't help at all. You could not go outside on deck and that worried me as I needed to watch the horizon, which I did for long periods throughout the crossing. Even from inside though, I was able to find windows through which I could look at it.

Sleeping was difficult at best and at times impossible. During the storm was one of those times. The tossing of the ship, coupled with the lack of fresh air, the cramped spaces we all had to deal with, and the sounds of soldiers getting sick (again) kept the vast majority of us from sleeping that night. What to do? Nothing. We could only wait it out and hope that the ship held together. I remember thinking, This too shall pass, and eventually morning came. Things were much better up in the lounge areas, where we could look out of the window, and by midday the storm was over.

We resumed our routine of eating, reading and waiting. I knew no one on the ship and made no friends during the crossing. I found no one with whom I had anything in common. Surprisingly, even sports talk didn't go very far. I think none of us were in very receptive frames of mind. I was delighted to hear, at lunchtime on the fifth day, that we were in the English Channel and that we would soon be passing the white cliffs of Dover. I had two reasons to be happy. First, I looked forward to seeing the cliffs, and second, of greater import, this meant that we were not far from Bremerhaven and the end of this most unpleasant episode. The cliffs lived up to their reputation as we passed them heading north. They did in fact look white and they were very impressive. For some reason, portions of what I knew about European history passed through my head as I stood by the rail and gazed at England. I thought of William the Conqueror and the Battle of Hastings in 1066, and wondered how William got his Norman army across the channel. I also thought of the Spanish Armada and its demise here in 1588 by the smaller, quicker, and apparently deadlier British Navy. And I thought of the Vikings who must have passed through the channel regularly on their epic voyages. I already felt I was experiencing interesting things. That my spirits were high was no doubt affected by the fact that Bremerhaven and the end were near.

In later years, I was to see and enjoy Bremerhaven, but this visit was limited – to say the least. A few hours after the ship docked ('formalities' given as the reason for the delay), we started to disembark in two, long, single-file lines. Name and serial numbers were double-checked as we passed onto the dock. Then we walked 100 yards and got onto a waiting train. Hearing the railroad workers speaking German reconfirmed that we were indeed in Europe now.

As had been the case on the ship, accommodation was not first class, but tolerable. We travelled in what the Europeans call second-class carriages leased for this particular journey, and headed for France. We made almost no stops, but still didn't make very good time. Our 'troop' train commanded very little priority, and we were regularly shunted onto sidings so that express trains could pass us. Our route took us through Holland and Belgium before entering France. I was fascinated by just about everything. Signs in foreign languages, posters, clothes, cars, rail stations, you name it and I thought it was worth looking at. I spent most of the trip standing between the cars looking at the passing sights. I was excited at the newness of everything and didn't really mind the delays. I can remember being particularly intrigued, after we had passed into France, by watching some French railroad workers who were talking with cigarettes in their mouths. The cigarette would move a little as would their lips, but the cigarette never fell out.

I was pulled out of the crowd when we arrived at Orléans and taken to my temporary quarters in an old château. This was definitely more to my liking. Each CIC agent had a private room with all basic amenities either in the room or readily available and a private shower as well. Compared to Leonard Wood, or Holabird, or the bloody ship, this was very definitely a step in the right direction.

The other newly arrived agents were all good guys with whom I had much to discuss and speculate about. On all of our minds was the question of where we would finally be assigned. Being in the CIC and being at the 66th Headquarters were certainly good, but the next step in the process would seal our fate for the next two years in Europe. There was general agreement that the further from the Headquarters complex in Orléans that one could be assigned, the better would be the assignment. In fact, one could be assigned to either Germany or France. I definitely wanted a French assignment, but would have been hard pressed to articulate why. We didn't have long to wait. The day after my arrival, several of us got our assignments and I got Bordeaux. I was thrilled.

I stayed several days in Orléans to carry out the required processing and was there for Christmas Day 1958 – my first Christmas away from my family. Despite my excitement at being in Europe and my joy at having been assigned to Bordeaux, I recall Christmas 1958 as the least enjoyable one of my still young life: no church, no gifts and no family contact. The Army tried to help. There were about six of us and they farmed each of us out for Christmas dinner with a military family living in Orléans. It was a sensitive gesture on their part and the family I ate with couldn't have been nicer, but it was just not the same. It was only a temporary downer, however, and we all survived. Two days later, I left for Bordeaux.

It was just past noon on a grey and chilly day in late December 1958 when I got off the train at the *Gare Centrale* in Bordeaux. (To those of you who read *Peanuts* and are amused at this passing resemblance to Snoopy, let me just say that it *was* a grey and chilly day in late December.) I had been travelling with two other young CIC agents, also en route to their first post of assignment. One had disembarked in Poitiers and the other in Angoulême, so I was alone for the last part of the trip. Since I spoke no French and had never been outside the United States before, I must confess that, at the age of twenty-three, I felt a little inexperienced and uneasy about what the future would hold for me in the south-west corner of France. Of more immediate concern was contact with my base in Bordeaux.

To my considerable relief, although I certainly tried to hide it, two colleagues were waiting for me at the end of the quai. Introductions accomplished, we went directly to a small café for lunch.

Hank Boyer, a captain in charge of the CIC's Bordeaux office, and Dick Rock, a lieutenant who ran the base at Camp Bussac, north of Bordeaux, had greeted me warmly at the *gare* and the warmth was sustained over lunch.

During lunch, I was told that I would be the number two officer at Camp Bussac, a supply and logistics depot with huge stores of gasoline and petroleum products. It was part of the string of supply bases stretching, at the time, from the German border to just south of Bordeaux. Planning at that time for the defence of Western Europe, in the event of an attack by the Warsaw Pact, was to meet the attackers in central West Germany and try to hold a line. Withdrawals, if necessary, would be through Germany and France towards Bordeaux. This string of supply bases was part of the overall strategic plan and the bases themselves were placed to provide the Army with road and rail access to the front line. As a port, Bordeaux would receive the supplies and begin to move them to or through the string of bases. Bussac, like all the other supply depots, had a key role to play in the event of hostilities, and the security of all these bases was of paramount importance to the Army.

Other incidents such as a labour strike by the base workers' union that would affect the smooth functioning of the base also had to be carefully monitored. The same was true for actions such as sabotage of supplies or penetrations of the base to supply classified information to an enemy. It was the job of the CIC to check and report on these security issues and it would be my role at Bussac to develop contacts and French liaison ties that would enable me to do this. I was eager to take on the challenge.

I also discovered that since I would not be permitted to wear a uniform for my work, one of my allowances would be for clothing. That I would be obligated to wear civilian clothes caused me no pain at all, none. The military was not to be my life's career and I had no particular liking for the tedium of a peacetime army.

I was, therefore, delighted with what I considered my great good fortune. I had actually found a little niche, about as far from the US Army command structures as one could possibly get. Things had worked out very well – so far.

FOUR

RED WINE
KILLS GERMS

1958–60

Before I started looking for a modest apartment, or 'efficiency', around Bordeaux, I moved in with another CIC agent, Lawrence P. Jepson III. I've always remembered his name because I've never met another man entitled 'The Third'. It was good of him to offer, but I was soon to learn that CIC officers and agents were very close and it was not unusual for one of them to make this kind of a gesture. Larry and I became good friends.

I discovered that finding a place to live in France was not easy for a kid just arrived from the Midwest who spoke no French at all. Newspapers were of precious little help unless you wanted to live in Bordeaux itself. I had decided that morning traffic problems would make a commute from Bordeaux to Bussac unacceptable, so I was looking north of the city and concentrating my search in small towns along the Route Nationale 10. Word of mouth was the only way. Asking around in cafés, bars and restaurants usually prompted leads. After looking for two weeks, I found a place that I thought would be just fine.

My find was located in St André de Cubzac, a typical little French town along the Route Nationale 10, midway between Bordeaux and Camp Bussac. Everything was quaint to me, of course, and this town was no exception. I considered myself lucky to have found this little apartment situated fifteen minutes' drive from the city and the base. The Route Nationale ran right through the middle of St André de Cubzac, and was the lifeblood of the little town, keeping up a steady flow of customers to the bars, cafés, restaurants and hotels.

In the middle of town was a small bar called Bar Centrale and I would stop in after work for a beer, red wine or other aperitif, and to practise my French, which improved measurably over the ensuing months.

Soon, I became a regular customer, and would stop there several times a week for an aperitif before dinner. I had never done this before in my life, but it was an established custom in France and I tried to fit in. Mme Duveaux, the owner, was very patient with my early efforts at the language. Another attraction was Mme Duveaux's daughter, Mimi, who worked part-time at the bar. Mimi, who was slender, blonde and attractive, was much less tolerant of my poor French and that greatly inhibited my efforts to initiate a friendly relationship with her. She was polite, but it was difficult to communicate. We did have one 'date' when I took her to the only theatre in St André de Cubzac. It was small and poorly ventilated, and the odour of garlic was so strong that, having been in France just a short while, I could hardly believe it. I tried to hide my reaction, but Mimi might have noticed and been either surprised or upset.

My small apartment, just opposite Bar Centrale, was on the first floor of an old, corner building. It had a private entrance, toilet and two rooms, plus a small kitchen. The couch in the second room was also a bed so I could accommodate visitors. Parking was easy and readily available. The location couldn't have been better and it was to be my home away from home during my tour in France.

The task of exploring the area around St André de Cubzac was a pleasant one and the area became, and still is, my favourite part of France. Bordeaux lies on the south bank of the Garonne River at a point where the Gironde estuary splits into the Garonne and the Dordogne Rivers. The south banks of the Gironde and the Garonne create one side of the Medoc peninsula, one of the finest wine-growing areas in the world. The entire area around Bordeaux, of course, features wonderful vineyards. While not up to the historic grandeur of the Loire River valley, there are many beautiful châteaux along the Dordogne River valley to the east of Bordeaux, where prehistoric caves abound. Those at Lascaux, with their remarkable drawings, are perhaps the most well known. I was indeed fortunate to be able to visit those caves in 1959 before they were sealed off to the public to preserve the drawings.

To the west and north of St André de Cubzac is Blaye, a fortified city built by the Romans. And, of course, a few hours' drive south of Bordeaux lies the Pays Basque with its unique culture and gregarious people. Along the Atlantic coast there is Arcachon, featuring towering sand dunes and wonderful oysters, and further south is Biarritz, Bayonne, and, just below the Spanish border, San Sebastien. Clearly, there was a multitude of attractions for a young man whose previous travel experience had been to Wisconsin on family vacations and the East Coast on a college basketball trip. I took full advantage of the opportunities on offer.

At work, I was doing less challenging and therefore less rewarding tasks than I had hoped. Still, I did all that I could to make a solid and favourable impression on the CIC hierarchy starting with Dick Rock at Camp Bussac. There were a series of routine tasks that were bureaucratic and boring, such as security threats at the motor pool where local employees with access and motive might, for example, put foreign products into a petrol tank, tamper with brake lines, or disable a steering column.

More to my liking and definitely more interesting was our responsibility for 'taking the pulse' of the situation on and around the base. To do that, I set about making a wide range of contacts on and around Camp Bussac and quickly became one of the most prolific reporters in the region. I very much enjoyed the learning and the research that was a part of what it took to produce good reporting.

The current political situation – labour union activities, Soviet Bloc activities in the area, port and road network developments – were all potential subjects for reporting. I particularly liked, especially when my French had improved to a level where I could carry on routine conversations, meetings with French liaison counterparts who were members of the Renseignment Générale or the Direction du Surveillance de la Territoire – both French internal security organizations. I travelled from time to time to Toulouse and Perigueux to meet liaison officers to discuss, for example, the travel and activities of members of the Russian and

Polish Consulates in Toulouse and the movement of Bloc ships into Bordeaux port.

Soon, a pattern developed. Work on the base itself was tedious; work in the immediate area or the region was interesting and enjoyable. That pattern would persist throughout my tour in France. I again counted myself lucky to have ended up in a job in the military that had a positive aspect to it. Indeed, it would set a direction for my life in that I became very interested in intelligence work and living abroad. Both were to become integral parts of my thirty-five-year career with the Central Intelligence Agency.

Eating also became an enjoyable part of each day. With no criticism intended, it can certainly be said that my background defined me as a 'meat and potatoes' kind of guy. In my apartment, I always prepared something that passed for breakfast and actually got pretty good with a fried egg sandwich. But lunch and dinner were another story. I quickly adapted to the wonderful French cuisine. Many of the tastes were new, but very good. Eating with courses one after another was also new, but easy to accept. For lunch, I sometimes ate on the base, but looked forward to the more palatable lunches with liaison counterparts. Dinner was usually with a friend at some local restaurant in either Bordeaux or St André de Cubzac. In Bordeaux, there were dozens of great little cafés from which to choose and I was rarely disappointed in the quality of a meal.

Over time, I grew to know the chef, Jacques, at the little restaurant at the Hôtel de la Poste in St André. I often had dinner there and was sometimes alone having just come directly from work. Jacques took it upon himself to try to educate the 'barbarian' American in the finer points of French cuisine and wine. I was having no trouble adjusting to the latter and liked it better all the time. Prior to arriving in Europe, the only wine I had ever tasted in my life had been communion at the Lutheran church I attended with my parents. Now I was having wine at least once each day with lunch or dinner. Jacques felt it important that I understand *why* I was drinking wine. So he took the time to explain to me how a particular wine was better suited to a particular dish. And he made it clear that wine was actually good for my health. '*Le vin rouge tue les microbes,*' he said once. 'Red wine kills germs.' I never have forgotten his certitude. 'Moreover,' he added, 'red wines from the Bordeaux region, especially the Medoc, are the healthiest of all.'

I was young, knew nothing about wines at all, and had no reason to doubt Jacques' expertise, thus I became a convert to red wine from Bordeaux. I still prefer it although I've become much more open-minded about other wines. And I know now that the Napa valley in California has some great wines too.

Jacques also expanded my diet. I always ordered the same thing – steak and frites with a green salad. He was unaware that as my French was so weak, I couldn't say anything else, much less read and understand it on the menu. I was soon eating chicken, pork and fish as well as vegetables, fruit and cheeses.

Over time, Jacques addressed some of the finer points of eating a French meal. With my salad the waitress would always furnish vinegar and oil with which to prepare the salad dressing. I had had no idea what to do, and simply watched other customers in the restaurant and tried to imitate them: a little of this, a little of that, and some salt and pepper. Some nights it wasn't bad; others it wasn't good. It was a hit-and-miss technique. One slow night Jacques came over to lecture me on how to prepare good, consistently good, salad dressing. By this time, my French was getting stronger, but I still had some trouble with cooking and cuisine vocabulary.

'*Il faut regarder les bulles*,' he began. 'Look at the bubbles. The number and size of oil bubbles in the vinegar dictates the quality and taste of the dressing.'

This was difficult for me to grasp, but after he had demonstrated and I had a chance to actually see the bubbles (with the proper light angle), I got the point. And, subsequent to that little lesson I've always been able to produce pretty good salad dressing.

In February 1959, about eight weeks after my arrival in France, a colleague, Pete Wilson, invited me to go skiing in the Pyrenees. I had never seen a mountain except in pictures. Nor had I ever been on skis. I had no equipment or clothes and my French was still weak, but I accepted without hesitation and thanked him for thinking of me. We travelled south in a van, accompanied by three

French girls who were friends of his. They all spoke some English, but communication was laboured at best

We left on a Friday evening, first to Tarbes, and then onwards into the mountains to a small ski station called La Mongie. I do remember passing through the town of Roquefort, famous for its cheese. Not surprisingly, it was noticeable because of the strong odour a kilometre before we passed the factory. I have, over the years, grown to like Roquefort cheese, but that first introduction was unpleasant. All of the girls tried to convince me that I shouldn't be put off by the smell. I listened politely, and feigned agreement, but thought, Ain't no way any of that stuff is going to pass my lips!

A couple of days before our departure, Pete had informed me, to my great surprise, that the US Army would supply its members with just about anything one might require for leisure activities. For a $1.50 rental fee, we each picked up skis, boots and poles. The selection process was truly a case of the blind leading the blind. The sergeant behind the counter at the base knew less than either of us about which skis would be suitable. And I knew nothing. Pete, who had already been skiing a couple of times the year before, said we should hold up an arm, cup the hand, and the ski should be that long. That was probably the rule of thumb at that time for Olympic skiers, certainly not one to use with a first-time skier as the longer the ski, the more difficult it is to control. Since none of us knew any better, however, that was the length of ski I took. There was no quick release mechanism for boots at that time – just a type of heavy boot that was lashed onto each ski. I went to a local department store and bought a cheap pair of salopettes and was, therefore, outfitted for my adventure. I had no proper gloves, no goggles and no ski jacket, but I was ready and more than willing to give it a try. Happily, as it turned out, the weather was bright, sunny and mild.

We arrived at La Mongie just after ten at night and checked in at a small pension. To my *great* surprise, we were all to sleep together in a large dormitory type room with two rows of single beds. This struck me, with my background, as somewhat unusual. Pete told me not to worry. About what? I thought.

'Where do we change?' I asked when we arrived in the dormitory.

'Right here,' one of the girls responded.

I hesitated, but nobody else did.

The girls, all already wearing long underwear, simply took off their outer garments and jumped into bed. I thought sleeping in long underwear even stranger. Then I noticed how cold it was in this unheated, top-floor dorm and started to get the picture. I also figured out why the girls had made a bee-line for the beds around the chimney flue in the middle of the room. The stone was hot and generated a bit of heat close by.

Nobody else seemed the slightest bit embarrassed so I thought I'd just try to fit in. I went to the bathroom, down one level, and returned to find that the lights were already off. Fine with me, I thought as I took off my trousers and slipped into bed. Thankfully, there were plenty of heavy blankets and I slept very well despite, according to the girls, Pete's snoring.

I was in the bed on the end of a row. It was furthest from the chimney, but next to a small window on the end of the building, and so I awoke to a glorious day featuring a beautiful blue sky. Then I faced the same (for me) dilemma – how to get up and get dressed in front of all these girls. Pete must have had previous experience as he jumped up without hesitation and started getting dressed. If he can do it, I can, I figured, and I gave it not another thought. It was all part of the process of understanding and accepting things different from all I had previously known. I actually enjoyed the differences and such was to be the case in many other places I would visit or live in throughout the world.

After a 'continental' (read Spartan) breakfast, we gathered up our gear and headed for the lifts, just a short walk away. I discovered it was no fun walking in ski boots lugging skis and poles, and appreciated the location of the pension, as well as the cost of our unheated dorm.

On the way, I questioned Pete about which lift I should take. He wasn't much help. Nor were any of the girls. Because I was a complete novice, they were hard-pressed to judge what I might be willing or able to take on. One suggested that I take lessons, but that seemed unnecessary as well as too expensive for my limited budget. Finally, I decided that I'd get the most practice on the longest *piste*, which was also the highest. This was not a brilliant decision, but I didn't know it at the time. The others chose lesser practice runs, so we were separated right away. Pete voiced some concern about where I was headed (he had never been up that run), but seemed content to let me learn the hard way. I was probably too dumb to be concerned and was actually very much looking forward to getting up to the top. I had been watching people coming down the various runs and was perfectly confident that I would catch on quickly. Of course, it turned out to be harder than I had expected.

I boarded a *télé-cabine*, which should have given me a signal, but didn't, and up we went. It was truly a beautiful sight for me. Rising slowly, the *télé-cabine* made its way to the very top of the mountain, bathed in morning sunshine. With a clear, blue sky and pleasant temperature, it was just perfect. One of those days that all skiers long for and I was lucky enough to have it on my first outing.

When we got to the top there was no messing around. All the others had their skis on and had disappeared over what looked to me like a cliff, before I had had a chance to absorb the enormity of the moment. There I was on top of a mountain in the Pyrenees, looking one way into Spain and one way into France, on an absolutely gorgeous day. Impressed, I thought about how far I was from Elmhurst, Illinois, and from family and friends. I had in fact 'crossed the Rubicon'. Eventually, however, I had to start thinking about how I was going to get down.

It dawned on me that, for a novice, skiing down this run was going to be a demanding task. Had I bitten off more than I could chew? By this time a second *télé-cabine* had arrived and disgorged its complement of experienced skiers, all of whom disappeared in turn over the same 'cliff' that was the start of the run. I watched carefully to get some idea of how to approach the 'jumping-off' point – no pun intended. I had my skis strapped on and couldn't think of any reason for further delay. To me, the angle of descent at the starting point seemed outrageously steep. It was. It was not intended for a novice like me. Even though I was traversing, I promptly fell and slid about twenty metres downhill. I had not been leaning into the mountain and the edges of my skis got no grip on the hard-packed snow. As I picked myself up, no mean feat with those bloody skis strapped onto my feet, I noticed yet another *télé-cabine* arrive, and soon another stream of skiers started downhill.

This time I had a different (and better) view of their techniques. I got some good pointers. It was clearly going to be some time before I could parallel ski like the best skiers and I watched how the less accomplished skiers attacked the slope. Traverse, traverse, traverse. I started to make my way down. I traversed to gain ground and then, either while standing or having fallen (there were to be many falls), I would change directions and do it again. Happily, the descent became much less steep after the first fifty metres or so and I was able to cope. It didn't take long, however, before I started to tire and slow down. My technique was poor, and that caused me strain. And getting up after the many falls was a struggle.

An early hurdle was learning how to turn while moving. I had thought that would pose no particular problem, but it was proving to be tricky. Again, by watching the lesser skiers I noticed them using (what I was ultimately to learn) a stem christie. I began trying to imitate and soon was achieving some success, especially in areas with well-worn ruts to follow. For half an hour, I slowly, very slowly, wended my way down the mountain.

Then, suddenly, I realized that a part stem christie felt a lot like stopping on ice skates. I had played ice hockey as a kid in Elmhurst and had become a fair skater. Quick stops were necessary all the time while playing hockey and I could feel the same type of muscle co-ordination. Needless to say, I was overjoyed at this discovery.

There remained the matter of getting to the bottom. By this time, I figured I was about halfway down with just the occasional skier whipping by. There followed a lengthy period of further descent during which I diligently practised turns and stops. Finally, the bottom appeared in the distance and I had reason to believe I would actually make it down in one piece. I continued and soon could see the little restaurant at which we had agreed to meet for lunch.

Ignorant and overconfident, I had planned to meet up with my friends after the fourth or fifth run down the mountain. I checked my watch and found that it was almost 12:30, the agreed lunchtime. And I was just finishing my first, my only, run. The restaurant was situated so that you could ski right up to a terrace where many people were eating in the fresh air. I spotted Pete, who had just taken off his skis, but who had not yet seen me. The slope was gradual by this point and it was easy to ski right at Pete. I shouted a greeting and slid to a stop right next to him. He was surprised – and impressed.

'Are you sure you've never skied before?' he said.

'Never,' I replied, trying to act matter of fact, but inwardly marvelling at my good fortune. I did not bother to explain to Pete that it had taken me *three* hours to make my one and only run and that a significant portion of that time I had spent on my butt. He didn't ask.

Lunch on the sunny terrace was pleasant. We had a great vegetable soup and ham and cheese sandwiches on portions of a baguette. During lunch, Pete and the girls praised the run they had been on in the morning hours and suggested that I join them for the afternoon. I didn't see much point in talking about the run I had taken that morning and simply said that would be fine; doubtless my best decision of the day.

That evening, after a tasty and hearty dinner, we had a few beers in a crowded basement café nearby. That was nightlife in La Mongie. There was music and a small dance floor and it was very noisy. Lots of popular songs blared out including one called '*Chérie, je t'aime*', which seemed to have an Arabic lilt to it. The war in Algeria was a big issue in France at that time and I was a little surprised at the enthusiasm with which everyone sang along.

Sunday was more of the same: a beautiful day, great snow conditions and a wonderful temperature. So exhilarated was I as we stepped out into the cool fresh air, that I decided to go up to the top again. No one elected to join me. There was the same *télécabine,* the same glorious view on the way up, and the same splendid panorama at the top. Also, unfortunately, the same journey down. Having attained the 'I can make it down this mountain' level on the day before, and having convinced myself that I could now manage (barely) turns and stops, my decision to try this run again seemed sensible. In fact, it had been driven by hopelessly ill-founded confidence. I did make it down, but not without some problems. Early on after the initial 'cliff', I was traversing and inadvertently attained more speed than I could handle. With a ravine fast approaching, I attempted a sharp left turn to reverse direction. It didn't work. I ended up spread-eagled and face down with skis dug deeply into the snow. And I hit hard. Both legs hurt and I feared that I had actually done myself some serious damage. Luckily, I hadn't. How to extricate myself was the next question.

I took stock and determined that everything worked and nothing seemed to be broken. My arms were free, but both skis were well dug in and I couldn't move either leg. I was too embarrassed to call out to any of the few passing skiers for help and decided to solve the problem myself. Eventually, using the ski pole both to dig and to gain leverage, I managed to stand up. I had been forced to unstrap one of my skis in the process. I got my ski back on and continued downhill. This, my first 'great' fall had its consequences however. I was now skiing with significantly increased doses of caution and prudence. Happily, that didn't last long and I concluded that falling is a part of skiing. Even the best skiers go down from time to time. This time, the run only took an hour and a half, which was encouraging. I spent the rest of Sunday on less difficult slopes and managed to avoid serious falls, but I was absolutely hooked.

By mid-summer 1959, the newness of France had worn off and life at Bussac had taken on a routine that was less than stimulating. Still, I had only to look around me to confirm how lucky I was to be doing CIC work as a resident agent. I could have ended up working in a motor pool or as a company clerk or some other deadly dull Army peacetime job. There were monthly reports to write, status reports about the situation on the base and in the area, and we were responsible for the security of classified information at Camp Bussac – of which there was precious little. That meant that I had to routinely change combinations on the safes that housed classified documents. Each company and all of the various staff offices on the base had one or two classified documents and that meant that every couple of weeks I had a combination to change at some place on the base.

Changing the combination was much easier than it seemed although I never explained that in any of the offices I visited. The safes were relatively primitive. Once opened I had only to take out three discs that had inserts with numbers on them. I shifted the inner disc to the numbers for the new combination (dates of birth not allowed), put them in order and resealed the lock box on the inside of the safe door. I then had to test it a couple of times before closing the door and spinning the dial, *et voilà*. The new combination was set.

We also kept track of some of the physical security concerns, which meant that I occasionally rode the perimeter fence with a military police patrol to see if there were any places that would afford entry to an infiltrator. Sabotage? I strongly doubted it but we had no choice.

I routinely visited the barrack that housed the Polish guards. After the Second World War, thousands of Polish refugees and former military personnel were recruited, trained and organized into guard units that were assigned to the various American and NATO bases scattered throughout Western Europe. We had a company assigned to Bussac whose duty it was to guard the base perimeter at night. Actually, they did a terrible job, but it was not all their fault. No one had looked at their situation seriously in years. Morale was poor and, as I came to understand their position better, understandably so. They were alone; few had any contact with their families and if they did it was suspect because Poland was a member of the communist Warsaw Pact. The war had been over for almost fifteen years, yet they had little hope of ever returning to Poland. Some had French girlfriends or wives, but mostly they were a pitiful lot. They drank too much, argued incessantly and searched for ways to spend off-duty time. But they were nice guys who, for geopolitical and historical reasons not of their making, were miscast and misplaced. I made a couple of friends in the Polish company and tried to stay in touch. Our fear, of course, was that someone would attempt to exploit their discontent in some way against the Army's best interest. But apart from an occasional drinking or fighting incident, they never posed any problems.

Most interesting to me were the reports I obtained from my sources on and off the base. I had been given the names of several longtime contacts when I arrived and I saw them regularly. I was also making links of my own. I hesitate to call these people 'agents' because our efforts were not nearly so sophisticated as that. They were carefully selected people, unpaid, who knew what was going on in circles of interest to us (the employees' union at the base, for example) and were 'pro-American' enough to take the time to talk discreetly with us. No real tradecraft was ever employed. Subjects of interest included, for example, whether the Confédération Générale du Travail (CGT), a Moscow-oriented, French Communist labour union, was trying to gain influence; if any of the officials of the Russian Consulate in Toulouse were active in the area; might the fallout from demonstrations about the Algerian War affect the base in any way; if riots by supporters of agrarian reform could close roads and hinder normal operations at the base.

Gathering and then compiling this information into reports was interesting for two reasons. Firstly, collecting it enabled me to move around and, increasingly, use my French. Official liaison contacts were a part of this effort. Secondly, it was quite clearly a learning process. In my discussions with French contacts and in the reading of the local press (an increasingly useful source of information as my comprehension improved), I was gaining a better understanding and appreciation of the French and their culture. Living abroad was very much to my liking. Doing so, however, as a member of the US Army did have its drawbacks. Still, I continued to be thankful for the opportunity. Great good fortune I thought then, and still do.

Dick Rock and I worked out of a two-room office in a single-storey frame building that also had a staff office in the other end of the building. Our office had a private entrance and both Dick and I had keys. We also each had a quasi-private vehicle for our daily use. Mine was a two-year-old French-made Simca and his was a Renault, although we often traded for one reason or another. The base motor pool was responsible for maintenance of our vehicles so whenever we needed something, including gas, we just stopped by the motor pool. There were, of course, forms to fill out and mileage charts to keep, but the convenience was well worth it. I often drove the Simca back and forth to work if I had evening meetings with contacts or something work-related to do in the morning. Nobody hassled us, nobody monitored what we were doing, except Headquarters far to the north, and Dick Rock was a pleasure to work with. My reporting totals were always among the highest in France and that kept our reputation high – and attention from those higher up low. Bottom line was that our lives were more than tolerable. Rock planned a career in the Army and viewed the Bussac posting as a pleasant interlude for himself, his wife and three children.

Near our office on the base was a recreation lounge that had a table-tennis table. Once in a while, in late afternoon, to kill some time before a meeting with a contact, I would stop by to try to pick up a game. I was never in uniform and moved freely around the base – including the officers' club. (Under a military version of 'cover', I had Department of the Army civilian rank and was a member of the officers' club.) No one was quite sure how to treat me and so it was usually done with care. This particular area was frequented mainly by enlisted men on free time for some reason. The winner kept the table so I would just get in line waiting for a game.

I had played quite a bit of table tennis in both high school and college, and in high school had in fact won some local tournaments. When I would get to the table, I would assess the other player as we warmed up. There were none I ran into at Bussac that I couldn't beat. Early on, I admit that I took a malicious delight in pitty-patting the ball back and forth until just before we started the game when I let fly a couple of forehand and backhand smashes. When they got to know me, however, my little psychological ploy dropped out of use. I always enjoyed those breaks even though playing table tennis in a jacekt, tie and street shoes was not ideal. In the first few months I also visited the base gym several times and played pickup basketball. I always enjoyed it and considered joining the base team. It soon became clear, however, that the practice time and the travel time to other bases in France for games would require a much bigger commitment than I could make.

Periodically, civilians were allowed onto the base in controlled areas in order to sell their 'wares'. These included everything from suits and fine china to cars in a parking lot. While closing the deal for a VW convertible I bought as my personal car, I made the acquaintance of an American, Tim Lawson, who made his living as a car salesman. He was the kind of a guy that you instinctively don't trust much and I have no doubt that he was making money in other ways as well – including some that were illegal. He had served in the Army in the mid-1950s and was stationed at Bussac from 1955 until 1957. He decided to stay in France after his discharge and found his car salesman job after bumming around for a while. He was living with a French girl, and seemed to have lots of French friends and know a lot about what was going on in the little towns around the base (although sorting out rumour from fact was always a problem) and for that reason I would occasionally have a cup of coffee with him.

I can't remember how it came up, but on one of those occasions he launched into a long tirade about the 1956 Hungarian uprising. I had been in college at the time and, though I did remember it, I was certainly far from well-versed in what had happened. Shortly after the uprising began, he told me that he and some other soldiers in the motor pool (where he worked as a truck driver) heard, via short-wave radio, the Hungarian freedom fighters calling for help from the United States and Western Europe. Send them weapons and they would do the rest, they said. As the situation became worse and the Russian intervention seemed imminent, the freedom fighters were literally pleading for help.

He was so agitated and so frustrated, he said, that he actually considered taking a truck and driving to Hungary to fight at the side of the freedom fighters, and he insisted that others, including some young Frenchmen he knew, would have gone with him. In the end, of course, they didn't go. The Russians sent in troops and the uprising was crushed. The freedom-fighter broadcasts stopped abruptly and it was all over. He had no feeling for or understanding of the international politics that were involved, nor did I, but he was still outraged three years later.

He had two reasons for his anger and they were the obvious ones. Why would President Eisenhower, a military man, refuse to act and leave the freedom fighters to be slaughtered – especially since he knew that the Europeans would not act without American leadership? And secondly, how could the Russians be so brazen as to openly intervene in another country when the people were so clearly opposed to their government? Certainly I was no expert, but given the Cold War and the geopolitical situation that prevailed, the answers seemed obvious. The political and military assessments carried the day. But Tim would have none of that and said he still felt pain for the freedom fighters decimated by Russian tanks.

That conversation with Tim Lawson had a major effect on me in that I began to think about subjects I had not until that point thought much about. In my early twenties, I hadn't given much serious thought to the Cold War, communism, or the international situation in general. I was very patriotic and believed that the American position was right – whatever it was. Communism was bad. Russians were bad. What had happened in Hungary was just awful and reinforced my negative feelings about communism and its efforts aimed at exporting their system.

The West must strongly resist, I concluded. And the groundwork for my decision to spend a career in intelligence, living abroad and working to counter the communist ideology wherever possible, was being laid though I didn't realize it then. To say that I was haunted by that conversation is too strong, but it crossed my mind frequently for several weeks. It made me feel differently about why I was in Europe and why a base like Bussac was needed. If the Russians were ever to attack Western Europe, there would clearly be a role for all the bases strung out through France. The army was needed and it was doing its job – without much enthusiasm or efficiency, it must be said, but after all, we were at peace and the threat then didn't seem that real.

In July 1959, with Lawrence P. Jepson III and another friend of mine, a Norwegian college friend called Olav, I headed for Pamplona in Spain. We planned to participate in (not just attend) La Fiesta de San Fermin there, one of only a few remaining events at which fighting bulls were run through the streets of the town to the Plaza des Toros, the bullfight area. Why? Certainly the adventure and excitement were a part of the reason. The potential danger we either ignored or weren't smart enough to figure out.

I had written to Olav in Oslo several months earlier and he had immediately accepted my proposal to run with the bulls at Pamplona. He and Larry seemed to hit it off just fine so we were a compatible and exuberant trio as we departed. I was driving my little VW convertible and, as the weather was great, we put the top down.

We travelled south from Bordeaux to Bayonne and crossed into Spain at San Sebastien. From there, it was an easy shot east to Pamplona, a typical Basque town (except during the seven days of San Fermin).

The festival, which starts every year on the seventh hour of the seventh day of the seventh month and lasts for seven days, was to start the next morning and there were already crowds all over the town. There were already groups of people dancing the *jota*, a Basque folk dance, in the streets and squares. We had sleeping bags and planned to sleep on the ground near the car, so began to look for a nice park or field on the outskirts of the town where we could leave the car and have easy access to town. But many people had the same plan and were already camped out in a field on the edge of Pamplona. We occupied some space under a big tree on the edge of the field, locked the car and sauntered into town.

Everybody seemed to be doing the same thing – just strolling around. We joined right in and soaked up the ambience of the festival. It quickly became apparent that we each needed one of the red San Fermin neck scarves that all men were wearing. We stopped in a local shop to make the purchase and got instructions at the same time on how to fold and tie the scarf. They weren't expensive. In fact, the Spanish peseta was weak then so our dollars went a long way. We then had a few drinks and the beverage of the day was local red wine, at about seven cents. It didn't taste at all good, but that fact dimmed after a few glasses. It was strong to say the least.

We sat down at a café in a small square to think about where we would eat dinner and watched people go by. There were lots of very attractive girls, but none seemed to be unescorted and we weren't sure how to break the ice. I was the only one of us who spoke Spanish, but it was certainly not strong enough to get us very far. Eventually, about 10 p.m., restaurants started to open and we decided it would be smart to have something to eat. Despite the after-dinner coffee, we were uninhibited enough to join in with a group dancing the *jota*. One didn't need a partner. Standing in a circle, dancers, in this case mostly young men, would raise their arms with elbows bent and then alternately raise each leg (in time with the music if possible) bending it at the knee and pointing the foot forward.

By now it was about midnight and things were livening up after the dinner-time lull. People were very friendly and strangers frequently offered us drinks. They would simply hand you their *boda* and invite you to take a drink. This was easier said than done, however. The *boda* is a leather pouch with a thong to carry it on your shoulder and a spout on the end. In Pamplona they were all filled with red wine, the seven cents variety. To take a drink, you had to hold the *boda* above your head and squirt the red wine into your mouth. It was simply not done to put the spout into your mouth. Missing your mouth, of course, had predictable results – which always caused great amusement for onlookers. And many missed including all three of us. So the wine flowed – literally. And flowed.

Dancing erupted spontaneously almost everywhere we turned. By this time, the wee hours of the morning, the vast majority of the crowd was young people. All were determined to have a good time. Larry, Olav and I loved every minute of it. It occurred to me at one point that there were very few girls around. The crowd, the dancers and the onlookers were almost all young men – drunk young men – engaged, as I later understood, primarily in a ritual of preparation.

By about 4 a.m. everybody was tired. The almost frenzied level of activity dwindled noticeably and some even dozed fitfully on benches or in cafés. Instead of singing and shouting there were now conversations, quiet but focused, about the bulls. I had a moment of reflection and may even have questioned in my mind the wisdom of running with fighting bulls (I had seen these animals lift and toss horse and rider picadors with the strength of their necks and I knew they were bred to fight and die). The courage of the *boda* quickly blotted out any doubts, however, and I felt more than ready. Hell, that's why we came, I thought. Let's get on with it! Like clouds gathering for a storm, the groups of men began drifting, almost imperceptibly, towards the starting point for the run. Those who were rookies, like us, just followed. Still, there were short bursts of the *jota* here and there. Still, the *boda* was passed around. But definitely there was now a purpose to our movements. We were going to find, and then run with, the fighting bulls. Who thought this up anyway? I wondered. At this point, it felt like a part of the Inquisition that had somehow survived the centuries.

With dawn came the sun, which hurt my eyes. We stopped at a public fountain in a small plaza and splashed cold water over our faces. We all agreed that there had perhaps been too much red wine. In a just opening café we found and drank coffee.

It was by then 6.40 a.m. and the excitement level was building. We found ourselves in a long and narrow plaza on the edge of Pamplona. Already partly filled, it was now receiving a steady inflow of young men. Several strong-looking policemen (Spain's answer to a crowd control unit in 1959, I guess) were holding a rope and blocking access to the street leading towards the bullring. No one would start, they made clear, before the appointed hour – 7 a.m. All other streets leading into the plaza had been or were now being barricaded with heavy timbers. Crowds were gathered. They were waving flowers and red scarves. We had, in fact, moved into the plaza just as the street we were walking down was being closed.

The mood was quite festive again. For the men in the plaza though, it was laced with some uneasiness. By 7 a.m., no one was allowed out over the barriers. We were all, like it or not, at this point, committed to run. Climbing over the timbers, to get in or to get out, was strictly prohibited.

Nobody inside the plaza was talking much. But then, I noticed a definite surge in the crowd towards the opening that led away from the bulls. It was clear now that the bulls would be released at the far end of the plaza. How far behind us would they be? I found myself wondering. Excitement, now tinged with anxiety, was at a high level.

Then a cannon thundered. It was 7 a.m. Let the fiesta begin! The crowd roared its approval. The policemen holding the line were more than pleased to give way and the mass of men started down the street heading for the bullring. Some were running, some jogging, and some made a show of not moving much at all. The latter were no doubt the experienced ones who planned to run right among the bulls. These guys have to be nuts, I thought as I went by.

The cannon scared the hell out of me, but also sharpened my senses. I looked at Olav and Larry, raised my arm and shouted over the din, 'See you in the ring,' and started jogging into the street opening that was the only way out. They joined me and at first we were jogging along together. This isn't too bad, we were all thinking.

It had taken a couple of minutes to get out of the starting plaza. Once into the street headed for the bullring, we jogged a couple more minutes and passed an intersection, noting that it was closed with a heavy timber barricade. A runner who had apparently had second thoughts was trying to climb over to get out of the street. Not done, *hombre*! The crowd wouldn't let him climb over. Then we all heard it. The cannon crashed again to signal that it was 7:05 a.m. The bulls had been released and were running through the starting plaza and onto the street behind us. How fast would they run? How far ahead was the arena? What might distract them? *Why are we here?*

Two things happened to me after I heard the second cannon go off. Firstly, although I claim no expertise in bloodstream phenomena, I'm sure that whatever alcohol was left in my bloodstream was overcome by a surge of adrenaline. And secondly, I suddenly had a very clear goal in mind – to get into the arena and behind the fence that would protect me from the bulls. The pace at which I was moving very definitely increased.

I lost track of Olav and Larry. It was impossible in the crowd to avoid being separated. They were making their own decisions I was sure. Soon I started glancing behind me to see if any bulls were in sight. I saw none. I also began looking for places I might wait in as the bulls went by. Any port in a storm, but the narrow doorways I was passing didn't tempt me at all. I could have stood in one, but what if a bull noticed me? Not a pleasant thought. My pace quickened. A Spaniard next to me tried to hand me a rolled-up newspaper – why he had two I don't know. I didn't understand and refused. Not in the best of shape, I started to get tired, but kept moving. I tried to spot my friends but couldn't.

A shout went up from the crowd on a barricade and I looked back to see two bulls about fifty yards behind me. They looked enormous and it seemed as if their horns were almost as wide as the narrow street we were running in. They weren't moving all that fast, but fast enough, because they appeared to be closing the gap between us. While I was gaping at those two strong, beautiful, yet dangerous animals, a young man in white pants and shirt and wearing the traditional red scarf around his neck, darted out of a doorway. He ran alongside one of the bulls and started swatting it on the side of its head with a rolled-up newspaper. The guy is berserk! I thought, understanding now what the Spaniard who offered me the rolled-up newspaper had had in mind.

Despite my increasing fatigue, the sight of the bulls caused my pace to quicken again and, since I was looking behind me and not where I was going, I bumped into another runner and fell down. He did too and cursed me in Spanish. I was on my feet again so quickly that I think I may almost have bounced back up. Concern for my well-being had kicked in strongly at this point. I took off down the street as if it was a fifty-yard dash or a fast break in basketball. To my great joy, I almost immediately emerged into the Plaza des Toros and could see, directly in front of me, the entrance to the bullring. Without wavering, and with the vision of those two bulls still fresh in my mind's eye, I headed straight for it. Little did I realize that another tradition was unfolding there.

Just in front of the entrance, which was wide enough for a horse-drawn wagon to pass through, and not too much more, a bunch of men would all lie on the ground and form a big pile of bodies. The bulls approaching the entrance would, of course, notice this pile and mill around for a minute not knowing what to do. At that point the pile would spring to life, shout at the confused bulls and run into the arena. This was considered a really cool thing to do and some would say that it was my great good fortune to be arriving at the entrance just as the pile was forming.

Unaware of the tradition, I didn't see it that way at all. Here I came, cruising towards what was to me the finishing line, having already seen two of the mighty bulls, and all I saw was a group of men blocking access to the finish and safety. Of course, I couldn't figure out what was going on. Were they all crazy? There was no way I was going to be part of this. Without ceremony, I put a foot on a visible butt for leverage, and went up and over the pile. From that point it was only a few yards into the ring and safety. To say that I was relieved would be an understatement.

I looked around the arena. Despite the fact that it was early morning, the arena was half-filled with spectators, many dressed in the traditional white with red scarves. The narrow inner passage around the ring, which was protected by a stout wall with slits only wide enough for a man to slip through, was filled with men who had just finished the run. The sun was low in a clear blue sky, but bright. A small Spanish band was blaring out bullfighting songs. A warm, friendly, and still very festive atmosphere prevailed.

Where I was, in the narrow passage, bravado was mixed with relief at having finished without encountering, at close range, any bulls. A sudden roar caused me to look over the fence. The fighting bulls had entered the arena and were passing through to the temporary holding pens. A few of the 'crazy ones', as we came to call them, were actually out in the ring as the bulls passed through. I was later told that the dangers were considerably less if one knew something about a bull's vision, reactions and mobility. I remain unconvinced. Soon after the bulls were penned, the ring was filled, with mostly young men.

Tradition has it that after the bulls have passed, a young bull with padded horns is set loose in the ring. I was unaware of this tradition too, and was taken by complete surprise when suddenly the throng near me parted to reveal the young bull bearing down upon me. Young, my eye! This was a big animal and I certainly didn't want him running over me. Big eyes, wide open with a look of confusion. Legs churning. Horns, even padded, that looked ominous. With only an instant to react I, like many others around me, dived out of the way. He charged right by and I got up trying to figure out what the hell was going on.

Then I spotted Olav, who ran up and shouted a greeting over the din. He had also been surprised by the sudden appearance of *el toro*. The bull was half-frightened half-furious as he charged around the crowded ring. Like a motor-boat on a still pond, he created a wave, as men were diving one way or the other and then immediately getting up again. Some tried to fight like a matador, holding up a shirt or jacket and challenging the bull. It was no contest. He either ran over or knocked over anyone in his way. By watching the wave, we could see him coming and on his second pass we were out of his path and didn't have to hit the deck.

Spectators were, of course, enjoying it all. Most were singing, dancing, or shouting. Soon, the young bull grew tired and, on cue, a cow was led in. The cow had a calming effect and the bull, by this time exhausted, meekly followed her out of the ring. His departure seemed to signal the end of the morning's festivities. A few diehards tried to stir up some dancing, but most of us had been up all night and had been expending lots of physical and nervous energy since 7 a.m. Enough was enough, we agreed, and Olav and I started to look for Larry. The crowd in the ring was thinning out by now and within a couple of minutes we saw him standing near the fence.

As we wandered back to where we had left my car, shops and stalls were just opening for the first day of the week-long fiesta. Greetings were shouted back and forth. We stopped at a bakery to buy an assortment of rolls and ate them with some orange juice on the way back to the field where the car was.

The field, probably a pasture in non-fiesta periods, had lush green grass and a small stream ran along one edge, and really did look inviting. It was still cool although the sun was shining brightly. The little VW was still under its tree near the stream and there was a fresh, clean, country smell with a hint of clover. We tried to calculate how the sun was moving in the sky and positioned ourselves and our bags near the car and the tree for maximum shade, and dropped onto the ground. In the end, we got about five hours' sleep and were back at the Plaza des Toros at 4 p.m. for the start of the day's fights. The matadors were first-class and the spectacle lived up to all expectations. As we looked at the individual bulls, we discussed the wisdom of running with such animals, but with no regrets.

After the bullfights, there was a repeat of the scene we had found upon our arrival: strolling around, drinking lots of red wine, dancing the *jota*. At a small café in one of the squares where we stopped for a drink, we saw a large man at a small outdoor table drinking coffee. He was, a waiter whispered, Hemingway. I have read since that 1959 was his ninth, and last, visit to Pamplona.

After dinner at about midnight, we were once again ready to run and passed the rest of the night wandering through town and joining in the traditional preparatory ritual. We ran again the next morning and all three of us were safe arrivals into the ring. Fatigue, however, was starting to take its toll. It was a great experience, we all agreed, but it was time to head back to France.

Les Landes is a *département* of scrub pine flatlands along the Atlantic coast from Bordeaux south towards the Pays Basque and the Spanish border. At a point right on the coast about where the Medoc peninsula ends and Les Landes begins, lies the town of

Arcachon. The town has the typical beach resort air to it, with lots of beautiful homes placed among the abundant pine trees that dot the coastline. And of course there are dozens of good restaurants, many of which offer fine oysters cultivated and harvested in the area. There is also a large marina that hosts dozens and dozens of beautiful and sleek sailboats. Sailing there is very popular and one can often see rainbow clusters of sailboats racing along – spinnakers billowing out in front and shining in the sun.

My first visit to Arcachon was suggested by Raymonde, a girl I had met at Camp Bussac where she worked as an assistant in the finance office. She was pretty and full of life, with dark hair, eyes that really sparkled, and even, white teeth. There were, of course, many other young French girls working on the base, and some dated Americans, but none interested me. After seeing her a couple of times, Raymonde did, however, and I wanted to introduce myself, but could contrive nothing natural. I was too shy to simply walk up to her, so I just watched from afar. Finally an opportunity presented itself. At lunchtime on a warm summer day, as I was coming out of the Base Exchange, the base's small department store, I literally bumped into another girl from the finance office with whom Raymonde was walking. I apologized more than was necessary and told them that I was in deep concentration as I was on my way to my French lesson.

They were gracious and friendly so I pressed on and asked them to help me by explaining how to pronounce *Les Etats Unis*. They asked that I try, which I did, and they both smiled. They agreed to help and there ensued a short conversation that broke the ice admirably. I don't know whether or not Raymonde had noticed my interest, but if so, she had not been put off by it and was pleasant and charming. Thereafter, I was able to greet her whenever our paths crossed and gradually to learn more about her. She lived alone in Bordeaux and commuted each day out to Bussac. Her father was French and her mother Israeli, which, in my eyes, only made her more attractive. She spoke Hebrew, Arabic, French and English and was an avid reader in all four languages. I couldn't speak Hebrew and Arabic, of course, but I could see that her French was fluent, as was her English. Our friendship grew and I asked her occasionally to the snack bar for coffee or a coke. Our conversations were innocuous; she didn't like to talk about herself and avoided subjects that might lead to discussion of her background. Meanwhile, I was blurting out my whole history. Once that had been thoroughly covered, I steered our conversations towards things French and asked about things to see in the Bordeaux area. We talked about Blaye, the fortified town built originally by the Romans, St Emilion, Bordeaux itself, and Arcachon. She said it was beautiful and that she was sure I'd like it.

'*Avez-vous jamais mangé les huîtres?*' she asked. 'Have you ever eaten oysters?'

'Are you kidding?' I responded. 'I'm from the Midwest, remember?'

'You'd probably love them as much as I do,' she said with a bright smile. 'And the season is just starting.'

With this clear opening in front of me, I immediately jumped in. 'Well, if it's that great, why don't you show it to me?'

She smiled, thought for a moment, and said, 'OK, I will.'

I was delighted with the prospect of not only seeing a new place, but seeing it in the company of a pretty and charming tour guide.

'Great,' I said. 'I'll pick you up on Saturday morning and we can have lunch in Arcachon and then climb the dunes.'

The following Saturday morning, with the directions Raymonde had given me in hand, I drove into Bordeaux and, with only a couple of wrong turns, found the town house where she had a room. Raymonde was waiting in the foyer. She seemed happy to see me and I felt sure we were going to have a great day together. And so off we went, the top down on the VW. Her long, black hair was pulled back, but still blew in the wind. I was as happy as a clam.

As we chatted, we got onto the subject of what we did on weekends. I rattled off a range of activities including visits with friends, tennis, dinners, and made it clear that I was delighted to be in France learning about and seeing new things and making new friends.

Hers was a different story. She hesitated, but finally admitted that her weekends were pretty limited. She had few friends, virtually no close ones, and her activities were confined to small domestic chores in her room and an occasional movie. I didn't believe that someone as vivacious and attractive as she could be so isolated, but I let the subject drop. She certainly didn't strike me as a loner. I was puzzled and hurt that she had not responded to my openness. She apparently was of the opinion that her personal life was just none of my business and I thought it was perhaps just one of the cultural differences between us.

At Arcachon, we passed on the Saturday morning market, which was in full swing, and headed straight to the magnificent dune of Pyla. It was much higher and bigger than those I'd seen on the south-east coast of Lake Michigan and had a wonderful view out to sea. Raymonde could see that I was impressed and that seemed to please her in turn. She took off her shoes and start wading in the surf. I wished I'd brought a camera. We stayed there for about an hour and then took a ride around the immediate area before heading into Arcachon to find a restaurant. I was enjoying her company; all the more so perhaps because our previous contacts had always been limited at Bussac.

Our search for a restaurant was interesting and more involved than I would have expected.

'Do you really want to try oysters?' Raymonde asked. 'You don't have to,' she added.

Not wanting to appear timid, I confirmed that I certainly did want to try them.

She first assessed the 'look' of the place and if it passed that test she reviewed the menu posted either in the window or on a billboard in front of the restaurant. By a little after one, she had selected a restaurant and we were seated at a table with a view of the harbour. We decided to share a platter of oysters – a sensitive suggestion on her part and, as it turned out, a very sound decision on mine.

When they served the oysters, I realized immediately that they were raw. I don't know what I had expected, but not these filmy-looking things lying in their shells. Growing up the only things we ever ate raw were certain vegetables and fruit. I didn't like to appear squeamish, however, so I knew I had to eat them. I watched Raymonde eat the first one and was appalled to see that she barely chewed it at all. Just sorta slipped that devil down.

I don't know if Raymonde sensed my pre-first oyster anguish. If she did, she ignored it and chatted away happily. Oysters are, in my opinion, an acquired taste. I didn't like my first beer either. And over the years, I've grown to like oysters very much and even have favourites – like those from Zeeland and Brittany. But sitting there that day in 1959 knowing that I was going to have to put six of 'em down, my taste buds were not exactly filled with great anticipation. Dread would have been a better word. Trying to be helpful, I think, Raymonde handed me my first one. I got a hold of the slippery little thing and threw it down. For good measure, imitating the guy at the next table, I then drank the water left in the shell. Don't ask me why.

'*C'était très bon, n'est-ce pas?*' she asked.

'*Formidable,*' I replied.

The rest of the meal was delicious. Last, as is tradition, came the salad course. Here was my chance to employ the skills I had learned from Jacques in St André so, trying to sound natural, I suggested that I prepare the dressing. Raymonde seemed at once surprised and amused. '*Avec plaisir,*' she said. Happily, or luckily, as the case may be, I got a good ratio of bubbles of vinegar in the oil and appropriate portions of salt and pepper. Raymonde tasted her salad and lauded the high quality of the dressing and we toasted the fact that this young man from the middle of the United States had already learned something practical in France. The oyster anguish melted away.

As we were leaving, I told Raymonde that she had been right. I really did like Arcachon and I thanked her for her suggestion. A little impishly I thought (I was driving and didn't see the expression on her face or the look in her eyes) she said she was glad that I had enjoyed Arcachon *and* the oysters. We got to Bordeaux in the early evening and I parked so I could walk her into her building. I told her how much I had enjoyed the day. Raymonde smiled and I sensed that she felt the same way. She said she'd had more fun today than in months. I was pleased and just about to leave when she leaned towards me and gave me a little kiss on the cheek.

'*Merci beaucoup,*' she said over her shoulder as she went up the stairs.

'We should do it again,' I said quickly.

'*D'accord,*' was her response and she was gone.

It had been a great day, I thought as I was driving back to St André de Cubzac. And Raymonde had made it. She had ample doses of charm, wit and intelligence. She was easy and fun to spend time with, and she was pretty as well. It was true that I'd seen a very nice town on the coast, but the companionship she added really made the difference. How pleasant would it have been had I driven out there alone? I was at least somewhat smitten by Raymonde and I certainly wanted to see her again. In the week following our visit to Arcachon, I saw her twice for coffee. I tried to steer our discussion towards another outing somewhere, and eventually she agreed to go out to St Emilion the next Saturday. It was another enjoyable day and we capped it off at dinner in a small restaurant in Bordeaux. However, she was still reluctant to talk about herself. I concluded then that it was more than a cultural thing. But if she wouldn't talk, there was little I could do.

Over a couple of months, I saw her at least weekly and we always seemed to have a good time. We went a few times to the opera in Bordeaux and to the movies. I liked her more and more and was increasingly perplexed at the unspoken, but apparent, wall she had erected between us. I'm not sure what prompted it, but one day, while walking in a park in Bordeaux, she sat down on a bench and said she wanted to talk to me.

'About what?' I asked.

'About me and about us,' she replied.

I became very attentive, wondering what would come next.

'*Je suis mariée*,' she said. 'I am married.'

I could hardly believe her. 'Why didn't you tell me?' I demanded in a stronger tone than I had intended. I felt utterly betrayed.

'The marriage has not worked. We are separated. There will be a divorce soon,' she blurted out in a rush. 'And I was afraid to tell you. I know I should have and I'm sorry.'

'I don't know what to say,' I admitted.

'You must tell no one,' she pleaded.

'But why?'

'Only a few people in Bordeaux know, and it is better that way.'

'When is the divorce?'

'Soon.'

'But what should I do? Why are you telling me this now?'

'Because I like you more and more and I know you like me. I wanted you to know.'

I was trying to think, but couldn't digest this news and I said little more as we walked back to her house. When we got there, she just smiled, kissed me and said goodbye. I watched her go upstairs. That night I slept fitfully.

My dilemma dragged on. I continued to see Raymonde over the next couple of weeks, but something had definitely changed. She continued to insist that everything would be all right soon. I had my doubts and cursed myself for having let myself get into such a situation. I rationalized and convinced myself that, in the end, this would all be a bad memory. Still, her news had changed things despite how I felt about her. I had strong doubts and struggled with questions about what to do. Just not see her again until the divorce is final? Insist on specifics about when the divorce would be final? I just didn't know.

My dilemma ended abruptly. I returned to my apartment one day to find a letter. Normally, I received my mail through the military post office, so it was very unusual for me to receive a letter in St André de Cubzac through the French mail. Maybe it was from Olav, I was thinking as I picked it up. My landlady had put it on the stairs leading up to my small apartment. It wasn't from Olav. It was postmarked Oran, Algeria, and I didn't know anyone there. I double-checked to be sure it was addressed to me.

The letter was from Raymonde's husband. Written in clear, blunt, French it made one basic point: You, Mr Holm, must stop seeing my wife. I read it and re-read it. It came like a thunderbolt out of the blue. He was a paratroop officer in Algeria.

How could this be? How could he know me? Or my address? Didn't he know that I didn't know of the marriage? What about the impending divorce? I was stunned.

I never saw or heard from Raymonde, or her husband, again. I tried to see her the day I received the letter, but she wasn't at home. She wasn't at Bussac the next day either and then I heard that she had resigned. I didn't know what to do. Months later I heard from one of her friends at the office that she had, at her husband's request, gone to Oran to join him. Not a note, not a call did I receive from her. The experience left me troubled and wounded. Sadder, but wiser and perhaps more mature, I concluded my tour in France several months later and returned home.

Excluding the fateful relationship with Raymonde, my experiences in France, and most especially the taste of intelligence work that I gained, caused me to think seriously about similar work after I finished my military service. Returning to Hallmark Cards now held little appeal. Intelligence work, albeit at the low levels I had practised as a CIC agent, was much more attractive to me, as was the possibility of living and working abroad. I was, moreover, strongly motivated by a sense of patriotism. What had happened in Hungary and in Eastern Europe was wrong. Communism was wrong and the Cold War we were fighting was important. I wanted to contribute in defence of American values and ideals.

And so it was that in the fall of 1960 I wrote to the Central Intelligence Agency and applied for employment. Soon I received their response. It sounded bureaucratic, but it didn't dim my enthusiasm. For security reasons they couldn't talk with me while I was overseas, but I was invited to meet them in Washington.

My return trip was easier in that I travelled by plane rather than ship. I said my goodbyes to friends. Then I took a train back to Orléans, where the typical military processing was accomplished. I did experience a problem, of my own making, in that I hadn't touched my uniforms for the two years I was in France, and when I took them out of the closet I discovered that the trousers had shrunk. I considered the possibility of poor storage conditions, but finally conceded that it might have been the French cuisine that had caused the problem. Thankfully, there were no inspections.

On landing back on American soil, I got my discharge papers at Fort Dix, New Jersey. My military service was over.

FIVE

JOINING THE CIA

1961

With the CIA's return letter in hand, I simply turned up at the Agency's recruitment office on 16th Street, Washington, DC. Interviews and a battery of tests followed, and I was offered a position in the Agency's file rooms. I would start on a night shift, I was told, and with satisfactory performance I would soon have opportunities for advancement. I was disappointed and pointed out that I was a college graduate with military experience.

'Oh, this is standard,' was the response from the interviewing officer.

'Well, it isn't what I was hoping for,' I said. 'Are there any other possibilities?'

'There is the Junior Officer Training, the JOT programme,' the officer said, 'but I'm not sure there are openings just now.'

'What's that programme like?' I asked.

He explained and I could see right away that that was what I'd like to do.

I also learned, however, that standards for acceptance into the JOT programme were high. I regretted some of the hours I had spent playing basketball and bridge in college instead of studying. My grade point average hadn't set the world on fire. I had done well on the graduate record exam though and had been accepted for a Masters at Washington University in St Louis before my military service. I hoped that would help my chances.

Six months and a comprehensive security investigation later, I started my training along with twenty-five other JOTs. It was

June 1961. In April, I had received a phone call telling me that I had been accepted. A separate letter a week later gave me specifics about where and when to report for training. My parents were uneasy. I was elated.

I drove straight through from Kansas City to Washington, DC, in my new Triumph TR3 in British racing green. I had recently purchased it in England (at a dealership in Berkeley Square in London) while on a trip to Europe with a friend and I was very proud of it. My prospects were looking good. I had been accepted into the programme I had wanted and I was looking forward to my initial training and the start of a career.

I stopped by the JOT office to check in. I was given some leads on housing and was soon established in an old house on MacArthur Boulevard in north-west Washington. I lived with three other young men, two of whom were also Agency officers. The fourth man was an Air Force officer. Two other JOTs joined us shortly thereafter so, of the six living in the house, there were four of us starting in the same class. That made many things much easier as we travelled together both in Washington and subsequently to our training facility in south-east Virginia. With many things in common, we made friends easily and those friendships have lasted over the years.

The first six weeks of training were spent in the Second World War era 'temporary' buildings near the reflecting pool in front of the Lincoln Memorial. Right on the Potomac River, it was a beautiful setting, despite the buildings, which were singularly unattractive.

My fellow JOTs were a very impressive group of twenty-four young men and three women. Word was that JOTs were the 10 per cent of applicants to the Agency, which, with the Foreign Service, had the highest standards in the government. Each of us had a list of class members and I perused mine with interest. Almost all had military experience (that was pretty much standard because of the draft), many had graduate degrees, and the range of majors studied in college was broad. Excluding four of us from the Midwest and a couple from the West Coast, all were from East Coast schools. It was a very high calibre group and I was lucky to be a part of it. My bachelor's degree, with a major in economics, from Blackburn College in the middle of Illinois had landed me in a spot I had never thought of while in school.

They started, naturally enough, at the beginning and gave us background about the origin of the Agency and Second World War intelligence issues. We got detailed briefings on the Agency itself and the four Directorates into which it was divided – Plans, Intelligence, Science and Technology, and Administration.

We all were destined for the Plans (Operations) Directorate. A detailed look at the intelligence community and how it served policy makers was next, followed by a review of post-Second World War events and the origins of the Cold War that dominated the world scene at that time. The confrontation between the free world, led by the United States, and the communist-inspired totalitarianism practised by the Soviet Union, China and their satellites, was the main reason all of us were there. I remember thinking again about Hungary and was very focused during those lectures.

There ensued several weeks of classes on international communism presented from a scholarly and historical perspective as well as from the intelligence and operational view. I had studied communist and socialist economics, but had read little about the politics. Learning about the inner workings, for example, of how a communist cell functions and is organized, gave much food for thought, and we discussed it among ourselves during breaks. It was a lousy system, we all agreed, and it needed to be resisted. Despite our varied backgrounds, there was a consensus on the subject of communism – it had no merits.

We also began the process of learning how to write intelligence reports. There was, of course, an accepted style, and we had to learn it. It was a little like newspaper writing, but with emphasis on precision and detail and no opinion unless clearly labelled as such.

To explain some of the nuances of reports writing, evaluation and dissemination, we were treated to a lecture by Wally Deuel. He also covered the 'requirements' process and its impact on field collectors – which we would all be one day. The requirements process is more formal now than it was in 1961 and has been refined and restructured in order to make it more responsive to policy makers. In the early 1960s it was the process whereby officials (at various levels) in the executive branch who were responsible for formulating policy would articulate their requests (requirements) for specific information about a vast array of subjects. Those requests would be staffed out and passed to that part of the intelligence community most likely to be able to collect the information.

Of special note at the time was the fact that Wally's son, Mike, was one of our classmates. With Mike's dad at the lectern, interest was high and we were not disappointed.

Wally Deuel started his professional life by accepting a post at the University of Beirut, in Lebanon. While there, he met and married his wife, Mary. He later joined the *St Louis Post Dispatch* and became a foreign correspondent for that paper. He had been posted in Rome during the early and mid-1930s and in Berlin during the late 1930s. He was intensely anti-Hitler and left Germany in 1939 to return home where he wrote a book called *People Under Hitler,* published after the war. During the war, he worked in the OSS and he later helped to write a history of that organization. He subsequently saw a need to resist another totalitarian movement and joined the newly established CIA to help stop communism from taking over Europe. A background like that would have been enough, but Wally Deuel was also an articulate and very entertaining public speaker. Obviously an expert on his subject (he had written many of the regulations that governed reports writing), he had a wry sense of humour. His presentation was a great success and headed some in the class towards reports officer careers or analysis. I'm sure Mike was quite proud.

On Sundays during those early weeks in Washington, groups of us (mostly the bachelors) would congregate on the mall or ellipse to play touch football. Other young men would come as well. I mention this because of the distinctions that surfaced. We would choose sides, and almost invariably it would be an Agency team against a Foreign Service team. Granted, some of us knew each other, but there was more to it than that. There seemed to be an intangible difference. All were bright, well-educated, personable young men, but our respective choices for career paths revealed different viewpoints and approaches. Agency officers (especially those aimed at the Plans Directorate), in general, were more action oriented, while the Foreign Service officers seemed to be more reflective and analytical. I say that to make no particular point other than it was a difference that registered – not only on me.

It was a distinction that would plague us throughout our respective careers. In my experience Agency officers and Foreign Service officers rarely saw eye to eye on specific issues. A mutual lack of trust and confidence consistently limited our respective efforts. Competition for the President's ear contributed to the problem as did a lack of real understanding of the other's role, but much of the cause I believe was (is) that we are simply different kinds of people. For that there is no ready solution. It is not a problem unique to us; the British and the French, for example, lament the same problem.

Early in the Washington portion of our training, we were scheduled to meet with the Director of the Agency at the time, Allen Dulles. He had a wonderful reputation, of course, and this was to be quite an honour for us. Many in the Agency never had such an opportunity. We were ushered in, en masse, one morning to his conference room. I knew little about him at the time except that he had a fine wartime record and that he was highly respected in Washington. His brother had been the Secretary of State under President Eisenhower. He spent twenty minutes welcoming us to the Agency, telling war stories and emphasizing the need for good intelligence during this critical time of the Cold War. No mention was made of the disaster suffered in the Bay of Pigs covert operation just months earlier. Then his secretary came in and announced that the President wanted to see him at the White House. We were all very impressed. That his secretary may have done the same thing each time a group of young JOTs was meeting him neither occurred to nor would have bothered us – at all. I liked Allen Dulles and believed him to be sincere in his efforts to sustain a strong intelligence community and an active clandestine service. I cannot say the same for some of the other twelve Directors for whom I would serve, Deutch, for example, or Turner.

Soon, with the groundwork laid, we were dispatched to the Agency's training facility in south-east Virginia, known within the Agency as The Farm. About three hours' drive from Washington, The Farm was to be our home away from home until Christmas. It was located on a former military base with a large river forming a part of its perimeter. There were few amenities. We were assigned rooms in a hut with a fan in each room. Spartan would be a good word to describe the furnishings and the one bathroom we shared, but we were too busy to complain about accommodation that we used only seven or eight hours a day.

Standard dress was military fatigues and combat boots and we ate in a mess hall that served copious amounts of food. We had no complaints there either. There was a gym a short walk from our quarters where we did required physical training each morning. Some took the PT in their stride; others did not. I didn't mind it as, excluding the two years in France, I had always tried to stay in good physical condition. If time permitted, a group of us would play basketball in the gym before dinner.

Apart from the PT and an occasional basketball game, there were no distractions. The facility had a patrolled and fenced perimeter and no unauthorized individuals were allowed on base. We were isolated and purposefully so. The setting was serene and we were expected to concentrate on one thing – our training. We did just that and, in fact, time passed swiftly. The range and depth of subjects we covered kept us busy for up to eighteen hours a day for the length of our stay. The art of 'tradecraft' – the methods employed to manage a clandestine intelligence operation, and I argue that it is an art because of the nuances that are involved – is not easy to learn. Some, lacking the required personality traits, can never learn it. And it is not acquired in five months of training, which provides only a framework. Actual experience running operations is essential. A Swiss banker isn't handled like a Jordanian camel driver although, in a given situation, both can provide vital information to satisfy policy makers.

The training itself, interesting because it was new and different from anything any of us had ever experienced, took on a life of its own. Blocks of time were allotted to specific subjects and we ploughed through each one: agent recruitment, agent handling, clandestine communications, surveillance and counter surveillance, report writing (good writers, we found, really had a distinct advantage), cover, security, liaison operations, covert operations, counter intelligence, debriefing and eliciting, etc.

Lectures covered philosophical, ethical, psychological, or academic aspects of every subject. However, training was always a hands-on effort. Lectures were followed by practical exercises. You had to actually do, several times at least, everything you were taught. Each class member had a mentor, an experienced operations officer, who monitored his or her progress. Strengths and weaknesses surfaced and were promptly addressed. If your eliciting or debriefing skills were not up to par, for example, extra practical exercises were arranged. Standards were pre-set and high. To successfully complete the training, every person had to meet, at least, those standards. With agents' lives and diplomatic incidents detrimental to our country's best interests possibly at stake, we were serious even in a training situation. This is not to say, however, that humour didn't creep in and those light moments helped relieve tensions.

During the fall of 1961, while we laboured at The Farm to master the principles of tradecraft, leadership of the Agency changed. A respectful seven months after the failed Bay of Pigs invasion Allen Dulles resigned. Dutifully, he took the rap. Following an intensive search to find 'the right man', President Kennedy named John McCone to succeed Dulles. McCone, a staunch Republican, was appointed, it was said, to emphasize Kennedy's belief that the Director of the CIA was not a political position. Like Kennedy, McCone was a Roman Catholic and an intense Cold Warrior. To him communism was an evil. We heard about it, of course, and some lamented Dulles's role as scapegoat, but it had minimal impact on our busy lives. Like a frog looking up from the bottom of a well, our view was somewhat limited.

The final exercise, during which we were expected to employ the full range of clandestine tradecraft techniques we had learned, was held over a period of three days in Baltimore. Acting in our traditional role of intelligence collectors, we were pitted against FBI officers in a counter-intelligence mode as our opposition. Stressful at times, it was also fun, partly, I think, because it signalled the end of our training. With one exception, the entire class completed the course, with strengths and weaknesses duly recorded in our respective files. The exception was a young man who dropped out of his own volition shortly after we started. He left the Agency to become an Episcopalian minister, a decision that puzzled the rest of us because of the difference between the two career paths.

Late in our training period, we were given a brief look at covert and paramilitary operations and how they fitted into the range of support the Agency could provide for the President. I found it very interesting, especially the paramilitary operations. Young and single, I thought this would be exciting. During that phase, we were given the opportunity to volunteer for an intensive four-month paramilitary training course, to include parachute training. Concluding that the additional training, and perhaps a short stint in paramilitary operations, would be worthwhile, I volunteered, as did eight other members of my class.

After a week's leave at Christmas to visit my family and several weeks at Headquarters in Washington, I reported back to The Farm in early February 1962 for paramilitary training. A couple of my MacArthur Boulevard housemates had also volunteered, and to prepare for it we had been running each morning before work during January and early February. It wasn't much fun. Part of our incentive, I have to say, came from the fact that a neighbour-ing house of girls, with whom we had struck up a friendly relationship (destined to go nowhere because of our frequent absences) had invited us for coffee each morning after our run. They were nice girls, two of whom were very attractive, and we enjoyed seeing them – even at 'oh dark hundred' on a January morning. The exchanges over a cup of coffee were entertaining as we tried to live our 'cover assignments' (Department of the Army civilians) and explain our absences. It was not an easy task. And they weren't buying our story, but never made a fuss about it.

For the duration of the paramilitary course, physical training was required and at our first session we met Burt Courage, who would be one of our instructors. We were impressed as Burt demonstrated pull-ups and push-ups – with one arm. He was, needless to say, in very good shape. Quiet and unassuming, he was a big, strong guy. We liked him, or respected him at least, and that helped us get through the strenuous PT sessions that always ended with a several-mile run. Our early morning runs had been worth the effort.

Our instructors were all highly skilled men. Each had several years' military experience and many had years of Agency experi-ence in the field as well. Each taught a speciality in which he was particularly expert. The goal was to familiarize us with a wide range of military skills that could be used in selected situations later in our careers. Much was made of the fact that, in many parts of the world, military officers were in control of governments or deeply involved in politics. Recruiting them as assets for our station would be an important task and familiarity with the military could only help. Moreover, paramilitary operations were being run in several countries at that time (Laos for one) and the Agency needed officers with the qualifications to run them. This training would help to prepare us for those tasks. This training was to be more blunt than tradecraft. Paramilitary operations are not an art.

Weapons training was an important part of our training and in it we were familiarized with, and fired, a whole range of US small weapons. Rifles, pistols, machine-guns, rocket launchers and mortars all got a turn as we spent many hours on the firing range. We also saw and fired many foreign weapons including those manufactured in Russia, China and Czechoslovakia. In the army M-1 rifle training, I had been awarded a Marksman medal. But I was not particularly comfortable in this block of training and more or less tolerated it rather than enjoyed it. Nor was I very good at it. Since it was designed only for showing us the weapons and letting us fire them, it didn't matter much whether we liked it or not. It certainly served its purpose and for me personally it was helpful in later assignments in Laos and the Congo.

Small unit tactics was another important block and much time was allotted to both the theory, citing Mao Tse Tung, Che Guevara and others, and recent uses thereof in various parts of the world. We used standard US tactics as our guide and, following the lectures, we spent many days in the woods and swamps on the base practising what we had been taught. To this day, I question the value we derived from wading waist-deep through cold swamps in February and March. But we did it and, I guess, got tougher in the process. Leadership was always emphasized and we rotated as platoon leader in our practical exercises. Everyone did well. Knowing that their turn would come, we were all very co-operative and helpful in both the planning and the execution phases of our exercises. With the best of intentions, however, things can still go wrong.

We had had two planning sessions to prepare for a simulated raid on an enemy camp. Timing, deployment, weapons and personnel were all decided. We had everything under control – we thought. The plan was to hit the camp at noon while they, the enemy, were eating. What could go wrong? We had it covered. At about eleven, the instructors dropped us off about half a mile from the target site and we started approaching, carefully. We had the co-ordinates and we had studied the terrain on our maps that morning. Up and down a couple of ridgelines and we would be there.

We went up and down a couple of ridgelines. Then up and down a couple more. Then we retraced our steps. Then we sent out small patrols. Clearly, we wouldn't be hitting the camp at noon.

To make a long story (afternoon) short, let me just say that we never did find that damn camp. We couldn't have missed it by much, but we missed it. The terrain all looked the same, but that wasn't an excuse. Most of us had had previous experience in similar settings, but that didn't help. It was embarrassing as hell, that's for sure, and the instructors didn't let us forget it for the rest of the course. But the learning point was clear and I would bet that none of us ever forgot that day and the camp we missed. Our first brush with Murphy's Law: if something can go wrong, it will.

A block was also allotted to parachute training. The lecture period was short. There isn't that much to say about throwing yourself out the door of a plane at 2,500 feet. Again the instructors were excellent, with much experience and hundreds of jumps on their records. Our physical training was intensified for this block. Lots of running and sessions aimed at teaching us to do the parachute-landing fall, the 'PLF'. Hours were spent practising PLFs by jumping into a sawdust pit from a six-foot platform. Next came our first jumps from a sixty-foot tower. This was standard training at the time and was intended to instil confidence in jumpers as well as to condition them to obey the jumpmaster's commands. It was not fun and few in the group liked it, but it was a necessary evil. A cable was attached to the tower just above the door used by jumpers. Each man strapped on a parachute harness that was snapped onto the cable. Once out the door, a jumper would slide down the cable to a soft landing about fifty yards from the tower. Simple. Actually, it is not.

The first tower jump was the worst. We jumped in 'sticks' (the military term for men in a line ready to jump) just as we would from a plane – four men to a stick. I was to be second man out the door and I remember thinking that I'd rather be first and get it over with. I climbed the tower without much enthusiasm, resigned to the fact that this had to be done. On the top, we entered a small room with metal walls and a cable leading out the door on the side of the tower. The instructor who was jumpmaster was standing there waiting for us. He knew, of course, that we were not looking forward to this. It was to be a preview of jumps from a plane so his commands were the same. We strapped on the parachute harnesses and stood in a line waiting.

'Hook up,' the instructor called out. We dutifully complied by snapping our harness line to the cable leading out the door. 'Get in the doorway,' he ordered, and the first man shifted to the door and put a hand on each side of the doorframe. Knees bent in a ready position, he waited for the next command. It seemed as though minutes passed.

'Go!' the jumpmaster shouted. And out the door he went. I watched as he took the initial shock of the cable and then slid down to the landing point without problem. (Contrary to the real thing when the stick would go out the door in quick succession, for training purposes the tower jumps were done one at a time.)

Then it was my turn and, almost without thinking, robot-like, I shifted into the doorway and grabbed each side of the doorframe. Then I did start thinking. I could plainly see the ground sixty feet below. I don't really want to do this, I thought. I tried to look at the horizon as instructed, but the ground was right there. Stop thinking, I tried to tell myself. It didn't help. As if waiting for the pilot's signal that we were over the drop zone, the jumpmaster hesitated. What was probably about eight or ten seconds seemed like for ever as I crouched, freezing, in the doorway.

'Go!' he shouted in my ear, over the noise of the make-believe airplane's engines I guess. I was startled, hesitated for a split second, then jumped out the door – contrary to all my instincts. The harness tightened as the cable caught my weight and then I slid down to land. I had made it! Only two more tower jumps, I thought. No question in my mind that they were the least enjoyable experiences I had during all of my training.

With the PLF mastered and the tower jumps behind us, the day for our first jump arrived. It was sunny and warm with few clouds in the sky. This day had been on our minds for months. We moved by truck to the airfield, where a two-engine C-47 awaited. We strapped on parachutes, the military T-10 model. We assembled next to the plane for the final briefing and chatted nervously among ourselves. After the briefing we started boarding the plane. The cable to which we would fasten our static lines looked almost ominous along the ceiling of the plane. In stick order we sat down on benches along each side of the plane. The parachute and the reserve were bulky and it was uncomfortable, but no one noticed. Each man held the hook on his static line in his right hand. Everyone tried to act casual, but the tension was readily apparent. We took off and made a large circle as the pilot gained altitude. He levelled off and straightened out.

'We're on final,' the co-pilot shouted back. We all waited for the next command. We had practised this many times on the ground in a mock-up plane. Everyone knew exactly what to do. No variations on the theme.

'Stand up!' the jumpmaster shouted authoritatively. On command, the four men shuffled forward and Mike Deuel, the first jumper, swung into position at the door with one hand gripping each side of the doorframe. He was gripping the doorframe very hard. I sat almost hypnotized by the drama unfolding before me. This was to be our first jump, not an everyday event. The assistant talked quietly and calmly with the first stick.

'Your first jump will be the best one ever,' he told them. 'Enjoy it.'

The jumpmaster was leaning out of the door waiting for the drop zone to come in view. We knew it was close. He stood up straight and the jump light flashed on.

'Go!' he shouted at Mike, swatting him on the butt as he jumped out the door. It all seemed to happen in an instant. The rest of the stick shuffled forward, swung into position at the door, and at the jumpmaster's command jumped, each receiving the swat on the butt, all in about six or eight seconds. The rest of us were transfixed. The first stick was gone. We couldn't see anything but sky. The four static lines were hauled back in by the jumpmaster (they had done their job of deploying the four chutes) as the pilot circled for another run over the drop zone. When he straightened out the cry came again, 'We're on final.'

'Stand up,' the jumpmaster intoned. The second stick, my stick, stood with hooks in hand. I was the number three man. We had serious, intent expressions. That's because we were serious and intent.

'First jump will be great,' the assistant repeated. I barely heard him as I strained to hear the next command.

'Hook up,' said the jumpmaster and we all snapped our hooks onto the cable. I gave mine a hard jerk to confirm that it was snapped on firmly. It was. We checked each other. I looked at the door. Soon, I thought, I'm going to jump right out of here. Imagine that!

Same scenario exactly. The jumpmaster shouted, 'Move to the door.' Automatically, we shuffled forwards. The number one jumper swung into position at the door. I wasn't even thinking at that point. I just reacted.

'Go!' came the next command and the first jumper leaped out of the plane receiving the standard swat as he left. The command and the swat were almost simultaneous. The rest of us followed. It was just like the practices. I moved forwards quickly, planted my left foot, pivoted on that foot and swung my right foot right to the edge of the door. Just as I grabbed the doorframe, I got the command and the swat, and I jumped out the door. No thinking was involved, just discipline and practice. It was over in an instant.

The wind draught caught me immediately and I was swung sideways. There was no sensation of falling. I saw the tail of the plane go by and disappear. The chute deployed behind me and I fell gently under it like a pendulum. It was quiet. I looked around, realized that everything had gone according to plan, and felt good. I could see the whole base and the river on the far side. I saw the drop zone and was happy to conclude that I was headed for the middle of it. This really was great, I reflected.

As I descended, I started thinking about my first real PLF. How would it go? We drifted slowly down towards the landing zone and it was clear that the jumpmaster and pilot had done their jobs well. We would be landing right in the middle of the large field that was our target. It was a splendid day, no wind at all. Later, I was told that the instructors on the ground had been talking to me, number three man in the stick, via loudspeakers. So intent was I on making this a good PLF that I didn't hear them at all.

'Loosen up, bend your knees, relax!' they yelled. Apparently I was locked up stiff as a board, but didn't realize it. As my stick neared the ground, they got more insistent. Nothing penetrated. I was staring straight ahead waiting for my toes to touch the ground so that I could smoothly roll into my perfect PLF.

It wasn't perfect. In fact, it was terrible. Exactly wrong. I came in backwards and hadn't touched the shrouds to try to control my direction. Heels hit first, wrong. Butt next, wrong. And then, with a thud, the back of my head banged onto the ground. Thank goodness for the helmet I was wearing, which no doubt prevented a concussion given the force of my landing. I was down. Yes, there was a ringing in my head, but I had made it. Nothing was broken and I gingerly got up. One of the instructors was 'in my face' as they say.

'Dammit, Holm, don't you listen?' he shouted.

'To what?'

'To me, when I give you instructions,' he yelled back. I could see that he was agitated.

'Sorry,' I said sincerely. 'I didn't hear you.'

'Well, next time listen up, goddammit.'

About half of the group had similar PLFs although mine may have been the worst. Nobody did the perfect PLF we had all hoped for. On the other hand, nobody was hurt on landing. The only injury was sustained by Bob Manning, a well-liked guy with great potential as an operations officer. Inexplicably, despite the checks and double checks, Bob got his static line under his arm as he hooked up. As he went out the door and the static line caught the chute to deploy it, his arm was jerked upward to clear the line. Happily, the angle was such that it did no serious damage. He had a nasty bruise on his upper arm, but it didn't stop him from making the rest of the jumps and completing the programme.

We completed four more jumps, including one at dusk. There were no incidents to speak of and things got progressively better. I listened and actually made some passable PLFs. There were no injuries and, as hoped, since that was the objective of the training, our confidence grew with each jump.

Following the parachute training, we were transported by plane to a secluded base in North Carolina, near the ocean, for training in explosives, and small boat operations and deployment.

In the first PT session there, it was the usual except for a few new exercises introduced by a new instructor. In response to our questions, he explained that they came from his training as a frog-man and were designed to strengthen the upper arm and chest muscles you needed when placing magnetic limpets on the hull of a ship. There were no more questions, but it gave us food for thought.

After breakfast that followed the PT, we went out to a demon-stration range and met the men who would instruct us in the use of explosives. They were all highly experienced and competent in their field and we were very impressed. One, John Ward, was also terribly entertaining. He could easily have been a stand-up comic. His stories and jokes were delivered with ease and good timing that captivated our whole group. He was wonderful in the club in the evenings, but he very definitely knew when to get serious and draw a line.

We were given a demonstration aimed at showing us the power and efficiency of relatively small amounts of plastic explosives. I wasn't at all sure that I wanted to mess with that stuff, but resolved to keep an open mind. The secret of efficient use of these explosives, we were told, was 'shape' charges. That is to shape and place your charge where it will attack the structure of your target. With a small charge, for example, you could drop a large tree right across a road or trail. Or bring down a bridge. There would be classroom instruction, but mostly this would be hands-on training to give us familiarity and comfort with the use of explosives.

Safety was the highest priority and we got very precise brief-ings on what to do and what not to do. It started with primer cord, an explosive itself, which is used to detonate the plastics. The primer cord had to be lit with a match and a cry of 'fire in the hole' was absolutely mandatory whenever you lit a cord. That alerted others to move to safe areas or bunkers. Timing was, of course, quite important and we practised diligently to acquire the skill needed to light the cord and know when the plastic charge would go off – not easy to do. It wasn't too bad with small lengths that would explode in seconds, but to give yourself minutes to move away from a bridge, say, that would come crashing down, was more of a challenge. Practice makes perfect, and after several days we all got pretty good at setting up charges that would explode within a few seconds of when they should. From count-downs of ten to boom, we got to within a few seconds of boom. Obviously, one would err on the side of more time rather than less.

With proper techniques learned, we practised on various targets: trees, pieces of steel, houses, vehicles. Along with instruction about structural engineering, which helped tell us where to place charges on specific targets, the practice built our confidence by showing exactly how a charge would affect a given target.

Interspersed with the explosives training, we received training on how to operate and manoeuvre a small boat. In this instance we used small, black, rubber boats powered by powerful, silenced, outboard motors. Even with three men plus equipment, those little boats would really move. They were the same boats used by Navy Seals and others to infiltrate teams at night to target areas. Apart from the initial familiarization with the boats and motors, which was quickly done, much of our training in the boats was done at night. It is easy to lose your sense of direction on the water at night so practice sessions concentrated on giving us pointers on how to stay on course. Sometimes we were towed out to a certain point and dropped off, and other times we moved out along the coast on our own. We got the idea. Planning, as usual, was an important part of the effort.

Our final exercise involved a raid at night to destroy an 'enemy' command post that was (according to the exercise script) unguarded at night. Our planning was accomplished as a group. We would bring in three small boats at a designated small cove. Each boat would carry three armed men (faces blackened) and explosives. After a rendezvous, six men would move to the target, while three others would guard the boats. At the target, two men would set up watch posts, while four entered the target and set the charges. Our instructors would be observing the whole thing. After the cord was lit, all would move back to the boats and beat a hasty retreat.

I drew the 'guard the boats' detail. It seemed to take much longer than it should for the attack team to get their job done and return – it always does. Finally though, we heard an explosion and saw fire in the direction of the target. Done, I thought. They should be back here in a couple of minutes.

'Let's get the engines started,' I whispered (I don't know why I was whispering) to the other two guards.

'What if someone hears them?' one of them responded.

'But there is no one here,' the third retorted.

'At least we will be ready and can get the hell out of here,' I said, pulling the start cord on my boat's engine. It sprang to life and purred softly. The cove had a small dock and we had positioned ourselves so that the returning team had only to slip into the boats and we would pull away into the darkness. I heard a second engine start and begin idling quietly.

'Shit, mine won't start,' was the next sound that penetrated the night.

Christ, I thought, that can't help anything. 'Keep trying,' I told him.

'I am, I am,' he shot back just as the attack team appeared out of the tree line at the end of the dock. They moved quickly to the dock and towards the boats. Two jumped into each boat – and waited.

'Let's move,' one of them said.

'Engine won't start,' was the response.

I don't know if this was built into the exercise as a test or not, but clearly we had to react and we did.

'We can't stay here. We'll tow you. Pass us a line,' I said quietly. They did and we moved slowly but steadily out into the blackness of the estuary. We followed the other boat that was ahead of us with everyone trying to keep as low a profile as possible. No problems developed and the field expedient worked out well. We had no complaints from the instructors, who may or may not have realized that one of the boats was being towed. So much the better.

It was a good exercise with enough realism to show us how difficult and dangerous a raid like that could actually be. Imagine being in that position on an enemy coast and having to limp out with failed equipment. It was also a good block of training. We didn't become expert in either explosives or small-boat operations, but we learned and practised enough to be effective later in our careers where the situation demanded paramilitary expertise.

The culmination of the paramilitary training course was a two-week session at the Army's Jungle Warfare Training School at

Fort Sherman in the Panama Canal Zone. We had heard about how demanding the training down there was and we looked forward to the challenge. We were in strong physical condition and had honed our skills in weapons training, map reading and cross-country movement, parachute training, small-unit tactics, explosives and small-boat training, and guerrilla warfare tactics and exercises. We felt ready.

It was late morning on a pleasant, sunny day when we landed at a US military base in the Canal Zone. It had been a long flight aboard the Director's private plane, which we felt lucky to be able to use, with one refuelling stop in Tampa. We were happy to touch down. We tumbled out of the plane and stretched our legs while we waited for the bus that was to pick us up.

'What's that?' Bob Manning said, gesturing at a sleek, black, single-engine plane that was taxiing towards the end of the runway we had just landed on.

'Don't know,' I answered. 'Never seen anything like that. What are those things under the wings?'

'I think it's a U-2,' said Ralph McLean. He was a Marine Corps officer assigned to the Agency in a special programme – as was Mike Deuel. I figured he had seen one before at some military base.

'Yeah, I think you're right, Ralph,' someone else said. By now we were all watching intently as the plane moved onto the end of the runway. Cameras came out, including mine. We all wanted a picture of this plane, which had gained such fame when Gary Powers was shot down over Russia in the spring of 1960. The pilot started his take-off and the plane moved quickly down the runway. As the plane gained speed, the wings, which could only be described as floppy, lifted and the struts beneath them fell off. It was a design feature for use in take-offs. For efficiency in cruising at high altitudes, the wings were much longer than usual for a plane that size. It was almost as if they could flap like a bird's. As soon as he had wheels up, the pilot must have given it full throttle because the angle of ascent was steeper than I had ever seen. It shot up into the air and was soon out of sight. We were mightily impressed.

We were assigned a small wing of a large concrete barracks at Fort Sherman, nothing fancy but adequate, especially since we would be spending so little time there. We were joining a group of 100 military officers sent to Panama from all over the US to take this course – given only twice a year. Excluding our group of fifteen and a small platoon of Navy Seals, all were young Army officers. We were surprised to learn of our minority status and of the size of the class embarking upon this two-week course, but no less anxious to get started. I'm not sure why, but we sensed that others were looking askance at this unlabelled group of civilians intruding into a military training programme. Would they be able to keep up? That, of course, piqued our competitive spirit and we resolved to make a good accounting of ourselves.

After dinner the first evening, we were assembled behind the barracks for what was billed as administrative briefings. At the end of the briefings, however, they announced a brief introductory exercise into the nearby jungle. It was dusk, nearly dark. Just a walk through the jungle to a nearby clearing, we were told. Some milling around ensued while groups were lined up one behind the other.

'OK, let's move out,' an instructor announced as he starting leading the first group into the jungle. We could barely see them as it had suddenly, as is the case near the equator, become night. It was dark. Other instructors were positioned along the line as we started moving forwards. As we left the barracks and entered the jungle, it became almost black.

'Hold hands,' an instructor told us. No one argued.

'I can't see a damn thing,' said Bill Watkins, a former Marine Corps helicopter pilot.

'It's like walking in a bottle of ink,' another said.

'I hope all the snakes are asleep,' someone else muttered, and everyone chuckled.

We were half stumbling through thick undergrowth up and down small knolls, and holding on dearly to the hands in front of and behind us. The trees had sharp needles. There wasn't much conversation; a few curses as people fell or hit trees, but otherwise pretty quiet. Soon we were in another clearing and out of the 'bottle of ink'. It was a relief.

It was, of course, a set-up, but it was an effective learning experience. The instructors knew that our inability to see while trying to move in the unfamiliar jungle surroundings would have an impact. It did. They moved us directly from the well-lit clearing behind the barracks into dense jungle. Our eyes had no chance to adjust to night vision and the brief walk didn't allow time to adjust either so we were left with a memorably negative impression about night-time movement in the jungle. It was a false impression that would be corrected over the two-week training course we would start in the morning.

'Just be sure to keep a firm grip just behind his head,' the instructor told me as the two-foot constrictor threw a couple of coils around my arm and started to hug.

The snake was not big enough to hurt anyone – after all, this was just a demonstration. We had been shown that there was a spot just behind the head, which would cause the snake to go limp if you squeezed. I was getting my hands-on shot at seeing how it works.

'Can I squeeze now?' I asked.

'Go ahead,' he instructed and as I did I could feel the coils loosen and fall off my arm. I handed the snake to the instructor, and was pleased to do so, wondering if I'd really wanted to pick up that bit of information about constrictor snakes. How the hell would I get hold of the head of a big one?

The constrictor demonstration was part of a morning of useful briefings we were given on the first day about the jungle: animals, birds, snakes, trees, plants, what is edible and what is not. It was interesting as well as informative. It would be of practical use to us over the next two weeks, as well as useful to those of us headed for South-East Asia.

One doesn't normally think of repelling (abseiling) in a jungle setting so the fact that we were to do it came as a surprise to most of us. Many of the military officers had advance knowledge of what to expect during these two weeks and knew it was coming. The rest of us knew nothing and took each day as it came. Fortunately though we had practised repelling techniques regularly at The Farm and become pretty competent. The repelling was included not so much as a skill for jungle warfare, but for individual confidence building.

We loaded onto trucks and drove inland. After dismounting, there was a half-hour walk to the top of a precipice that overlooked the Chagras River. It wasn't a waterfall, but here and there it was slippery because of water coming out of the rocks and falling down to the river below. You couldn't see all the way down until you got to the edge where the ropes were secured. It was about 150 feet down and about two-thirds of the way there was a rock shelf where we would change ropes. (At The Farm we practised on a twenty-foot tower where some of us got good enough to make the ground in one or two jumps. This looked considerably more challenging.)

The sun shone down on us as we waited in line for our turn to repel down.

'Looks neat. Should be fun,' Bob Manning announced as he got close enough to the edge to actually see down. He was first in our group.

'I never did like heights,' Mike L., another member, responded from further back in the line.

We moved forward until it was Bob's turn.

'Throw the rope over your shoulder and between your legs,' the instructor explained.

'Yeah, I know,' Bob answered as he took the rope and moved to the edge. He had been a pole-vaulter at Princeton and had done some rock climbing in New Jersey. He had also practised a lot with us. He knew how to repel.

'No, the other shoulder,' the instructor said sounding alarmed. (Bob is left-handed)

'OK, thanks,' Bob yelled as, without further ado, he went over the edge.

Several of us, including the instructor, watched as Bob more or less swooped down the cliff. We weren't surprised. The instructor was.

I was tempted to say it was his first try, but didn't. My turn was coming.

'Throw the rope over your shoulder and between your legs,' the instructor repeated for the umpteenth time that morning as I stepped into position with my back towards the edge of the cliff. He looked me over, then I pushed off backwards, less forcefully and boldly than on our tower at The Farm, watching the rock below me for my first touch. I bounded outward again, feeling more comfortable now that I was on my way down. Once my foot slipped and I bumped against the rocks, but I swung clear again right away and continued down. Once I got down to the shelf I had to walk over to the second rope where another instructor was waiting. He had been watching me, as he did everyone coming down, and knew I could repel, so he just handed me the rope and said, 'Move on.' I looked up towards the top of the cliff. The rugged natural beauty certainly added to the pleasure of the day. Bob was right, this is fun, I thought.

More confident now, I pushed off to finish the second, shorter, leg. Shove off facing backwards and downwards. Let the rope run freely over your shoulder and between your legs (making sure, of course, that it was placed on one side or the other). Squeeze the rope a bit to control your speed and catch yourself with your feet as you swung back into the rocks. Pay attention. Try to touch on flat solid spots to avoid slipping again. I got more aggressive as I neared the bottom and covered more vertical distance with the last several bounds. There were no mishaps. Everything worked fine and I quickly covered the remaining distance, slipped off the rope and handed it to a waiting sergeant.

I guess they thought our confidence needed some more building because the next exercise of the day was a river crossing. The terrain on our side of the river was higher than on the other side and the river was about 200 feet wide. A crude platform had been built in a tree about 30 feet up from the ground. I watched as those in front of me crossed the river. There was a long cable hung from the tree on our side to another tree on the opposite bank. Hanging just below the cable, fixed with a roller, was a two-foot metal bar. From the platform, you could reach up and grasp the metal bar. At that point you were well over 40 feet above the river looking down to the other end of the cable on the other side.

'Just hold on tight,' I heard the sergeant on the platform tell Bob Manning, who was ahead of me in the line and was on the platform ready to make his crossing. 'And drop into the water when you get to the other side,' he added. Bob let out a yell, leapt off the platform, slid down the cable (much as we had from the tower when we did our parachute training), and dropped into waist-deep water on the other side. He waded ashore, all grins.

When my turn came, I climbed onto the platform as the instructor was pulling the bar back from the other side. I had watched a couple of others in our group follow Bob. The difference between this and the tower jump, I noted, was that from the tower you jumped with a parachute harness securing you to the cable and just slid down. Here, you had to hang on as you slid down and then drop off at the right time. There were instructors on the other side, I also noted, who yelled out when it was time to let go. I can certainly handle that, I concluded.

'You got the bar?' the sergeant asked, when it was my turn.

I nodded. You bet I've got it, I said to myself and gripped the bar firmly. It was, literally, a white-knuckle ride.

'So fly away, man,' he ordered. I jumped out off the platform and started down the cable. I quickly gained speed and felt like I was rocketing towards the opposite bank. It all happened quickly and there wasn't time to worry. I dropped off just as I heard the instructor tell me to let go. Relieved, I waded to shore and climbed up the bank. It wasn't so much fun as the repelling.

Four or so behind me in the line had been Dan Farley, the oldest man in our group. He was from the Office of Medical Services and, after receiving an assignment to South Vietnam, had volunteered to take the paramilitary course. He was a pleasant and likeable guy and we all admired his grit. He wasn't in as good a physical shape as most of the rest of us, but he hung right in there on our field exercises. We were sort of half watching from the other side of the bank as each man made the slide down the cable and Dan was coming now. Something didn't look right. Watch out! we thought collectively. But it was too late. He froze, didn't let go in time and crashed heavily into the bank. We rushed over to see him. Two instructors were already there.

'Relax,' one of them ordered. Dan was lying half in the water.

'I think I broke something,' Dan said. He was in obvious pain.

'Don't try to stand,' said the other instructor. One of Dan's legs was clearly broken. A third instructor was already on his radio asking for a chopper. Carefully, and with considerable effort because Dan was a big man, they lifted him up onto the bank and tried to comfort him as best they could.

'I suppose this means you're going to poop out on us,' joked Bill Watkins.

'Nah, I'll be back after lunch,' Dan kidded right back.

'Tough break,' Bill said more seriously. 'But heck, one week in this steamy jungle is probably enough anyway.'

We all knew that Dan would be sent home as soon as possible. It was hard for him, but he had a harder moment coming. Because of the broken leg, his assignment to Vietnam was postponed. He did go, however, and he was in the Embassy in Saigon the day it was bombed. Like many others, Dan caught glass splinters in his face and eyes. As a result, he lost his sight and was medically retired. His grit came through again though and he made a terribly difficult adjustment look easy as he pursued life vigorously despite his blindness.

In the afternoon, we moved back to the Chagras for another river crossing. The technique would be different. This time we would cross on a single rope stretched across the river tied to trees on either bank. It was horizontal and six or eight feet above the water. More confidence building, although this one was more practical we all thought. To make the crossing, you would lie on top of the rope letting one leg dangle for balance and hooking the other leg, at the ankle, over the rope, and grasp the rope with both hands in front of you. To move forward, you pulled with your arms and pushed with the leg hooked over the rope. That made you slide along on top of the rope. The key, of course, was to keep your balance. If you lost balance, you would find yourself hanging under the rope just above the water. (To make the exercise realistic, we were told the current was so strong we would be carried away and that there were crocodiles in the water.) If you fell under the rope, you had to make your way across pulling hand over hand with your legs hooked onto the rope above. It was tough work. There was strong incentive, therefore, to try to keep your balance and stay on top of the rope.

My turn came and I just followed instructions. By then I had seen about a dozen others make the crossing and was aware of the pitfalls. Don't get the rope swaying sideways. Pushing with the hooked over leg more and pulling with your arms less produced better results. I started slowly and I finished slowly. I made a slow crossing. But I was very focused and I didn't fall off.

This was not the case for Andre LeGallo, who was two behind me. In the middle of his crossing, the rope started swaying sideways and Andre fell under the rope.

'You can't get back up,' the instructor behind shouted to Andre, who hung there in the middle as he let the swaying stop.

'Just come ahead hand over hand,' another instructor yelled.

Born in France just before the Second World War, Andre had been raised in Paris where his family, originally from Brittany, spent the war years. They emigrated to the United States in the late 1940s and settled in northern New Jersey where Andre's father, an excellent chef, ran a restaurant. Andre had been a varsity wrestler and had very strong arms and upper body strength. Either he hadn't heard the instructors, or he had elected to ignore their counsel. It was clear that he had decided to get back on top of the rope. With shouts of encouragement coming from both banks, Andre calmly hoisted himself back up, a feat requiring both strength and balance, and finished his crossing. Bravo, Andre. Neither instructor voiced any concern. Both were impressed.

Andre's notoriety was not over. One night early in our second week, we made camp in a clearing near the river. As usual, it had been a physically demanding day. The heat and the humidity took a lot out of us. Our packs and web belts contained a few personal things (underwear, socks, dop kit) and some field gear – shelter half, which is one half of a pup tent, *pancho*, entrenching tool (a small shovel), and a machete for clearing a way through the jungle. We paired up and, using two shelter halves, set up rows of pup tents to sleep in. *Pancho* doubled as a ground cloth to sleep on. There were no sleeping bags. It was not comfortable, but no one complained. We were too tired to worry about it. Moreover, this was in the middle of the jungle so we expected hardship. We ate C-rations as dusk came upon us. There were a couple of flashlights, but once it was dark there wasn't much to do except try to get some sleep. The camp quietened quickly as fatigue took its toll. Suddenly there was a loud cry.

'What the hell is that? A bat?' Bob Manning shouted. Bob and Andre were sharing a pup tent. Both were over six feet tall and didn't quite fit into it, and Andre, for the sake of some fresh air, was sleeping with his head just out of the open end of the tent.

'I don't know. Is that blood?' Andre said. Somebody produced a flashlight. It was blood. We were all awake now.

'There are two small holes on the top of your forehead,' Bob told Andre.

'The bat?' Andre asked.

'A vampire bat!' Bob exclaimed grabbing everyone's attention. The bleeding stopped quickly. You could plainly see two small holes on Andre's forehead where the bat had bitten him.

No one knew, of course, if it had actually been a type of blood-sucking bat, but that didn't matter. Andre had been attacked by a vampire.

Would it come back? As the camp quietened again after the commotion, there was a general shuffling as we all, despite the stuffiness in the closed end of the tent, shifted around so that our heads were inside the tent and our feet were at the open end. Someone mentioned the possibility of an infection, but it was soon forgotten. I don't think Andre even put a band-aid on the holes. In preparation for the Panama trip, all our shots had been updated and that may have helped Andre ward off any problem.

But the story spread quickly and Andre became famous.

Unfortunately, the next day was a particularly tough one and many of us were under-slept to face it. 'Living off the land' was the theme of the day. We did, however, have a field kitchen hot breakfast to help get us started. We were to divide into groups and each group would build a *bohio* (Panamanian Spanish for a small hut constructed from trees and thatch) in which they would sleep that night. Our group – now fourteen because of Dan Farley's departure – formed into two groups of seven. First, however, we would do some compass-reading exercises. That meant lots of walking through the jungle.

With one man ahead with a machete to clear a path – the point man – and two behind him with compasses to keep him on course, we took off at about seven thirty. We found one checkpoint after another and moved quickly along our assigned course. Our practice at The Farm came in handy. It wasn't difficult as an exercise, but it was wearing physically. We rotated our point man regularly as that was the toughest spot. By noon, we had finished the course and came into a large clearing, where the field kitchen was set up for lunch. Hungry and tired, we looked forward to a good meal of some sort. It was not to be as we quickly noticed that the lunch was stacks of C-rations containing several small cans and boxes of prepared (but cold) food. Usually it was a type of meat dish, some fruit, cookies or crackers, maybe some chocolate. Trading always ensued.

'What's your fruit?' Mike Deuel asked me. 'I got peaches.'

'Fruit cocktail,' I responded. 'Want to trade?'

'Nope,' he said. 'I'm looking for pears.'

'I got apple sauce,' Bob Manning chimed in. 'And beef stew. Anyone want this beef stuff?'

'Got to be better than ham,' Ralph McLean said, handing Manning his meat dish. 'I hate this ham.'

'I don't like it much either,' Bob said, 'but I'm sure tired of beef stew.'

It was always the same. No one was ever happy with what he got. It was fuel for the engine, however, and we always ate it all.

After lunch we gathered for a briefing on the afternoon's *bohio* building. The briefing was short and simple. 'Go ye forth and build tonight's dwelling, a *bohio*,' said the instructor. 'One more thing,' he added loudly over the din of preparation. 'Pass by the trucks on your way into the jungle and pick up dinner. See you here in the morning for breakfast at six thirty.'

We walked over to the trucks. Lines had formed and we fell into one of them. Looking ahead, we could see what was being handed out for dinner.

'They're giving 'em chickens, live chickens!' Watkins half shouted in disbelief.

'And yucca roots and rice,' Andre added.

'So that's dinner?' Manning asked, not really wanting an affirmative answer.

Each group got the same thing. Two live chickens, a handful of rice, and some yucca roots to boil. We collected ours and headed off to construct our *bohio*.

'Anybody ever kill a chicken?' Ward Warren asked of no one in particular. No one responded. 'We'll draw straws for the honour tonight,' he continued with a laugh. Ward, a graduate of the University of Michigan, had studied Chinese Affairs and spoke Mandarin Chinese fluently. He was an 'internal', meaning that he had joined the JOT programme from a position elsewhere within the Agency.

Of varying sizes and degrees of sophistication, a *bohio* is nothing more than a platform several feet off the ground (away from snakes, bigger animals and vermin) with walls around it and a roof over-head. Walls and roof would be palm branches (no corrugated tin available) spread over a wooden frame. There was at least no short-age of trees. We picked a site under some large trees and started planning the structure. To sleep seven, we figured the *bohio* plat-form would have to be at least twelve by twenty-four feet. None of us was an engineer of any sort. We had only machetes and entrenching tools. This would be no mean feat. Happily, the ground was not hard so the holes for logs to support the platform's frame would not be too difficult to dig. Three men got started with that. The rest of us, machetes in hand, set out to bring back suit-able trees. Happily, the trees in the jungle were softwood and we were able to bring down trees with a waist-sized trunk diameter in about fifteen minutes of hacking. Then the branches had to be trimmed off before carrying it back to the *bohio* site. Where possi-ble, we selected trees with a sturdy 'V' in the trunk somewhere into which we could lay other trees as we built up. Some were lashed into place with vines stripped down with our bayonet knives.

Little by little, as the afternoon wore on, the *bohio* took shape. It wasn't going to win any prizes, we could see that, but it would serve our purposes for one night. By dusk we were spreading palm branches onto the roof. The bloody thing was done. Ill-propor-tioned and uneven, lacking stairs to get in, and with a roof that would be unlikely to stop much rain, it was, nonetheless, sturdy. We were delighted to have it completed and wondered how many other groups had actually put one up. Very tired, we turned our thoughts to dinner and looked at the two chickens staked to the ground next to the *bohio*.

'So who wants the honour?' Ward asked. We were clearly city kids and no one was anxious to kill and clean two chickens. Finally, Bill Watkins stepped into the breach.

'I'll kill the damn birds,' he growled, obviously not happy about the task ahead of him.

'I'll help,' Ralph McLean announced to Bill's satisfaction and they walked towards the chickens.

'Do it somewhere else,' Bob Manning offered. 'Blood might attract snakes.'

Watkins glared at him, but agreed and they started off into the jungle with the two squawking chickens.

'Let's get a fire started,' I suggested. 'We also have to boil the rice and the yucca.'

'Easier said than done,' Andre commented. 'It's hard to find dry wood.' He was right. Since it rained so frequently and since sunlight didn't penetrate the canopy in many places, dry wood was not plentiful. But it had to be done and we spread out looking for anything that would burn. Eventually we got a fire started – not a very hot one, but a fire.

'Anyone ever boil rice?' Ward asked. 'Do you put it into the water before or after the water boils?'

'After,' Bob said. 'I think that's how my mom always did it.'

'It doesn't matter,' Andre interjected. 'It's not minute rice from Uncle Ben. We'll just cook it until it's soft enough to eat.' We all thought that to be a good idea.

It was dark by now. Very dark. The squawking of the chickens had stopped. We used our metal canteen cups to boil the rice and the yucca roots – which didn't look appetizing at all. We rigged up a crude spit for the chickens to roast on (nobody thought about boiling the chicken in pieces) and set the canteen cups on rocks as close to the fire as we could. Lord only knew how long it would take for the water to start boiling. We were very tired.

'Here they are,' Bill announced as he and Ralph returned with the hacked-up chickens.

'We threw the insides as far away as we could,' Ralph added.

'Many thanks, you guys,' I said. 'Couldn't have been much fun.'

'Wasn't,' Bill mumbled.

We stuck the chickens on the makeshift spit over the fire. We waited. And we waited. Nothing was happening. The fire simply wasn't hot enough. We waited some more. We were exhausted. Finally, the water boiled, barely, and the rice cooked a little. Same with the yucca, but that remained hard. In the end, fatigue won out. We ate a couple of mouthfuls of half-cooked rice, chucked the yucca, and threw the still raw chickens as far into the jungle as we could. Nobody wanted to wait for what might have been hours to cook the food. Sleep seemed a much better choice.

We climbed into the *bohio*, which did not fall down I am pleased to report, settled ourselves on its hopelessly uneven floor surface, and tried to get some rest. It was very uncomfortable, but I fell quickly into a deep sleep. The others did as well, and nothing bothered us until dawn. We had dug holes, felled trees and laboured to construct our *bohio* for over seven hours. We felt the effect.

In the morning, the field kitchen produced a hot breakfast and it was delicious – mainly, of course, because we were very hungry. I noticed that everyone attacked breakfast with gusto and wondered how many of those chickens had actually been eaten. Not many, I suspect.

'Wonder what this fine day has in store for us,' Andre said. It was now the middle of our second week and we were sitting in the back of a truck headed, again, into the jungle. And it was a fine day – bright and sunny.

'Who knows?' I answered. 'We'll know soon though, the trucks are slowing down.'

We piled out of the back and found ourselves next to Gatun Lake, actually a part of the Panama Canal. The shore was sandy and the water looked very inviting. At least thirty large, black rubber boats were floating in shallow water. A stack of paddles was on the shore. The head instructor faced the lake and we were facing him.

'Each group should get a boat and paddles,' he announced. 'We're going to do some work on the water today. This exercise is going to familiarize you with how to handle a small boat. No big thing, you just co-ordinate your paddling.' He hoisted up a paddle and demonstrated where to place hands and how to pull forward. 'Across the lake and back,' he continued. 'Just go around the orange buoy on the other side.' He seemed to be taking a lot longer than necessary to explain something that was pretty simple. 'Two more things,' he went on. 'First, this is going to be a race.' That got everybody's attention. 'The first boat back wins. And second, it starts right now!'

We leapt to our feet and started running for the boats.

As we ran, we could see that the rubber boats had been shoved out into the lake. 'Devious bastards,' someone said. They were now floating about twenty-five yards from shore and the paddles were floating in the water around them. There was confusion and some hesitation, but only for an instant. We ran right into the lake, the water felt great, and started swimming towards the boats. Over one hundred men headed for thirty boats. Lots of yelling, pushing and shoving was going on. We were among the first to get to the boats.

'Shove him in,' Andre ordered as he and I pushed Bob Manning into one of the boats.

'I am, I am,' I replied.

'Grab some paddles', Bill Watkins said, 'and throw them into the boat with Manning.' What a circus. Men were thrashing around everywhere. Bob pulled me and Monty Rogers, another Midwesterner, into the boat and Andre scrambled in too. This would be our boat, we concluded, and shoved others away as they tried to get in. Some weren't too happy. It was pandemonium. But we were in good shape. We spotted Ward Warren and Mike Deuel, hauled them on board, and got ready to head out.

'Grab another paddle,' someone yelled. 'And get lined up on either side.' It was Bill Watkins and he became our coxswain of the day – more by default than anything else. We didn't have time for an election.

We started for the other side of the lake, noting with pleasure that we were the first boat under way.

'Great!' Watkins yelled. 'We're way ahead. Most of them are still in the water.'

We were lined up, paddles in hand, on both sides of the boat. We chanted in unison and pulled as hard as we could. We had been together for a long time now and were organized. That was not the case for any of the others. We now had a big lead.

'Where are the Seals?' Monty asked. For the whole of the course, the only group we worried about was the Seals. They were in great shape and had lots of stamina as well. We had great respect for their ability – individually and collectively.

'They're coming,' Watkins answered. 'Paddle hard.' He wasn't a great coxswain, but he kept us headed in the right direction and we were making good progress. 'Right side paddle, left side hold,' he repeated. Our forward motion slowed as we righted our course and compensated by pulling less hard on one side or the other to keep our direction straight. Bob Manning was left-handed, strong, and he had experience paddling a canoe. 'Pull,' we shouted in unison to keep in synch. We were humming and very confident as we neared the orange buoy.

'Seals are coming,' said Watkins, who was the only one in our boat who could sneak a glance behind us. 'They are clear of the mêlée and paddling hard.' None of us doubted that. We knew they wanted to win this race for the sake of their pride. They wouldn't be deterred by the fact that we had got off to such a big lead. Unspoken, but clear, was the fact that we, the 'unlabelled civilians', also wanted to win this race. We pulled even harder.

We rounded the buoy and, for the first time, had a clear view of our position in the race. The Seals were about thirty yards behind, but closing. The rest were strung out behind the Seals and looked like a band of marauding pirates. Men were shouting, standing in the boat, waving paddles. The Seals went right by, headed for the buoy. They weren't wasting any breath or strength with emotional outbursts. They looked serious and determined. We tried to pull even harder and maintained our rhythm.

Some in the oncoming horde had decided that since their chances of winning the race, by catching and passing either us or the Seals, were nil, they would become spoilers. Several of the boats altered their course with the quickly obvious intention of intercepting us. We, of course, viewed their decision and their actions in a most unfavourable light.

'Never mind, we got 'em,' Watkins shouted as we came clear of the offending boats and were about halfway back to the beach. The Seals had rounded the buoy and were steaming back. None of the other boats bothered them, thinking, I suppose, that they had done enough already. We were running out of breath and had given up the chant, but we were in good synch and continued to pull hard.

'Pull harder!' Watkins implored. He sounded less confident. The Seals had narrowed the gap. We were nearing the beach. We urged each other on with whatever breath that could be spared.

We won! In fact, we hit the beach, got out of the boat, and hauled it out of the water, before the Seal boat arrived. They had narrowed our lead, but not enough. It was our great start that carried the day – and the fact that, at that time, we all were in good physical condition. We savoured our victory, inwardly. We said nothing to the Seals or to anyone else. (Now that I think about it, maybe we were too out of breath and tired to speak.) Nor did anyone mention the victory to us.

'OK, into the trucks, we're headed back,' the senior instructor said after the last boat had been beached. Maybe we surprised them.

Word got around, that the last exercise was really tough. The next to last day dawned like all the rest, clear, sunny and hot. Tomorrow evening we would be flying back to Virginia. How bad could this get? We were to find out.

We were finished with breakfast and on our way to the field by 0730. It was a longer ride than usual, I noticed. The trucks carried us to almost the far end of the peninsula. The red clay road followed the shoreline along the peninsula to the headquarters and barracks area. There were only a few roads. Four or five cut across the peninsula. When we got out of the trucks, we were eighteen miles from the end of the peninsula. We were in a large clearing halfway up a large hill. There was both anticipation and uneasiness in the air.

An instructor, who was standing on a small platform in the middle of the clearing, began. 'Today will feature an escape and evasion exercise and I'm going to give you the ground rules. Listen carefully because I don't want any screw-ups. Here's the scenario. You're in an enemy area and have just pulled off a successful raid on their headquarters compound. They are pissed off and have alerted all their forces to find, apprehend, or kill you. The plan calls for you to be exfiltrated by submarine from the point at the map co-ordinates you are now being given. A reception team will meet you and that will signal the end of the exercise. The exercise will start soon. [There was a general sense of rising tension.] There are more ground rules. We, my friends and I, will function as the pissed-off enemy. All roads will be patrolled and guarded. Road crossings will be risky and must be accomplished with care. If you are caught, you lose points. If you are caught more than once, you don't pass the exercise. If you try blatantly to escape capture, you will be considered killed, which also means you don't pass the exercise. Is all that clear?' There were no questions.

It was straightforward. We had to cover eighteen miles through the jungle, avoiding enemy patrols, to our pick-up point for exfiltration on the beach.

'There's more,' the instructor continued. 'The submarine can't wait past noon tomorrow, so unless you get there by then you won't be exfiltrated. That also means you don't pass the exercise.'

We were carrying light packs and M-1 rifles. To cover eighteen miles through the jungle, even though we were much more comfortable in it now than we had been on that first night down here, was not going to be a picnic. Still we had almost twenty-seven hours to do it.

The instructor continued. 'The exercise gives you a grace period of fifteen minutes during which you will, if you're smart, get the hell out of here and make tracks for the rendezvous point. After the fifteen minutes, the enemy will react on sight. Clear? The exercise starts when I drop my hat.' He dropped his hat.

All hell broke loose. Men were running in every direction trying to put distance between themselves and the clearing. Enemy patrols would be starting in fifteen minutes and they knew we'd be heading east along the peninsula. Try to get across the first road as soon as possible, we were thinking. We, in this instance, included Andre LeGallo, Mike Deuel, Monty Rogers, Mike L. and me. It wasn't planned, it just worked out that way. We had been standing together listening to the instructor's briefing and took off in the same direction when he dropped his hat. Nobody took off alone that I could see. Groups ranged in size from two to about five or six. I have no idea what the optimum would have been. We ran straight east along the road for almost ten minutes and then cut into the jungle on the spine of the peninsula. We saw a couple of other small groups, but soon we were alone in the jungle. It was still early morning, but the heat was rising and we were in a heavy sweat from our run.

We stopped to try to gather our thoughts and figure out where we were. We had good maps and it didn't take long to pinpoint our location. Our sprint along the road gained us about a mile so we still had seventeen to go to make the beach and the exfiltration.

'If we can make two miles an hour, we could be on the beach just after dark,' Mike Deuel said.

'Yeah, but hacking our way will slow us down,' I responded.

'Whatever,' Andre said. 'We need to start walking if we're going to get there.'

'I'll start on the point,' Monty said and we picked up our gear and fell in line behind him. He handed me his rifle (he couldn't carry it and use his machete at the same time) and headed east.

Within a couple of hours, we came upon a road that we'd have to cross. We heard a truck pass and assumed it was an enemy patrol. How often did they pass? we were wondering. We approached the road carefully after having located it on the map. Our progress had been slow, we noted, despite a steady pace and few breaks.

'Likely there will be foot patrols or outposts along the roads,' Monty said.

'You're probably right,' Mike Deuel noted. 'Let's get a good look at things before we try to cross.' We all agreed.

Our caution was rewarded after only about five minutes. We got lucky. We had fanned out along the road, a red clay ribbon about fifteen feet wide running through dense jungle, trying to spot a good place to cross while at the same time watching for possible guard posts. As Andre and I looked down a straight stretch, we saw another group try to cross the road about fifty yards from where we were hiding. Whistles blew and an enemy patrol appeared suddenly out of the jungle on the far side of the road and stopped them. 'Busted,' I heard one of them yell, probably to others in the group still hiding on our side of the road.

We moved off silently in the opposite direction and regrouped. Nobody else had seen anything, but all had heard the shouts and whistles. We briefed them on what we had seen. Getting across this bloody road was going to be more dangerous than we had anticipated. We moved further away from the patrol. Now, with a curve in the road between their location and us, we prepared to cross. We knew that the enemy patrol was taking the names of the men it had stopped and that soon they would be on patrol again. Move now, we thought.

We decided to cross the road just one at a time with a short interval between each man. We would regroup about twenty yards into the jungle on the other side. Everything seemed quiet. We certainly didn't want to wait until dark. We'd just have to chance it. Mike L. would go first and we would follow one by one if all went well. We knew we wouldn't be spotted by a vehicle patrol, but weren't sure that the other side of the road wasn't hiding a static lookout post.

In the end, our luck held. Mike L. dashed across the road and dove into the jungle on the other side. There was nothing but quiet as we collectively held our breaths. We followed one by one. As I went across, running as low to the ground as I could, I saw that a ditch ran along the road on the other side. The others had seen the same thing of course, but couldn't warn me. As they had done I suppose, I half slid into the ditch (it was too wide to jump over) and scrambled up the other side. It was no real problem, especially since all my senses were on full alert for the crossing. We regrouped as planned and set off again. One road-crossing down and, according to our map, only two more between us and the beach.

'If the other crossings take that long, we'll never make it to the beach today,' Monty remarked as we walked. It had taken us quite a while to scout out a crossing site and finally get across that last road. We had lost lots of time.

'Doesn't really matter,' Mike Deuel said, 'we have to just push ahead.'

We did and made a second road crossing without incident mid-afternoon. We came to a small stream shortly after the crossing and stopped to fill our canteens. The water was clear and cool and I almost didn't put in the purification tablets that were mandatory. I splashed the water onto my head and face. It felt good. The others did the same thing. All were perspiring heavily and our fatigues were heavy with sweat. We took ten minutes to eat some C-rations. Nothing great, that's for sure, but it would keep us going and it was a welcome break.

It was quiet and pretty under the jungle canopy. We had come to an area where we were higher and there was much less under-growth so the point man had very little hacking to do. All we had to watch was our compass. Go east, young men. Good thing we're all in good shape, I thought. Nobody was showing any sign of fatigue yet and we had covered about half the distance to the beach. Things could be worse, I concluded. And they were about to be, as it turned out.

It was almost five when we approached the last road we would have to cross. There seemed to be more activity and we assumed that lots of groups had made about the same progress as we had and would be at about the same point. The instructors knew that of course and, acting in their role as the enemy, they would be out in force to make things as tough as possible for us. We found a good vantage-point, decided to wait for a while and just watched. It would serve as a good break for us as we had been pushing ahead steadily all day. Sure enough, there was more traffic on this road than we had seen on either of the others. The noose was tightening as the 'raiders' were funnelling into a smaller and smaller area. It was built into the exercise. It increased the stress level – as intended. We talked quietly about our next moves.

'Hell, I think that curve', Monty said gesturing to our right, 'will give us enough time to get across. I say we move out. We're losing time again.'

'Monty's right,' Deuel said, 'unless they are right across the road, we'll have time to make it. We can hear jeeps or trucks well before they get here.'

'Agreed,' I said. 'The only difference this time is more traffic, but Mike's right, we can hear them coming.' Andre and Mike L. nodded. We would make the crossing now.

We moved up to the road carefully, listening for any sign of a presence on the other side. We heard nothing. Monty was first to cross this time and Mike Deuel was last. At Deuel's signal, Monty jumped out of the covering jungle and took off across the road. I began just as he disappeared on the other side. I saw them just as I finished the crossing. An eight-man patrol had Monty and now me. I yelled a warning, but Andre was already coming. Bad luck for sure. They got us all and we had to give them our names before we could continue. We had stumbled right into an area they had just covered. We cursed our bad luck. There was nothing left to do then except make it to the beach in good time. We wouldn't get caught again, of that we were confident.

We figured that there were about six or eight miles left and only a couple of hours of daylight. We had to make some decisions. We were well away from the last road by now and noticed that the terrain was getting rougher. Small hills, ravines and thick undergrowth were common now. What to do?

'If we push on, we can be on the beach sometime after midnight,' Mike Deuel said. 'But covering this terrain in the dark won't be much fun.'

I was torn, but worried about someone slipping into a ravine. 'I'd love to get in tonight,' I said, 'but I guess discretion may be the better part of valour this time.'

'Yeah, we don't want any injuries,' Monty added.

'Well, let's at least make it as far as we can before dark,' Andre said, 'and we can see what it would be like to continue.'

'So we move out briskly,' Mike Deuel concluded with a grin. We did and the terrain didn't get any better.

Dusk came and went. Mike L. was on the point. Finally, he turned and almost hit a tree. It was time to call a halt for the night we all agreed. Despite the fact that our comfort level while moving in the jungle was much higher now, there were limits. This terrain was difficult in daylight. At night it just didn't seem smart to keep moving. We would get some rest and finish the last miles starting at dawn. The decision taken, I leaned my rifle against a tree, took off my pack and sat down. It had been a long, stressful and demanding day and I suddenly realized that I was dead tired. We started spreading out *panchos* to sleep on and then got out some C-rations to munch on. It must have been around seven in the evening. Suddenly we heard noises behind us – in the direction from which we had come. A patrol looking for us? Another bunch headed for the beach? We didn't know. There wasn't time to do much. I reached for my (unloaded) rifle just because it seemed a sensible thing to do.

Suddenly three men we thought were from the Seal group, ran, yes ran, right by us. We watched in amazement. What the hell are they doing? we were all thinking. How long had they been behind us? Was this just for effect? We didn't have any answers, but were duly impressed. The Seals just kept right on going and we later heard that they had arrived first on the beach – well before midnight. However imprudent it might have been, watching them run by served to raise our already high regard for the Seals.

Despite the conditions – hard ground, bugs and intermittent rain – I slept pretty well. Fatigue will do that for you. Someone shook me lightly just before dawn and I rolled out and started to dress – put my boots on that is because we all slept in our fatigues.

Much to the concern of the rest of us, Mike L. had not taken off his boots. He said he was having trouble with his feet and didn't want to look at them until we got to the beach. We all argued that some air and dry socks would be a good thing, but he wouldn't listen.

We were already walking as it started to get light and our spirits were high. This would be the last day of the course and the end of a tough two weeks in Panama. The sleep, fitful for some, had done us all good, and there was a spring again in our steps. Mike Deuel took the point and he set a good pace. We all wanted to get this over with so no one complained. There was a pretty blue sky appearing over the jungle canopy and it was clear that we were going to have a sunny day – again. The terrain got less difficult as well as we approached the end of the peninsula. It took only a couple of hours to cover the rest of the way and we were on the beach checking in by 0830. It was a relief and I looked forward to a long hot shower and some food.

We had been watched and graded for the whole two weeks in Panama. The military had its standards and needed records for personnel files so, even though we were civilians, we had been included. And, as it turned out, happily so. We had done very well both individually and as a group. Points had been awarded for performance in each of the exercises in the course and the total points dictated how you finished. Above certain levels, distinctions (with badges) were awarded. The best you could do was a 'Jungle Expert' badge. That badge meant you had performed at high levels throughout the course. I left with a Jungle Expert badge, as did all but five in our group. The badge aside, I also left with a much greater appreciation of what is in a jungle environment and how to deal with it. What I learned and experienced in Panama would serve me well both in Laos and later in the Congo.

SIX

LAND OF A MILLION ELEPHANTS

1962

We were on our final approach to Hong Kong's Tai Tak airport. The mountains on both sides were pretty, but, at dusk, menacing. As we got nearer the city, the hillsides seemed covered with lights and buildings, and the harbour with hordes of boats. It was quite a sight. We had been travelling for the better part of two days and even in first-class, which we loved, it was starting to wear us down. There's a limit to how much good food and wine you can consume in a limited period. Still, we were excited to be nearing our destination, Bangkok.

Andre LeGallo, Mike Deuel, Ralph McLean and I had been together now for just over a year. After our CIA training together, we had volunteered for six-month, temporary assignments to Laos, where the Agency, in support of President Kennedy's decision to hold the line against communist expansion, was trying to help the Laotians maintain their territorial integrity and their 'independent' government. It was July 1962 and early evening as we landed in Hong Kong for an hour's rest and refuel.

Hoping for a little fresh air and a look at another new city, we were standing at the plane's door as they opened it. The heavy, humid and foul air hit us like the proverbial ton of bricks. A muggy Hong Kong summer evening, with no air moving and with rotting fish and garbage in the harbour waters only a couple of hundred feet away, produces foul odours indeed. The combination of our travel fatigue and the air in Hong Kong compared to that on the plane, made us feel as though we were stepping from

America to Asia in one step. I took a look at the lights shining on all the hillsides around the airport and remember thinking that, despite the awful smell, Hong Kong seemed intriguing and inviting. I made a mental note to come back sometime.

It was after midnight when we arrived at Don Muang airport in Bangkok. We were all tired, but excited and curious. Administration officers were there to meet us and it didn't take long to clear customs and get ourselves loaded into their van. I was travelling with a large duffel bag, a suitcase and a wooden, Jack Kramer tennis racket, all of my worldly possessions at that time. I had left my car, the British racing green TR3, with my dad for the duration of my assignment. The administration officers took us straight to a rest house not far from the Embassy, where we each had a room to ourselves.

Bangkok met all of my expectations. The Thai were a very attractive people and friendly as well. I liked them right away. Many of the girls were very pretty. The Buddhist temples, the *klongs* and waterways filled with small boats, the death-trap three-wheel taxis and frenetic traffic were, for me, another world.

A day later we were headed for Vientiane, the capital of Laos. Still travelling together, my friends and I boarded a Second World War vintage DC-3 and lumbered north.

We landed in Vientiane a little before noon and taxied to the area reserved for Air America operations. As we climbed down the door ladder and stood in a group next to the plane, three men approached us and we realized we were about to meet our bosses, Bill Lair, Pat Landry and Tony Poe. Each of the three had a reputation for having accomplished numerous acts requiring courage and toughness. We all had heard the stories about them and had been much impressed. These were men's men. Willing to take on challenges anywhere and anytime, they were the heart of the Agency's paramilitary efforts in Laos.

Bill Lair, who was in his late thirties, stood just under six feet and was a strong-looking man. A graduate of Texas A and M University, Lair had come to South-East Asia in the early 1950s and had spent that decade in Thailand organizing and training the elite Thai Police group called the Police Air Reconnaissance Unit (PARU). Wearing khaki trousers, a sports shirt and glasses, he was the Chief and was highly respected. His unassuming, almost shy demeanour masked a mental and physical toughness that we would come to know well. Anticipating we didn't know what, but certainly something new and different, our excitement level had grown as we had neared Vientiane and the end of our long journey. We waited for their first words of welcome.

'Jesus Christ, we asked 'em to send us more men and they sent us a bunch of kids. They look as green as grass,' Tony Poe growled. Tony, a bull of a man, looked, at a guess, to be about thirty-five. He was wearing fatigues and combat boots. He was balding prematurely, but at six feet tall looked as strong and tough as his reputation. He wasn't smiling. Tony, according to the stories we had heard and later confirmed, had almost taken up professional golf, which seemed a real anomaly. He landed on Iwo Jima with the Marine Corps when he was still a teenager and later served in Korea. He had also worked in a training programme with groups of Tibetans. He and Landry, serving in Indonesia during the late 1950s' communist rebellion, had been cut off, almost captured and eventually exfiltrated by submarine.

'Damn, they must not be reading our cables. We said we wanted experienced officers,' Pat Landry said in a loud voice. 'How the hell do they expect us to run this operation?' he asked of no one in particular. Pat was also a graduate of Texas A and M and with his stocky build he could have played guard on the football team. He wore cotton slacks and a sports shirt, and carried a swagger stick. It wasn't hard to picture him handling tough and dangerous situations.

'Well, we're just going to have to make 'em into something worthwhile,' Bill concluded. Now they were all smiling.

To say that we were deflated would be putting it mildly. Our bubble burst? I'd say so. But none of us reacted. We didn't say that we all had military experience and had earned high praise in the Agency's paramilitary course – run by men who were their cohorts. They would have known that anyway from our files. We just grinned at them, shook hands and repeated how happy we were to be there to work with them. And we were. I suspect that this was an oft-repeated scene for new arrivals, but they did make their point. We were indeed the greenest of the green. We would learn in a hurry, however, as responsibility was to come quickly.

'No sense messing around,' Lair told us. 'I want you four to go up to Sam Thong [an operational site not far from the Plaine des Jarres] in the morning to take a look at what we're doing. Meantime we'll sort out where each of you is going to be assigned.'

'I guess I can take one of 'em up to Sam Neua [a province near North Vietnam],' Tony said in a gentler tone.

'About time for some lunch,' Pat announced. 'Any of you guys old enough to drink beer?'

That comment confirmed for us that we were truly being needled and it prompted loud shouts of feigned outrage. We went off to a little French restaurant, where we enjoyed a very nice meal complete with baguettes and red wine – not beer. Rapport was established quickly. We definitely liked what we saw and they seemed favourably impressed also. Bonds that, in some cases, would last a lifetime began to be formed. It was a great start and I was confident that the work would be both challenging and rewarding. It certainly was.

The Agency's paramilitary efforts in Laos, headed by Bill Lair with Pat Landry as his active deputy, were divided roughly geographically. There were separate programmes in North Laos (where I would initially be assigned), Central Laos, also known as the 'Panhandle' (where I would later be assigned), and South Laos. In each programme, we worked with different groups of people (mountain tribal groups such as the Hmong in the north and the lowland Lao who lived mostly along the Mekong River). And while each had separate goals, the objectives were complementary: to monitor and impede, or at least harass, North Vietnamese efforts to support the Laotian communist party's efforts to overthrow the King and the Lao government in Vientiane, and to use whatever portions of eastern Laos they wished to support the war they were waging in South Vietnam.

For geopolitical reasons and for reasons of his own as well, I'm sure, President Kennedy had decided to draw the line in South-East Asia. That is, it would be US policy to resist communist global expansionism and South-East Asia was a case in point. Kennedy, with former President Eisenhower's blessing (indeed Eisenhower had so advised him), was firm on this decision. No 'dominos' would fall. Rather than introduce US military forces in Laos, however, Washington, in its wisdom, elected to use aid programmes, advisors and ultimately 'covert action' means to support the government. South Vietnam, of course, was to be a different story.

Kennedy's decisions triggered the Agency's planning that put Bill Lair into Laos to establish its programmes. Hundreds of other Agency and non-Agency Americans were to participate in what would become known as 'The Secret War in Laos'. In fact, as will become clear, there was very little secret about what we did.

The biggest, and most active, of four programmes at that time was the one in North Laos supporting the Hmong tribe. (In 1962 we knew them as the Meo. It was simple ignorance on our part. In later years, I was to discover that, in fact, Meo was a pejorative term that meant 'barbarian' in Chinese. Ultimately our successors figured that out. The Meo/Hmong knew, however, that we were not malicious, just dumb, so, in these early years, they didn't make an issue of it.) My colleagues and I arrived at the early stages of the programme and an expansion effort was under way. The Hmong were (still are, I hope) a mountain people, pushed into Laos long ago from southern China, who rarely lived below about 2,000 feet in the mountains that cover North Laos. Tough, proud people, they were not afraid to fight for what they wanted, which, basically, was to be left alone to pursue their traditional existence. Theirs was an agriculturally based economy with slash-and-burn methods employed to grow mountain rice and vegetables – and poppies for opium whenever possible. Ideology was not an issue.

The average Hmong could not have distinguished between communism and capitalism and certainly could not have cared less about either. They felt threatened, however, by the Lao communist movement and by the Vietnamese support thereof. They had decided that they would fight to preserve their autonomy and all they asked of us was financial and material support. Lair struck the first agreement at a meeting with Hmong leader Vang Pao in December 1960. At that meeting, Vang Pao made their position clear: Lao communists will push the Hmong off their lands if they didn't fight. If the Americans gave weapons and support, they would resist. For the Hmong, more than a decade of fighting and dying was sealed by that decision.

For purposes of managing the programme, Hmong country, that is, Northern Laos, was divided into regions. The regions were numbered, but often were known by the name of the province they were in or by the name of a main village in the region.

The protagonists in the North, and elsewhere in Laos, were the Royal Lao Army (known in French as the Forces Armées Royales, the FAR) to which we were allied, and the Lao communist forces known as the Pathet Lao (PL) or Lao People's Army. The latter force, ill-organized and poorly trained and equipped, was supported by North Vietnam whose units were known as Vietnamese communists or VC. The VC enjoyed a strong reputation as a result of their victory over French forces at the end of the colonial period. They were known to be tough, smart and aggressive fighters.

The Hmong units we were arming and organizing were opposed to the PL and, by extension, the VC. They accepted, rather tolerated, the FAR, but only for practical purposes – they had a common enemy. Actually, the Hmong did not like the Lao and the feeling was mutual. Finally, into the alphabet soup of opposing forces in Laos at the time one must add the name of Kong Le, an obstinate Lao captain, who commanded a battalion of parachutists. Kong Le, angry at politics and politicians in Vientiane, staged a coup and broke away from the FAR to form what he called 'neutralist' forces. His forces, known as KL, fought the FAR, but not the PL or the VC. They were not very neutral in fact. That was the mix with which we were faced in trying to support the Hmong programme.

Our trip to Sam Thong the day after our arrival was our first visit 'upcountry'. In fact, everything north of Vientiane was considered upcountry. It meant we were headed for a different world. There were no, and I mean no, amenities. We knew that and were not bothered in the least. This was what we had been looking forward to for months. We were all wearing field clothes now, including jungle boots we'd acquired in Vientiane. The mountains of North Laos, ranging from 2,000 to 8,000 feet, have an unusual beauty and we drank it in from the helicopter. Enormous walls of *karst* – limestone outcrops – rose straight up out of the ground at random. Soon we were circling to land at Sam Thong's dirt strip. There were already a couple of small planes on the ground.

After landing, we found out that a Special Forces trained Hmong battalion was going to graduate that morning and we would watch the ceremony. The Special Forces units, known locally as 'White Star', had been sent into Laos to help with training as the programme was getting under way. They were accepted, I thought, for political reasons. Most Agency officers were not convinced that they really belonged in such a programme. We took note of the White Star camp. It seemed to be a large unit with tents, latrines, drinking water purification systems, mess facilities, movies at night, mail deliveries – and peanut butter. It required logistics and daily flights from Vientiane to keep them supplied. These didn't seem to be the snake-eating live-off-the-land warriors we had heard about. To me at least, they were not what was needed to train and organize the hit-and-run guerrilla forces we envisioned.

The ceremony was, in fact, a parade to be reviewed by the White Star commanding officer, who was flying in from Vientiane in late morning. It went as planned and I remember thinking how inappropriate it seemed to have guerrilla fighters parading in front of an American officer. The Hmong were not much as marchers and their ranks were rarely straight. But they did it. Unfortunately the Hmong leader, Major (later to be Lieutenant General) Vang Pao, was all but ignored by the Army brass in attendance. As an afterthought, he was acknowledged as the march-by was concluding. We all thought that a serious faux pas by our White Star comrades. Despite what anyone may have thought of how the ceremony was handled, the Hmong unit did finish with uniforms, boots and weapons (including machine-guns, recoilless rifles and mortars), and good training on how to use them.

When the festivities were finished, we had a chance to roam around the village to size up the kind of place we would be living in for the next several months – minus the White Star amenities. The Hmong were clearly a different people and not at all like the lowland Lao we had seen in Vientiane. With sharper features similar to the Chinese, they were small of stature, but strong and energetic. The village, like other Hmong villages I would see, was basic, almost primitive: thatched huts with dirt floors; latrine area outside the village. Water was available from streams that were, if you were lucky, a short walk away. Women and girls hauled water, cooked, sewed and washed clothes. Men farmed, hunted and lolled around. Those were first impressions, but I confirmed them in every Hmong village I was to visit.

We were introduced to Vang Pao, or VP, as he came to be known to us. He looked upon each of us sternly and seriously as we were introduced. His English was weak, although it would improve greatly over the next decade, so we spoke in French. He had been a non-commissioned officer in a French army unit several years earlier. Plainly, he was aware of the fact that we would be assigned, separately, to Hmong regions and he thanked us for coming to help his people. I thought he was an impressive man. We had lunch with him, Hmong style: sticky rice, pieces of chicken, some kind of green vegetable and fruit. Since this was a special day and Sam Thong was well supplied, we also had a can of Japanese beer. Cooled in the nearby mountain stream, it tasted pretty good. It had been an interesting first exposure to upcountry and, as we flew back to Vientiane, I was more eager than ever to find out where I would be assigned and when.

I didn't have long to wait. We got back to Vientiane at dusk and went straight to the 'Motel' (at least a version thereof – it was the only one in Laos and even had a swimming pool), where Bill and Pat lived. We met in the bar, had a couple of drinks, and Bill or Pat called each of us aside for a private chat. Pat spoke with me and, eschewing small talk, got directly to the point.

'We want you to go up to Ban [the Lao word for village] Na,' he announced. He frequently seemed to announce things. There was to be no debate or even discussion.

'That's great. Where is Ban Na?' I asked.

He smiled. 'What if I said just outside Dien Bien Phu?' (The site of a famous battle in which French forces were defeated by the North Vietnamese in North Vietnam.)

'You wouldn't send me unless you thought I could handle it.'

'Right you are, lad,' he said smilingly. 'Ban Na is just west of the Plaine des Jarres and it needs a longer landing strip. We can only land single-engine planes or choppers up there and we need a capability to land larger twin-engine planes. You run the region, which is established and is quiet for the moment, but concentrate on getting that landing strip lengthened. Any questions?'

'People with shovels are the earth movers, right?'

'Right again. I could send up some cratering charges if you know how to use them.'

I hesitated a moment, thinking about the explosives training we had had. 'Yeah, send them up,' I responded. 'When do I go?'

'In the morning,' Pat replied, looking me straight in the eye. 'I know you didn't come all the way out here just to hang around Vientiane. Be at the airport at oh seven hundred.'

'I'll be there. What about some field gear and a weapon?'

'You can pick up what you want at our airport warehouse in the morning. Don't take too much. You have to carry whatever you take,' Pat said.

There was no talk of the enemy and no talk of danger. That would come soon enough, I thought.

About a week ago I had been saying goodbye to my parents in Kansas City as I boarded the plane for San Francisco. Now I was standing next to a short, dirt landing strip in a Hmong village just west of the Plaine des Jarres in Laos, half a world away from Kansas City. Incredible, I was thinking as I watched the single-engine helio-courier disappear over the ridgeline. The helio, as we always called it, was designed for use on short strips. Known as a Short Takeoff and Landing (STOL) aircraft, it did yeoman service for Air America and the Agency throughout the years that we operated in Laos.

As planned, I had arrived at the airport in Vientiane at 0700 and was sent directly to the logistics officer in our warehouse. Air America and another contract airline shared a large compound at one end of the airport. In it were hangars, parts shops and maintenance facilities. They had a big operation and it was getting bigger all the time. The Agency had a small office and a warehouse next to the compound.

'What do you think you'll need?' our logistics officer asked.

'I really don't know,' I told him. 'What are the guys upcountry carrying?'

'Well, they all start out with too much and end up turning in excess gear,' he said. 'First choice I guess is what kind of weapon you want. Nobody carries a sidearm upcountry so the choice is really either a carbine or an M-1. Carbine is lighter, but is less reliable and has less range than an M-1. What's your pleasure?'

I tried to weigh the pros and cons of each weapon. 'I'll take an M-1,' I said finally. (I would later change my mind and exchange the M-1 for the lighter Carbine after walking in the mountains upcountry for some time.)

'You want a backpack?'

'Guess I'll need something for some extra clothes,' I replied. 'But only a small one.'

'That's all I have,' he said, 'this isn't L.L. Bean. What's more, the Hmong are all little guys so most of the gear we have is small.'

'OK, so give me a small backpack,' I told him.

'Most guys carry a web belt,' he went on. 'Makes it easy to carry your emergency radio.'

'My what?' I asked.

'Nobody flies around upcountry without carrying an emergency radio for use in case something happens. Here's yours,' he said, handing me a small transmitter/receiver that I, like all others working upcountry, would end up carrying everywhere I went. It would fit into a pouch attached to a web belt and it became my most important piece of gear.

'You should have a couple of extra clips of ammo and a small first aid kit too,' he continued.

I also picked up a bayonet knife and stuck that on the web belt as well. It seemed a good idea, but wasn't, and I soon returned it in favour of a multi-blade jack-knife, which was much more practical. 'That should do it unless you have an extra pair of nine and a half jungle boots,' I said.

'Not likely, but I can order them up from Bangkok. I'll let you know when they come in.'

'Many thanks,' I told him as I picked up the gear and headed for Pat's office. And I meant it. He had been a pleasure to deal with. No forms, no signatures, no bureaucracy. Just good advice and generosity with whatever he had. If you needed something to get the job done, he'd give it to you. And if he didn't have it, he'd get it. That was a hallmark of our support system the whole time I was in Laos. It was reassuring for those of us who lived and worked upcountry.

At Ban Na I watched the helio disappear, and I have to admit that I felt as if I was at the end of the world, and it was lonely. I turned to speak to Panit, the leader of the small PARU team that would work with me in Ban Na. He and his three colleagues were members of the élite unit that Bill Lair had spent the last decade organizing and training. Hand-picked by Lair and a couple of Thai Police officers, they had been selected from hundreds of applicants. Three hundred strong, all were at least high school graduates and most spoke a language from a neighbouring country in addition to Thai. They were trained (at a jungle camp in central Thailand that Allen Dulles had once visited) and organized more or less like the US Army's Special Forces. Counter-guerrilla tactics were one of their specialities.

In addition to their general training, PARU personnel all had specific capabilities designed to enhance small-unit operations. Panit, who headed my team, was a weapons man, which meant that he could handle (provide training, employ, assemble, repair) the whole range of weapons we were providing to the Hmong. With him on the Ban Na team were a medic, a radio operator (very important as he was our link with Vientiane) and an explosives expert. In fact, all four could provide basic training. All PARU were jump qualified.

As we landed, I had noticed that work was under way to lengthen the landing strip. A bunch of villagers were out there digging. 'How are things going on the landing strip?' I asked Panit. 'That's one of the things Pat Landry has asked me to focus on.'

'I know it's important,' Panit said. 'And we are working on it. It's hard work, sir. We could use some explosives.'

'Landry is sending up some cratering charges.'

'That's good news, sir,' Panit said, smiling. 'The Hmong will be happy.'

We had been standing at the end of the landing strip and the cluster of bamboo and thatch huts that made up the village of Ban Na was just below us. Panit headed up the mountain towards a couple of huts above the landing strip. The other three PARU were waiting and I was introduced. Just the look of the team I would be working with impressed me: clean, strong, bright-looking young men who exuded confidence and a willingness to get things done. I was to find that all of my first impressions were accurate. Two huts stood there more or less side by side. One of them I would share with Panit. We went inside where there were two bed-sized bamboo platforms about eighteen inches off the dirt floor. One of them would be my bed. An old parachute served as the sheet and blanket. The thatched walls would keep out wind and rain and hopefully the ceiling wouldn't leak. Panit put my backpack next to my 'bed' and said he hoped I'd be comfortable.

The PARU had hung a bright orange parachute over the area between the two huts and constructed a wooden table under it. That, clearly, was the dining room. It doubled as the living room as that's where we sat to discuss things and read at night. A lantern hung over the table.

The bathroom was another story. For a shower one walked to a cold (really cold, but eventually I got used to it) mountain stream. Standing in it about waist-deep, one washed. That was it. We carried and heated water for shaving although I was the only one who shaved every day. The latrine, not quite as far but in the other direction, was a hut perched over a hole in the ground. It did not feature a board with a hole in it. A balancing act was required. I got used to that too. Looking around, I repeated to myself that this certainly was a long way from Kansas City.

Panit took me down to see the village. Forty plus huts were perched on a flat outcrop of the mountain. There were no streets per se, just lanes between the huts. More or less in the middle of the village was an open area that served as a town square. As we got there a Hmong pony, quite obviously male, was doing his best to mount a less interested female and a group of Hmong kids were giggling and pointing. Nobody did anything. We kept on walking. I was the object of lots of interest and everyone was smiling. Dressed in traditional garb, black dresses with multi-coloured bands on their heads and waists, the Hmong women looked strong and hardy. Like the men they were small in stature and most had sharp features. Pigs and chickens made their presence known and the small ponies were the largest animals I saw. The Hmong didn't keep water buffalo because they weren't agile enough to move around in the mountains (many of the trails, I would discover, were narrow and precarious – at least, I thought so) and because their techniques for rice growing did not require paddies. The views, in almost any direction, over the valley that lay below were incredible.

After lunch Panit took me down to see the landing strip. In effect, we were removing a big hump in the middle of a sloping area. Without the hump the strip would certainly take larger aircraft. A group of villagers were working with crude hoes and shovels, and carried away the dirt in wicker baskets slung on a pole. What we really needed was a bulldozer, but cratering charges would help.

'If we get some cratering charges, we'll be done in two weeks,' Panit boldly predicted. 'Just moving it after the charge goes off is a lot easier than having to dig it out.'

The next day Panit showed me the five outposts around Ban Na. They formed a semi-circle facing the Plaine des Jarres, as it was from there that any enemy patrols would come. From each one there was a good view of the western portions of the Plaine, a prominent, and unusual, geographical feature in North Laos. Nestled among the mountains, it is actually a plateau covering a little over thirty square miles. Located midway between Vientiane and the border with North Vietnam, it has rolling grasslands dotted with woods and streams. Roads ran from it to Vietnam to the east and Vientiane to the south-west. At this time, July 1962, the Plaine des Jarres, so named by the French colonialists because of the enormous earthen jars that were strewn all over the plateau, was in the hands of the PL and the KL, who had taken it in 1960. There were KL and PL units on the Plaine and the VC, of course, had free run. Truck convoys from North Vietnam arrived regularly during the dry season bringing all types of supplies for the PL and KL units.

I looked down on the Plaine wondering if there were any VC units down there. None of us worried much about the PL or the KL, but we, and the Hmong, had respect for the toughness and the tenacity of the VC fighters.

Our outposts were placed to observe and to block approaches to Ban Na from the Plaine. Each had a small, low shelter in which the Hmong ate and slept, and mortar and machine-gun emplacements. About fifteen Hmong guerrillas manned every one. Panit, the weapons man, a Hmong officer and I arrived at each. Obviously we were expected as everyone was 'standing tall' by their weapons. I was introduced. A few of the Hmong spoke French. We inspected their emplacements and weapons. For some reason, the head space on the 50-calibre machine-gun was frequently neglected and almost always needed to be adjusted. At this early stage, the Hmong didn't really appreciate it, but this was a serious problem. Without going into too much detail (I haven't seen a 50 calibre for a very long time), because of barrel blowback (recoil) one must, using a special tool, adjust the head space by about three clicks. Without the right adjustment, expended shells might not be properly ejected and the weapon might jam. The 50-calibre machine-gun is a 'no kidding serious weapon'. It was used in Laos and Vietnam primarily as a perimeter defence weapon. It was not easily portable. Were it to jam during an attack on the outpost, it would be a distressing development for the defenders.

We also looked at maps so that everyone could make it clear to me why this particular outpost was placed where it was, chatted for a few minutes and moved on. We left early in the morning and didn't get back until just before sunset, a long day. Happily, because I was not yet used to either the altitude or the mountain trails, no stretch of walking that day was more than about an hour and there were rest periods at each outpost.

My life in Ban Na featured few highlights. Days were spent working on the hump in the airstrip, training the Hmong, and walking to nearby outposts and small villages. They were all the same, weekends passed unnoticed, and often we forgot what day of the week it was. In the evenings, we would sit around and talk, but communication was difficult as only Panit spoke good English and none of the PARU spoke French. The village went quiet when the sun went down and we didn't go down there very often.

Dinner was always an adventure as they tried to prepare things I would like. There really wasn't much choice: pieces of chicken or pork (sometimes beef or horse-meat), boiled rice because the Thai weren't that fond of sticky rice, and green vegetables, boiled or stir-fried over a wood fire. Dinner always produced conversation about what we were eating. It was always hot, spicy hot that is, as both the Thai and the Hmong love red peppers. Initially, it was so hot I could hardly eat it. I got used to that too. We usually went to bed early, due to a combination of fatigue from active days outdoors and the fact that there wasn't anything else to do. Often I would read for a while or study maps, but that never lasted long. I always slept well.

Our goals were straightforward. We were to help the Hmong in any way we could to defend their territory. In this case that meant Ban Na and the sector immediately around it – just off the western end of the Plaine des Jarres. Ban Na wasn't really a region, I came to find out, but an important spot for watching what the enemy was doing on the Plaine. And, since it was quiet, a good place to put a new kid to see how he would do. My responsibility was to manage the operations of my PARU team (not a difficult task since they knew much more about what was going on than I did) and, most important, serve as the link with our logistics base – Pat and Bill in Vientiane. Whatever the village or my team needed to do their job, it was up to me to see that they got it. It made me a key person and they all knew it.

I met regularly with the Nai Ban (the village chief, in this case he was also a Nai Khong, chief of a group of villages) to discuss needs. Since most of the men were fighters now, agricultural activity was almost at a standstill. Therefore the village needed food supplies regularly to augment the meagre amounts they were producing. Periodically, I would send a cable to Pat and request a rice drop. Our system was amazingly efficient. I could always count on prompt responses to my cables. I didn't have to duck after the cable was sent, but almost. Within one or two days, sometimes within hours, the drop would arrive. One or two hundred sacks of rice would land on our drop zone, the landing strip. Three or four sacks of salt would always be included.

Early in the programme, I heard that some poor Hmong would actually try to catch a sixty-or eighty-pound double-sacked bag of rice dropped from altitude. The result was predictable. He was crushed. I never saw that happen. Ban Na villagers stayed away from the drop zone until the drop was on the ground. We also dropped uniforms, boots, tools, and whatever else was needed. For now, weapons and ammo came by helio, chopper, or parachute. One of the reasons we wanted the longer strip at Ban Na was so that we could bring in more supplies and build up Hmong defences on the western end of the Plaine des Jarres. It was my responsibility to get all of those things on the ground in Ban Na. I was also responsible for keeping Vientiane aware of enemy activities on the western Plaine. We sent out patrols and individual villagers regularly to watch what the enemy was doing. I sent regular reports down to Vientiane.

July being the rainy season, enemy mobility was greatly decreased by impassable roads. That left us, with great off-road mobility in the mountains, in the driver's seat until the next dry season started in October or November. The enemy didn't want to take on the Hmong in Hmong territory. It left us the opportunity to conduct typical guerrilla warfare: hit-and-run attacks on their roads and supply points. We were still early in the programme and were building our capabilities, but offensive actions were increasing. An ultimate goal was to retake the Plaine des Jarres, thereby relieving pressure on the Hmong territory around it. It was a cat-and-mouse game that became more deadly as the 1960s unfolded.

The scenario was always the same. They were strong and would push upward in the dry season, and we would attack and push them back in the rainy season. In the later stages, air power used in support of the Hmong offensives was extensive, but that didn't happen while I was in Laos.

True to his word, Panit had the hump removed and the length of the landing strip almost doubled in just over two weeks after we got the cratering charges. With the end in sight, the villagers, mostly women, worked steadily after the charges simplified their task and the job was completed early. There was still a roll in the middle of the strip and the whole thing sloped uphill, but the Air America pilot who came to check it out did not mind and gave it his OK. Rolling uphill after touch down would help planes stop, he said, and going downhill on take off was also a plus. 'We planned it that way,' I lied, smiling. Ban Na's strip could now handle a Caribou, a Canadian-made STOL aircraft with great stability at low speeds, which can land on relatively short strips – not much longer than those used by the helio. But, with two engines and a rear-opening ramp it had a much greater payload. Bringing it into Ban Na meant getting more supplies closer to the Plaine des Jarres, a strategic step forward.

A few days later, the first Caribou landed without problem at Ban Na with room to spare, as the pilot told me. I had been in Ban Na less than three weeks and had adapted quickly to the routine, knew the sector well by having walked all over it, and was truly absorbed in and enjoying my work. I felt I was really contributing something tangible. But a cable the previous day from Pat advised that I should come back to Vientiane for reassignment. I thought about asking them to reconsider, but concluded that my baptism by fire had apparently gone OK. I was going to be moved and that was that.

By now I had heard that Mike Deuel was with Tony Poe in Sam Neua province, Ralph was on the eastern edge of the Plaine des Jarres, and Andre had been given a region north and east of the Plaine to handle. We were all gainfully employed. I wondered what would come next.

I went straight from the airport to Pat's office on my return from Ban Na. He was reading cable traffic from Headquarters that he apparently found of little interest, as he seemed to welcome the interruption my arrival occasioned.

'So, kid, how was Ban Na?' he said with a smile.

'Great. We got the strip lengthened and I got a good look at the whole sector.'

'I know,' Pat noted drily. 'That's why you were up there.'

'Panit's team is really first rate,' I added.

'I know that as well,' Pat responded. 'And Panit likes you too. That's good.'

'Well, I'm pleased to hear that, but I have to tell you those guys are not hard to get along with. They know what the hell they are doing.'

'But you come out with high marks and that's excellent,' Pat said. 'Makes it easier for me and I like that.'

'How about some lunch?' I asked. 'I need to grill you about what I'm going to do next.'

'Never eat lunch. Makes me fat and sleepy,' he responded. 'Not sure yet where you are headed. I have an idea, but I want to confirm it with Bill.' He abruptly changed the subject. 'How long would it take to walk down to the Plaine des Jarres from Ban Na?'

'That I didn't do,' I responded, 'but the Hmong say about six hours – less than a day. It would probably take a full day coming up from the Plaine. Why?'

'Because I'm just thinking about us walking down there and taking over some day, that's why,' Pat said. 'We're getting stronger all the time.'

'I'd like to be back up there if we're going to do that,' I told him.

'Not for a while, kid, not for a while.'

I sensed that our conversation was over and got up to leave. 'OK, so I'll see you later. When might you get a chance to talk with Bill?'

'Stop by about eight tonight. We'll have a couple of drinks and then eat somewhere close by. I'll have some word by then. Now go relax somewhere and get a hot shower.'

Vientiane, especially after nearly three weeks in Ban Na, was quite a change. It was, at the time, an 'open' city. Sprawled along the Mekong River (still the longest un-bridged river in the world) with Thailand on the opposite bank, it was the capital and largest city in Laos. The Lao, lowlanders who lived in valleys and along the rivers, made up the majority of the three million inhabitants of Laos. There were also, however, large numbers of foreigners who lived in Vientiane and other cities in Laos. Mostly in commercial endeavours, they included Chinese, Indian, Thai, Vietnamese and French, the former colonial masters.

It was very definitely the latter group, the foreigners, which created the activity and the hustle and bustle evident in some parts of Vientiane. Mostly because of the great infusions of money and aid supplies coming into Laos to help it withstand the threat from Vietnam and its own communist insurgents, there was much money to be made in Vientiane and these merchants were there for exactly that purpose. Graft and corruption of all sorts thrived. Working discreetly (sometimes openly) with Lao politicians and military officers, the merchants siphoned off huge sums of official money into their pockets. We knew this, of course, but few wanted to take on the job of trying to control it. Live and let live seemed to be the motto followed by everyone in the city – Americans included. Little of what was going on in Vientiane bothered me very much. I was fully involved in our programme, and saw our efforts as something apart from the mess in Vientiane.

Building architecture, street names, certain stores and restaurants, bars and cafés, and even a partially built 'Arc de Triomphe' were reminders of the city's colonial past. In better days it could have been a small city in the South of France. Sadly though, it was decaying. Most streets were littered, and neither the residents nor the government showed much interest in cleaning them up. Still, it was an intriguing and enjoyable place and I spent some pleasant afternoons walking around. Close by were some of the several nightclubs that were doing a flourishing business. And a few kilometres to the south and east was the official crossing point into Thailand. Nong Khai, on the opposite bank of the Mekong, was where travellers from Bangkok, or elsewhere, cleared Thai border formalities and crossed into Laos by boat. In fact people could, and routinely did, cross the Mekong anywhere and anytime – causing angst within Thai officialdom.

What was going on in Lao politics at the time would have been grist for Shakespeare's mill. He could have written a great play about the daily machinations and intrigue that plagued Vientiane in particular and Laos in general. A king without power, royal princes working towards opposite goals, corrupt politicians selling influence and position, and graft-seeking military officers manipulating the system relentlessly could all have featured in what surely would have been subtitled 'A Tragedy in Asia'. I knew little of what was transpiring. Nor did any of my colleagues. Worse, I could not have cared less. We were there with the noblest of intentions. We were going to push back the red tide and save Laos; not only Laos, but, if one believed the domino theory so popular at the time, the whole of South-East Asia. Freedom and liberty were not just abstract words. I was strongly anti-communist, anti any authoritarian system, and was more than willing to oppose them whenever and however I could. Helping the Hmong to resist and secure the north of Laos was a step in the right direction and it deserved all the support we were giving.

Clearly though, arrogance (and ignorance) was widespread among the Americans serving in Laos. 'Just do what we tell you and stay out of the way' was a common approach. It was not a malicious arrogance, but one that, in the end, served us ill. In retrospect, it seems obvious that a greater understanding of what was going on in Laos would have enabled us to work more effectively and perhaps spared some of the pain the country experienced. But I emphasize that we were serving and supporting US policy and we believed in it.

I took a taxi back to the compound after my conversation with Pat. I sometimes wondered what the taxi drivers thought as I headed upcountry with my pack, web belt and gun, but I never got any questions. I read several books on rice growing in South-East Asia, paddy and mountain variety, to be able to support my cover, but it never came up in any conversation.

I stopped to pick up a paper and magazines, starved for news of what was going on in the world. I was particularly interested in the talks about Laos that were under way in Geneva. In fact, the first thing I read was that the Geneva Accords were about to be signed. I knew that would signal significant change for our efforts in Laos. The US representative, Ambassador Averell Harriman, was prepared to sign the Accords promising that the US would pull all but diplomatic and specified Aid personnel out of Laos. The communists (Russia, China and North Vietnam) said they would follow suit. We would have until 7 October to comply. What would happen? Would we be sent back to Washington? I hoped not, but had no idea what to expect. I looked forward to talking with Pat and Bill. Surely they had word from Headquarters or the chief in Vientiane. Maybe that was why Pat pulled me out of Ban Na and was unsure what I would be doing next.

I cleaned up and wrote a letter to my parents – who probably thought by now that Asia had swallowed up their eldest son. I also got the maid to wash all my clothes as, due to the lack of hot water and soap, they hadn't had a proper wash in Ban Na.

Our group of JOTs had been the second to arrive in Laos. Four months earlier, four young officers from the paramilitary class before us had arrived in Laos as the first contingent. They were now considered veterans with four months' experience. All were assigned upcountry. One, Vint Lawrence, happened to be in Vientiane that evening and joined us for dinner. It was standard practice that when any of us from upcountry were in Vientiane (or Bangkok), we would spend lots of time together. As I had hoped, we quickly got onto the subject of the Geneva Accords after we sat down with our drinks. And, as expected, Bill Lair was able to give us lots of information. Unfortunately, political decisions were yet to be made so there were gaps regarding the future of our programme. But we had until fall at least before anyone had to leave. That was welcome news, but prospects seemed ominous nonetheless.

As was always the case, the evening with Pat and Bill was enjoyable. Bill was soft-spoken and quiet, but one sensed a man who was reflecting on issues and when he came to conclusions you knew they were well-considered. Pat had a gruff exterior, but was in reality a very considerate and, I thought, caring man. He worried about his subordinates, especially the 'kids' he was sending upcountry. Both, in their own ways, were great guys and splendid to work for. Before we left, Pat told me to show up at his office in the morning. 'And bring your gear,' he added. 'I don't want you just lolling around Vientiane.' To me, that meant that I'd be going back upcountry in the morning and that was good news. After dinner, Vint and I went to a nightclub for a couple of hours and drank a few beers while we shared upcountry experiences and other thoughts. We were both immensely pleased with what we were doing.

'Ever heard of Phou Song?' Pat said when I walked into his office the next morning.

'I know that *phou* means mountain but that's about all,' I responded. 'Is it in Hmong country?'

'Yes, it is,' Pat said and he seemed more serious than I had seen him before. 'It's north of Ban Na. We're expanding the programme into that area and I need you up there to keep things organized. Panit can handle Ban Na now that the strip is finished and we're more established. Phou Song has a PARU team and I want you to work with them to expand the whole programme up there. Phou Song also has a difficult Nai Ban and I think you can deal with him. Remember to listen.'

'Just two questions,' I said. 'What are the bad guys doing around Phou Song, and when do I go?'

'You go this morning,' Pat said. 'Not that much action yet,' he went on, 'but I am worried about what the PL units nearby have on their minds. Best keep on eye on them.'

'What's the problem with the Nai Ban?' I asked.

'Ornery and greedy,' said Pat, who was often a man of few words.

SEVEN

THE ELEVENTH MAN

1962

Phou Song was bigger than Ban Na, and occupied a plateau halfway up the mountain after which it was named, near the edge of a precipitous drop down into the valley. From anywhere in the village there was a truly spectacular view. Because of the large open space next to and behind the village, Phou Song had a very nice landing strip that would easily accommodate twin-engine STOL aircraft. It also had a large drop zone next to the strip.

Our landing had been an interesting experience. As we dropped down from altitude and entered the valley in between Phou Song and the mountains around it, we reached about 3,000 feet – well below Phou Song's 7,000 feet peak. To make our landing, the pilot simply turned left, started to crank down the flaps (done manually on a helio-courier), and headed for the strip. One minute we were flying high above the valley and the next we were landing – an unusual approach.

Take offs were also a kick and some of the pilots delighted in scaring selected passengers. They would take off, head towards the valley and the precipice, and get only enough air speed to more or less fall off the end of the landing strip. On these occasions, the plane, seen from the other end of the strip, would actually drop out of sight. Then, as it 'fell', it picked up air speed and the pilot would climb up and out of the valley. Since they were already at 3,000 feet when they left the end of the strip, it was not dangerous, but it got the attention of some unsuspecting passengers.

The village was safer than Ban Na since the only approaches were relatively easy to monitor and block. The nearest enemy (in this case PL) camps were at the far end of the valley. Courtesy of the aid programme there was a warehouse, built with planks and a tin roof, where rice, clothing and other material that was regularly distributed to nearby villages were stored. The majority of the men from the area were fighters and Phou Song was a focal point for the programme's efforts in the area.

The PARU team leader, Prasert, seemed friendly and I had the same favourable impressions when I met the other team members. They would be easy to work with I was sure. I got myself installed and then Prasert and I took a walk around the village. It was built on flatter ground than Ban Na and there seemed to be more symmetry. The Nai Ban's house was the biggest in the village. In and around it there were signs of wealth, comparatively speaking: more animals, tools and materials obviously brought in from Vientiane. I made no comment to Prasert, but noted to myself that the Nai Ban was prospering in these tough times. In the several weeks I spent working at Phou Song, I did take note of what the Nai Ban was doing and concluded that he was, as Pat had said, certainly greedy (more so than ornery). He was a man heavily engaged in an effort to feather his own nest. While I was there, I was able to curb this, but there was no telling what happened afterwards.

There was more to do than had been the case in Ban Na. There were the routine jobs like logistics and training, but now I was obliged to move around more. To do that, I cabled regularly for air support. Early on, Prasert frequently went with me, but, after I got to know the region, I often went alone. On those occasions, much depended on the availability of French or English speakers. In the villages I visited, we would talk about what nearby enemy units were doing and about needs – of all kinds. We supplied everything from weapons and ammunition to schoolbooks, medicines, rice and salt, uniforms, building materials and money. For some of these things I was simply the middle man. I would make arrangements for a delivery to a given village. Every so often, I would get fewer reports on enemy activity than I wanted, but there were always requests for food.

It didn't happen regularly, but sometimes there would be no

plane available or there was no landing strip nearby. Then I would take a Hmong patrol and a couple of the PARU and walk. We limited these walks to distances that could be covered in less than two days. More than that simply took up too much of my time. Those walks were both physically and mentally demanding. From Phou Song, very little of the walking was along ridgelines – unfortunately. The bulk of it was up and down. It was the middle of the rainy season when I arrived and the frequent rainstorms made the mountain trails muddy and slippery. Those were challenging days and everyone watched to see how the *farang*, the foreigner, would handle the trails, but they always made it as easy as possible for me. (It was after the first couple of walks that I traded my M-1 for the lighter Carbine. I didn't need the longer-range firing capability as on these trails you could never see further than the next turn or rise.) The Hmong soldiers, all of whom were smaller than me, carried packs plus their weapons and food and water. I never slowed them down, I made sure of that.

One morning, six young Hmong, Prasert and I left early and headed for a small village that didn't have an airstrip. It hadn't rained for a couple of days, but it was sunny and humid – even at 3,000 feet – and the air was heavy. We made steady progress on a difficult trail and were getting ready to stop for some lunch when we came to a small stream. A couple of small pools looked very inviting and all promptly agreed that a little dip before lunch would be very invigorating. We were all hot and sweaty and were still in a safe area so concern about enemy patrols was minimal. However, one of the Hmong was posted to watch for any unexpected visitors.

The Hmong were in the water in what seemed like seconds while I was still looking for a place to put down my weapon. I hurried, but was the last one into the water. Prasert and the Hmong were already sitting neck deep in one of the pools. I was standing about ankle deep in the middle of the stream trying to pick a way to the pool when another type of unexpected visitor arrived. Swirling downstream was a snake. It was thin and maybe eighteen inches long. What kind or how dangerous it might have been I had no idea. How it got there I didn't know either. It all happened in a blur. Just as I saw it, the snake saw something to throw a coil or two around to save itself – my left leg just above the ankle. I don't like snakes and it scared the hell out of me. I shouted and lashed out my left leg to get rid of it. My leg was slippery. He was slippery too and couldn't hold on. With all eyes now focused on me after my shout, the rest of the group saw the snake go flying in one direction and me lose my balance and fall over backwards into one of the smaller pools. The snake landed back in the fast moving water and was carried downstream. The Hmong and Prasert found the scene terribly amusing and a great howl of laughter came from all of them. I stood up, bowed deeply to my audience, and jumped into the larger pool.

We arrived at our destination a few hours after lunch (strips of dried meat and sticky rice) and were, as usual, welcomed by the Nai Ban of the village. As the honoured guest, I was given slices of fruit and a drink of the Hmong-made whisky. It was awful stuff, but there was no choice – you had to drink it. He explained, over the next hour, what his village's needs were and how willing they were to fight to protect Hmong country from the communists. I refrained from asking him what he thought a communist was. The distance from Phou Song was just too great to make a round trip in a day so, as planned, we had dinner with them and spent the night.

We took the same trail for our return so we passed the same little stream a couple of hours after leaving the village. No one suggested another dip. There was lots of smiling and laughing, however, and one of the Hmong did an imitation of the 'great leg kick' I had demonstrated the day before. We continued downhill and were crossing the level ground when it started to rain; not heavily but steadily. It rained the rest of the day and made the climb back up to Phou Song all the more tedious. I was happy to have the jungle boots because their cleats gave me added traction. Still, climbing up a rather steep mountain trail in the rain was less than pleasant. We stopped a couple of times to rest, but only for short periods. We didn't eat lunch, hoping to get back to the village sooner. It was early afternoon when we arrived. We were all soaked to the skin and were tired and hungry as well. Back at altitude, I felt a chill, but thought nothing of it. I dried off, changed clothes and stood by the fire sipping tea. The next day I felt lousy. It turned out to be more than just a cold.

As the day wore on, I felt worse and worse. By mid-afternoon, I had serious chills and a fever and couldn't eat without vomiting. I didn't stray from my hut. Prasert brought me soup and hot tea. By evening, I felt really weak and could barely get up to go to the latrine area. Prasert and I talked and decided that we had best call for a plane the next day so that I could see a doctor in Vientiane and get some medicine. The PARU team medic gave me aspirin, but didn't know what else to do. I got very little sleep and felt even worse the next morning.

The weather persisted too and we were still looking at heavy clouds and periodic rain. Prasert had sent a message the night before and we were waiting for word from Pat. His reply said that they were concerned about my condition and would send a plane as soon as possible to get me to a doctor. Bad weather all over North Laos, however, had flights grounded for the time being. 'Will come when we can,' the cable ended.

Word had filtered around the village that I was sick. There was not much anyone could do, but they all expressed concern and the Nai Ban stopped by to see me. I tried to put on a brave face. 'I'll be fine tomorrow,' I told him. He didn't say much but studied me carefully.

Later that morning the village Shaman showed up. Prasert was uneasy and that made me uneasy.

'Send him away,' I told Prasert.

'It's not that easy,' he responded.

'What do you mean?' I asked. 'Tell him I'm going to see my own doctor as soon as a plane can get in here. There really isn't anything he can do. And I'm tired.'

I could see that Prasert was having trouble getting through to the Shaman. 'The Nai Ban sent him,' Prasert said. 'We can't be so rude as to refuse to let him ward off the evil spirits that are troubling you. He won't leave.'

'Evil spirits? Don't be silly, I've got a fever.' But I was thinking as I said it that we would be obliged to accept the Nai Ban's gesture. Prasert watched me. 'OK, OK,' I said, 'but I'm not taking any potion from him.'

Prasert explained to the Shaman, who nodded.

He was dressed in traditional Hmong garb – black trousers and black shirt with a leather belt – had long hair, and a coloured scarf around his neck. On his shoulder was a leather pack, which he took off and set on the floor after Prasert told him he could 'treat' me. From it he produced two gourds with rice grains or beans inside. For some reason, Prasert left. Then it was just the Shaman and me.

He mumbled softly as he took some other things out of his pack. I couldn't see what, as he was standing at the end of my bed platform and they were on the ground. He never looked directly at me and his eyes seemed a little wild. I still had the fever, I was tired and weak, I sure didn't need this guy messing around the end of my bed. Why me? I thought.

Suddenly he started chanting loudly and swaying as he shook the two gourds. I started with surprise and half sat up in bed. He paid no attention to me at all, just kept chanting. Now I was very concerned because I recalled reading about Shamans in a book at Headquarters while we were getting ready to come to Laos. It came back to me vividly. He was chanting to rid me and the hut of the evil spirits that were, he thought, certainly the cause of my illness.

I had read that there was no organized religion among the mountain tribes and most were animistic. Spirits were very much a part of their beliefs and, while trying to treat the sick, Shamans would ward off spirits when possible. When their efforts did not seem to be working, however, they had been known to leap upon the sick (in this case me) and stab them repeatedly to make holes for the evil spirits to get out of their bodies. Can this be happening? I thought. What can I do? Where the hell is Prasert?

I don't know how long this went on – me, weak and tired, but watching him carefully, and him just chanting and waving his gourds. Would he actually try to stab me? I wondered. I'd certainly fight him. My Carbine was on the wall. I couldn't shoot him. I may have been delirious by that time and I think I passed out several times. Each time I was conscious, I focused on him. He was still chanting. The medic came in to give me some aspirin and I told him to send in Prasert. 'How long must this go on?' I asked. Prasert told me that it was evening now and that he thought the Shaman would be leaving soon. Obviously I had been in and out of consciousness all day.

'Don't leave me until he is gone,' I instructed Prasert.

'OK, sir, I'll stay,' he replied.

Soon thereafter was the grand finale. The Shaman became very excited and chanted faster and louder. And instead of just swaying, he moved around the bed, which scared me at first. Then he abruptly stopped chanting, half bowed in my direction, and left. I was greatly relieved. If nothing else, he had certainly taken my mind off the fever, which was, however, still there. Prasert insisted that I eat some soup and boiled rice.

I woke the next morning to discover that the fever had broken. I felt weak and even hungry. I dressed and went outside. Some villagers were passing and saw that I was up. I'm sure the Shaman took full credit for my recovery.

I wrote a message to Pat to allay concerns in Vientiane about how I was doing. I was not feeling great and spent the day resting. The Nai Ban stopped by in the afternoon to check on me. He didn't say anything, but I imagine he was thinking how clever he had been to send the Shaman. It had been three days now since I got sick. The weather broke that night and early the next morning we heard the sound of an approaching helio. Although I was starting to feel better, having had a good night's sleep, it was a welcome sound and I looked forward to seeing an American doctor later that day.

After a few days in Vientiane, I felt like new and was anxious to get back up to my region. The doctor said it was probably a type of dengue fever that I had picked up. God knows where. I flew back upcountry and found that things were busy in Phou Song. We had training under way and several patrols scouting the area to our east. Sometimes we would air drop the patrols the supplies that they needed. Dropping supplies by parachute requires a lot of co-ordination to be sure you are dropping to the right guys and to leave avenues for the patrol to get to safe areas again after the drop has pinpointed their position to possible enemy positions or patrols. The PARU were doing their usual good work and I just dug in to help.

Shortly after I got back to Phou Song, I scheduled a plane to take me to three villages in our region. At one of the villages, I noticed a plane already on the ground. That wasn't all that unusual as we sometimes overlapped with neighbouring regions and simply co-ordinated our efforts. When we landed, I realized that Vint Lawrence was standing by his helio waiting for me. It was always good to see a colleague upcountry. Vint was working closely with the Hmong leader, Vang Pao, and was very well-informed about what was going on since he co-ordinated all efforts under Vang Pao's command – in effect, the whole Hmong programme. And he was doing a great job. As I walked towards him, I noticed a look of concern on Vint's face.

'Hey, Vint, how are things?'

'Not good, we've got a problem,' he replied.

'What's up? Can I help?'

'There's a helio down. Pilot may be hurt. I think it's Tom Dieffenbach, a good guy. He was alone in the plane and we don't have much to go on. A Hmong patrol thinks they saw where he hit the side of the mountain.'

'You got a message to Pat yet?'

'Tried but he wasn't in his office. Don't know when we'll hear from Vientiane.'

This was a serious situation. Even as the new kid, I knew the unwritten but strong code we all followed. It didn't take long to figure it out. If a plane or chopper went down for whatever reason, every possible effort would immediately be made to rescue those aboard. We all knew that if something happened, our colleagues would come after us. It was the same for everybody – Agency officers, Air America pilots, anybody. It became the highest priority and other activities would stop if necessary to free up men or aircraft to carry out rescue missions.

'Can't we do something?' I said.

'I was standing here trying to decide what to do when I heard you coming,' Vint answered. 'I was thinking that I could take a patrol and get up there.'

'No question. He may be hurt. I'll come along and I say we take off right now,' I blurted – not having assessed the possible downsides. 'We can send Pat a message and tell him what we're doing.'

'He won't be happy,' Vint answered. 'We're supposed to stay out of sticky spots.'

'But this is an emergency.' I could tell that Vint wanted to go. He was just talking himself into it. I was prepared to defer to

Vint because he had been there first and knew more than I did. Plainly though, I thought we should try even though, as it turned out, discretion at that point might have been the better part of valour.

'You're right,' Vint said. 'Pat will understand.' He took out a pad and scratched out a quick message to Pat. 'We, Dick and I, are with a patrol and hope to rescue the pilot,' he wrote. 'Will explain later.' Vint's plane was headed back to Vientiane and we gave the message to the pilot.

It was late morning when we headed out. Vint and I had only our web belts and weapons. Neither of us, of course, had anticipated what we were undertaking. I was wearing fatigues, jungle boots and a wide-brimmed Australian bush hat that proved valuable as we walked. Vint, taller and heavier, also had on jungle boots but was hatless and was wearing a short-sleeved shirt. We had no food and no extra clothing. I had matches in a pouch on my web belt and my jack knife. Focused on rescuing the pilot, we hadn't taken the time to consider what we should be taking with us. It would be a quick in-and-out effort, I thought.

There were eight Hmong with us, all wearing fatigues they had acquired after their initial training. I had no idea how good they were or what kind of experience they might have had. They seemed confident and they did know where they were going. Each carried a small pack and had a length of bamboo hanging next to it. In the bamboo, I knew, was boiled sticky rice. As needed, lengths of the bamboo were cut off and split to provide part of a meal. It was a very efficient way to carry ready-to-eat rice. I also knew that they would share with us, which was comforting.

There was a sense of urgency, as we all knew that the pilot might be in dire need of help. We maintained a fast pace and took few rests. The first couple of hours were downhill as we headed for the valley below us. The Hmong thought the plane was down on the far side of the mountain in front of us. There were PL positions on the other side of the valley, we were also told, so a chopper rescue wouldn't be feasible. In between was no man's land. Vint and I were silent. We continued downhill to the valley floor. I sensed right away that this was a lower altitude than any place I'd yet been in Hmong country. The jungle was thick. There was a trail of sorts, but little used and the undergrowth had almost closed it in. We had to cross the valley and head up the mountain in front of us before we could get to the downed plane. A Hmong with a machete took the lead and we all followed close behind.

I had read about leeches in the Laotian jungle, but had never seen one. Vint had, and he carefully briefed me on the procedure to be followed. Watch for leeches, he told me. Each man watches his own front and the back of the man just ahead of him. The last two men rotate positions often. This was simple enough, but important because leeches can become a problem if an infection starts. And that wouldn't take much in the humid, steamy conditions we were now experiencing.

The trail was better than it at first seemed to be, but still there were vines and branches to be dodged and that meant lots of turns and bends for all of us. Many of the branches and vines brushed against us as we passed. Strangely, I felt more vulnerable down here than I had ever felt higher up where the Hmong lived – and ruled. We were all tense as we pushed forwards. There was no talking. The heat was oppressive and I could feel the sweat running down my back and stomach. Because of the denseness of the jungle, it was hard to tell how far we had come towards the mountain we would climb. We came to a stream and all took long drinks of the cool, clear water. I didn't have a canteen with me and Vint didn't either so we were dependent upon what little water the Hmong were carrying or water from the streams we passed. Fortunately, water from virtually any stream in the mountains was clean and drinkable. We had few concerns about disease.

We waded across the stream and, once again, I was happy to have the jungle boots. Whoever designed the small holes in the instep and the padded insole that caused air to circulate, or in this case water to be pumped out, ought to get a medal, I thought, as we followed the trail. Soon the ground started to slope upwards and I knew that our climb had begun.

By now it was mid-afternoon. As we climbed, the jungle fell away from the trail and the machete found its sheath. The air became less heavy and less humid. I was less tense as well, but the sense of urgency was still there. We stopped for ten minutes to rest, having covered a lot of ground since late morning. Both Vint and I were in good shape and having no trouble keeping up with the Hmong. We hoped to find the plane, and the pilot, before nightfall but could not be certain. Distances are difficult to estimate in such a situation, plus the exact location of the crash was unknown.

We ended the rest and started up the mountain. One doesn't hurry up a mountain. But you can keep the pace steady and we did. With few respites, we climbed for about three hours until almost nightfall. It became clear that we weren't going to find the pilot that day and we looked for a place to spend the night. We were high above the valley by now and as the sun went down it was much cooler, especially wearing sweat-soaked clothing. We came to a clearing and at the far end saw a hut, where we decided to stay for the night. Four Hmong went ahead, cautiously, to see if there were any people around. There were none. The hut was not in good shape, which was not surprising since it had probably been abandoned long ago, but it had a roof and walls, which looked good to us at that point. It was, apparently, all that remained of a small Hmong village.

It was a pretty site looking out over the valley and it had probably been a pleasant place to live. We entered the hut, but no one sat down. Our first priority was to check carefully for leeches.

I stripped, systematically checking each piece of clothing and then hanging it on an old rack. I pulled off my T-shirt and checked my torso. Clear. I raised my arm to look under my right armpit and was shocked and disgusted to see a leech fastened to my skin under my arm. I had felt nothing and still didn't.

A leech fastens two fang-like teeth under the skin and starts to extract blood. Something on the leech's teeth deadens the sensitivity making it all but impossible to feel. This ugly bloodsucker had evidently fallen on my shoulder or neck escaping detection by the Hmong behind me and made its way to my armpit. I remembered now having pushed off my hat in the jungle so that it hung behind me. In Laos there was an accepted way to rid oneself of a leech. You apply heat – either a match or a hot coal from a fire. The leech, feeling the heat – literally – then rolls up into a ball, extracting the fang-like teeth in the process, and falls off. Using that technique precludes the possibility of breaking off the fangs in the skin thereby increasing the risk of infection. Thus you should not just grab the ugly thing and rip it off your body. All of that, of course, makes good sense.

But mine was a reflex action. I didn't think at all. And it happened in an instant. The moment I saw that leech under my arm, I just grabbed it, ripped it out and threw it on the dirt floor. Then I stomped on it. Filled with blood, my blood, it squished and became a small, red puddle. Well, that was dumb, I thought and glanced at Vint.

'Aw, you probably won't get infected,' he said. 'Let me look at it.'

'Ugly goddamn thing. I didn't even think,' I said.

Vint looked under my arm and said, 'Looks like you might have got the fangs out. Still, it wouldn't be a bad idea to take a couple of tetracycline when we get back to Vientiane.' (Tetracycline was the antibiotic of choice for all of us in Laos at that time. The doctors prescribed it for almost anything.)

'Did you find any?' I asked Vint.

'Nope, I was clean,' he responded. It turned out that I was the only one to find a leech. As a result, the young Hmong who had been behind me took some good-natured ribbing for having missed it.

'Too bad we didn't make it to the crash site,' I said to Vint, changing the subject. We were standing apart from the others as we put our clothes and boots back on.

'Yeah, I'm sorry too. But we'll probably find him first thing tomorrow morning,' Vint replied. 'Meantime, this is home for tonight. Got anything to eat?'

'Not a thing,' I told him. 'Maybe the Hmong will take pity on us.' But, as we had departed with such short notice, the Hmong didn't have much either.

'We'll get something, I'm sure,' Vint said. And in fact we did. The Hmong patrol leader gave us each a lump of sticky rice. That was all they had and we were thankful to have something at least. There was nothing to drink and I thought about retracing our steps to the last stream we had passed. It was night by then, however, and that would have been folly. Then a Hmong came in and handed us each a cucumber. He had found them, growing wild, in a patch maybe cultivated by the villagers that had lived here. I had never liked cucumbers, but that one was delicious and full of moisture and I've liked them ever since.

The hut was stuffy so we decided to sleep outside. From where we lay down, you could look out over the valley. It was a clear night and there were stars. I could make out nearby mountains. Despite the fact that the tension and the walk had left me bone tired, I didn't fall asleep right away.

As I lay there looking at nothing in particular, I thought about where I was and what I was doing. The answers didn't bother me at all. I was in Laos, more isolated and vulnerable than I had ever been, and I was doing what I definitely thought was right. I had no regrets about the decisions I had made and I felt lucky to have the chance that only a few ever have of actually making a difference. I was confident, perhaps without good reason, that I could handle whatever might come up and felt sure that the patrol would succeed. Ten young men were going to find and save the eleventh man, the pilot. Of that I was sure. We had to. I tried not to think about or assess what the enemy might be doing. Maybe it was simple over-confidence. I did, though, wonder what the next day might bring. Then I slept, soundly, on the ground, next to a hut on a mountain in North Laos.

I was awake early, the sun just rising. The Hmong were moving around. I nudged Vint, who was next to me, and we both got up. All things considered, I felt pretty good, but I was thirsty and hungry. Ever resourceful and ever considerate, the Hmong had made some early efforts regarding both of these problems. There had been no fire last night, but in the daylight they felt secure enough to start a small one behind the hut. Someone had discovered a small stream above the abandoned village, and returned with water, which was being heated in an old crock found in the hut. One of the Hmong produced some tealeaves from his pack and we had hot tea. I had never been a tea lover either, but that tea tasted great. And we got another wad of sticky rice – someone's load today would be lighter.

We started climbing again. Now the slope seemed less steep as we seemed to be going around the mountain as much as we were going up, as if along a ridgeline. And the walking was easier. We were only eight now because two Hmong had left at daybreak to carry out a reconnaissance above us. As we pushed ahead, I was struck by how dependent Vint and I were on the Hmong. We had no idea where the plane might be and no landmarks to use to get there – or back. They knew it, but they also counted on us for the support we could call in. There was great mutual trust and respect. Both sides needed to do their jobs. I knew the Hmong would do theirs and I was damned sure that Vint and I would do ours.

An hour or so after we started, the two other members of our patrol appeared. I could tell by their faces that the news was bad. They talked excitedly with the patrol leader and then he gave it to us in French. The pilot was dead, he said. He had probably died on impact as the front of the plane was smashed in. There had been no fire. The eleventh man wouldn't make it after all.

There was more bad news. They had seen activity far below them that caused them to think a PL unit might be moving up the mountain from the opposite direction to check out the crash site. We had no idea how many PL might be coming, but with the pilot dead (our two Hmong had hidden the body away from the crash site and could return for it later) prudence seemed to dictate that we retreat. We could always return with more force and more knowledge of what the enemy was really doing. The Hmong were going to defer to us. Vint and I talked it over.

'Rotten news,' said Vint, 'all of it. There isn't much we can do up there now except maybe get in trouble.'

'I agree,' I said. 'Be hell to pay if we get ourselves into a fire-fight. We can't help the pilot. Probably better to come back with more strength.'

'We don't really know that the PL are moving in,' Vint said. 'Don't know that they are not either and we don't know how many there might be.'

'True,' I replied, 'but with our guy already dead, is it worth the risk to find out?'

'No, it's not,' Vint concluded, 'so we might as well haul ass.'

'Makes sense to me,' I said. 'Back the same way we came?'

'Yep, at least we know the route,' Vint said. 'We should be back there by mid-afternoon.'

We explained to the Hmong patrol leader, who seemed relieved. We started back and the walking was easy since we were headed down and around the mountain at the same time. We passed the clearing with the hut in it where we had spent the night and continued down. Then we heard a helio, a welcome sound indeed. Vint pulled out his emergency radio and tried to make contact. The radios were line of sight, which means that there can be no obstacles to the signal you are sending – or receiving. The helio seemed to be just around the corner of the mountain. Suddenly it was in sight and the pilot must have had his mike open because he picked up Vint right away. Whoever was in the plane with the pilot, probably one of our colleagues, sounded very relieved to have made contact with us. Then there came another dose of unwelcome news.

Intelligence reporting that had not been available to us, but was available in Vientiane, indicated that PL units had moved into the valley we had come through and were now heading for. It was possible therefore that we were cut off and were no longer in no man's land. Nobody knew for sure yet, but Vientiane was taking no chances. Pat meant to get us out – the sooner the better, we were told. A chopper was now positioned at a nearby landing strip, in the air at first light this morning. It was still early.

'Same reporting says the PL has heavy weapons on the mountain opposite the crash site so we can't fly through the valley,' our helio link concluded. 'That's why we've been hanging around where we are.'

'So we need to get around to the other side to get picked up?' asked Vint.

'Not enough time. We don't want you down there that long.'

'Hang on,' Vint said. 'We've got to think.' To me he said, 'The clearing with the hut is right behind us. The chopper could certainly get in there. But would he come in with the possible PL guns over there?' he added, looking across the valley. We weren't far enough around the mountain for it to be safe for a chopper to land.

'Yeah, but look at the weather,' I said to Vint. It was what the weathermen call a partly cloudy day.

He looked out at the valley and across where the suspected PL gun emplacements would be located. The other side of the valley was just coming into view again after a large cloud had passed by. We were standing at between 4,000 and 5,000 feet and each time a cloud rolled by it obscured vision across the valley. It happened all the time in the mountains during the rainy season.

'Yeah,' Vint said slowly, mulling over the same thought that had occurred to me. 'And if we can't see over there, then they can't see over here.'

'Right,' I said with obvious pleasure. 'If the chopper came in while a cloud was out in the valley, the bloody PL wouldn't see a damn thing. They would hear it, but have no idea where it was.'

'Great,' Vint said, snapping on his radio again. Quickly and succinctly, he outlined our plan for a pickup. We would retrace our steps to the clearing above us and we would put out a marker. (The patrol leader had one in his pack that he used when taking parachute drops. Pilots making any kind of airdrop would do so only if the prearranged drop signal was spread out on the drop zone.) We would be in touch with the chopper pilot by radio, talk him in, and give the signal when a cloud had cut off PL vision to this side of the valley. Those in the helio understood and bought our plan. Risk would certainly be minimal and they were anxious to get us off that mountain.

'Sounds good. You get back up to the clearing you're talking about and we'll get in touch with the chopper and get them over here right away. With any luck he'll be in the air behind the mountain in fifteen or twenty minutes.'

'We're on our way,' Vint said. He turned off his radio. We briefed the patrol leader who passed word on to the others and we started back up the mountain. There was a sense of urgency again. We knew that this wasn't going to be all that difficult, but the uncertainties about where the PL units might or might not be was troubling. For all we knew, the patrol our two Hmong thought they saw could be coming down the trail we were now going up.

It took us only ten minutes to reach the clearing. We looked around first, then entered the clearing and put our marker in the middle. One of the Hmong was posted on the trail just above the clearing with instructions to come running when he saw the chopper coming in. None of us wanted the chopper on the ground for more than a couple of minutes. We called the helio and they told us that the chopper pilot was on board with the plan and was en route. He'd be in position in five or ten minutes. We waited – not without some anxiety.

'This got pretty complicated,' Vint said. 'I wonder if Pat and Bill are pissed.'

'Just a guess,' I said, smiling at Vint, 'but I don't suppose they are happy to be having to drag us out of here by chopper. Too bad we didn't have that intelligence reporting before we took off.'

'We had to make a call and we did,' Vint concluded. 'I'd do it again.'

'Me too,' I responded. We got a call from the helio that the chopper was in position.

'Hold on', Vint told them, 'till the gods smile on us and send a big cloud through the valley.'

The helio, at a high altitude and out of range of any PL attack, had already spotted the clearing and seen our marker. From their vantage point above both, they could see the clearing and the chopper. A few minutes later, after a large cloud had filled the valley and obscured vision, Vint told the helio to send in the chopper. They passed the message to the chopper, which was still out of our line of sight. It worked like a charm.

I had never liked choppers either. (I still don't but I readily concede that they are, in certain circumstances, uniquely able to perform important services.) The noise and the rushing air from the rotating blades always adds stress and tension for those not used to choppers – none of us were. People get confused. They can't hear. They do stupid things. With those things in mind, we had carefully briefed the patrol leader and insisted that he make our instructions clear to the other Hmong. In this instance, we were better versed and we were in charge. We were formed in a single file in the trees at the edge of the clearing, Vint first and me last. We were on the side closest to the direction our lookout would come from. We would board the chopper in order – one after another – clear to the rear, away from the door.

We heard it before we saw it. The pilot hugged the side of the mountain and swung around and touched down right in the middle of the clearing; he even had the door facing us. The Air America pilots were truly outstanding. They had plenty of skills and plenty of guts. This was not your run-of-the-mill type of flight and he knew it. He could have refused – but he didn't. They rarely did. Yes, they made a lot of money, but there was more to it than that. They knew what we were doing and they were fully supportive. When we needed them, we could count on them. They didn't let us down. I had then and still have great respect and admiration for the pilots I knew in Laos. I would fly with them anywhere and anytime.

Vint was sprinting towards the chopper as the wheels touched down. One by one, the Hmong followed. Our lookout had reappeared – he wasn't about to get left behind. I pushed him just ahead of me and held his arm until it was his turn. He took off for the chopper as I released his arm and I followed not far behind. He clambered aboard and Vint lent a hand as I climbed on. The pilot was lifting off as I got in – the rotors had never stopped. There was lots of noise as predicted, but everything went just as planned. In just a couple of minutes, we were all aboard and the pilot swung back around the mountain and headed for Vientiane. There were ten of us. The eleventh man was left behind. There hadn't been a sound from across the valley.

Pat and Bill were waiting on the tarmac as we arrived back in Vientiane. We weren't sure what to expect. Although it had made perfect sense at the time, the fact was we had taken off on what turned out to be a risky and dangerous mission without approval from our superiors. We had plain guidelines that we were not to place ourselves in combat or other dangerous situations. If an Agency officer fell into enemy hands, there would, we all knew, be hell to pay in Washington. The political repercussions would be widespread and in our ranks there would be ample grief. We didn't know it, of course, but as it became known the night before that we were out looking for the pilot, there had been lots of nervous people and concern for our safety.

We got off the chopper and headed over to Pat and Bill. As we approached, I could see that we were not in serious trouble. Both looked relieved and happy to see us.

'It was worth a try,' Pat growled. 'Never mind all the shit I would have had to deal with if something had gone wrong.'

'Thanks, Pat. That's what we thought,' Vint told him.

'Sorry to worry everyone,' I added. 'We didn't think we had time to wait for a message.'

Bill Lair hadn't spoken. 'Next time it wouldn't be a bad idea to wait,' he said.

Bill's typically low-key comment belied the concern and the responsibility he very strongly felt. Vint and I were two of eight young American officers for whom he was accountable. There were, at the time, an equal number of other Agency officers involved in running the upcountry aspects of the Agency's 'covert' paramilitary programmes in Laos. And Bill, with Pat's able assistance, ran the whole show. It was an awesome responsibility. It was also an awesome accomplishment. With fewer than a couple of dozen men, they were putting together an effective resistance force. We were spread thinly and we worked hard – but we wouldn't have had it any other way. We took our losses even in those early days – both Agency officers and the pilots who were supporting us – but we got the job done.

Friends, who worked directly with Pat in the office, later told me that Pat had been genuinely concerned and really torn as the situation developed. On the one hand he was frustrated and irritated that we took the decision on our own and left with the patrol. He knew that it would be dangerous. On the other hand, he was proud of us. That we didn't hesitate to go after a pilot in need pleased him. In the end, he was so relieved that we were back safely that he didn't yell at us. I don't know if a cable on the episode was ever sent to Headquarters. Tom Dieffenbach's body was recovered.

I spent a couple of days in Vientiane reading at our compound. The programme was expanding and we needed more emphasis on intelligence reporting to go along with the harassment operations that were increasing. One needed to complement the other. It was useful for me as I had a better picture of what I wanted from the teams we were sending out of Phou Song. I got to meet several of the officers who were working at the compound with Pat and Bill. I liked them all and gained respect for what they were doing to support those of us who were working upcountry.

Managing the daily flow of message traffic from upcountry was no mean feat and we all knew that the flow was going to get heavier as the programme continued to expand. They had to keep Washington up to date with activities and maintained an impressive map room that gave a constantly updated assessment of where friendly and enemy units were located. I also met the air operations officer, who provided the liaison between our office at the compound and Air America, and other offices at the Embassy.

Support and logistics also operated out of the compound offices as did finance. In total, a very complex and comprehensive operation was functioning very efficiently – a tribute to the organizational and managerial skills of Pat and Bill. I have to say that I never thought of either of them as a manager, but the proof was in the pudding. They had put together a small but strong team and been able to absorb a variety of additional officers, including the JOTs, and still be able to make the operation hum. Despite the major changes that were to come as a result of the Geneva Accords, the programme was strong and getting stronger.

One of the young officers working at the compound, who was not an operations officer but definitely wanted to be one, spent a lot of time with upcountry officers whenever we were in Vientiane. We had dinner one night and he related the following story about an experience he had, allegedly, had on a short visit upcountry to replace someone temporarily. I wasn't there and can't vouch for all the details, but it makes a good story.

While walking back towards the village from the latrine he had just visited (so far so good, as the latrines were always away from the villages), he spotted a long snake on the trail in front of him (also believable, as there were certainly plenty of big snakes in Laos). The snake seemed to be moving towards the village. He knew there were children and others in the village. He had an M-1 with him (being a former Marine, he preferred this gun). We often carried our weapons outside the village. He fired a round at the snake hoping either to kill it or scare it off. The snake, possibly as a result of the shot, started into a hole just off the trail. He ran towards the snake, why I wouldn't know, and arrived to find about two feet of the snake still protruding from the hole.

He couldn't then explain why he did what he did next. He stepped on the end of the snake and grabbed it with one hand to stop it from disappearing into the hole. And he yelled so that someone from the village would come to help. Help do what? So there he was, standing on the end of a large snake and holding it so that it couldn't get into the hole. It all happened quickly, he went on, and he didn't think.

Then he heard a hissing noise to his right rear. He turned to see the 'bad' end of the snake, a cobra he now realized because of the tell-tale hood, striking at his leg and missing because it couldn't move forwards – because he was standing on the tail end of the same snake. It was rotten luck that the hole had another opening so close. This was obviously a serious situation. The snake was very clearly angry. He was almost petrified with fear. What to do? Drop the snake and run? Could he even make his legs move? Kill the damn thing! He pointed the M-1, holding it with his free hand, at the snake. The snake was thrashing around wildly in its anger. He couldn't really aim. Suddenly the snake struck at the end of the rifle. He shoved the M-1 directly at the snake and it struck again. He then pulled the trigger and blew off the snake's head. He was standing there shaking as a couple of villagers ran up to him. They saw the dead cobra. He was a hero. He didn't feel like a hero. They pulled a 14-foot dead king cobra out of the hole, with much rejoicing, and carried it into the village for dinner.

On my way back to Phou Song, Pat asked me to stop at Sam Thong for a ceremony in a nearby village. The ceremony, a traditional one to welcome friends, was called a *bossi*. The village, Long Tieng, was an easy walk from Sam Thong and it was going to join the programme. Vang Pao would be at the ceremony and we needed to have a couple of Agency officers in attendance.

Mike Nolan, an older, experienced paramilitary officer assigned routinely to north-west Laos, and I arrived at Sam Thong early and were met by a couple of young Hmong who were to walk with us to Long Tieng.

I was impressed, as we crested the ridgeline between Sam Thong and Long Tieng, by the natural beauty of the valley. It was long with steep, *karst* sides. I could see a small stream running through the valley and cultivated patches dotting the floor of the valley. Long Tieng was a small village, but it looked more permanent than other Hmong villages I had seen. I could see why. Who would want to leave this pretty valley for a place perched on the side of a mountain?

We did not understand the Hmong politics of the situation, but certainly some were at play. Vang Pao was moving in and, as an emerging leader of the Hmong tribe, he must be welcomed in the traditional way. And for his part, he must demonstrate his power and influence. Beyond words, he would produce representatives of the American government that was helping the Hmong people. That was us, I saw right away. It started with an unusual dinner in that it was of a quality and quantity I had not seen before. A large, earthen urn was filled with locally made rice wine and guests were provided with long straws. It wasn't bad, but it certainly was not good either – until you'd had enough. We drank a lot with and after dinner when some Hmong girls did some traditional dances. Then the ceremony started: toasts and then the *bossi* itself.

After a chant intended to persuade good spirits to protect our souls and give us good fortune, the local Shaman (himself honoured on this occasion by our presence and that of Vang Pao) tied strands of white cotton yarn around the wrist of those being honoured. Each piece of yarn had a specific meaning and collectively they assured the wearer of good luck. The yarn ties in the soul and good fortune and one must never cut off the strings because that will bring bad luck. Rather, you leave the strings on your wrist until they come off naturally. I was so honoured three or four times while I was in Laos and each time I had the strings on my wrist for a couple of weeks before they fell off. Everyone knows what they are and wearers gain prestige and are looked upon with favour. We slept well that night and awoke to a beautiful day, considering the season: clear blue sky and crisp fresh air. A chopper was due to pick us up, but we had time for a walk around the valley. My favourable impressions of the previous day were confirmed. However, Long Tieng's location south and west of the Plaine des Jarres, and various geographical features (like the long flat area that would soon become an airstrip capable of landing cargo planes and even T-28 fighters to support Hmong operations against the VC and PL), also made it an ideal military location. It was destined to become the Hmong stronghold.

This valley and the Hmong living in it would witness dramatic change over the next decade. That change would include warehouses for vast supplies of food, clothing, ammunition and medicine, frame houses for senior officers and our advisors, and housing as well for the Hmong families dislocated by the heavy fighting to come. In addition, there would be a near constant stream of air traffic into the large airstrip that would be constructed. All of the effort required would change this valley and the village of Long Tieng for ever. And a terrible price would be paid after the fall of Saigon in April 1975, when the United States pulled out and cast the Hmong adrift. But none of this was foreseen by any of us on that pretty day in 1962.

I spent a few additional weeks in Phou Song working to expand our programme further, but time ran out on us. Political decisions were taken in Washington as a result of the Geneva Accords, and word came that military 'advisors' and Agency officers would be withdrawn from Laos. This was a bitter pill to swallow. All of our reporting and observations indicated that the VC had no intention of pulling any of their units out of Laos. On the contrary, their activities in eastern Laos, especially in the Panhandle area, were increasing. If they weren't leaving, why should we? There had been exchanges with Headquarters, of course, but to no avail. The State Department ruled the day and they were determined to live by the agreements of the Accords that Ambassador Harriman had signed. Despite the evidence we had supplied, they could not be swayed. There was no choice but to pull out.

I was most unhappy with this turn of events, as were my fellow Agency officers. We did successfully argue that it would be wrong to leave the Hmong high and dry. It was agreed that two advisors could discreetly remain at Long Tieng, Vang Pao's headquarters, to monitor the ongoing situation. Vint, because of his French-language capability and the relationship he had developed with Vang Pao, and Tony Poe because of his paramilitary experience, were selected to stay behind when we left. Theirs would be a tough assignment.

Initially, Bill and Pat moved their programme headquarters from the house near Vientiane's airport to Nong Khai, just across the Mekong from Vientiane but in Thailand. The move, bringing with it a gaggle of *farangs*, was a jolt to what had been a quiet and sleepy little Mekong town. The local population, however, adjusted quickly and welcomed the boost it gave to their economy. Sales figures for, among other things, the Thai Singha beer jumped noticeably.

At Udorn, a much larger town about 50 kilometres south, there was a large airport with a (US built) concrete runway. Udorn was destined to become a major US airbase and staging area for combat and supply flights into Laos in support of US efforts to aid the

Laotian government. A large US compound was constructed (including numerous permanent buildings), and Pat and Bill would eventually move their headquarters to Udorn. First dozens and later hundreds of Americans moved there with predictable results on the town. The sudden influx of money caused, as had been the case in Vientiane, vices of all sorts to flourish and prosper.

The last weeks at Phou Song had been a blur. While we had attempted to further our expansion plan, to all intents and purposes, regions started shifting into a gear much closer to neutral. As the 7 October date imposed by the Geneva Accords approached, fewer actions were initiated and we took a watch-and-wait stance. We all made quick trips aimed at making the preparations necessary to leave the programme essentially at status quo while developments were monitored.

The Hmong were none too happy either, but there was nothing any of us could do. I can't even remember where I went on my last trip upcountry, but I remember looking down at the Plaine des Jarres and speculating if the Hmong would ever retake it.

We all wondered, of course, what was to become of us. I was only three months into a six-month assignment and wanted very much to stay. Violations by the VC were already being documented and I felt sure we would be going back up to help the Hmong sometime soon. In late September, we all found out where we would be headed after we left Laos. While I was on a quick visit to Vientiane, Pat called me into his office.

'Lots of changes, kid, and you will be moving,' he said. 'We want you to take over the project in the Panhandle,' he went on. 'It's in its early stages, like the Hmong effort, and they will be moving from Thakhek, a small town right on the Mekong, to Nakorn Phanom, which is right across the river in Thailand.'

I was surprised. I hadn't expected to get a whole project to handle on my own and I would be working with ethnic Lao, not Hmong. I wasn't at all sure what the project was doing, but was confident I could manage it. And running the show was certainly an appealing aspect.

'I think I should say thanks, Pat, but I don't know enough about it to say anything. Mind telling me what they are doing and why you selected me?'

'They're just getting going. Tom Ahern [my predecessor] has got the teams started and now we need to start getting some intelligence about what the VC are doing. His tour is up and he's going to Saigon. I need a replacement and I think you can handle it. Got it?' As usual, Pat was not one to waste words. 'Ahern leaves next week, so you might as well get the hell over there. Bring in all your gear and luggage in the morning and I'll have a plane for you later in the day. They know you're coming. You should probably read a bit before you go. You can start that right now.'

I had dinner that night with Mike Deuel, who had found out that he would be moving to Nong Khai along with Andre and Ralph to work at the programme headquarters. He wouldn't be spending that much time in the field, and he wasn't all that thrilled, but at least he would still be working with the Hmong, for whom we all had great respect as fighters and as individuals.

EIGHT

OPERATION HARDNOSE

1962–63

'South Laos, if saved, can be the keystone connecting the pillars of Thailand and South Vietnam, and sealing off Cambodia from further infiltration. South Laos is the key to preventing Southeast Asia from being cut in two.'
Special Report by Task Force on Vietnam
19 June 1961

As we circled Nakorn Phanom before landing, the pilot 'buzzed' (took a low pass over) the Agency house to alert Tom that we had arrived. The pass took us out over the Mekong, wide and muddy at that time of year.

Nakorn Phanom was a quiet, pretty little town of several thousand inhabitants. It was clean, I noted, cleaner than Udorn or, certainly, Vientiane. Several streets were paved and there seemed to be a town square. With very few exceptions – Tom's house was one of them – the houses were of typical Thai style: tin roof and wooden structures about 4 to 6 feet above ground. They looked Spartan but sturdy.

Tom was a tall and slender man a few years older than I. 'Welcome to Nakorn Phanom,' he said. 'We've only been here a short time so I don't know many people, but the ones I know are all friendly and I'm sure you'll do fine.'

'Happy to be here, Tom,' I replied. 'How long do we have before you're out of here?'

'Four days and counting,' he said, 'and I need to bring you up to speed so we better get back to the house and get started.'

'Nice little town,' he continued as we drove, 'but quiet, so we tend to stand out. Everyone wonders what the *farang* is doing here. Many know that we moved here from Thakhek and that I have contacts across the river. They also know about the Geneva Accords. Word flows, even across rivers. If they don't already know, two and two will soon make four. Not much we can do about it. Nor does anyone ever ask.' That was the operative phrase. Nobody ever asked.

I was to spend almost twenty months operating out of Nakorn Phanom, and during that period no one ever queried what I was doing. Those who did know, knew enough not to ask questions, and those who didn't, didn't want to know. My cover was back-stopped only minimally, but no one seemed too worried – certainly not I. I had, without fanfare, moved from Laos to Thailand. The Agency took care of all the paperwork so I was not illegal, but the rationale was pretty thin. It simply was not an issue.

The VC violations of the Geneva Accords began to increase and were verified with photography and Sigint, or Signals Intelligence, which, at the time, was an all-encompassing term for intercepts of transmissions from target countries, installations, or units. Today the efforts are more sophisticated and there are many 'ints' from which to collect information. Even Ambassador Harriman finally conceded that they were not abiding by the rules set down. Accordingly, restrictions on us were less and less of a constraint. Early in my time at Nakorn Phanom, I had my team leaders come over to see me on the Thai side of the Mekong. Later, I began making trips into Laos at night. Finally, I crossed over into Laos regularly in broad daylight. I never carried identification or my passport. No one, least of all the border officials, either Thai or Lao, ever questioned me about what I was doing.

At the house, Tom introduced me to the PARU team and to the two assistants who worked with him. The latter two, Jimmie and Mr Ambrose (neither used their Thai names), had ties to the Thai Ministry of Defence, but those ties were never very clear. Both were very good in their work. Thais, from the government to the military, the police and the vast majority of the people, were afraid of the communist threat. They didn't really understand it, but feared it nonetheless. They welcomed the support and resources we were giving and they were more than eager to help in any way they could. Thus the PARU and others, all of whom were well-paid I should add, were of great assistance to us.

The PARU team, six young men, looked just like the PARU I had worked with upcountry in Laos. There was also a locally hired house-boy named Whet, who was responsible for cooking, cleaning and laundry, as nobody thought it a good idea to have a young woman in the house with nine men. Whet did a great job and seemed literally to leap through the door to serve or respond every time I called his name. We spent the rest of that first day checking equipment, signing the required forms about gear, administration matters and finance and looking around Nakorn Phanom. The latter didn't take up much time. We stopped by the officials' club, which had a membership of Thai government officials and selected private citizens of Nakorn Phanom. It featured one cinder-block building and three concrete tennis courts. In the building, there was a bar and a big room with a snooker table. Snooker, for reasons unknown to me, was very popular in the club and in Thailand generally.

We had dinner that night at Nakorn Phanom's only real restaurant, the Mekong River Garden. It was owned and managed by a Sino-Thai man who was also the cook. He was almost 6 feet, large by local standards. Bald with a protruding stomach, he always wore some kind of tank top. His restaurant, which was located right on the bank of the Mekong River, had a porch extending out towards the river that, at some times of the year, rushed by as you ate. Upon entering the restaurant, you passed by what served as the kitchen, where there were shelves, racks and a fire with a large wok on top. You would scan what was there (almost as if looking at a menu) and select what you wanted to eat that day. After chatting with the cook or the waitresses, you would ponder, point, then sit down on one of the little wooden stools that encircled each table.

Everything was fresh from around the town, even the fish. The waitresses, Lek and Deng, were both in their teens. They came to know us well and were always happy to see us. (We tipped.) Shamelessly overworked and underpaid, they were nonetheless cheerful and pleasant. I was to eat many meals in this restaurant and there was always a stock of very cold Singha beer on hand.

'Where should we start?' Tom asked the morning after my arrival as we got started with the operational aspects of his turnover to me.

'I've read the files,' I said, 'but more detail would help. Let's start with the current location of each team and your thoughts about the team leader. Where do these guys come from?'

'It's a mixed bag,' Tom said as he and Mr Ambrose started laying out some maps on a large desk. (There was also a big map board on the wall showing the whole of the Lao Panhandle, from just north of the Nape Pass through the Annamite mountain chain between Laos and Vietnam, to the Bolovens plateaux in the south. I became intimately familiar with the map co-ordinates of places in central Laos. Within months I could cite from memory the co-ordinates of specific towns or road junctions.) Mixed bag was an understatement.

From north to south, Tom briefed me on each team he had (more or less) organized and was now supporting. He had started from scratch and had been obliged to work closely with Lao military officers, who were also a mixed bag. All seemed to be corrupt (by our standards), but to varying degrees. Team leaders, often nominated by the military commander of a given area, were usually former military officers who had allegedly (we never really knew) retired. Some were refugees who had been Nai Khongs (or Nai Bans) from a key village in the area they were working. Makeup of the teams varied. All were local villagers. Some had been displaced by the communist takeover of the areas along the border with North Vietnam, while others were from areas along the Mekong. Some had been members of the FAR. The seven teams varied in size, from over one hundred to fifteen men. None, I noted, was located in a position that would enable them to make observations for intelligence purposes. Some intelligence was being provided, but it was irregular and of minimal use. It came primarily from sporadic patrols or villager debriefings.

The level of competence also varied widely from team to team. This, I would come to find out, was largely a function of the team leader. Each team had a radio and was in daily contact with us. Two of our PARU were radio operators and maintained the base station for our project. Each team member had at least rudimentary weapons training – all were armed and had uniforms and boots. We also supplied rice (drops scheduled by cable, first to us and then from us to Nong Khai and later Udorn) and medicines. And all were well-paid by Lao standards – more than Lao military personnel – according to rank or position. Payments were made in cash to the team leader, who then distributed (we always hoped) wages to each member of his team.

The team leaders each had strengths and weaknesses and Tom gave me a good brief on each one. (Mr Ambrose, who interpreted at each meeting with team leaders, also knew them well and would be a great help in months to come.) The briefing took the whole day.

The next day, unusually, a finance officer from Vientiane visited us. Tom's finances were out of balance. He knew the problem, but resolving it, to the satisfaction of our finance officers, was not an easy task. In the confusion that prevailed in the days when they were pulling out of Laos to move to Nakorn Phanom, payments had been made to some of the teams that couldn't be accounted for. No proper receipts of payment were obtained. Twice, team payrolls had been dropped to teams in isolated areas. No receipts were obtained here either. Papers had been misplaced. Amounts of payrolls hadn't been recorded.

They worked all day. Mr Ambrose, who knew the payments had been made, helped to clarify some of the outstanding problems. Most were cleared, but in the end, Tom was obliged to put some of his own money into the cash box to rectify the imbalance. I thought that was awful. But it was a clear lesson for me and I never forgot it during the rest of my career. This is not your money, I told myself repeatedly over the years, so take care of it. Even a scrap of paper or a note would have saved Tom his anguish, but none existed. The finance officer wanted to be helpful, but his hands were tied. There and then, I made it a rule never to open my cash box without making some record of what I had taken out.

Tom was preoccupied during the last two days with preparations to leave. We didn't talk much about his thoughts for the future of the project. He had been fully absorbed in getting things going. Similarly, Bill and Pat were seized with the Hmong programme and its future. I had received little or no guidance from them about where to take things. 'We need some intelligence,' was all Pat had said. So this was going to be whatever I could make of it. The project, still in its infant stage, had generated little attention at Headquarters and was not yet even known by some. It had no cryptonym. It was just there. Still, I was pleased to be in this position. There were challenges of course, but I could see room for both growth and increased reporting so I was eager to get started. But where to start? There were day-to-day activities required to keep things going, but what were the long-term goals going to be? Just how would we improve our reporting capability? And how much time would I have? My six-month tour was due to end in January. There was a lot on my mind as I said goodbye to Tom.

To develop a plan, I looked first at the problem. Geographically, I was looking at a specific area – the Panhandle of Laos. This area ranged from just north of Thakhek to midway between Savanakhet and Pakse to the south. It is bordered on the west by the Mekong River, also the border with Thailand. The Annamite mountain range, running from north to south, delineates the eastern limit and the border with North Vietnam. Coastal plains to the east of the Annamites are Vietnamese – in this instance North Vietnamese. Plains and the Nakay plateau, on the western side, up to the Mekong are Laotian. On the south-eastern edge of the Panhandle was the demarcation line between North and South Vietnam. This chunk of territory was of obvious, and strong, strategic interest to the North Vietnamese in their efforts to subvert the South Vietnamese government. We, the US government, were just beginning to understand the over-riding importance of dealing with the North Vietnamese use of this area.

Various ideas were considered, including one by the military to build a road straight across to the Mekong from the demarcation line. Then to fortify and defend that road to preclude any effort by North Vietnam to move men or supplies south through Laos on the increasingly well-known Ho Chi Minh Trail. The latter, so named in honour of the famous North Vietnamese communist leader on his birthday in 1959, was actually a network of dirt roads and trails running along the eastern side of the Panhandle from north to south. The military proposal was rejected.

The Ho Chi Minh Trail was my problem. In late 1962, I was not thinking of ways to cut the trail and stop the flow. I wanted simply to monitor the traffic to confirm that it was certainly the problem we all thought it was, and to see just how much was moving south towards South Vietnam. Later, my successors would deploy teams to harass and disrupt the traffic.

The road network in the Panhandle, carved out by the colonial French, was sparse. Two passes through the Annamites range provided access for roads. In the north of the Panhandle, Route 8 ran through the Nape Pass in a south-westerly direction to join Route 12 just east of Thakhek. Route 8 followed the western edge of the Nakay plateau. Route 12 passed through the Mu Gia Pass and headed along the bottom of the Nakay plateau west to Thakhek. Route 9 headed east out of Savannakhet across the Panhandle into South Vietnam at a point just south of the demarcation line. Route 13, the only north–south road in the Panhandle, ran on the Lao side of the Mekong all the way from Vientiane to Pakse. With a crushed laterite surface, these roads were all weather, but experienced flooding and other problems in the rainy season and were not reliable for travel.

Generally speaking, we believed that trucks were limited to these roads for transporting anything in the Panhandle. We would come to know better. Even as early as 1962, the North Vietnamese were building and improving road networks between Route 12 and Route 9 that would soon facilitate truck convoys. Off this limited network, jeeps and sometimes trucks could move into areas along the Mekong or between villages elsewhere, during the dry season. In the rainy season, movement off the all-weather roads was only accomplished on foot. Roughly, the western portion of the Panhandle was controlled by the FAR while the eastern portion was under PL and KL control. The VC had, and fully exploited, free access and movement in the eastern portion.

My goal was to position teams at key points to clandestinely watch all traffic along the roads and trails being used by the VC after they entered Laos via one of the two passes through the Annamites. To do that, I would have to train, motivate, and support the villager soldier members of my teams so that they would take the risks that were required to move into enemy-controlled areas and radio reports back to our base station.

Looking at my maps, it wasn't hard to select the points where I wanted to establish road-watch sites. The Nape and Mu Gia

Passes were obvious sites. More difficult, I knew, would be the task of getting teams onto those sites. It was going to take time and effort, of that I was sure, especially since I would be working from across the Mekong from the Panhandle. From a relatively passive, organizational stage, we would be moving into a much more active, and risky, effort.

During the first month in Nakorn Phanom, I met all but one of the team leaders. Each made the journey from wherever their team was currently located to Thakhek and then crossed over to Nakorn Phanom. Rarely did any of them miss the monthly contact. They were not so much in quest of the wisdom I imparted rather than the monthly payroll. But it did give me control and leverage, and gradually I was able to develop personal relationships with each one – some more so than others, of course.

At those first meetings, I spent a lot of time briefing each one on our collective mission. As expected, and as Tom had made clear, some reacted more favourably than others. Those who were hesitant were either comfortably near the Mekong and inside Lao-controlled areas, or fearful of moving clandestinely into enemy-controlled areas to the east. Much cajoling and motivating, or team leader changes, would be required to move those teams to selected areas. The others either didn't want to admit they were afraid or were actually ready to take the risks involved. It was about a fifty-fifty split. I knew that several would report promptly to their Lao military contacts, and I could expect questions. Why did I want to make waves? Because we all needed to know what the VC were doing.

Soon we made progress. A team in the northern sector was already located in a spot from which, with minimal effort and risk, they could send out small units to watch Route 8 – but only at a point inside Laos from the Nape Pass. This was good, but not good enough. Another team was able to move to the Nakay plateau and put watchers on the bluffs overlooking Route 12. Again though, it was too far west of the Mu Gia Pass. Traffic passing those two sites would only be carrying supplies for the KL and PL units in the area. It wasn't the Ho Chi Minh trail, but it was a start. Further south, along Route 9 and in the area between Routes 9 and 12, it was going to take more work.

In late 1962, Pat cabled that my six-month assignment had been extended by six additional months and did I have any problem with that? I had never been asked, but promptly responded that I was happy with the extension and would use those months to get things going. 'Get what things going?' he cabled back. By that time, Bill and Pat, with staff in tow, had moved to a building at the airport in Udorn.

I asked for a plane and flew over to Udorn to brief my plans in detail.

'Here's what I think we should do,' I said to Pat as I spread out my maps. 'If we're going to get some useful intelligence, we need teams a lot further east than we have them now. Risks yes, but they should be able to stay out of trouble, and they sure want to do that.' Pointing to the sites I had selected, I added, 'If we can put teams at these sites, with radios, we can get daily reports on what is moving into Laos via the Nape and Mu Gia Passes. We're not there yet but things are moving. It's going to take some time. These aren't the bravest guys in the world.'

Pat had been studying the map as I talked. I had piqued his interest. 'That's good, that's damn good,' he said. 'Think you can do it?'

'Yeah, I think so, and it's certainly worth a try,' I responded.

Pat, of course, read all the cable traffic from Headquarters and from Saigon station so he was much more aware of the growing interest in the VC use of eastern Laos than I was. He also knew that both Saigon station and the US military had proposed ways to start dealing with the problem of the Panhandle and the Ho Chi Minh Trail. Each had made tentative moves into the area without success. We could, he knew, make a major contribution if we could get regular reporting on the roads and trails that made up that network. Also he knew that it was, at this point, only a plan and that much work lay ahead. Still, if successful, it promised to pay off with solid intelligence reporting. Instinctively he knew that it would be well-received at Headquarters.

We spent a couple of hours going over specifics. I outlined what we had team by team, showing him the location of each. I was pleased that he was so interested and impressed with the depth of the questions he posed. Finally he said, 'OK, I want a cable for Headquarters outlining this whole thing.' (I had, until that time, authored almost nothing for transmission to Headquarters and I dreaded the prospect. Style and format were all but forgotten as I had written no cables since my training ended almost a year before.)

'Why don't you write it, Pat? You know the whole thing now,' I said. 'You'll write it so Headquarters will like it,' I added.

'They'll like it,' he responded, 'and you are going to write it. And as soon as you do, I want you to go up to Vientiane to brief Whitey [Charlie Whitehurst, the Chief in Laos] before we release the cable.'

Needless to say, I wrote the cable. I laboured for several hours and finally produced a draft that Pat liked. He did some editing, but the guts were all there and he was happy.

I stayed in Udorn that night and several of us went out for dinner and exchanged war stories. Collectively, our experiences were sometimes funny, sometimes harrowing, and always interesting.

Frequently, during these evenings, we played Liar's Dice. You rolled the dice, hid them from view, and passed them to the next player claiming (rightly or wrongly) a certain score. He believed you or called you a liar. Then he rolled. If you were caught lying, you were, of course, a loser. First loser paid the food bill and second loser paid the bill for drinks. It was better by far to pay the food bill if you lost. Drinks were as cheap as the food, for that matter, but the quantities consumed made the difference. After dinner and a couple more drinks we would visit one of several bars and nightclubs that flourished in Udorn. They were noisy, lively and overrun with young Thai girls practising the world's oldest profession.

Early the next morning, I flew up to Vientiane to see the Chief. Charles S. Whitehurst, or 'Whitey', as he was widely known, had arrived in the summer of 1962 to replace Bill Jorgensen. Whitey lived, with his wife Dottie and their two sons, next door to Souvana Phouma, a Lao prince of the royal family and the Geneva Accords-installed neutralist premier of the Lao Government. I had never met Whitey, but had heard the stories about him.

Despite his young age – he was about forty – he had quite a history. He was born in the south, Florida I think, and had been a semi-pro baseball player in his youth. Somehow, drafted into the military perhaps, he ended up in the OSS and parachuted into

North Vietnam with a team of commandos intending to blow up a key bridge between Vietnam and China just as the Second World War was ending. He later moved to Shanghai, met and married his wife, Dottie, and served there until the communist victory in China forced a move to Formosa (now Taiwan). He had been a Chief several times, most recently Singapore, before coming to Vientiane. Given his history and varied experience, we all expected him to be a good Chief. We were not disappointed. Pragmatic, smart and unpretentious, Whitey handled the varied programmes with aplomb.

I saw Whitey only briefly in his office. He was having a busy day as some crisis had erupted and invited me to his home for dinner that evening. I was surprised that he would invite such a junior officer, but accepted with pleasure. He and Dottie were gracious and welcoming hosts when I arrived that evening.

'Good to see you,' Whitey greeted me at the door. 'It'll be a lot easier to talk here. There will be no phones, no meetings and no flap to deal with. Come on in. How about a martini before we eat?'

'Sounds good to me,' I lied, as I couldn't remember ever having had a martini before in my life.

Sitting alone in the living room, as Dottie was supervising the preparation of dinner in the kitchen, Whitey and I talked in general terms first about my background, and then about the project in the Panhandle. I was impressed with the questions he asked, which showed that he already had a good idea of what the problems were and a feel for what it was like to deal with Laotians. Tall with thinning hair, Whitey showed the beginnings of what would become a larger than he wanted stomach to lug around. In time it would cause him back problems. He was affable and very easy, with an innate sense of what was important and what wasn't, and he made me feel comfortable right away. He focused on what should be emphasized in my cable to Headquarters, and told me that, with a couple of changes, he wanted it sent soonest. Not surprisingly, I was delighted.

Dinner over, Dottie excused herself to help their sons with homework problems and no doubt to give us time alone, and we retired to the living room again. Coffee and cognac in hand, we started getting into specifics about what I saw down the road and how much of the plan was I going to be able to accomplish. It was important, Whitey assured me, because the whole question of the Ho Chi Minh Trail and what to do about it was heating up considerably in Washington.

With maps in front of us, he again posed penetrating questions.

Where are the KL units? What about the PL? How far west do the VC operate? What kind of bridge is that? How high are those bluffs? Can they walk there in a day?

I responded with more detail and my responses prompted more questions.

'Are you guys having fun?' Dottie asked, as she entered the room, with a coffee pot in hand, and spotted us half sitting half lying on her living room floor poring over maps.

Towards the end of the evening Whitey said, 'I had no idea this skeleton existed. This could really work, Dick. We've got to get things cracking.' It was late when I left, but I was elated.

'What did you tell Whitey?' Pat asked me, as I entered his office the next morning.

'Same thing I told you,' I joked, 'that the sun doesn't just rise and set on the Hmong project, and we got things happening in the Panhandle too.'

'Don't get smart, kid,' he retorted. 'Well, whatever it was, he liked it. We're going to get the cable out of here today.'

The flight to Nakorn Phanom from Udorn is a straight shot east. You fly over Sakon Panom with its large, shallow lake, which, from the air, looks like a big puddle. Jim, my pilot for the day after my dinner with Whitey, was used to flying in the mountains in Hmong country in north Laos and this was tame stuff. He gave me the controls for a while after we had reached cruising altitude. As we neared the Mekong River and Nakorn Phanom, however, he took over and decided to add a little spice to our otherwise routine flight. We were well into the dry season by that time and the water level in the Mekong was way down. Indeed, at that time of year, there were places where one could actually wade across one of the world's mighty rivers. Jim took us down to about 5 feet above the water level. The river was so low that the banks on either side of us seemed to tower over us. It was like flying in a canyon or tunnel. As we came upon startled fishermen in their long narrow boats, some actually jumped into the river. That, I now sheepishly admit, caused us great amusement. Really feeling his oats by this time, he decided it might be fun to bounce his landing gear on the surface of the river but, perhaps noticing the look of dismay on my face, thought better of that idea. Soon, we were approaching Nakorn Phanom with Thakhek just on the other side.

Jim moved to the Laotian side until we got just abreast of Nakorn Phanom's clock tower in what passed for the town square. Still at about 5 feet over the water, we took a sharp right turn and headed directly at the bank below Nakorn Phanom. I was growing concerned. At the last minute, he pulled the helio sharply up and we passed directly over, barely, the Mekong River Garden restaurant. As we roared by, I could see the little waitresses, who had heard us coming, rush out on the porch to stare in amazement.

Our flightpath took us, almost immediately, right over our house, which alerted Jimmie to come to the airport to pick me up. Jim the pilot, with just a small grin, cranked down the flaps and we landed. While not exactly in accord with established flight rules for a landing, it was one of my more memorable arrivals at Nakorn Phanom.

Less than a week later, Pat cabled me in Nakorn Phanom to say that Headquarters had bought the whole thing: the concept, the goals, the plan itself, everything. Pat sounded happy and I sure was. It hadn't really occurred to me that the plan I had proposed was a perfectly logical extension of the project I took over or that it would have been difficult to be against what I wanted to do. Who could be opposed to trying to collect on the Ho Chi Minh Trail? Doubtless I didn't understand some of the politics involved, but it didn't really matter to me. They approved and that was the bottom line.

But with the approval came a request for a budget and some reporting requirements. I thought those to be ominous signs. Was this bureaucracy rearing its head? I was to find though that Udorn (Pat actually) shielded me from the bulk of the more onerous, to a field officer, reporting requirements for Headquarters.

This newly born Panhandle project had now been given an official cryptonym for use in cable traffic. Henceforth the project was to be known as Hardnose and the next time I was in Udorn,

Pat greeted me with, 'So, how are the Hardnosers doing? That's got a nice ring to it,' he went on. 'I love working with hardnosed people.'

'Who thought up that crypt?' I asked.

'I don't know,' he said, 'but I like it.'

My discussions with Whitey and some reading I had done while I was in Vientiane provided me with some useful background about the politics of the situation in the Panhandle and in South Laos. North Vietnamese use of the now three-year-old Ho Chi Minh Trail, and Washington's concerns about that use, had been increasing steadily since 1960.

The Pentagon had voiced its alarm in no uncertain terms and had proposed several different plans to address the problem. None were approved – primarily, it seemed to me, because of timidity at the political levels in Washington, Vientiane and Saigon. But clearly the interest level was high and there was a glaring need for intelligence on VC activities there. I now understood why both Pat and Whitey had been so favourably disposed to my plan.

Media reports from Hanoi in the mid-1990s, soon after the United States established diplomatic relations with Vietnam during the Clinton years, recount details of a conversation between a visiting group of American military officers and historians and senior Vietnamese military officers. Of note were the comments by the Vietnamese officers regarding the paramount importance they attached to their use of the Ho Chi Minh Trail. In unequivocal terms, they made clear that their unimpeded use of the Trail to move troops, cadre and war materials south through eastern Laos to destinations in South Vietnam and eastern Cambodia was critical. 'Without it,' their delegation leader emphasized, 'we could not have won the war.'

Thirty-five years later, we could only lament the fact that we, the United States, did not focus more attention on the 1961 Task Force report (an excerpt of which is quoted at the beginning of this chapter). One wonders, in fact, how many senior officials, during those early months of the Kennedy administration, even read the report.

The weeks after my meeting with Whitey were a blur. We were several months into 1963, my activities were limited by the constraints imposed by the Geneva Accords, and I had unsatisfactorily infrequent meetings with my team leaders. Those meetings, however, coupled with message traffic, started to produce some results.

I travelled to Mukdahan, a Thai town across the Mekong from Savannakhet, for meetings with two team leaders operating in the southern area of the Panhandle. And, periodically, as time passed and the constraints lessened, I slipped into Laos at night for additional meetings with my team leaders. Logistics, training, reporting, communications and, above all, team location were the subjects we discussed. All but the latter subject was discussed with no problem. Getting agreement to move teams into enemy-controlled areas to the east, however, was always touchy.

One particular trip to Mukdahan was a quick one. Road travel in the Land Rover over poor, rutted roads would have taken several hours each way and I didn't want to spend that much time. Moreover, it was sometimes risky as the road ran right along the Mekong in several places. So, I elected to fly, despite the fact that Mukdahan had no 'official' landing strip. I had been there previously and knew there was a large soccer field right on the edge of the town that would take a helio flown by a skilled pilot. I talked it over with Jim, my pilot for the day, and got his view: 'No problem, Dick. If you think I can land there, I can land there.'

Off we went to Mukdahan. The small river town's claim to fame is a beautiful and ancient Wat in which, it is said, there is a small holy vessel containing some of Buddha's ashes. Indeed, for that reason the King and Queen of Thailand visited Mukdahan (the first visit by a King of Thailand to the north-east of the country) in the spring of 1964 to pay their respects. By plane, it was a quick trip to Mukdahan and we were soon over-flying the town. Jim spotted the soccer field right away and noted, as did I, that both people and water buffalo were milling around on the field. Many of the people were gesturing at the plane, an unusual sight in Mukdahan. To signal our intent to land, Jim made a very low pass of the field. It worked. Soon it was completely cleared. With no further notice, Jim easily put us down with plenty of room to spare.

'Many thanks,' I said, as we rolled to a stop.

'At your service, sir,' he grinned.

'See you in a couple of hours,' I told him as I headed for my meetings.

About two hours later I returned. The plane was surrounded by a large crowd of locals who had probably never been so close to an airplane in their lives. Kids running around everywhere, young people, old people, it seemed as if half the town was on that field.

We were going to leave, I told the crowd, so please could they move away from the plane. All complied and we taxied out to the far end of the field. There was plenty of room for a take-off and no obstructions on either end of the field. The wind was coming right at us as Jim prepared to give it full throttle.

He looked at me and said, 'You want to make the take-off? It'll be an easy one.' (I had made several take-offs out of Udorn with Jim.) 'Good practice.'

I was sure he was pulling my leg and, besides, I had no intention of making a soccer field take-off. 'It's very thoughtful of you,' I responded, 'but why don't you just go ahead.'

He did and we left to the cheers and waving of much of the population of Mukdahan.

The problems with moving teams into the east of the country continued. One team leader, who crossed over from Thakhek, was particularly memorable. He was about thirty-five years old, slender like most Lao, but tall and avoided direct eye contact. Although I never liked using an interpreter, I had no choice at this point, and Mr Ambrose was with us. (After I got extended, I started to study Thai and became fairly conversant. Given its closeness to Lao, especially along the Mekong River where people spoke what they called Lao Thai, I also began to understand Lao.)

As was usually the case, our discussions on routine matters, like logistics and training, went smoothly. The team radio was down and he would be carrying back some spare parts to put them back on the air. We also discussed what the FAR was doing in his particular area – south and east of Thakhek. Then he provided some intelligence they had collected from a villager who had been in a village near the Vietnamese border to visit relatives. It was low level stuff, but of interest because we got very little from that area.

'That's good,' I exaggerated, 'but we really need to have steady reporting about traffic on the network running south from Route 12 towards Tchepone.'

'I know, but that's very difficult,' he responded.

This was a little dance we did each time I saw him. I decided to up the pressure. 'Tell me again why your team can't move further east,' I said.

Mr Ambrose knew the dance well and he smiled before he translated the question.

'Because it's too hard, sir,' was the answer.

'But I know that you are well-trained and brave, and I don't understand why you can't move east,' I persisted.

'Maybe we can move soon,' he said, hoping, I'm sure, that I'd drop the subject.

'But we really want you to move now so that you can report regularly. Where is your team located now?' I asked as I walked over to the map of the Panhandle on the wall.

'Our base camp is right here,' he said as he pointed to his south-eastern spot, 'but I send out patrols regularly to try to get information.'

'But I need you to be here,' I said pointing to a location much further east. 'We talked about this last month and we agreed that this location would be safe because you would remain hidden in the jungle.'

'You don't understand. That location has bad *Pi*,' he blurted out.

I had heard that before. I remembered the Shaman in Hmong country and, later in my life, I was reminded of it by the Lao officer at Walter Reed Hospital. Bloody evil spirits again, I thought. A couple of other team leaders had voiced the same excuse and I was initially perplexed. If they really believe that, I thought, we just have to reason with them and work our way through it. I can certainly be flexible and there are other spots from which they can watch the roads in the east. Soon, however, I came to realize, as of course did Mr Ambrose, that almost all locations in the eastern Panhandle had bad *Pi*. This was as opposed to places nearer the Mekong River – areas controlled by the FAR that were far away from the VC. Bad *Pi* was the best excuse they could think of for not taking the risk of moving into VC-dominated areas. I understood their dilemma, but this just wouldn't do. Other teams were moving, albeit slowly, east and his team must as well.

'OK,' I said, 'let's pick another spot nearby that doesn't have bad *Pi*. How about here.' I pointed to a location even further east. 'It's on a hill and *Pi* don't like high places,' I noted authoritatively.

He blanched, hesitated, and pointed to a spot between his team's present location and the original place we had discussed. 'We could move out to here. Would that be all right?'

'That will be a good first step,' I told him, making a mental note to myself that he was not going to work out as a team leader. In fact he did not work out and I was obliged to replace him.

One day in the spring of 1963, a member of another team named Bravo walked into Thakhek and made contact with us. One of my PARU met with him and was told that the team was falsely reporting its position. In the recent months, we believed that the team had twice moved east, but they were still having trouble collecting steady traffic reporting. The team member told us that in fact they were still located not far from Thakhek. I was irritated. I asked if he would lead us to where the team was located and he agreed. (We later found out that he and the team leader disliked each other intensely.) For some reason, I felt that my credibility and reputation would be strengthened by a straight-forward move and decided to walk into the camp and confront the deceitful team leader. It took some planning.

We had a boat, purchased in Bangkok, at our disposal. It was made of fibreglass and had a powerful Evinrude outboard motor with an automatic starter. It would move at high speeds and it was the only one of its kind in either Thakhek or Nakorn Phanom. It was not exactly low-profile. We used it to cross into Laos for delivery of various types of supplies. (There were never any customs or immigration formalities.) We kept it in a floating U-shaped boathouse on the Mekong that was built on ten empty, floating fifty-gallon gasoline cans, four on each leg and two across the top. We constructed a walkway over the floating drums and added walls, a tin roof and a wide swinging door that could be padlocked shut. Secured by ropes to either stakes or trees, it was sturdy, secure and efficient, particularly important given the dramatic seasonal changes in the Mekong's water level. At the height of the rainy season, you could see the boathouse as you approached the riverbank and a long plank afforded easy access to the boathouse. In the dry season, on the other hand, you couldn't see the boathouse until you reached the riverbank and looked down – sometimes way down. Towards the end of the dry season, the boathouse was easily 50 feet lower than the rainy season level.

We crossed at night. Since it was towards the end of the dry season, the water was low and the current was not strong. (Subsequent night crossings during the rainy season were, to say the least, harrowing. Very high water, surging currents, debris, including trees, carried downstream, and complete darkness presented a real challenge. Ultimately, as the situation changed, I was able to give those trips up in favour of daylight crossings.) There were four of us making the journey – the team member, Jimmie, who was driving the boat, a PARU and me. We had kept a house in Thakhek for meetings, supplies and contacts, and we stayed there that night. Via our contacts, we had rented a jeep (courtesy, I'm sure, of some corrupt FAR officer).

Early the next morning, we left Thakhek heading south-east along Route 13. The KL held Mahaxay, directly east of Thakhek, but our intelligence said that they did no active patrolling towards Thakhek so we weren't worried about them. 'Don't rock the boat' was their motto. About 25 kilometres out of Thakhek, we parked the jeep in some bushes and started walking directly east, the team member leading. The rest of us were watchful and, knowing that we were isolated and vulnerable, a little tense. It was easy walking on the relatively flat terrain and within two hours we came to a stream and could see the camp on the opposite bank. We were a way west of the location they had recently reported by radio message.

I saw no reason for a confrontation between the team leader and the team member, who had exposed the lie they had been living, so I instructed the latter to wait for us to return. We used a long, narrow *pirogue* to cross the stream and team members saw us coming. We walked directly into the camp and asked for the team leader by name. No one in the camp knew me except the team leader, but, harshly, my PARU made it clear who I was. The team leader appeared. He looked dumbfounded and sheepish at the same time. He looked at me, thinking, I'm sure, How could *you* be here?

'Where is your radio?' I asked sternly.

'I'll show you,' he replied, starting to walk towards a tent with an awning spread in front of it. There was a table under the awning.

'Show me your maps,' I told him.

He spread a map of the sector on the table.

'Please show me on the map the location of this camp,' I said.

'It's right here,' he said, pointing to our location on the stream.

Pulling his most recent cable from my pocket, I read out the co-ordinates given in the cable and pointed to them on the map. 'We cannot tolerate false reporting,' I snapped. 'It's impossible to work with people you cannot trust.' Only the team leader and the radio operator were within earshot as Jimmie translated my comments.

I was uncertain how many in the camp knew of the deception. Not too many I guessed. I didn't know if the team could be saved or not, but was convinced that the two before me had deliberately lied. They would be dismissed, but discreetly.

'I want to see you both in Thakhek in three days,' I told them. 'And bring all of your gear.'

Caught red-handed, there was nothing either could say and no defence was presented. I later discovered that only a few, including the team member who reported to us, knew of the deception. All of those who were culpable were dismissed and I broke the team down to a small unit by transferring several members to another team.

Had I been older and wiser, I probably wouldn't have been so blunt. I should have assessed the risks involved more carefully than I did. I had no idea, really, how the team leader was going to react. Happily he didn't get hostile or violent. Maybe the element of surprise worked in my favour.

That was the only time during my tour in Laos that I had to take such an action. It must be said, however, that we had a difficult time trying to confirm team locations for the whole life of the project. There was little we could do and we were obliged to take the word of our teams. We were well aware of the potential problem and did what we could to reconfirm whenever possible. With my surprise visits, I hoped word got around that you never knew when I was going to turn up.

Sometimes we could use collateral reporting to double-check reporting from our teams. If we had overhead coverage of the Mu Gia Pass for example, we could check it with reporting from a team along Route 12. Our colleagues in Udorn often did this for us. I was always pleased to hear that our team had reported a truck convoy on some route and air coverage on the same day confirmed the convoy was there. Occasionally, individual reports from villagers could also be used to confirm our road watch reporting. The parachute and rice drops also served to confirm team locations. No drop was made unless the proper signal was displayed on the drop zone and the team had to be there to display the correct signal. We changed the signals periodically to keep the teams' attention. They definitely wanted to receive the drops and were very careful about the co-ordinates they gave and the signals they were to use. It was a thorny problem, but I was confident we handled it as well as we could. Subsequent to my departure, when teams were inserted by chopper, we knew exactly where they were.

In mid-1963 the VC became increasingly aware of the fact that our teams were watching them, and counter-measures were employed. The VC actively patrolled areas along the roads they were using and planted sources in the villages in the area. Our teams sometimes discreetly purchased food from some of the villages (from trusted friends or relatives) and that, occasionally, proved dangerous. Once discovered by a VC patrol, our team could only run. They lacked the firepower to stand and fight. Later in the 1960s that changed as bigger teams with heavy firepower were inserted, but in the early years evasive action was our answer.

In their efforts to discover our teams, the VC sometimes used sniffer dogs to track us down. That caused many problems, which we dutifully reported back to Udorn and Headquarters. Included in one of our reports was mention of the fact that the presence of tigers in a given area made a difference. Our teams reported that VC dogs took off in the opposite direction if they smelled the excrement or urine of a tiger. We had no way of knowing if this was true. On the other hand, we had no reason to doubt it, so we reported the tiger story to Udorn and it was passed back to Headquarters.

Officers in Headquarters were perplexed, and the subject was discussed at several meetings. In their efforts to be as supportive as possible, an office in the Directorate of Science and Technology decided that we might use a counter-measure of our own on this problem. Could we, they reasoned, put a substance in the areas around our base camps that smelled like tiger excrement? If we could, the dogs would be rendered ineffective and our teams much safer. This seemed a good idea, but would it work? In the end it didn't, but the effort was appreciated. Coincidentally, when I retired in January 1996, I was talking to another senior officer, also retiring, and the subject of Laos somehow came up. Eventually it came out that he had been a young analyst in the office that had tried to help us. He remembered having sent some colleagues to the national zoo to collect samples of tiger urine and excrement so that it could be analysed. They did produce a substance that closely resembled it – but it didn't fool the dogs in Laos.

While I laboured happily in Nakorn Phanom, my colleagues, Mike, Andre and Ralph, were more or less stuck in Nong Khai. Office work on a routine basis was not what they had come to do, and they were, understandably, less happy. That there had been no choice after the Geneva Accords were signed was of little consolation. Pat and Bill understood, of course, but their hands were tied. They did try to give them short trips, whenever possible, to break the boredom of office work. Mike got to work frequently in Tieng Khong just across the Mekong from Laos in the far north-west area near the borders with Burma and China.

Working under the command of Bill Young, who as the son of a missionary, had grown up in the area and spoke several local dialects, Mike worked on the project that supported tribal groups like the Yao of north-west Laos who, like the Hmong, were strongly anti-communist. Mule trains carrying weapons, ammunition and other supplies were moved to the border for handing over to the guerrillas. By early 1963, constraints were lessening and both our government and the Lao government approved of these efforts. It was risky as the area had various groups operating therein, including nationalist Chinese who had been there since the end of the Second World War.

Mike, a Cornell University graduate and a Marine Corps officer, was an excellent and very action-oriented officer. In the summer of 1963, he returned to Headquarters to out-process officially from the Marine Corps. He spent almost eight months there and returned to Laos in early 1964. As a Far East Division officer, he was sent to Pakse in the south of Laos.

Andre, a former Army officer, was equally unhappy in a desk officer role and took every opportunity to get to the field. He visited me for a couple of weeks during early 1963 and helped me during the early organizational stages of Hardnose. It was doubly beneficial to me. I had help with the project and a good friend with whom I could discuss various subjects. My Thai was still very weak and my conversations in Nakorn Phanom were very limited. It was great to have him there. Andre also got to work in the southeast of Pakse. With his fluent French, he handled a French planter with whom we maintained contact. It was not like running regions in Hmong country, Andre said, but it sure beat the hell out of office work.

Andre had an interesting experience travelling by train from Nong Khai to Bangkok for some R and R. None of us had paid much attention to our actual cover status when we moved out of Laos into Thailand. Bangkok took care of everything for us. We were advisors was about all we knew. No one ever asked questions, so we didn't worry much about cover.

While on the train, Andre befriended a Thai family because of their attractive daughter. They had also boarded the train in Nong Khai, and I guess Andre figured they lived in Nong Khai and he might be able to meet the girl. The father, who turned out to be a general in the Thai army, spoke English. In response to a question about what he did in Thailand, Andre said, 'Advisor,' and the subject wasn't pursued. Small talk followed until a Thai immigration officer checking identity cards came to their compartment. The general and his family received a cursory check and then the official turned to Andre, obviously a foreigner, and asked to see his passport. Andre handed it to him, remembering that we had all given our passports to the administration officers for some type of stamp. Whatever was stamped in the passports was written in Thai and none of us could read it, but we weren't in the least concerned.

The immigration officer leafed through Andre's passport, came to the stamped page, read it and looked sharply back at Andre. Then, to Andre's great surprise, he snapped to attention and saluted. Somewhat taken aback, Andre nodded in recognition and the official handed him his passport, turned and left. There was a moment of awkward silence and then the general asked if he could look at Andre's passport. Hoping for some explanation, Andre handed it over. After a look at the stamped page, the general nodded knowingly and handed it back. He said nothing nor did Andre, who never did quite understand what had happened. The stamp must have identified Andre as a senior official or special envoy of some sort.

In February 1963, Andre returned to Headquarters where he was destined to work in Africa Division. (We had both been assigned to Africa when we finished our initial training and had been 'loaned' to Far East Division after we volunteered for a temporary assignment in Laos.) He had been called back by Africa after the six months and was sent to the former Belgian Congo on assignment. I don't know why they let me stay – possibly because I was handling a project. It was the luck of the draw.

Ralph also came over to Nakorn Phanom for a while and, like the others, welcomed the chance to get out of Nong Khai's office routine. A Harvard graduate, Ralph had joined the Marine Corps and been commissioned along with Mike before also being assigned to the Agency for two years. Ralph followed all reporting on order of battle in North and Central Laos and became quite expert in a short period. He returned to Headquarters in the summer of 1963, also to out-process from the Marine Corps, eventually returning to South-East Asia.

As the months passed, our Hardnosers became more aggressive and more effective. We were not stopping the red tide, but we were now positioned to watch it go by. 'Stay away from the enemy' was the message I preached to all of my teams. None of them had any problem at all with that concept. Find a spot away from the road with clear vision, on a hill or bluff if possible, and stay hidden. Rotate small teams from a base camp every couple of days and always stay out of sight. Move at night. Nothing particularly brilliant, just common sense, and slowly it started to work.

We handed out cameras and gave several days' training to team members in how to photograph passing traffic. We handed out laminated plastic cards identifying various kinds of trucks and other vehicles and systematized the reporting we were getting.

Soon, in addition to the written reports we received by radio on a daily basis – 'Four trucks carrying rice sacks passed grid WE 1467 at 10.30 a.m. on 7 July heading west on Route 12', for example – we started getting cassettes of film that we sent to Udorn. Our photo coverage got pretty good and some of it was useful in confirming VC presence, which, in turn, lessened constraints on us. We got photos of walking patrols, trucks, bicycles, and even elephants laden with sacks and cans. From the spring of 1963, our coverage of the Ho Chi Minh Trail network in the eastern Panhandle of Laos increased steadily in both quantity and quality. There were no firefights during my tenure, with full co-operation from our teams who definitely were not looking for trouble. In those early days of the project, we did not deploy teams by chopper, nor did we attempt to stop the VC traffic. The VC, while increasingly aware of and interested in the activities of our teams, saw minimal threat and started their counter-measures slowly. As our efforts became more aggressive, they reacted in kind.

As the end of my six-month extension neared in late spring 1963, Pat called me over to Udorn for discussions. He was expecting a senior visitor from Headquarters and wanted a current briefing on Hardnose, which I gladly provided. At that point, I was feeling better and more comfortable with how things were going. There were still problems, but steady progress had been recorded. We went over everything including the budget – a subject I didn't know much about. I asked for something and it appeared was all I knew. Pat took care of finance and administration. At the end, he seemed satisfied, even pleased and that, of course, pleased me.

I spent that evening with friends at a restaurant much like the Mekong River Garden. Vint, Mike, Pat and Ralph were all there and we had a splendid evening during which we consumed much food and much Scotch. The next morning I stopped by the office to see Pat before returning to Nakorn Phanom.

'Sounds like things are OK with your Hardnosers,' he said.

'Hope so,' I responded. 'It ain't easy, but we're doing everything we can think of.'

'The reporting is improving and I like that,' Pat went on.

'We have to do more between Route 12 and Route 9 around Tchepone,' I said. 'We're working on it.'

'Well, keep at it,' Pat said. 'And by the way, we want to ask Headquarters to extend you till summer 1964 and just make this a full two-year tour. That OK with you?'

It was typical Pat. Out of the blue. The proposal took me by surprise and I had to think before responding. The question of Africa Division, which was expecting me back, crossed my mind. But I didn't have to think for long. I was enjoying my work and felt like I was making a useful contribution.

My life in Nakorn Phanom took on a routine. There were periods of intense activity, some punctuated with clandestine visits to Laos, and periods of great calm verging on boredom. I had to find ways to occupy my time. Now that I knew I would be staying for two years, I bought a book on elementary Thai and started taking Thai lessons from, literally, the girl next door.

Our neighbour, of Vietnamese Thai origin, had an attractive daughter in her early twenties who was a schoolteacher. Arrangements to get started were difficult. I first met her little brother and was then introduced to her. Everything needed to be very proper. Her family was very sensitive to her contacts with me. Lessons in our house were out of the question. The venue we settled on was the library at her school during her free periods.

My first visit caused quite a sensation since I was the only *farang* in Nakorn Phanom. Thus a visit to the middle school to see Dara (meaning 'little star' in Thai) attracted special notice – students were all a-twitter. After it became a routine, the interest level subsided. She was a no-nonsense taskmaster and I learned a lot of Thai. The language has four 'tones' and initially that was a difficult hurdle to clear. Eventually I did, however, and it was a great help to me years later when I learned Mandarin Chinese, which has the same four tones. I also started learning to read the Sanskrit-based Thai. Our lessons, twice a week, were an hour long and were interrupted only if a plane buzzed my house, which I could hear from the school, announcing the arrival of something or someone from Udorn. I did my homework and, with

ample opportunity to practise, I was fairly fluent when I left
Thailand in the summer of 1964.

Wanting to stay in good shape, I also tried to get some exercise
each day. My PARU team members jogged and lifted weights,
but I didn't join them although I did follow a regime of exercise
in my room in the morning. One day, in search of more enjoyable
exercise, I wandered down to the local outdoor basketball court
hoping to shoot baskets with somebody. I got into a pickup game
and promptly noticed two things: the players were small, very
quick, and knew the game, and I was the big man on the court. At
Blackburn I had almost always been the smallest. I went up for
rebounds and I actually got them. I made tip-ins. I posted up to
the basket. I loved it.

They noticed something too. This big *farang* would be a great
addition to the Nakorn Phanom town team; not exactly a Wilt
Chamberlain, but for north-east Thailand in 1963, a real find.
They urged me to join their team. I was pleased with their interest and gratified by their praise, but alas, I was unable to commit
myself to regular practices and games. I did agree to do some
coaching as time permitted. They were a nice group of young
men and I enjoyed the time I was able to spend with them.

I also played tennis a couple of times a week when I could get
away in the late afternoon and became a member of the officials'
club, where, out of *politesse*, they always made a place for me when
I showed up. The Thai were always extremely cordial and did
whatever they could to make me feel welcome. My most enjoyable
tennis matches were with a wiry little Vietnamese tailor, who had
come to Nakorn Phanom after the Second World War. He was a
good player and a splendid person as well. Frequently I would
have a beer in the officials' club bar after a match and, as my Thai
improved, chat with Thai officials and sometimes play snooker at
their invitation. With smaller pockets and greater distances on
the table, snooker is (to me) much harder than the pool played in
the United States. I never got very good, but the Thai were very
tolerant and always loudly applauded my few successes.

Meantime, there were periodic trips to Udorn. On one of these,
I had had the controls for about the last half of our flight and,
when I could see Udorn, nudged the dozing pilot, Jim. We had
flown together many times and he apparently had some confidence

in my flying and navigating. I had been there well over a year by that time and, having logged many hours in a helio, I felt pretty confident in the air. This had been done 'unofficially', but all agreed that it was useful for us to know something about flying 'just in case'. We rarely elaborated on what that meant, but we all knew that the possibility of taking enemy ground fire that could disable the pilot was ever present. It therefore made sense for us frequent flyers to have some feel for what to do.

As Jim awoke, he said, 'It's about time you took a try at landing this thing. You up for that?'

'Yeah, I think I can get it down,' I responded cautiously.

'Just listen and do what I tell you,' he said.

I reduced the power and we started down while lining up with the *very* long runway. As we descended and lined up for our final approach, he told me to bring down the flaps. This is done with a crank in the middle of the ceiling just behind the pilot who sits on the left. Since I was sitting on the right, I had to crank with my left arm. It was hard, but I got the flaps down. With lowered flaps, we slowed down, but I was unable to judge the speed we were carrying. He started talking me in.

'Little lower, little lower,' he mumbled softly. 'Keep it steady, that's good.'

I listened and I tried, but my depth perception let me down. Or I was just impatient. I took the last 20 feet or so in one chunk and we bounced back up into the air.

He got a little excited.

'Still plenty of runway left,' he said. 'Just ease her in.'

Again I must have rushed it. Again we bounced back up into the air.

'Why don't I help?' he said. '*We* can do this.'

I certainly hoped *we* could and on the third try, with his help, I actually landed the bloody helio – on the second longest runway in South-East Asia. Landing an airplane, I concluded, is harder than it looks.

In mid-1963, we started thinking about moving back into Laos. That didn't happen while I was there but, in early 1964, we rented another small house in Thakhek and I sometimes stayed there overnight while in Laos for meetings. After I left in July 1964, my successor moved the whole base station of the project to Savannakhet, Laos.

As the situation changed, we were able to cross the river more frequently and travel by day instead of at night. I saw the senior Lao army officers more, but more for reasons of courtesy than anything else. We didn't discuss what our teams were doing, but they had a good idea anyway. Only a few times did they raise objections and then only indirectly. I travelled a few times to see their camps and strongpoints on the road leading into Thakhek from the east. My relations with FAR were good and, on a few occasions, I was able to help them with communications support or logistics. In turn, they helped me by providing selected men for our teams, transport, or approval to land at airstrips for resupply purposes.

In the late fall of 1963, I travelled by boat and on foot to see one of our teams positioned north and east of Thakhek near Route 8. In addition to seeing the team, which was doing a fine job for us, I wanted to get a first-hand look at the terrain. It was an area not fully secured and we rarely had the chance to over-fly it. Together with two of my PARU, and the team leader who had come to Thakhek to guide us in, I drove north along Route 13 out of Thakhek. At the point where Route 13 crosses the Nam Ngum River, we left our jeep and got into a waiting boat. Typical of the area, it was long and narrow with a long-shaft outboard engine. It took us all with plenty of room to spare. We were carrying small packs, as we intended to stay overnight, and weapons.

We headed upstream passing through increasingly rugged hills and rocks. Soon we could see a line of high *karst* far ahead, rising abruptly and almost vertically. Starting just north of Thakhek, it stretched for many kilometres and formed an obstacle to east and west travel. Climbing it would have been all but impossible without proper equipment and going around it meant walking many extra kilometres. There were a couple of points through which you could pass and they became strategic choke points in time of hostilities.

The scenery was truly astounding. Natural beauty abounded as we pushed upstream on what was a beautiful day. We passed no villages for a long period. It was calm moving up the river, a time to think. Again, I felt suddenly a little isolated and reviewed the decisions I had taken to get here. I was satisfied that they had been good ones.

Finally we came to a large village near the *karst*. The Nai Ban of the village had been alerted to my arrival and he, with several others, was waiting for our arrival. I was not happy about that, but hadn't thought to tell the team leader not to advertise that I would be in the area. With all the lectures he had heard about discreet travel, I never thought he would mention that we were coming. But he did and I was to get a special welcome. The village rarely received visitors of any sort let alone a *farang*. I was anxious to press on, but plans to serve us a special lunch were not to be broken. We stayed and ate. It was a pleasant time and all in the village were most gracious to us.

'Could you send some tools?' the Nai Ban asked, as we were finishing lunch.

I thought about what to say. 'I really don't have any tools,' I responded finally, 'but I can certainly check with the AID [Agency for International Development] office and see if they can help.'

But the Nai Ban pushed ahead. 'We need them badly to complete the fish farm we have constructed,' he said.

'Well, that's the kind of thing AID likes,' I said. 'I'll certainly pass along your request. How would they send the tools to you? By boat?'

'By boat would be easiest,' he replied, 'but we can come to Thakhek to get them if necessary. Or maybe you could drop them from a plane.'

I let the last comment go.

This was 1963 and already the Nai Ban of this isolated village was aware of the fact that he could ask for all forms of help from the Americans. I was the wrong one to ask in this case, but he didn't know that. And he didn't care. Over time I can only imagine that it got worse. 'We don't have enough so give us more' was the mentality that we created. Our efforts and largesse were certainly well-intentioned, but what good did they do? I'm doubtful. Primarily because of the waste and corruption I was to see around the world, not only in Laos but in the Congo, in West Africa in general, and in several countries in South-East Asia, I was never a supporter of large aid programmes. I saw enormous sums of aid

money expended with minimal, if any, results. The people bene-
fited almost not at all. When you work for it and do it yourself,
I'm convinced that you appreciate it more.

One night I was sitting in the small house we had rented in
Thakhek, working on some reports that I would send to Udorn
the next day. Quite suddenly, heavy gunfire broke out all around
me. I could even hear machine-guns. I had no idea what was going
on. Could it be a raid by PL or VC units, right into Thakhek? I
turned out the lights and grabbed my weapon. Crouching in the
darkness, I moved to the front of the small house. Only the screen
door was closed and I peered out. To my surprise, I saw people
firing weapons into the air, and others making noises with whatever was at hand – pans, pails, drums. What the hell was going on?
I didn't know anyone so was left to puzzle it out. I watched for a
couple of minutes, concluded that some sort of festival must be
under way, and went back inside to finish my reports. Eventually
it got quiet again and I went to bed. The next day, I asked Mr
Ambrose what festival had been celebrated the previous night.

'None that I know of,' he replied. 'What are you talking about?'
I explained. 'Oh, you mean the eclipse of the moon. The Lao
believe that an eclipse is actually caused by a giant frog jumping
on the moon. Loud noises will frighten the frog and then it jumps
off the moon making it visible again. It works every time.'

'You're not serious,' was all I could say to this.

In November 1963, we got a message from team Delta, a good
team, south of Route 12. The message read: 'We are sorry to hear
about your President and we send our condolences.' I had no idea
what they meant. I had a short-wave radio in my room and sometimes listened to the BBC for news, but, being away, not regularly.
Gleaned from a short-wave news broadcast, that was the first
word we had in Nakorn Phanom of President Kennedy's assassination.

By December 1963, activity was at a high level and reporting
had increased steadily. Almost all the teams were positioned well
for reporting purposes and were maintaining the low profile I
advocated. I was busier and busier managing the project and had
to keep several balls in the air at a time. Logistics, planning and
delivery, finance, training, and meetings now frequently held in

Laos, were keeping me very occupied. I was in regular touch with the base in Udorn ordering supplies, discussing intelligence reports and requirements, and asking for air support to move around. There was lots to do and, although Jimmie and especially Mr Ambrose were a big help, I had my hands full. Late in December, I sat down to organize the week coming up and cabled Pat with a request for planes on four consecutive days. His response came back:

Plane 23 Dec OK. Plane 24 Dec OK. Plane 26 Dec OK. FYI 25 Dec is Christmas Day. We are not flying on Christmas Day except in case of emergency. Cool it, kid.

I read his message standing in our office. I sat, read it again, and had to smile. I had been so tied up with what I was doing in this tropical Buddhist village that I had completely forgotten about Christmas. I thought of my parents and immediately sat down and wrote a letter home. Then I declared Christmas Day a holiday in our house and altered my planning accordingly.

Early in 1964, Pat and Bill sent reinforcements to Nakorn Phanom in the form of Dick Kinsman, who ultimately took over the project when I left. Dick, from upstate New York, was a Syracuse University graduate and had joined the Agency a few years earlier. He was a volunteer like the rest of us and had arrived at Udorn in the fall of 1963. Maybe the Christmas Day message caused Pat to conclude that I was losing my grip and needed help. Whatever, Dick's arrival was most welcome. He was a low-key guy and I could see right away that we would get along well. We did.

He sat in on all meetings with team leaders and frequently travelled with me when I crossed into Laos. Nothing we were doing was very complicated and Dick caught on quickly. Much of our success depended upon personal relationships and he established rapport easily. Persuading, even cajoling, or convincing the team leaders and sometimes the members as well of the wisdom of our suggestions was terribly important and Dick had a knack for listening and explaining without being condescending.

It was good to have someone with whom to discuss operational ideas. Dick and I talked through several possibilities for the future of the project including one that would move us into a more aggressive mode in the eastern Panhandle. To do that, our teams would have to be bigger and have more firepower. Company size, at least, units would be required if we hoped to mine the roads the VC were using, or otherwise disrupt the traffic, or ambush and destroy truck convoys. This was a big step beyond road watching and would have to be carefully planned. We were cautious as we considered the first steps. We would need to recruit and train more men and we would need more resources, including PARU support for the training. As was the case in neighbouring Vietnam, things were heating up and south Laos was becoming more critical, for both sides. We had, at that time, no hopes of impeding traffic on the Ho Chi Minh Trail, we wanted only to harass the VC and make their tasks more difficult. We sent an outline of our thinking to Udorn. They approved the outline, as did Headquarters. 'Go slow,' was Pat's guidance.

As a first step, we needed a place to do our training. Dick and I went to see the Thakhek military commander and explained our needs. Corrupt and ineffective as a commander, he nevertheless agreed to let us take over a former Lao army training facility just outside of Thakhek at a spot where a river crossed Route 13. Some repair would be needed, but otherwise we could get started anytime we wanted.

Recruiting new members for our teams was the next step and we put the wheels in motion for a recruiting drive. We didn't want just anybody, we made clear, and recruits would have to meet our standards. Being a cousin, brother, or family friend of a team leader was not necessarily a qualifying factor.

In our youthful zeal, and lacking experience, we came up with an ambitious plan.

With our sights aimed much higher than was reasonable at the time, we developed a plan to hit Route 12 just as it passed through the Annamites at the Mu Gia Pass. The VC would be shocked, we thought, to see the Mu Gia Pass closed to truck traffic. But, we found out, not nearly as shocked as our team leader when we explained the plan. While not overly risky in our view, it involved some complicated logistic efforts. It was the dry season so we knew boats could pass through the *karst* to a point near the team's location. We explained to him that we would send cratering charges, by truck and then boat to their base camp. Then a fifteen-man patrol, carrying twelve cratering charges, would walk across the Nakay plateau to the border where Route 12 entered Laos via the Mu Gia Pass.

They would pick a spot along a ravine or other vulnerable place, and, at night, plant all twelve of their cratering charges. The charges would cut the road for, hopefully, weeks. We didn't want to make an air drop en route, we explained, as we didn't want to risk compromising their position. There weren't many villages on the plateau, but still the patrol should avoid contacts with locals who might be in touch with PL units. As they got closer to the pass, we noted, they should move only at night to reduce any chance of bumping into an enemy patrol.

By this time, my Thai language skills were moderate, but I never tried to discuss serious subjects on my own so Mr Ambrose had been translating. (Increasingly, however, over the months, my comprehension had improved to the point that I could understand much of the conversation between Mr Ambrose and whomever he was talking to. This became a big advantage for me as it gave me additional time to think and consider my responses. They didn't know that I understood much of what they were saying. And Mr Ambrose was discreet enough not to reveal my newly acquired knowledge.) The team leader had been listening and his eyes were getting bigger and bigger. The look on his face as Mr Ambrose finished, and we all awaited his response, seemed to be a combination of amazement coupled with disbelief and panic.

He almost couldn't talk, but then started spewing out one reason after another why such an effort would not be possible. He had so many reasons he didn't even include bad *Pi*. As he talked we got the picture.

Asking our patrol to walk across Laos (carrying forty-pound cratering charges) to the Mu Gia Pass, the enemy's lair so to speak, to blow up a vital transport link that was probably guarded at key spots was asking a lot. Then to request that they elude the angered VC and walk back across Laos was probably more than we could expect. Actually, I had considered going with them, but feared Pat's ire if he found out. In a state of shock, the team leader pleaded with us to reconsider. In the end, we did and no such patrol was sent.

Years later, as I followed the war via newspapers and news reports, I learned that B-52 bombers had dropped tons and tons of high explosive bombs and cratering bombs all along the trail and in the strategic passes, including Mu Gia. The road was never cut for more than a few days at a time. The Vietnamese did an incredible job of repairing and/or rerouting in order to keep supplies flowing south. Our dozen cratering charges, even at that early stage, would not have been much of a statement.

The same officer we had talked with about the training site invited us to a local celebration of Lao National Day at a military base about fifteen kilometres south-east of Thakhek along Route 13 and near the road junction with Route 135 that led to KL-controlled Mahaxay. It was a gala affair that started in late afternoon.

We had crossed over to Thakhek in our boat, grabbed a waiting jeep and driven out to the base. Traditional dancing was under way when we arrived. We sat down to watch. As honoured guests, we were offered drinks. Soon a type of a cross-cultural skit was in process.

The Lao delight in getting guests drunk and from that moment on, we always had a drink in our hands. We danced the Lam Rhang, a traditional dance for couples. We didn't know how to do the dance, but that didn't matter. You never touch your partner, just move around each other. We drank. We chatted with Lao officers in English, French, or Thai. We drank. We participated in a *bossi*. And we drank. We drank Scotch, Mekong whisky (Thai-made that had to be drunk with soda or coke), and rice wine from large urns that had fermented for some undetermined amount of time. In fact, we drank too much, way too much, but so did everyone else and it was a glorious party.

It was dark when it ended and we had a dilemma. We rarely drank as much as we had that night and we knew we weren't exactly ourselves. Still, we could make it back to Thakhek, we thought. And none of our hosts had ever heard of the 'friends don't let friends drive drunk' line. We found our jeep and got in. According to Dick Kinsman, I insisted on driving even though I was in no condition to do so. (I'm sure I figured he was in even worse condition than I was.) As we left the perimeter of the base, it became pitch dark. I found the lights and turned them on.

The unpaved two-lane track in front of us looked like a tunnel through dense jungle and over-hanging trees. We each had weapons and Dick held his on his lap – why I don't know because had we found trouble that night, it would surely have been serious for us. We started towards Thakhek driving slowly and talking loudly.

Within minutes, Dick was shouting at me to stop.

'I dropped my M-1,' he told me after I braked.

'How the hell could you do that?' I asked in amazement.

'You drove off the road and the bushes grabbed it,' he shot back.

'The bushes grabbed it?'

'Yes, they did,' he repeated. (We were not communicating particularly well.) 'The barrel was sticking out and when you veered off the road back there it was pulled out of the jeep. We have to go back and find it.'

'Can't see a damn thing,' I told him honestly.

'But we have to try,' he insisted. 'Turn the jeep around. Be careful.'

With considerable luck, I turned the jeep around without hitting anything or going into the ditch at the side of the road. We went back and stopped. With the lights left on, we got out and started looking for the missing M-1.

Somehow, Dick found it. I turned the jeep again and we made our way back to Thakhek. We left the jeep, found our boat and got in to head back to Nakorn Phanom. Happily, it was a clear moonlit night and we could see the lights of the town across the river. All we had to do was head in that direction. Even a drunk could have made it.

It was the dry season so the current wasn't bad and soon we spotted our little dock and boathouse. We made it in, on about the third try, and locked everything up. It was a memorable night and I'm glad it was a rare event.

We were proud of our work in the Panhandle and, as a function of this, enjoyed an ongoing and good-natured needling relationship with those officers in the Hmong programme. Shortly after I left Nakorn Phanom to return to Headquarters, Dick told me that I'd just missed the arrival of a small box, which had been sent to us from Tony Poe in Long Tieng, via Udorn. Inside there were what appeared, at first glance, to be dried apricots. They were, in fact, dried ears. The Hmong, in lieu of a body count and for traditional reasons, sometimes cut off the ears of dead enemy soldiers and bring them back as proof of their prowess and courage. In the box was a note from Tony that read, 'My men up here are real fighters.' This was meant, we knew, to be a slam at the lowland Lao with whom we worked.

Then, a newly arrived officer had a bright idea. One of the PARU was sent to the local abattoir, where he collected the genital organs of a large, just slaughtered, male water buffalo. It was long and imposing. They custom-made a long narrow box and secured the water buffalo penis and testicles into it. A note was included: 'We are fighting real men down here.' The box was sent back to Udorn addressed to Tony in Long Tieng.

However, inexplicably, someone in Udorn, instead of waiting for the next helio direct to Long Tieng, sent the box on to Vientiane. The people who handle Agency mail are required by regulation to know what is in each package or envelope. Much laughter followed. The story flashed around like wildfire. No one was upset except, that is, the Ambassador. He was not amused and ordered the box destroyed. Tony never received his gift.

Tony was an exceptional guy. Intensely patriotic, he apparently slept with an American flag over his bed, loathed the communists, and fought them for most of his adult life. Allegedly he single-handedly carried out an air raid against a VC column in early 1963, which was unheard of during this period. Vexed at VC advances on one of the villages in his Sam Neua region, he decided to retaliate. With a colleague (whose identity never surfaced), he stuffed several dozen empty glass jars with hand grenades. As the lids were put on the jars, they pulled the pins so that the grenades were 'live'. Since the handle couldn't fly upwards while the grenade was wedged into a jar, however, the grenades would not explode. The jars were carefully packed into several cardboard boxes. Then Tony convinced one of the Air America pilots to be a participant.

Acting on current intelligence, they caught a VC column completely by surprise. Theirs was certainly a brash and unexpected move. The pilot approached from behind the convoy at tree-top level. Those in the convoy, which consisted of a few trucks and a

couple of companies of walking troops, could only watch in disbelief as the small plane roared overhead. No one reacted quickly
enough to mount any effective defence. As they passed the length
of the column, Tony and friend threw the glass jars down onto the
column as fast as they could. As the jars hit the ground and broke,
the grenades exploded. That sent the troops diving into the jungle
on either side of the road. Tony was hanging halfway out of the
door cheering as the pilot banked away to safety. Gutsy, but not
crazy, they made only one pass.

Tony also had flaws – don't we all? Sometimes he drank too
much, perhaps as a way to deal with the ever-present stress and
danger, and that had predictable affects on his judgement. Once I
met him in Bangkok, where we both were enjoying a couple of
days of rest.

'Tony, how the hell are you?' I greeted him.

'Not bad, I thought I needed a break,' he responded.

'How long have you been here?'

'Eight hundred dollars.'

I was a little puzzled. 'So how long are you staying?'

'Fifteen hundred,' he replied. That was Tony.

Never concerned with formalities, he had just decided he needed
some time off – or some companionship, or both. He just told Pat
he was going to Bangkok. And he did, taking fifteen hundred
dollars with him. He didn't mess with requesting leave or filling
out any forms. With a voracious appetite for Thai girls (*any* girls
actually) and whisky, he would consume the pleasures of Bangkok
and return to work when the fifteen hundred dollars was gone.

Shortly after Dick Kinsman arrived in Nakorn Phanom, work
began on a new air base about 15 kilometres west of Nakorn
Phanom. A US Navy construction battalion, the Sea Bees, arrived
one day by road – a long convoy, we were told, of heavy machin-
ery, all sorts of trucks and jeeps, and even some Land Rovers. The
site selected was strategically located to serve two purposes.
Firstly, the Thai would gain a first-class air base in their under-
populated and vulnerable to communist insurgency (they thought)
far north-east provinces. Secondly, it was well-located for United
States purposes of supporting the air war against North Vietnam,
North Laos and the eastern Panhandle of Laos. The base was to

become extremely active in search and rescue missions for US pilots downed over North Vietnam or Laos. It was as close to the critical danger zones as the US could get. Coupled with the major efforts under way at Udorn's air base to construct new facilities and improve existing ones, it would support a strong US air capability to employ against North Vietnam.

We went out to the site about three weeks after the Sea Bees had arrived to meet and welcome them. The construction site near Nakorn Phanom was largely covered with dense jungle and their first task had been to set up camp. Rows of large tents with plank flooring were already in place, as were several buildings housing offices, the mess hall, and motor pool. Clearly, these guys weren't messing around. We met the commanding officer and his deputy, who were surprised to hear that two Americans were living in Nakorn Phanom. We explained that we were 'advisors', and, at that point, they weren't sure what that meant, but never pursued the subject. They were tasked, they told us, with building a 10,000-foot, pierced steel planking runway as quickly as possible. Taxiways, parking areas, hangars, maintenance facilities and a security perimeter were all part of their project. It was a major undertaking. They assured us that it wouldn't take long. And it didn't.

We stopped to watch them work for a while. It was impressive. They had connected an enormous type of chain between two enormous caterpillar bulldozers. In the middle of the chain was a huge steel ball that rolled the chain forwards. With a bulldozer on each end, and one pushing the ball, they would drag the chain through the jungle and level a swath about 100 foot wide. We were fascinated. The bulldozers had steel cages protecting the drivers from falling trees and things falling from the trees – like snakes. They killed several snakes a day, we were told, and most were large and poisonous. The bulldozer just crushed them. At the rate they were going, it seemed like 10,000 feet wouldn't be much of a problem, and we could see why they were optimistic about finishing quickly.

Included in the expansion and modernization efforts at Udorn had been the construction of a new building to house the headquarters area for Bill and Pat. No longer just the Hmong programme (although that remained by far the priority), the whole effort had grown dramatically and could no longer function out of a rented house in Nong Khai. The increased levels of activity in North-West Laos, South Laos and the Panhandle were part of the reason for the increased workload. The newly constructed building, on a restricted access compound at the Udorn air base (which also facilitated Thai Airways flights for civilian use), answered the need. It made little difference to me. Our regular contact was by radio message and we just changed the address line. My periodic trips to Nong Khai, which had been relatively infrequent, were to discuss a wide range of subjects pertinent to Hardnose. Now those trips, which gradually became more frequent as our activity and reporting levels grew, were to Udorn instead. The move marked the start of a new phase, though, for paramilitary operations in Laos. Centralized now out of Udorn with a large and efficient headquarters staff and well-established air and logistics capabilities, momentum was growing palpably. By that time, constraints occasioned by the signing of the Geneva Accords in July 1962 were a fading memory. The VC had ignored those Accords and now we were doing the same thing. Souvana Phouma, the Laotian neutralist premier, practised *realpolitik* by requesting increased levels of covert support for his government's struggle to exist. Our programmes were responding to his requests. The Accords had become a hollow shell existing only on paper. For geopolitical purposes, all paid lip service to them, but on the ground they were ignored.

For the remainder of 1963, significant progress, including in my project, was recorded and prospects were bright for 1964. Just let us get back into Laos, we told each other, and we'll really get things on track. Attitudes were positive and our confidence was high. To a man, we were pleased with where we were, what we were doing and what we had already accomplished. The original gameplan – small, well-trained and mobile units for use in hit-and-run operations designed to harass and tie up VC units – was only then starting to shift incrementally towards more ambitious tactics aimed at actually seizing and holding ground. None saw the dangers that portended.

Understandably, I believe, the high level of confidence bred great optimism for the future of our projects. We would definitely give the VC fits. Of that we had no doubts. At the policy level in

Washington, newly installed President Johnson was equally convinced that the United States would prevail and he increased overall US support for South Vietnam. Both in Washington and in South-East Asia, despite political machinations in Saigon and Vientiane, Americans were looking at the situation through rose-coloured glasses. That a world superpower could be tied down and ultimately rendered impotent in its conflict with North Vietnam was inconceivable. Some harsh political lessons were yet to be learned.

On one of my trips to Udorn in May 1964, Bill called me in for a chat. This was unusual as he mainly concerned himself with the Hmong programme and let Pat handle the others. I was curious as I walked into his office.

'What are you going to do when you get back to Headquarters?' Bill asked.

'Go to Africa Division I guess,' I replied. 'I was supposed to go there before I volunteered to come out here.'

'Happy out here?'

'Love it,' I told him quite honestly.

Like Pat, Bill didn't waste a lot of words. 'If you'd like a home leave and return to Laos, we would like to have you back here,' he said.

This was unexpected and I tried to gather my thoughts. Certainly I was flattered. For Bill to make such a proposal meant a lot to me. I knew he wouldn't have made it if he weren't completely happy with what I'd done. I also knew that Pat must have agreed and may have been the instigator. That these two men, for whom I had great respect, looked favourably upon me, and my efforts for them, was gratifying. I had thought about this question in recent months and been unable to come to any definite conclusion. I was sure that, if Far East Division wanted me (and now it was clear that they did), they had the priority at that time to win the bureaucratic battle. But did I want them? I wasn't sure. Bill's offer was tempting and I certainly enjoyed what I was doing. But it was a major career decision. It would mean that I would run paramilitary operations in the future rather than the classical intelligence operations that I had envisioned before coming to Laos. Young and still single, I wondered if I could have it both ways. Not likely, I concluded.

'Thanks very much, Bill,' I responded eventually. 'Coming from you, that's a real compliment. I've been breaking my head about this exact question and I don't have an answer yet.'

'I could have guessed as much,' Bill said. 'So now you know we're happy and we'd like you back to keep running Hardnose.'

'It's very tempting, Bill,' I said, 'but I don't feel right committing myself until I've talked to people at Headquarters. Let's just say that I'd like to come back, but I don't know if I can.' This sounded wishy-washy I had to admit, but it was the best I could do.

'It's your call, Dick,' Bill said. 'But you don't want to go to Africa. Those people are uncivilized. They'll eat you.' We both laughed, neither suspecting how prescient his comment was, and he waved me out of his office as the phone rang.

Pat was aware, of course, of my conversation with Bill. 'You won't come back,' he predicted. I started to protest, but thought better of it. In the end, Pat was right.

I left Nakorn Phanom in July 1964, travelling to Bangkok via Udorn, and met my brother, Bob, in Europe, where we toured several countries for three weeks before flying to New Jersey where my parents now lived. Bob, a Marine Corps officer, was just returning from a tour with a forced recon unit in the 'I' Corps Region of South Vietnam. It had been a tough and dangerous duty and we had a splendid time unwinding together in southern Europe.

I was happy as I returned home, happy with the previous two years, about prospects for the future and to be returning home to see my family. I felt that I had been part of a worthwhile effort. And beyond that, we had been productive and successful. I had met many officers that I liked and respected – none actually that I didn't like – and my career, I thought, was off to a good start.

Now, thirty-five years later, as I reflect upon what we did in light of developments in Laos after I left, I lament many of the unintended results of our efforts, but I point no fingers. I just feel sorry that we, the United States, couldn't have been smarter about our policy decisions. 'Too soon old, and too late smart' applies to our policies in Laos from 1961 to 1973. The ignorance and the arrogance of Americans arriving in South-East Asia (especially Laos from my perspective, but likely Vietnam as well) during that period were certainly contributing factors. We came to help, and of that there should be no doubt. But we had only minimal understanding of the history, culture, or politics of the people we wanted to help. The discussions in Geneva were about big power issues rather than Laos or Vietnam. Our own policy interests and decisions were superimposed onto a region and a country wherein our President had decided to 'draw the line'. And we would do it our way. For over a decade we poured in manpower and resources, unable to see, or maybe to accept, that it simply wasn't working.

The ways in which we used our airpower and exploited our complete air superiority are an example of that policy flaw. To illustrate, I include a paragraph I wrote several years ago as part of a review of *Shadow War: The CIA's Secret War in Laos,* a book by Kenneth Conboy and James Morrison about the Agency's efforts in Laos:

An interesting aspect of the book that readers may want to consider as an issue in its own right is that of the use of air support. The author carefully describes the extensive role played by US airpower. From cargo planes delivering troops, war materiel, and food to reconnaissance planes, helicopters, ground support fighters, and even B-52 carpet-bombing runs, virtually every US airplane in Southeast Asia was deployed in support of the war effort against the Communist forces. It is probably not an overstatement to say that never before and never since has an irregular 'guerrilla' force been so intensely supported by the full range of a superpower air force. Dealing with their vulnerability to attack from the air presented the North Vietnamese with an enormous challenge. They responded with nighttime attacks and major offensives launched during periods of bad weather that curtailed the effectiveness of total US air superiority. In the end, that air supremacy did not carry the day in Laos or in Vietnam. While airpower can tilt the playing field and postpone the inevitable, it will not win wars. The foot soldiers, who seize and hold territory, are ultimately the victors, a point clearly made during the 1960s and 1970s.

The fact is that we didn't learn, we didn't adapt and we lost. Worse yet, the lessons seem still to be unlearned. Witness the policies we have recently employed in Iraq and Kosovo. Scholars and policy makers, far brighter than I, will no doubt keep gnawing on these problems. Hopefully we will, one day, get it right.

In Afghanistan we got it right. We got it very right and have in fact broken new ground in terms of the ability to project air power. A new, extremely powerful and ruthlessly efficient warfighting capability was born in our Afghan campaign. The following point made by *The Economist* in March 2002 sums it up: 'America's war there brought new refinements unheard of even a year ago, in the art of delivering deadly firepower at long range with devastating accuracy.' Facing a completely new kind of foe, in a land-locked country far from our shores, required us to implement innovative strategies and employ flexible, common-sense tactics. We did exactly that. Our ability to fuse intelligence gained from multiple sources with real time air attacks and ground assaults destroyed an enemy that showed itself only rarely. Potential adversaries the world over must now accept the fact that not only our technological superiority, but our ability to employ that technology, cements our position as a world superpower.

While there are many things that might have been done differently in Laos, and while I concede without debate that hindsight is always 20/20, I will cite two examples of policy initiatives that had far-reaching impact. One was a sin of omission and the other a sin of commission. Could either have been avoided? It doesn't really matter now, does it?

In 1961, the Pentagon voiced great concern for South Laos and subsequently presented a plan to build a defensive barrier running from the Gulf of Tonkin, at the demarcation line between North and South Vietnam. It was described as a strategically key area because of threats to South Vietnam and Cambodia, and even Thailand, if you adhered to the domino theory. The Pentagon presented a plan to build and defend a road from the Gulf of Tonkin to the Mekong River. Starting at the parallel dividing North and South Vietnam, it would end at Savannakhet and more or less follow Route 9. (Actually, in early 1964, Dick Kinsman and I, unaware of the earlier Pentagon proposal, came to the same conclusion one night while we were

College graduation photo, 1957.

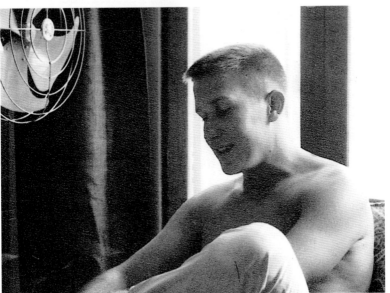

Nakorn Phanom, Thailand, 1963.

With a PARU Team Leader
and a Nai Ban, Hmong
country, North Laos, 1962.

With Lao guerillas,
Hmong country,
North Laos, 1962.

Receipt of medal for
work in Laos, 1964

Arriving in Stanleyville, the Congo, 1964.

Our wedding, 1968.

Hong Kong harbour from our balcony, 1971.

On a friend's boat in Hong Kong, 1972.

Judy at home in McLean, 1973.

Suzanne, Alison, Danika and Pia in McLean, 1974.

Alison, Danika, Pia and Judy in the Swiss Alps, 1987.

In Rome, 1981.

With Vice President Bush after receiving a commendation, May 1986.

With DCI Jim Woolsey in his office for the presentation of the award for (Classified) Operational Accomplishment, fall 1994.

With Judy and DCI Deutch for the presentation of the Distinguished Intelligence Medal, 1996.

With Dr Tim Miller – who cared for me after the Congo crash – in front of the statue of 'Wild Bill' Donovan in the Headquarters' lobby, 1996.

working in Nakorn Phanom. We sent our idea to Udorn. It died.)
Coincidentally, also in early 1964, in Hanoi the Communist
Party's Politburo came to its own conclusion regarding the Ho
Chi Minh Trail. Declaring the Trail of absolutely critical impor-
tance to its war effort, the Politboro tasked the Army to refine,
expand, exploit and protect the Trail at any cost.

The plan was the result of a careful study of the situation made
by a task force of military officers. It made good sense in that it
would preclude further North Vietnamese support of insurgency
in the south. No supplies, no men, nothing would move from
north to south. Armour, artillery and air forces could all be effectively employed. Our naval power would control the Gulf of
Tonkin and we could also patrol the Mekong to prevent attempts
to flank the barrier. An air base, Seno, existed near Savannakhet
that could be expanded to facilitate resupply. And, as of early
1963, the newly constructed air base at Nakorn Phanom was in a
position to provide all kinds of support. The Pentagon estimated
that approximately 200,000 troops would be required to defend
the barrier. That number could have included, or been augmented
by, Allied troops such as the Australians or the Koreans.

The plan was feasible and could definitely have been implemented. There were many advantages. Our force would have been
centralized in one place. The advantages of our superior air,
artillery and armour firepower could have been effectively
employed. Our troops, assuming we manned the barrier, would
have been fighting from fortified defensive positions and therefore
have been less vulnerable. Forcing the North Vietnamese to come
to us, as opposed to chasing them around the jungles in South
Vietnam, would doubtless have been preferable to the tactics ultimately employed. We'll put up this barrier, the plan said, and
leave the problems in South Vietnam to the South Vietnamese.
And the South Vietnamese, recipients of all the aid we gave them,
fighting only 'home-grown' insurgents, might well have prevailed.
But, as history has recorded, the plan was rejected. Political decisions, taken without vision and without a clear understanding of
what was actually happening on the ground, foiled an effort that
would have struck at the core of the problem in South-East Asia
at the time. It was a sin of omission. Instead, the same political
leaders, who backed away from a decision to put 200,000 troops

across Laos and Vietnam in late 1961, adopted a policy of incrementalism and ultimately deployed over 500,000 troops into the jungles of South Vietnam. In retrospect, one has to question how we let that happen.

Second, and I have already alluded to it, is the disaster that befell the Hmong as a result of US policies in Laos. Unknowingly, Vang Pao's discussion in late 1960 with Bill Lair was the beginning of more than a decade of warfare and hardship for his people. Neither man could have foreseen, at that time, what was to happen.

From its origins as an effort to organize and train a people, the Hmong, to resist communist encroachment via guerrilla, I repeat guerrilla, tactics, the programme grew, incrementally, to become a direct challenge, not just to the PL forces in Laos, but to North Vietnam. It was a mismatch. Despite our best efforts, and despite the employment of the full range of our superpower air support, the Hmong were slowly decimated. No one wanted it to happen, but it happened. It came on the heels of one decision after another, from the mid-1960s onwards, which upped the ante and pushed the Hmong further onto the point.

More training, larger units, increased firepower and air support, all were introduced little by little. US policies in South Vietnam drove decisions in Laos. The Hmong must have seen what was happening, but they carried on. Vang Pao not only agreed to these decisions, he actually pressed for many of the offensive actions taken as the conflict wore on. But his decisions were clouded, I think, by the 'stars' around him: his own, as he was promoted up to lieutenant general, and those of the generals and ambassadors with whom he now was an equal. He believed that US power ultimately would save him, and the Hmong.

Long Tieng, although under intense military attack in 1972, never fell. Yet when the war ended in South Vietnam in late April 1975, it also ended in Laos. We accepted a political agreement that allowed the communists to seize power. And then we left; we simply walked out. This was a sin of commission for which the Hmong, our staunch allies for more than a decade, are still suffering. Was it unintended? Yes. Would that it had been handled differently. Was any lesson learned? Ask the Kurds in the north of Iraq.

NINE

THE BAMBOO CURTAIN

1969–73

It was the same approach I had made in 1962 on my way to Laos. We came in from the South China Sea, over Tung Lung Island and through the corridor formed by Hong Kong Island and the mainland. Again we flew over the waters of Hong Kong harbour until touchdown at the end of Kai Tak airport's long main runway, which jutted far out into the harbour.

But it was now March 1969 and things were dramatically different for me this time. Judy and I had married on 1 September 1968 in Bulpitt, Illinois. (One of Dr Duffy's last operations left me with a large bandage on my right hand that was in the photos and went with us on our honeymoon.) Suzanne, now a delightful three year old, clearly emphasized how much my life had changed. Moreover, Judy was, in biblical terms, great with child.

I was arriving to fill a position in our Hong Kong office headed by Charlie Whitehurst. This would be my first tour as a case officer. My career was, finally, back on track. The crash in the Congo had precipitated a long and difficult period of 'getting ready' to get back to work and I was anxious to find out what, exactly, my tasks would be.

The Hong Kong office's primary and dominant focus was China. (The same was true for the State Department's officers, who were housed in the Consulate General building on Garden Road on Hong Kong Island.) We were China watchers. And China watching was an all-consuming task, a task greatly complicated by the 'Bamboo Curtain' China had erected on its borders.

The Cold War was beginning its third decade. China's communist ruler, Mao Tse Tung, was running a country that was completely cut off from the rest of the world. And, at the time, China was in the midst of the Great Cultural Revolution (1966–76), which, ultimately, took a terrible toll on its people.

The British Crown Colony of Hong Kong, which had been wrested from China as a result of the Opium Wars in the mid-nineteenth century, was both a listening and watching post for the West. For China, it functioned as a window to the West. For want of any alternative, the American Consulate in Hong Kong (technically a Consulate of the Embassy in London) functioned like an Embassy. Our office in Hong Kong was tasked with running clandestine operations to gather intelligence for US policy makers on political, military and economic developments in China. Given the circumstances, it was a difficult task. China was, in our parlance, a 'denied area'.

After returning to work in the spring of 1967, I had worked on a desk, providing basic support for operations. It was Headquarters at its worst, but since I was a junior case officer, I could expect nothing different. The work was minimally challenging, but it was important that it was done thoroughly and carefully. Many of the safeguards built into the Clandestine Service's system are dependent upon the quality of work accomplished at desk level. Name traces, operational reviews, collection requirements, counter-intelligence guidance, budget preparation and cover issues were all part of the desk officers' daily effort. Despite the tedium involved, I knew that experience working on a desk in Headquarters was important and it was essential that field operations officers understood fully what types of support Headquarters could provide. Still, it must be said that work at Headquarters was the main reason behind the desire of the vast majority of operations officers to serve in field stations abroad. Being in 'front line' field positions was where the action and excitement were.

By January 1968, I was getting restless and figured that I had had about as much of this 'valuable' experience as I required. I wanted to get out to the field on a regular operations tour. My only field experience to date had been in paramilitary work and I needed, I thought, to get some experience running clandestine operations in the field. As was the case with operations aimed at the Soviet Union (also a 'denied area'), the efforts of China Operations were global so there were many options open to me as I considered what to ask for as a field tour. I wanted to be as close to the target country as possible. Hong Kong was my first choice. That would certainly be feasible, I was told, but what about the language? China Operations preferred its operations officers to have solid Chinese language skills. Despite my eagerness to get to the field again, I knew that it made sense to be language qualified so I agreed to sign up for the two-year Mandarin Chinese training course. It consisted of one year in Washington and one year in Taiwan. I had mulled it over for a couple of weeks. It would prolong the 'getting ready' phase, I knew, but in the long run it would be worth it.

While I was weighing the field tour, and related language questions, Judy made her announcement about a tour in Taiwan for her, with the results that I have already described. I proposed marriage and she accepted. It was definitely an eventful month that was to shape the rest of my life.

I started Mandarin language-training in July, and after Judy and I were married in September we moved into an apartment near the language school in Rosslyn (just across the Potomac from Georgetown) in anticipation of moving into a new house we had purchased in McLean, which would be completed in early fall.

Chinese came easily to me for reasons I can't really explain. Part of it was the fact that I was well grounded in Thai, also a tonal language. But Chinese grammar is not particularly difficult and the effort boils down to memorization and hard work. It also takes a good ear for languages, I think, and the fact that I also had Spanish and French probably helped. I progressed rapidly and tested high for the first period of our training. Then came a decision point.

I found out that there was a vacant position in Hong Kong for which I would be qualified. Should I continue the Chinese training by moving on to the school in Taiwan, or should I go directly to Hong Kong and start working? I was given a choice and I discussed it with Judy. In fact, I knew what I wanted to do and she sensed it right away. I wanted to go to Hong Kong and start working. I had a good jump on my Chinese, I reasoned, and I could continue my studies with a tutor in Hong Kong. 'Let's go,' I said. Judy agreed.

As soon as the decision to go to Hong Kong had been taken, we told Wally and Mary Deuel, whom we had continued to see regularly. They particularly enjoyed seeing Suzanne and delighted in each new phase she entered. They understood our decision, but were nonetheless saddened at the prospect of the separation. Neither of them enjoyed good health and the future was uncertain. We enjoyed a departure dinner with them and then visited our respective families as we headed for Hong Kong.

The welcome we received upon our arrival in Hong Kong was, I thought, especially warm. The support staff had been particularly thoughtful and the problems associated with settling in were minimal. From the selections open to us, we picked an apartment on the South China Sea side of Hong Kong Island at Repulse Bay. There had been massive civil unrest and rioting during 1967 and 1968 caused by the start of the Cultural Revolution on the mainland and as a result we were all required to live on Hong Kong Island to preclude the possibility of being cut off during a time of crisis.

An oft-repeated story about decisions taken after the 1968 rioting is worth relating. In earlier periods, many Consulate personnel, especially those with families and small children, enjoyed living on the Kowloon peninsula. In its wisdom, the US government had purchased literally dozens of pleasant little houses not too far up the peninsula from Hong Kong harbour. It provided what was, to some, a welcome alternative to living in a high-rise apartment on Hong Kong Island.

Shaken by the disruptions and unrest caused by the 1968 riots, however, that same wise government reassessed its housing policy and a decision was made to move all personnel onto Hong Kong Island. The question of what to do with the government-owned houses then arose. Keep them and rent them out until things settled down? No. A Consulate administration officer was heard to brag about the fact that he had sold ('unloaded') forty-three houses. In the depressed real estate market of early 1969 he lost money on the sales, but following Washington's orders, he felt it was a great effort on his part. Just a couple of years later, those houses would have been worth a small (no, a large) fortune and many people would have loved the option of living on the Kowloon side of the harbour. Today, with the Consulate renting 'apartments' for upwards of $10,000 per month, those houses would be a godsend. One questions why some decisions ever get approved.

I was anxious for my first meeting with Whitey as he had given no hint of my assignment in the cable traffic. We met at nine o'clock on my second day in the city. After welcoming me to Hong Kong, we got down to business.

'I have some problems,' he said, 'and I'd like you to sort things out.'

I was a little puzzled. What kind of problems could I help with? I still had a way to go with my Mandarin, and I had no field experience yet with classical intelligence operations. And there were no paramilitary operations being run in Hong Kong, at least that I knew of.

Whitey continued. 'Our operational support structure is way out of whack, Dick, and it needs some careful attention.'

I'm sure he saw the look of disappointment that appeared on my face as I replied, 'But what could I do with that?' Operational support is the nuts-and-bolts part of running clandestine operations and was not at all what I had hoped for. I wanted to get into the operations themselves.

'Don't fool yourself, Dick,' he quickly replied. 'Operational support is the backbone of our effort and it's also where we get tripped up from time to time. It demands close scrutiny and I want you to take it over. It won't be for ever, just get things squared away. We're bloated as a result of the last two years and the turmoil Hong Kong has experienced.'

There wasn't a whole lot of choice. When the Chief speaks, we listen and we comply. 'I'll give it my best shot, Whitey,' I said with as much enthusiasm as I could muster.

'Good, I'll appreciate it.' He got up to shake hands and showed me out of his office.

I met next with the Deputy Chief, Jim Lilley, whom I also knew from earlier times. Jim knew, of course, what Whitey had told me and that I would be less than pleased with that assignment. He tried to take out some of the sting.

'Whitey's right, you know,' he said. 'We need to trim down and restructure our operational support capabilities. He remembers what you put together in Laos and he thinks you are the right man to get the job done.'

'I'm a little worried that I don't know enough about Hong Kong yet,' I offered, hoping he might pick up on that point. 'It's a pretty complex place.'

'Initially you'll have to understand the problems and that will be done inside the office. You'll have time to figure things out. You're a fast learner.'

Clearly, I was facing a united front and they wanted me in the operational support job. 'I'll do the best I can,' I said.

'Down the road, you'll appreciate this experience,' Jim replied. 'And we appreciate the obvious delight with which you take on this chore,' he added to pull my chain a little. In fact, Jim was absolutely right. In subsequent tours, I would look back on the two years in Hong Kong doing operational support work as a strong base for my tradecraft skills. And when I ran offices of my own, I always paid special attention to the nuts and bolts of operational support that were, all too often, relegated to the most junior officer in the station – as Whitey had done with me.

My assignment was announced that afternoon and I reported to the offices that housed the operational support section I was to head. The man I was replacing, a mid-level officer nearing retirement, was getting ready to finish his tour and transfer back to Headquarters so there was no animosity. I didn't know if he knew how the Chief and Deputy felt the programme was doing and I wasn't about to raise it. His secretary, who was to become my secretary, was a wonderfully competent individual. I was blessed to inherit her. And one other officer, even more junior than me, also worked in the section.

As I listened to the briefings my predecessor provided, a couple of thoughts crossed my mind. It was apparent that he was burned out and, consequently, unenthusiastic, even uninterested, in his job. I had no idea why and didn't pursue the subject with him or anyone else. Second, the briefing lacked organization and structure. I was soon to discover that that was because the programme itself lacked organization and structure. For reasons difficult to trace, it had grown too fast. The programme was barely meeting needs and I quickly understood why Whitey was worried about it. Reshaping the entire programme presented a challenge I hadn't expected. Maybe doing this, for a while, would be tolerable.

Since it was a broad programme, my job quickly exposed me to the entire range of operations being run. I had been impressed while supporting Hong Kong's efforts at the Headquarters level. Now, on the scene, I was even more impressed. I worked closely with all the Branch Chiefs and felt good about the professional approach all took towards their operations. And I was pleased with my initial exposure to something other than paramilitary operations in the field. I knew several officers and had done my early training with one so I felt comfortable. Knowledge of my marching orders was widespread and all felt it important that I get on with my efforts. I had wondered how it would be to serve in a field job other than a paramilitary one and had harboured some concerns about what it would be like. The acceptance I was feeling eased those concerns.

Operational support, as any Le Carré novel will reveal, is the sum total of the adjunct operations that are required to support an ongoing clandestine operation, whether that operation be for intelligence gathering, influence, or counter-intelligence purposes. The operational support efforts, it needs to be remembered, must also be clandestine. Mistakes cause compromises, which are the worst nightmare of any field station. (For interest, many CIA agents do read novels about espionage and other intelligence subjects. As I've said, tradecraft is an art – a combination of common sense and imagination. It is also pragmatic and sometimes what we read would produce ideas that we used in the field.)

Included in the array of operations labelled operational support are 'safe houses' and accommodation addresses. The latter is an address secretly provided by an agent who likely has no other task or tie to us. It can be an apartment, a post-office box, or some variant thereof. Unopened and untampered-with mail is passed to the case officer running that operation. Obviously, the agent must have a cover story for sending something to that particular address. Hence the need for a large number of them. Basically, it is a clandestine communication channel. Also included in operational support are listening posts, surveillance teams and others, depending upon the type of operation being supported. As I took over, it was plain to see that we had a surplus of safe houses, too few reliable accommodation addresses and a weak surveillance capability – at least according to the incomplete records that existed. So I had the problem figured out. Solving it would be another matter.

For safe houses, my first goal was to reduce our holdings by half. But that decision was the easy part. Which ones would go and which ones would continue to be operationally useful? That would be harder and would require some careful analysis. A part of the information needed to make rational decisions was knowledge of the city itself and specific neighbourhoods. There were, for example, parts of Hong Kong where Caucasians were rarely seen. Going to a safe house in such an area would arouse unwanted interest and could prompt a security problem. Except for our ethnic Chinese officers, we would avoid such areas. In essence, I needed to be sure that our safe-house inventory blended as closely as possible with our operational needs. That would take some doing considering the numbers I was looking at.

It was time for me to get out on the streets of Hong Kong to see what was going on. It was not going to be easy; Hong Kong was bigger and certainly more complex than it seemed on a map. The city was like a large onion. The more layers you peeled away, the better you got to know the city, but, especially for a non-Chinese, there were always more layers. But it had to be done. In fact any operations officer must have a thorough knowledge of the city and region in which he or she works, but I felt that with my particular responsibilities I should be a reference point and therefore needed a lot more knowledge than my colleagues.

So I started a systematic scouring of all parts of the colony, both the Hong Kong and Kowloon sides, that we might possibly use for an operational venue. I rode every bus, trolley and ferry line in the colony. I also used taxis and mini buses to move around. Then I started walking through neighbourhoods and would stop for tea, lunch, shopping, or some other reason just to get a feel for that particular area. Which dialect of Chinese was spoken? (It was usually Cantonese, but other dialects were used in specific places.) Were there any English speakers? Blue-collar working-class or could others mix in? Criminal elements, gangs? Did any Caucasians live in the neighbourhood? Actually, it was quite interesting and, over time, I became very familiar with most areas of the colony. Few questions came up that I couldn't answer or find the answer to. For months I allocated several days or half days per week to this effort. I felt it paid off. In my discussions with operations officers, Branch Chiefs, or even Whitey and Jim, I could present solid reasons for keeping, acquiring, or dropping a particular safe house.

The database I built was equally useful when preparing cables and dispatches for Headquarters as I could pre-empt questions and concerns about security. There were few problems with Headquarters, however, as they were pleased with Whitey's decision to scrub our operational support holdings. Given the number of related issues that were involved – length of leases, cover, life of a given operation – it took the better part of my first year in Hong Kong to reach the point where I felt comfortable with the safe-house picture. At that point, we had fewer than half the number of safe houses we held when I arrived. Whitey was pleased as was the new Deputy Chief, Bob M., who had replaced Lilley in the summer of 1969.

With the other operational support 'tools' we had a different problem. Too few accommodation addresses was something that needed to be addressed and the answer was simple. We needed more assets in our stable. While I would be able to weed out over-used or inappropriate addresses, acquiring new ones was a pressing need. Whitey held regular staff meetings in his office with his deputy, the Branch Chiefs, reports chief and support chief in attendance. Given my responsibilities, even ones so lacking in glamour as operational support, I sometimes attended and, at one of those meetings about six months after my arrival, I voiced my concerns about the accommodation address issue. Further, I proposed a priority effort to bring on board some new agents. Pretty routine stuff actually, but the response was only grudgingly positive. It was clear they were thinking, *like we don't have enough to do already*. But Whitey deemed it a worthwhile proposal and the others fell into line. Part of the issue was that we also supported other field offices and Whitey took that responsibility seriously. Our programme took an upward turn, but even after twenty months, when I left the operational support job, I was still not satisfied with our holdings.

Any office in the field can profitably employ a good surveillance team and Hong Kong was no exception. In fact, the enterprising and imaginative fabricators in Hong Kong, and there were many, made our needs all the more pressing. Well aware of the thirst for information by China watchers of all stripes, there were those in Hong Kong who were more than willing to co-operate (either overtly or covertly) by providing information. Many, however, simply fabricated reporting, documents, photos, or tapes to hand over as authentic information about China. Given the difficulty of verifying the information caused by China's closed borders and total censorship, these 'fabricators' were a constant worry. They are anywhere, of course, but the circumstances in Hong Kong exacerbated the problem. All of which is to say that we needed a better surveillance team and I took steps to build such a capability – a far more difficult task than I had anticipated.

There was a host of problems and obstacles to be overcome, but before I left the operations support position, we did have a team of young men that we could deploy on demand. After recruitment, weeks of on-the-street training, photo and communications training, and vetting had been required. But ultimately it paid off. On one occasion, the team supplied us with clear, unmistakable photos that unmasked a would-be fabricator. The product of their efforts allowed us to break off contact without having been hoodwinked. It was seldom that easy and the photos were invaluable.

While all of my initial impressions had been favourable, as I spent more and more time in our Hong Kong office, I grew ever more positive. I found my colleagues, be they peers or senior officers, to be almost uniformly competent, well motivated and professional. We were very serious about our tasks and our responsibility to provide solid intelligence to the policy makers in Washington. Most, including Branch Chiefs, spoke good Chinese. (My own Mandarin, with the help of a tutor in the Consulate, continued to improve, but it had been a mistake, I concluded, to avoid the year in Taiwan. I would not attain the levels routinely reached at that school.) Our ethnic Chinese officers spoke more than one dialect, and that made them particularly effective. Despite varied backgrounds, we had no problems working together. There was competition, of course, some of it fostered and some not, but I found it to be a healthy and positive competition.

There were, however, some troubling aspects to what we were tasked to do. I found it difficult, for example, to support the covert action programmes. While covert action certainly had been effective in post-Second World War Europe (many examples had been described to us in our training), I had my doubts about the effectiveness of influence or media operations in Hong Kong. The Chinese I knew in Hong Kong worried about economics. Making a living and saving enough money to get out of Hong Kong if necessary was the focus. Politics in general, including the conflicts between capitalism and communism and the merits of one or the other ran far behind. Articles about those subjects would find, I thought, few readers and were not worth the resources expended.

And the goals of the programme aimed at China itself 'to light prairie fires of discontent across the plains of south China', as a Headquarters' colleague put it, were unrealistic. Hopelessly unrealistic, I thought. Resources spent on those programmes were, in my view, ill-spent. Some of my colleagues agreed with me, but Headquarters was unmoved by the few sounds of disagreement that reached Washington. The covert action stalwarts were well entrenched at Headquarters despite the ongoing debate within the Service about the merits of covert-action activities.

This was not, of course, a new issue. Debate had been ongoing since the Agency's creation and events such as the Bay of Pigs débâcle in 1961 had enlivened the arguments of both sides. Explanations aplenty had been provided, but no closure was reached. I should make clear, I think, that even in my initial training I was one who questioned the value of some covert-action operations. I'm still in that camp.

And I speak here of two basic types of covert actions. One is designed to influence the thinking of a specific portion of a target population. To accomplish the desired goal (often either political or economic), a specific individual or placements in various organs of the mass media can be used. The second features a more direct approach and, like the Bay of Pigs, or the 'Secret War' in Laos, is designed to change the landscape. Either one envisions activity in that grey area between diplomacy and military force. Covert action is an option that has been employed by many presidents. I doubted in my training days and in Hong Kong, and thirty-five years later I still doubt, the efficacy of 'influence' operations, especially in Third World environments. On the other hand, operations like the effort in Laos, or the support rendered to the mujahidin in Afghanistan during the 1980s, can produce results directly responsive to the tasking we had been given.

The action-oriented operations, however, raise perplexing questions, such as: What are the chances for success? Why should the Clandestine Service be tasked? The answer is that a carefully planned and well-executed covert operation can, in a given situation, provide exactly the alternative (to diplomacy or military force) that a president needs. And, given the need for secrecy (or at least plausible denial), the Agency, in particular the Clandestine Service, is the only arm of the US government that can carry out such operations.

While I think that both parts of my answer are correct, I also think they only tell part of the story. It is the aftermath of such efforts that is sometimes frustrating and even harmful. If a covert operation goes well, nothing is said; nor should anything be said. But if one of these risky operations is compromised or fails, the Agency and the Clandestine Service suffer serious criticism and the 'rogue elephant' line springs forth. (This phrase, used to describe CIA activities as 'wild' and 'out of control' was first coined by Senator Frank Church during the initial phases of his committee's investigations of the Agency during the mid-1970s. The press loved it. Interestingly, when the investigation had been completed, Church retracted his characterization of the Agency as a rogue elephant. He had concluded, he said, that with few exceptions the Agency acted only on the orders of the President and the National Security Council. Church's retraction got less press play. Unfortunately, the label stuck and critics still use it when it suits their purposes.) I'd like to stress this: a Presidential Finding, the full knowledge and approval of the National Security Council, and a congressional briefing (oversight committees since the mid-1970s) are all required to initiate an operation.

The foreign policy community, which originated, or applauded, the idea for a covert operation and approved its execution, simply melts into the background leaving the Agency to explain, as best it can, what happened. This is par for the course in Washington, but that doesn't lessen the frustration for the Clandestine Service. We are the arm of the government that can execute these operations and we are not in a position to say, 'No, Mr President, we won't accept that tasking.' It's a dammed if you do and dammed if you don't dilemma for the Agency. This is an issue that has arisen often over the years. I have no answers. Will Washington politicians voice the courage of their convictions? (If they actually have any and I know that some do.) That is not likely. But that covert operations, to which we devote about 10 per cent of our efforts on average, should cause 90 per cent of the grief we experience continues to be troubling.

Apart from covert action, towards which I harboured serious doubts, I was fully on-board with our operational efforts. Directing the bulk of our resources towards the high priority target of China was perfectly logical and we pursued those efforts vigorously. But it was a hard slog. A portion of the effort was aimed at developing relationships with individuals who had direct access to the mainland. They were a wary group and arduous work was required to ferret them out, meet them, and then try to develop a relationship. Meticulous security procedures at Lowu, the border crossing point into China from the colony, alerted anyone entering China to the potential dangers they would risk by running afoul of the Chinese security services – an obvious possibility if they agreed to co-operate with us.

Chinese, other Asians and Europeans were essentially the group with which we tried to establish contact. The efforts produced regular successes and provided a steady flow of intelligence information on China. Despite my primary responsibility for operational support activities, I was also tasked with attempting to develop intelligence-collection operations and I spent lots of time doing just that. As things turned out, I had successes in the operational support arena mainly with Chinese and in other areas with Europeans. In the latter area, I was able to develop several close relationships that produced a steady flow of economic information about what China was buying and what little they were exporting. I was also interested, of course, in diplomats who were serving in China. Many of them visited Hong Kong regularly and were therefore accessible for discussions or debriefings.

In late 1969, I discovered that a French diplomat due for a posting in China during the summer of 1970 was going to give a course in contemporary French history, in French, at the University of Hong Kong starting in January 1970. It piqued my interest right away. First, I would no doubt learn from the content of the course. Moreover, I might get to know him personally, which would facilitate discussion about China whenever he visited Hong Kong. And lastly, it represented an opportunity to refresh my rusty French-language skills. I enrolled.

It was a once a week evening class. His lectures were interesting and happily, his French was clear and moderately paced. The period we were looking at started in 1870 and he covered some interesting subjects. I made a point of going up to see him after the classes to ask some question or compliment him on the content of that particular lecture. He was pleasant and approachable. That I had lived in France, and was interested in French history, were points in my favour. And I knew my French was improving. So far so good.

The course progressed and we came to the First World War. His emphasis, logically enough I thought, was on the French role in the combined effort to defeat the Germans. But I was surprised at what I perceived to be his exaggeration of what the French did – he seemed to downplay the contribution of the American and English forces. I chalked that up to French pride, concluding that, although I thought it was skewed, it was his view. I said nothing to him about my thoughts. His lecture about the 1920s and early 1930s in France was mostly new to me and informative. It seemed designed to set the scene for what was to follow.

Then came his lectures – there were two – on the Second World War. I was startled at how distorted they seemed compared to what I had learned and read. At the same time, I found it interesting to listen to someone articulate a different version of history than that described in American history books. For him, it was 'La France' ever glorious, triumphant, Charles de Gaulle, the Resistance movement, the liberation of Paris. Oh yes, there was that landing at Normandy and the Americans and British did help some, but in essence, he made clear, the French flat-whipped Hitler's butt.

Glossed over, or unmentioned, were issues such as the Vichy

government's co-operation with the Germans, the questionable record of the Resistance movement and its penetration by communist elements that later posed problems in post-war France. The deportation of thousands of French Jews and France's total reliance on the Allies for the war material with which to participate in the battle against Nazi Germany were also unmentioned. It really did seem to be too much this time. So, knowing that it might have been against my own best interests to rock the boat, I still could not resist approaching him after the second lecture to pose some pointed questions. Predictably, he became prickly as he explained his version and interpretation of what I thought were clear facts. The issues I pointed out gave emphasis to the wrong things, he concluded. Sensing that I had already done harm to our relationship, I didn't press my points. Two weeks later, I called him to propose lunch together and discovered that his assignment had been cancelled for budgetary reasons and he was returning to France. So much for twelve lectures on the history of contemporary France. I missed out on what might have been interesting discussions about China whenever he visited Hong Kong, but I did learn a lot about France and that made the effort worthwhile.

Just over three months after our arrival in Hong Kong, in July 1969, Judy gave birth to a beautiful baby girl, Danika Marie. We were elated. The birth was at Canossa Hospital, located just above the American Consulate in the 'mid-levels'.

Inexperienced in such things even in my early thirties, I had been very concerned when Judy told me one morning that we'd best go to the hospital. The Catholic nuns took over as soon as we arrived and I was directed into a waiting room. Soon the doctor came in to see me. He was Portuguese, recommended to us by colleagues upon arrival, and Judy had found him to be both competent and experienced.

'Would you like to assist at the birth?' he asked.

I was taken aback. I had never thought of such a thing. I had never *heard* of such a thing. Moreover, I wasn't sure what he meant by 'assisting'. A look of shock must have crossed my face. He was sympathetic.

'Do you mean be in the same room when Judy has the baby?' I responded. My thoughts were jumbled. What earthly good could I be in there? It never occurred to me that Judy might be pleased to have me there to share the experience with her. Me, in the delivery room? Nope. Couldn't fathom such a thought.

'Yes, that's right,' the doctor replied.

'No, thanks. I think I'll just wait out here,' I muttered.

The morning after Judy gave birth, I went to the hospital to visit her and the baby. We were going to decide on a name. I had been playing early morning tennis. An accidental fall on the gritty public clay court had left me with scratches on my elbow and my knee that actually looked worse than they were. It was July and it was hot. I was wearing a short-sleeved shirt and Bermuda shorts so the scratches were exposed. One of the nuns, all of whom were conscientious nurses and delightful individuals, was with Judy when I arrived and she spotted my wounds.

'It's nothing,' I told her as I approached Judy.

'But it looks terrible,' she gushed. She left and promptly returned with another nurse in tow. They made a fuss over me and insisted on cleaning and bandaging my knee and elbow. I was embarrassed.

Judy watched sympathetically for a while, then asked, 'Who's in the hospital anyway? How about some attention over here?' She was just kidding. I think.

My work was all-consuming during the first years in Hong Kong; actually my work was all-consuming throughout my career, and that was fine with me. I spent long days on research and reports writing, or on the streets involved in operational efforts and evenings in meetings with agents or work-related social activity. Often, weekends were also given over to some work. Judy understood and was not only tolerant, but helpful. Aware of my desire to further a particular relationship, she often deftly managed to give me time alone with that individual for in-depth discussions.

It was not all work, however, and we did enjoy living in and getting to know Hong Kong. We went to the beaches with the kids, who were thriving, rode ferries to the outer islands for picnics and hikes, drove up to the new territories for visits to special restaurants or hikes on the coastline, and explored the intricacies of the numerous shopping districts. Many featured specific items such as antiques, rugs, jade and other precious stones, and Oriental art. There were an almost endless number of things to do in Hong Kong and we tried to take advantage of as much as possible. We both like Oriental rugs so throughout our time in Hong Kong we learned about, shopped for and purchased many beautiful rugs from various parts of Asia and the Middle East.

We also purchased, and it would be hard for me to explain all the reasons why, a royal blue Morgan sports car. It had a leather top that required two men and a boy to put on, hence we left it off for months at a time and could sometimes be seen driving with an umbrella covering the opening between the *tonneau* and the windshield. It had a wooden frame (to give a stiff ride I guess), a sheepskin strap over the 'bonnet' ('That's the hood,' I explained as we read the owner's manual), a Triumph gearbox and engine, and everything else Morgan features. It was a great little car and Judy not only indulged me, but also enjoyed the Morgan a lot. It was actually a practical car (except for the top and the 'side curtains', which got tedious) for driving in Hong Kong where the roads were narrow and curvy and one rarely attained speeds above forty-five miles per hour. The back seat was actually a leather bench. On it, we put Suzanne and Danika and, with a long black leather strap built into the frame, secured them into place. We loved that little Morgan and enjoyed it immensely during our entire tour. It worked fine even after our third daughter, Alison, was born. All three small children fitted nicely onto the bench in the back. After being strapped in, they couldn't move, but all the trips were short ones so nobody complained. When Pia was born at the end of our fourth year, however, we knew the Morgan would have to go. Reluctantly (and foolishly) we sold it before we left Hong Kong. We both later regretted leaving it behind and wished we'd brought it home with us.

In the winter of 1971, some Chinese colleagues invited Judy and me to a 'snake dinner' in Wanchai, a district that stretches along the harbour in the middle of Hong Kong Island. It was an interesting experience. It was February, which, according to Cantonese custom, is the best time of year to eat snake because it raises the body temperature and keeps you warm in cold weather. For Hong Kong, it was indeed a cold day with the temperature in the forties. Dinner was to be in a large dining room on the second floor of a Cantonese restaurant. It had been pre-planned and would feature snakes from several different areas of south China prepared in several ways. Judy and I were the only non-Chinese, a fact not unnoticed by most who passed the table where we were seated with our friends. We started with a hot soup accompanied by a drink made from snake bile that had chrysanthemum petals floating on top. The soup wasn't bad. The drink tasted just like what you'd think snake bile should taste like – awful.

There followed a series of dishes featuring different kinds of snake that were grilled, boiled, chopped, ground up, filleted, fried and I can't remember what else. I lost count. Most weren't bad, with a taste and texture something like chicken, but the idea that one was eating a snake was hard to get out of your mind. It was tolerable if not really tasty, to our palate at least, but an experience we are unlikely to repeat.

As is inevitable if you live in a foreign culture for an extended period (unless you resist, which we definitely did not), you learn a lot about that culture. For me, it started as I began to study Mandarin, but in Hong Kong we all learned about such varied events as Chinese New Year celebrations, Dragon boat races and lion dances. It's not a conscious effort; it is simply absorbed as time passes. And it is not forgotten.

The first two years in Hong Kong passed quickly. Midway through I was offered the option of a second tour in Hong Kong after a home leave. I asked for the second tour and Headquarters approved. Early in 1971, I left the operations support position and moved into a Branch headed by Bill D. I was named as his Deputy. Our Branch was responsible for recruiting and running agents who had direct access to China and our total focus was on China. All of our officers (including Bill and excepting myself) had strong Chinese-language skills and an extensive knowledge of the political, military, and economic situation on the mainland. I was pleased with the move and eager to get into the fray, but the first couple of months in that position sped by and it was soon time for me to go on home leave.

At a party just before we left, the Deputy, Bob M., took me aside to compliment me on the results of my first tour. He was pleased, as was Whitey, he told me, with our restructured operations support capability and, in addition, I had one of the best recruitment records in the office. I was gratified to hear that my efforts had been productive – and recognized.

I had been fortunate, I felt, to serve in Hong Kong for my first tour. Whitey was an outstanding leader and his Deputy, Bob M., had been both a motivator and a teacher for me. Moreover, my colleagues and peers were, I thought, strong, ambitious officers. Years later, I was to realize how prescient I had been. We did have an exceptional group gathered together in Hong Kong at that time. Two ultimately led the Clandestine Service. At least a dozen others (that I can remember) rose to the Directorate's senior ranks and headed major Divisions, staffs and stations. Indeed, only a few did not. The success that the group as a whole achieved was exceptional and I am hard pressed to explain why it happened. I have heard of a similar phenomenon involving Berlin Base during the 1950s and wonder if there were any comparisons. Both places, however, involved intense effort against (at the time) one of the Agency's most difficult targets and perhaps those who accepted that challenge were a different breed and destined to be rewarded. Home leave, eight weeks rushing around the United States visiting our respective families and many friends, was a whirlwind of activity. Judy, pregnant, left early because of airline regulations and went straight to her mother's home in central Illinois. She took Suzanne and Danika with her for what was a gruelling trip of over twenty hours. She left in April 1971 and I followed in May. Shortly after my arrival in Illinois, Judy gave birth to another beautiful baby girl. Alison Lee was born in Springfield, Illinois. After a couple of weeks, we headed towards the East Coast.

We spent time in Washington, where I went to work for several days to check in on a variety of matters both administrative and operational. It was enjoyable to see many old friends and to compare notes on phases in our respective careers. I was behind the curve, I found, largely because of the Congo incident and its aftermath. I had gained little experience between fall 1964 and spring 1967, when I started preparing for the Hong Kong tour. So be it, I thought, I'll just have to catch up.

Discussions at Headquarters were detailed and interesting as the desk officers sought to gain a better understanding of the operations I had been handling during my first tour. The chief of the desk expressed his agreement with and admiration for the operational support restructuring and the fine-tuning I had accomplished and I told him that Whitey had made me do it. And I got some briefings on agent communication developments in anticipation of my tasking in Hong Kong. I didn't have many spare minutes while at Headquarters.

Heading back towards Hong Kong, we stopped to visit my family and managed a few days of pure relaxation (as much as is possible when travelling with three young children, one a new-born baby). It was an eventful, hectic and tiring home leave for all of us and we were actually relieved to land once again at Hong Kong's Kai Tak airport.

Events in 1971 dramatically changed the politics of Sino–American relations. The visit to Beijing of an American table-tennis team and a subsequent secret trip to China by Secretary of State Henry Kissinger were to set the stage for a visit to China by President Richard Nixon. While these events did not signal the end of the mutual suspicions and hostility that had prevailed since 1949, they did usher in a period that would feature face-to-face discussion of and debate about differences.

The Cultural Revolution raged on, however, and hard-line communists retained firm control of all aspects of life in China. And, to our regret, the Bamboo Curtain remained firmly in place. There was no loosening of the stringent security controls ever present throughout China. The increased policy level interest brought with it increased demand for intelligence collection on China. Our job would be just as hard – perhaps harder. Still, we felt somehow encouraged by what had transpired and more than willing to redouble our efforts. Now that we were talking with China, we reasoned, our policy makers needed, more than ever, good intelligence upon which to base their decisions.

Running an agent into China from Hong Kong in the early 1970s was a difficult undertaking; no less difficult than it had been before the visit of the ping-pong team. Identifying individuals who could obtain first-hand information on China required constant laborious sifting through our wide range of contacts and agents, then initiating contact through a variety of different ploys, developing a relationship of understanding and trust, and ultimately recruitment to service our requirements were obligatory steps. Essential tradecraft training was next. We felt a great sense of responsibility for the security of our agents and none would be asked, or permitted, to enter China without full testing for reliability and training for survival.

On the one hand, we knew how vulnerable we were to fabrication and deception by the conmen operating in Hong Kong. We employed as much operational testing as possible to confirm our agent's identity, background and intentions. But there were built-in limitations. At best, we might be able to confirm that an agent had entered China. Beyond that we had no capability and had to employ analysis and research to verify what we were told by the agent.

On the other hand, it was unthinkable to send in an agent without having provided all the training and necessary equipment we could to protect him while penetrating the Chinese security blanket. It started right in Hong Kong where we knew the Chinese security and intelligence services operated actively. Compartmenting our operations from scrutiny by any other service, friendly or not, was of paramount importance. Careful use of various tradecraft methods was imperative. Training the agent often required long hours of repetitive execution of a certain technique such as microdot retrieval. There were no short-cuts. These were issues we dealt with on a daily basis. In sum, they amounted to what it takes to run a clandestine operation into a denied area. It's a difficult and complex activity with, literally, life-and-death consequences. The high risks involved served as a great motivator to the operations officer running the case. While an agent, who accepted our tasking for ideological or financial reasons, made his own assessments of the level of risk involved, we never lost sight of the fact that imprisonment or execution faced the agent who was ill-prepared or made a stupid mistake.

And we did suffer the loss of agents. Not often, but each one caused sadness and much reflection, and prompted efforts on our part to discover and understand what had gone wrong. Typically we would become aware of the arrest by the Public Security Bureau (the PSB, China's internal security organization) by reading a mainland newspaper. However we acquired the information, it was a terrible day – especially for the officer who had dispatched that agent. Cables, including our best analysis of what had caused the compromise, had to be prepared for Headquarters. The analysis was usually thin. Since the compromise and arrest had taken place on the mainland, behind the Bamboo Curtain, information about it was almost impossible to obtain and only rarely did we know much about what had happened. Conclusions drawn were not surprising. We must ensure, we wrote, that the training provided and the technology employed be of the highest level in order that each agent be capable of defeating the PSB's comprehensive security network.

There were, we knew, many Chinese communist officials and sympathizers living in the colony. Some worked in companies associated with the Chinese government, and some were journalists, intelligence officers and bankers. Another Branch was tasked to initiate operational activities aimed at identifying those individuals. Because of their access to information about the Chinese government, they would become targets for recruitment as agents. These individuals were well aware of our presence in Hong Kong and extremely wary of any approach. The officers working in this Branch faced a challenge every bit as difficult as we did. In fact, as we moved around Hong Kong, each of us was on the lookout for individuals of possible interest to our programmes in general. Sorting out which Branch would handle him could be done in due course; the priority was to establish the initial contact. Various methods like club memberships, newspaper ads and access agents were used to enhance our efforts.

We had to be careful with the selection, vetting and initial development of new contacts. No matter which Branch handled the contact, it was essential to determine just what actual access he might have and what the dangers were that he was either a fabricator or was controlled by another service hoping to penetrate our programme. File and name checks were standard vetting procedures for the initial data we obtained, but always the first contact had to be accomplished and that was often telephonic. A meeting site was agreed upon and our officer must then make that meeting. Counter-surveillance, to rule out knowledge by another service that we were making contact with that person, was imperative – and, in Hong Kong, difficult. I recall my first efforts.

For starters, my training in counter surveillance was eight years old. Moreover, that training had been less than sophisticated. Compared to current training, it was like the difference between an eighth-grade education and a Ph.D. I don't say this critically because my trainers did the best they could. It was simply a fact of life. We have learned much over the ensuing years and we are vastly improved.

I sought some advice from colleagues and ventured forth. Clearly, my knowledge of the streets and transportation networks in the colony was of great value, as was the time I spent training our own team. Even so, when an operational contact is on the line, you can't be too careful. Leaving the office, my first mistake I would later learn, I proceeded into the central district with the goal of determining if I was being followed. The odds were against me, and my colleagues faced the same problems. Central District just below our office was, at almost any time of the day, stuffed with people. The crowds were everywhere. And they were 95 per cent Chinese. They were mostly the same size, with black hair and even similar clothing. No way could I single out a suspect surveillant. The narrow streets, heavy traffic and numerous alleyways compounded the problems.

One possible solution was to move a lot. I took ferry rides, taxi rides, tram rides and shopping excursions, always with a watchful eye, and sometimes spent a couple of hours making my way to a meeting site. At times, however, the press of work precluded spending that much time and on those occasions I was likely so obvious in the precautions I was taking that I would have signalled to a surveillant, had there been one, my concerns about surveillance. I was, however, always 'clean' when I made a meeting – or at least I thought I was.

We carefully practised our tradecraft techniques despite the obstacles Hong Kong's environment presented. We did not have, during that period, any indications that our activities were being watched by another service. This in spite of how hard I thought it was to run counter-surveillance routes in areas teeming with Chinese, who, at that time, all looked the same to me. Over time, I became much more discerning as I scanned crowds of Chinese and other Asians.

Our second two-year tour in Hong Kong was every bit as enjoyable as the first. Shortly before our home leave we were invited to join a very nice tennis club located in the 'mid-levels', the Ladies' Recreation Club. We had applied for membership immediately upon our arrival in 1969 so we had waited two years for our chance to come. Knowing that we were coming back for two more years, we jumped at the chance to become members. Featuring nine tennis courts, two swimming pools, dining rooms, bar, reading room and other first-class facilities, it was a super club that would become a great place for us to spend weekends. The kids loved the pools and when there was time, Judy and I got to play tennis. Located less than five minutes from our apartment building (we had by then moved to the 'mid-levels' from Repulse Bay), it featured a wonderful view of Hong Kong harbour.

Aided by my detailed knowledge of various areas of the colony, we systematically continued our exploration of Hong Kong. We knew many people who owned boats and often accepted invitations to spend a day on the waters of the Crown Colony. We had a wide circle of friends, Chinese and other Asians, Europeans and other Americans, and many also had young children so our kids were often a part of the weekend social activities. It was a good life.

From my tennis activities, I got to know M.W. Lo, an elderly Chinese man who was a fixture in Hong Kong social circles. He had been educated in England and subsequently enjoyed a successful career as a lawyer in Hong Kong. He had retired in the late 1950s, but was still physically and mentally active. His son carried on the family business. M.W. loved tennis and had reportedly played doubles at Wimbledon in the 1920s. He was in his late seventies when I met him and he still played an acceptable game.

M.W. lived in a large house overlooking Stanley, a small fishing village on the south side of Hong Kong Island. The house was built halfway up the mountainous spine of the island and terraced next to and below it were three grass tennis courts. All had a view out over Stanley Bay, which, on weekends, was usually filled with fishing and pleasure boats. It was a beautiful setting for tennis and I was lucky enough to become part of a group that played there on Sunday afternoons.

In addition to the tennis, which was always good, I met lots of interesting people and was able to develop some productive relationships. It was the best of two worlds. M.W. always took the best player there on a given Sunday as his partner. Those sets would be enjoyable, but tame. M.W. could only play two sets though and often sat out while others took over the court.

Much to our collective surprise, Ken Rosewall, the world-class Australian player who was in town for the Hong Kong Open tournament, showed up one Sunday to partner M.W. As honorary head of the Hong Kong tennis association, M.W. had lots of clout in the colony's tennis world. We were duly impressed. M.W. played a good set with him and then sat out. To my great delight, I then got Rosewall as my partner. As we walked onto the court, he asked if I wanted the forehand or backhand side to receive serve. Although I usually played backhand, I told him I thought it best to defer to one of the best backhands in the world. He just laughed and said that would be fine.

'How shall we play this?' he then asked me.

'Well, if I don't win with you as a partner, I'll never get invited back here,' I responded without hesitation. 'So we better win.' We did, with him not trying to intimidate anyone, just making the shots as necessary. It was quite a thrill for me to play with a player of his calibre who was also a true gentleman.

Also through tennis (which was to be a valuable icebreaker for me throughout my career), I met Jean Ingles, the private secretary to the Governor of Hong Kong. Jean, a typical British civil servant, had lived in Hong Kong for years and been secretary to several governors. A delightful person, whom we came to like very much, Jean invited us to play mixed doubles regularly on the three clay courts at the governor's mansion. The governor didn't play and she had access at any time she wanted it. Again it was great for two reasons – the tennis and the people we met. Although slightly less so in this instance because the mixed doubles we played was less demanding, and the people we met were all European. Still, the conversations we had when we broke for 'tea' were always interesting and informative.

I have to say that neither Judy nor I could understand more than about half of the conversations at tea when we first started accepting Jean's invitations. We simply couldn't pick up the accent of the mostly British people who were there or the nuances of word usage. We were shocked at not being able to understand 'English' and they were amused by our American 'dialect'. Soon, of course, we tuned in and had no problems.

I should also record that Judy, perhaps in self-defence and to be able to go with me instead of saying, 'Have a nice game', took up tennis (in between having babies) during our first tour in Hong Kong. As with most other things she tries, she picked it up quickly and within a year she had a very respectable game. She was strong, athletic and had good hand–eye co-ordination (having been a tomboy softball player in her youth) so her progress was swift. She had started out in 1970 (using a butterfly brand bamboo racket made in Shanghai), taking weekly lessons from Charlie Chan (that was indeed his name), a freelance instructor at a local public court, and by late 1971 was playing regularly at the club and elsewhere. She's an impressive lady.

In January 1973, fortunes for the Agency took a definite downturn and, although we didn't know it at the time, several years of turmoil began. In late November 1972, after having been re-elected in what politicians and pundits like to call a 'landslide', President Nixon fired Dick Helms, our Director. I now know that their relationship had been strained for a long time because of differences over Vietnam and Helms's reluctance about deeper Agency involvement. In addition Helms had refused when Nixon asked him to cite national security reasons as part of his (Nixon's) efforts to cover-up the Watergate burglary. That refusal was apparently the last straw.

At the time, however, as a mid-level officer in the field, I was stunned. Why? I asked myself. Partly I'm sure, because of the role he played in my Congo adventure and his visit to Walter Reed to see me, but also because I respected his ability and his leadership, I liked Helms, as did my peers and I think most in the Agency. He was one of us. What could have prompted Nixon's decision? Vietnam and Watergate were the answers, but I couldn't put that together at the time. A general uneasiness set in.

Within a short time, Nixon named James Schlesinger to be our new Director. He would be my fifth. Schlesinger? Who is Schlesinger? we asked each other. What does he know about intelligence? He's a career bureaucrat, a political decision. Doubt, dismay and concern were voiced throughout the office. James Schlesinger took over as Director in early February 1973.

It didn't take long for our questions to be answered. Even far from Washington and even from my distant view of the reins of power, effects of Schlesinger's 'reign' were soon felt. The Directorate of Plans, the Clandestine Service, would be renamed,

Schlesinger decreed. Henceforth it would be the Directorate of Operations to recognize the true nature of its activities. (None of us liked the new name – mostly, I think, because it was Schlesinger's idea. Had Helms done it, few would have complained.) Worse, he announced a drastic reduction in force for the Agency. More than 1,500 people were fired or forced to resign or retire. Of that total, over a thousand would be cut from the Clandestine Service. Again we were dismayed and, as panels set to work to determine who would go and who would stay, tensions mounted. None would be let go from field positions we assumed – or hoped.

Our hopes were dashed when word came from Headquarters that two of our officers would leave the service. Morale fell to the lowest point I had seen in my twelve years of service. The decisions regarding our two officers were appealed, but the appeals were rejected and, within months, both officers departed. As word reached us via the grapevine, it became clear that Schlesinger planned to shift priority (and resources) to 'technical' operations as opposed to the human source operations we were running in the Clandestine Service. Morale sank even lower. Schlesinger was flat wrong, of that we had no doubt at all. But we were powerless, as was our Directorate. (In this instance as well, I think, the fact that it was Schlesinger calling the shots made it particularly hard to take. Many realized that our involvement in Vietnam and Laos had left us with more officers than we needed. Had it been Helms mandating the cuts they would have been more readily accepted. But coming from Schlesinger, especially given his stated intention of reducing the size and importance of the Clandestine Service, it was hard to swallow.)

Then Schlesinger moved to reorganize the Agency. That would entail more drastic change. The 'Contact Division', an overt intelligence collection operation responsible for debriefing Americans who had travelled abroad, would lose its separate status, Schlesinger decided. Instead, it would be moved into the Directorate of Operations! Mix an overt office with the Clandestine Service? What sense did that make? This man is a real disaster, was the conclusion most reached. Other moves followed. None were to our collective liking. To say that Schlesinger was unpopular, especially within the newly named Directorate of

Operations, would have been a considerable understatement. From our perspective he didn't understand the Agency, he didn't like the Agency, and he didn't give a damn about the Agency's future. That he was able to make such a negative impression in such a short period of time is actually quite remarkable.

In addition to our woes with Schlesinger, 1973 opened with a number of other body blows to the Agency in general, and to the Clandestine Service in particular. In January a *New York Times* profile about Cord Meyers, one of our stalwarts, was published and its thrust was negative. Daniel Ellsberg's trial, the famous Pentagon Papers trial, started in January. Ellsberg, a Pentagon analyst, strongly disagreed with US policy in Vietnam and decided, on his own, to make public a batch of classified Pentagon policy papers. *The New York Times* published those papers and the government took Ellsberg to trial. A retired CIA employee, Howard Hunt, was involved in a break in at Ellsberg's psychiatrist's office. The Agency was accused of some kind of plot and in early March, when Schlesinger's personnel cuts were announced, the press speculated about a possible connection with the Ellsberg trial. In April, a book titled *The Politics of Lying* by David Wise, an Agency critic, was published and it added to the cascade of negative press and feeling about the Agency. There were others that I won't list, but suffice to say it was a miserable period for all of us. I was happy to be in the field, but knew that come summer I would be returning to Headquarters.

In April 1973, just months before we left Hong Kong, Pia Kristina, yet another beautiful baby girl, was born in Canossa Hospital. We were delighted, as were her sisters. Not so the waiters at the Chinese restaurant in Happy Valley where we regularly went for dinner on Sunday evenings. They watched as we arrived in Hong Kong with a daughter and soon had two. Then we returned from home leave in 1971 with another daughter. They were polite, but plainly distressed and felt sorry – for me. Now we walked in with another baby and they flocked to see it. Another girl! This time they couldn't conceal their disappointment. How awful it wasn't a boy, they told me. It was a clear reflection of the cultural gap that existed between us. We had a perfect baby and couldn't be happier. They, on the other hand, just couldn't bear to see me without a son. Never mind, one of them finally consoled me, now you have the four legs of the table, next time you will get the top. I nodded sagely, and proceeded to order dinner.

That was spring 1973. Judy and I visited Hong Kong again in the fall of 1997 and stopped to eat in the same restaurant. The waiter who consoled me was still there and recognized me. At another favourite restaurant a few years earlier, the Spring Deer, on the Kowloon side of the harbour, the *maître d'* came running up and said, 'Oh, Mr Holm, I not see you for a long time.' It had been seventeen years. He had quite a memory. And of course, thanks to my Congo experience and the scars it left, people don't easily forget me.

Also in the spring of 1973, in May, William Colby, the Agency's number three leader as the Executive Officer, and General Vernon Walters, the Deputy Director of the Agency, visited Hong Kong. I was invited to cocktails at the Chief's house and met with them both during the evening. Colby was congenial and willingly answered questions we posed about what the hell was going on at Headquarters. Walters was also friendly and lived up to his reputation as a raconteur.

It was during that evening that word came in an immediate cable that Schlesinger had been named Secretary of Defense and would be leaving the Agency within days. We literally cheered the news. But there was more. Nixon had nominated Colby to replace Schlesinger. This was super news indeed. One of 'us' was in charge again. Certainly Colby, who would be my sixth Director, could stem the tide and repair the damage Schlesinger had inflicted, I thought.

In the course of that trip to the Far East, Colby the subordinate to Walters became Colby the Director. Strange are the ways of Washington, I remember thinking. But Nixon finally got it right. Again I had no idea that it was the tightening Watergate noose that likely prompted Nixon's decision. For us though, Schlesinger's brief, February to May, tenure had been a nightmare and we were delighted to see it end. But our problems were far from over.

We left Hong Kong in July 1973. The challenge of travelling almost halfway around the world with four young children taxed us, but we managed (the girls were great) and I felt that everything was on track for me. I had been promoted to GS-13 in 1970 and was staying abreast of my peers. Back-to-back tours for four years in Hong Kong had gone well and I felt comfortable with all aspects of my work. I liked the field case officer work, which was what I had originally intended. I had managed, I thought, to make up for lost time and I felt lucky about that. Prospects were bright as we left Hong Kong in July 1973 for our next tour – in Headquarters.

Out of ignorance (maybe I just didn't have a complete enough picture of what was happening in Washington), or naivety, or some combination thereof, I had no fears about the future of the Clandestine Service. This despite the almost incessant bad news we had received since Helms's firing. We had continued to do our work and felt that Headquarters would just have to sort out those problems. It was a bad phase but we felt that 'this too shall pass'. Even now, many years later, I am hard pressed to remember, let alone explain, how I felt about the issues we were confronting. Maybe it speaks to how highly motivated we were. We'll be OK, I had concluded. Colby – who at the time was in the midst of a very tough confirmation process – will put things back on track.

TEN

THE AGENCY
IN TURMOIL

1973–76

Nothing much had changed at Headquarters and I didn't mind being back. Many of the same people were still around – the Headquarters cadre. And many friends, including colleagues with whom I had started my (now twelve-year-old) career, were also assigned there.

As I entered the building on my first day back, I read again the biblical quote carved into the marble wall of the main entrance to Headquarters: 'And you shall know the truth, and the truth shall make you free. John 8:32.' I remembered how impressed I had been when I read it in January 1962. I had been full of the spirit of adventure then and it was different now. The quote underscored a sense of far deeper responsibility. Laos and the Congo had provided about as much adventure as I needed, I guess. The serious business of providing high quality intelligence to our policy makers was more important to me now. And I did have a wife and four children.

The building was also unchanged except somebody had the bright idea of adding more colour in the hallways. As a result, doors were pastel coloured and there were pictures and posters on the walls to make things cheerier. Parking was still a pain. Even though I was now a mid-level officer instead of a junior one, I parked in the hinterlands and had a long walk to the building. In many ways, I felt lucky about our situation. Friends working for either the FBI or the Department of State were forced to drive daily in horrible traffic into the city, scrounge out a parking place and contend with the bureaucracy at close quarters. We were blessed, I thought, to have our wooded compound in the suburbs that offered some insulation between us and the dreaded political problems that abounded in the city. We had Allen Dulles to thank for that and we were all grateful.

We moved back into our home in McLean (which had been rented during our absence), this time filling all five bedrooms. My commute to the building was about ten minutes and our adjustment was relatively painless. We joined a country club in Vienna, a nearby suburb, and started using its tennis and swimming facilities.

In the first few months back at Headquarters, I renewed old acquaintances and established new ones. As I moved around the building, which housed not only the Clandestine Service but major portions of the three other Directorates as well, there was only a hint of the trials and tribulations the Agency had been, and still was, suffering. The issues came up in conversation, but few expressed any real concern for the future. Most felt that the storm would pass. Colby suffered nasty allegations about his background, stemming primarily from programmes he conceived of and ran while he served in Vietnam and the ongoing debate about US policy there. Many of us were frustrated and irritated that some in Congress were questioning his fitness to lead the Agency, but Colby handled the grilling with aplomb. He was no stranger to difficult and challenging situations. During the Second World War, Colby had served with distinction in the OSS and had led a small group on one particularly perilous mission – a mid-winter parachute jump into German-occupied Norway. Trained to operate behind enemy lines, they linked up with Norwegian partisans and skied, mostly at night, to a key railway line, which was in heavy use by the Germans to move crack troops from Finland, via northern Norway, back to Germany to counter invading Allied forces. They blew up the line in several places and the mission was a success. Courage, stamina and determination were required and Colby was generously endowed with all of those characteristics. In the end, allegations about him were resolved and Bill Colby was confirmed as our Director.

Don't get me wrong. It was painful for us all to read the articles and books attacking the Agency and to hear the criticisms of men like Colby and Cord Meyers. But we all believed strongly that the Agency was innocent of the charges being levelled against it and that our motives, in following the orders of a given President (or not doing so as Helms had demonstrated), were beyond reproach. The truth will out one day, we hoped, and if not, at least we know better. There was a high level of motivation in us all. We had a job to do for the country and we would, by damn, do it. That may sound corny to some, but I really think it's a fair representation of how we felt at the time.

As a China Operations officer within the Far East Division, I had been assigned to China Operations itself. My Headquarters job would be different this time, however, and promised to be more interesting. As opposed to working as a desk officer supporting a station, I was now assigned to a Branch responsible for supporting, globally, operations targeted against China or Chinese officials. The Branch was divided geographically in line with Divisions in the Directorate and, because I had French I guess, I was assigned to the European section.

In fact, I *was* the European section. I received (with copies to the relevant desk) all cable and dispatch traffic about cases being run in Europe against the China target. I was responsible for assessing the traffic, doing whatever research was required and then preparing a response to the field. This Branch was definitely a service organization designed by China Operations to encourage and support operations against the target for which we were responsible, anywhere in the world. The China target, just as difficult elsewhere as it had been in Hong Kong because of the wariness of Chinese officials to make or sustain contact with us, was being vigorously pursued, I was pleased to note. The Branch had 'referents' for each area Division including Far East Division, and we held regular staff meetings to discuss trends and operational ideas that might be suggested to the field.

Book cables (sent to all stations in the world) were prepared regularly for transmission to stations and bases worldwide. They contained background information on various aspects of the China target and suggestions on how to approach a given subject. They were general in nature as opposed to the specifically tailored guidance we would give relating to a given operation. We also met regularly with our reports officers to discuss and evaluate reporting on the China target received from stations worldwide. These were always interesting meetings, I thought, because of the substance involved. We were getting some excellent reporting, which in turn encouraged us to sustain our efforts.

The upshot of all this was a very busy day for me and I found myself working long hours including, frequently, Saturdays till about noon. Happily though, it was almost all focused on operations. Only a minimum amount of the more tedious aspects of Headquarters support were required and that was fine with me. My day would begin with a look at the traffic that had come in overnight. It was a ritual of the desk officer. As with a dairy farmer who must milk his herd daily, a desk officer, like it or not, feels compelled to read incoming traffic promptly. It was an important part, critical even, of supporting a station or operation in the field, and it simply had to be done conscientiously. Often, however, a cable did not get answered on the same day it was received so there were always issues waiting to be dealt with. And that was what filled up the rest of my day.

Meetings with European desk officers to explain or justify a cable I wanted sent out were common. I also met frequently with colleagues to mull over progress in a certain operation. And there were mountains of material to read and digest. My knowledge of the military, geographic, economic, political and social affairs in China grew significantly – and this was in addition to what I had amassed while in Hong Kong. I now had a much broader picture of what China was doing and, to the extent that I could understand it, why. China's policies were simply wrong, I concluded, and only caused suffering for the Chinese people. My anti-communist feelings, already strong, were reinforced.

There existed during that period (before and after as well, but I was more conscious of it at that time) a competition between Soviet Operations and China Operations. Both were global targets, but Soviet threats being more tangible, there was consensus that their target had a higher priority. That never sat well because we thought China was an equally serious issue for our policy makers. Debate within our Directorate about resources given over to our respective targets was low-key but persistent. It became more intense when budgets were discussed. We felt that Soviet Operations was condescending and lacked understanding. We tried to have our support to individual stations reflect the level of concern we had about the need for a strong operational programme against the China target. It was hard to say whether or not the Directorate as a whole noticed our efforts, but it made us feel better.

As had been the case in Hong Kong, I liked and respected both my peers and my superiors. The Chief of China Operations, Jim K., who had flown as tail gunner in a B-24 over Europe during the Second World War and served in Berlin Base during the late 1950s, was a gruff but likeable man. Dedicated to his work, he spent long days in the office and was adept at managing the Headquarters bureaucracy. His Deputy, Harry S., a University of Michigan graduate, had served in both Europe and the Far East and brought much experience to the job. Calm, patient and competent, he was universally well liked and respected. He later would head up Far East Division. I car pooled with him for a while and grew to know him well. And the better I knew him, the better I liked him.

My fellow referents, all at about the same grade level, were mostly China Operations officers on Headquarters tours. We all worked hard, thought we were productive and looked towards our next field tour, wherever that might be.

The Agency was enduring hard times. I had returned to Langley just as Colby was confirmed and installed as Director. For the rest of 1973 and for all of 1974 and 1975, there was enough grief to make his tenure as Director tedious indeed. Press attacks prompted President Gerald Ford (by then, Nixon had resigned over Watergate) to name his Vice President, Nelson Rockefeller, to head a commission to review accusations of wrongdoing on the Agency's part. Despite administration desires to the contrary, Congress soon took up the trail. Committees in the Senate, headed by Senator Church, and the House, headed by Representative Pike, were formed to hold hearings about Agency operations, which I have already referred to.

Hoping to head off publicity and distortions, Colby had compiled what became known as the 'family jewels', or the 'skeletons' – specific, secret, unpublished, and at that time not briefed to Congress, details about politically sensitive operations – and reported to the Rockefeller commission. Research conducted in our early years, or domestic covert actions involving student groups who opposed the Vietnam War, for example, were revealed and then thoroughly investigated by Congressional staffs. Pressures grew as Congress opened its investigations, and there was considerable 'sound, light and fury'. Assassination planning came to light – Patrice Lumumba in the Congo, Fidel Castro in Cuba – and Congress howled. These were all subjects that (while a few selected individuals on the Hill had been briefed) the executive branch (a given president actually) had until then held very closely.

Through it all, Colby took the heat and plodded onwards. Some felt many of the wounds were self-inflicted, but, except at very senior levels, few (certainly not me) had the basis to make informed decisions and no consensus was reached.

In the ranks of the Clandestine Service, these were difficult times, but the turmoil had minimal effect on our work. We knew that Colby and some of our senior (Division level and above) officers were intensely engaged with first Rockefeller and then Congressional investigators, but those activities were (effectively from my point of view) compartmented from the rest of us. We did our jobs while struggling with the substance of some of the revelations. A very small number of officers had actually been involved in the efforts under attack, so the majority of us knew little or nothing about the accusations. I either didn't believe them, or I felt they were distorted by opponents of the Agency. I rationalized. They were not subjects of much conversation and when they did come up colleagues tended to think much the same.

Books have been written on those years and the difficulties the Agency and Colby suffered and it is not my intention to labour the subject. I would only make the point that, through that awful period, the service carried on its work, albeit knowing that the Agency's image had changed in some intangible way.

As a direct result, I think, two oversight committees, one in the House of Representatives and the other in the Senate, were established to keep tabs on CIA operations. The Agency's very existence had been questioned. At the time, none of us liked it but it's a reality we have learned to live with.

I took several trips to Europe during the three years of that Headquarters tour. Each was designed to further support specific operations under way in Europe. Face to face discussions, we believed, were always better than reading a cable. When an operation had progressed to a particularly promising point, a visit would be scheduled. Usually I would stop at three or four offices just to profit from the fact that I was in Europe. Typically, travelling alone, I would make contact with the office after my arrival in the city where it was located. Then I would visit that office and have detailed discussions with the case officer running the operation that was the reason for my visit.

Often the Chief, knowing that I was there, would ask me to host an informal seminar about China Operations. I was always pleased to do so as I was eager to encourage additional effort on 'my' target. Based on my pretty solid background on the subject and my four years in Hong Kong, I was able to pass on lots of useful information. I enjoyed those sessions. I took one such trip through North Africa in the temporary absence of the Middle East referent and visited Morocco, Algeria and Tunis. For Judy, life was full and she had almost no time off from running the household and raising our 'platoon' of daughters. A break seemed a good idea and this trip offered the possibility. We got Judy's mother to come and take over the household and made plans to have Judy accompany me. It was to be the only time during my career that she went along on a business trip.

We had friends in Rabat, Andre and Cathy LeGallo, with whom she spent days while I worked and on a weekend we were able to visit Fez in the Atlas Mountains, a few hours' drive from Rabat. Judy then flew to Tunis for a few days in the Hilton hotel while I went to Algiers. I'm sure her trip was much more enjoyable than mine. Algiers was a hostile place and I marvelled at how our officers could get much done at all. But all were enthusiastic and my visit was well received. They had no active contact with the Chinese but assured me they were going to give it a try. I must add, however, that I left Algiers without much optimism about prospects for a strong China programme. Even with (or perhaps because of) my US diplomatic passport, I was hassled at the airport during my departure. I thought about the Algiers described to me by Frenchmen I knew in Bordeaux in 1959, and wondered what they would make of this decaying and hostile place. While regretting what was happening to a once beautiful city, they would probably have been as happy as I was to leave.

It was a short flight to Tunis and, as planned, I found Judy at the Hilton Hotel. She was lying in the sun beside the pool. With bright sunshine and a pleasant temperature, it would have been a perfect day but for one problem – the wind was blowing steadily at about forty miles per hour with gusts even stronger. As Judy sat up to greet me, her sunglasses were blown off her head into the pool. Tunis was experiencing a Sirocco wind. As far as I could understand from explanations given to me at the time, a Sirocco is hot air coming off the Sahara desert. It blows steadily, day and night, for several days. Not the best timing, but there was nothing to be done about it.

That evening we were invited for dinner at the Chief's residence. We took a taxi over to his house and arrived at dusk with the Sirocco still blowing. A pleasant and interesting man with considerable experience in North Africa, he was the perfect host. I wasn't that senior, but he and his charming wife went out of his way to make us feel welcome and there was very little shop talk. In fact, it was (still is) common in the field to welcome and entertain our visitors. It was something I always liked and I thought it another indication of the high calibre of people I worked with. In later years, I always took steps to see that visitors felt welcome – especially when I was a part of station management. It's harder in large stations, but we always did it.

After drinks and hors d'oeuvres, we had a delicious meal of North African specialities including roast lamb. Conversation continued during and after dinner and their strongest recommendation to us was to visit the site of the ancient city of Carthage and they offered to take us out there on the weekend.

With the Sirocco still blowing and Judy shopping at the souk, I spent the entire next day with colleagues. Despite their small number, the Tunis officers had interesting developmental contact with some Chinese officials. I briefed them on general subjects about the China target and then spent several hours with each of the two officers who were in touch with Chinese officials. Both posed good questions and tabled ideas about how best to proceed. I had done some homework at Headquarters and I was able to put some thoughts on the table in response. I was impressed at how they were approaching the problem of deepening their relationships. Good planning is essential and they were certainly doing it.

It reconfirmed in my mind the value of face-to-face meetings as opposed to cable traffic.

I also spent an hour or so with the Chief and his deputy discussing operations in general and, inevitably, what was going on at Headquarters. It was and still is the responsibility of officers visiting from Headquarters to fill in field officers on events at home. Promotions, assignments, budgets, reporting and many other subjects are fair game and the visitor just fields questions and responds as best he can. It was a long but thoroughly satisfying day.

Sometime that night, a Friday night, the wind stopped. The weather was beautiful on Saturday and Sunday. We got our chance to see the ruins of Carthage and an artists' colony at the port of Tunis.

The next week I was on leave, and we looked forward to a vacation as we hit Madrid and rented a small car. We spent a couple of days seeing sights and shopping, then travelled down to Toledo to see some of the ruins left by the Spanish Civil War in the 1930s and the beautiful steel knives and swords produced by local artisans. We also went to the Valley of the Fallen, a spectacular memorial to the dead of both sides of the Civil War. Neither of us has forgotten the beautiful cathedral carved into solid rock.

Next was north to San Sebastien, where I took Judy to places I knew from my visits in the late 1950s. A highlight was a small Basque restaurant, the Aita Marie, which overlooked the beautiful and picturesque harbour filled with fishing boats and sailboats and served wonderful seafood and Spanish wine. Then onwards to Bordeaux and Saint André de Cubzac, where I introduced Judy to Mimi, who still worked in the Bar Centrale. Neither seemed particularly impressed with the other.

Our vacation ended in Paris – Judy visiting the city for the first time. She had had her first real vacation, and break from the kids, for five years.

Another such trip, in late November 1975, minus Judy and the vacation, took me to Rome and Athens. Both were interesting and productive visits, but the Athens visit became painfully memorable.

On the last day of my visit, the Chief, Richard Welch, called me into his office in the afternoon to discuss my views on their

China programme. He had asked me to do a seminar and I did so with pleasure. All in the station had been receptive and anxious to exchange opinions. They welcomed the ideas I was able to present. My comments about the programme were positive.

Dick Welch and I had a pleasant and substantive conversation about China. He lamented having never served in Hong Kong, then moved to another subject.

'Have you seen the tourist spots here in Athens?' he asked.

'Actually, no,' I responded. 'I've been too busy. Maybe another time.'

'Well, you must at least see the Acropolis,' he announced. 'There is time right now. You don't leave till tomorrow morning, right?'

'That's right, but I have some cables to write . . .'

'You can write them at home. This is something you shouldn't miss. My driver can take you up there now. I'd go with you except that I have to see the Ambassador.'

I could see that he wasn't going to take no for an answer and I did want to see it. His secretary made the arrangements and, in his car, I was soon on my way up to the Acropolis. The driver dropped me off and I joined the crowd strolling up the path to the ancient ruins. It was a pleasant day and I was feeling pretty relaxed. It had been a good trip and it was almost finished.

I was relaxed, but I wasn't asleep. I always tried to stay alert to things around me. The years in Hong Kong, I guess, made me almost instinctively aware of people around me. Most Clandestine Service officers are the same. Not really believing it at first, I thought I picked up surveillance on me. It didn't seem likely, but there it was. Not knowing, of course, who the hell it could be, I tried (as unobtrusively as I could) to confirm what I thought I was seeing.

How could this be? I was thinking. I don't know anyone in Athens except people in our office. And nobody knows me. But half an hour later – by this time I was on top of the Acropolis wandering through the ruins of the ancient temples – I was convinced I was right. At least three men were watching my movements. Not aggressively, but I was certain it was me they were on. Why was a big question in my mind, but at the time, how to get rid of them was a higher priority.

I had sent the driver back to the office when he dropped me off, having told him that I could catch a taxi back. Had these guys seen me arrive? Did they expect me to return to the parking lot area to get picked up? I mulled over these questions, trying to decide what to do. I asked an attendant if there was another way down apart from that taken by the tourists and he directed me to a small path next to the building housing public bathrooms that went down the 'back way'. It was worth a try, I thought as I looked at the path he had pointed out.

I went to the bathroom and was pleased to see that none of the surveillants followed. Expecting me to descend with the flow of tourists to the parking lot area, I guess, they kept their distance. They had no line of sight to the entrance of the men's room and would simply wait for me to reappear. Without stopping, as soon as I was out of their sight, I headed straight for the small path. I half jogged most of the way down and entered a tourist shop at the bottom. From inside, I could see the end of the path. None of the three appeared and after fifteen minutes of browsing I bought some coasters and left.

Immediately after my return, I went directly to Welch's office. I was clearly agitated.

He didn't question what I had seen and tried to ease my concerns. 'Dick, I'll bet it was Greek police,' he said. 'Whenever they see a new face in town with any tie to our office they just check things out. Not to worry. How was the Acropolis?'

'Maybe it was the ride in your car that fingered me,' I noted, and let the subject drop.

On 23 December 1975, less than a month later, Dick Welch was murdered on his doorstep by unknown terrorists. News of the murder hit heavily at Headquarters and we were all shocked and saddened. I thought immediately of my recent visit to Athens and of the surveillance I had reported to him. Now there was good reason to believe that it had not been Greek police I had spotted, but the terrorists. I immediately reported the event to European Division officers handling the Greek desk and the investigation. I did not tell Judy.

On 25 November 1975, just before my visit to Athens, Dick Welch's name and address had been published in the English-language *Athens News*. The report was the result of information

printed in the anti-CIA newsletter called *Counter Spy*. Philip
Agee, who had formerly worked for the Agency, provided information for *Counter Spy* and contributed to the exposure of many
Agency officers worldwide. Agee denies it, but many, including
me, hold him responsible for Welch's death. It is painful to think
that he has never been held accountable for his treachery

My Headquarters tour laboured onwards but it wasn't all work
and no play. In January 1976, Dick Kinsman and his wife had
invited us to dinner. Dick, who had replaced me in Laos in 1964
and subsequently returned to Headquarters, had joined Latin
American Division. A graduate of Syracuse University and subsequently the masters programme at the Thunderbird School in
New Mexico, Dick spoke fluent Spanish. All at the dinner were
Latin American officers.

Soon I was taking a bit of good-natured kidding about why I
hadn't been smart enough to join LA Division instead of Far
East. I responded in kind, of course, and the conversation drifted
onto language skills. They were so good, they told me, that they
could sing Spanish songs without problem. Could I sing Chinese
songs? In fact, could I sing the Chinese national anthem? one
challenged me. I had had about enough kidding by that time and
I'd also had a drink, maybe two.

'Of course I can,' I shot back.

'So sing it,' he said, smiling at me like a Cheshire cat. Judy, who
wasn't at all sure I could sing anything in Chinese, let alone the
national anthem, looked a bit uneasy. I can pull this off, I was
thinking. None of these guys speaks a word of Chinese so it'll be
a piece of cake.

I launched into a spirited, Chinese-sounding song. I was using
Chinese words randomly and what I was saying made no sense at
all, but, as I had suspected, no one challenged me. There were
some fishy looks, but all just listened. As I was finishing, I was
running out of words and got a little concerned about making the
ruse work. I glanced around the room and noticed a bowl of nuts
on a small table. With gusto, since by then I was sure no one
understood anything, I concluded with '*yao guo ji ding*', which
means chicken and cashew nuts in Mandarin. I thought I had it
made. There was silence.

Just then Judy, who speaks very little Chinese, but having eaten so often in Chinese restaurants, knows the Chinese names for many Chinese dishes, blurted out, 'Chicken and cashew nuts?' It blew the whole thing. Suspicious anyway, the LA officers knew immediately that I had been bluffing and there was lots of abuse.

A month or so later, in February 1976, with my Headquarters tour well into its third year and both Judy and I starting to think about a field tour, I was called in to see Harry S. I knew him well by that time and considered him a good friend. After some small talk, he told me that the Division, Far East Division, thought it was time for me to get back to the field. He knew I was more than ready to go out again, but China Operations, acting in the interests of my career, wanted to be sure it was to a good job.

I had been promoted to GS-14 in July 1974 and things had gone well for me since then so I was in line for a good assignment. He said he could only tell me that I had been approved for a good job in summer 1976 so I should start thinking about going out. I tried to pump him for more information, but he resisted saying that it would be announced soon.

The next week I was named as Deputy Chief in Kuala Lumpur, Malaysia. I thought it more than I could have hoped for and was delighted. Judy was pleased as well and looked forward to living in Kuala Lumpur – she had visited while she worked in Bangkok. And as if that wasn't enough good news, I was promoted to GS-15 in the spring before we left. I was elated and threw myself energetically into preparing myself for another field tour. The weeks and months flew by and soon we were packing to leave. The Headquarters tour, despite the problems for the Agency that the period had witnessed, had certainly been a good one for me and for my career. Prospects continued to be bright.

In January 1976, President Ford asked Bill Colby to leave his position as our Director. Political realities dictated the decision. Ford hoped to be re-elected President in the fall and Colby, who had been the subject of much controversy, was clearly a liability. It didn't matter that the operations in question were historical, and didn't happen on Colby's watch, Colby would have to go. There were mixed feelings in the Agency. In the senior ranks, Colby's strategy had generated debate. Some felt he had exacerbated our problems by the tactics he employed. They were not sorry to see him leave.

I was disappointed to see yet another Clandestine Services officer dismissed for clearly political reasons. What we don't need now, I thought, is more change. I didn't know enough about the substance of what had transpired over Colby's tenure to be critical of what he had done. Much of the debate centred on issues that had been closely compartmented. Scapegoat is a word that came to mind. Most, I think, were saddened.

Ford named George Bush to replace Colby and Bush, my seventh director, took over in February 1976. Most thought Bush's nomination a political one designed to mark a new beginning for the Agency. Bush himself was relatively unknown to most of us and was received with neutral feelings. That would soon change – all of our initial impressions were positive.

I can't remember exactly why, an effort by Bush to meet officers at all levels maybe, but I was introduced to him sometime in the spring of 1976. I was impressed, first that he was meeting with an officer of my grade, and second because he seemed to be genuinely interested in the Agency and me. I came away from that meeting a strong fan. If we had to have an outsider as Director, I concluded, this man had been a good choice for the job. Nor was I alone in that conclusion. The Agency as a whole welcomed Bush, perhaps as a harbinger of better times to come.

ELEVEN

A CULTURAL
CROSSROADS

1976–78

I pulled into the underground parking area of one of Kuala Lumpur's several shopping malls one Thursday afternoon. Ostensibly, I was there to do some personal shopping in my lunch hour. And, as I always did, I shopped for about twenty minutes buying, this time, several birthday cards to send home.

In fact, I was there to receive my first pass from my key agent. The turnover meeting had gone well a few weeks earlier and we had agreed to continue the operation as it was. I had no reason to suggest any changes. He was comfortable with how things were going and we assessed things as being secure (acceptable level of risk, that is). I liked him and thought our relationship got off to a good start. There needs to be mutual confidence and we were on the right track early on.

Often, the simplest plan is the best. No one forgets his role. On previously agreed dates and times, I would park my car (he had the description and licence plate number, which meant that in this case – since there was no option – he knew my true name) at a place also prearranged. I had given him a key. After I had parked the car and gone up into the mall to shop, a perfectly natural thing to do in the event anyone happened to be watching me, he would pass by about ten minutes later.

In the space of a few quick seconds, he would open the trunk and place the small package on the floor. Then he was gone. About a quarter of an hour later (we left time for unforeseen events, also known as Murphy's law), I would return from my legitimate, and readily explainable each time, shopping outing, get in the car and leave. The package, which routinely contained cassettes of film and short handwritten notes, was vulnerable for the brief period between when he placed it in the trunk and when I returned. It was a risk we had considered and were willing to take. No clandestine operation is risk free.

On this occasion, a first pass in an operational environment with which I was as yet unfamiliar, I was trying to act naturally, but I felt stressed and nervous. On my return I eased out of the parking place (don't need an accident at this point, I was thinking) and headed for the exit. I noticed nothing unusual. Parking in this lot beneath the mall was free so there was no attendant to worry about. I pulled out into traffic that was heavy during the noontime hours, and headed back towards the Embassy. Since this was billed as a short shopping trip, there would be no diversions or counter surveillance effort. I headed straight back to the parking lot next to the building that housed our office. There was still nothing unusual and I breathed easier, hoping that all had gone according to plan.

I routinely kept my briefcase in the trunk so as not to tempt petty thieves. At the office parking lot, I got out with the small package of cards in hand and opened the trunk. His small package, I was pleased to note, was right next to the briefcase. I leaned in, opened the briefcase, and put in the cards and the small package. Everything had worked according to plan.

Using the film cassettes, which we developed that afternoon, and the short note my agent had included, I was able to write several intelligence reports. That system of passes, with periodic variations, worked well in that operation for the whole time I ran it and it produced a consistent stream of intelligence. We limited, for security reasons, our face-to-face meetings to about three a year. It required a lot of prior planning, but that was to be expected and was readily acceptable to gain extra security. The agent was comfortable in large part because he had decision-making powers. He decided whether or not to make the pass. Alternate dates were built into the plan. And he could, via an innocuous phone call, trigger an unscheduled meeting if something came up to prevent him from making the pass.

The operational plan was tailor-made for that agent and that operational environment. For other agents in other places it might not have worked as well. I had great respect for this man who was taking considerable personal risk for largely ideological reasons. Receiving that pass had been my first operational act in Malaysia.

With our daughters in tow, and me keeping track of six passports, six tickets and fourteen pieces of luggage, we had departed for Malaysia in late July 1976. We transited Hong Kong before landing at Kuala Lumpur's international airport, which lies due west of the city. Our Chief and his wife plus the Deputy I was replacing and his wife were there to meet us, as was a support officer with, happily, a large van.

They made us feel welcome and whisked us to the first-class hotel where we were to stay until we found a suitable house to rent. It had been a long trip, but the kids had handled it well and were excited to be in a new place. How can we make friends? Where will we go to school? Is it always this hot? Can we go to the hotel pool? Clearly, they were none the worse for wear. Judy and I were happy to have finished what had been two very hectic weeks.

First thing the next day I went to our office, located in the top couple of floors of a tall building in central Kuala Lumpur, to check in. Ed B., our Chief, was at a country team meeting chaired by the Ambassador. The Deputy was meeting an asset, so I introduced myself to the two front office secretaries (both of whom were outstanding employees) and then settled in with the support officer to take care of a number of administrative matters. Soon, Ed returned and we went into his office so I could get my initial marching orders. A senior officer with tours elsewhere in Asia and in Paris under his belt, Ed was an experienced and competent professional. He had been raised in West Virginia and enjoyed the outdoors. He and his wife were avid golfers, she a better golfer than he. He was a big man, strong looking and tanned. His welcome was genuine and I found him to be an easy man to work with.

He first briefed me about our operations. Since I had done a lot of reading at Headquarters, I was familiar with what he was describing and able to pose some pertinent questions. I was happy to be back in the field, back where the action was. From operations he went on to personnel, logistics, finance, reporting – we covered it all. Not in any detail, but enough to give me a good picture of how he saw our programmes and staff. I was impressed, not only by his grasp of our activities and his plans for the future, but also by the position I was about to assume.

With plenty of food for thought and lots to digest as I got started, I left Ed and stepped into the adjoining office. It was the Deputy's office, soon to be mine, and he had just returned from his meeting. He was a former Marine officer and looked it physically. He had a square chin, looked solid and strong, and carried himself erectly with a firm handshake and direct eye contact. I liked him right away. As we spoke, I quickly perceived that, apart from the look, he didn't seem Marine-like at all. That is, he was soft spoken and reflective – almost academic in his approach. I don't mean that critically because he was competent and effective and you could almost see decisions and comments being formulated in his head.

We got down to the nitty-gritty, including the cases I was going to take over from him. One which was particularly productive and sensitive (in terms of potential for negative political and diplomatic reaction in case of compromise) demanded special attention. I had, of course, digested the files, both operational and production, while at Headquarters, but this face-to-face discussion with the man who had handled the case for the past three years was of great value. I peppered him with questions about the agent's motivation, personality, family origins and plans for the future. His responses were clear and concise and the session did us both good. From his point of view, you always feel better about turning over an agent if the receiving officer is knowledgeable and positive, and from my point of view because I had greatly enhanced my picture of the agent I would soon be handling. We scheduled the turnover meeting in a room rented in alias in a busy downtown hotel, for two days hence. We also discussed a couple of other agents I would take over and, again, I felt that the direct conversation was a big help. These cases were not as sensitive with less 'flap' potential (CIA slang for a diplomatic tizzy) and production.

And I then got the Deputy's impressions of the other case officers in our office. They were a mixed bag, according to him, and I would ultimately come to the same conclusion. Each handled about half-a-dozen cases, but there was a definite paucity of developmental activity. What could we do about that? I asked. He just shook his head. That was not a good answer, I thought, and I made a mental note to address that issue as soon as possible. We broke for lunch in a nearby Malaysian restaurant and our conversation shifted to more personal matters.

Life in Malaysia was good, he told me. He and his family had enjoyed their three years and had been able to travel to both Singapore and Thailand. He also told me that the schools to which three of our daughters would go were very good.

The International School of Kuala Lumpur was located on the south-eastern edge of the city in an area called Ukay Heights. His house would not be available for us to rent, but there were plenty of nice houses on the market. He highly recommended his two servants, one Chinese and one Malay. They had been good workers, he told me, and he was confident we would like them both. I thanked him and said we would certainly like to meet them soon. Ultimately, after Judy and I looked around for several days, we rented a house in Ukay Heights. And we hired the two servants, whom we found to be delightful and everything he said they would be. Lai, who was Chinese, could do almost anything, was a willing worker and a fine cook – both Western and Chinese and Malay. The other, Azma, while less intelligent and less productive, did the tasks assigned to her and was always cheerful. Both were very good with our children.

All my first impressions were positive and it looked like this was going to be a very good tour, both professionally and from a family point of view. It was not exactly the centre of the Cold War world, or even a hot spot of any sort, but Malaysia was an interesting country for lots of reasons. Plus it offered a wide assortment of officials of foreign governments of high interest to us as recruitment targets.

Unspoken about, except in private, was the ethnic tension in Malaysia that lay just beneath the surface. According to government census data (disputed by many ethnic Chinese), the population was about 45 per cent Malay, 40 per cent Chinese, and the rest mixed Indian, Aborigine and other. The tension, and conflict, existed between the Malay and the Chinese. Several years before our arrival, the confrontation had got out of hand and there were beatings, killings and extensive rioting. A tenuous compromise had been hammered out that seemed to be working. In effect, the pie had been carved up, and because of Malaysia's tremendous natural resources and wealth the pie was big enough to give almost all a large piece. (Malaysia had a significant share of the world market in palm oil, tropical hardwoods, rubber and, from the mid-nineteenth century when it was discovered, tin. The latter prompted an influx of European investments. More recently, oil deposits and natural gas were added to the list.)

The Malay controlled the government, the military and the police, while the Chinese controlled the economy and business sector. The Malay, often none too subtly, tried to use their political control to gain economic advantage, but the Chinese were usually one step ahead of them. The average Malay seemed less motivated, had a weaker work ethic and often gave the impression of being short-sighted – at least, that's how I saw it. Those were early, but in the end, lasting impressions. I have tried to follow Malaysia's progress over the ensuing years and little has happened to change those views.

Adding to their differences was the fact that the Malay were Muslim and the Chinese, if religious at all, Christian. This was a manageable difference because neither group was prepared to make religion an issue. The only exception to that rule was when the Malay tried to use Islam to justify some move with economic implications. That was rare in my experience and it never really worked. On the political front, there were periodic Malay efforts to pass laws (called '*Bumiputra*') favouring Malay businesses, but the Chinese always found a way to get around them and continue to prosper.

Language presented another dilemma. The Malay absolutely refused to learn Chinese. The Chinese refused in turn to speak Malay even though, according to our language school where I studied six weeks of Malay part-time and gained a rudimentary understanding, Malay, an offshoot of Indonesian, is the easiest language in the world to learn.

As a consequence, English, a holdover from colonial days, was the lingua franca in Malaysia – unless one was deep in the countryside populated almost totally by ethnic Malays. The little Malay I had learned was of use now and again, but good English was widespread so I used that most of the time. In parts of some cities or in Chinese restaurants I used Mandarin or my basic

Cantonese, but English usually carried the day. The fact that both groups were so stubborn about the language question made it much easier for us and other foreign government officials. Officially, Malay was the country's language, but that was simply ignored in daily life. We were to experience similar linguistic divisions when we lived in Belgium and in Switzerland. The Swiss were by far the most sensible and tolerant in dealing with the problem and speak two or even three of the languages used in the country.

Soon after our arrival, we joined the Lake Club, a well-known local club that had several tennis courts and a large swimming pool plus luncheon snacks and a nice dining room. There was also a bar and a small gambling room with slot machines. As a diplomat, I was able to join immediately.

This would not have been the case with the Royal Selangor Club, which had a splendid (I was told) golf course in addition to tennis courts, swimming pool and many other amenities. Its dining room, in which I ate several times on business-related lunches, was first class. The Royal Selangor was exclusive in its membership and had a long waiting list that effectively ruled out diplomats because of the relatively short periods of time they lived in Malaysia. It was a Malay enclave with membership heavily biased towards ethnic Malay individuals.

Not being able to join the Royal Selangor Club caused us no problem since the Lake Club served our purposes very well. With fine weather year round, Judy used it almost daily with the girls and became active on the tennis circuit. The atmosphere was warm and friendly. And since many of its members were also foreign diplomats, there were positive professional benefits as well. Many of the diplomats we met there were of interest as sources of information, especially the few who were from the Soviet Bloc countries. A couple would later become advanced developmental contacts.

My interest in tennis would, again, be helpful from a work perspective. Judy and I both played regularly and met a wide range of people as a result. And we often played mixed doubles for the club team. In the latter activity, we met people from other clubs and within about six months we had quite an active tennis and social circle of friends. The Malaysians who were members of the Lake Club were mostly ethnic Chinese, because most of the Malays preferred the Royal Selangor Club. We enjoyed their company and spent many evenings at social gatherings or dinner with them. In moments of candour, they would relate their side of the story about ethnic conflicts in the country. More in sadness than in anger I often thought. The Europeans we met, including a number of French businessmen and diplomats, were also an entertaining lot. There were few other Americans in the club and we were viewed with interest at first and then warmth and friendliness.

In November 1976, just a few months after our arrival in Malaysia, President Ford lost his bid for the presidency to Jimmy Carter, an unknown (to me at least) former Governor of Georgia. Carter promptly signalled his intent to change Directors at the Agency and in January 1977 we lost George Bush, who had served as Director for only a year. Again I was distressed to see a Director go. I had liked Bush and had high expectations for where his leadership would take us. Many of my colleagues felt the same way and we all disliked the political nature of decisions being taken about 'our' Agency. We wanted to be left out of the political equation, but Watergate, which in the end had dashed Ford's hopes, changed that for ever.

To replace Bush, Carter named Stansfield Turner, a Navy admiral with whom he had attended the Naval Academy. There was apprehension within the service. The grapevine immediately lit up with efforts to ferret out, from Navy contacts, information about Turner. His reputation was suspect (inflexible and mean-spirited) and some thought that the only thing worse than an inexperienced politician was an inexperienced military man. Turner, the eighth Director of my sixteen-year career, arrived in January 1977. Word that filtered out to the field indicated that he walked in with several staff officers in tow and wanted to make things 'shipshape'. It was an ominous beginning, I thought.

We can call him Igor, which is not his true name, and I met him playing tennis at the Lake Club one day. He was a known member of a Soviet Bloc intelligence service and a pretty nice guy as it turned out – just on the wrong side of things. Under the circumstances, we were more or less obliged to be nice to each other (two other club members had arranged the doubles game), which was fine with me because I considered him an attractive contact.

After the game (as a player he was strong and enthusiastic, but inconsistent and lacking in knowledge of tactics), we had drinks on the verandah and, cautiously, probed each other's background. He either knew or suspected that I was also an intelligence officer, but that didn't seem to bother him. He seemed intrigued and was more forthcoming than I had expected.

Cold War rhetoric often put a damper on conversations with diplomats from communist countries, but things had gone so well that as we prepared to leave, I suggested that we have lunch together. To my surprise, he accepted immediately and we made a date for the next week. We exchanged cards. I told him I would call to remind him and he said that would not be necessary. Did he not want me to call his office? I didn't know or at that point care.

Lunch the next week at a steakhouse called the Anchor in the middle of the city was both interesting and enjoyable. Igor had an engaging sense of humour. The chemistry seemed good. We avoided political discussion that might lead to conflicts. It was a promising beginning.

Over the next nine or ten months, I saw Igor regularly. Initially, our meetings were at the club, but after he got to know Judy, he and his wife joined us with groups of friends for dinners at local restaurants. I grew increasingly interested in him as a possible recruitment target.

I knew that Igor spent time in the club's gambling room playing the slot machines. That and other traits he showed made me think that he was not the ideal communist man of Lenin's dreams.

Using a tennis film I had requested from Headquarters, which included matches played by a player from his country, I invited Igor and his wife for dinner at our home. He was tempted I could tell, but hesitant. He would check, he told me, and I didn't press him. Was he checking in the office? Would his office permit him to come? I didn't know. He called the next day and accepted. It was a very successful evening during which our girls absolutely captivated him and his wife. Dinner, the film, and the girls combined to put them both at ease.

During the evening, conversation drifted to music and the piano. I remembered that Igor had told me he could play and he suggested that we should have a piano so that the girls could learn. Whereupon the girls and Judy, who also plays beautifully, thought that was a great idea and I suddenly found myself under strong pressure. To a smile from Judy and cheers from the girls (who had not considered the hours of practice this would mean), I said, 'OK, OK, we'll look for a piano to rent next week.' Igor smiled as well. I had thought that the whole subject came up innocently, and maybe it did – but there is more to the story.

Kuala Lumpur had only one store that sold or rented pianos and we were there the next Tuesday at lunchtime. We looked at the whole selection – me less enthusiastically than Judy. First she convinced me that we should buy one not rent. That way we could keep it as the girls grew up and we moved back to the US. Then, it became clear that only a grand or baby grand would suffice. I figured out that this was a battle I wasn't going to win.

We settled on a Weinbach, a beautiful baby grand piano that had been made in Czechoslovakia. The decision taken, we approached the counter to talk with the owner.

'We would like to buy a piano,' I said.

'Very good, sir,' he replied. 'Which one?'

'The Weinbach baby grand that costs the same as a Volkswagen Golf.'

He smiled. Judy frowned.

'Fine, I'll need some information for customs papers and so that we can deliver it. Your name, sir?'

'Mr Holm.'

'Ah yes, Richard L., is that right?'

Alarm bells sounded loudly in my head. How could he have known my name? I just nodded and said nothing.

'And your address?' he went on without a blink.

'Here's my card,' I said. 'My address and phone number are listed.'

He took it and scanned it. 'You are a diplomat, Mr Holm?'

'That's right,' I confirmed.

'That should make things much easier. No taxes.'

My mind was working hard as we left the store. I wanted very much to know how he had been able to rattle off my first name and middle initial after I told him my family name. I could hardly wait to get Judy's input but said nothing until we were in the car with the motor running and the radio on. Was I over-reacting?

Before I could say anything Judy said, 'How did he know your first name?'

'I've been trying to figure that out.'

'Seems very strange,' she muttered.

'Who knew we would be in that store?' I asked.

She thought a moment. 'Only us and the girls.' She paused. 'And Igor.'

My fear, of course, was that Igor, knowing we would be looking for a piano (and perhaps aware as well that there was only one piano store in Kuala Lumpur), had been there before us and bribed or recruited the owner. His goal would have been to gain access to whichever piano we chose before it arrived in our house and plant a microphone. His service could then listen to all conversations in the room in which the piano was placed. Moreover, given the open configuration of our house, with which Igor was familiar, listening to conversations on much of the ground level would also be possible.

Well, it's a double-edged sword, I thought. Given the same set of circumstances in reverse, I would have at least considered doing the same thing.

Back at the office, I did some checking on both the shop owner, whose name I had from his card, and the company. We had no traces. I cabled Headquarters asking for their checks while explaining what had happened. The response, two days later, was that they also had nothing on the name or the company. They shared my concern, they said, but seemed less agitated than I was. I discussed the incident with Ed, and we concluded that, to be safe, we would have to have the piano, which had been delivered the day after we purchased it (also very unusual for Kuala Lumpur), checked out by our technicians. We asked Headquarters to concur. They did, and the visit was set for early the next month – they couldn't make it any sooner.

The piano had been delivered while I was at work and the kids were in school. Pia was in nursery school and she got home first.

'Why is the piano way over in the corner?' they asked, almost in unison.

'I like it over there,' Judy responded, 'it's nice near the windows.'

In fact, although uncertain herself, Judy knew how concerned I was and had the movers put the piano as far away from where we talked as was possible. I was pleased that she did so. Because of the climate, the piano had a heating coil built in to reduce the possibility of damage from humidity. But, to deny power to a possible transmitter implanted in the piano, I reasoned, we didn't plug it in. Our maid, Lai, thought that strange, but said nothing about it.

More and more, I convinced myself that I had been had, and I was determined to avoid the snare, so to speak. Even without power supplied via the heating-coil cord, there remained the possibility of a battery pack concealed in the piano that could power a transmitter. So we had to remain vigilant until the piano was checked. Once we had confirmation of what, increasingly, I believed, we could consider our next steps.

Where, I wondered, could they have established their listening post? It had to be a low-powered transmitter with a range of about 200 feet. One of the apartments in the building just above us on the hill? It was impossible to tell. Maybe they had a more sophisticated transmitter? There was no way to know that either.

I thought about my colleagues posted in the Soviet Union, or other opposition controlled places, where it was just assumed that your home, whether it be house or apartment, had audio devices implanted in it, and your telephone was tapped. We expected it in those places. It was unusual for Kuala Lumpur although we took the same precautions they took and never discussed sensitive subjects outside of secure areas. While I viewed it as part of the business, and on the one hand I was pissed off that Igor would have set this up, I was also resigned to it as an occupational hazard.

We spent a couple of weeks carefully avoiding the area the piano was in and ventured near it only for playing and listening to it. There was an amusing incident involving an indoor pool near where we had placed the piano. Such a pool was not unusual for houses in Malaysia that are designed to be open to allow air to circulate. When we moved in, the pool was dry with only decorative rocks and plants therein. One of us had the bright idea of filling it with water. Wouldn't it be nice to have fish swimming around in our pool? we thought. We filled it and stocked it.

Within a couple of weeks, it was filled with frogs that 'sere-naded' us at night – all night. No one could sleep and we soon emptied the pool of both fish and frogs. Now we knew why it had been empty when we arrived. Amusing to me though, was the thought of someone sitting somewhere listening to the transmitter fill his ears with the sound of croaking frogs.

Finally, our technicians arrived. I don't know if they were buying the story or not, but they were there to do the job. I briefed them carefully and made plans to invite them over to our house for dinner that night. It had to sound normal. We didn't want to alert anyone that we were on to the implant. All went according to plan. After dinner, we chatted casually while they started carefully checking out the piano. After about an hour, they shrugged their shoulders and indicated that they had found nothing. Outside as they were leaving, we agreed that they would come back the next afternoon, with special pieces of equipment, for an even more thorough check. I was perplexed.

To cut a long story short, they almost disassembled and rebuilt that bloody piano and found – nothing, nothing at all! I was even more perplexed. Judy laughed. In my mind, the pieces all fitted and I was convinced that Igor had tried to exploit a target of opportunity. But it just wasn't so. There was no transmitter in that piano. How had that clerk known my first name and middle initial? I never did find out. Maybe they just couldn't put the operation together. Who knows? But the incident was a head-breaker for me as I tried to outguess – nobody. Was I seeing bad guys behind every tree? Maybe so and one must guard against that because it is also a part of the business.

(We still have the piano. All the girls learned to play it and Judy still produces beautiful music from it regularly. Sometimes we joke about the transmitter hidden inside.)

On Thai National Day some months later, we were at a cocktail party. These occasions were all the same, but they did facilitate making contacts, which was the primary objective of most attendees. I saw friends in the crowd, but hadn't yet spotted Igor. The plan was for a group of us to go out for dinner after cocktails, and it was at the dinner that I hoped to begin probing about his country's political system, gently, but unambiguously.

We all dutifully toasted the King of Thailand and people

started to leave. I still hadn't seen Igor. Something must have come up because he had confirmed that he and his wife would be there. We joined up with our friends and left for dinner hoping that they might join us there. They didn't.

To our considerable disappointment, we found out several days later that Igor had been abruptly reassigned back to his country. The news came from a brief conversation in a grocery store between a club member and one of Igor's friends. Using other local sources, we were able to confirm the, for us, bad news. Why had there been such an unusual move? We had no idea. Was it his routine of gambling and too much drinking in the Lake Club, which would have been known to other Bloc diplomats? Or could it have been his relationship with me? We would never know as it turned out. We did pick up some reports (which we couldn't confirm) that his wife had blown the whistle on his 'behavioural' problems. The bottom line for us was that they were just gone and their abrupt departure brought closure to what I had considered to be a promising developmental operation.

The record of my efforts and the information about Igor that we had amassed would rest in the file on him for use in the future if one of our officers ever made contact with him in the future. Of all the Bloc officers I met during my career, he was the most fascinating and I still wonder sometimes about what happened to cause his re-assignment, and how he fared after that.

About midway through our tour in Malaysia, my dad visited us for about a week. Mom had died several years earlier of breast cancer. During his visit, I took some leave and, without the kids, we all went up to the Cameron Highlands, several hours north of Kuala Lumpur by train, for a brief visit. The Cameron Highlands' claim to fame is that they lie at the Malaysia peninsula's highest point. The weather is almost always cooler and less humid than anywhere else in Malaysia and it is a favourite vacation spot.

Our rustic old hotel with a British ambience faced a large clear plateau on which there was a nine-hole golf course. Dad suggested a game the afternoon after our arrival, but my post-Congo manual dexterity ruled it out and I demurred. Although rusty from lack of play, Judy promptly volunteered to play with Dad and they played the course – twice.

At dinner that night, Judy confessed that the golf had caused a severe blister on her hand. It had broken and now it seemed to be infected. We thought little of it and told her to be sure to clean it thoroughly that night. She did but it didn't stop the infection and by morning she had angry looking red streaks going up her arm and a lump in her armpit. It looked serious and I was alarmed. Checking with the hotel, I got directions to the nearby clinic, where the only doctor available worked. Immediately after breakfast we walked there.

We registered with the nurse and sat down to wait. We were the only foreigners there and thus the focus of some attention. We were used to that and just waited patiently. The next patient to arrive, however, caused us all to take notice. An Aborigine about 4 feet tall, he wore only a loin cloth and was carrying a long bamboo blowpipe – from which small poison darts are blown to bring down game. He had a small quiver over his shoulder. Still holding the bamboo blowpipe, he sat down and the blowpipe was taller than he was. Seemingly oblivious to the rest of us, he sat there staring straight ahead. He was just your average patient, I guess, but we had never seen an Aborigine before and couldn't help looking at him. Now, almost a quarter of a century later, I wonder how the Aborigines of Malaysia are faring. Not all that well, I would guess. Before he, or anyone else I hope, noticed our focused attention on the little man, the nurse called our name and we went into the doctor's office.

He asked a few questions and then told Judy he recommended a shot of penicillin right away. 'Then I can give you some penicillin tablets to take for a few days,' he went on, 'but I think we should get on this right away with a shot.'

'I guess there isn't much choice,' Judy responded as she nodded agreement.

'I have to tell you', the doctor then said, 'that I have no American penicillin. I have only Polish penicillin. It's equally effective, but it goes in harder.' Neither of us picked up on what he meant.

'Let's just go ahead,' Judy replied.

He prepared the shot that Judy was to take in the upper thigh. Soon we understood what he had tried to tell us. The Polish penicillin was visibly viscous and only with obvious effort could he push it into her butt. And it hurt, according to Judy.

As I have already mentioned, Malaysia wasn't exactly a hot spot on the Cold War map, but as a charter member of the South-East Asian Treaty Organization (SEATO) it played a role in regional politics and that was of interest to our policy makers. The countries of SEATO (the Philippines, Thailand, Singapore, Indonesia and Malaysia – later to be broadened and become the Association of Southeast Asian Nations, ASEAN) were all in the Western camp. Of interest as well was the fact that each was concerned about internal subversion carried out by communist sympathizers or actual insurgents. In Malaysia, we monitored the activities of a small group of insurgents operating in the far north near the Thai border. They posed little threat.

Economically, the region's enormous natural resources promised growth and prosperity. How SEATO (ASEAN) handled its economic policies and trade agreements was monitored by our office and by the Embassy's economic section. Political reporting, to the extent that it could impact on economics or internal security issues, was also forwarded to Washington.

But little of this reporting was earth shaking. Rather it was grist for the mills of analysts in Washington trying to follow or discern trends of interest or importance to the United States' interests in the region. We produced fewer intelligence reports than had been the case in Hong Kong and that was something I had to get used to. I came to realize that Kuala Lumpur was simply not a place that would produce like Hong Kong.

As the Deputy, I was also the de facto reports officer and I was ill-prepared for that responsibility. Ed also followed our reporting, of course, but he deferred to me for much of the editing and many of the decisions about whether or not to disseminate a particular report. I worked very hard in the first weeks to bring myself up to speed. It required lots of reading for background on the range of subjects we were following and exchanges with Headquarters concerning the requirements for reporting that they levied on us. The reading was helpful, essential really, in my work in the office and was also beneficial to me on the cocktail and liaison circuits where it helped sustain interesting conversations. Still, I longed for the expert and competent reports officers I had dealt with in Hong Kong and at Headquarters. They represented an integral part of the system and my respect for them as a group was career long. Their detailed knowledge of the subjects we reported on and the mechanics of our reporting system, coupled with their ability astutely to assess the access of each reporting asset, consistently, in my view, enhanced the quality of our reporting. As any of my colleagues would have been able to do, I was able to fill the shoes of a 'real' reports officer, but it must be said that reports officers at Headquarters regularly picked up some slack. In sum, it was a good experience for me – and in some ways a humbling one.

Our primary interest, given the lack of priority attached to the kind of reporting we could produce, was in recruiting new assets for reporting on subjects accessible to that individual. Kuala Lumpur was a good place for this effort in that the pace of life was slow and casual and the diplomatic circuit offered opportunities for contact with numerous people who were of interest as possible sources of information.

As a consequence, all station officers were active on the cocktail circuit. It was an incessant merry-go-round that you could jump on, or off, as you liked. As with anything else, some are better or more comfortable with it than others. A couple of our officers were good at it; others were less comfortable and therefore less productive.

Over the years, I never developed any strong feelings one way or the other about attending those events. Some were enjoyable and productive. Others were a bust. But I was convinced that we had to go because there were few better ways to expand your circle of contacts. It was proved many times over. There are other ways to make contacts too. Tennis was always a good way for me to meet people, but not everyone plays tennis.

On one occasion, we were as usual circulating in the crowd. We had drinks, snacks and toasts – the same old story. We turned to greet an acquaintance who was talking to an Asian who wore on his lapel a pin with a likeness of Kim Il Sung, North Korea's leader. Following the script for these affairs (it was almost a duty), our acquaintance introduced us to the North Korean diplomat. He mentioned our names, but did not tell the North Korean that I was a US official.

'How do you do?' Judy smiled. I followed suit, adding his name, Mr Lee, as I shook his hand.

He was a slight man with close cut black hair and the

inscrutable look we talk about for Asians. He avoided direct eye contact, but had a firm handshake. He had the features of a North Asian and I might have picked him out as Korean even without the pin on his lapel.

'Who is that?' Judy asked, gesturing at the pin.

He seemed (or at least feigned) surprised. 'That is our great leader,' he replied.

'What is his name?' she persisted. I watched, not knowing what she was up to.

Now looking a little flustered, he quickly answered, 'Kim Il Sung.' Who is this woman? he may have been thinking. Could she be serious? Does she not know who Kim Il Sung is?

'So what country are you from?' Judy continued.

Now he really looked perplexed. You could almost see the wheels turning in his head. Was she taunting him? She looked innocent enough. After a moment's hesitation, he apparently made his decision. 'I am from North Korea,' he declared.

'That's nice,' she said. 'I've never been there.'

He nodded and glanced nervously at me, wondering, I suppose, what I had made of the exchange just completed. I smiled. I had been watching, partly in awe, and partly in amusement. With the exception of the Chinese or the Russians, the majority of foreign diplomats at the time found North Koreans notoriously difficult to approach. Innocently, or deviously, I didn't know which, Judy had disarmed him beautifully.

'We are Americans. I am a US official,' I told him. It was a calculated move on my part. In other circumstances, I might well have left those comments unstated for a while as I tried to probe a little and establish some rapport. North Koreans were by far our most difficult target and flatly refused contact with Americans of any stripe. The story was the same worldwide. As soon as they were told they were speaking to an American, a North Korean diplomat would abruptly, often rudely, turn and walk away. Given, however, that Judy had left him so nonplussed, I had decided to strike while the iron was hot and he was off balance.

'I don't know many Americans,' he said cautiously. That was probably a gross understatement.

There followed a five-minute conversation on totally innocuous subjects – the weather, how we each liked Malaysia, where we each had been posted. Inwardly I was delighted. Just to engage a North Korean diplomat, any North Korean actually, was a coup and even this brief contact led me to think he was different. It was probably wishful thinking. In any case, as he indicated that he was going to break off the conversation, I decided to push on.

'Well, it's been nice talking with you,' I said handing him my calling card. 'Do you have a card?'

Acting as if he was taking a rotten fish, he accepted the card, muttered, 'I don't have a card,' and moved away towards a couple of Russian diplomats.

I don't know why he stayed to talk and must conclude that Judy's seemingly innocent interrogation must have had something to do with it. Unfortunately, nothing ever came of the contact. Neither he nor any other of the few North Koreans assigned to Kuala Lumpur was a regular attendee on the diplomatic circuit and I saw him only one more time, at an occasion at the Russian Embassy. We made brief eye contact as I was walking by. He quickly moved away and I never saw him again.

Judy and I had been separated earlier and I found myself standing alone in the garden. Not for long though. As I glanced around looking for either Judy or some acquaintances to greet, Vlatko Cosic, the Yugoslavian Ambassador to Malaysia, shouted out a greeting and came over to where I was standing. At about 5 foot 10 inches and 180 pounds, Vlatko looked a little round. He wasn't fat really, just wide around the middle. Balding and being out of shape made him look older than he actually was. Surprisingly, when I had run traces on him, I discovered that we had been born on exactly the same date, he in Sarajevo, Yugoslavia, and me in Chicago. I never knew, or at the time cared (a Yugoslav was a Yugoslav), if Vlatko was a Croat or a Serb or a Muslim. If the latter, he certainly bent lots of the rules. Vlatko was a friendly guy who got along with everyone. Not a communist ideologically, he had simply adjusted to realities in his country and done quite well for himself. He didn't talk about politics and that was that.

We had met and become friends via contacts at the Lake Club, where he also played tennis – after a fashion. The chemistry between us was good and contacts with him, and his wife, were always enjoyable. Whether he admitted it to himself or not, and whether he did it purposefully or not, Vlatko had been a big help to me. He regularly included Judy and me in affairs he hosted at his residence, in local restaurants, or at the Lake Club. And we, of course, tried to reciprocate although it was difficult for me to invite an ambassador. Routinely at those affairs, I would meet people of interest because Vlatko's circle of friends was primarily in the communist grouping. I met a number of Russian, Chinese and Eastern European diplomats. I pointedly thanked him several times indicating how much I appreciated being able to meet people I would otherwise have no access to. He brushed off my thanks, but I think he knew what he was doing – acting, albeit informally, as a social broker for me.

One story about Vlatko merits telling. Playing tennis one day at the Lake Club we made history. I was playing with Igor against Vlatko and a Malaysian Chinese club member. We put Vlatko on the defensive and he hit a lob. (Vlatko was known for hitting very high lobs and since his game featured nothing else of note, he nurtured his notoriety.) He smacked the ball straight up into the air. About two counts later, a dead bird fell at his feet. There was a moment's stunned silence and then shouts and laughter. Vlatko smiled broadly and bowed. Soon the whole club had heard the story and Vlatko's lob had become even more famous.

Work continued with, it must be said, more inside the office than outside of it. That was not something I particularly liked, but I put that down to my new management responsibilities. More time spent on monthly and annual reporting, budget planning, personnel ratings and intelligence reporting was something I had not had to do in my Hong Kong tour. It did not occur to me that I would spend the rest of my career in management jobs.

It's ironic that we, operations officers, start 'on the street' recruiting and running agents and as soon as we prove we can do that well we are promoted to management jobs. From that time onward, we stop 'on the street' activities and sit behind a desk. It is a well-known phenomenon, which doesn't make much sense, but we never figured out an answer.

I should say here that the work I was doing was made enormously more palatable by the performance of our two secretaries. It was in Kuala Lumpur that I started dictating – with lousy manual dexterity, I am a poor typist – because I now had my own secretary to call upon; and Ed's as well in times of need. Each young woman was skilled, highly so, in all of the things one would expect from a secretary. But it went beyond that. They were always one step ahead of us in things that needed to be done. They both had initiative, and plenty of it. Each was pleasant, helpful and liked by everyone. Willing and able, they accomplished a wide range of secretarial, administrative and financial tasks for us all. There is little question that without them our efficiency level would have decreased sharply. They were a really professional pair and we were blessed to have them.

I will add that such was the case in virtually every overseas office I ever worked in, headed, or visited. Our Directorate has been unusually well served by a strong, competent and dedicated secretarial corps for, certainly, the three plus decades I can comment on. Their contribution merits much more praise and recognition than it has ever been given.

Life in Kuala Lumpur was good for us. The pace of life was tolerable, the climate was pleasant and our living conditions were very comfortable. Two servants, a gardener and a watchman (he could not have been described as a guard) left us with leisure time to spend with the girls. And they were doing just fine. As reported, the elementary school was good so Suzanne and Danika were appropriately challenged. Alison was to start kindergarten and Pia was in a Malaysian pre-school.

On a daily basis after school during the week, Judy and the girls would go to the Lake Club. All the girls, even Pia at age three, were strong swimmers and thus water safe. That made the club visits much less stressful than had been the case in Hong Kong. Judy had almost daily tennis games and soon Suzanne and then Danika started hitting balls. Both seemed to like tennis (we tried not to press them) and both had promising games. Often on weekends we were able to visit nearby tourist sites and the girls were wide-eyed at the beautiful beaches, lush jungles, and neatly manicured plantations.

Pleasing to us as well were the various types of cuisine available in Malaysia. There were excellent Malay, Chinese (our favourite) and Indian restaurants at which we could eat. And Lai provided excellent meals on a daily basis. A wide variety of excellent fresh fruit was always on the table. In fact, we could pick bananas, from our verandah looking out on a hillside, and other fruits that grew in our yard. I'm painting a rosy picture because that's just how we saw it; a wonderful two years that we were reluctant to see end.

Less than wonderful, however, was an incident that occurred one day as we returned from a visit to the Lake Club. We pulled into the driveway in front of the garage and, as usual, there was lots of milling around as everyone got bags with swimming suits and towels, tennis rackets and balls unloaded from the car. Then we went into the house, each one heading for their particular room to put things away. It was a ritual. All the bedrooms were on the second floor.

Suddenly, Suzy bolted out of her room, slammed the door and ran down the stairs shouting about a snake in her room. We tried to calm her – she was eleven years old at the time – and get a clear story. Quickly regaining her composure, she explained.

Wrapped around the wires of the shield for the blades of the large post-mounted fan at the foot of her bed, she told us, was a thin, bright green snake. (An adage from Thailand, the brighter the colour the more poisonous the snake, flashed through my mind.) When she threw her racket on the bed, it moved and she noticed it as it started down the post. She screamed in fright, ran out of the room and, happily, had the good sense to slam the door. In theory at least, the snake was trapped in Suzy's bedroom. What to do?

Lai had heard the commotion, understood what was happening and told us to do nothing while she got her husband, Louie. I don't know what I would have done anyway so we waited until he arrived on the scene.

'No problem,' he told us when he showed up a few minutes later. 'We'll just kill the snake.'

'How?' Suzy blurted out. 'We don't know where it is.'

'I've killed snakes before,' he explained. 'You just wait down here.'

He was carrying a tree branch no thicker than his finger, about 3 feet long and flexible. He snapped the floor at the top of the stairs before he opened the bedroom door, and I could see the utility of his weapon. It would deliver a sharp blow across a broad area. Lai, and now Azma as well, also armed with switches, stationed themselves in the hallway in front of the bedroom as he prepared to open the door.

For no good reason, I thought I should be involved so, with tennis racket in hand, I went up the stairs and stood with the two women in the hallway. They all probably knew that I would be of little or no use, but none wanted to tell me to stay out of the way.

'The snake can move quickly,' Louie told me, 'so watch out.' Then he opened the door cautiously. Seeing nothing, he slowly entered the room – still nothing. The snake wasn't on the fan. Louie was carefully scanning everything in sight. He bent down and tried to see under the bed. He couldn't and decided, wisely I thought, against getting down on the floor. Positioning himself carefully, he jerked the bed away from the wall.

Without warning, the thin, bright green snake (Suzy had been very accurate) darted out from behind the bed and headed for the door. In rapid succession, Louie delivered three quick hits just behind the snake's head and it lay still. Two more hits for good measure and we were all convinced it was dead.

While not all that unusual to Lai and Louie or to Azma, the incident left the rest of us somewhat shaken. Happy that it was over, I expressed sincere, very sincere, appreciation to Louie.

Regrettably, this was not an isolated incident. I came home from work one day to great excitement in the household. The girls were all abuzz with the story of how Azma, having discovered a snake behind the washing machine, had first lured it out and then killed it.

And there was the Komodo Dragon that regularly lounged in the sun on the brick wall behind our house. No one ever got close to him. No one *wanted* to get close to him. Actually we didn't know if it was a Komodo Dragon or not, but it was a large (about 2 feet long), ugly, nasty-looking lizard that made regular appearances on the wall. He didn't bother us and we certainly didn't bother him. After our departure, we heard from friends that, because of 'nests of cobras' found beneath our house, the Embassy did not renew the lease.

While life in Kuala Lumpur for me, and certainly for Judy and the girls, was good (Kuala Lumpur, at that time, was famous for being a good family posting), I felt a little frustrated at work. This was a new feeling for me. Until that point, all my feelings about work had been very positive. Kuala Lumpur was simply not in the mainstream. As a result, and despite our best efforts, I didn't think that either the quality or the quantity of our reporting was up to the standards I wanted to see.

Nor was our recruitment record all that strong. We had a few promising developmental efforts under way, but not enough of them had really jelled. I couldn't articulate anything specific, but I had the impression of a lot of wheel spinning without enough forward motion. In retrospect, I can see how naive I was. My career to that point had hardly been average. Laos, the Congo and Walter Reed all consumed time in my career, but each period was different from what I had expected my career to be. I had judged Kuala Lumpur far too harshly. It was not Hong Kong and not Headquarters. It wouldn't offer the same type of priority or activity level. Progress in places like Kuala Lumpur is incremental and is dependent upon lots of factors that are out of our control. You win some and you lose some. Being in the right place at the right time makes a big difference. If an opportunity arises, one's exploitation of it makes a mark. For the eighteen months I had been in Malaysia when I sensed the feelings of frustration, nothing much was possible or worked. It wasn't necessarily anybody's fault, but that didn't occur to me at the time. I simply urged my colleagues to work even harder.

Early in January 1978, our Division Chief, Bill Graver, visited Kuala Lumpur. It was not often that a Division Chief, or any other senior officer from Headquarters, visited a small (by Far East Division standards) office like ours. We were pleased, of course, but couldn't help wondering what may have prompted the visit. We had been picking up vague rumours about some management problems in Hong Kong, but didn't really know much. Ed speculated about a possible connection but, again, we had nothing specific.

After a private conversation with Ed, Graver came into my office, closed the door and said he wanted to talk with me about an assignment. That surprised me and it also got my attention.

'I know you have asked for a third year here in Kuala Lumpur,' was his opening shot, 'but I need you elsewhere. I'd like to move you to Hong Kong this summer.'

His comment really caught me off-guard. Part of Ed's speculation had been that if there were problems in Hong Kong, he might be transferred (he was in his third year in Kuala Lumpur) there to take over. I would be left, he went on, to take over in Kuala Lumpur. He was a super grade (senior) officer and I was a GS-15, and he reasoned that we were 'top heavy'. It had sounded logical to me, but Graver's statement shifted the ground.

'Hong Kong?' was all I could think of to say in response.

'You would be Deputy,' he went on. That completed the surprise. I had not expected it at all.

'I'd love it,' I quickly replied, 'but I'm going to have to talk with Judy.'

He knew Judy and posed the question cautiously. 'Any problem there?'

'I don't know. I honestly don't know,' I told him. 'Remember that her memories of Hong Kong are not as positive as mine. She had three babies during our four years there and was busy as hell. It didn't sit all that well. She was cheering when we took off on the last day.'

'I'll talk with her,' he said immediately. 'We're talking about the needs of the service here and I'm sure she will understand.'

I smiled, 'I'm glad *you* are,' I said. 'You'll have your shot tonight at dinner. By the way, does Ed know about this?'

'Yes he does. I just told him before coming in here,' he responded. 'He seemed disappointed. I guess he just doesn't want to lose a good deputy.' I said nothing.

I gave Judy the news when I got home from work. She was surprised and initially not all that pleased. Reluctant you could have said. 'Don't make a hasty decision,' I told her. 'Bill wants to talk to you about it tonight. It would be great for my career,' I added. She knew that.

In the end, as I had hoped (in fact I knew she would), she bought the plan, although she made clear that, as had not been the case when we left Hong Kong, she would definitely regret leaving Kuala Lumpur after only two years. There were two factors, I thought, that likely influenced her decision to accept something she wasn't much in favour of. Three maybe. First, she knew I was delighted and more than ready to help run our office in Hong Kong. It was a real step up for me. Second, she knew we weren't going to have any more babies. And finally she also knew that, and I was delighted to have had the foresight, our lifetime membership in the Ladies' Recreation Club meant that we would simply walk in the door when we got back to Hong Kong. Life in Hong Kong this time would be great, I assured her. She smiled. What a honey!

I did my best to stay focused on our activities and operations, but word of my summer transfer to Hong Kong changed things. From that point on, there lurked beneath the surface what is commonly known as a 'short-timer's mentality'. I continued to follow all of our ongoing efforts (we were already in touch with Igor's replacement), but inevitably planning for our departure had to begin.

My replacement was soon named and we began corresponding with him and his wife. He would assume handling responsibilities for the sensitive asset I was handling. That case, by the way, had been running smoothly and productively since I had taken it over. I kept the number of personal meetings to a minimum for security reasons, but given his long-time status as a clandestine agent, it had no adverse impact on our relationship with him. At one point, I was able to slip down to Singapore for a two-day meeting with him, which we both enjoyed as we were able to get a better feel for each other.

The office took the news calmly. All saw the move as a good step, and many offered congratulations. They realized it was a positive move and were pleased for me. Ed more or less shrugged his shoulders and said he had known we were top-heavy and it didn't surprise him that one of us was being pulled out.

With the best of intentions, I had tried to bring along one of our officers with a carrot-and-stick approach. The stick had been a less than sterling fitness report (which he fully deserved) and a long talk about making himself more effective. I fully expected him to improve over the next period as I thought him a potentially strong officer. My departure, however, would mean that, from me at least, he'd only get the stick and not the carrot. I don't know if he was pleased or disappointed to see me leave.

At home, there was much to be done. We had been expecting a third year in Kuala Lumpur and the upcoming move to Hong Kong was going to require new plans. Housing in Hong Kong would be no problem, nor would movement of our household effects – including the infamous piano. But this time we would have to think about schools and make some choices. Even Pia, our youngest, would be ready to start school in September in Hong Kong.

'But happily there's the Ladies' Recreation Club,' we both exclaimed (possibly for slightly different reasons) periodically.

And the home leave promised to be as hectic and stress filled as the last one had been. There was no way to avoid that as we simply had to see both families and I had to go to Washington for some briefings and introductions. The last months of our tour in Malaysia were indeed busy ones. But they passed quickly and uneventfully.

There were, as is the norm, many cocktails and dinners given to mark our departure. We had cut a wide swath through Kuala Lumpur and the number of departure events attested to the number of friends we had made. Both in the diplomatic community, including Vlatko, and in the local Malaysian community people were kind enough to honour us with events of some sort. There was a most pleasant, and large, dinner given at the Lake Club at which I was asked to give a short speech. I did so saying, truly, that we regretted leaving Malaysia, but that it was a part, albeit an unpleasant one, of the career I had chosen. I did not mention how much I looked forward to getting to Hong Kong and the 'mainstream'. I also said how pleased Judy and I had been to meet the King of Malaysia. (Judy and I had been selected to play a 'friendly' mixed doubles with a team from the Royal Selangor Club in the summer of 1977. The King sponsored the match and presented each player with a pewter plate as a memento of the occasion. In fact, he was, at the time, the 'acting King', as the elected King was away on vacation, a term which greatly amused me. How could one be 'acting King'? You are or you aren't.)

We managed to complete all the parties and events, and the introductions for my successor (both to agents and to liaison). And then our pack-out (which reminded me of just how much one can accumulate in just two years – we are *not* shipping those rocks, I had to remind the girls), and travel plans. It had been a good, if unspectacular, tour for me; lots of learning and honing of skills in a new set of responsibilities. I was ready, I thought, to take on both the problems and the challenges in Hong Kong.

By the time of our departure from Kuala Lumpur, 'Admiral' Turner had been our Director for about a year and a half and he had made his presence felt. For starters, he insisted on being called Admiral, which most of us found annoying. (As Director, call yourself the Director. If you want to be an Admiral, go back to the Navy.) Also he seemed (not surprisingly) too military, too bureaucratic and, even eighteen months after his arrival, untrusting – especially, we thought, of the Clandestine Service.

I never met Turner because I was overseas during his entire tenure. From comments I picked up, however, I got an impression. His negative view of the DDO, his attitude towards being our Director (just another job) and, perhaps most of all, his 'militaryness', were factors that made him one of the least likeable Directors we had ever had. He and Schlesinger were running neck and neck in office polls.

TWELVE

RETURN TO
HONG KONG

1978–81

We arrived in Hong Kong in the summer of 1978. It hadn't changed all that much during our five-year absence. There were new office and apartment buildings, and the harbour tunnel had changed traffic patterns, but the people and the hectic pace of life seemed the same. It remained a vibrant, dynamic city – and it was still hot and humid in July. We arrived in early evening after the gruelling, fifteen-hour flight from Los Angeles. We were met as we cleared immigration and taken to our hotel.

We were at the end of several busy months and were relieved to be at the end of our travels. Our home leave had been a series of enjoyable but wearing trips around the country visiting family and friends. Our girls handled it all with aplomb and we were proud of them. The two eldest, Suzanne and Danika, remembered Hong Kong and were excited about coming back. Relatives promised they would visit us and we welcomed them, but doubted that they would actually come. A stop in Washington had given me some idea of a 'personnel issue' in the Hong Kong office, but there were few details.

I was soon told that the problem involved inappropriate behaviour on the part of the Chief, Jack G. Rumours were running rampant and they greatly exaggerated the story. He was alleged to have had an illicit affair with one of our female employees. Obviously, that was unacceptable and he was withdrawn as soon as Headquarters became aware of the situation. In addition to the damage he did to himself and his marriage, the terrible example he set and the poor leadership and judgement he demonstrated seriously harmed morale. For reasons of privacy, I never received a briefing on the matter. But it wasn't difficult to piece together at least the outline of what had precipitated the management changes in the station.

One of the unfortunate casualties of this unseemly situation was the man I was replacing, Charlie K. He had been caught up, unfairly so in my view, in the turmoil caused by the Chief's actions. A Korean American with a long record of loyal and exemplary service in the Directorate, he had been my Branch Chief at Headquarters in the mid-1970s. He had been a conscientious and hard worker and his assignment as Deputy in Hong Kong was in recognition of his abilities and contributions. I liked and respected him greatly and wanted to talk to him about the situation. That was not to be, however, as he left, feeling disgraced, before my arrival. I felt then and still feel today that his difficulty had a cultural origin. He was simply more supportive and loyal than was warranted under the circumstances. My view was that he either didn't know about, or more likely didn't believe, the stories about the Chief, and as a consequence found himself isolated and in an untenable position. I don't know who made the decision to withdraw him short of tour, or why it was made – certainly no one could have questioned his integrity. I saw him as a victim and I know that the shame of what happened hurt him deeply.

Arriving on the same day as me, from Seoul where he had also been the Chief, was Bob G., Hong Kong's new Chief. I had never met him before despite his long record of service in the Far East Division. Our paths had just never crossed. I knew of him, had neither positive nor negative views, and I looked forward to getting to know him. An Irish American from Boston, as were a large percentage of his generation of Directorate officers, he was reputed to be energetic, hard working and fair. He was staying in the same hotel and we had arranged to meet on the morning after our arrival. I went up to his room to meet him.

'I've heard lots of good things. Glad to finally meet you,' he said with a warm and sincere smile after opening the door. He wasn't dressed and had been in the middle of shaving when I knocked. He was in his early fifties, and at about 5 foot 8 inches and 160 pounds, he looked to be in pretty good shape. He waved me into the room. 'Sit down a minute,' he said. 'Sorry I'm late. I'll be finished in a minute and then we can have some breakfast. We've got lots to talk about.'

I sat down in a chair by the window looking out across the harbour towards Kowloon.

'What do you know about why Headquarters sent us here?' he said from his stance in front of the bathroom mirror.

'Not much at all,' I replied. 'Mostly rumour. It seems to be personal and they are holding it pretty close. I was in Headquarters two weeks ago and got almost nothing. Just briefings on what we're doing work-wise. I didn't press anybody.'

He came out of the bathroom and started dressing. 'Well, I've heard that Jack was messing around where he shouldn't have been and Headquarters found out. They had to recall him. Charlie just got screwed by the situation. And I've also heard that one reason it's you and me is that we both have reputations as strong family men.'

I knew that he had friends who were senior officers, so I figured he had pretty good information. 'I feel sorry for Charlie,' I said. 'I know he wouldn't have done anything wrong. I hoped to talk with him, but he's already gone I'm told.'

'Yep, I think he left two days ago. Jack's gone too. We need to get in there and raise the comfort level.' He studied me carefully for an instant. 'You know Hong Kong,' he said. 'That's going to be a big help.'

Our officers had known the changes were coming and many of them knew one or the other of us, so our entry on the scene caused few ripples; probably more behind the scenes than I imagined, but outwardly we were welcomed. Many hoped we would bring a stabilizing influence and I hoped to do just that. The sooner we put the disruption behind us and got back to a total focus on work, the better. I know Bob felt the same way.

While Hong Kong itself had experienced little change in the years since our departure in 1973, the situation in mainland China was dramatically different. The changes in 1976 were particularly momentous. In January of that year, Chou En Lai, China's respected and revered Prime Minister, died. Then, on 28 July, a stunning earthquake centred in the city of Tang Shan, in northeast China, left over 250,000 dead. The city, a coal-mining centre about 200 miles north-east of Beijing, was left in rubble and has never been rebuilt. Finally, with the aftershocks of the terrible earthquake still felt, Mao Tse Tung died on 9 September after a long illness. The totality of the events in 1976 caused many in China to fear that '*Jung Gwo*', the Middle Kingdom, had lost '*Tian Ming*', the mandate of Heaven. Mao's death signalled the end of the Great Cultural Revolution, which must have been a great relief to China's masses. Given the different climate it would bring about on the mainland, it also portended changes in our approach.

As if that suffering wasn't enough, the 'Gang of Four', Mao's wife and three other opportunistic hard-line communists, seized control of the party after Mao's death, and with it political control of the country. There was continued turmoil until the Gang of Four was arrested and Hua Guo Feng took the reins of power. He lasted only until early 1978. At that point, Deng Xiao Ping, who had been disgraced and removed from power during the Cultural Revolution (for, among other things, being a bridge player), manoeuvred his way back to the top and gained full control of the party and the country. The years since my departure, especially the last two, had been eventful indeed for China.

We didn't know it at the time, of course (I doubt that Deng himself knew what was coming), but Deng was to introduce reforms that would have profound and lasting effects on China and on its relations with the rest of the world. Those same reforms were to have an impact on us as well. For many reasons, but most importantly for trade and economic reasons, China under Deng was to become a more 'open' society than it had previously been.

We could see change coming in the summer of 1978, but we didn't see it going as far as it has. The changes we envisioned were welcomed mostly for the easing of the security environment that might result. Deng's reforms, which started in the country-side as collective farms began to be systematically dismantled in favour of private plots, prompted another surge in interest in China among Washington's policy makers. There was, in turn, a surge of requirements levied upon us as change in China gener-ated questions at all levels. Pressure for increased production of intelligence fell heavily upon our office. Clearly we were going to have to both augment and fine-tune our programmes.

Despite increased openness, however, the Bamboo Curtain had not been lifted. Heartening to us, though, was the fact that the greatly increased level of travel into China, including American businessmen and diplomats, would augment the pool of people we could talk to about what was going on inside China. As these changes occurred however, the bar measuring the level of intelligence we were tasked to collect was raised. Certain kinds of information that had been obtainable via carefully planned clandestine operations were now available by overt means. Our tasking pushed us up the scale towards intelligence information that was ever more difficult to obtain. With all of these things in mind, Bob and I started trying to improve our collection programmes across the board.

We blended back into life in Hong Kong quite easily. In some ways, it was as if we hadn't been away at all. Some others had the same feeling. Shortly after we had reactivated our membership at the Ladies' Recreation Club (one of the first things we did), I ran into a member who had been a casual acquaintance in 1973.

'My goodness,' he said, 'I was just thinking that your home leave had been a long one.'

Many of our old friends were still living in Hong Kong and we resumed our contacts with ease. Judy moved back into some regular tennis games and, at her vastly improved level, was promptly invited to play on the club team. As opposed to our first arrival, we knew where to go for various household purchases. Driving on the left side of the road presented no problem. We moved into a nice apartment on Bowen Road in the mid-levels. It was nicely located at the end of the road and offered immediate access to Bowen Path, where I jogged most mornings. And the living room was big enough to accommodate the baby grand piano we had shipped from Malaysia. Two of the girls shared a bedroom, but that presented no problem either. Soon, we felt right at home again.

After some discussions with friends, we decided to put the girls into the Hong Kong International School, located on the other side of the island in Repulse Bay. It was run by a Lutheran missionary group, but didn't press religion on its students. The majority of the students were from the American community in Hong Kong, but there were many Chinese and European students too. The fact that it used American techniques and standards influenced our decision. We felt it would preclude problems of adjustment for the girls. The International School of Kuala Lumpur had also used the American system and they would likely be returning to school in the United States after this tour.

Within months, however, we began to doubt our decision. It started with Suzanne, then aged twelve. Her reports of how things were going in her classroom were, to us, disquieting. We were similarly worried by reports from Danika and Alison. One thing led to another and we found ourselves questioning what educators at the time called the 'open classroom' method. The final straw came while I was escorting a visitor from Washington on a tour of the school. In one of the large, open classrooms, there were about 100 students.

It was noisy, I noticed. In fact, it was Bedlam. Kids were milling around everywhere. I greeted the teacher and introduced my visitor.

'It's too bad we got here during the recess period,' he said. 'I was hoping to watch some classroom sessions.'

'Oh, it's not recess period,' she told him. 'It's just that the children have more freedom and choice in our system. This is the classroom. There are no smaller rooms. That teacher', she gestured towards a woman sitting in a cluster of children, 'is teaching now.'

My visitor looked surprised. I was shocked. How the hell could anyone learn anything in a place like this? We looked around for a few more minutes and then left.

'I'm not that impressed with the open classroom system,' was all he said when we got outside. Neither was I.

We decided to withdraw our children from the Hong Kong International School as soon as possible. Unfortunately, only Suzanne could transfer after the first semester. The others were forced to wait until the following September for openings.

When he learned of Suzanne's withdrawal, the Principal asked to see me. Our conversation was, I suspect, satisfying to neither of us. After some initial sparring, I came directly to the point and levelled some strong criticisms of open classroom teaching. He tried to explain and I rebutted his explanations. Finally, exasperated, he said, 'You just don't understand.' He was right. But I note for the record that the open classroom system was soon scrapped as being unworkable and bad for students.

In contrast to this chaos, our girls thrived at the Swiss German International School, run through the European system, where discipline, structure, homework and classes of no more than twenty were standard. It was more demanding, but all my girls have fond memories of their time there.

The office, a large one, had a strong complement of officers and support personnel. My initial favourable impression of our officers, gained while I was at Headquarters, was confirmed as I met each one. All but a few spoke good Chinese. Several were Chinese American officers who spoke at least two dialects of Chinese. Each of our Branches looked to be well-staffed and functioning smoothly. For several reasons, including my recent experience in Kuala Lumpur, I was particularly happy to see that we had two excellent reports officers. One was a man who had formerly been a case officer (he would be replaced the next year by an even stronger reports officer), and the other a young woman with only Headquarters' experience who was on her first tour. They were a strong and competent section.

Our support officers also performed admirably, handling personnel, administrative and budget logistics, and a myriad other things that come up unexpectedly. And, as was the norm in my experience, we had strong secretaries. All met every demand we placed on them.

I met each employee in the office privately, as did Bob. For me, all the vibes were positive and indications were that the sooner we put the unfortunate failings of the departed Chief behind us and got on with our work, the better all would feel. Bob made that precise point at the first 'all hands' meeting and in the staff meetings. Within weeks, the unscheduled changes were just history.

The upheaval, tempest in a teapot I'm tempted to say, had little discernible impact on our operational activities. I had reviewed the status of our operational programme briefly while I was at Headquarters and I was favourably impressed. Now, on-the-scene discussions with each of our Branch Chiefs left me optimistic about the contribution we would be able to make. Branch by Branch I could see that promising developmental efforts were under way and ongoing agent operations were producing solid intelligence for Washington. Even more heartening was the fact that the operational Branches were particularly active. I was pleased to note that the component handling covert action activities was smaller and its objectives seemed to be more sensible. One Branch, which focused on South-East Asian and, to some extent, European matters, was certainly holding its own, but lacked Chinese speakers. No matter what your target was, an inability to speak Chinese was an inhibiting factor in Hong Kong. By now, of course, we had a presence inside China, but it was labouring under severe security constraints and just getting established. Hong Kong remained, as it had for two decades, a primary collection point for China and the 'flagship post' for China Operations.

Overall progress, I noted, had been substantial. Each Branch was aggressively pursuing several promising efforts aimed at the future while running ongoing operations to sustain our level of production – which was good. There were a number of reasons for the progress recorded during my five-year absence. Clearly we were getting better and better at running denied area operations. That steadily improving savvy, and the increased levels of sophistication and applicability evident in the technical and communications gear that had been developed for use in these operations, was doubtless paying dividends. Our confidence was up.

Another reason, I assumed, was the degree of change in China. The years since the table-tennis team's visit in 1971 had witnessed considerable social and political turmoil and change and much of it had worked in our favour. The death of Mao and the end of the Cultural Revolution signalled a lessening of the xenophobia that had gripped the country since 1949. The Gang of Four was gone and far-reaching reforms were in place. Diplomatic relations between China and the United States had been established and we had an Embassy in Beijing. The number of people entering China was overwhelming by comparison with the early 1970s and the internal security network was, in turn, stretched. They couldn't possibly maintain the same level of scrutiny as had previously been the case. The operational climate, while by no means favourable, was 'less unfavourable' and we had shifted our approaches to more productively exploit the new environment. I made a point of complimenting the Branch Chiefs and reported my impressions to Bob. I also made note of those impressions in a long cable to Headquarters.

I do not mean to gloss over what happened in Hong Kong in the months before my 1978 arrival. The offences committed and the behaviour of the Chief, details of which are still unknown to me, were not trivial. Nor could they have been ignored even if someone had wanted to. Our Director at the time, Stansfield Turner, did not like the Agency and was particularly suspicious of the Directorate of Operations. Seeking to upgrade the morals of those serving abroad, for reasons never clear to me, he had dispatched a crony, Rusty Williams, to numerous overseas stations to investigate and report on family life. Many were offended by the accusatory approach he took and neither Turner nor Williams enjoyed much respect or popularity. It may be an overly harsh judgement (as I've said, I never met the man), but I view Turner as one of the worst Directors the Agency has ever had.

What happened in Hong Kong only added fuel to Turner's fire of criticisms of the Directorate's overseas complement. He was, among other things, wrong and naive in his views. I do not excuse the comportment that prompted the withdrawal of a Chief. But it should not have been expanded into a general critique of the Directorate of Operations and I hasten to point out that the sins he lamented are not limited to officers serving overseas. They are sins committed by people in all walks of life. Indeed, a President of the United States was accused of adultery and sexual misbehaviour, and *was* excused.

Human beings are weak and they sin. The fact that our cadre is so carefully selected, tested and vetted, and is of such a high calibre, does not mean that some will not violate trust. It would be silly to think otherwise. But Turner had his own optic and that may explain his actions. Rusty Williams is reputed to have been appalled to learn that operations officers in Europe (as is the case globally) sometimes left their wives and families in the evening to go and meet agents. Since evenings and weekends, when they are not at work, are the only times the vast majority of agents can be met, there was (is) no choice. Wives of our officers around the world understood and accepted it as a demand of the service – an occupational necessity. Most didn't like it, Judy certainly didn't, but they understood why it had to be done. It shouldn't have been that hard for Williams, or Turner, to figure that out.

The months passed quickly and soon it was spring 1979. I stood in front of the window in my office and looked down on the traffic passing down Garden Road towards central district. It was late afternoon and there was lots of traffic, but I was looking without seeing. I was thinking. One of our Branch Chiefs and our senior reports officers were sitting in my office. We had been discussing how we intended to respond to the latest cable from Headquarters that raised, again, questions about one of our operations. They thought we were getting flawed information. I was perplexed, maybe even irritated, and standing in front of the window gave me time to weigh what I would and what I would not condone in our response, which the reports chief would write.

'So, Headquarters is still convinced that our guy is giving us bum skinny,' I said as I turned and sat down again at my desk.

'That's right,' the Branch Chief responded, 'and I'm dammed if I know why.' The incoming cable had frustrated us all.

'What do you think, Mary?' I asked the reports officer. She was excellent and had lots of experience.

'You know what I think, Dick,' she quickly replied. 'I would not have recommended dissemination of the intelligence if I had any questions about the agent's access or reliability.'

'I think they are way off base on this one,' the Branch Chief interjected. 'Matt [the case handling officer] has done all his homework. We've got independent confirmation of his activity. Plus we saw him get on the train to Lowu. He makes the trips.' He slapped his knee.

'I think that much is clear even to Headquarters,' I said, 'but the reporting is what they are questioning. Is this a stalemate or is there some way we can convince them that it's good stuff?'

'I'm not sure, but we have to try,' Mary volunteered. 'Let me draft a reply for you to look at and we can meet again before we send something back.'

This was not an unusual meeting. The case had been the source of a series of cables back and forth to Headquarters for the past several months. We had recruited this particular agent and vetted him carefully, trained him thoroughly and dispatched him to the

Chinese mainland. First missions, as usual, were for testing purposes as much as for intelligence collection. To us, he looked good. We also tested him in Hong Kong and he passed there as well. Matt had elicited a lot of background information about him and his family in China, and it all hung together. Part of his motivation was abuse suffered by his family during the Cultural Revolution. Another part was financial; he wanted to send his children abroad for an education. Mary assessed the access he claimed and it squared with the information he was reporting. We felt we were on strong ground.

But some at Headquarters questioned both the access he claimed and the information he was reporting. They were reluctant to disseminate it to the intelligence community until their doubts were resolved. As the exchanges continued, flashes of frustration appeared in some of the cables. This, despite efforts on both ends to keep the exchanges civil and substantive. I held the major portion of that responsibility at our end and I was determined to avoid letting emotions or frustration colour our presentations.

In the end, Mary wrote an excellent draft cable that struck just the right tone. Bob agreed and we fired it off to Headquarters. I knew that the leader of the Doubting Thomas group at Headquarters was a particular senior reports officer who had served previously in Hong Kong. I respected her professional competence and I knew she could draw upon her experience in this type of operation and reporting. But still I disagreed with her assessments and felt she had developed a bias against this particular operation. It was the human element in any system and I see it more dispassionately now than I did in the late 1970s in Hong Kong. In their response, Headquarters not only rejected our arguments, but raised more questions about the intelligence. In the end, the exchange ground to a halt and we dropped the case. We were not happy, but that was how the system worked.

That case was but one of many similar exchanges and it was a function of the system at work. It was the responsibility of officers at Headquarters to review field operations and intelligence to assure reliability and accuracy. And it was the responsibility of officers abroad, in response to requirements received from Headquarters (the intelligence community as a whole that is), to generate new operations and to authenticate them to the satisfaction of Headquarters. When both sides were doing their jobs, the system was working as it should. The final say, however, rested at Headquarters. We in the field could only continue to press our points and attempt to convince our colleagues at Headquarters that the operation in question was a good one.

There is little question that in the case of an office running operations into a denied area, like Hong Kong at that time, the issues were more difficult to resolve. Our ability to verify what happened to an agent once he or she crossed the border into China was minimal and left many questions unanswered. We could only make informed decisions and there was always the danger of bias in favour of what were, in fact, our own operations. We were aware of that, of course, and strove to make solid balanced calls. Almost always, Headquarters accepted our judgements and the intelligence was disseminated to the community. Sometimes it was not.

Later in 1979, in July, I was enjoying a rare respite from the mountain of office work my job demanded. I saw Stig before he spotted me sitting at our reserved table. He was often late as lunchtime was a busy time of the day for him. I was sitting in the American Club in the St George's building, a newly built skyscraper in Central district and an easy walk from the office. This was a relationship based entirely on personal friendship with a Scandinavian I'd known since the early 1970s, so I made no attempt to ferret out possible surveillance. Despite its name, the American Club had a mixed membership. Less than half the membership was American and the other half was Chinese and European. It was a prestigious place, which offered excellent lunch and dinner service. Mostly it was a lunchtime rendezvous spot for businessmen working in Central. I often used it as a place to meet and develop contacts of interest. My Scandinavian friend, who worked in the transportation sector, had lots of contact and dealings with Chinese officials.

'Stig, over here,' I called out as he approached. I stood up to shake his hand. 'How are you?' I asked. We exchanged pleasantries for a couple of minutes.

As our waiter approached the table I looked at Stig. 'What do you think? Should we have the usual?' I asked.

Without hesitation, he replied enthusiastically, 'The usual.'

Over the years of lunching together at the American Club, we had fallen into the habit of always having the same thing. We both liked it. I ordered two Bloody Marys to start. Then two avocado, stuffed with baby shrimp and covered with a thousand island dressing. Then steak tartar for two. It was easy for the waiter.

'Let me guess,' I said, 'you were late because you had a call from Europe.'

He smiled. 'No, not this time,' he replied. 'I had a meeting with a visitor from Beijing and he wouldn't stop talking.'

'Well, is Deng still in charge up there?' I asked with a smile.

'Yeah, I think so,' he said. 'And according to this guy, everyone is happy as the reforms crank along.'

'Well, I'm going up there next month. I hope they are so busy with the reforms that they don't bother a poor China watcher from Hong Kong.'

'Ah, but for you there will be a special welcome,' he grinned.

Although I had not admitted otherwise and he had not pushed the point, I knew he wasn't buying my 'China watcher' cover. No matter, as it never affected our relationship.

'Seriously though, Dick. Are you going up there? That would be an interesting trip. Can you believe that I've lived in Hong Kong for over twenty years and I've never set foot on the mainland?'

'Sure I can believe it. There are lots of people in Hong Kong that have never been into China. But things are changing and for someone with your contacts it would be easy to set up a trip. You ought to think about it.'

We had finished the avocado cocktail and the waiter approached the table to prepare our steak tartar. It was always done with flair. How would we like it today? he would ask. Like you always make it, was the standard response. He started by breaking a couple of raw eggs into the large bowl in front of him on the small table he was using. Then he put in some condiments, followed by the raw steak. Then he mixed things up for a while and added some salt and pepper and a few other spices. Having finished the ceremonial preparation, he presented us each a small taste of the final product. 'Does that meet with your satisfaction?' he would always ask. 'Just right,' we would always respond. I don't really know what he put in, but I would not have disputed the club's claim that they served the best steak tartar in Hong Kong.

As we ate, Stig and I discussed a wide range of subjects that we both followed. We always covered investments and finance. He had money in the stock market and precious metals as well. We also hit international affairs, usually region by region. Politics blended right in and he voiced his deeply held Conservative views. Carter caused him great pain and he was delighted when Reagan was elected President. He was intensely anti-communist and had left his home country because of the increasingly socialist and leftist policies pushed by the government there. The United States, he often told me, was the world's best hope. Even with a President as naive as Jimmy Carter, he added, after my return in 1978. Chemistry between us was good and we agreed on most subjects so the conversations were always congenial.

After we had finished the steak tartar, and after rationalizing the decision, we both ordered apple pie *à la mode*, another speciality of the American Club. Neither of us normally ordered dessert, but at the American Club we both made an exception for this. Then came coffee and it was usually over coffee, after many patrons had left, that we fell onto the subject of his dealings with the mainland Chinese. Sometimes he would just say that there was nothing new. Other times he would raise the subject himself. By this time, he knew what was of interest to our analysts and, speaking quietly but clearly, he would fill me in on recent developments. I would pose questions from time to time. He would answer. Sometimes I would take a few notes. Always our conversations on this subject were interesting. Intelligent, observant and articulate, he was able to provide me with valuable insights into what China was doing in the shipping sector. Intelligence reports I prepared from information he provided were well received by Headquarters. One in particular was singled out for special praise because of the history and insights it contained.

For me, the meeting was not only interesting but a welcome respite in a day often filled with work inside the office that involved meetings, decisions, cable writing and other management chores. In Hong Kong, the situation (the internal service there would not be easy to fool) and the operational climate dictated that I would not handle any agents. This kind of a meeting, an innocuous one with an old Viking friend, was as close as I could get to 'on the street' operational activity. Otherwise, I had to be content, in an operational sense, with vicarious rewards.

Later in the week after my lunch with Stig, I was back to the regular routine and getting a briefing about a troublesome case.

'The meeting was in our safe house in Wanchai,' the Branch Chief was explaining to me. Mary, the reports officer, and Mike, the case officer, were also there.

'Which one?' I asked.

'It's in the building right on the corner of Hennessey and Fleet – on the fourth floor. You can see the whole intersection from the window in the living room.'

'Harbour side of the intersection?' I asked.

'That's right,' he replied.

I could picture the building in my mind. We had had a safe house there when I took over our operational support section in 1969. It had been terminated and this was a new one. It was a good building for our purposes. It had entrances (and therefore exits) on two different streets, and there was no caretaker monitoring who came and went. It was easy for a Chinese support agent to rent an apartment and access was clear all day while the agent was at work. There were Europeans living in the building and most apartments in the building offered a good look at traffic in the intersection in front of the building. Hennessey Road itself was a major thoroughfare running east–west along the north side of Hong Kong Island. There was heavy traffic most of the time – cars, buses, mini buses, taxis and trucks in abundance. It offered easy, quick access for agents and case officers alike.

'Why don't you review what happened?' I said.

'I had scheduled the meeting for eleven this morning,' reported Mike, 'and Lynx [the cryptonym used for this particular agent] arrived just a couple of minutes late. I saw him get off the mini bus coming from Central. The meeting went about as planned. He didn't have much intelligence from his cousin, but said he'd have more after his cousin's trip to Shanghai next week. As you know, we've had some questions about his reporting,' Mary nodded, 'so we set up surveillance to see what he would do after the meeting.'

'So, what did he do?' I asked.

'He came out on the Fleet Street side, looked around quickly and headed down Fleet for the Harbour. He made a short phone call, then turned east on Lockhart Road. Three blocks down Lockhart he met Au Sap Chung, who was waiting on the corner. Brazen little shit! I think our guys got a good photo of the two walking together.'

'I knew it!' Mary almost jumped out of her chair. 'He's nailed.'

Au Sap Chung was a known fabricator, and catching Lynx with him immediately after a meeting with us was all we needed to resolve our doubts about his intelligence production. It was a coup and evidence of solid tradecraft by Mike.

'Bloody well done, as the Brits would say,' I told them. 'It's like dodging a bullet when we dig one of these creeps out of the woodwork.' Thinking of cases in my previous tour, I added, 'We've had to do it before and we'll no doubt have to do it again.'

Mary and Mike had worked closely together to set up this test that Lynx failed so miserably, although he didn't know it yet. This was just how teamwork should turn out and I was pleased. In the near future, we would cut off contact with Lynx citing some plausible reason. We would not let on to him what had happened or that we knew of his contact with Au Sap Chung. That pained Mike, who wanted to confront Lynx with the photograph. But there were other fabricators out there we knew about and, from our perspective, neither Lynx nor Au had any 'need to know'.

'And what is the reason for your trip?' the immigration official at the train station in Kowloon asked.

'Tourism,' I responded. It was true. It was October 1979 and I was embarking on a familiarization trip to add some sense of reality to the target country on which I was devoting most of my waking hours. I would undertake nothing smacking of collection or operational activity. To strengthen my case, I had hoped Judy would accompany me, but she declined, not wanting to leave the girls under servant care for two weeks. Upon hearing that, my dad, who for years had wanted to see Shanghai, jumped into the breech and volunteered to accompany me. I accepted with pleasure.

All of the travel arrangements had been made with China

Travel Service (CTS), the official Chinese government organization responsible for dealing with tourists to China. CTS guides (watchdogs?) would accompany us for much of the time. We were among the first wave of tourists into China since the reforms initiated by Deng Xiao Ping in 1978 had opened the floodgates.

I was particularly interested in the customs and immigration checks at Lowu, as we crossed into China. Years earlier, I had tried to prepare agents for this moment without knowing how it worked, and since then I had read numerous reports about what could happen.

At Lowu, we disembarked from the train and walked across the border to enter the customs hall. The checks we experienced were cursory. The customs officer glanced at our luggage and waved us through. Nor was there any question or comment when our travel documents were scanned. I hadn't been sure what to expect. I had to assume that as an American diplomat on vacation I would draw some attention, but didn't know how much. These guys couldn't have cared less. I also had to assume that by now the PSB, China's internal security service, had me spotted as a China watcher in Hong Kong and suspect intelligence officer. Would I, as a result, be put under surveillance or harassed in any way? That remained to be seen. Certainly there was no hint of any interest in me at Lowu as we crossed into China.

We left the customs hall at the opposite end from where we entered and boarded the train waiting on the Chinese side of the border. An uneventful trip to Canton followed. There were few non-Asians on this train, so it must have been easy for the CTS guide to spot us as we got off the train in Canton.

Approaching us with a big smile, she asked in good English, 'Are you Mr Holm?'

'Yes, I am,' I smiled back and introduced my father.

'Welcome to Canton,' she said. 'Please follow me.'

First we picked up our luggage which had been off-loaded into the station, then boarded a small mini bus and drove to Canton's airport about twenty kilometres north-west of the city. We would be visiting Canton on our return trip. Today we were headed straight to Shanghai by plane.

We were met as we deplaned and driven straight to our hotel. It was a decent, not deluxe, hotel located in what used to be the

German quarter before the Second World War, just outside the centre of the city. Then, to my surprise, the CTS guide left us on our own with nothing but a schedule of travel arrangements. Three days to visit Shanghai, as we wished, day trips to Hangchou and Soochou and then to the airport for a plane to Beijing.

With the benefit of this unexpected freedom of movement, we spent three days wandering around Shanghai visiting all the tourist sights and taking a cruise on the Huangpu River. It was truly enjoyable for us both and I marvelled at much of what I saw, much of which was not at all what I had expected. I was delighted to be able to use my Mandarin. I couldn't understand the Shanghai dialect, but many people spoke Mandarin as well as their dialect and most understood me. A few were dumbstruck to hear a '*yang gweidz*', a foreign devil, speaking 'the mother tongue of the central kingdom'. In a couple of cases, I think I might have been the first foreigner the person had ever seen.

On the river cruise, I joined many others in taking numerous pictures including some that had Chinese navy warships in the background. Before the reforms, such photos would have been strictly forbidden. I was amazed at the lack of any controls. We visited the Yu Gardens and the famous teahouse (hundreds of years old) therein and the Friendship Store, where we bought some jade and stone carvings.

While we were walking along the famous Bund, a walkway along the Huangpu River, built in the 1930s by German contractors, we were approached by a Chinese man who addressed us in English.

'Are you American?' he asked. Until that point, there had been no surveillance and no particular interest in us at all, and I had asked myself how we could be moving around so freely. When he addressed us, my guard went up. I nodded.

He was well dressed, wearing a suit and tie, and trim looking. He must have been about Dad's age, late sixties.

'I used to be in the United States Navy,' he announced proudly. 'I almost became an American citizen, but the war changed everything here. My name is Wang.'

'In our Navy?' I asked. 'Where did you serve?' Dad was intrigued but said nothing.

'I worked on a Yangtze River gunboat in the thirties,' he

replied. 'I did some training in the Philippines and I had almost ten years of service when the Japanese attacked. I couldn't get out of China.' It sounded plausible enough. My concern ebbed.

He walked with us along the Bund. We chatted about some of his experiences and he had had quite a life. He was retired now and obviously had been able to save some money to support himself. We didn't talk about any family he might have had. We both felt more and more at ease with him and when he suggested a cup of tea together we agreed. We had been walking for quite a while and I knew Dad would enjoy a break.

As we chatted, he declared that he wanted his family to meet two real Americans and he invited us for dinner at his home that very evening. I hesitated. We were free, but was this legitimate? I considered the possibility of a provocation engineered by the PSB. But to what end? We were doing nothing wrong. I discounted that possibility and accepted. Dad was delighted, seeing this as an exciting experience.

The taxi driver looked incredulous when I handed him the small piece of paper on which Wang had written his address. I'm sure he was thinking, what would you two guys be going there for? We had no idea what part of the city it was. We had tried to look it up, but the street was too small to appear on a tourist-style map. After a twenty-minute drive into and through the centre of the city and then to the north-east, he dropped us off on a dark corner and pointed up a small lane.

There was hardly any light and we hesitated to get out, but there was little choice. The driver spoke Mandarin and he confirmed that the building just up the lane was our destination.

Even in the quiet darkness, you could sense that the neighbourhood we were in was old and decrepit. There was no one in sight as we started walking slowly up the lane towards the building the taxi driver had pointed out. I had some second thoughts about the wisdom of being in this situation. I didn't let on to Dad, and I did not start whistling in the dark.

'I can't see anything, Dick,' Dad said. 'You sure we're in the right place?'

'I'm pretty sure we are,' I replied. 'Taxi driver said it was this building.' We were walking in the lane along a wall that separated the lane from the buildings. Just then, we came to an opening.

The gate was broken and hanging open, on rusty hinges. There was a small, dim light on a pole inside and it illuminated the number on the front of the building. 'That's the right number,' I said as I spotted the sign.

'He said fourth floor, right?' Dad asked.

'Right,' I replied as we entered the front door of the building. Still we had seen no one. We were alone in the small lobby (or at least what passed as the lobby) of what had, at one time, been a nice apartment building. Now it was literally falling apart. There was no elevator. We headed for the stairwell in the far corner of the lobby. For reasons I couldn't put my finger on, I still felt uneasy. I tried not to let on or make Dad nervous.

'Well, do you feel like walking up four flights of stairs?' I said. 'I don't see any elevator.'

'No problem,' Dad replied as he started up the stairs. I followed. Even if we find Wang, I was thinking, how the hell are we going to get out of here?

There were doors on either side of the fourth floor landing. Fortunately for us, there was a readable sign on one that bore the number Wang had given us. We knocked. To my relief and delight, the door was opened immediately to reveal Wang smiling broadly. He ushered us in and introduced us to his two sons who were waiting in the living room. One spoke a few words of English and the other spoke Mandarin. There were some women present as well, but they stayed in the background. With precious few amenities, we sat down in the adjoining dining room and the women started bringing in food.

Several courses were served and it was clear that Wang wanted to impress us with his hospitality. He did. I know the meal was a costly one and I felt almost embarrassed because I had no idea how much money this family could afford to spend entertaining complete strangers. The *pièce de résistance* was a course of hairy-legged Shanghai crabs, a speciality in Shanghai. They were delicious and I'm sure expensive as hell. Good Chinese beer was served throughout the meal. The entire family treated us as honoured guests and the evening was enjoyable in every sense of the word. Rightly or wrongly, my fears, which had been just below the surface during our protracted arrival, and my concerns about our being there, evaporated after the first course and the first beer.

As we prepared to leave, I asked Wang for some directions. He waved my questions aside as we said goodbye to his family. He and a son insisted on accompanying us downstairs, where we found that a taxi was waiting in front of the building. Obviously, prior arrangements had been made. In the Shanghai dialect, Wang instructed the driver on where we were staying. No problems at all and soon we were home safe and sound.

The question remains; why did Wang insist on hosting such an affair? His memories of the American Navy must have been good. We exchanged addresses and he said he would write to Dad. He never did. Not knowing his situation, and fearing a possible security problem for someone receiving mail from an American he didn't really know, I never wrote to him either.

Visits after Shanghai to Hangchou, Soochou, Beijing, Nanking and Canton were both interesting and enjoyable and we left China on a hydrofoil from Canton port to Hong Kong. This was a remarkable ride during which I thought about Clavell's character, Tai Pan, in the book by the same name. In a particularly exciting part of the book, Tai Pan makes the same voyage, from Canton to Hong Kong, also at night, but sailing alone on a battered junk so laden with gold that it is almost sinking, and being pursued by several thugs. Our journey was not quite so hair-raising.

The trip admirably accomplished its goal of giving me a better picture of the county I reported on and read about on a daily basis. There is little question that much of what I saw and experienced greatly enhanced my understanding of and 'feel' for China.

As a family, we prospered during the three years of my second tour in Hong Kong. Because of the earlier tour, we adjusted quickly and had almost universally positive experiences. All but five-year-old Pia started playing lots of tennis. (Even Pia by the age of eight, when we left, was hitting lots of tennis balls.) They all seemed to like it and each one did well. We were delighted. Especially so when Suzy, via her success in junior tournaments, was asked to join the Hong Kong junior Davis Cup team. Danika also enjoyed success in junior tournaments, but was too young to make the same team. They all still play – and they all beat their dad regularly.

Alison, while in grade three at the Swiss German school, entered a colony-wide public-speaking contest. This after overcoming the objections of her British teacher, who was highly critical of Alison's American accent. One can imagine how proud she was, and also the rest of us, when she won in her district and was placed high in the colony finals. (To her credit, Alison's British teacher was gracious about Ali's success although she made clear it was *her* work with Alison that had carried the day.) Pia, striving to stay up with her sisters, was ahead of herself in many areas. All four played in piano competitions, practising on the infamous piano from Malaysia. It was a period of rapid and solid academic and social growth for them all.

In January 1980, about eighteen months after our joint arrival, Bob G. was called back to Headquarters to become Chief of East Asia Division. It came as a surprise to all of us and it left me in the position of Acting Chief until Bob's replacement could be named and arrive on scene. Still at the GS-15 grade level, I could not have hoped to be named myself, so I would just have to wait and see who would be coming.

Bob left in February and his replacement didn't arrive until summer. The months that I spent in an acting capacity were enjoyable and demanding. My desk was truly where the buck stopped. Days were filled with the full range of decisions that had to be taken in order to keep everything functioning. The highest priority, of course, was operations, but personnel, budget and administrative questions among others surfaced all the time.

It was, for example, (still is, of course) important to prepare annual appraisal reports on our officers and other personnel carefully and thoughtfully. Either writing or, as is required in our system, reviewing appraisal reports took up many long hours. Happily, our officers were strong and that made the task that much easier. Collectively we all faced the same challenge.

On another occasion, Ron, our administration officer, presented me with a draft state department administrative cable to be sent to Washington. It had to do with budget matters and shared costs. The state department functioned as the manager, so to speak, and other government departments and agencies, including mine, contributed to the operating costs on an annual basis. I refused to sign this one.

'But Dick,' he said, 'we've been signing it for years. What will I tell the administrative officer?'

The cable I was refusing to sign had us contributing to the general fund for, among other things, 'office equipment and furniture'.

'Let me explain, Ron,' I said. 'I first arrived here in early 1969. I was here for four years and I knew all the offices. Our premises are exactly the same. And so is everything else. There is no new furniture or desks, and no new typewriters. We have nothing new at all. Everything in this office and our other offices is the same as it was in 1969. So why the hell should we pay anything when we get nothing?'

'I didn't know,' Ron replied. 'They aren't going to be happy. This is pretty standard stuff.'

'That's just tough. We're taking it off standard. Just say we won't pay for what we don't get,' I declared. 'And tell them that I'm writing to our Headquarters and laying out the problem. They can hash it out in Washington. I'm not signing till I hear from home.'

'OK, OK, I can see that you have a point,' Ron said. 'I'll explain to the admin officer.'

I knew I was making life difficult for poor Ron, but it just wasn't a fair deal. I didn't know how long we had been doing this, but I meant to stop the boat – or at least express some displeasure.

In the end, there were discussions at the Washington level and a compromise of sorts was reached. We did make a reduced contribution. And we also got some new typewriters and office furniture. About time, I thought, as it was arriving, and enjoyed seeing a cable to various offices in East Asia Division alerting them to the issue of goods received for contributions made.

In May 1980, the Deputy Director for Operations, John McMahon, visited Hong Kong. I met him at the airport upon his arrival and took him to his hotel – standard *politesse* for a visiting senior officer. I recall being impressed at how informal he was and yet how professional he seemed. He walked out of customs carrying his own bag. He had no entourage. Next morning he came in and we provided extensive briefings about our activity. He was already well informed and posed lots of questions. The morning passed quickly and at noon he and I headed for a lunch hosted by some local officials. We discussed issues ranging from global operations targeted against China to Agency relations with Congress and the newly created oversight committees. We found their demands intrusive and doubted that Congress could keep a secret, but it was a train no one could stop. McMahon's counsel was that we must learn to live with it.

At 0900 the next morning, John and I reported to the small Royal Air Force airbase in Kowloon for a helicopter ride around the colony. The helicopter was waiting and, within minutes, we were airborne. There were no doors, I noticed right away, which meant that one not used to such rides would feel a bit vulnerable. Certainly, John and I both did. As we ascended and made our first turn I looked out, and inwardly questioned the wisdom of whoever took off the doors. Better vision, we were told. I pulled my seat belt with shoulder straps even tighter and noticed that John was doing the same thing. Soon, in light of the sights we were seeing, the openness was forgotten.

Most interesting was the border area, where we saw Chinese guard posts and military positions. They were there to keep people in not out, I remember thinking. We flew at very low altitudes most of the time, so we got exceptional views of everything. Also interesting was the container port in western Hong Kong harbour on the Kowloon side. Large already, it was the scene of extensive new construction and it was plain to see that it would someday be an enormous port. In fact, it was then, and still is today, one of the largest container ports in the world. John was leaving that afternoon to continue his Far East trip, but we had a few private moments before he had to go to the airport.

'How long will you be here?' he asked.

'At this point, it looks like we're here until the summer of 1981,' I replied. 'Then it will have been five years overseas and Judy is anxious to get back to the States for a while.'

'What will you do when you get back?' he queried.

'Hard to tell. I guess East Asia Division will want me to take over a Branch or something like that,' I responded.

'Typical narrow operations officer response,' he said. 'There are other things to do back there, you know. Would do you good to get out of the line for a while and see something new. Have you ever thought about that?'

I hadn't. 'Not really,' I said. 'What kinds of things do you mean?'

'There are staffs, there are seventh floor jobs, and in the intelligence community a guy like you with overseas operations experience would be a great find. What about congressional relations?'

'I had never really considered jobs outside the DO,' I admitted.

'Well, open up your mind a little', he said, 'and think about it.' I did think about it. And I realized that I had my head stuck so deeply into the trench, so to speak, of line operations that I was largely ignorant of most of the rest of the intelligence community. I resolved to do something about that when I forwarded my reassignment request to Headquarters. Ultimately, I did take a job in congressional liaison, a major career decision, and in his absence thanked John for, in effect, dragging me out of that trench.

With Bob's departure, I was asked to extend for a third year. There was little choice, as the new Chief would need some time to fit in and the transition needed some continuity. Rarely did we (or do we now) move both Chief and Deputy at the same time and this was to be no exception. We had planned, considering the two years in Malaysia, to return home in 1980. The needs of the service intervened. I was prepared to salute, and Judy agreed. Life was good for us in Hong Kong and one more year would be easy to take we thought.

The new Chief and his wife arrived in July 1980. Also an Irish American from Massachusetts, John G. was quite different from Bob. I had briefly met him once before when I passed through Brussels on the way to the Congo for my ill-fated airplane ride.

Stocky and red-faced, he seemed unhappy. He smiled only rarely and kept his own counsel. He was much less outgoing than Bob had been and harder to talk to. I could never quite put my finger on it, but there seemed to be some quirk somewhere that affected his personal relationships. He was an intelligent man and had experience in both Europe and Asia. I did the best I could and our professional relationship was tolerable, but we did not become friends, which was unusual for me, and our social contact was limited to affairs to which we had both been invited. I didn't dislike him, but he was one of only a few people I worked with over my entire career who struck the wrong chords.

As an example, in the fall of 1980, I was promoted into the Senior Intelligence Service, the highest level in the Directorate. As was normal, John saw the cable first (cables about personnel matters were marked as sensitive traffic). He called me into his office. The front office secretary, Peggy, a wonderful and very experienced woman who had been an enormous help to me while I was Acting Chief, had seen the cable and knew what was coming. She said nothing to spoil the surprise, but I sensed her excitement.

John, almost grudgingly, handed me the cable and said, 'They have made you an SIS officer.' He didn't stand up or shake my hand. 'Maybe it's your reward for being Acting Chief out here. Seems a bit early, but I'm glad for you.' That was it. He started reading other cables.

I was, of course, tickled to death. I came bounding out of his office and hugged Peggy and the other front office secretary, Judy. A big celebration ensued. But that more or less typified John.

A new officer, Graham F., arrived to take over one of the Branch Chief jobs. He came from Kabul in Afghanistan, where he had been Chief of a one-man office. An officer of the Middle East Division, Graham spoke Russian and Turkish and had had several tours in small Middle East posts. We had been surprised at his assignment to Hong Kong. What experience did he have? How would he fit in? The cables before his arrival informed us that he also spoke Chinese, and had learned it on his own while developing his contact with a New China News Agency journalist. Officers who had spent two years working full-time to achieve fluency in Chinese were sceptical.

To cut a long story short, Graham lived up to his billing, did an outstanding job and was moved up to replace me when I left in the summer of 1981. He took over the handling of a valuable and sensitive agent who spoke only Chinese and soon dispelled any doubts that lingered about his ability to speak the language. He also had a deft touch operationally. He quickly sensed openings in the developmental operations being run in his branch and cleverly orchestrated the recruitment of several fine agents during his first year. A small, wiry man, he was intelligent and academically oriented in some respects, but also pragmatic and realistic. No ivory tower for him. The blend of his talents produced an exceptionally strong operations officer.

Thinking back now, I realize that our complement of ethnic Chinese officers never received the full measure of credit they deserved. This had been the case in my earlier tour in Hong Kong as well. It wasn't that they weren't appreciated and respected – they certainly were. In many ways the backbone of our operational cadre, they were an enormous asset to our programmes. With fluent spoken and written Chinese, they could move freely and inconspicuously in the colony, handling any kind of operation. The same was true when they served in other posts in Asia.

However, much of the problem of lack of credit came from their weaknesses in written English, their second or even third language. Operational or intelligence writing required editing before it could be submitted to Headquarters. Candid, but probably unfair, mention of that weakness routinely appeared in appraisal reports about them. Unintentionally, it diminished the totality of their contribution. It was a flaw in our system that caused them to be less competitive, despite their operational successes and strengths.

Ultimately, we recognized the problem and worked to resolve it. It was not solved overnight, but eventually progress was achieved. Several of our Chinese American colleagues rose up into the SIS ranks. One came back to be the Deputy Chief in Hong Kong and another rose to become Chief of China Operations.

Before leaving Hong Kong, I worked towards getting all appraisal reports done before my departure. As Deputy, I had to write more than a dozen appraisal reports and it was not something I liked. It was essential that it be done conscientiously, however, and I wrote each one with care before submission to John for his reviewing comments – a standard procedure. One was for Mary, our chief reports officer. Since I thought her a strong and highly competent officer, who was serving us admirably, I gave her high marks across the board. And, since her tour would soon be ending as well, my narrative remarks included an assessment of her tour, as I knew it. Growth and solid contributions the whole way through, I wrote. I sent it, in draft form, to John.

I was stunned to get it back the next morning with John's reviewing comments attached and a note to me. John, who had at that time been in the station for about eight months, had assessed Mary's work to be 'acceptable' and in some areas only marginally so. I should consider revising my draft, the note said. Taken by surprise, I didn't know what to think. I thought things over for a few minutes. Then, with no intention of changing anything I had written, I went to see John. I thought that surely he was confused about something and that I could clear things up for him so that he could write reviewing comments that more accurately rated Mary. It didn't happen. He voiced criticisms of her that 'came out of the blue'. I disputed him, to no avail. I had never been involved in such an argument before. Nor would it ever happen again in my career.

We both had dealt with Mary daily. We had talked about her work regularly. Headquarters assessed our intelligence reporting regularly and had consistently given it high marks.

'Mary is doing a fine job,' I told him.

'You don't see things that I do,' he responded. For a Chief and his deputy to have such a profound difference of opinion on anything, let alone the performance of a key member of the office, was unheard of.

In the end, we came to no agreement. Mary's appraisal report was transmitted to Headquarters with obvious, and serious, disagreement between the rating and the reviewing officers – a highly unusual submission. Mary was, of course, shocked when she read his reviewing comments. She came to see me and asked the obvious question, why? I told her what had happened and confessed that I simply didn't understand his action.

'What shall I do?' she finally asked.

'Nothing,' I counselled her. 'I'm sure Headquarters will focus on what I wrote. They know what you have done and you won't suffer because of the reviewing comments.'

We heard nothing from Headquarters about the appraisal report and its disagreements, which was also unusual. Mary was promoted the next year. That told me that Headquarters had indeed discounted John's dissent – also unusual. The incident served to put further distance between John and me.

'Does she think he would take money for making the deal?' I asked.

'I haven't specifically asked that yet,' Jan replied. Jan, one of our Chinese American officers, was handling a female agent, the mistress of a senior officer, who was heading an office in Hong Kong of a country of high interest to us. He had direct access to Communist Party policy makers and, if ultimately recruited, would be the source of high-level intelligence. Via a couple of access agents, we had discovered his relationship with the woman whom we then approached. She agreed to help us.

In his early fifties, the official was married, but his wife was not with him. The woman, Chinese, was in her mid-thirties and attractive. She had previously worked in a bar as a prostitute. Pragmatic, she was a retired hooker still willing to ply her trade for sufficient compensation. The money we provided, in return for her secret co-operation, effectively doubled what she was receiving from the official for 'services rendered'. Economics motivated her. Politics did not.

We were meeting in my office to plan our next steps in what was a promising operation. With me were Jan, the case officer, and Don, his Branch Chief.

'Well, we need to ask her that at the next meeting,' Don interjected. 'If he will take money for doing nothing in a deal we have rigged up, we'll know that greed moves him. It would be a good step forward.'

'Agreed,' I said and added, 'Can she influence him to look the other way and accept the deal? Does he listen to her or is the relationship just sexual?'

'Again, I'm not sure,' Jan replied. 'She claims she has influence over him, but we don't have any way to confirm it.'

'This ought to be a good test,' Don asserted.

'I'll certainly press her on it when I see her next week,' Jan said.

'Can we get audio into his apartment?' I asked. 'Then we'd have independent confirmation of what they talk about and whether she has any influence or not.'

'We're looking at that,' Don responded. 'Not easy though. We don't have any access to get in without her. We're checking apartments next to his that might have a common wall.'

An audio operation would also give us transcripts of his conversations with other visitors. Maybe some intelligence would be produced.

'We're on it,' Don continued. 'I'll keep you posted.'

Our efforts against that official were ongoing as I departed from Hong Kong. The woman was quite savvy, we discovered, and did in fact manipulate the official into accepting the first deal, a bribe actually. We were optimistic about our chances. We knew full well that bribes are a way of life in Asian business and politics and that many Asians would accept one if he thought it was 'safe'. If confronted at some point with the fact that we were involved, however, the official would be looking at a much tougher situation. One we might be able to exploit. It was what is defined as a 'target of opportunity'.

In late fall 1980, I submitted my request for reassignment. In it I outlined what I would like to do if appropriate assignments were open and if East Asia Division would let me take what was called a rotational tour (i.e. outside of your home Division). I had thought long and hard about John McMahon's advice and concluded that it would indeed be smart to broaden my knowledge of both the Agency and the intelligence community. With that thought in mind, I asked for jobs I would never have thought about in earlier years.

My promotion to the SIS level meant that I was no longer home based to a specific Division, but was a 'Directorate asset'. I was pleased to hear in the spring of 1981, just months before my departure, that I was going to work in our Congressional Affairs office when I returned to Headquarters. That ought to be interesting, I thought, and promptly wrote back, thanking Headquarters for the decision.

By that time, Ronald Reagan had been elected president and he had named a new DCI, William J. Casey, to replace Admiral Turner. Casey would be my ninth Director and that was just fine with me. I had no problem seeing Turner leave. In fact, few tears were shed over Turner's departure. Casey, with experience in the OSS during the Second World War, was welcomed as a supporter and an activist.

One of the people Casey brought in with him was Billie Doswell, a Virginia politician, whom Casey named to be the head of our Congressional Affairs office. Others shared my concern that Doswell, with no experience at all in intelligence matters, would have difficulty adequately representing the Agency's best interest on the Hill. That remained to be seen, I thought. I'll meet him in September and will judge for myself how well he does.

For the first, and only, time in my career, I used a combination of stored up home leave and two weeks of annual leave to take eight weeks' leave between our departure from Hong Kong and my return to Headquarters. We had planned a trip through Europe to expose the girls (now aged eight, ten, twelve and fifteen) to historical sites and to their 'roots' in Sweden and Italy. We ordered a Volkswagen van that we picked up in Frankfurt, Germany, our first destination on the flight west from Hong Kong.

We drove first through northern Germany (Suzy's German was strong and a big help in hotels and restaurants) and into the three Scandinavian countries. In Sweden, we visited the small church in Ljungby, central Sweden, where my great-grandparents were buried in the adjoining cemetery. As we signed the visitors' book in the church, we discovered that, by sheer chance, my father's cousin, who lived in California, had visited the same church two days earlier with his immediate family.

We drove in a great circle through Stockholm and Oslo and then down the coast of Norway where we stopped to visit a friend who had a beautiful home on an island. From there, we took a ferry to Jutland in northern Denmark and then proceeded southwards through Germany and into Switzerland.

While in Hong Kong we had purchased an apartment in the French-speaking area of Vaud in the Swiss Alps. We stayed there for a few days, and hiked and played tennis – Judy and Suzy faced each other in the women's finals of a small tournament we entered. (Suzy won.) Thence onward to Italy where we first visited the small village near Turin, in the Piedmont, where Judy's grandparents had once lived. We continued south to Rome for several days of sightseeing. Then Florence, Venice and Switzerland, and ultimately back to Frankfurt, where we turned in the van, which we had decided to keep, for shipment home. We boarded a flight to the States the next afternoon. It had been six great weeks. Every day had been an adventure and I think none of us will ever forget that trip. The girls, I must add, did mention that they had seen enough cathedrals and churches to last them the rest of their lives. They exaggerate.

THIRTEEN

COUNTER TERRORISM

1981–85

In early September 1981, I had my first meeting with Billie Doswell, who had been in his position for about eight months. The initial amenities had been covered and we were now getting down to specifics.

'Are you a lawyer?' he asked, revealing that he had not read my file and knew little or nothing about me. A bad start, I thought.

'No, I'm not,' I replied. 'I'm an operations officer on a rotational tour.'

'But if you're not a lawyer, what can you do in this section?' His question betrayed a serious lack of understanding of the Agency's relationship with Congress. This was an understandable gap in his knowledge considering the short time he had been at the Agency, but a red flag nonetheless. There was indeed a need for lawyers to deal with specific issues like reviewing legislation or writing proposed bills for Congress to consider. But our contacts went far beyond that. Hadn't anyone explained to him that there was a thirst on the Hill, especially in our oversight committees, for basic knowledge about overseas operations?

'Well, the Deputy Director for Operations assigned me here to answer questions that regularly arise in the oversight committees about what we are doing overseas,' I replied. 'I understand that Pete [a DO officer who had just left the staff for an overseas assignment] did just that while he was here and the staffs loved him.'

Billie seemed to be unsure of himself. 'Well, we can certainly give that a try,' he said. 'We'll put you in the House branch.' The

Office of Congressional Affairs had a front office and support group plus one branch dealing regularly with the Senate Select Committee on Intelligence (SSCI) and one dealing with the House Preferred Select Committee on Intelligence (HPSCI).

This wasn't how I had expected to be welcomed into our Congressional Relations office. John McMahon's admonition about rotational tours briefly crossed my mind (he was now the Deputy Director to Casey), but I forced it out and concluded that this would work out fine. And it would be both interesting and broadening for me.

My first chore was to attend a three-day seminar in downtown Washington about how Congress deals with the whole budget process – badly was the obvious answer. In preparation, I reviewed some books, both in the office and at home, about how Congress functions. It had been a long time, I discovered, since the basic government courses I had taken in high school and college. But it all came back quickly and the seminar itself served to put everything back into perspective.

My introductions to HPSCI went smoothly and I was heartened by the reception I got. It seemed to confirm what I had originally understood about what a DO officer would do on the Hill.

On the one hand, the ensuing weeks were rewarding. I became aware of a host of subjects on which we (the Agency) provided briefings to both oversight committees. The bulk of them were done by officers from the Directorate of Intelligence and concerned what we call 'finished intelligence', an all-source analysis, written or presented as the final product of the entire intelligence community. Specific committees in the House, not just the oversight committee, could (and did) request these briefings and it was the Congressional Affairs office's responsibility to make the appropriate arrangements and then take the briefer down to the Hill.

The subjects of many of the briefings were completely new to me and I was fascinated by the range, particularly scientific or technical, on which we could brief. For example, briefers from the Directorate of Intelligence or the Directorate of Science and Technology might discuss missile research, satellite developments, telecommunications or the economic impact of a drought.

The substance of each briefing would be tailored (sometimes to a specific foreign country) to provide background about policy issues.

And as predicted, there were, from day one, lots of questions for me from various staff members. How do you pay agents? How do you task media agents? What do you tell liaison? Why do you tell liaison anything at all? How do you function inside the United States? Why do you need so many safe houses? Most interesting, and surprising, to me in the informal sessions with various HPSCI staff members was the ignorance that was exposed. Ignorance laced, unfortunately, with a tendency to be suspicious of, and to attack or lay blame on, the Directorate of Operations. In those weeks, I certainly helped to defuse many problems – simply by being able to provide honest, candid and informed responses.

On the other hand, I felt frustrated. I felt that I could actually do much more if the section would use me more effectively. As just a member of the Branch, not the Branch Chief, I was being tasked in the same way that junior staff employees were tasked. I was spending many hours doing things that any low-graded employee could do – making the arrangements for a given briefing, accompanying the briefing personnel down to the Hill to sit and listen to their presentation, for instance. This was time taken away from dealing with the myriad of issues that I was uniquely well prepared to handle. The answer, of course, was Billie Doswell. The red flag I saw early on was coming back to haunt me. Billie, who had no experience at all of intelligence community matters, let alone espionage abroad, simply didn't know what to do. He was running his office as if it was operating in Richmond, Virginia, where he did have some experience with executive branch dealings with the legislative branch. Things were just not working out.

I voiced my concerns, first to Billie (he drew a blank I could tell, but he said he'd see what he could do), and then to others on the seventh floor. By now it was mid-December and knowledge of this dilemma was more and more widespread. No one seemed to know how to progress the situation.

Finally, I was called to the office of the Deputy Director of Operations (the DDO).

'Well I haven't noticed that the Congress is any friendlier since

September, have you, Bob?' John Stein, the DDO, joked as I entered his office.

'Nope, same problems and same static,' Bob M. replied. Bob had been the Deputy in Hong Kong during the better part of my first tour there and I considered him a good friend. His current job was as Chief of the International Affairs Division (IAD), a large Division with responsibility for global operations ranging from covert action to paramilitary operations and terrorism. It was a big job, fraught with the potential for hostile press or political reactions to some of the operations we were tasked to run. As an intelligent and outgoing activist with lots of ideas, Bob was up to it and word at Headquarters was that he was doing a great job. He dealt frequently with William Casey and with the oversight committees. He was happy to pull my leg a little too.

'Come on,' I threw back, 'it's only been four months. Rome wasn't built in a day.'

'That's true, Dick,' John said, 'but we're running out of days. In fact, they are all gone.'

I glanced at Bob. 'What's that supposed to mean?'

'Let me explain,' John continued in a more serious tone. 'We've been following the situation in Congressional Affairs and don't like it at all. We can't afford to have one of our SIS officers with solid operational experience working up there as a staffer.'

'It is a pain,' I interjected. 'I've been complaining and trying to get things changed. No luck.'

'Frankly, the problem is Billie Doswell,' he confided. 'And there is little we can do about it. As soon as Casey realizes that his old buddy is miscast, Billie will be out of here. But we aren't going to wait him out.'

I said, 'What *are* we going to do?'

'Bring your rotational tour to a screeching halt. I've already told them that we are pulling you back to the DO. We have an important job for you to take over.'

'Aren't they going to be pissed off?' I asked.

'No, because everybody but Casey knows that Billie is way off base.' I saw that the decision had been taken. No one was inviting comment from me.

'Not much of a rotation,' I kidded. 'John McMahon will be on my case. He's the one who told me to take a rotational tour.'

'He knows the story,' John said.

'So what is this important job?' I asked. I was only halfway serious as I thought he had used that as his excuse for pulling me out of a rotational that clearly wasn't working out.

That was the signal for Bob to get into the conversation. He had said nothing thus far and came directly to the point. 'I want you to take over the terrorist group in my Division,' he told me. 'I knew this was coming', he went on, 'and I got here first. I have a crying need for a good operations officer to take over what is going to be a tough job. I know you, congratulations on the promotion by the way, and I asked John to let me make this proposal to you.'

As was always the case during my career, it just never occurred to me to say no. If Bob had specifically asked for me and if the DDO was on board, I wasn't going to be coy. But I could at least be honest. I had no idea what the terrorist group was or what it did. 'It's the only element in the Directorate that follows and works against global terrorism,' Bob explained. 'It's not big now, but that is what I want you to do, build it up. Terrorism is a serious problem and is going to get a lot worse before it gets better, if ever. The Hill is asking what we are doing about it. So far, *you* are what we are doing about it,' he concluded.

'But I don't know a bloody thing about terrorism except what I read in the papers,' I responded.

'I'm confident you'll learn quickly,' Bob said, smiling. 'That's what operations officers do.'

'The quicker the better,' John said, signalling that the meeting was over.

I went back to the Congressional Affairs office to announce my departure. Nobody seemed to care at all. They had their own problems. I thought the change would be quick and painless, but that was not going to be the case. Another issue would intervene and delay the move.

Plans had been made for the chief of the HPSCI staff budget office to tour North Africa and Europe in early January 1982, before Congress reconvened. He would be inspecting and visiting several of our stations as well as several military bases in Europe. It would be a two-week trip. He had asked that I be the accompanying officer and the entrée to our stations. With the change in my status, I saw no reason for me to go. There was plenty of time for someone else from the Congressional Affairs office to step in and replace me. I asked that someone else be named.

They were uneasy. Gingerly, they raised the question with the budget chief. He rejected it out of hand. Heavy-set, balding and pleasant, he was a very savvy, retired Army colonel. The choice was between me and someone else in our office, who had never been overseas. His choice was me, period. No one argued.

In late 1981, just a few years after the oversight committees had been established, there remained a latent fear of somehow displeasing them – and that applied to staffers as well as representatives or senators. This was especially true of people who were key to us. And the man who generated our budget and could add or delete millions of dollars with the stroke of his pen was defined as a key person. Even John, the DDO, agreed that I should go as planned. So I went.

We flew first to Madrid. (First class, of course, as befits servants of the people.) After an overnight, we were picked up by the military and headed for North Africa. I should explain what I mean by 'we were picked up'. An executive jet with a crew of four was put at our disposal to fly us to all our destinations. Their job was to take care of us while we were in Europe. The jet, a small sleek plane with all amenities on board, was perfect for the small hops we would be making. The crew was completely attentive to our needs including handling our luggage through all formalities. I packed my bag before we left each place and left it in my hotel room. I saw it again at the next hotel room, military bases, or Bachelor Officers' Quarters. Our schedule was their schedule. Bottom line: we were outrageously spoiled.

The Pentagon was miles ahead of the DO in terms of how to curry favour on the Hill. No effort, or expense, was too great to keep the Hill happy. The budget chief was, of course, pleased with the preferential treatment he was accorded. Interesting, I thought, that while we were focused on ways not to *displease* the Hill, the Pentagon was sparing no effort to go one step further and do everything possible to *please* the Hill. We had some learning to do.

Our first visits were to several cities in North Africa. At each location, the chief provided a complete briefing that always elicited the same questions from the budget chief. His questions were well fielded and, since I had some idea where he was coming from, I was often able to elaborate. I quickly realized that if this man was going to be out in the field making this type of visit (in fact, the need for his visit was not at all clear to me), then someone like me (a DO officer with field operational experience) ought to be with him. He was gaining a much better feel and understanding of how the DO works in the field than he would have if I had not been there.

Next we visited some military bases in Germany and Italy, where I got my first dose of military briefings. Much more formal than ours had been, they featured officers whose sole job was to present these briefings to visiting dignitaries. Lecterns, microphones, slides and overhead projectors produced a flow of information that put listeners in a position sometimes described as having to drink water from a fire hose. The format seemed always to be the same. First they would tell you what they were going to tell you. Then they would tell you. Then they would tell you what they had told you. Too much to absorb and I even suspected that it was done intentionally because, when they finished, you were so overwhelmed with information you couldn't formulate any questions.

That wasn't always the case, however. At one unit, a military intelligence battalion, we were briefed on their cross-border efforts into Eastern Europe, a denied area. Candidly, I have to say that the briefing wasn't impressive at all, but I said nothing – until asked. Towards the end of our discussions, which were more informal on this occasion, the budget chief asked what I thought of a certain group of operations. They were being run to provide 'early warning' of any attack from the Soviet Bloc.

'Did I understand you to say that your communications link with these agents is via secret writing on postcards and letters?' I asked the briefer.

'Yes, sir, that's right,' he replied.

'I may just be splitting hairs,' I said, 'but maybe these operations should be ones that provide early "indications" of an attack, like stockpiling of ammo and fuel for example. Warning of an actual attack is probably another thing. If they attack, and if your agent sends us a postcard warning of that attack, there would be a question of which would get here first, the Russian tanks or the postcard.'

'I understand your concern,' the briefer said. I'm not sure he did, but I wasn't going to press the point.

'Maybe you should try to get some radios in there,' I suggested.

One of the large air bases in Germany that we stopped at had a young air force captain named Holm – Greg, my youngest brother, who had been assigned there in 1980. The commanding general of the base, with several of his deputies, hosted a marvellous luncheon in the splendid officers' club (the air force officers' clubs are all splendid, I have concluded) after the morning briefings. When the budget chief mentioned that my brother was assigned to the base, the general immediately sent for him.

I had planned on surprising Greg, and his fiancée, Becky, an army nurse who was also a captain, because I hadn't been sure till the last minute that I would actually be coming on this trip. He was indeed surprised. Ten minutes later, as we were finishing coffee and cognac, Greg was ushered in 'to see the commander' and when he spotted me, his jaw dropped.

When I had returned to Headquarters from Hong Kong in September 1981, I could see that our new Director Casey had already made his presence known. And what he was doing met with widespread approval in the Agency, including the Clandestine Service.

On a couple of occasions while I was in Congressional Affairs, I assisted Casey when he delivered briefings to the HPSCI. They were difficult sessions, partly because Casey mumbled and was difficult to understand and partly because the HPSCI sensed (accurately) that Casey harboured an 'attitude' towards the Hill. I'm not telling you any more than I absolutely have to, was the impression he gave. I saw him to be tough, single-minded and determined to rebuild the Agency – especially the Clandestine Service.

The Church and Pike committees' hearings in the mid-1970s, which had spawned the oversight committees Casey had to brief, had, in his mind I think, ushered in a dark period for the Agency. Following on the heels of the Watergate affair, in which the

Agency was falsely implicated, thanks to Nixon's attempts to use us as part of his defence and despite Helms's best efforts to keep us out of the line of fire, the revelations dramatized by (especially) the Church committee tarnished the Agency's reputation and weakened its ability to serve the nation. The years under Carter with Turner as our Director did little or nothing to help clear the air or rekindle the 'can do' spirit we once enjoyed.

President Reagan had decided to face down the 'evil empire', as he described the Soviet Union, and to do that he wanted to employ every tool at his disposal and that included the Agency. To do that, the Agency needed to be strengthened and Casey was determined to do it. He had initiated efforts to rebuild at all levels. My colleagues in the DO and I were in complete accord.

On the Monday morning after my return from the European trip with the budget chief, I went first to visit the offices of what was then known simply as the 'Terrorist Group'. On the door, there was even a sign that read 'Terrorist Group'. I don't know how long it had been there. Certainly no one had intended any harm, but I immediately had problems with it. It was insensitive to the current political climate, I thought, and subject to considerable misunderstanding. Moreover, I thought, I don't really want to go home and tell Judy that I now head up the CIA's Terrorist Group. We're against it, I thought, and made a mental note to rename this group. We became the 'Counter' Terrorist Group (CTG). Bob agreed and that was my first official act as Chief.

To set the scene for my assignment and the DDO's decision to strengthen our capability to fight global terrorism, we must recall that in the early 1980s a spate of terrorist incidents had heightened concerns in Washington and in Europe. A US Army General named Dozier had been kidnapped from his residence near a NATO base in northern Italy by the Red Brigade, a Marxist-oriented group that routinely employed violence, including assassination, in support of its ends. The kidnapping had occurred in mid-December, just before I was recalled from Congressional Affairs. In addition, Libya under Qaddafi had sponsored several anti-American terrorist incidents and had threatened to kill President Reagan.

Worse still, in 1979, the events in Iran (the occupation of the Embassy in Tehran) had highlighted a new phenomenon – state sponsorship of terrorism – to an already dangerous situation. As the incidence of terrorist attacks mounted, Washington reacted. And the bureaucracy's reaction was a typically American one: throw more resources at the problem. It had worked before (except in Vietnam), so why not try it again? Throughout the executive branch, agencies and departments were either establishing or augmenting an office of terrorism. We were, of course, no exception, except that we had long followed the subject (the 'Terrorist Group' had been established in the mid-1970s) and were already running operations against some of the terrorist organizations. But we would do more – and soon.

After twenty years in the service, this was to be my first real management job at Headquarters. I was in charge of a group, albeit a small one for the time being. And I was the Directorate's point man for the increasingly serious and sensitive issue of global terrorism. I was eager to get my teeth into the day-to-day operations run by the group. We were a total of seventeen, of whom only a few were operations officers with overseas experience. (I viewed that with some concern because I hoped, naively, that we would become actively engaged in supporting or running agent operations targeted at specific terrorist groups. In fact, it wasn't going to be that simple.) The rest were intelligence analysts with, for the most part, only Headquarters experience. A mixed bag really, but all seemed eager to do their jobs. I had been given great leeway in terms of what I could do, but I had to learn my account before I could contemplate any major changes.

I set about learning about terrorism by reading as many studies as I could get my hands on and listening to briefings given by members of the group or by terrorist analysts working in the Directorate of Intelligence. A couple of the latter were particularly good, I thought, and I would be seeing lots more of them as the group expanded in size.

One of the operations officers in the group, Chris F., had been one of our platoon on the paramilitary course in the spring of 1962. When I went to Laos, he (as a member of Latin American Division) went to Florida to train Cubans involved in boat infiltration operations. He had been in the Counter Terrorist Group for a couple of years and was knowledgeable about all of the known terrorists that concerned us. He was, in fact, the resident expert.

Groups of interest to us included groups in the Middle East, assorted Palestinian and other Arab groups, and groups in Latin America, Europe and Asia. We had a few agent operations and liaison efforts under way, but for the most part the programme was moribund. Not surprising because we had many other things to do and, until then, terrorism had not been considered a front burner issue. But it was now and we, along with numerous other executive branch departments and agencies (the FBI, the Department of State, all branches of military intelligence, the Department of Energy, the INS and the Secret Service), had been energized by recent events. A larger and stronger national capability to fight terrorism was under construction.

(In today's world some things have changed and some have not. A number of the groups we combated, in Europe, Asia and Latin America no longer exist, and the issues they fought for have been resolved. There has been little change, however, in the Middle East. Ever present, the problem of terrorism simmers and sometimes boils. What happened to us on September 11 attests to the enduring animosity that we face. The names of the groups have changed but the members are still angry, hate-filled, and dissatisfied Muslims.)

As if on cue after Bob's prediction that the terrorist problem was going to get worse, the US military attaché in Paris, Lieutenant Colonel Ray, was assassinated in January 1982. I had, almost literally, just walked in the door of the Counter Terrorist Group. An Arab group, the Lebanese Armed Revolutionary Faction (LARF), claimed responsibility for the murder. We worked closely with the French internal service, the DST, in an effort to gather details about the incident. Also in January 1982, Italian counter-terrorist forces rescued General Dozier safe and sound from a 'cell' in a Red Brigade safe house in northern Italy.

During 1981, in addition to Dozier's abduction, there had been incidents in Germany, Latin America and elsewhere, and on 6 October President Sadat of Egypt had been assassinated by a group of Muslim fanatics. After the killing of Lieutenant Colonel Ray, 1982 was to see a surge of terrorist incidents. Indeed, the total of 794 incidents in 1982 was second only to the total of 838 in 1978. The 1978 total included fewer attacks directed against American interests.

Deadly attacks by the LARF against Israeli diplomats, one in Paris (April) and a second in London (June), prompted an incursion by the Israeli army into Lebanon in June. Despite questions about the role played by the Palestinians, Israel decided to act and their forces moved all the way to Beirut, ultimately forcing the Palestinian forces there to flee to Tunisia. In retrospect, the assassinations must have been like waving a red flag in front of a bull.

'The Director wants you to go to Saudi Arabia to brief Prince Turki,' Allen W., the London Chief, said. He was reading from a cable that had come in that morning. It was June 1982 and, after less than six months as Chief of CTG, I was in London, the last stop on my first series of visits briefing local counter-terrorism officials. I had visited France, Germany and Belgium. It had been a successful trip during which I had explained our heightened interest in combating global terrorism. I had secured promises of increased levels of co-operation from each. The Europeans made clear that they were pleased to have us more actively engaged. This was by no means a new initiative. Co-operation had long been active. I was trying to instil a sense of renewed priority.

'What the hell am I going to tell the Saudis that they don't already know?' I asked.

'That will certainly be your call, Dick. As the cable says, you are our counter terrorist expert and that's who the Director wants to send to see the Saudis,' he said with a smile. He knew this was totally unexpected and that it was a tough assignment. He also knew – as did I – that there was no option. As instructed by the Director, I would go to Jeddah as soon as possible. It was (is) highly unusual for the Director to instruct a tasking like this. I assumed that Bob had tried to talk with him, but to no avail.

'Could I see that cable?' I asked

Allen handed it to me. 'We'll make the plane reservations and get your ticket. Will you want to fly directly home from Jeddah? You'll need some money too. I'll sign to approve an advance.'

I read the cable carefully. Headquarters had done their best to give me some background about the trip. Apparently, the Director had just met with the Saudis (not specific) and they talked about terrorism, especially Arab terrorism. The Director was seeking increased levels of co-operation, he had told the Saudis. Their non-committal response was to agree and that we should perhaps start with an exchange of information. Reportedly, the Director had promised to send his man over the next day. That was it and those were my marching orders. Headquarters knew what a difficult position this put me in, and to help, they sent an outline of topics I would want to cover and suggested some studies I might quickly review to give me some additional background. I had worked hard to get a good feel for our holdings on Arab terrorist groups (the highest priority threat at that time), which were considerable, and was confident that I knew them well. And the analysts' briefing had done much to put things into perspective. Also, Arab terrorism was a subject that had come up frequently during my recent exchanges. So I was as ready as I could be at this stage in my counter-terrorism role.

My flight, direct to Jeddah, was the next day and there was a near disaster. At least that is what it seemed at the time. I had obtained my visa for Saudi Arabia and it was stamped into the diplomatic passport I was carrying. Wishing to be as helpful as possible, the Chief tasked his driver with picking me up and driving me out to Heathrow airport. This was a kind gesture as I was feeling stressed – because of the nature of this mission I guess. I had called Judy the night before to tell her of my delayed return. I couldn't say much over an open phone line. 'I'll explain when I see you.' She wasn't too happy.

We had plenty of time when we arrived at the airport, having arrived early. I wanted to be sure nothing went wrong. He dropped me off and we took my bags out of the trunk. I thanked the driver, picked up my bags and headed for the check-in counter. Then it hit me. My shoulder bag, the one I carried onto the plane and the one with my tickets and passport was still sitting on the back seat of the car. I could picture it in my mind. Shit! I thought. I won't lose the bag, but I'll surely miss this plane. I headed for a phone to call Allen's office and explain what had happened.

Just then, the driver appeared in front of me, my shoulder bag in hand. 'I figured you'd probably need this one too,' he said with a big smile. What a relief! I could have hugged him. Maybe I did, I can't remember. He had spotted it on the back seat, parked the car and set off to find me. It could be said that he made my day.

We landed in Jeddah, which is located on the Red Sea coast along the Kingdom's western border, just before midnight. Formalities were routine. No one was there to meet me. I caught a taxi outside the reception hall and headed for my hotel. The driver, a large, strong-looking man who spoke decent English, seemed anxious to talk, but I was tired and had little to say. He gave up after about five minutes.

The next morning I went to the office and checked in. The Chief had been aware that I was coming and he welcomed me into his office. He didn't know, he told me, when the Prince might be available. The Prince did know I had arrived.

'When do you think we'll get to see him?' I asked.

'No idea,' he responded. 'Sometimes it takes days to get in there.'

'Days?' I said. 'But I thought this was all laid on. The Director specifically sent me to brief Prince Turki. Wasn't it set up at a high level?'

'Yes, it was, but that doesn't mean much out here. The Saudi Royal family operates on its own schedule. You'll see him. I just don't know when.'

As I listened, my reaction was something between frustration and irritation. 'So what the hell am I supposed to do in the meantime?'

'Just cool your heels,' he replied sympathetically. 'Sorry, but there's nothing I can do.'

I sat around for three days. I borrowed a racket and shoes and played tennis once in ninety-degree heat – but only once. I figured that there must be better things to do and read in my air-conditioned hotel room growing increasingly frustrated. Finally, at about 10 p.m. on the third evening, the Chief called to announce that we would see the Prince at midnight, at his residence. He would pick me up, he continued, at eleven-thirty. I didn't really understand, but figured that this must be a cultural thing. I didn't complain and I didn't argue.

The royal compound was dark as we approached it just before midnight in the Chief's car, except for a lone light just over the gate in the wall. Not surprising, I was thinking, at this time of night. But as we passed through the guard post and entered the interior courtyard, there were lots of lights. I saw groups of armed men loitering around several Mercedes limousines. They were dressed in civilian clothes, but many carried Uzi machine-guns. The Prince was in charge of internal security for the Kingdom, so the civilian clothes were no surprise. Nor were the weapons for that matter. We parked, were welcomed by an aide who knew the Chief, and were led into the Prince's reception room.

The room was large and dimly lit with several low sofas scattered around it. Each had three or four big pillows. We were directed to one of the sofas and sat down. A servant appeared with cups of thick, sweet mint tea. The Chief sipped at his. I did too and guessed that it must be an acquired taste. I didn't like it.

Shortly thereafter, the Prince came in and sat right across from us. Three or four men appeared at the same time and lurked in the background. They weren't taking any chances. Prince Turki had been educated in England and his English was good. He was gracious as he welcomed us into his home – if one could call that place a home. So, after all the preliminaries, I was going to brief this guy.

It soon became clear that if there was ever a case of taking coals to Newcastle, this was it. There were limits, of course, on what I could say, so much of what I laid out was generic information about the various terrorist groups we were following. Per guidance from the Director, I focused on the Arab groups. All, certainly, were well known to him. I posed questions several times only to receive polite put-offs – 'I'll have my staff look into it.' He was pleasant. He asked simple, non-contentious questions. We were equally pleasant. It all went smoothly and in the end it was worth just about nothing. I said as much after we had departed the compound.

'I'm sorry, Dick, but I'm not surprised,' he said. 'To be honest, this was not a good idea from the beginning, but I could hardly argue with Headquarters. He was nice, but you're certainly right. Not much got done.'

An intriguing case began in the fall of 1982. In the early stages, CTG was getting only information copies of the incoming cables. And we weren't getting all the traffic because some was coming in the back channels and didn't have the CTG 'slug' on the header line. Gary, one of the best operations officers in the group, followed the case as closely as he could. Much of its interest derived from the fact that Rome had received and was working with a walk-in claiming to be Libyan. He had been encrypted Spider-1 (S-1). His story took a while to unfold. Initially, he had claimed contacts with a group that had access to fissionable materials. Gary, right away, smelled a scam and resolved to follow the case.

Within a couple of weeks, things changed, and so did all the priorities. Two new developments pushed S-1 way up the scale of interesting cases. One was his recent notice to his case officer that he was a Libyan intelligence officer working outside his country's Embassy. Secondly, the cast of players on our side grew dramatically after his announcement and after he reported that the target of a Libyan assassination plot was none other than President Reagan.

'Have you seen the cable from Rome?' Chris asked, signalling that it was not your average cable. He had a copy of it in his hand.

'Not yet,' I replied. 'I just got back from the staff meeting.'

'Take a look.' The cable described the recent meeting Rome had with S-1, wherein he alleged he was a Libyan and a member of the Libyan intelligence service. And further that he was under non-official cover, that is, he was not a member of the Libyan Embassy in Rome. It raised lots of questions that would have to be answered, but it was potentially a big breakthrough. He claimed knowledge of *modus operandi* employed by the Libyan service that, if true, would be of great interest to us. Moreover, he gave us a sketchy outline of a plot to kill Reagan. And, for good measure, information about the movements of the infamous international terrorist, Carlos.

'Who has seen this?' I said.

'Near East Division got their copy, so did Europe Division,' Chris replied. 'For here, just you and me so far.'

'I'm not sure where this might go,' I told him, 'but for now, let's hold this pretty tight. Just you and Gary.'

The cable hit Headquarters like a ton of bricks. Knowledge of it was tightly compartmented, but those aware of it were keenly interested in follow-up information. The Libyan Chief called while Chris was still in my office and we arranged to meet in an hour to discuss the response to Rome. At that meeting, there was general agreement that a clear priority in handling this individual should focus on verifying his bona fides, that is, to carefully check out his documentation and all the information he had provided.

Our response, written by the desk and co-ordinated by the Counter Terrorist Group, told Rome how pleased we were to be in touch with S-1, a potentially valuable agent. At the same time, we added, much remains to be done to confirm he is who he says he is and has the access he claims. There followed, in Rome, a series of meetings with the would-be agent that produced information that was tantalizing, but hard, even impossible, to confirm.

Given the substance of the assassination plot information, we promptly informed the FBI and, because of the threat (even though still unconfirmed) to the President, the Secret Service. Given the climate that prevailed at the time, there was considerable high-level interest. The latter services, as well as the White House Security Office, became involved. With the Chief of the Near East Division, I began attending weekly meetings in the White House at which the FBI and the Secret Service were also represented. The purpose of the meetings was to carefully disseminate the information we were collecting and to co-ordinate what the US government's response would be and who would take what steps.

The information kept coming and it kept Headquarters off balance because of the cast of players involved. For example, S-1 reported that Carlos would be transiting Paris by air in the last weekend in November. There were serious doubts that Carlos would be so bold, reckless even, as to pass through Paris, where the French services were so anxious to get their hands on him. A debate ensued at Headquarters. Finally, we agreed that we couldn't risk *not* acting on the information and we informed our contacts in Paris. Without specifics, the French were obliged to cover both international airports in Paris, Charles de Gaulle and Orly, for three days. Heavy resources were expended. Carlos never appeared. He had changed his plans at the last minute, the agent responded when he was next met. We were disappointed – and some of us were suspicious.

Despite stronger and stronger urging from the Washington end, Rome had not yet seen the individual's basic documentation. He provided one excuse after another for not producing his

ID card and his passport. Memories of the fabricators we had dealt with in Hong Kong surfaced in my mind. I smelled a rat. Chris and Gary were having similar doubts.

As the weeks passed, the FBI and the Secret Service also became suspicious. But there was just enough checkable information to keep the operation going. For example, the agent provided the names of three Americans who, he told us, were involved in the plot against the President. We checked the names. They existed. Indeed two of them lived in Washington DC. The Bureau and the Secret Service started digging into their backgrounds, trying to confirm or deny the allegations.

A polygraph test was ordered and conducted. The results were ambiguous. The FBI and the Secret Service were frustrated – we were too. Rome did obtain and forward to Headquarters photos taken of the individual claiming to be a Libyan intelligence service officer.

As time passed, a split developed between the CTG and the branch. 'Something is wrong,' we insisted. 'Step one is to check bona fides and documents and here we are, months into this operation, and we haven't seen anything.'

'You just don't understand Libyans,' they responded. 'They do things differently. He doesn't have a diplomatic passport.'

'But we haven't seen anything at all,' we responded. 'He has to have some kind of documentation to be in Italy.'

The FBI and the Secret Service sensed the differences we were having. My meetings at the White House had resulted in close relationships with many of their officers, and I was honest with them about my increasing doubts about the operation.

At one of the weekly White House meetings, I arrived alone and Stan, my FBI counterpart with whom I had grown quite friendly, was also just getting out of his car.

I joined him and we headed for the guard post at the gate.

'This damn case,' he said. 'It's driving me nuts. We have to pin him down soon.'

'I agree,' I told him. 'Believe me, we're doing everything we can.'

We approached the guard, a uniformed Secret Service officer, and showed our passes. He recognized us from previous meetings. That didn't matter. He systematically followed procedures.

'You carrying?' the guard asked Stan as we stopped in front of the gate. Odd question, I thought, not making any connection. What's he talking about?

Stan didn't blink an eye or hesitate at all. 'Nah,' he said, 'I'm just a Headquarters hump.'

'You're not, are you?' the guard said looking at me.

'Not what?' I asked.

'Not carrying a weapon,' he replied. It was a random check. Stan was amused and related the exchange to our colleagues at the meeting. (With the exception of Laos and the Congo, I never carried a weapon while working.)

Over the several months of this effort, I had become friends with many of the FBI and Secret Service officers with whom I was working so closely. I liked and respected them all. Our office had few problems in our liaison with them. They said they felt the same way.

One afternoon Chris and Gary burst into my office. 'We got the little bastard,' Chris almost shouted. 'Look at these.' He put two photos on my desk.

I looked at them. They were both of the agent who claimed to be a Libyan, I thought. 'So that's him, isn't it?' I asked.

'One is,' Gary said with what was a triumphant smile. 'The other is a Lebanese fabricator named Jabril. I had some suspicions, we all did, so I've been scouring a pile of files I got from Near East Division and I found him. Near East should have done this homework, but never mind. This does it.'

I was elated, but still cautious. 'Let me see the files?' I asked. Gary had them with him and he handed them to me. 'Great work, Gary,' I told him when I was sure. 'They are sure as hell the same guy.'

'Can we tell NE right away?' Chris asked.

'Bloody right you can,' I responded. 'They should know soonest. And start working on a cable to Rome too,' I added.

We had been breaking our heads for several months and now Gary had found what amounted to the needle in the haystack. Superb work on his part and we all owed him.

'Mary, get Stan Klein on the phone,' I called out to my secretary.

I knew, from our last meeting, that Stan was going to ask a judge for court approval to initiate phone taps on the two US citizens as a result of the information we had provided. It was a serious step, but one they couldn't avoid while there was a possible threat against the President.

'Stan, do you have the court order yet?' I asked when I got him on the phone.

'Not yet,' he responded, 'I just got all the paperwork together.'

'Well, cancel the whole thing,' I told him, relieved that we had broken the case before he had approached the courts.

'You sure, Dick?' Stan asked. 'For us this is serious stuff.'

'Stan, I know. It's serious for us too. I'll explain in detail when I see you, but for now just be aware that the subject [I didn't give any detail on the open line] is phoney – a fraud. And we've got proof.'

'Great news, Dick,' Stan said. 'When can we get together?'

'First thing tomorrow, Stan,' I replied. I was terribly pleased. The Lebanese, he was not Libyan, had been very clever, but some solid work by Gary had carried the day. I was doubly pleased that Gary got a special achievement award for his work.

Since I found it so interesting and since it is textbook stuff in terms of how to authenticate and check operations, I questioned Gary about how he had proceeded. Early in his career, he told me, he had been working on Cuban operations. He was deceived, he said, by a team that falsely reported details of their mission. They had been afraid to proceed, he discovered, and wouldn't admit it when confronted. Once burned, twice shy, he decided and since that time he had developed a career long interest in counter-intelligence efforts.

On his own initiative, he had ordered files of old operations and had scoured them carefully. He had all Arabic-language portions translated. He checked all passport data. He checked all references to other operations. He reviewed each photo. It was careful, methodical and professional work, and in the end he found that haystack needle that was to break the case. After literally months of being led down the garden path by a clever fabricator, we were able to confront the individual and end the ordeal. Gary fully deserved the praise he received and I still admire the example of solid deskwork that he provided.

'This would mean giving the DI guys access to our raw cable traffic,' I said to John Stein, the DDO.

'What's wrong with that?' John McMahon, who had just come in, demanded. 'What are you talking about? Why can't Intelligence read that stuff? Typical DO bias is what it sounds like.'

'Settle down, John Stein,' the DDO said soothingly. 'We're just talking about bringing Directorate of Intelligence officers into the Counter Terrorist Group and we both think it's a good idea. In fact, Dick proposed it. But we have to smooth the way so the bureaucracy can handle it. It's not been done before you know.'

McMahon relaxed. 'Oh. Well, for the record, I think it's a good idea.'

The idea had been gaining support for several months. As we had worked more and more closely with the Directorate of Intelligence's terrorist analysts, most of us had become increasingly convinced that joining forces would make sense. Often their analysis of operational developments, or of the aftermath of a terrorist incident, strongly enhanced the end product.

Ultimately, everything fell into place (although it was much more complicated than I had ever imagined it could be) and we more or less combined forces with the element in the DI that worked on terrorist analysis. We were stronger for the move.

One must bear in mind that this was a major step to be taking in the early 1980s. One of the strongest elements of the Agency's culture had been, since 1947 when the Agency was established, a separation between the operational and the analytical Directorates of the Agency. Both Directorates risked 'pollution of their product' by collaborating too closely with the other, we all thought. The Directorate of Operations in particular had a deeply engrained bias against opening up its traffic to DI (or anybody else's) eyes. That we were able to take the steps we did spoke more strongly to the high priority accorded to combating terrorism than to any real change of sentiment. Ultimately, significant change would come, but only much later and only by fiat.

The size of our group grew steadily from early 1982 onwards as we expanded our capabilities across the board. Part of the increased size was the addition of the Directorate of Intelligence element (almost a dozen), but there was much more to it than that. In early spring 1982, Bob had asked if I had any objection to moving the VIP protection unit from the Special Operations Group (paramilitary) to the Counter Terrorist Group. 'It just seems a better fit,' he reasoned. It made sense to me as well, and the unit, fifteen officers, was transferred.

Soon thereafter, we hired on contract two retired Secret Service officers to upgrade our skills base and strengthen the VIP protection-training course we were offering to foreign liaison services. More operations officers, more Directorate of Operations intelligence analysts and technical specialists also joined us. And we brought on board officers from the Office of Technical Services and the National Security Agency to augment the package of skills we could bring to bear in response to a terrorist incident.

We established an Incident Response Team (IRT) that we subsequently dispatched upon request to field stations dealing with terrorist attacks or incidents. It was a big step and turned out to be a great success. Updated versions of the IRT exist to this day. It enabled us to swiftly and significantly augment the capability of a given field station with tailored means to react to a wide range of terrorist incidents.

As our numbers grew, we were able to expand the services we provided. We began producing a small publication (classified) for the whole community about terrorist groups in general. It summarized the status of various ongoing investigations and provided background on the subject of terrorism in general. We formed, and I chaired, a counter-terrorism committee for the entire intelligence community. Over a dozen agencies, departments and military services sent representatives. Via the committee, we were able to co-ordinate various bureaucratic and operational efforts being undertaken by the various members of the intelligence community. We also began the effort (years would be required to complete it) to organize, co-ordinate and, to the extent possible in view of classification issues, disseminate to the intelligence community the existing database on terrorists and terrorist groups. If resources could help in the battle against terrorism, none would be spared.

Much of my job in the Counter Terrorist Group involved close liaison contact with numerous foreign intelligence and security services. Those contacts were in addition to our ongoing contacts with the FBI and Secret Service and the rest of the services in the intelligence community. As a result, I travelled much more than I had expected or wanted. Rarely did a month go by without a liaison trip somewhere. Given the fact that the majority of terrorist incidents, and therefore demand for our attention, were in Europe and the Middle East, the majority of my travel was to those areas. Services with which we had contact in Europe were dealing with internal terrorist groups and most believed that those groups maintained ties with Arab terrorist groups.

Moreover, many people felt that the Soviet Union and its minions in East Europe were, at a minimum, providing training and logistical support to various terrorist groups. I was not alone in that assessment. In her book *The Terror Network: The Secret War of International Terrorism* (Weidenfeld & Nicolson, London, 1981) Claire Sterling states:

> It was never part of the Soviet design to create and watch over native terrorist movements, still less to direct the day-to-day activities. The Phantom mastermind co-ordinating world-wide terror from some subterranean map room is a comic book concept. The whole point of the plan was to let the other fellow do it, contributing to continental terror by proxy.

Politics, as much as intelligence requirements, dictated that particular priority be given to trying to discover just how much support the communist bloc was giving to terrorist groups targeting Western interests. President Reagan, Secretary of State Alexander Haig and Director Casey were all keenly interested in the question. Without any inappropriate reference to classified data, I think I can say that we found no 'smoking gun'. Yes, the Soviets and their Bloc allies were more than willing to help 'nationalist' (a term very broadly defined by them) fighters by giving them weapons and training or money; or by allowing unmolested travel through their countries. But no, the Soviets weren't orchestrating or directing a global network of anti-Western terrorist groups. It was quite simple: problems (including those caused by terrorist groups) for Western governments were fine with the Soviets and their allies.

Frequently, other CTG officers, including DI officers, who had expertise about a specific terrorist group, would accompany me on a liaison trip. Typically we would visit three or four countries during a one-or two-week period. In a seminar type environment, we would discuss with each service (sometimes two or more in each country) issues about various terrorist groups. Believing that the more each friendly service knew about the *modus operandi* of given terrorist groups, the better each could defend against and combat that group, we shared as much as we could. The exchanges were mutually beneficial in that information obtained from these visits and seminars was as useful to us as our information was to them.

We also advocated training for personnel in security services and willingly provided some of the curricula we had developed for various courses. VIP protection, crisis management, hostage rescue and other disciplines tailored for counter-terrorist operations were among those in which we gave either advice or actual training. We were warmly welcomed at virtually every stop and were encouraged at the depth of the relationships we were establishing and maintaining. Liaison relationships in general were strengthened by our visits and our own stations were also grateful for the visits. The menace pushed all of us closer together.

Regrettably, the liaison side of our efforts was stronger than the unilateral side. Our stations were trying, of course, but penetrating terrorist groups by recruiting members of those groups was (it still is) extremely difficult. Terrorists are, almost by definition, fanatics of one type or another, and finding ways to motivate one towards recruitment presented all but insurmountable obstacles. Just identifying one and establishing contact was a true challenge. Our unilateral agent stable was small during those years and we were constantly working to expand it.

In some cases, our own regulations and restrictions governing source use and protection added to our problems. If, for example, one of our limited number of assets was asked to participate in a terrorist attack (an obvious and standard test for members of groups, especially new ones), executive order dictated that we veto his involvement. By effectively pulling him out of the planned attack, we would be putting him at risk of retaliation – he had failed the test. Partly perhaps to compensate and partly because we were trying hard, we did succeed in recruiting agents on the fringes of the terrorist movements. Many were recruited and, coupled with technical collection activities, they enabled us to prevent many terrorist incidents. And this was done without the terrorist group knowing what had gone wrong with their plan. 'The dog that didn't bark,' as Bob M. put it, borrowing a line from a Sherlock Holmes mystery.

An equally difficult and sensitive side of the problem of recruiting agents was on the political front. Our friendly relations with a particular country versus the issues surrounding terrorism in that country could put us between a rock and a hard place. One man's terrorist is another man's freedom fighter. Awkward, even untenable problems were sometimes the result.

As we expanded, I was delighted to have Bill Buckley, who joined the Counter Terrorist Group in the spring of 1982 with other members of the Protective Security Branch from Special Operations Group and who became my deputy. A former army officer, he had a strong record of service and achievement since joining the Agency. He had served as a paramilitary officer in Laos in the late 1960s.

Serious and intelligent, Bill had a military bearing and insisted at first on calling me 'sir'. It was just the normal thing to do for him, but we got over it after I convinced him that we were in fact colleagues and 'sir' made me feel uneasy. We had skills that complemented one another and strong mutual respect grew. He was highly professional, dependable, loyal, fair and easy to work with. He quickly won support and respect from members of the group. I sought and valued his judgements and listened to his views on both operational and personnel matters.

In early October 1982, I found myself looking down out of the helicopter at the deep blue Mediterranean. It was sunny and clear and we were flying, eastwards, at a low altitude. So low that I thought I saw a school of dolphin, or shark, swimming in the opposite direction.

At 0700, we had taken off from Larnaca on the south central coast of Cyprus headed for Beirut, Lebanon's embattled capital. I was travelling with my old friend Andre LeGallo and we were headed to Beirut for a series of meetings with Lebanese authorities. There was a crew of four aboard the chopper and two carried AK-47s. It was not a pleasant flight. The choppers were old and noisy and I found myself planning what I might do if we had to go down. No life jackets were visible in the cabin; the plan would have involved a lot of swimming.

Lebanon was in turmoil. The Israeli forces that had invaded Lebanon just months earlier, in an attempt to eliminate the threat of terrorism in their northern territories, had just pulled back to the slim corridor they intended to occupy in south Lebanon. They had been replaced, shortly before our trip, with a multi-national force, the result of negotiations that had ended the crisis – or, more accurately, were 'intended' to end the crisis.

As a participant in those negotiations, the United States had agreed to provide assistance to the weakened, but still functioning, government of Lebanon. Caught between the bold and powerful Palestinian force that had acted with impunity in Lebanon before the Israelis invaded, and the Israeli armed forces, the Middle East's strongest, the government of Lebanon did what it could. It was largely ineffective, however, because it had almost no real control over its territory. The Syrians, the Palestinians and several infamous terrorist groups ran roughshod over Lebanese forces. Adding to the difficulties and complexity was the religious split, Muslim versus Christian, which literally divided the country and its capital.

The aid provided by the United States would be in the form of advice and material support to organize, or strengthen, Lebanon's ability to police and control its own territory, and to establish and maintain law and order. Training to police, security and intelligence organizations was a key part of the plan. And, lest anyone conclude that we weren't serious, someone had to get out to Lebanon quickly to get talks, action even, started. Andre, as Chief of Operations for our Near East Division, would initiate efforts to start some training programmes and, given that Beirut was a hotbed of terrorist activity, I had been asked to accompany him for separate discussions aimed at building a strong counter-terrorist capability in the process. Our goals were completely complementary. We found ourselves as the point men for a security programme with prospects for success that were mixed at best.

Beirut's airport had been forced to close during the hostilities associated with the Israeli invasion and it had not yet been reopened. Politics surrounding the conflict ruled out either Damascus or Tel Aviv as jump-off points and we had finally settled on Larnaca. We flew there by commercial air and were picked up by the two Christian militia helicopters. The eastern part of Beirut and portions of the north of Lebanon were under control of the Christian militia. We maintained contact with the Christians as well as with elements of the (mostly Muslim) Lebanese government.

We came in along the coast and got a good look at Beirut before passing the port and landing nearby at a little after 0800. It was a military compound and Jim, one of our officers whom Andre knew, was waiting next to the landing pad with two black sedans.

It was a short ride to our hotel. East (Christian) Beirut, where we had landed, showed few signs of the recent conflict. We crossed the Green Line that divided the city. In West (Muslim) Beirut, signs of battle were everywhere with burned-out or badly damaged buildings in most parts of the city.

Our hotel had been spared serious damage, but it was operating on a limited basis. The phones worked and there was hot water (sometimes), but staff was limited, as were services. As we didn't plan to spend much time, there it didn't bother us. Located on a street that ran along a ridge above the coast, it offered a view of the Mediterranean and the coastal road. It was a beautiful view, even in these difficult times. On the coastal road just below our hotel was the three-storey office; no frills and not very attractive. We didn't have much to do in our office itself. We would simply explain to the Chief, Ken, that Andre's local meetings would be to discuss training programmes for their personnel and mine would be to discuss terrorism and the groups operating out of Lebanon. I also had a meeting with an agent that we had been able to schedule for the next day. But we wanted to visit and exchange views with the Chief on a number of issues. Moreover, it was a courtesy that we would not have failed to extend to him and his staff, especially in these troubled and difficult times.

Ken lamented and cursed, as he recounted what had clearly been a harrowing period. Many things were described as a 'bug fuck'. He had been under much stress and, not surprisingly, he was letting out some of the tension. He had needed someone with whom to share his frustrations and we happened in at just the right time. We listened sympathetically, offering up expressions of support where possible.

The climate they had been operating in had been exceptionally difficult and dangerous, Ken explained, and his officers deserved lots of credit for what they had been able to accomplish.

We were soon to discover that they all, in varying degrees, were feeling the stress of the situation in Beirut. Operations officers, in particular, although there weren't many, were feeling the effects of trying to carry on in the face of numerous obstacles. Just moving around in the city was difficult, dangerous and sometimes impossible. Curfew and the confusion that abounded over who was actually in charge, made it extremely hard to schedule or conduct agent meetings. We had expected stress and frustration, but not to the extent that we found. From the Chief down, there was clear evidence of fraying of nerves as our colleagues struggled in an extremely hostile environment. We were both struck by what we found. Andre, of course, reported our findings back to the Chief of the Near East Division with a recommendation that R and R travel be scheduled for each person in the office to give them a break from the tension of living in this ravaged city.

After concluding our discussions and after lunch at a nearby Lebanese restaurant, we visited the Embassy's security officer. A state department employee, he was a career security officer who had been in Beirut for only six months. We reviewed physical and personnel security issues with him and each of us came away with the impression (which we later shared with the Chief) that security for the Embassy needed some tightening up. Part of our concern was about access from the highway that ran right by the front of the building. 'Couldn't something, even fifty-gallon fuel drums filled with sand, be placed in front of the building?' we asked the security officer. The discussion was a delicate one in that we had no authority over Embassy security matters. We could only ask pointed questions and make (hopefully) subtle suggestions. We did the best we could, but neither of us felt good about it when we left.

The day after our arrival in Beirut was another bright sunny day. I was in the eastern, Christian, part of the city, standing on the balcony of the apartment looking down at a playground full of children. There was a basketball game going on and, at the opposite end of the playground, younger kids were playing soccer. You would never have guessed what turmoil was going on in the other half of the city and in the rest of the country. Here, everything seemed pleasant and normal. One of our counterparts had dropped me off a few minutes earlier and I was waiting for the man who would take me to the agent I hoped to debrief. I wasn't sure why I couldn't have been taken directly to the agent, but we didn't have any control over the arrangements so I had to accept their terms. We had to trust the Christian service or not see the agent.

Soon there was a knock on the door and I let in the intermediary. I had a name and a description and both seemed to fit. I doubt it was his true name, but it didn't matter much. We left immediately and went down to his car, which was parked right in front of the apartment building. We headed towards the outskirts of the city. He was using the rear-view mirror to convince himself that we were not being followed.

'See anything?' I asked.

He smiled. 'Nothing,' he said. 'There won't be any problems.' His English was good.

Before long we were in foothills north-east of the city. We stopped in front of a well-tended, two-storey house built into a hillside. Could this be the agent's home? It didn't matter. We went inside and the agent met us in the living room. He was elderly and looked Middle Eastern, but I couldn't tell much beyond that. I never knew if he was Armenian, Lebanese, or something else.

The subject of our discussion – he also spoke good English – was going to be the Armenian Secret Army of Liberation, known as ASALA. A group that some Armenians sympathized with and supported, ASALA employed violence (assassinations and bombings) against Turks and Turkish interests, worldwide. They staged attacks in Europe, in the United States, in Canada, in Latin America and elsewhere. Innocent bystanders were often injured or killed and, to us, ASALA was a terrorist group that needed to be stopped.

Why have discussions about ASALA in Beirut, a city awash with Arab terrorists? It just so happened that a large community of the Armenian diaspora lived in East Beirut and someone was willing to talk about ASALA with a CIA officer. (Actually, there is also a sizeable Armenian community in Los Angeles. As a result, the worst job in the Turkish Foreign Service is Consul General, Los Angeles. Many of them have been attacked and several killed.) ASALA was a group watched closely by the FBI and by most of our European liaison counterparts and the opportunity to collect information about its *modus operandi* or personnel was not to be passed up.

The agent was wary but polite and forthcoming as we started talking about ASALA after initial amenities were accomplished. My companion sat and listened. He said nothing. He refilled our teacups from time to time. For three hours we covered subjects like factional infighting in ASALA, organizational history and structure, background and whereabouts of key individuals, and how weapons and explosives training was accomplished. ASALA links with other terrorists groups was touched upon as well. The agent seemed to relax and warm up to the task at hand as we talked on and on. I found myself wondering why he was doing this. What motivated him to give us this information? I probed, but he deflected my questions. In the end, I could only thank him sincerely for the information he had provided and offer to reimburse him for the time he had spent with me. I didn't really expect him to accept any payment and he didn't. I reiterated how much we appreciated his co-operation and joined my companion who was already outside.

Back at Headquarters, using my extensive notes, I was able to write two lengthy intelligence reports about ASALA. Both were well received in the community and large portions of both were shared with several European liaison services. There were many unanswered questions about the agent. There still are. But the information was good.

From the meeting with the agent, I was taken directly to the Headquarters of our Christian counterparts. Andre was there and we spent the remainder of the day discussing training programmes. We talked about schedules, logistics, curriculum, personnel, funding. They were eager to have whatever we could (or would) provide so the discussions were open and friendly. Interspersed, there were lots of interesting comments about Palestinian and other Arab groups operating and training in Lebanon. Time passed quickly and soon it was early evening. The discussions completed, we prepared to take our leave and drive back to East Beirut. They wouldn't hear of it.

Just before midnight, 'some drinks and food' ended. Our hosts had been gracious and relaxed throughout and that put us at ease as well. We probably had more of the drinks than we needed, but it wasn't noticeable. I didn't notice it, that is. Nor can I remember what was said as we left the restaurant and headed back to our hotel in East Beirut, but I was happy to have had two cups of strong coffee before we left. Our colleagues knew we were headed back across the Green Line and they knew what time it was, but they didn't seem to think there was any problem. They just gave us some last-minute directions and waved us on our way.

It was a cool night with no moonlight. Andre was driving. It was a strange city to us both. We headed west along the coast road for about ten minutes. Then the road was blocked and we were obligated to turn south. The road wound in a generally west-ward direction. Andre was driving cautiously, as we didn't know exactly when the demarcating Green Line would appear or what would be there. There were few streetlights in the neighbourhood we were passing through and it was difficult to see very far ahead. Suddenly, there were no lights ahead of us at all and a makeshift barricade blocked our way.

'Must be the Green Line,' Andre muttered, staring intently in front of us.

'I'm sure you're right,' I said. 'Who mans it now? The Lebanese government?'

'Don't know,' Andre said. We stopped near the barricade.

We were alert, uncertain what would come next and decidedly uncomfortable to be in the position we were in. I wished the Israelis were still in control. At least they were predictable. We doubted there were any multi-national forces here and certainly no Christian militia. Maybe there was no one around.

No such luck. Without warning, a couple of men appeared out of the darkness to our front left, on Andre's side of the car. Looking in that direction, we then spotted, about thirty yards away, a fire next to a burned-out building. Several men were standing around it. All, including the two now approaching the car, were carrying weapons. Bad news, we were both thinking. Who the hell are these guys? As they came close enough so that we could get a good look at them, I felt even more uncomfortable. They were not wearing complete uniforms and didn't appear to be part of any government unit.

Short and stocky, both had scraggly dirty beards and unkempt black hair. Their clothing was tattered and hadn't seen a washing machine (or the local equivalent) for a long time. They wore black combat boots and one had a scarf wrapped around his head.

Andre's window was open and they approached that side of the car.

'Where are you going?' one of them asked in French after he noticed that we were both foreigners. His tone was gruff, almost as if he was irritated because we had bothered them so late at night.

Andre speaks fluent French. And he thinks quickly. In French, he responded, 'Sorry to bother you, we got a little lost in the dark. We're trying to get back to our hotel just above the American Embassy. Does this road go through?'

The gruff one paused a moment and then exchanged a quick phrase in Arabic with his companion. He looked back at Andre. 'Who are you?' he asked.

There was no option. 'We are American diplomats,' Andre said.

Another pause. Someone by the fire shouted something in Arabic and the gruff one responded. By now we could tell that all of them had been drinking. Those by the fire probably still were.

'We must see your passports,' he said. Andre looked at me.

'They look like goddamn thugs,' I muttered under my breath. 'And they are drunk.'

'We can't tell them to bugger off,' Andre pointed out. 'There isn't much choice. It's their barricade and they are armed.' He was right. I handed him my passport.

'Mr Gruff' took the passports and walked over to the group at the fire. The leader of this group, presumably, was over there. His partner waited about 15 feet to the left front of our car.

We were perplexed and not just a little nervous. We discussed the situation briefly as we waited and concluded that as American diplomats we wouldn't be bothered by these guys. We would talk our way through. Briefly, the thought of just driving around the barricade crossed my mind, but I knew it was too late for that. We both wondered exactly who these guys were and whom they represented. The three or four minutes we waited seemed much longer. Finally, we saw the gruff one start back towards us with the passports in hand.

'*Allez*,' was all he said to Andre as he handed him our passports. His partner pulled the barricade off the street in front of us and, with considerable relief, we crossed the Green Line into West Beirut. We were, at that point, not far from our hotel and we arrived there without incident.

Most frustrating, and ominous, for us had been the fact that we had no control over the circumstances. Without warning we had stumbled into the roadblock and found ourselves in what could only be described as a dicey situation. It was in fact the reality of being in a city wherein only the slimmest thread of law and order prevailed, and where signs of deep-seated hatred were everywhere.

I relate the above because it was one of our experiences in Beirut. I relate it also because the episode flashed into both Andre's and my mind when, months later, Islamic terrorist groups began taking Western diplomats and senior officials in Beirut hostage. Armed terrorists broke into homes and offices or ambushed cars to kidnap their victims. Many were held for several years before their release. Some were executed or died in captivity. It was hard for us to escape the thought that we had certainly flirted, albeit unknowingly, with disaster that night as we crossed the Green Line.

Beirut airport reopened that day. The Embassy managed to get us seats on one of the first flights out – happily so, since that would preclude another ride in that bloody helicopter. The negotiations required to reopen the airport had been contentious and the situation there was tense as we arrived. Government control, although tenuous, prevailed, however, and after several delays our Air France flight took off for Paris. We had mixed emotions. We were delighted to be getting the hell out of there, but also felt genuine concern for our colleagues (indeed any foreigners required to stay there) and the perils they were confronting. We took a last look at the visibly war-torn city as the plane took off.

The year 1983 would see a slightly reduced total number of terrorist incidents. From the perspective of US national interests, however, it would be one of the deadliest years on record. A total of 387 Americans, 267 in Beirut alone, died in 1983 at the hands of terrorists. For the Counter Terrorist Group, the challenge intensified. Terrorism was widespread and Western interests were under attack on many fronts. Obviously, the attacks directed at US interests were the focus of our heightened efforts, but co-operation with allied services facing threats of their own also increased.

On 18 April 1983, the United States Embassy in Beirut was bombed. A member of a fanatic Muslim terrorist group, committed to suicide, drove a truck filled with explosives into the ground floor of the Embassy. It was detonated by either the impact as it hit the building or a remotely controlled signalling device, something like a garage door opener.

The explosion collapsed much of the building causing numerous wounded and sixty-seven deaths. Fifty of the dead were local employees of the Embassy, and seventeen were Americans. Included in the American dead were Ken, our Chief, Jim, who had met Andre and I at the military base, Jim's wife, and a senior DI analyst who was visiting. These heavy losses were hard to accept. I thought immediately of the concerns Andre and I had about Embassy security standards. Most especially, I thought about the unimpeded access from the road just in front that we had talked about during our recent visit. Who would have guessed? Indeed who *should* have guessed? Hindsight is always 20/20.

Even more devastating was the attack we suffered later in 1983. As one of our trips was ending in Madrid in late October 1983, we got news. We had just finished breakfast. I was travelling with Bill, an operations officer, and John, a DI analyst. As we left our hotel and began the short walk to the US Embassy, Bill stopped to buy a *Herald Tribune*. It provided details about a devastating terrorist attack in Beirut the previous day, 23 October. We had heard a reference to the attack on the morning news but it gave few details.

Our feelings of grief, sadness and frustration mounted as Bill read the article about the attack. A suicide bomber, driving an explosives-laden truck, had destroyed the US Marine barracks claiming 296 lives, 243 of them US Marines. Almost without knowing it, we began assessing the details that were available and trying to figure out which group was responsible for this, to us, senseless carnage. We got nowhere. Anything useful would have to wait until we were back at Headquarters where complete detail would be available. For the moment, the news certainly underscored the magnitude of the danger terrorism represented.

Bill, the operations officer travelling with me, had joined the Counter Terrorist Group in the fall of 1982 following the acquisition of some first-hand experience about how terrorism works.

A former Marine Corps Aviator with combat experience in Vietnam, Bill had left the military to seek a graduate degree. After getting a Ph.D. in American Government, he joined the Agency. He did well in our training programme and in due course was dispatched to his first field tour – Tehran. His timing was lousy in that he arrived there just weeks before rampaging Iranian students, with full support from the government of Iran, invaded and ransacked the American Embassy and took all Americans therein hostage.

According to newspaper accounts, the Iranians pieced together shredded documents, a tedious task at best, enabling them to discover that Bill was a CIA officer. That prompted 'special' treatment for him and he spent nearly fourteen and a half months in solitary confinement before negotiations secured his release along with the other hostages. It was a dreadful experience, which he handled with great inner strength. He credits his military training for much of his success, but there is more to it than that. Generously endowed with determination and common sense, Bill coped pragmatically with whatever each day dealt him. He is not overly fond of Iran, but he carries few scars as a result of his life-threatening brush with raw terrorism. He was a welcome and ultimately highly productive member of our group. I admired how quickly he put that behind him and got on with his life. He is a truly stout fellow.

That same year, 1983, also witnessed a series of deadly attacks by ASALA against Turkish interests and citizens. The attacks, in North America and Europe, killed a score or more, including innocent bystanders. Major efforts and resources were committed to neutralizing them.

Arab terrorist groups continued to be active against Israeli and other Western interests. North Korea attempted to assassinate South Korean officials in Rangoon, Burma. In December, as the year was ending, there was a potentially deadly, but largely unsuccessful, attack against the US Embassy in Kuwait. There were also some successes in 1983. On 5 June, a group of aid workers near Boma in the south of the Sudan was taken hostage by a dissident group. There were several deaths in the attack. Two Americans were among the hostages. It was an unknown group and may not have met the standard definition of terrorist, but the tactic they were employing was enough to prompt our response. The Counter Terrorist Group was alerted and we raised the issue to the intelligence community as a whole. Following close consultations with several sister agencies, and some liaison services, an Incident Response Team was dispatched to organize and implement a rescue effort.

Within a couple of days, everything was in place to send in an attack force. From excellent overhead coverage, we knew where the base camp of the dissident/terrorist group was located and that the hostages were being held there. I'm confident that they had no idea they had incurred the wrath of several Western governments who were more than willing to respond in kind – especially so quickly. Arriving by helicopter at dawn less than a week after the catalysing incident, a highly trained hostage rescue force routed the terrorists and rescued all of the hostages. Losses: good guys none, bad guys many.

The complete success of the operation confirmed the value and efficacy of the IRT concept and, needless to say, we were very pleased. Soon there was even more to please us. Part of our co-ordinated effort to employ any possible resource in support of the IRT and its rescue effort had been to solicit priority coverage from overhead assets. And we got it. Indeed, we were presented with real time photographic coverage of the rescue team's dawn attack. It was as if we had been in a plane circling above as the assault took place. Plainly visible were rocket blasts, choppers approaching and landing, individuals running on the ground and vehicles trying to escape.

It was a lucky break as timing had to be just right, but it was nonetheless an impressive achievement for our overall capability.

Bill Buckley prepared and delivered, to Director Casey, an excellent briefing about the successful rescue that featured the real time photography. His briefing was well received and no doubt raised the profile of our group on the seventh floor. And a higher, favourable profile at senior levels didn't hurt our efforts aimed at continued augmentation of our staff. Nor did it hurt at budget time.

In late spring 1983, I was called up to Director Casey's office. That was unusual. I called Bob to see if he could shed any light on why the Director wanted to see me. He couldn't. 'Let me know what he wanted,' he said.

Soon after my arrival, Chuck Cogan, the Chief of our Near East Division, joined me, and we were shown into the Director's office by the secretary.

'Hi, Dick,' Casey said. 'Have a seat. Hello, Chuck.' A man I didn't know was sitting in an easy chair near the Director's desk.

'Let me introduce you to Bob Woodward,' the Director said, reciting both of our true names to Woodward. 'He works for the *Washington Post*.' Both Chuck and I knew that. Woodward's role in the Watergate affair that brought down Nixon was well known. 'He is going to do a three-part series for the *Post* on terrorism and he would love to talk with us about the groups operating in the Middle East.'

What the hell? I was thinking. We don't usually deal with the media at all, let alone be introduced to a journalist in true name.

'Terrorism is a key issue', Casey said, 'and I wanted to be as helpful as possible. You two are the best guys I could think of to talk with Bob so I told him we could give him a briefing. He's going to Beirut next week.'

'This is just for background and will be off the record,' Woodward, who may have sensed our uneasiness, said right away.

There was little choice, none really, for Chuck and me. We spent the next hour answering Woodward's questions as best we could while striving to protect our sources and equities. Woodward was good. He understood our position but was nonetheless eager to exploit this occasion as best he could. It all went pretty well and we were able to satisfy many of his queries. We also alerted him to some potential problems he should watch out for in and around Beirut, the Bekaa Valley for one. Finally it ended and, with gracious thanks, he left. Casey never seemed to sense the discomfort both Chuck and I felt.

'Bill would make a fine Chief, especially in that stress filled environment,' I responded.

The question: what did I think about naming my deputy, Bill Buckley, as Chief in Beirut, had been posed by Chuck. The position had been filled on a temporary basis since the April bombing when we lost Ken, our former Chief.

'It is, as you well know, a damn tough and dangerous job. There aren't many people I would consider sending, but Bill is tough and I think he could do it,' Chuck went on.

'I'm confident he can do it, and I know he'll say yes if you ask him,' I said.

It was summer 1983 and Bill was in fact named as Chief in Beirut. After several weeks of various types of training, Bill reported to Beirut in early fall. As predicted, the job was tough and required hard work for long hours seven days a week. Bill thrived despite concerns he had voiced about a lack of experience in some areas. And, as we all knew, it was dangerous.

On 16 March 1984, barely six months after he got there, an armed group of Arab terrorists captured Bill as he was leaving for work in the morning. His car was blocked by two cars carrying heavily armed terrorists. He had no way to escape. The attack had been carefully planned and, in a few short moments, Bill was forced into a waiting car and driven away.

We have few details about his captivity. From debriefings of other hostages who were released, we know that Bill got sick and received little or no medical attention. We also know that ill treatment contributed to his failing health. We don't know exactly when, but Bill died in captivity after many months of suffering in solitary confinement. His killers are still unpunished. I was serving in Brussels when I heard of Bill's death. Shock and grief were followed by great sadness at the loss of such an outstanding colleague and patriot. On the Agency's wall of honour, there is a star for Bill. There is also one for Mike Deuel. For me those stars are a painful personal memory of losses suffered for causes and beliefs we shared.

The United States hosted the summer Olympic Games in 1984 in Los Angeles. Heightened by the surge in state-sponsored and supported terrorism, and by attacks suffered in 1982 and 1983, concerns about security at the games prompted high level attention in Washington. As a result, all of the offices in Washington dealing with terrorist issues, many of them only recently created, were ordered to focus resources on security measures for the Olympic Games to ensure that those measures would be strong enough to discourage any terrorist group from attempting an attack.

As the 'lead agency' for domestic terrorist incidents, the FBI headed the effort, but as I would soon learn there would be many other players. Our role, an important one, centred around the collection and dissemination of relevant intelligence. We became very involved and expended heavy resources in support of the security goals that were established. Overall, I was told later, the US government spent more than $95 million on the effort to provide security.

Planning and initial meetings began in the fall of 1982 – that's right, 1982. Much work needed to be done, I soon realized, just in terms of organizing the groups and communications channels that would be needed when the games began. First there was the effort in Washington itself. We had no problem with the FBI's leadership, but there were internecine squabbles that arose elsewhere within the intelligence and security community. Fortunately, the FBI enjoyed a strong reputation for competence and efficiency. This was especially so, we believed, among foreign terrorist groups that had thus far been afraid to challenge the FBI on US territory. We were more than pleased to enhance wherever possible the FBI's image of being 10 feet tall. Soon the Washington end fell into place with basic guidelines having been established.

We were in touch, of course, with our stations and bases worldwide and all had been alerted to the need for immediate attention to any intelligence that might relate to the security of the upcoming games. That was on track. Next came the meetings in Los Angeles. As the Agency's senior representative, I was invited to attend a series of planning meetings in and around Los Angeles. I flew out there with Wayne Gilbert, a senior FBI officer who headed the Bureau's activities, to gear up for security at the games.

'Who the hell are all these people?' I asked Wayne as we arrived together for the first meeting.

'All represent police and security organizations that will be involved when the games begin,' he responded. 'State police, county police, city police, park police, hostage rescue units, crisis management experts, and maybe beach police for all I know. Lots of people with a finger in the pie.'

'I'm glad they are going to be your problem and not mine,' I said with a smile.

'Thanks, Dick, I'll remember you for that,' he grinned back.

The meeting started with briefings about the potential threats to security at the games. The men doing the briefing went on and on with comment about virtually every known terrorist group. There were then talks about the various venues and what was around them. I was surprised to find out then that the Iranian and Armenian communities in Los Angeles were the largest outside of Iran and Armenia. Planning for the security of Turkish athletes and officials would certainly have to take into account the large number of Armenians resident in the area and the potential pool of individuals willing to co-operate with ASALA that they represented. What the large number of resident Iranians meant from the perspective of security for visiting Iranians was less clear.

As I listened, I realized what a complex effort this was going to be and why serious planning and organizational activity had begun more than eighteen months before the games. And I was pleased to see, and feel, the spirit of co-operation that prevailed. Wayne and other Bureau officers were careful and sensitive in their handling of various issues that arose.

I named a small unit, to work on all aspects of what was required from us, to support the overall effort. Within the Agency, we worked closely with the DI and with the various geographic divisions and, as had been the case in Los Angeles, we enjoyed high levels of co-operation across the board.

The only problem I can recall in our effort to support security for the Olympic Games concerned the dissemination process for the raw intelligence we would be collecting. For finished intelligence about terrorist groups or security threats there was an established mechanism and no problem. But for our so-called 'raw' intelligence, debate erupted over what could be sent directly to FBI units operating on the scene in Los Angeles. My background of working with the Bureau and my respect for their professionalism put me in the position of being the advocate for direct dissemination. Some (on one of our staffs that was the watchdog for dissemination channels) objected and insisted that there should be no exception to standard dissemination channels. The debate was short-lived. Logic and pragmatism soon won out and I was given authority to establish channels for the dissemination of relevant intelligence directly to Agency elements established in Los Angeles for passage to FBI and other security elements.

Organizing and ultimately implementing security for the 1984 games was a lengthy, complex and costly effort. As had happened in other areas of my job, it was much tougher than I had anticipated. Literally thousands of security and intelligence officers were involved over an extended period before and up to the games themselves and millions of dollars were committed. By the standard set, however, total safety for all events, athletes and spectators, the effort was a complete success.

I was Chief of the Counter Terrorist Group for well over two years. It was an exciting time – and often stressful. Our workload and our size grew steadily during my tenure, especially during the two years that were marked by high levels of terrorist activity directed against US interests and those of our close allies – 1982 and 1983. I had worked closely with sister US agencies like the Secret Service and the FBI and I had established close contacts in several European liaison services. At times frustrating and at times gratifying (when we could invoke the dog that didn't bark line), the period had its successes and incidents that had to be labelled failures. Most frustrating was the difficulty we had in penetrating the inner core of the groups committing the attacks. Without enough agents on the inside of these groups, it was difficult for us to take the initiative except in terms of training and implementation of security measures. We did all that we could, but the initiative was in the hands of the terrorists (Abu Nidal, Abu Jabril, Carlos and others) who planned and executed the attacks.

There were close to eighty people in the Counter Terrorist

Group when I left it. Analysts, communicators, technicians, paramilitary officers, operations officers and reports officers were included in the increases. We were headed towards a 'stand alone' capability that could work to penetrate, monitor, or respond to terrorists and their organizations. The surge in state sponsorship of terrorism, whether for religious or political (or some combination of the two) reasons, added a new dimension to the problem with a corresponding need for policy initiatives. The latter was an area in which we could only make recommendations since it was State's prerogative to make policy for the administration. The group was destined to grow much more. Our efforts had given direction, a blueprint if you will, to that growth and within two years of my departure, the group was designated the Counter Terrorism Center and its size increased to over 200 people. As a 'center' it operated (and operates today) in the name of the entire intelligence community.

My assignment had been rewarding and broadening. It had included a wide range of tasks and contacts in many agencies and disciplines. It ranged from visits to Congress for testimony as the Agency's terrorism representative or briefings to members and staff, to visits with liaison services from Europe to Asia and the Middle East. As usual hard work and long hours had been required, but I accepted that as the norm and didn't mind. It was a watershed assignment that would put me firmly into the management camp. Operational activity was definitely a thing of the past.

The end of my assignment was seriously clouded, however, by my great concern about Bill Buckley's fate. His seizure by an unknown terrorist group had only just occurred at this point, but we knew it was a grave incident and we feared for his safety. We spared no effort, of course, to try to discover who was holding him and where, but the trail yielded little to work on. Unaware that our worst fears would one day be fulfilled, we could only pursue every avenue of possible access to information about his whereabouts in the hope of launching a rescue effort. We did not succeed.

Late in the fall of 1983, I was named as one of the Agency's two representatives to the Department of State Senior Seminar, a prestigious academic year of exposure to a wide range of foreign and domestic policy issues. I was pleased to have been a nominee and even more pleased to have been selected. It would be yet another opportunity to broaden my horizons. The class would start in late August 1984 and conclude in early June 1985. Subsequently, in January 1984, I was named as Chief in Brussels starting in summer 1985. More planning would be required.

The senior seminar was as good as advertised. I had heard from several people, including a good friend who had taken the seminar in 1981, that it was a most enjoyable and informative experience. That's precisely what I found it to be. For starters, it was a definite (and welcome) change of pace. There was a schedule of speakers for each week. And each week was given over to a close look at some specific domestic or foreign policy question. There was time before the first speaker began for reading the paper (a real luxury), or reviewing articles or studies about the subject at hand. After a relaxed lunch it was the same thing, some reading and then a speaker. After their tailored presentations, the speakers opened the floor for questions and we had the opportunity to follow up on any issue we liked. By far the majority of the subjects we looked at (immigration, education, welfare, agriculture, national labour policies, drugs and the environment) were of high interest, so most of us did preparatory reading before hearing that week's speakers.

One week a month we spent travelling in the United States for a first-hand look at one of the subjects we were studying. For example, we went to Texas to look at immigration problems, to the north-west to see forestry programmes at work, and to Minnesota to stay on dairy farms and talk with the farmers about their views of government policies. Especially for someone like me, who had spent so much time abroad in recent years, it was interesting to re-examine domestic policy questions. I hadn't thought much about most of them for a long time. The only requirements were threefold. Firstly, you had to show up every day and for the trips. Not too taxing. Secondly, each of us was assigned the responsibility for setting up the speakers for one of the blocks of study. That meant reviewing the subject, deciding on whom to invite to speak about it, and then making the calls and writing the letters to set it up. Journalists, academics, businessmen and government officials were all possible speakers depending upon the subject. Most of those invited were happy to come. And thirdly, we all had to write a lengthy paper on any subject we chose. The subject had to be approved, but that posed little problem. With the luxury of knowing my next assignment, I selected the European Union as the subject of my paper. My research included visits to the various embassies of EU members and a trip to Brussels to visit the headquarters of the EU.

The visit to Brussels was a good chance for me to get a look at the office I would soon head and to discuss EU issues with experts at the organization's Headquarters. Writing the paper, which was accomplished between January and early April, gave me a head start on a subject that would be of high interest once I got to Belgium.

All aspects of that academic year were positive, and I considered the time well spent indeed. It served to recharge my batteries, so to speak, and, as a bonus, it gave me a chance to do some preparing for my next assignment. It capped off what had been an interesting four years at Headquarters. I was more than ready, however, to get back to the field. Judy and the girls were ready too and we were all looking forward to life in Europe. True, we would be leaving Suzanne behind in college, something we had been dreading, but she had already spent her first year at Swarthmore College, away from home, and was confident that she could handle the separation (I was less confident that Judy could.) She had grown up in what seemed like just a few years after we got back from Hong Kong. To our considerable distress, her siblings would soon follow suit.

FOURTEEN

TO CATCH A SPY

1985–88

Of course I was very much looking forward to my first posting as Chief. I had read over the personnel files of the people in the Brussels office so that I'd have some idea about the strengths and weaknesses of the staff I inherited. Pretty solid, I thought, although there weren't enough case officers with operationally useful language skills – a common failing of the service at the time, unfortunately. We had several good French speakers, but only one officer who could speak Dutch. None had any capability in Flemish.

My Deputy, Jack A., was a strong officer with lots of experience. He was highly respected for his solid operational skills and his ability to deal with Headquarters and other bureaucratic problems that were a part of our life. I liked him from the start. Jack was rough cut and a little jaded and frustrated with his career track, but that had no effect at all on the quality of the work he turned in. Divorced, he was living alone in Brussels. Or so I thought for a long time. Ultimately Jack told me that he and one of the intelligence analysts in the station were living together. They were married a few years later. I was no doubt the last one to know of their relationship, which was a function of the fact that no one tells the boss anything about such matters. It caused no problems. Jack made sure of that. Indeed there was one operation wherein, working as a team, Jack and Becky did an outstanding job clandestinely passing a note to a KGB officer.

My arrival in Brussels was slightly clouded by the non-standard turnover of leadership. I will explain. During my March 1985 trip to the city for research on the paper I wrote about the EU, I had met my predecessor, who shall remain nameless. For one of the few times in my career, I found a fellow officer unlikeable. His career background had been in the Middle East Division and he was openly critical of how some things were done in Europe Division. He made no secret of the fact that he considered himself to be the only really competent case officer in the office – a claim that won him few friends. Whether or not there was merit in any of his critique, it obviously would have been smarter to tone down his bad-mouthing of the Division in which he was working. I had quickly observed that he was not liked in the office.

Nor was he liked outside the office. He wore a cape instead of an overcoat, which many thought a bit much, and it seemed that some Belgians were upset and irritated at his attitudes. It was rumoured that after his departure, his household belongings were 'mistakenly' sent to Cape Town, South Africa, instead of Baltimore. The locals stuck to the story that it was a mistake, rather than payback.

All things considered, I concluded that a clean break was probably a good idea. It meant that I would have no personal turnover and would have to arrange to meet people on my own. That was less desirable, but I wanted to be 'untarnished' by his reputation. I talked it over with Judy, who had also met him, and she agreed with my decision. I have always trusted her assessment of people and her agreement confirmed my intention not to have a normal round of cocktails and personal introductions. Most of all I wanted to start out on the right foot. As diplomatically as possible (there was no reason to alienate him), I pleaded personal and family problems that would preclude our arrival until after his scheduled departure.

The first Ambassador for whom I would work as Chief was Ambassador Allen Schwabe, a political appointee. Well heeled from his ownership of a large department store chain in California, he was an original member of President Reagan's 'kitchen cabinet'. He was also a big contributor to the Republican Party. In his middle sixties, Schwabe was a shrewd and likeable man. My initial dealings with him went well, which was a great relief to me since the relationship with the Ambassador often dictated how relations with the Embassy would pan out. Our relationship turned out to be positive.

Initially, my relationship with Schwabe's number two, Deputy Chief of Mission Ron Ward, was less positive. The problems started shortly after we both arrived in Brussels, he in his first DCM slot and me in my first assignment as Chief of our office.

In due course, there was an issue. Ward called me to his office and asked that I brief him on various activities including covert action efforts. He knows I can't and won't do that, I thought. So what's the angle this time? Testing, I suppose, to see just how far he can push. I told him I couldn't brief him and pointed out that I had already briefed the Ambassador.

'Did you give him specific details?' he asked.

'No, I did not,' I replied. 'Nor can I.'

'Well, we'll just see about that,' he announced.

He then explained that he needed to know about everything that was happening so that he could properly manage the Embassy's affairs. He would cable Washington, he said, to clear up this issue. Was that supposed to be a threat? I didn't bite.

'First of all, it is not a problem,' I told him. 'It is simply that I have no options. There is a law that forbids me from revealing sources and methods to anyone. But cabling your superiors is a good idea,' I added. We parted amicably I thought. We agreed to disagree was how it turned out. I waited.

In the meantime, I cabled Headquarters to explain what had happened and to give them a head's up that they might be receiving a query from State. Headquarters responded promptly confirming that my response had been appropriate and thanking me for alerting them.

A couple of days later, the Ambassador called me to his office. 'I understand you and Ron are having a problem,' he said after some initial small talk.

'Nothing serious, Ambassador,' I said. 'We'll get it ironed out.' I wasn't sure if Ron had explained the issue or not. 'There are limits to what I can tell him. I can brief you, but no one else in the Embassy.'

'Well, I want to be sure that you two are getting along and working together,' the Ambassador said. He must have told Ron that he was going to call me.

'I can assure you that I'm trying hard,' I told him.

'It'll come, Dick,' he said, 'you know how some of these State guys are.' That last comment was music to my ears.

Neither the Ambassador nor Ward ever raised the issue again. I did not brief Ward. I suspect that State simply explained the ground rules to him. Or that he knew them full well, never actually cabled Washington and was just probing for a reaction from me. He got one.

Part of what was driving Ward, I concluded later, was frustration about his status in Belgium. There were three American Embassies in Brussels and most agreed that the one accredited to Belgium was low man on the totem pole. The Embassies at the Common Market (soon to be European Union) Headquarters and at NATO commanded higher priority in the grand scheme of things. US relations with tiny Belgium didn't measure up to the issues and concerns emanating from the other two Embassies. Ward then was number two at the third-ranking Embassy, although he would never have admitted that openly. A cable from his political section about a strike in the coalmines around Liège would have been a typical concern for him, not an earthshaking issue in Washington.

To make matters worse, my office, which had responsibilities in support of all three Embassies in Brussels and for the major military presence (SHAFE) in Mons, Belgium, was bigger than Ward's State Department complement in the Embassy. That probably gnawed at him, as did the fact that he knew I had regular dealings with all three Ambassadors and the Commanding General at Mons. In fact I joked at the time (not to Ward) that I worked for three Ambassadors, a Lord (Lord Carrington, who was head of NATO) and a four star general (the commander at Mons). I met and briefed each of them regularly about various, often counter-intelligence, subjects. Looking back, I must admit that I too would have been frustrated had I been in his place.

Despite the early hiccups, my relationship with Ward developed reasonably well. I tried to make things work and did brief him whenever I could about local issues we sometimes came across. He appreciated my efforts, I think, and we managed to overcome the initial problems. I discovered that he played tennis and suggested a game. He accepted and we played a few days later at a nearby local club. A great rivalry ensued. I thought myself a better tennis player, but our matches were invariably very close and he won as many sets as I did. He was fiercely competitive and tenacious as hell. I've never been accused of lacking a competitive spirit either and I rose to the occasion. Usually, we would skip lunch and play for an hour or so at noon and always the matches were tough battles. I don't remember ever telling him so, but I admired the tenacity and guts he displayed every time we stepped on court.

The office in Brussels, a large one by European Division standards, had zero requirements concerning Belgium. There was simply nothing going on in the small country with a population of ten million people that generated any interest among our policy makers. But there were issues that involved individual Belgians that were certainly of interest. Terrorism, or the grey arms market, or violations of trade agreements – computers or electronics being sent to countries not permitted to receive them, for example. So we did have interest in some Belgians, especially those in positions that would give them access to information in areas of interest, or a Belgian working in some capacity for a target country, like Libya.

Belgium's history is complex. Brussels, for example, was once the capital of Spain. It has been overrun many times during the wars that are a part of Europe's history. The result leaves Belgians with many problems. Ethnic, cultural and linguistic divisions run deep and tensions often run high. Little love is lost between the French-speaking, the Walloon, half of the country (in the south) and the Dutch-oriented, Flemish-speaking northern half. There is also a small German-speaking enclave near the German border in the east.

Naturally enough, the politics of the country are equally divided. All parties have French-speaking and Flemish-speaking wings. Disagreement over a myriad of subjects is a constant feature of running the government. While we did not become involved directly with these issues, the differences that were a part of daily life for most Belgians were something always to be kept in mind.

The office was a platform from which to operate against and report on a wide spectrum of intelligence community requirements. Some, like terrorism and arms sales, I've already mentioned.

Predominant among the others was the activity of the various Soviet Bloc intelligence services known to be operating in Brussels. Our efforts in support of our NATO and Common Market Embassies were heavily focused on counter intelligence. Working closely with the security offices of both those organizations and with the Belgian and various European security services that had representatives in Brussels, we monitored as closely as possible what the Bloc services were doing. And they were busy little beavers.

We monitored a surprisingly large number of operations being run by Bloc services. And certainly there were others about which we had no information. Most were being run against NATO and we kept the NATO security office apprised of the hostile activities we were aware of: Russian (both the civilian KGB and the military GRU), Czech, Polish, Romanian, Bulgarian and even Chinese intelligence officers were active. They also targeted the Common Market Headquarters located in central Brussels.

A favourite tactic used by most of the hostile services was to attack NATO's secretarial staff. Typically, access agents would help, say the GRU, select a specific secretary with confirmed access to highly sensitive documents. Usually she was unmarried and not the subject of much male attention. Then the GRU would identify an access agent. Invariably, he was handsome, suave and available. Using a variety of ploys, arrangements would be made to put the 'couple' into direct contact. From there, nature would, or would not, take its course. The objective was to manipulate the secretary into a position where they could either exploit her affection for the access agent or to blackmail her about the relationship. Either way she would begin providing copies of sensitive documents. Despite briefings and warnings to the secretaries and other NATO employees, this tactic worked several times during my three years in Brussels – and probably before I arrived and after I left as well.

The Russians achieved successes against men working in NATO too. One, which we discovered as a spin-off of another operation, caused us great concern because of the access to sensitive documents of the GRU agent.

Brussels' involvement started when, in the fall of 1986, I opened a pouch marked 'Eyes Only Chief'. It contained photographs taken by the surveillance team of a European station, and a memo outlining what had been uncovered. I was impressed. Our colleagues had done excellent work. The photos of the agent and of a known GRU general, and of the two together, were clear – indisputable. And we were confident that neither the GRU nor their agent, a senior Belgian officer, knew anything about our success in uncovering their relationship.

It was a coup, but with the success came serious and difficult questions. Headquarters had posed several and others occurred to me as I read the memo. Foremost among the questions, not surprisingly, was what to do with our information. Certainly we wanted to expose and terminate the GRU operation that was doubtless providing them with a steady flow of sensitive NATO information. But there were lots of equities at stake. We had to protect the source (our own operation and assets) of our information while prompting the effort that would be required to expose and ultimately to arrest, the Belgian agent.

I knew that we didn't have the access that would be required to pull off a success in this type of an operation. Lots of manpower and free access to the agent's offices (one at NATO Headquarters and another in a Belgian military compound) would be necessary. We would have to work via a NATO service, but which one? Who should we tell in NATO? How much could we tell? Should the NATO security office become involved? I had my own answers to these questions and they would carry considerable weight because I was the Chief on the scene. I responded by cable to the memo I had received and opened a dialogue about the questions. Convinced that the best interests of all concerned had been served, I was pleased with the outcome.

We elected, logically enough, to inform the Belgian military service. I made contact with the service's commanding general, who was Flemish. He was likeable and competent, a no-nonsense army officer.

One issue – the possibility of a Russian or Bloc penetration of one of the Belgian services who would alert the GRU agent to our knowledge – weighed heavily on our minds. No choice would be risk free and two points argued for the military service. First, we believed that a Bloc agent recruited inside their service was less likely and second they had the major advantage of access and flexibility in investigating a military officer.

Along with a senior officer visiting from Headquarters specifically for that purpose, I briefed Lord Carrington, the Secretary General of NATO, and then the Commanding General of the Belgian military service. For Carrington, the briefing was sparse and generic: 'You have a Soviet penetration of your organization.' He was distressed, of course, to hear our news, but he agreed to the plan we outlined for him. Fortunately, he clearly understood that many equities were involved that precluded us from providing specific detail on the one hand and necessitated very strict compartmentation on the other. Carrington gave us *carte blanche*, and asked that we keep him informed. We did.

The briefing for General Raymond Van Calster, chief of the military intelligence service, was necessarily detailed. We showed him the photos and explained what we had. Van Calster and his deputy listened carefully as we outlined our case.

After we had finished, Van Calster glanced at the photos that I had laid on his desk. Picking them up, he said, 'This is serious, Dick. It's awful. But I'm sure you know that we'll need more than these pictures to get this guy.'

Then came the obvious question: 'How did you get the photos?'

We had known that this question would be posed and we had discussed how much we could say in response. It would be tricky. To assure that the GRU agent was arrested, we wanted to provide as much as we could, but we had to protect how we got portions of our information. Where to draw the 'need to know' line was the question.

'I can't tell you everything, Ray,' I responded, 'but I can tell you the city in which the photos were taken and the dates the agent was there. You'll need to check travel records to confirm that the agent was gone in the right time frame.'

'You sure about this, Dick?' Ray asked. 'We'll need special court approvals. Serious business.'

'We're sure, Ray,' I told him. 'That's your man on the left and that is the GRU General, Boris Konstantin, on the right. I can't think of any innocent reasons for them to meet clandestinely in another European city. It's agent and case officer.'

'OK, we'll do some checking and I'll get back to you,' Van Calster said. 'I'm not sure if I should say thank you or not.'

'Sometimes things get nasty,' I told him as we got up to leave.

Our initial traces had revealed that the GRU agent, by virtue of his NATO position, travelled periodically to the United States for meetings with American counterparts. He attended conferences at US Air Force bases and thereby had access to sensitive classified information. Since there was no doubt that he was passing that information on to the GRU, our concerns were further heightened. Van Calster had been right. This was serious business and this agent had to be stopped. I thought of my Air Force officer brother and other American officers working with the agent and sharing information with him, unaware of the fact that the information was headed for the GRU case officer to whom he was reporting. Cauterising the wound, soon, was essential.

We heard from Van Calster a week or so later. I was asked to visit him for a briefing. No subject was given, but I knew what we would be talking about. Their checks started to flesh out the picture of the agent. An Air Force colonel, he was divorced and lived alone. There were no blemishes on his record and he was on track to make general in the not-too-distant future. It was hard to believe that he was a traitor, Van Calster told me, but judgement would be reserved. The agent's rank and reputation increased sensitivities. There would be hell to pay if we were wrong. In addition, the agent was good looking and smooth, and was reputed to be something of a ladies' man. That, as it turned out, would be at the heart of some early doubts about the investigation of his activities.

In deference to the sensitivities involved, Van Calster held information about the GRU penetration of NATO as tightly within his service as we were holding it in ours. Still, the requirements of an effort like this one (surveillance team members, analysts, techs) meant that around a dozen officers knew about it.

Also in attendance at the meeting in which Van Calster briefed me on their early findings was his service's top counter-intelligence officer, Claude Van Miert. In his late fifties, Van Miert, also Flemish, was a stocky man with a full head of grey hair. I had never met him before, but, given the brief outline of his career Van Calster provided as he introduced him, I was not surprised to see that he was running the show. I had no reason to doubt that

Van Miert was, in Van Calster's mind at least, Belgium's premier 'spy catcher'. Events would prove that his confidence was well placed.

In full charge of the investigation, Van Miert's first step after a thorough check of files and travel records (the latter revealed that the agent had in fact been out of Belgium in the time frame we had reported to the Belgians without permission required by military regulations) was to initiate around-the-clock discreet surveillance, a costly and politically sensitive effort. He put the agent's phone and mail under scrutiny as well. Special court approvals had been sought and obtained. We were pleased to see Van Miert operating precisely as we would have in a similar situation. It justified, I thought, the confidence in and respect for the military service that had made us choose them to carry out this operation.

On one of the first days of their coverage, the surveillance team noted clear surveillance consciousness on the part of the GRU agent. Teams are trained to be particularly aware of such action on the part of their quarry and they were excited to see it so early in the game. The colonel drove out of Brussels, doubled back and parked in a roadside rest stop, obviously scanning traffic behind him. The team handled the manoeuvre flawlessly, probably questioning in their minds the poor tradecraft training provided by the GRU. The agent made no other move and returned to his home. What had he been up to? On its face, the agent's move was an indicator of interest in clandestine activity. The report generated interest and concern. Coverage continued.

Within a couple of weeks, surveillance coverage, coupled with the phone taps, revealed that the colonel was having an affair with a married woman, the wife of a fellow Air Force officer. And he was fearful that the husband might be following him. He believed the husband to be jealous and violent. So much so, in fact, that he dubbed the husband 'Rambo' after the movie character of the same name. He was frightened of the husband, but continued the affair. I was reminded of the story that avers that God gave men a brain and a penis, but only enough blood to run one of them at a time.

We were amused, but there was a downside to the story. The agent's concern about 'Rambo' explained what we all had taken to be a sign of involvement in clandestine activities – the kind of interest to us. It raised doubts in the minds of some on the Belgian side. Nothing else had surfaced during the several weeks of close discreet surveillance that consumed big chunks of manpower. Coverage continued.

Then small signs began to appear. At work, the agent requested documents to which he would not normally have access or on subjects for which he had no 'need to know'. And he was spotted making copies of sensitive documents. Why? That, and confirmation of his travel to the city we had reported during the same time frame we had given, prompted Van Miert to take another step. He ordered a search of the agent's house. The agent lived alone and the search was easily accomplished leaving no trace of the team's activity. It yielded the best evidence yet of espionage activity. Spy gear – including a miniature camera and a communications plan – was found concealed behind a bookcase. Now Van Miert was in full chase. We knew the agent was spying for the Russians, but Van Miert had to build a case that would stand up in court if necessary. Coverage continued.

As many FBI officers who have been engaged in the same effort will tell you, compromising an agent working for a hostile intelligence service is arduous, often boring. Such was the case for Van Miert's officers, but they were confident they would crack it. Finally they did. One team member noticed a red poster that was routinely on the shelf behind the back seat of the agent's car. Most of the time the red side was up, but occasionally, he noticed, the agent turned it over or put it on the back seat, out of view. In surveillance activities, seemingly insignificant actions matter and that observation led to a breakthrough. We were ultimately to discover that the agent was using that poster to signal his GRU case officer that a dead drop was pending. The team got photos of the agent making a drop.

The agent was scheduled to attend a conference at an Air Force base in the United States and we were concerned about what he might learn. I went to see Van Calster and Van Miert.

'Is there a way to prevent the trip without alerting the agent?' I asked.

'Not to worry, Dick,' Van Miert said. 'We're ready to move.'

'You've got your case?' I asked.

'We do. The colonel and I are going to have a talk tomorrow,' Van Miert said with a broad smile.

The agent confessed early on. In their totality, the information and photos that Van Miert had carefully amassed left the colonel with no option. His motive, he told Van Miert, was greed. The GRU paid him well for the documents he gave them. The GRU officer was expelled and the colonel is, I trust, still serving time in a Belgian prison. To our knowledge, he never did have to confront 'Rambo'.

The Belgian military service did an excellent job and I congratulated Van Calster, passing on kudos received from Headquarters. Van Miert had been patient, meticulous and professional in all aspects of what had been a highly sensitive and difficult case. It's true that our information got the ball rolling, but the Belgians picked up that ball and ran with it. Co-operation and mutual trust were key factors and I was pleased to have played a role, even a minor one.

It was January 1986 and my patience had run out. I finished the cable I was dictating to Headquarters: 'I regret then that we will be forced to terminate the operation.'

I was referring to an operation of high sensitivity about which I had been carefully briefed before I left Headquarters. I had, at that time, raised questions about how the product of the operation was disseminated and exploited by analysts and users. The answers had been disquieting. I was told that it was being put together. That wasn't enough and I had pursued the subject after my arrival in Brussels. I had always believed that the primary objective of our presence abroad was to produce intelligence for policy makers. I still do. Counter intelligence and covert action are also important, but running operations to produce intelligence is paramount. A cardinal sin, in my view, would be to run operations just to run operations; in effect, to take risks without gains.

At the time, we were running a highly sensitive operation that produced rooms full of information. It was interesting information, but not intelligence unless collated and analysed so that it made sense and was of value to policy makers. The problem at Headquarters was in deciding if the resources required to process the information were justified by the value of the end product.

Headquarters components were arguing that question. It was a moot point to us because, in the meantime, we were taking high risks and expending considerable resources to collect the information. It wasn't intelligence until or unless it was processed at Headquarters and disseminated within the intelligence community.

I had pursued the question for several months only to be put off by requests that I be patient. In fact the operation had been running for over a year before I got to Brussels. I'm not going to belabour the nuts and bolts of my dialogue with Headquarters on this subject. Suffice to say that I had had enough. After I sent the cable, I took the steps necessary to stop the operation and eliminate the risks, at least that part of them, to which we were exposed. Without an intelligence product, I simply wasn't willing to risk a possible compromise – one that would bring grief to the Directorate and us. There is little doubt that if something had gone wrong, blame would have landed in Brussels and in the Directorate of Operations. Our vaunted 'can do' attitude would have come back to haunt us – again. 'Now let me get this straight,' a senator or the Inspector General would ask. 'You were running this operation, with all its risks, without getting an end product?'

There was barely a ripple from Headquarters. Few questioned my decision. The components that had been discussing the resource questions simply let the whole thing drop. It seemed as if they had been saying, 'If you'll keep taking the risk, it's fine with us. If not, so be it.' I was happy to have pulled the plug. The requirement for a particular type of information is generated in the intelligence community. The Directorate of Operations is then tasked. Brussels was running, flawlessly, a sensitive operation. So far so good, but it was the big picture that got cloudy. In fact, we had overwhelmed the system with information that it was unable to process into intelligence. This kind of a situation is an ever-present danger and Chiefs ought to focus on it for their own protection as well as for the good of the system.

Our family thrived in Brussels. In late February 1986, we (Suzanne was back at college after her Christmas visit so we were five) drove down to our chalet apartment at Alpes des Chaux in Switzerland. The chalet housing our apartment was literally a few metres from a slope and lift so we would put on our skis as we walked out the door and ski down to the lift. On the second morning, Danika announced that she was going to take Judy and me to the 'top of the world'. As we were less adventurous, and less competent as skiers, Judy and I stuck close to home on familiar slopes and had never ventured to the area Danika was proposing. 'You'll love it,' she said confidently. Ali and Pia had already been and sided with their sister (no surprise there). The T-bar lift near us carried us to the top of the mountain. From there one could descend and climb again via numerous different slopes. With Danika in the lead, followed closely by Ali and Pia, we descended towards a valley lying between us and an adjoining complex of ski trails. Instead of ascending again, as we usually did, we traversed the valley and started up the mountain on the other side. Several different lifts thereafter we arrived at the top and stopped for some hot chocolate. Danika assured us that we weren't there yet and pushed us on to a chair lift, which carried us to a high point well above both Villars and Alpes des Chaux, where we drank in a truly spectacular scene: bright sunshine in a clear sky reflected on the icy mountains, all of which seemed to be below us. 'This is the top of the world,' Danika announced with certainty and none of us disagreed.

Suzanne visited Brussels a couple of times a year and worked in a local office for one summer. She wasn't overjoyed with the work, but enjoyed being in Brussels and liked speaking French. She rapidly became a fluent speaker. After a year at the University of California, Santa Cruz, she had returned to finish her last two years of college at Swarthmore and she seemed happy to be back there. Especially after she met Steve, her husband to be.

After considerable thought, we selected St John's International School for the three other girls. Located in Waterloo, a small suburb of historical note just south of Brussels, it was reputed to be an excellent school. Their first day was memorable.

For starters, they mistakenly got on the wrong bus and ended up at the military high school north-east of Brussels near NATO Headquarters. They discovered their mistake en route, but could do nothing about it. They were embarrassed as the other students got off the bus giving them a fish-eyed look; then off to St John's, where they were, naturally, late.

General, first day of school, assembly was in session when the three of them arrived. The only empty seats were, of course, right in the front so they had to tramp down the whole aisle. Their arrival prompted whoever was speaking to stop while they got into the first seats they could find. At the ages of twelve, fourteen and sixteen, they were embarrassed. Stares, sniggers and unwanted attention followed them down the aisle. It's safe to say that their arrival at St John's did not go unnoticed.

Recovery from the trials of that first day came quickly. Soon they were fixtures in the middle and high school. That came as no surprise to me, the proud but objective father, since each was attractive (even beautiful), talented and intelligent. St John's, smaller than other schools they had attended, offered an environment in which they could blossom. And blossom they did. They excelled in both the academic and sports side of their activities. They played volleyball, basketball and tennis and the fortunes of St John's in those sports rose noticeably during the years of their attendance. They were particularly strong in tennis.

There was a conference of international schools in Europe and each sports season ended with a big tournament. With its central location and access at an indoor tennis club (at which we happened to be members because it was quite close to our house), St John's hosted the conference tennis tournament the second year we were in Brussels. To our great delight, and to the great surprise of many, the St John's girls team swept the championship tournament and took all honours.

Danika and Alison won the doubles without a loss. (In fact, they never lost during the two years they played in Europe before Danika returned to college in the USA.) Another St John's girl, displaying considerable intestinal fortitude (guts), lost her first singles match, but went on to win the singles championship. Even Pia, still in middle school but drafted to the high school team, contributed a couple of wins before being beaten. The coach's strategy of playing Danika and Alison in doubles instead of singles (one or the other was the rule) had paid off. I tried to be as modest and gracious as I could, but it was hard.

There were similar successes in basketball. In her last year in middle school, Pia was the star of the girls' team and St John's middle school girls' team had a spectacular season winning all of its games. The boys' varsity coach, a good friend of our family, harangued his team with stories about Pia's scoring. I had played basketball in both high school and college and I thought I knew something about the game. I tried to understand why almost every shot she threw up went in. I never did. She dribbled with either hand, but that didn't explain it because she scored from all over the court. The girls' high school coach could hardly wait for Pia to play the next year.

But, inexplicably, in the change from middle school to high school, Pia stopped shooting with two hands and began one-handed jump shots; apparently this was a much cooler style of playing. She did well in high school, playing guard along with Alison, but her prolific scoring dropped off considerably.

The academic standards were high at St John's and, as the grades came in, we were pleased that all were doing well. The girls grew in many ways during those three years. We watched as they matured socially and grew more confident while recording life successes. St John's, Judy's choice with which I had agreed, had provided the environment and to our relief, as we struggled with the challenge of raising a platoon of teenage daughters, they took advantage of the opportunity.

It was also while we were in Brussels that our youngest two daughters became aware of the fact that I worked for the CIA. We had talked about it, and reasoned that we didn't want to burden them with a cover story until they were old enough to deal with it. Each CIA family facing cover issues deals with the problem differently. It was our decision to wait. As each left for college, we had decided, we would let them know. Suzanne's first reaction (we were living in our home in McLean at the time and my commute time was about eight minutes) was, 'I wondered how you could get home so fast after I had talked with you on the phone and you were at work in Washington.' I told Danika when she left for college after our second year in Brussels. Then there was a bend in the road.

As a little background, I should record the fact that in 1986 I got a cable from Headquarters alerting me to the fact that my name had appeared in a book recently published by Bob Woodward – of Watergate fame. The book, called *The Veil*, was about terrorism. In it, Woodward names Chuck Cogan and me as

CIA officers who briefed him on the subject of terrorism before one of his trips to Beirut for research for the book. I immediately recalled the briefing Director Casey had set up. I also recalled that it had been clear that the briefing was 'off the record' and that Chuck and I were members of the Directorate of Operations and were under cover.

I was irritated and shot off a cable to Headquarters voicing my concern. Nothing could be done, I was told. Woodward's response, they reported, was that he didn't know we were still active. It would have been easy for him to have checked. I found Woodward's action irresponsible, especially given the subject he was writing about. The bottom line, however, was that we had to hope that the brief reference to Chuck and me would go unnoticed – especially by the wrong people in the Middle East or Europe.

As further background, I played tennis a couple of times a month with another parent of a St John's student, Ray Jenkins. An American businessman, he was in charge of the sale and distribution of Levi jeans in Europe and was based in Brussels. He travelled frequently, but in between his trips, or mine, we would get in a tennis game. We would usually have a cold drink of some sort after we played and one day while we were having a drink he asked if he could pose a question.

'I've been reading a book written by Bob Woodward,' he said. 'It's called *The Veil*.'

I could see it coming. 'I know the book,' I replied, buying a little time. 'I've read it. What prompts you to read about terrorists?'

'Nothing special,' he responded. 'I picked it up at the airport because I'd heard of Woodward. But my question is, are you the Dick Holm mentioned in the book? You never have seemed much like the average diplomat. I'm not trying to be difficult. Just curious.'

I had been quickly mulling over what to tell him. 'Well, there are two answers to that question, Ray,' I said. 'One is that there must be somebody else named Dick Holm. The other is, yes, I briefed Woodward. Obviously I'd rather go with the first answer and leave it at that. Woodward had agreed not to reveal our names and should not have done so. But that can't be changed at this point.'

Ray studied me for a moment and then, with a sympathetic smile, he said, 'No problem, Dick. It must have been another Dick Holm.'

That incident left me with a dilemma. I talked it over with Judy. If Ray, of all people, could pick up the book and read about me, then anyone could. Apart from the issue we didn't want to talk about (some fanatic seeking me out), there was the question of what, if anything, to tell Alison and Pia. Certainly I didn't want one of them to be confronted by a classmate or a teacher. We decided that they must be alerted to that possibility so they wouldn't be vulnerable to an unpleasant incident. To impress upon them (in the event it was quite unnecessary) the seriousness of the subject, I decided to bring them to my office to tell them.

On the following Saturday morning, I invited them to come with me to work. Right away, their ears perked up.

'I want to talk with you about something,' I explained.

'Is Mom coming?' they asked.

'She doesn't need to,' I said. 'She already knows.'

'Is this going to be a lecture?' Ali asked.

'No, no lecture,' I replied. 'Let's go.'

We drove up to Brussels. They had been in my office before. They were expectant.

I wasn't sure how to start, maybe because I didn't know how they would react. I decided to mince no words. 'Well, I have to bring you two up to speed. Suzy and Nika already know what I'm going to tell you. I wouldn't be doing this now except for some problems that have developed. It's a serious subject.' I definitely got their attention. Both looked at me expectantly.

'It's about my work,' I replied. 'I work for the Central Intelligence Agency. I am the Chief of its office here in Brussels. I can't tell people that. I tell people that I am a special advisor.' Both girls were wide-eyed and digesting. Obviously, neither had harboured any suspicions.

'So you'll never be an ambassador?' Ali finally asked.

'You do all that James Bond stuff?' Pia blurted.

'No, Pia, I don't. That stuff is greatly exaggerated. Most of my work is pretty normal.'

Both were still digesting.

'And we shouldn't tell anybody, right?' said Ali.

'Right,' I replied. 'You two just say what you have always said, that your dad is a special advisor. Don't be worried. I know you both can handle it or I wouldn't have told you.'

'There won't be any problem, Dad,' Ali said. 'Right Pia?'

'Right,' Pia responded promptly. 'Boy, Dad, this is exciting! We can talk to Mom, right?'

'Yeah, you can talk to Mom,' I told her, adding, 'My name is mentioned in a recent book called *The Veil*. I didn't want you to be surprised by a question from someone who might have read it. Otherwise, I would have waited until you were older. But you two will deal with it just fine, I'm sure.'

Judy and I liked the Belgians and had many local friends. Tennis was, again, an icebreaker for us. We joined the Waterloo tennis club and became active members. Judy was more active than me because of my lack of enough free time. I was able to attend dinners from time to time and lunches on the weekend, but couldn't get free for as much tennis as I would have liked.

Judy, on the other hand, did join the ladies team and was a great success. Playing both singles and doubles, she led the Waterloo senior ladies' tennis team to the finals of the Belgian national club championship. That they lost in the finals (although Judy won her match) was only a minor point. Waterloo's team had never advanced beyond the district level, so making it to the national finals was a great triumph. Judy, deservedly so, got full credit for the team's success. She was widely known in the club and in Waterloo. In that milieu, I was known and introduced as 'Judy's husband'.

Among our friends was a couple we met on the diplomatic circuit, Jackie and Jean Paul. Walloons, they lived east of Brussels in what became known in our family as 'the pink château'. It was a large château (its aged stone façade had turned light pink) situated on a large tract of land that had been in the husband's family for many years. They had links to Belgium's royal family and he had a title of some sort, but was unpretentious. We had many enjoyable evenings with them, but I particularly remember one Christmas Day we spent together.

It was our first visit to their home and Judy was reading me the directions as we headed east out of Brussels. The girls, all four since Suzanne was home for the holidays, were, I think, excited at the prospect of visiting a country home and having dinner with some Belgians. Within half an hour, we had found, and missed, the entry road to their estate. Doubling back, I entered a long driveway lined with tall poplars. At the end, was the wall and the entrance to the château. We drove through, past a pond with ducks and geese, and caught sight of the château. It was an elegant, hundred-year-old structure and we all were impressed with its beauty.

Introductions took a while. Their three sons, who were all older than our girls, were there and seemed bemused, I thought, to meet these four young American girls. They were nonetheless extremely polite and attentive. A little shy at first, the girls warmed up to the occasion as we settled in the drawing room and started to chat. Though a little stilted at first, conversation soon flowed smoothly. Jackie was quite gracious and pleasant and the girls warmed to her quickly. The oldest son served champagne. We made no objections (nor did they) when the girls were each given a small glass. Jean Paul toasted the occasion and Jackie announced that dinner would be forthcoming. Her announcement signalled the departure of the three young men who left to serve dinner. The girls were impressed, I'm sure.

Soon thereafter, we trooped into the large and impressive dining room. One of the pretty murals that covered the walls had recently been cleaned and restored. The others, in dire need of the same effort, would soon get the same treatment, which was, however, very expensive. The large and elegant table easily seated us all and one of the sons served wine while another served pieces of a baguette. The girls were taking it all in. Each glanced at the first course, a piece of rich pâté, on a small plate in front of them. It was a generous portion. Then, after a brief toast, Jackie, for reasons I never did figure out, presented a lengthy and graphic description of how this pâté had been made.

'For starters,' she said, 'one must be sure to stuff as much corn as possible down the throat of the goose. Usually you have to hold the neck and just shove the corn down.' Jean Loup, their youngest son, graphically demonstrated. Our girls listened and said nothing. 'That's so you can make the goose's liver as large as possible,' she went on. 'Then when you cut out the liver to make this delicious pâté, you get the best taste.'

Finally, I sensed that the girls didn't really need, or want, all the detail. None were happy at the prospect, I was to learn later, but they all ate the bulk of their first course. I was proud of them. Judy had tuned in much more quickly and discreetly urged that all plates needed to be cleaned. That hurdle having been cleared, we went on to have a delicious dinner that all enjoyed. We still remember occasionally the dinner at the 'pink château'. And someone always mentions the pâté.

One of our highest priorities, throughout my stay in Belgium, was counter espionage. We knew that the Belgians and other European services were also focused on the same problem, but many lacked the manpower, funding and expertise to counter effectively the hostile activities of the Russian services and their Eastern European allies. The Chinese were also active in Brussels, but most Western services focused little attention on them, believing them, we guessed, to be of minimal threat.

Necessarily, because of Brussels' unique position as the site of the Headquarters for both NATO and the European Union, we all maintained contact with the security offices of both those organizations. This was sometimes contentious and frustrating because of the personalities of some of the people involved and their sensitivities about 'turf'.

One of the 'personalities' that contributed to many of the problems was an individual with whom I worked. Slightly built with grey hair, Alfred R. was always well dressed and very dapper. He was an intelligent man who spoke Dutch, French, English, Spanish, Italian, and maybe some other languages. His English and French were both excellent and I have no reason to doubt that his fluency in the other languages was also strong. He had been active in security matters since the late 1970s.

Outwardly, my relationship with Alfred was always positive and friendly, but he maintained a wall between us that prevented me from ever considering him someone in whom I could have total confidence. Not that having such a feeling is any standard for a relationship like ours was, but I never knew what to expect from him. Allegedly, he had a terrible temper, but I never saw it. Always helpful and even gracious, Alfred was consistently the picture of willingness for working together – but nothing ever got done.

Alfred took the late train from his home every morning and was met by his chauffeur. He would arrive in his office at about 10.30 and start with a cup of coffee. His desk was constantly stacked with files and memos that begged for, but only rarely received, his attention. His secretary, young and attractive, literally rejoiced when she got a memo signed and was able to move it on. Soon he would prepare to leave for a 'working' lunch. I have vivid memories of my lunches with Alfred.

Opportunities to have a private session with him were always rare so I would prepare carefully and be ready to raise and discuss issues of mutual interest and concern. We met for lunch about every six weeks. Alfred was always the host. His secretary would call, propose two dates and, following my response, tell us where and when the lunch would take place.

Always we lunched at an excellent restaurant and Brussels boasted dozens in that category. One of his favourites, I found, was the Maison du Cygne, which was located right on the Grande Place – a really super restaurant, it was also one of my favourites. Despite every tactic I could think of, the scenario never changed. I would arrive prepared to discuss current issues and problems – not Alfred. He simply did not respond to any subject I proposed and he raised only innocuous ones. For three years, we met and discussed subjects such as our respective daughters, the wine and the food.

Conversation would, literally, stop after we had carefully examined the menu, listened to the special dishes of the day and ultimately made our choice for lunch. The break would enable Alfred to study the wine list in order to assure that he ordered just the right wine for what we were going to eat. He often ordered a white for the oysters, which we always had in the right season, and something else for the main course. I would start trying to get him talking about something work related. I almost never succeeded.

I got lectures from him on wines, various special dishes, such as game, eels, and fish, and regular explanations of some historic place or event, but I got precious little about our mutual efforts. Bear in mind here that this was a most unusual experience for me: my first tour in Europe and my introduction to the man who happened to be the most extraordinary character in Brussels. It never changed and I came to accept it as a 'duty' and one of my responsibilities as the Chief. It is true that I learned a great deal about wines, oysters and fine cuisine, but it was the last thing I expected – or wanted. It's also true that I liked Alfred. Following a 'working' lunch (minimum two hours), Alfred would return to his office to once again peruse the stacks on his desk. Little would be touched and he might have a quick meeting or two. Then, oblivious to the fact that he had come in late, he would depart early to catch the train back home. That was pretty much a standard day for Alfred and he got away with it for years. To my knowledge, he maintained his position for some time.

The following is an account of an operation conducted by a sister station. I include it because it is an example of a problem we all faced in attempting to monitor the aggressive activities of the Soviets and their minions. One of my officers, who had the required language, went to that station to help. He provided the following:

'Our reporting began pointing to a steadily increasing level of activity by the KGB, just one of the hostile intelligence services we were watching. We needed a source of information on the kinds of people that service was targeting and courting. An observation post, with a clear look at the Russian compound, would provide us with the grist we needed in the form of photos of both the visitors and their licence plates. This would be easier said than done, however.

'Finding and renting the right place would not be easy. Two access agents were carefully briefed and tasked. Neither knew of the other's involvement. They were directed to opposite sides of the compound. From the right apartment in any of several buildings, we could set up photo coverage of the parking lot and the entrance to the office we wanted to monitor. Weeks passed. Then one of the access agents got a lead on a promising apartment in a building directly across the street from our target. Acting quickly, the case officer and the access agent were able to confirm that windows in one of the bedrooms of the apartment would afford us a clear, direct look at the area we were interested in. We had a couple, moreover, who could plausibly rent the apartment and use it as a city residence – they lived north of the city in the countryside. We moved ahead.

'Within a month we were acquiring pictures of all visitors and of their vehicles. Over a period of time, this was to be a most useful counter-intelligence tool. However, our efforts to acquire and establish the observation post had taken place in the late fall and winter. Spring, naturally enough, brought foliage and we soon discovered that our view was going to be partially obstructed by the leaves on a tree near the street in front of the apartment. We had taken note of the tree and this had been considered a possibility, but not a serious problem. It would not put us out of business, but it was a nuisance and limited some of what we could cover. We didn't want to be limited.

'The problem was resolved within several weeks when the tree "died". Neighbours may have found it strange that the tree should die so suddenly, but no "autopsy" was conducted and there were no questions in our minds. The tree had died because of the poison that was injected into its root system late one night after the leaves started coming out. There was never any indication that the hostile service's security officers noticed the sudden demise of that tree. The operation carried on smoothly and productively – with an unobstructed view.'

The years I spent in Belgium were hectic ones for my colleagues in Washington. They witnessed the end of an era at CIA in January 1987 when Bill Casey died. Casey had been an activist as our Director and much good came from his efforts. Significant increases in our budget that he fought for (Reagan was a strong supporter) enabled us to rebuild both operational capabilities and our personnel strength.

But there was a downside as well. His relationship with the Hill, and the oversight committees in particular, had never been a good one and we paid a price for that in the years after his death. Subsequent Directors faced closer scrutiny across the board. Moreover, our involvement, of which he was aware, in the Contra Affair that came to light in 1987 led to a series of problems and many changes at the senior levels of the CIA, not the least of which was Casey's replacement, Judge William Webster, who had previously been the Director of the FBI.

(As a reminder, the Contra Affair began as a political argument. The Reagan administration strongly supported covert aid to the Contras in Nicaragua, who were fighting a communist government. The opposition Democrats, who controlled the House of Representatives, disagreed and authored an amendment prohibiting the use of funds for military aid. To outflank the Democrats, Oliver North, and others, made secret contact with Iranian officials and negotiated the sale of missiles to Iran. The monies from those sales were then used to provide weapons to the Contras. When details of this funding mechanism became known, Congressional Democrats strongly attacked the administration. Several Agency officers became embroiled.)

'Judge' Webster, as he liked to refer to himself, took over on 26 May 1987. He would be the tenth Director for whom I would work. While the media tended to compare, and generally equate, the two jobs, many (myself included) knew that being Director of the CIA was very different to being Director of the FBI. Regrettably, Webster never really fitted in at the Agency, but he was nonetheless a good choice for the job at the time. The waters had been stirred up and we had needed a stabilizing presence at the top.

Concerns at the time ran high as Oliver North as well as several Agency officers were implicated and indicted for the Contra activities. Could Webster calm the waters? Few ventured any guess. Optimism was not running rampant. Those were troubling times for the Agency in general and for the Directorate of Operations in particular.

It was clear that the Deputy Director for Operations, Clair George, would have to be replaced. Selecting the new DDO would be one of Webster's first tough decisions. Surprising us all, Webster, in January 1988, selected Dick Stolz to replace Clair George. It was, in my view, an excellent choice. Stolz had retired seven years earlier after a long and distinguished career. An obvious choice to be DDO when Casey took over in 1981, Stolz had retired in frustration after Casey selected an obscure businessman friend.

Stolz carried none of the 'baggage' George had accumulated during the Casey years. And his arrival reassured a Directorate staggering under the attacks generated by the Contra Affair. His reputation as a professional, intelligent and fair operations officer gave the Directorate confidence in his leadership and our collective future. I would grow to know Stolz well and I have great respect and admiration for him. He very ably led us through a hazard-filled period that included the enormous changes that came with the end of the Cold War in 1989.

In early 1987, when he was still at the FBI, Webster visited Brussels to attend a meeting of the NATO Security Committee. It was a committee composed of internal security services thus the FBI was representing the United States. The Agency sent an officer as an observer who sat in the background. I didn't attend the meeting, but I was invited to one of the social functions associated with the event. I was also invited to play tennis with Webster and his top aide. Webster was (likely still is) an avid tennis player and always tried to get in a game when possible. I played with the NATO security chief. Both were better than average players, and we had two good sets – starting at 0630 one morning. In the process of my contacts with him I gained some impressions of Webster – none from a professional perspective. I found him to be a pleasant and friendly man, and liked him. I remember thinking though, how different he was from Bill Casey. With a very different background, Webster seemed to lack Casey's toughness and shrewdness. Those thoughts came back to me after Webster was named as our Director.

In early 1988, shortly after his recall from retirement to become the DDO, Stolz made a European trip to visit major liaison partners. It was the traditional first trip for a new DDO. During his trip, he cabled me to ask if he could stop by Brussels to see me. I'd be delighted, I promptly responded. I had never met Stolz and was anxious to do so. I would be finishing my tour in Belgium and returning to Headquarters in less than six months and I assumed (rightly) that we would talk about what job I would get upon my return. I had been promoted again in 1987 and I felt ready to take on a senior position. It would be an interesting meeting.

I had been thinking about what I wanted to do at Headquarters and was pretty much open to any proposal the DDO would make. But I was unprepared for Stolz's proposal.

'I want you to take over the Career Management Staff,' Stolz announced.

'What? Why me?'

'Think about it, Dick,' Stolz said calmly. 'I consider it one of the most important jobs in the Directorate,' he went on. 'There aren't too many people who could do it and I want you to take it on. I want a senior officer with an operations background in the job. I think one needs operations and overseas experience to do the job and you've got both. You on board?'

I had never considered the job and wasn't at all sure I'd like it. It was a staff rather than operational job, but I would not have refused. I could have said no and held out for a line job, but despite my misgivings (which would ultimately be borne out) I just thought that if that's what Dick Stolz wanted me to do, I'd do it.

The months left in our tour following Dick Stolz's visit passed quickly and uneventfully. Danika, who had graduated from high school at St John's the previous year, was awaiting our return. She had just finished her first year at Mary Washington College in Fredericksburg, Virginia, where she had played varsity volleyball in lieu of tennis.

Suzanne graduated from Swarthmore College in May and Judy and I returned home for the commencement exercises. The amphitheatre in which the ceremony was held was a beautiful setting and Suzy, to the delight of her parents, graduated with honours. She had recently, and belatedly, announced that she would take a Masters degree at Bryn Mawr College, a few miles from Swarthmore, where Steve would be finishing his degree. How much that had to do with Suzy's decision was unclear to those of us who were a continent away. A lot, I suspect.

Alison, with only one year left in high school, was troubled at the prospect, but everything worked out well for her. She made friends quickly and she joined the girls' tennis team that won the state championship. Pia was happy to return to our home in McLean, where she had three years of high school to go.

Brussels had been a splendid tour in all respects. We bade our farewells in July 1988 and left in high spirits. We looked forward to being closer to both Suzanne and Danika. And at the age of fifty-three, with twenty-seven years' worth of experience in the Directorate, I viewed a Headquarters job with much less foreboding. I was returning to a key senior position and I looked forward to working with Dick Stolz, who had already demonstrated a strong and steady leadership style.

FIFTEEN

THE ENGINE ROOM

1988–92

It didn't take long to confirm that this was going to be a very different kind of job. I had known that it would be. Still, I was surprised by what I found. Managing, for the entire Directorate, the broad spectrum of issues that fell under the responsibility of the Career Management Staff (CMS – it has since been renamed Human Resources Staff) was definitely going to be quite a task. I had a lot to learn. Happily, I inherited two highly experienced and competent deputies.

One, Mike M., I had known of as we had both been China Operations officers early in our respective careers. His reputation in the service was very good. Mike managed about half of our staff of some forty people and was responsible for handling our promotion panel system, counselling at all levels (except in the Senior Service, which was my responsibility), senior field and Headquarters assignments, and the recruitment of new officers. There were peripheral issues as well so Mike had a full plate, which he handled without ever missing a step. Imbued with uncommonly high levels of common sense and integrity, Mike was a senior, experienced operations officer. Excellent in his dealings with people, he inspired great confidence and trust.

My other deputy, Peggy, whom I had known little about before taking over CMS, was equally talented and competent. Peggy's side of the office was responsible for budget and administrative matters, training programmes, the grievance system, the manning table (how many people we could hire or promote was derived from the manning tables), and our formal ties to the Directorate's staffs and geographic divisions. An 'Agency brat' who had (like Mike) started her career as a junior employee in our file rooms, Peggy knew the Directorate, and Headquarters in general, intimately. She was exceptionally well-qualified for her job and was handling it beautifully when I walked in the door. Truth be told, in her areas of responsibility she knew far more than I did. She conducted herself gracefully, however, (which is to say that she never dwelled on how much I did not know about some Headquarters matters) and we developed a positive and friendly relationship. I had great respect for her abilities and it took only a few weeks for me to realize how lucky I was to have her in that job.

Meetings, I soon discovered, would be the bane of my existence. There had been lots of meetings, of course, when I was Chief of the Counter Terrorist Group, but this was an entirely different level and the pace of my working day quickly showed it. Each component Chief (Division or staff) met at least weekly with Dick Stolz – imagine *his* work day – and I was no exception. Indeed, because of the myriad of issues that came up regularly, I met with him far more often than that. And I met frequently with Division Chiefs to discuss assignment, promotion, disciplinary, or other issues. The same thing for chiefs of our major staffs – especially the Operational Resources Management Staff (ORMS), which handled money for the Directorate much the same way I handled personnel.

In addition, I was the Directorate's representative on a host of Agency-wide committees, which decided recipients of Agency medals, scholarships, disciplinary actions, nominations to prestigious schools and seminars (recall my own nomination to the State Department's Senior Seminar in 1984, others included the National War College), management of the Agency's Language Incentive Programme (LIP) – I was chairman of that committee – and the Family Liaison Office. There were others, but that is a representative sampling. Most days I carried a schedule to get me from one meeting to another. My secretary, who was highly competent and professional, was an enormous help in keeping me on track.

The above is not a complaint. It is just a statement of fact. I took those responsibilities seriously and did my best to represent strongly the interests and the employees of the Directorate of Operations. There were Headquarters' and inter-Directorate politics, of course, and I quickly tuned in to the process of reaching what we all felt was a fair decision or result. I admired and respected the representatives of the Intelligence, Administrative, and Science and Technology Directorates with whom I worked on these committees. With few exceptions, I felt that we all had the best interests of the Agency at heart. I don't mean to say that there weren't disagreements. There were and many were inspired by loyalties to specific Directorate employees or goals – or the result of ignorance of another Directorate's mission in a particular area. Comparing, for example, the career of a scientist to that of an operations officer or an analyst to determine which Agency medal should be recommended, was not easy. But we found solutions, accepted one another's explanations and carried out our roles. It had always worked that way so we were no exception. It was, nonetheless, a new experience for me. It was a far cry from running a station abroad or managing street operations.

Peggy came into my office one morning to announce that the Directorate of Operations had no candidates running for the Board of Directors of the Agency's government subsidized Health Insurance programme.

'Is that something a DO officer would think much about?' I responded. 'Most are either overseas or want to go overseas so it's not something they would react to. Should we be surprised?'

'You're right, but that's wrong,' was her immediate reply. 'DO officers and staff have the same interest in our health insurance as anybody else so why shouldn't we have some say in how it's run? We ought to have a DO officer sitting on the Board of Directors.'

'I can't argue with that, but what can we do?' I said. 'I can't really order someone to be a candidate, and even if I could who would it be?'

'What about you?' Peggy said with a smile, perhaps revealing the real reason she was there.

'I don't know a thing about insurance programmes or how they are run,' I immediately countered.

'Doesn't matter. No one does when they first get on the Board. You could learn,' she concluded.

Clearly she had taken me by surprise. I thought about just

refusing. Well, maybe it wouldn't be that bad, I then thought. Wouldn't get elected anyway and at least the DO would have someone on the list of candidates. I hesitated. Then, uncomfortably because I saw this as an uncharted area, I said, 'All right, put me down as a candidate.'

'Good decision,' Peggy said with a smile. 'You'll probably win in a landslide,' she added as she left my office.

'Spare me,' I replied to an empty doorway.

Three weeks later I got a pile of votes and was elected to the Board of Directors. How I'm not sure. There was no campaigning. Employees who were members of the health programme were simply given a list of candidates and sent in their vote. As the only DO officer on the list, I must have garnered votes from DO members. Anyway, it was a done deal.

Soon I received several volumes of books to study before the next meeting of the Board. Just what I needed, I thought. Lest I mislead anyone though about my acceptance of the responsibility I had been given, albeit to my considerable surprise, I did study the material and I served my two-year term without missing a meeting or a debate. Headquarters employees were well represented, I thought, and always had been. I considered myself a representative of many employees who were serving overseas and took special interest in issues that would affect them. Other board members welcomed my input and I was pleased to witness several positive steps taken to facilitate and upgrade benefits for employees abroad. I learned a lot and, in retrospect, valued the experience. Now, I thought at the time, I am truly a Headquarters bureaucrat!

Training was an issue that took up much of my time, which was fine with me because I had always been partial to strong training programmes and was pleased to be in the position to support it. The subject was a broad one including training given to the Directorate's new employees, periodic training designed to hone and upgrade various skills, and language training. I met, and developed a close working relationship with, Paul Erikson, the Chief of the Directorate of Administration's Office of Training and Education (OTE).

A frequent bone of contention was the status and the curriculum of the DO's training programme at The Farm, our training installation in southern Virginia. Notice I said 'our' installation. The DO had, for decades, viewed the installation to be one dedicated to goals of the Directorate of Operations. Others might use it from time to time, but its primary function was to work in support of training for the DO, we believed. It was ours. Times were changing, however, and others, including Erikson, believed that the DO should loosen up a bit in its imagined hold on the installation. Some of the problems were personality driven and both Paul and I recognized that. Still, the changes that were afoot were not making the DO happy.

The problem was exacerbated when, I think in all innocence, the OTE 'dared' to make some suggestions about how and what to teach in the basic operations training course. Experienced operations officers were outraged.

There was more smoke than fire really and, as is almost always the case, there was middle ground. As professional training officers, they made some suggestions that made perfectly good sense and once we got people to sit down and actually talk over the subject, things calmed down.

It is safe to say, however, that many DO officers, especially those assigned to The Farm as instructors, were chagrined at the unwelcome intervention into 'our' business. The fall of the Berlin Wall and resultant collapse of communism and end of the Cold War had prompted calls for a change in our training and we were, at the time, modifying our programmes. The problem was that few thought that ideas from the Directorates of Administration or Intelligence would be of much use.

The issues involved were discussed at the highest levels, but negotiations and problem solving were left to Paul and me. Usually common sense and pragmatism prevailed. Certainly those years, the early 1990s, witnessed much change for the better in our training programmes. To my knowledge, the trend has been a steady one and new operations officers now receive excellent initial and periodic training. There will always be debate, of course, but I think most would concur in that assessment.

Language training was an equally important issue, and in this area as well there were differences of opinion. But there was less to mess with. The goal was to produce 'operationally' fluent speakers and readers of foreign languages – not an easy task.

Nuances that prompted questions spurred debate. How does one define 'operationally fluent?' (Good enough to recruit agents, is the quick answer.) How important is good grammar? Isn't speaking more important than reading? What kind of a vocabulary should be presented – political, military, or economic? All of the above was the answer. Should work on cultural and historic affairs be included? You get the picture. I met frequently with the head of the language school and often with groups of teachers. In our assignment process, we strongly favoured the assignment of a given officer to a given country only if he or she spoke the language of that country. In practice, though, we didn't always succeed and that was a constant frustration. So I worked hard to press the Divisions to ensure that officers selected either had or would be fully trained in the language of the country to which they were being sent. In principle, most agreed and the percentage of language-qualified officers being assigned abroad went up. There were practical problems however. Taking a year or more out of an officer's career to ensure that he spoke good Dutch, for example, was tough to do. It would serve him for one, maybe two tours and then what? (Moreover, many people in Holland speak good English.) It wasn't like learning French, Chinese, or Spanish, which could be used throughout a career. Compromises were part of the process.

And speaking of compromises, the LIP prompted many. The idea, a sound one, was to encourage employees to learn, use and maintain solid foreign language skills. The programme provided cash awards for attaining a certain level when first learning a given language and for raising that level in subsequent testing. Cash awards were also given for using a language in the field. In addition, an award was available for individuals who maintained their language skills, in off-duty hours, while serving in Headquarters, where regular use of their language was precluded. It was not an easy programme to administer. Inevitably, questions were posed to the Board I chaired about some aspect of the programme.

Not surprisingly, one that often came up concerned testing at the language school. Complainers usually alleged that the testing was flawed. That the instructor (almost always a native speaker) had somehow misunderstood or been too subjective or demanded unreasonable standards. Others claimed that a given student didn't speak as well as they did, but got a higher grade. Often the complaints came from people who had not attained the level required to get their award. I talked frequently with the language school and they made several modifications in the programme designed to make testing as objective as possible – by using several instructors and taping the tests, for example – but still there were some who complained.

The use award also generated questions that bubbled up to the board. Did someone stationed at Headquarters who travelled TDY once a month to some place where they used their language skills to meet with and debrief an agent, merit a use award? The whole award? If not the whole, then what percentage? Or, did someone stationed in Stockholm who was using Spanish to develop a Latin American diplomat deserve the use award? And what about officers (the vast majority of whom were native speakers) hired specifically because of their language skills whose job it was to translate documents or transcribe tapes? Did they deserve a use award on top of their salary, earned only because of that skill? These were thorny issues that we hashed out one at a time. I was not always comfortable with the decision we reached, but was reluctant to press too hard with my biases that were, of course, DO oriented. Board members from the other Directorates often presented convincing arguments in support of a claim from a member of their Directorate.

Even more troubling to me was the maintenance award. My view was that since it was (or should be) a critical work skill, an individual should be motivated enough on their own to maintain that skill. The LIP had provided awards for learning and using the language and benefits were there for use in the future. Awards for maintaining skills that were a part of their job seemed too much to me. I was in a minority on the Board.

My philosophical problem with maintenance awards was worsened when, to me, particularly egregious cases were brought to our attention. I'll cite an admittedly unusual case, but it makes the point. An officer from the Directorate of Intelligence does analytical work on countries in South-East Asia – perfectly solid work. The officer is of Polish extraction and learned Polish as a child. He still speaks it well enough to pass the language exam. He can't get, and doesn't apply for, an attainment award. He can't get a use award because he never has (and very likely never will) used it on an Agency task. Should that officer be given a maintenance award? Some supported his claim. Absolutely not, was my answer, and in the end I won.

On a Monday morning, several months after my arrival in CMS, Peggy and a colleague, Betty, came into my office. On their minds was a proposal to make a major change in the personnel structure of our Directorate. They had been mulling over and modifying the idea for some time before my arrival.

The DO was structured to ensure, to the extent that we could, fair competition for limited promotions. To do that, my predecessors, with Directorate management approval, had categorized employees doing the same (or similar) work so that our promotion panels (made up of DO officers at higher grades than those being reviewed) could compare and rank them against each other. The goal was to compare apples with apples, and not apples with oranges.

Perhaps the most clear-cut example was the category for operations officers (Category B). All operations officers at a certain grade were ranked annually against one another for promotion to the next highest grade. Depending upon headroom (the total number that could be promoted at that time), a specific number of those ranked highest were promoted. It sounds easier than it was. Even within the relatively homogeneous Category B, panels were faced with difficult questions. What is the relative value of work accomplished by an operations officer in the field, who may have recruited several agents or written numerous intelligence reports, compared to an operations officer serving a Headquarters tour who is working on a desk or in a staff? Or an operations officer who has just finished a year of language training? It was not a perfect system. The grey areas in Category B were as bad or worse in other categories. And some of the other categories were peopled by a variety of skills that made comparisons that much more difficult to make. Reports officers, for example, were competing in a category that included a wide mix of skills. Consequently, I discovered, the value of their contribution was diluted and they were promoted less often than seemed fair. Change was overdue. The proposal Peggy and Betty were advocating was to begin making that change. They were well prepared and I was soon won over. To begin the process, they proposed that we create a new category, Category O. For people in Category O, distinctions would be sharper, and competition would be limited to others doing similar jobs, and therefore would be fairer. We hoped employees would see this change as an effort to modernize our system. They would be happier and more motivated. It was a tall order, but we were optimistic.

After giving him a thorough briefing, I obtained Dick Stolz's approval. As Chief of CMS, it then fell to me to introduce the change. That I did at a general meeting in the Agency's auditorium – known to us as The Bubble. To some it was a bold, unnecessary move. The system wasn't actually broken, they argued, so why did it need to be fixed?

The vast majority of those who would be affected by the Category O change spent the bulk of their careers at Headquarters. Many of them came to the noon presentation. It was 11 January, and so, in my introductory remarks, I made reference to Caesar's decision to cross the Rubicon on the same day in 49 BC. Category O was born on that day and was the first of many subsequent changes. It thrived and met almost all of the goals we had set for it. Several months later, after much discussion, a Category I was introduced for reports officers (who, for reasons I could never quite fathom, but didn't want to argue about, wanted to call themselves intelligence officers). A Category L was formed for language officers – mostly translators and transcribers. Others followed and in each case it facilitated the ability of our panels to make sharper comparisons between officers doing similar work. Space for promotion was carefully monitored and divided among categories on the basis of the population in a given category. If that population were 20 per cent of the Directorate's total, that category got 20 per cent of the headroom. Those changes were the first in many years. They were followed by many others throughout the 1990s.

Life at home had changed. Why wouldn't it? The girls weren't girls any more. They were now young women. Pia was the only one still living at home. Given the super experience we had had at St John's in Brussels, we thought a parochial school in McLean would be a good idea. After a year, though, Pia could see that it simply wasn't the same and she transferred to the public high school near our home, Langley High School. Pia excelled at tennis, basketball and softball and amassed a 3.4 grade point average. There were no problems there and we were very proud of her.

Alison, after a successful senior year at Langley where she had helped the girls' tennis team win the Virginia state championship, received early acceptance at William and Mary College in Williamsburg, Virginia, and started there in 1989. She spent part of her junior year in the South of France studying French and European affairs. She met her husband-to-be, Tom, at William and Mary. Astutely, in my view, Tom spotted Alison when they first met in her freshman year and he was tenacious, and ultimately successful, in his courtship of her.

Danika, already at Mary Washington College in Fredericksburg, Virginia when we returned from Brussels, continued there until her graduation in 1991. She played volleyball for Mary Washington and elected to major in geography, which, I was to learn, was more than 'state capitals'. After graduation, she went out to California for a year and then to graduate school at the University of South Carolina.

Suzanne finished her Masters degree at Bryn Mawr and, to no one's surprise, announced that she and Steve were engaged. They were married in August 1990 and spent their honeymoon at our apartment in Switzerland. And immediately thereafter, they moved into a small (I mean really small) apartment in Paris, not far from Notre Dame. They spent an academic year teaching English in two French high schools. It was a great year for them, during which they were able to see much of France and visit other European countries as well.

Judy and I weathered, perhaps not as gracefully as some do, the process that brought us to the 'empty nest' stage in our lives. After Pia graduated at Langley and headed for Mary Washington College, we began to think about one final overseas tour. I had been promoted again and was one of the most senior officers in the Directorate so I hoped for a Chief's job abroad. Judy and I discussed possible places and, with strong urging from me, agreed to try for Paris. A tour alone, minus any of the girls that is, would no doubt be different, but we looked forward to getting into the field again.

By mid-1990, I had been in the CMS job for two years and I was definitely ready for a change. It was not to be. Dick Stolz asked me to stay on and I agreed. It was a hectic and change-filled period. The collapse of communism in the fall of 1989 ushered in a time of great turmoil as the Directorate of Operations sought to understand the ramifications it would bring and to set in motion the changes that would be imperative. Under the adept guidance of Dick Stolz, about half a dozen of the Directorate's most senior officers formed a core group to tackle the problems. We met frequently and wrestled with alternative solutions to the problems we had identified. This was not an easy task as it would bring about a degree of change never before experienced by the Directorate.

Heretofore, our mission, and related operations, had been targeted at Cold War issues – the dynamic of communism versus capitalism. That was history now, we knew, and things would surely be different. But few, if any, of us envisioned the amount of change that would come.

Weeks of meetings and debate were required, but ultimately we put together a strategic plan for the next decade. With a consensus achieved and modifications in place, we gained Dick Stolz's approval. There was, of course, a myriad of areas that would be affected. Shifting operational priorities to reflect the new requirements of policy makers was first and foremost. The policy makers were definitely slow off the mark, however, and specifics regarding what intelligence would be needed in support of the 'New World Order' were not readily available. They did want a 'peace dividend' they made clear, but beyond that there wasn't much guidance. We did discern that economic intelligence would be increasingly important and adjusted accordingly. Terrorism, narcotics and weapons of mass destruction were also subjects that had to be covered and the new priorities would dictate changes in recruiting of new officers, training, assignments, promotions and budgets.

Before we could begin implementing our new plan, we had to sell it both within the Agency and on the Hill. Inside the Agency, Dick Stolz accomplished much of the effort. His relationship with

Judge Webster was strong and our homework had been well done. The other Directorates were briefed, mostly out of *politesse*, useful mutual insights were gained and the other Directorates began preparing strategic plans of their own. Having been first off the mark, we were well ahead of the curve and were able to nudge others in directions we had taken. Overall, the planning activity was a highly useful and, given the global changes we faced collectively, obviously necessary effort.

Our presentations to both the HPSCI and the SSCI oversight committees were well received. There was a solid consensus on each committee that major change was required and they welcomed the vision our plan presented. There were, inevitably, some who did not agree, but the majority view supported what we planned to do. Opposition, primarily within staff elements, came from would-be operations officers who had changes of their own in mind. In the end, however, we prevailed and we assured members of both committees that prompt steps would be taken to begin implementation of the plan.

In early 1991, with Dick Stolz's support, I was approved as the next Chief in Paris. This was splendid news indeed and it helped to motivate me through an additional year plus in CMS. It was a time of great challenge to us all. The changes being implemented as a result of our strategic plan were tearing at the very fabric of our culture and everything that had been so carefully constructed through the decades of the Cold War.

Where CMS was concerned, there were cries for change in almost all areas of our personnel structure. Areas cited for change included (in no particular order of priority) faster promotions, an end to the long cherished (but resource demanding) panel system, more diversity, a modernized training structure and the removal of the 'glass ceiling'. Also a more open assignment process, honest and insightful Performance Appraisal Reports (this was a great irritant), a revised category system that would rein in the elitism of Category B, recruiting priorities that would reflect needs outlined in our strategic plan and greater accountability. And please have the changes in place by next Monday morning.

We heard those cries, of course, and we were trying. But expectations were greater than the ability of an entrenched culture to change. Cultures resist change and many within ours were fearful.

My frustrations mounted as one seemingly intractable issue after another came my way. Thinking back now, I suspect that the hectic pace of change simply took its toll. Four years in a job like CMS had limits. I was eagerly looking forward to getting back out into the field.

By this time, Mike had been named our Chief in Hong Kong and Peggy had moved on to a different assignment.

Mike was replaced by Glen, an operations officer returning to Headquarters from a job as our Chief in Finland. Glen brought seniority, experience (mostly in European Division jobs), and an exceptionally high level of energy and competence to his new job. With a University of Virginia Law Degree in his background, he also brought a very disciplined approach to his work and a level of integrity that was beyond reproach. He understood the Directorate and he made judgements with both fairness and compassion. Mike suggested Glen as his own replacement and a review of Glen's file left little doubt that he was an excellent choice. I was pleased when he accepted the job and more than pleased with the work he accomplished. I have great respect for his straightforward approach to his relationships with people both above and below him in the hierarchy. Peggy's replacement, Nancy, was a senior, highly respected DO reports officer. Like Glen, she did not hesitate to put in long, hard hours researching a particular issue to ensure that no point about it eluded her. I had complete confidence in her judgements and in the objectivity with which she approached contentious issues – of which there were many. Her proposals reflected lots of common sense and a spirit of compromise when necessary. Changes occasioned by the new strategic plan (in our budget, training, manning table and hiring among others) had a greater impact on Nancy's side of the office than on Glen's and she met the challenge with aplomb.

Almost by definition, the people-oriented deputy jobs in CMS require exceptional officers who can generate high levels of trust and confidence. Assignments and promotions, as well as the related activities that support our personnel structure, touch at sensitive and sometimes raw nerves of individual employees. Thus the officers selected for those jobs need a wide range of attributes. Such was the case during my tenure as Chief. One of my committees involved disciplinary actions. A vast majority of the cases we judged were the result of sexual misconduct or excessive drinking. In one such meeting, I couldn't help remarking that if we could just control bottles and zippers we would solve the bulk of our personnel problems before they got started. The group met bi-weekly to be briefed and make judgements on violations of Agency regulations. Why I asked, when we took such pains to select and hire the highest calibre people, must we regularly face these problems? No one, at the time, offered any response and I haven't thought of one in the interim. These problems are not unknown in the rest of our society so why should the CIA be any different?

A particularly frustrating case (which did not involve either sex or alcohol) involved an operations officer whose work and comportment fell well below the standards we expected. Serving in a European post, he had produced questionable accountings, demonstrated bad judgement and practised exceptionally poor tradecraft. He was a relatively senior officer and we had every right to expect much more from him than we were getting. Complaints from other officers generated an investigation by the Office of the Inspector General. It was at the conclusion of that investigation that the case was raised to my attention.

Accompanied by the Chief of the European Division, I was invited to the Inspector General's office to be briefed on the results of the investigation. In its totality, the information collected and presented by the Inspector General painted a picture of an officer failing in his responsibilities, his duty. Since the Inspector General does not mete out punishment, it would be up to the Directorate to decide what to do next. The European Division Chief and I were given copies of the Inspector General's report to study as we deliberated what we would recommend to the DDO.

We met several days later to discuss our conclusions. We agreed immediately that the report was damning and that the officer's performance had been unacceptable in all respects. There was solid evidence, much of it irrefutable and some the officer had admitted. We discussed the possibility of dismissal. He deserved it, we concluded, but, as was so often the case, his PARs had not adequately reflected the poor quality of his work and would not support such a strong step. After further discussion, we decided to propose a memo for his file, signed by the DDO, which would preclude any future field assignment for this officer or any in a management position. The Directorate had lost confidence in his judgement and his integrity, the memo went on, and he could either retire or spend the remainder of his career in a Headquarters job under close management scrutiny. The DDO, Tom Twetten, who had by this time replaced Dick Stolz, accepted our conclusion and signed the memo. (Tom, an old and current friend who had been a member of my original JOT class, had been hand-picked by Stolz and, given the far-reaching changes under way, he stepped in at a particularly difficult time. Also of Viking heritage and a Midwesterner, Tom's high level of competence and years of experience in the Clandestine Service stood him in good stead.) Tom's signature, however, was not the end of the story.

The offending officer, who was of Hispanic origin, challenged the Inspector General's report claiming he had been discriminated against because of his minority background. People didn't like him, he claimed, because he was a Latino. They had therefore lied to the Inspector General, he alleged, which then produced a flawed report. Neither the European Division Chief nor I was ever contacted as a result of his suit. The Directorate was not involved. But he won the case and, with his victory, a cash award. This despite the fact that we had clear evidence of his failings that had nothing to do with any allegation from a co-worker. The Inspector General's report had weaknesses that some clever lawyer exposed and exploited.

Distressing to me was the fact that the Directorate was now saddled with an officer we knew had violated the trust that is the foundation of our system. (If you can't trust an operations officer to report truthfully what transpires at an agent meeting, the entire reporting cycle is at risk.) And by exploiting the failings of an apparently flawed Inspector General's report, he appeared to be vindicated. All the while, the Directorate of Operations was not involved. The issue was taken out of our hands and all the efforts expended by the Chief of the European Division and by me were for naught. I'm not so naive as to believe that life is always fair, but in this case the bureaucracy simply dropped the ball. Regrettably, there were other similar cases and most were equally distasteful — and disappointing, in that they were a periodic reminder that even in our barrel of carefully selected apples there were some bad ones.

In August 1991, Webster decided that four years was enough (no one I knew disputed his decision) and retired as Director. In November, President Bush named Robert Gates to be our next Director. Gates, a career intelligence officer, would be the eleventh Director of my career. That he understood intelligence and was an Agency officer was good, but he was from the DDI, not the DDO, and that worried us. Intelligent, professional and well plugged in to the inner circles in Washington as a result of an entire career in the city, Gates was uncomfortable, I thought, with the Clandestine Service. We hoped, in the end, that his familiarity with Washington's ways, and ability to work his way through the ever-present minefields, would redound to our overall benefit.

Time marches on and soon it was early 1992. Tom had identified my replacement and I was eager to begin preparations for my tour in Paris. The CMS job had been a difficult one and I left it with few regrets. There would be time to read personnel and operational files, visit various departments and agencies in Washington that had ties in Paris that I would be involved with, work yet again on my French to improve my fluency, and put family affairs in order. More than three and a half years away from operations managing the 'nuts and bolts' of the Directorate's personnel structure had been a long and tedious time.

Writing about this period of my career has been difficult. I think it is because I never really liked the substance of the job. I was able to derive pleasure or satisfaction from only a few of the things I did during this time. I sometimes felt like I was the chief in the engine room of a battleship. We provided the resources, the energy to keep the ship moving, while Dick Stolz and Tom Twetten steered on the bridge. It had been unlike any previous job. Judy sensed my frustration and mentioned it more than once, but I never realized what impact the job was having on me. I was gratified and honoured when, upon my departure, Tom presented me with the DO's highest award for service rendered, the Donovan Award. I had done my duty as best I could and it was now up to a colleague to take up those chores.

SIXTEEN

PARIS CHIEF

1992–95

Sans the children, Judy and I arrived at Charles de Gaulle airport on a sunny morning in late August 1992. We had decided to finish our language training with two weeks of total immersion at a school in Provence, so we picked up a car and headed south. I hoped also to take the pulse of political realities in the provinces, thus we planned to drive south via the west coast, to Bordeaux and the foothills of the Pyrenees.

Charlie T., our administrative officer, met us as we came through customs and welcomed us to France. An outstanding and experienced officer, who was also a very likeable person, Charlie would prove to be a strong performer as he carried out his responsibilities in our office and in the Embassy. He had arrived in Paris only a few months earlier, and prior to leaving Headquarters had stopped by my office. He passed us the keys to the car we would use for our trip to the language school, wished us good luck at the school and left to return to Paris.

We hadn't slept much on the plane. I was excited at the prospect of getting back to the field, and Judy doesn't sleep well on planes. We had no particular itinerary in mind and simply headed west out of Paris. Before long, discretion seemed the better part of valour and we decided to stop and spend the bulk of our first day resting rather than driving.

We drove only as far as Chartres, a couple of hours' drive west of Paris. A delightful city, its claim to fame is the magnificent Gothic cathedral that is visible from miles around. Particularly striking are its incredibly beautiful stained-glass windows. We spent our first night in France in a hotel there. I was more than pleased. Our tour was under way.

For the next week, we made our way through La Rochelle, Bordeaux and Toulouse en route to the school in Provence. There were frequent stops along the way and I used every occasion I could to engage the French with whom we came in contact in conversations about a wide range of subjects. Not only was that good for my French, it also started to flesh out impressions I had gained from extensive reading about numerous political and economic subjects. I was eager to deepen my understanding of what made the French tick.

A subject of no small import at the time was an impending national referendum on the extent of France's participation in the European Union. My conversations along our route plus a look at editorials in local newspapers helped me understand the contentious issues being debated. In the end, the government's argument for greater involvement with the European Union prevailed with a slim majority.

The school, located in Pont St Esprit near Orange in Provence, was housed in buildings that had formerly been a monastery on a rural site just outside of the town. Everything had been restored and modernized, so our accommodation, while modest, was comfortable. Classrooms and the dining room were on an upper level and easily accessible. The dining room served non-gourmet but acceptable meals that were eaten family style with a French instructor at each table. There was a large open room on the lower level that was used for breaks and, in the evenings, for cultural programmes. Two tennis courts were located below the main building. In barely usable condition, they afforded the only distraction available and we used them a few times between afternoon classes and dinner.

It was a no-nonsense setting in which total emphasis was placed on improving one's French-language capability. Since that's why we were there, we had no problem with that. Agency students had studied there before and had also studied at the school's branch in Spa, Belgium.

French was spoken twenty-four hours a day Monday to Friday. Weekends were free. Judy and I were placed in different classes because of our respective levels in French. Judy, who had actually studied more French than I (including courses at the Alliance Française in Hong Kong years earlier and in Belgium during our tour there) was clearly stronger in vocabulary and grammar. We were both well served over the course of those two weeks. It was an excellent jumpstart to our arrival in Paris.

There was one bizarre incident during the second week. It started when I was asked to give a talk as part of an evening session. Each night we were required to attend some type of speech or lecture. Local politicians or teachers were invited and presented their views on a variety of subjects, after which we asked questions. For this session, I had been asked to talk about the life of a diplomat. (I was attending in my cover capacity.) I was reluctant because the thought of giving a talk (of any kind) in French was less than appealing. But I finally agreed. I spent a couple of hours preparing my remarks. That wasn't difficult because I certainly knew what Embassy officers spent their days doing.

Then, as we entered the dining room the morning of my talk, Judy spotted a handmade poster someone had put on the bulletin board in front of the dining-room door. 'Come to Hear James Bond Talk' it announced in bold letters. A drawing of a pistol with an American flag protruding from the barrel was included. My first reaction was one of irritation. Who would have done that? Why? I took the poster down and stuck it in a nearby wastepaper-basket. Less irritated after breakfast, I had to decide what, if anything, to do next. Judy counselled restraint and ultimately the wisdom of her view carried the day. I gave my talk as advertised and it went as planned. There was nothing untoward and no questions about anything except diplomacy. I never discovered who put up the poster, why it was done, or what prompted someone to suspect that I was not a real diplomat.

Paris had always been an active and important place for the Agency and my tour there would be no different. I was delighted to finally be in place and I eagerly commenced a series of meetings with colleagues to gain an on-the-scene sense of what was going on.

As had been the case in Hong Kong, Kuala Lumpur and Brussels, I first focused my attention on our operational support structure. Some changes would be required. I was conscious of what some might think, so I made it as clear as I could that this was simply a 'thing' for me. We all had our own style and worrying about operational support was a part of mine. I meant no criticism towards any of my predecessors. Counter intelligence worries were at the heart of my interest in the operational support mechanisms. Often left in the hands of our most junior and inexperienced officers and only rarely reviewed, operational support operations had in the past caused compromises and the resultant political grief. Often supporting valuable and sensitive operations, safe house keepers and agents who provide accommodation addresses need the same careful handling afforded to all other agents. I knew of instances where handling of those types of agents had been lax and we had suffered the consequences. I wanted to avoid any such problem.

With concern quickly assuaged, I turned attention to a host of subjects of high interest to policy makers. As an international crossroads, Paris offers access to and information about a range of issues that is truly global in scope. The Middle East and Africa were particularly well represented. Information available in the city would satisfy many, if not most, of the intelligence requirements levied upon us by Washington. Our job was to carefully, and selectively, construct the operational activities that would produce that information. As I had already been aware, the job was in train. I was assuming command of an active and productive office. But there would, of course, be obstacles to overcome and the first one was just ahead.

Just after Thanksgiving 1992, a cable from Headquarters announced that our budget for the fiscal year that had started on 1 October, almost two months earlier, had been cut – by 50 per cent! The news stunned us. No one had seen this coming. Congress, on a whim I can only suppose, had decided to cut the Agency's budget dramatically and our options seemed to be to live with it, or – to live with it.

One of my first thoughts was about the planning we had accomplished at Headquarters in 1990 and 1991. It was all for naught apparently as Congress, contrary to agreements reached at the time, now wasn't buying our arguments, a key one being that as the United States was reducing its diplomatic and military presence in the world we would need a stronger not a weaker global intelligence capability. These cuts would be a part of the 'Peace Dividend' to be harvested from the end of the Cold War in 1989, I concluded. But how were we, and our colleagues elsewhere in the field, to accomplish our jobs? It was a bitter pill and not the best start in the world for my tour in Paris.

Charlie and his assistants briefed me on the full extent of the problems this drastic cut in our budget would cause. With commitments already made for the first quarter of the fiscal year, heavy cuts across the board were going to be imperative, he told me. Seeking some clarification and hoping for some wiggle room, I asked him to send an immediate cable to Headquarters. He drafted the cable including a last line along the lines of 'if we don't get some relief, the last guy out will turn off the lights'. It was a bit of levity that was apparently lost on Joe D., the European Division Chief at the time. The grapevine reported back that Joe complained about the quip and admonished us to be more serious. In fact, we were quite serious.

The Headquarters response made it clear that I was going to have to make do with half of the budget that had originally been submitted, and approved. The Agency budget had been cut and, illogically, the comptroller convinced the Director, Bob Gates, to spread it out equally among the four Directorates. No effort was made to determine the impact such cuts would have on individual programmes. Nor was any consideration given to the fact that elements operating abroad would face far greater problems and crippling blows to their efforts.

So, in a time of great uncertainty, as the nation was struggling to find its way in a dramatically different world, the country's Clandestine Service was being not just reduced, but slashed. Many of us had recognized that fewer resources would be available and we had planned with that reality in mind, but we had not anticipated this tactic – it made little sense. As our British colleagues would say, 'at the end of the day', we lost in a budget battle on the Hill and our ox got gored.

I asked Charlie and his assistant to pull together a draft of a new budget, underlining where they would recommend we take the cuts that were now unavoidable. With a real sense of dread, I reviewed what they had produced before meeting my deputy and our Branch Chiefs. I wasn't happy with what they presented, but

I knew it was realistic. They had done a good job. At our meeting, we discussed the issue in general terms and then I gave everyone a copy of the draft and scheduled a meeting three days later at which the tough decisions facing us would be taken. They should all study the draft, I told them, and be prepared to argue their respective cases as we focused on reducing the scope of our activities. It was not a happy group.

The subsequent meeting was a long and tough one during which we scrutinized all of our efforts and ultimately agreed upon which ones should suffer the axe. The pain would be considerable and emotions ran high, but I was pleased to see that a strong spirit of co-operation prevailed. We were all in this together. Cuts in the administrative and support areas were mostly a nuisance that we could live with, albeit with some belt tightening and complaints. But the drastic cuts in our operational efforts hit directly at our *raison d'être*, questioning why we were there and what we would be doing in the future. The subject itself generated additional fears because a follow-on personnel cut was envisioned. The episode hammered morale.

Without intending to belabour this budget-cutting exercise, I will take the opportunity to point out that I saw it as a symptom of alarming uncertainty at the national level about how a single superpower world should run. And, in turn, how that superpower should conduct itself. From some there were cries of a need to cut military and intelligence budgets and focus on domestic issues. It was a surge of isolationism, according to some pundits. Others pointed out the danger of doing what had been done after the end of the Second World War, and the First World War as well. I certainly would agree that reductions were warranted, but, as is so often the case, the pendulum swung too far. In the case of the Directorate of Operations, excessive and ill-considered cuts, especially to our capabilities to operate abroad (which is what a Clandestine Service is for), were carried out for several years. Now, as I write more than a decade after the Cold War ended and communism collapsed, there is a realization that the cuts were too deep. The world is not the benign place some had unrealistically hoped it might become. There is indeed a national priority for a strong and vibrant Clandestine Service and efforts are under way to rebuild the service that was so recently crippled. It takes time, but usually common sense prevails.

I was blessed in Paris with another strong Deputy. Charlie D. commanded great respect within the station. He was fair and objective, and had an unusually strong grasp of tradecraft. His counsel on operational matters was widely sought, including by me, and his judgements were consistently solid and accurate. So strong was his reputation that Headquarters sometimes called upon him to handle particularly sensitive operational activities in other places. The opposite of flamboyant, Charlie dealt easily with easy decisions and took hard decisions head on. No procrastination was allowed. I felt lucky to have had him as my Deputy for the first two years of my tour. I wish he had been there at the end.

Initially there were three Branch Chiefs, but eventually the personnel cuts that we had feared came to pass and I was forced to reorganize our complement. Our new structure had two Branch Chiefs and both were, I thought, exceptionally strong. Each, one was male and the other female, was hard-working, fully committed and had broad operational experience in their backgrounds. Both were personable and well liked by the officers working for them. (There were a few exceptions – there always are.)

The female was one of the strongest operations officers, male or female, I ever had the pleasure of working with. In addition to strong management of her active branch, she handled some particularly sensitive operational activities. The male Branch Chief, fluent in several languages, had denied area operational experience and was a strong mentor for several of our younger officers. Our office was big by any standard, but we had lots of work to do. The recruitment targets and the information were there. Our job was to recruit and collect.

Righting the ship, that is accomplishing all the changes that the crippling December 1992 budget cuts forced upon us, took several months. In the operational arena, each cut had to be viewed with counter intelligence and operational security in mind. When an asset is told that his or her services are no longer needed, the reaction is difficult to predict. Care had to be taken in each case to ensure a soft landing that would prompt no problems. This is easier said than done, and our officers merit praise for having weathered the storm with no known incident or breach of our operational security.

In January 1993, just three plus months after my return to the field, Bob Gates was relieved of his position as Director. This was a function of Bush having lost the 1992 election to Bill Clinton, the former Governor of Arkansas, who took his state from forty-seventh to forty-ninth place nationally in education during his tenure. How he ever beat Bush is beyond me, but he did. I suppose Ross Perot is the most likely answer. With a plurality, not a majority, of the popular vote, Clinton took charge and decided to put his own man at the Agency. The political nature of the choice of Director at the Agency was firmly established.

To replace Gates, Clinton named James Woolsey, an experienced Washington bureaucrat. The twelfth man to serve as our Director during my career took command in early February 1993. Few of us knew much about Woolsey and reaction seemed pretty neutral. He would certainly be better than other candidates that had been mentioned. We'll just wait and see how he does, was the general conclusion.

One morning in early 1993, in the midst of the budget-cut-prompted turmoil, I arrived at my office to find a large manila envelope on my desk. Addressed to the Ambassador, it was stuffed with documents – or, more precisely, copies of documents. It was the content that had prompted the Ambassador's office to send the envelope to me.

Inside the envelope was a stack of documents that had been purloined from the files of the Direction Générale du Surveillance Extérieure (DGSE), France's equivalent to the CIA. The documents, which had been altered to make them appear to be more current than they actually were, appeared to be an outline of a DGSE plan to collect technical and economic information clandestinely in the United States, the United Kingdom and Switzerland. From information also included in the packet of documents, we learned that the same documents, or at least a portion thereof, had also been sent to newspaper offices in those three countries. Left unclear was whether or not other intelligence services were in possession of the packet. For us it was at once a bombshell and a potential tar baby (i.e., that once involved, it is very hard to extricate yourself). We were wary of addressing the problem though we knew we had to do something. There was a host of questions to be answered as we focused on what steps we would take and how we would react.

First we puzzled over who had sent the packet and why it had been sent. There were some obvious answers and some less obvious. Surely it was someone who disliked, and wanted to stir up problems for, the DGSE; someone who was angry and vindictive. Either a member, or a former member, of the DGSE, who would have had the access to documents as sensitive as these, or who co-operated with a second party to acquire the packet. Exactly what that person hoped to accomplish remained unclear.

In our immediate cable exchanges with Headquarters, opinions were given and theories postulated. No real answers were forthcoming. We reconstructed the recent history of DGSE activities in the United States. A careful review of the documents in the packets revealed not only the subtle changes that had been made to try to make them appear to be current, but also that the documents were actually relevant to a specific earlier period. An operation directed against American interests had been compromised and the DGSE had been asked to explain and clarify its actions. Following some sensitive and delicate conversations, an understanding had been reached. In effect, the issue had been resolved. Furnishing us, and the British and Swiss, with the current doctored packet seemed to be an effort to reopen an old wound for the DGSE – and then pour salt into it.

And it worked. There was much consternation and lots of fretting about exactly what to do. We couldn't just ignore it because articles had appeared in British, Swiss and, despite our best efforts, American newspapers heralding DGSE plans to conduct industrial espionage in friendly countries. The articles didn't generate much follow-up. Still, the perpetrator must have been pleased to see that the packet was causing embarrassment and problems for the DGSE.

I had briefed the Ambassador. We certainly didn't want him blindsided when the newspaper articles were published. Moreover, it was a development he needed to know about. He deferred to me on what action to take with the DGSE and offered any support I might need. Our exchanges with Headquarters finally produced agreement on what to do. I would take a copy of the packet to the DGSE and ask for an explanation. After considerable research and rumination, we were going to adopt a very straightforward approach. We had heard nothing from either the British or the Swiss, but how they decided to react, we concluded, was up to them.

The packet affair and its aftermath raise some interesting points about the nuances involved in contacts with foreign intelligence services, especially ones between friendly and allied nations. What the policy makers dictate is undertaken to the fullest extent possible. There are activities of each service that are 'compatible'. During the Cold War, for example, we worked with all our allies against the Soviets (and their minions) and we co-operated where possible. But sometimes activities are *not* compatible and one side doesn't like what the other is doing, as was the case outlined in the documents. For many reasons, including political ones, that causes inter-service problems that require delicate handling.

To handle those problems, discreet discussions are the preferred course of action. Contain the problem and avoid publicity that inevitably prompts posturing by politicians and ill-informed journalistic sermonizing. These are unwritten, but closely observed, rules of the game. The end of the Cold War, however, prompted major changes that have greatly exacerbated the sensitivities that are involved.

The far-reaching changes that started in late 1989 brought about a vastly different world for those of us in the intelligence business. Among the changes was a different optic in 'friendly' relationships. Gone were the 'good guys and bad guys' days that had been an acceptable guideline during the Cold War. The new environment demanded a new (and more difficult) assessment of activities that would previously have been viewed as 'compatible'.

Another change was the upgraded priority given to economics as a collection requirement. And on that subject, our staff officers wrestled with definitions. What's the difference between economic intelligence and industrial espionage? It depends on where you're coming from, is the answer.

The thrust of the documents in the packet, theft of our technology, caused no surprise to intelligence professionals. Information shared by the FBI and our own counter intelligence reporting (much of which has been published by newspapers and magazines) had made us well aware of French efforts to collect economic information in the United States. Nor are the French alone in this endeavour. For any country, friendly or hostile, seeking cutting-edge technology, the obvious place to look for it is the United States, the world's leader in research and development. And many countries, including friendly ones, are doing just that. It's a reality we must face and the real challenge is to ensure that safeguards are in place to protect our secrets and in turn our competitiveness. That task is complicated, however, by a mentality in the corporate world contending, 'We can invent new technology faster than they can steal it.'

As the packet episode and the budget-cut period were ending, the Embassy was preparing to receive the new Ambassador. The November 1992 election of President Clinton, warts and all, presaged a change at the Embassy too and now it was coming. The Ambassador, dutifully, submitted his resignation and it was accepted. As a Republican appointee, he neither expected nor wanted to stay in Paris. There was, of course, much speculation about who would be named Ambassador to what was considered one of the plums of Europe. Soon after the new administration took over in January 1993, we had our answer.

Clinton named Pamela Harriman, the well-known Democratic fundraiser and widow of Averell Harriman, to be the United States Ambassador to France. I was taken by surprise. Her name had been mentioned during the speculation period, but I didn't take it seriously. I knew her to be 'the hostess with the mostest' in Georgetown circles and doubted that she could handle the diplomatic chores in a country as important as France. And I fretted about her ability to absorb sensitive briefings and render judgements. My doubts and concerns, I would ultimately discover, were unwarranted.

Along with Avis Bohlen, the Deputy Chief of Mission, and several Embassy counsellors, I met Ambassador Harriman at Charles de Gaulle airport early one morning in May 1993. I remember marvelling at the time at how bright and attractive she looked (at the age of seventy-two) after an overnight flight from

Washington's Dulles airport. There were brief introductions before she was whisked away to the Ambassador's residence on Rue St Honoré, just behind the Embassy.

My first professional meeting with Ambassador Harriman occurred a few days later when I was asked to brief her on my office's activities and programmes. Part of the introductory schedule called for each senior officer to brief her and I was, of course, no exception – except that for my briefing, she and I were the only ones in the room because parts of the briefing included 'Ambassador Only' material. I gave her a candid comprehensive briefing and was surprised at the depth of understanding her questions revealed. She had been well briefed at Headquarters, I concluded. (I was not yet ready to simply give her credit for being an unusually smart and savvy individual. That would come soon enough.) The session went quite well and, despite my nagging concerns, I was impressed at her easy manner and seemingly sincere interest in intelligence matters. I liked her, I later told Charlie. He harboured doubts.

I suggested to Ambassador Harriman that I brief her a couple of times weekly on selected pieces of intelligence that, from my understanding of current priorities, would be of interest to her. She liked the idea and accepted, asking that Avis Bohlen be included in the briefings. That posed no problem for me as I had come to have a high regard for Avis's in-depth knowledge of France and her professionalism. We decided on twice weekly briefings and they were built into the Ambassador's schedule. I was pleased for several reasons. First the briefings gave me regular contact with the Ambassador. And, based on my experience, I was able to deepen her understanding of reports received from outside of France. The selection of reports we briefed on included our own reporting as well as sensitive reporting from other places. In addition, I was assured that my primary 'customer', the Ambassador, was a regular recipient of the product of our efforts. Also it enabled me to stay attuned to the issues she considered of highest priority importance.

One of the members of our office was a senior analyst from the Directorate of Intelligence and it was his responsibility (among his many others) to review systematically, on a daily basis, all clandestinely acquired intelligence and select items for the Ambassador's attention. He accompanied me to brief the Ambassador and usually gave the briefings. In a sense, because of the insights he provided from his analytic experience, the Ambassador was receiving raw and finished intelligence at the same time. Although I tried to schedule around these briefings, there were days when I couldn't attend. The system continued regularly, however, with our senior analyst ably carrying on. Overall, these briefings were beneficial for both sides, with perhaps a bit of a plus on our side of the equation. I consistently enjoyed them and was particularly happy that they gave me the opportunity to know Pamela Harriman, a talented and charming woman. I never got to a 'Hi Pamela' stage, which would have been unacceptably informal, but we became good friends and mutually appreciative of the other's abilities. Evidence of the depth of understanding achieved came on the occasions when she let her hair down, so to speak, and rendered candid views on specific individuals or problems. She pulled no punches. 'So and so is a lightweight jerk', or 'That guy [politician usually] simply has no balls.' I almost always agreed with her assessments and noted that she didn't spare members of the administration. My only real problem with her was her prominence as a Democrat and her support for President Clinton. He has been a great disappointment. Ambassador Harriman was popular and respected inside the Embassy, and the same was true outside. Her background was spicy and intriguing. She spoke French. She was attractive, intelligent and charming. The French accepted her with open arms and, in spite of my initial misgivings, I ultimately assessed her to be an effective Ambassador.

Ambassador Harriman once referred to the dominance of senior female officers of the Embassy's state department as her 'all girl band'. It was an innocuous comment that left me uncertain if she liked or disliked the situation. With few exceptions, senior state department officers in the Embassy and each of the three consulates general (located in Bordeaux, Marseilles and Strasbourg) were women. Most believed this was the result of a class action suit against the Department of State in the early 1980s. As I understood it, female employees launched the suit to protest against the 'glass ceiling'. The settlement afforded females preferential treatment in the assignment process and positions, such as the highly sought-after ones in France, were bid upon and often awarded to women.

As had been the case in previous tours, terrorism seemed ever present – at a simmering level. But spikes in terrorist activity, usually prompted by some political event or issue, are cyclical. As an example, consider the Algerian national elections in the early 1990s that were annulled by the Algerian military after it became clear that an Islamic party was about to take control of the government. The 'stolen' election prompted militant Islamic groups to launch a deadly wave of terrorist attacks that continues to this day. Given the history of Franco-Algerian relations, the terrorism in Algeria quickly spread to French soil. United States policy opposed the terrorist acts in Algeria and we were quickly thrust into a position of supporting, in any way we could, the French efforts to combat Algerian terrorism.

Terrorism had been an ugly reality on the world scene for several decades and all intelligence and security services knew that disparate bits of information, sometimes obtained via a liaison channel, often were the key to bringing a given terrorist to justice. The file stays open until it can be closed with the confidence that those responsible for a specific terrorist attack have been hunted down and will face their fate in a court. We have not forgotten those who murdered Richard Welch in Athens in the middle 1970s or those who murdered Bill Buckley after he was taken captive in Beirut. One day we will find them and they will pay.

Many foreign services, including the French services, feel the same as we do, and from time to time co-operative efforts generate a shared success. In one such instance, the French obtained, from a friendly service, a piece of information concerning the whereabouts of Carlos, the infamous international terrorist, who had been on the run for many years. Reluctant at first to believe the information (innumerable false leads had been run down over the years), the French expressed their appreciation and said they would check with sources of their own. Nothing came of their checks.

Carlos had, among many other murderous attacks, killed three members of the French internal service. The French were keenly interested in bringing Carlos to justice. Given my abiding interest

in terrorism as a menace to society (which was no doubt strengthened by my tour as the Chief of our Counter Terrorism Group),
I monitored the effort to apprehend Carlos with great interest.

Confident of its information, the friendly service dug even
deeper and within weeks gave the French specific information
pinpointing Khartoum, Sudan, as Carlos's hideout. Having been
forced out of several other Arab countries, the Jackal had been
forced into Khartoum's relative oblivion. This time the data really
rang the French bell and they eagerly set up to pursue what now
was an extremely promising operation.

Close co-operation between the two services ensued. Rémy
Philippe, a respected and highly professional senior officer, took
the lead for the French effort. No resources would be spared, he
made clear. A quiet, unflappable man, who exuded competence,
he had served, as a young military officer, with reconnaissance
units in Algeria during the latter stages of the French Algerian
War. There was an inner toughness clearly detectable in him. He
had many years of experience dealing with terrorist and Middle
Eastern affairs and was a virtual encyclopaedia of knowledge on
terrorists and their supporters and collaborators. It was clear to
most people that if he wasn't 'Lawrence of Arabia', he was the
closest thing to it in French terms. He worked steadily to sift
through the minutiae of the stream of reporting that was being
collected. There were high points when the effort seemed poised
for success and low points when the activity seemed hopelessly
stalled. But he persisted and urged collaborators to continue their
efforts.

Three months into the investigations that seemed to be tightening the noose around Carlos, information was obtained
indicating that Carlos would be travelling to a North African city
in two days. Co-operative authorities in that city were immediately notified and they set in motion a plan to intercept the Jackal
at the airport. A determined effort turned up nothing. Alas, the
report had been based on inaccurate information.

Two weeks later, Philippe received a similar report. It was a
difficult decision, but he concluded that, despite questions about
the source's access, he couldn't afford *not* to act. Again colleagues
were mobilized and they waited at the designated city's airport. It
was another no show.

These were disappointments of course, but by now Philippe was more determined than ever to bring the operation to fruition. The quarry was bracketed and he wasn't about to give up efforts. Numerous planning sessions generated various plans for achieving the final objective. Each was carefully evaluated, bearing in mind political and operational realities. Would political and diplomatic pressure carry the day? Could he organize and then carry out a covert paramilitary operation to 'snatch' Carlos from his hiding place in Khartoum? Each option assessed carried with it obstacles and risks and producing a definitive decision was difficult indeed.

I suspect that intense, behind-the-scenes diplomatic pressures ultimately made the difference. Buttressed by the information they had amassed, the French were able to make a strong case that was finally accepted by the Sudanese Government. A carefully planned secret turnover was arranged and the French took custody of Carlos. In accordance with the plan, Carlos, who had just undergone a surgical procedure to override a vasectomy, was strapped to a gurney and transported straight to a waiting French team at Khartoum airport.

As he became aware of what was happening, Carlos was at first terrified that his captors were Israelis. After a long plane ride during which not a word was spoken, he seemed almost relieved to discover that he was in the custody of French officials. He knew that the Israeli justice system includes capital punishment, and that his punishment would have been swift and severe. The French do not employ capital punishment, but Carlos's trial assured that he would pay his debt. He now languishes in a French jail and, I fervently hope, will remain there for the rest of his evil life.

As the product of many months' worth of effort and close co-operation between the two services, the apprehension of Carlos was a classic example of co-operative activity at its best. With an established level of trust, confidence and professionalism, they were able to meld together the ingredients required to accomplish a shared goal. Would that it could happen more often – especially in the field of counter terrorism.

We moved into our 1920s' town house in Neuilly-sur-Seine, a western suburb, just before Thanksgiving 1992. With newly refinished parquet floors, modernized bathrooms and a complete repainting, it was as good as new; terribly comfortable, yet with the character and ambiance you would expect in a European home. It even had a nice first-floor terrace with a stairway down to a flower-filled back yard. And best of all perhaps, because of the parking problem that was a constant in Paris, it had a connected two-car garage with a remotely controlled steel door.

My commute took me along the Bois de Boulogne and through a large circle called the Porte de Maillot. Then up Avenue Charles de Gaulle, and across the Etoile, with its Arc de Triomphe in the middle. It must be said, and I think that most Parisians would agree, that the Etoile presented traffic planners with a real challenge. With twelve major streets and avenues feeding into and out of it, negotiating it was a formidable task. Until you figured out the system. Then it flowed rather well. Always I was amazed during rush hour at how efficiently the whole thing worked.

From the Etoile, my commute would take me straight down the Champs Elysées. It was broad and strikingly beautiful, and it led to the almost equally famous Place de la Concorde, where, in 1793, Marie Antoinette, Louis XVI and other members of the aristocracy were beheaded. And just off the same corner of the Place de la Concorde where the guillotine once stood was my daily destination. Yes, some mornings I had meetings and would go elsewhere and yes, in deference to security concerns, we did vary our route using other streets, but that was a frequently used route and it never got old. It had beauty and history at almost every turn.

Our house was literally fifty metres from the Bois de Boulogne, an enormous wooded park on the edge of Paris. Lakes with ducks and swans, beautiful flowerbeds and well-tended paths made it pleasant year round and we took full advantage of the proximity. I jogged in the Bois most mornings and Judy took daily long 'power' walks. There was a stable in the park within earshot of the house and we were often awakened in the morning to the sound of horses clattering by with riders on their morning outing. Security had, as always, been a consideration before I decided on where we would live. With my experience in counter terrorism and knowledge of what had happened to Buckley and Welch, how could it not have been? There were, of course, a host of factors to consider. In the end, the way to be completely secure would be to stay in the United States. I had long ago discarded that option. As was usually the case overseas, with incomplete knowledge of all relevant factors, one had simply to weigh pros and cons of a given situation. In this case, the house we moved into offered more pros. The strongest one being the fact that an armed French policeman was on twenty-four hour a day duty at a post ten feet from our garage door. Our two neighbours were considered possible terrorist targets by the French and therefore afforded protection. Frequent patrols by vehicular teams augmented the guard post. There were no guarantees, of course, but we felt more secure and were comforted by the police presence and activity.

Paris, every bit as fascinating as Hong Kong although in different ways, was enjoyable in virtually all respects. The frequent strikes (of all kinds) were a drag, I must admit, but they didn't seem to bother the French very much and we got used to them. Parking was an ever-present problem, but I became quite creative in finding places to leave our car. I don't remember ever getting a parking ticket in Paris. The museums, the restaurants, the parks, and just exploring some new part of the city, all occupied our leisure time. Our first Christmas in Paris was, despite the logistics required, a family affair. All of the girls came to visit. United Airlines loved us, I'm sure. So did the girls. They were delighted to spend ten days in the city of light.

With four bedrooms, our house accommodated everyone without problem and we had a splendid time. There were to be other visits while we were in Paris, but the first one was particularly pleasant. The days usually started with one or a couple of the girls jogging with me in the Bois. Happily, the hooker, who regularly plied her trade with men on their way to the office, was nowhere to be seen. She was taking her own Christmas vacation, I suppose. Following the run, we would visit museums, or perhaps the weekend flea market, and enjoyed some wonderful meals en masse. It was a memorable family time.

Inevitably, I suppose, in a place as large as our office in Paris, there are a few difficult, even contentious, personnel issues. We were no exception. As I have often said, even in our barrel of superior apples some are bad, or go bad with time. And sometimes there are oranges misplaced in the apple barrel.

Sometimes, the origin of these problems is a function of weaknesses in our rating system. We do it to ourselves with an unwillingness to provide each other with candid assessments. Officers responsible for rating a given employee were simply unwilling (even unable) to give honest evaluations of performance. Fear of a face-to-face confrontation with the employee meant that in effect they were protecting him or her and hiding from the rest of us the flaws and weaknesses they didn't record. Sometimes, a given individual simply didn't belong in a field position or perhaps in the Agency at all. In those instances, our screening mechanisms failed us. Management in a field station, more so than would be the case in Headquarters, is complicated when there are inconsistencies in the quality of personnel. This was not, of course, new to me, but that made it no less vexing. To illustrate the distraction and overall strain on efficiency and effectiveness these problems cause, I will cite some examples. How could they have been avoided? Beats me.

Shortly after my arrival, a highly regarded minority woman with strong credentials was assigned to our office. This was her first field tour. After having assessed her record and discussed her case, we (my deputy, both Branch Chiefs and me) agreed on where she should be placed. In deference to her newness, she was given a light workload. After six months or so, her Branch Chief reported concerns about both the quality and the quantity of work she was producing. We discussed the problem and concluded she needed more time. The Branch Chief counselled her and worked closely with her to provide hands-on guidance. After another six months, the problem was, if anything, worse. Her French was still weak and she was doing nothing to strengthen it. Her writing was also weak, which complicated her reporting chores. Her workload was minimal, and her number of hours of work per day was far below the norm. We put her in the other branch hoping for a spurt of interest and product.

Her new Branch Chief, also a female, had some heart-to-heart talks with her and encouraged her to 'show her stuff', to get out into the city and make contacts. In short, provide us with some sign of your interest in and ability to be an operations officer. The deputy talked with her. I talked with her. A second year passed with no improvement noted. By then it was difficult to attribute the weaknesses to newness. And she took umbrage at comments in her annual appraisal citing the inadequacies in her work. She had, by then, expressed criticism of her Branch Chief. There was favouritism, she insisted. Increasingly, she carped and complained about management in general. Our standards were too high, she contended.

We never succeeded in our efforts to change her, and things went from bad to worse. Everyone knew of the problems (if they didn't, she told them) and her relationship with management stuck out because it was so out of the norm. Given the effort we had expended trying to help her, the situation was both sad and frustrating. In the end, one couldn't escape the conclusion that an unwillingness to put in the effort required for whatever reason, and a related lack of confidence, were at the root of the problem. In our parochial terms, however, it boiled down to a woefully inadequate return for the position she occupied. She was sent home.

Another example, also involving a female officer, had apparently simmered for several years. She was in the office when I arrived and had had previous field operational experience. Intelligent and competent, she was highly regarded for the excellent work she did in her cover capacity. For reasons that never did become clear to me, she became increasingly critical of the Agency and what it was asking her to do. Her husband, also an operations officer, but in fact a closet academic specializing in central Asia, had, by the time of my arrival, also decided that he didn't want to work for the Agency. He resigned a year later after finding other employment. We were aware that she was also seeking other employment, but she never admitted it.

Needless to say, neither the woman nor her husband added much to morale in the work place. Endlessly critical of both Headquarters and field decisions, they were both jealous of officers who moved ahead of them in grade. She also alleged favouritism within her branch and was highly critical of her female Branch Chief. But her work and reporting were consistently strong and that was reflected in her appraisals. In fact, however, she would have been far happier, and probably even more productive, working for the Department of State instead of the Agency. Finally, she also resigned but not without having been a real burr under our collective saddle. Why or how did she join the Agency in the first place? we wondered.

There was a third example, a male officer in his early thirties, who was married and had several children. He had a previous tour in the Soviet Union and fashioned himself to be a very strong operations officer. In fact, he had strengths, but they weren't in the field of operational tradecraft, where he was no better than average. His strong area was in the technical field. A good operations officer must, above all else, develop and recruit sources of information that will satisfy the requirements generated within the intelligence community. He had done none of that at his previous post and didn't realize (nor did the system, of course) how much he disliked the whole idea of recruiting agents. Moreover, he had decided that his evenings and weekends must all be his own. His workday ended at five in the afternoon. That, of course, made him useless for many of our most important activities and caused us to lose the production we expected from a key operations officer slot. No amount of explanation, cajoling, or even direct orders could dissuade him and all he did was handle established cases. He was good at that, but it was only half the job we expected. He was a likeable and pleasant enough officer, but the totality of an operations officer's work was simply more than he had bargained for. He finished his tour, after a fashion, and then resigned from the Agency. He now has a nine to five job in the Washington area – involving technical matters. Things just didn't develop as either he or the Agency had expected.

It shouldn't take a lot of analysis to conclude that when an individual officer isn't pulling his or her weight the office, as a whole suffers. This is especially true when your most valuable asset is the individual officer. I cite the above examples not necessarily to criticize those officers or the system that assigned them to field positions. Rather I cite them to put into better perspective the importance of each individual in the chain we construct to accomplish our mission overseas. Ours is a special craft and accomplishing it requires special people.

One of the highlights of celebrations, in June 1994, to commemorate the D Day landings in Normandy in June 1944, was a presidential visit. Most field officers, I think, dread a presidential visit and this one was no exception. Whether or not you like a particular president, the fact is that the administrative, logistical and security support required for his visit will mean long hours and much frustration for most officers in the Embassy. Our involvement for President Clinton's visit in June 1994 was primarily in the security field.

Starting several months before the actual visit, we met with Secret Service officers to begin planning for the support we would provide them. Over a dozen of our officers would ultimately be involved. The meeting went well and in the end so did the President's visit. Our role was a limited but important one. Others worked as hard or harder than we did and the end of the visit signalled a 'wheels up' party celebrating both the success of the visit and the departure of the whole Washington crowd that had accompanied the President. For some, however, it was just the beginning.

The office of the military attaché, which had been heavily involved in the President's visit, was now called upon to attend celebrations of each city (and town) liberated as the Allied army moved across France after the 1944 Normandy landings, pushing the Germans back. It was a demanding time as, for many months, the officers and the enlisted men in the office attended event after event where they gave speeches and presented our colours. I became involved in one such event that had a slightly different twist. It took place in the South of France in March 1994 and it commemorated an Office of Strategic Services (OSS) operation in March 1944.

Planning for the Allied invasion of France in 1944 included plans to activate and exploit agent networks operating clandestinely in France. Real time reporting from those networks, it was felt, would be of enormous value to the Allied effort on D Day. Thus on 17 March 1944, Jean Gitteray dropped into the South of France with the mission of contacting one of the agent networks and initiating intelligence reporting by radio.

Gitteray had been a part of the French Resistance in the early years of the Second World War. For reasons unknown to me, he made his way out of occupied France and joined the Resistance movement headed by General Charles de Gaulle. He was based in Algeria in 1944 and was picked to return to France for an important mission. He was to contact agent networks to report on

German transportation and logistics activities in north-west France. Such information would, of course, be of great value to the invading Allied force.

The operation was supported by the OSS, which was to deliver Gitteray into France. On 16 March, a US Air Force B-24 carrying only its crew and Gitteray took off from Algiers headed for a drop zone just west of Pau in the foothills of the Pyrenees. On instructions from the pilot, Gitteray positioned himself above the open small round hole in the plane's belly, ready to drop out of the plane on command. Overcast skies, however, prevented the pilot from seeing the ground signals from the waiting group of Resistance fighters. The mission was aborted; back to Algiers.

On the next day, they tried again. That time the pilot saw the signals and gave the command Gitteray had been waiting for. Instantly, he dropped through the belly hole into the dark night sky. Everything worked as planned. His main chute deployed and the pilot's experience in airdrops was confirmed as Gitteray dropped right into the arms of the waiting Resistance team. Those receiving him had made careful plans and they immediately moved him to a safe house, where he was kept in seclusion for two days. Subsequently, he was provided with forged alias papers. He then made his way north, where he was able to establish the contacts he needed to provide well-received intelligence reporting. As I digested the details of what Gitteray had done, I reflected on the amount of courage, determination and patriotism needed to succeed at such an undertaking.

Fifty years after his clandestine arrival in the Pays Basque, Gitteray was a well-known journalist writing columns for *Le Figaro*. He had been closely involved with the French political scene over the years and, while near retirement, still wrote insightful articles on current political matters. His many contacts in political circles afforded him access to information that, coupled with his analysis, produced consistently interesting commentary.

I first met Gitteray at his office early in 1994. Then in his mid-seventies, Gitteray was a dynamic and impressive man. I liked him right away and my favourable impressions grew to great respect as I learned more about his exploits during the Second World War. I introduced him to the Ambassador and her reactions were similar. We discussed plans for a commemorative ceremony that would take place at the site near Pau where Gitteray had landed. Gitteray invited me, in recognition and appreciation of the role played by the OSS, and a member of the military attaché's office, to attend the ceremony, and I accepted with pleasure. The event was to be sponsored, we were told, by an organization of veterans of the French Resistance movement called Orion.

The invitation included spouses so Judy accompanied me and we flew first to Pau where we rented a small French car. After I figured out how to put the bloody car into reverse, which took about ten minutes, we drove into the city. Arrangements had been made for us to stay at a beautiful old hotel in Pau's central district and we met the officer from the military attaché's office and his wife shortly after we checked in. The next morning we drove for about thirty minutes to the small village nearest the actual field Gitteray had landed in. We were touched by the warmth of the welcome we were given. Genuine appreciation for what the United States had done during the Second World War was clearly evident as one French official after another thanked us for coming.

A small church nearby was the site of the opening ceremony and it was filled to overflowing with visitors from Paris and local residents. Many people wore Second World War uniforms. A village band played badly, but loudly and enthusiastically. Seats had been held for us and, soon after we sat down, the ceremony started. Short but emotionally moving, the ceremony provoked many memories among those gathered in the church. Most especially, I'm sure, for Jean Gitteray.

Following the church ceremony, all were invited to the military base in Pau for a luncheon. Pau was and still is the home and training site of France's parachute units. And, as a local Resistance hero and an early practitioner of parachuting, Gitteray was a natural as honoured guest at a commemoration banquet. It was a splendid affair and, after a great meal, guests assembled by the drop zone next to the dining hall to watch a combat training drop of recent recruits. Everything went according to script and the drop signalled the end of festivities. It had been an exhilarating experience for us and I said as much to Gitteray as we said our goodbyes. He expressed his gratitude for my having come and presented me with a medal issued by Orion for the occasion, a memento of an experience I won't forget.

One morning early in 1994, a stunning report hit the front pages of newspapers throughout Europe. We received a cable from Headquarters the same morning. To our collective great surprise, we read that the FBI had just arrested Aldrich Ames, one of our officers, on charges of espionage and treason. It hit us all with great force. A traitor in our midst, inside the Clandestine Service, had been all but unthinkable. Now it was a reality. The investigation of the reasons behind losses suffered in the middle 1980s had been under way for years and finally, the spy had been found. Ames, a career Clandestine Service officer, had volunteered his services to the KGB in the mid-1980s and had provided them with highly sensitive information for the ensuing period. Numerous agents had been compromised and several were executed. Tenacious counter-intelligence work, much of it in co-operation with the FBI, led to his downfall. Convicted in a federal court, he will spend the rest of his life in prison. For many, the death penalty, which he gave to several of our agents, would have been a just sentence.

Predictably, the Hill raised a cry for accountability and an investigation by the Inspector General was launched. Masses of data collected during the lengthy effort that had ultimately uncovered Ames was reviewed as a part of the investigation. It was difficult to pin down individuals who were to blame but many, especially on the Hill, wanted to see blood on the floor. By late summer, a report was provided to Director Woolsey. Striving to be firm but fair, Woolsey reprimanded a number of Agency officers, almost all of whom were members of the DO. Many people, both inside and outside the Agency, felt it was not severe enough. Under intense pressure as a result of his 'failure' to handle the Ames affair, Woolsey resigned in December 1994. Ames had been his undoing and the Agency was leaderless (and cowed) in the troubled aftermath of the turmoil the affair had caused. The Clandestine Service was chastened.

For five long and unnerving months the Deputy Director, Admiral Studeman, went through the motions of running the Agency while the President worked through a series of potential new Directors. Studeman did all he could, but events worked against him. Attacks on the Agency multiplied and the climate grew increasingly hostile. Finally, Clinton 'persuaded' John Deutch to leave his post at the Defense Department and replace Woolsey. Deutch was clearly a reluctant dragon and many felt he accepted a post he didn't really want because he saw it as a stepping-stone to bigger and better things.

Deutch took over as the Agency's new Director in May 1995. He would be my thirteenth and, as it turned out, last Director. As had become standard over the years, he brought senior staff officers with him. One of their top priorities, Deutch and his staff made clear, would be to 'rein in' the Clandestine Service. They would dismantle the 'old boy network' and change the culture of élitism that prevailed within the DO. An ocean away, I shuddered at the thought of what was to come.

SEVENTEEN

HAZARDS AND PROSPECTS

1995–2002

What any CIA Chief in the field dreads, almost more than anything else, is an operational compromise. It ranks right up there with the worst things that can happen in an intelligence career. Simply defined, an operational compromise is the discovery, by the internal service in the country in which you are working, of an 'incompatible' operational activity. As already explained, an incompatible operation is conducted unilaterally, at the behest of the government for which you work. Obviously, the host government, if and when it becomes aware of such an operation, objects. And just as obviously, conducting incompatible operations entails risk. It could be defined as an occupational hazard for intelligence officers.

In the latter part of my career, I was to learn the consequences of an operational compromise. All compromises, of course, are serious and, depending upon the circumstances, have their own twist.

This particular case began when the Ministry of Interior told our Ambassador that activities of several diplomats were 'unacceptable' and must stop. It was a carefully choreographed meeting. The Minister produced photographs to support his contention (none were given to the Ambassador) and a list of five officers who had been involved in the – to him – objectionable activities. None of the officers would be declared *persona non grata* (i.e. that a government is formally expelling a foreigner), he said, but his government would like to see them leave the country – soon. It wasn't a long meeting. The Ambassador, taken by surprise, was in an awkward position. Having never dealt with such a situation (few Ambassadors have), he wasn't sure what would follow but sensed stormy weather ahead and some rain on his parade.

When the Ambassador reported this conversation, we knew immediately that the Minister had announced an operational compromise. Our security perimeter had been breached. Details would emerge over time. I was the Chief at the time and this was to be my only involvement in such a compromise in my entire career.

Thanks to a decision taken in the Minister's office to release internal service dossiers to the press, the twist in this instance was fulsome and critical media coverage of the incident for several weeks. We took a distinctly dim view of that decision, as did the frustrated and angry internal service concerned. The source of their irritation was twofold. Firstly, the dossiers contained complete operational details of what had happened (which they certainly did not want published overtly), and secondly, the publicity amounted to a violation of the unwritten inter-service code that dictates discreet handling of such matters. Regrettably, the decision had been taken out of their hands. Why? The Minister's political party was in the latter stages of an intense political campaign with the country's presidency as the prize. The Minister had just been accused of exploiting some illegal wiretap operations to his party's benefit and was under heavy criticism in the local media. We believed, as did many others (including his political opponents), that he announced, and then facilitated media coverage of, the weak link in our security chain as a diversionary tactic designed to take the heat off himself. The Minister made no comment that I can recall. It was an unfortunate sequence of events for us, but it worked for him. (After the presidential election, the story died.)

Apart from the informed media coverage caused by the Minister's release of dossiers, the operational compromise itself was not unlike others the service had suffered. It was not the first, nor would it be the last. As dictated by standard procedures, we launched an immediate investigation into the cases and circumstances involved – as we knew them at the time. Our starting point was based on the information, including the names of our officers, that the Ambassador had been given. We were able to put together a solid picture of what had been compromised – 'blown' in our jargon. Working in concert with our Headquarters desk, we initiated a thorough review of each piece of information we had. It was important that we discover how and when the compromise had occurred.

I gave the Ambassador a detailed briefing of what, as best we knew at that early stage, had happened. He understood the issues and nuances of what was involved and was supportive. 'We will simply have to weather the storm,' he said. I appreciated his support then and I would appreciate it even more as the ensuing months passed. (Later, the Ambassador wrote a letter to our Director and in it voiced strong support for my handling of 'a difficult and sensitive situation'. He advised him not to seek out a scapegoat for this, by now, highly publicized contretemps. This advice was not heeded.

To our collective dismay, there was extensive media coverage, both locally and in the international press. In the flood of articles, there was distortion, conjecture, inaccuracies and outright falsehoods. The press had a field day. Also included, however, thanks to the release of dossiers, were many specific operational details. Added to what we had already pieced together, those details enabled us to confirm our understanding of what had happened. The initial compromise, we now knew, had occurred at least two years earlier, shortly after my arrival on the scene. In that earlier period, one of our agents had been 'doubled' by the internal service. (Doubled means that an intelligence/security service discovers that an individual is working for another service and then recruits that individual to work for them without informing the first service. Thus the agent is working for two services. One of those services, in this case us, is unaware of the other and comes out on the short end in that its activities with and tasking of that agent are all known to the other service.) That was when our security perimeter had been breached. We didn't then, and still don't, know how the internal service knew that he was our agent. Once they knew, however, it was not difficult for them to pressure this citizen of their country to co-operate fully – without letting us know. A thorough review of the tradecraft employed by the officer handling the agent at that time would be imperative, we concluded, but in the turmoil that ensued it never happened.

Why the internal service, and the Minister of Interior, had elected to just hold their knowledge of the agent and not promptly confront us was, and is, a mystery. I can only speculate about their motives. Once they had control of the agent, and after having exploited their operational advantage, they instructed him to cease operational contact with us, which he did. The operational effort involved was a low level one and perhaps the internal service didn't think it worth the dust that a confrontation would raise. It is also possible that they were holding the card for play at a time of their choice – when reacting to the fallout of an operational compromise they might suffer in our country, for example. Or they could have been trying to use their knowledge to expand the breach in our security perimeter. If it was the latter, they were only minimally successful in that over a two-year period only a couple of other cases were lost. Clearly, once the breach is made, the internal service holds all the cards as it is in a position to monitor all aspects of an operation that is thought to be clandestine. Although the final report on this incident made no reference to it, my officers should have been commended for the effective tradecraft and counter-intelligence measures they practised during that lengthy period. They kept our losses to a minimum.

At a second meeting with the Ambassador, the Minister added two further names to the list of officers who should promptly depart the country. Of the original five named, three were not in the country having long ago left for reassignment. (Until the complete picture had emerged, we had been puzzled about the fact that three of those named were already departed.) I was distressed to learn that my name had been added to the list as well as that of another officer. As the Chief it was at least logical (though unprecedented) that my name would be added, but we never understood why the other officer was named.

Our careful scrutiny of the operations involved was under way and, from a counter-intelligence perspective, we were taking a careful look at the full range of our activities. In the overseas environment hazard is ever present. Poor tradecraft employed by the handling officer or a brief careless moment may well have been the cause of our problem. Despite our best efforts, those kinds of weaknesses can produce the kind of compromise we suffered.

We reported the results of our review and our conclusions about what had caused the compromise. The next step was for our Headquarters desk to complete the review and draw the final conclusions. It was at the Headquarters end, in this instance, that the whole process ran completely off course. I write about it here partly for the record and partly in the, perhaps naive, hope that it will not happen again.

Not long after the Ambassador's first meeting with the Minister, but before the dossiers were released and the media barrage had erupted, a senior Headquarters officer briefed both oversight committees of Congress. In response to our tasking, he told them, we had been running an operation that, for reasons still unknown, had been compromised to the internal service. We were piecing together the history of the operations involved, our briefer went on, and we would brief them again when we had the full story. Neither committee reacted adversely and the thrust of their comments, paraphrased, was 'go get 'em' and 'keep on doing your job'. Following the onslaught of the media coverage, however, the climate changed, negatively. At a subsequent briefing, there was posturing, press statements from the committees were released and 'concerns' were raised. What was just fine when unpublicized, had somehow changed in the light of public exposure. We needed accountability, they now thought; we needed a thorough review (one was already under way they were told, to no avail) and, now in full cry, we needed an investigation by the Agency's Inspector General.

The Inspector General (IG) at the time, who had previously had a short stint as an operations officer, promptly announced that he would initiate an investigation and, within days, he named a team to carry out the investigation. It was an unprecedented effort on his part. (An operational compromise is, by definition, an operational matter – it is not fraud, malfeasance or corruption, which are standard matters for IG concern. Routinely an operational compromise and its ramifications have always been handled by the Directorate of Operations.) We were alarmed to see that only one member of the team named by the IG had any operational experience at all and his was minimal. The others, including (perhaps especially) the team leader, had neither overseas experience nor operational experience. In essence, the deck was stacked and, although I didn't realize it at the time, the result was to be a flawed and politicized investigation.

The IG investigation (the normal detailed operational review carried out by the field and the Headquarters desk having been overshadowed by media play and political reaction thereto) was undertaken in a climate that can only be described as hostile. It was a period in which we faced criticisms from many fronts. There were many reasons for the hostility. Certain parties harboured doubts about the degree of actual change that had been accomplished by the Clandestine Service since the end of the Cold War. We had been asked, among other things, to reduce our size, close some of our stations, decrease our spending, increase support for the military and refocus our priorities. Why couldn't more be done? those people demanded. There was also fall-out from the Ames affair that left the Agency leaderless at a difficult time. A fracas over a 'human rights' issue, stemming from an operational activity in Central America, generated a cause célèbre. There were detractors of the Directorate of Operations, including some from within the Agency where latent jealousies had long existed, who were simply happy to see the Clandestine Service facing problems. All joined in a chorus of cries for accountability and 'punishment'. What followed was a thirteen-month débâcle after which the IG team ultimately published its report.

In addition to the IG team, another, billed as an 'accountability team', was named to investigate the compromise. I was appalled. I argued with the then Deputy Director for Operations who had named the team making it clear to him that as the Chief, I was accountable – for the good and for the bad. We all knew that and we didn't need another bloody investigating team to tell us what we already knew. He feared allegations of a cover-up, he told me, and my argument fell on deaf ears. In the end, that three-person team, which included an operations officer with overseas experience, produced (in a few months) a solid well-reasoned report. Working independently, it focused on issues relevant to the compromise itself and made objective conclusions. Some of the latter were debatable, but the end product would certainly have been of value to senior management and the Director. Regrettably, however, internal pressures from the IG, who insisted that his report took precedence and must be the first one published, precluded formal publication of their report.

Then a third team was formed (this was turning into a circus) to investigate the same operational compromise. The third team was composed of five to eight (the numbers changed) individuals from the Division's counter-intelligence (CI) office. Few had any operational experience and several, casting a negative spin on whatever they wrote, demonstrated precious little objectivity. The team leader and his deputy, who had ties to the handling officer directly involved in the compromise, seemed unaware of the risk of conflict of interest. Some on the CI team presented theories about issues completely unrelated to the compromise that had been suffered. They attempted to paint a picture that featured a member of the internal service behind every tree in the capital city. Wild speculation contributed to what became an exercise in futility. It was a sorry and unprofessional state of affairs.

All three teams visited the field and all had the same mission – to investigate the compromise and discover the reason for it. None found it. The accountability team did its job. They interviewed officers who had been involved and drew their preliminary conclusions. Then they left. The members of the other two teams strayed far afield and posed questions about totally unrelated issues and operations. They questioned every member of the office and asked about issues that had nothing to do with the matter at hand. They are just looking for dirt, several officers reported to me. A finance officer was asked what he thought about the counter-surveillance practices of a particular operations officer – a feckless and inappropriate question since he had no basis on which to respond. I explained (on two occasions) to the IG team leader what types of cover we employed. She simply didn't understand. What is this woman, who has no clue what goes on in an overseas operational situation, doing out here investigating us? I asked myself. The IG and CI teams had, summarily, broadened the scope of their inquiry to include virtually everything the office was doing. It was far beyond their mandate and it was being done in an unprofessional manner. The visit of the latter two teams was a severe blow to morale.

Not long after the visits of the IG and CI teams, I returned to Headquarters. With my name on the Minister's list, my effectiveness had been impaired. In addition, the distressing visits we had just experienced raised concerns in my mind about how the investigation was being handled. I had not yet sensed just how slanted and politicized it had become. Leaving the office, in its wounded condition, was difficult but there seemed to be little choice. The new Director had just been named and there was tension in the air. A political appointee lacking experience in intelligence matters and therefore credentials, he had already made clear, as I've said, that one of his priorities was to 'bring to heel' the old boy élitist ethic of the Clandestine Service. That didn't bode well. My concerns were heightened.

Soon after my return to Headquarters, having gotten the lay of the land, so to speak, I sought out a meeting with the Inspector General himself. I had few illusions about how the meeting would go, but I was determined to raise some serious concerns. It was not a pleasant meeting.

First I registered my shock and dismay at the composition of the team he had named for the investigation. They lack the competence to do the job, I argued, and cited specific examples. You wouldn't send coal miners to investigate a bank fraud case, I pointed out. Nor would the military ask submarine officers to investigate an airplane crash. I guess he got the point, but he rejected it. 'They are smart people [a point I didn't contest] and they can do the work,' he said. 'Questions completely unrelated to the compromise are being asked,' I then pointed out. 'We didn't find enough related to just the compromise,' he responded, 'so I decided to do a complete investigation of the office.'

'Then you must send a team with the competence to do so,' I retorted. He ignored this too.

Raising another issue, I reported to him that the IG team and the Division CI team were colluding on their respective investigations. They were meeting together and sharing the results of their queries. Polluted and biased conclusions would be the result, which was both inappropriate and unfair. He agreed and said he would look into it. I don't know that he did, but in my view the damage had been done.

Finally, I asked when the report would be published. It had

already been six months since the compromise. Soon, he responded. But it was not soon. After announcing a publication date seven times, the IG finally issued his report thirteen months after his investigation began.

During the, many, months after my meeting with the IG, the two unfinished teams continued their effort in fits and starts. Drafts were written and rewritten. Numerous people at Headquarters level were interviewed. Also during that period a new Deputy Director for Operations was named. A new arrival into the Operations Directorate, he had spent the vast majority of his career as an intelligence analyst. He had almost no operational experience and had never served overseas. In my opinion, he lacked the requisite talents and his appointment was certainly a mistake. Coupled with John Deutch's stated intentions, it was an ominous development. A 'dark age' for the Clandestine Service began with that appointment.

Finally, I read the IG report. It was so replete with distortions and inaccuracies that I could hardly believe it was about the office I had headed. I felt that it clearly reflected the lack of competence of the team members about which I had complained. With only passing reference to the actual origin of the compromise (its age and the handling officer), the report focused instead on alleged tradecraft weaknesses of selected officers – not including the handling officer. Moreover, it alleged that far-reaching mismanagement and 'a lack of concern' for counter-intelligence matters had been the crux of the problem. Keeping to the political line of the time, the long awaited and frequently rewritten report seemed more intent upon criticism (heaps of it) of how the Clandestine Service functions overseas than anything else – like getting it right! Bottom line – it was a stinging critique of my professionalism. It hurt deeply.

Most egregious and most shocking of all (in a report, mind you, literally filled with errors and distortions) was the allegation that the station lacked concern for counter-intelligence matters. It came out of the blue. Neither team had raised the subject with me during the interviews I had. And it was utterly untrue. As I've said, I was consistently concerned with our security perimeter. Dating from my arrival, I had initiated over a dozen specific steps aimed at shoring up our counter-intelligence posture. Everyone in the office knew about most of the steps we had taken and it must have come up during many of the interviews. None of those measures, however, were mentioned in the report. Indeed, a close reading of the report revealed that nothing positive had been included in the text. It was all negative.

The allegations (I'm tempted to say charges) against me were general ('he managed his office poorly'). Allegations against several other officers, however, were more specific. The level of distortion and inaccuracy was such that we elected to rebut. Other officers and components, equally frustrated by the report, said they wanted to join in our rebuttal. Our decision faced obstacles raised by the IG. Having taken thirteen months to prepare his report, which totalled over 380 pages, he ruled that we would have one week to review it and respond. He was anxious to have the report made public, he told me when I saw him to protest. He relented and gave us one additional week. In the two weeks afforded us, we, and others who disputed IG facts and conclusions, prepared a 340-page rebuttal volume. How could they get so much wrong? one might ask. We wondered the same thing. That a report of 380 pages could generate a 340-page rebuttal from the very people who were the source of much of the information in the report speaks volumes. The story goes on. When finally published, the IG report was distributed to selected senior managers and to both oversight committees. Copies of our rebuttal were not included – until after I had protested, again.

It won't surprise readers when I say that the period I have described was a difficult one. I was treated like a pariah in my own Directorate. I had no real job and more or less languished while Rome burned and the office of the Inspector General fiddled. The new Deputy Director for Operations was 'too busy' to see me and in any case, he sent word, there was nothing he could do. For a senior officer in his Directorate who was Chief of a major overseas office under his command, there was nothing he could do? Not even listen? Didn't he want to hear what I thought about what had happened in the office I had managed and about the travesty that was under way in the office of the Inspector General? Did he not care about morale and operations in the field, about relations with the Embassy, and about reactions within the local security services? My colleagues and I had every right to expect much more support than we ever got from our Directorate's senior management. I feel that the new DDO, a miscast individual, was cowed by the new Director, who had voiced his intention to 'lay one on' the Clandestine Service. Cowed also by the executive director and the IG, he displayed precious little backbone.

I can understand (and could at the time) that once the media was ignited politics would come into play and that would (and did) affect standard procedures. So be it. In that event, you just take your lumps. What I couldn't and still don't understand, or accept, was how shabbily my colleagues and I were treated by the Inspector General and by my Directorate's most senior officers. We had been sent to the field to do a tough job. Risk is, I repeat, inherent when we operate overseas. Yet when a Headquarters' approved operation was compromised (for reasons still unknown), we were left hanging in the wind. And worse, some even helped to hang us out there. The DDO, with no experience in this kind of problem, could at least plead ignorance. He just didn't know any better.

A fairer target for criticism was his deputy for counter intelligence, who did know better. He never met with me to discuss the compromise despite the fact that he was, theoretically at least, responsible for CI matters in the Directorate. After I read the IG report and its allegations of a lack of concern for CI issues, I insisted on a meeting with him and showed him the list of CI steps I had taken – a list that cut the ground out from beneath any such allegation. He read it and said, 'I didn't know that.' It was his *job* to know that, as it was to monitor closely any CI investigation in the Directorate. He and other senior officers had been shockingly obtuse, while colleagues were sacrificed in the IG investigation.

Also reprehensible was the leader of the Division CI team. With long-standing ties to someone key to the initial compromise, he should have let someone else handle the matter. Instead of seeing those ties as a conflict of interest, however, he led an investigation that veered sharply away from premises that involved that officer. His report downplayed that officer's role in the compromise and highlighted instead the erroneous contention that we all lacked sufficient CI awareness – an issue he never discussed with me. Knowingly acting as he did not only skewed the conclusions of his own report but also tainted those of the IG report.

At this point it should be clear that my experience with an operational compromise was not a happy one. There were two basic problems (apart from politics about which we can do nothing): IG methodology and leadership in the Operations Directorate. The handling of the compromise we suffered was a prime example of a process run amok. The IG report on the compromise was seriously flawed and painted an almost totally inaccurate picture of the office's counter-intelligence profile. As a result, the Directorate was ill served. In addition, DO leadership failed to live up to its responsibilities. It made no effort to understand what had happened or to make an independent judgement. Consequently, the Directorate's officers were ill served as well. Numerous reasons exist for these shortcomings and I have outlined only the main ones.

Since it is relevant, I include here a paragraph written by one of my colleagues as the episode was coming to an end. It sums up our collective feelings. It is sad that we felt obliged to remind those in charge at the time of a basic tenet of the Clandestine Service:

> With the clarity of retrospection, we would like to offer our thoughts on the lessons learned from the operational compromise now being investigated. Central to our reflection on the topic is the premise that *preventing all future compromises is impossible* [the italics are mine]. No amount of process, oversight, or structural reconfiguration will result in risk free operations, especially those directed at a sophisticated host country target. By their very nature, clandestine operations are a continual process of compromise between risk and gain. The officer and the station conducting those operations are called upon daily to take calculated risks based on imperfect knowledge. At best, these are judgements, and while guidance from Headquarters or more senior officers is necessary and welcome, it is not possible to establish 'rules' to cover every contingency. And while no stint of effort to mitigate those risks can be tolerated, it must be expected that, occasionally the officer/station will misjudge. However, for any operation to have a chance of

success, the case officer and the station must be encouraged to make those risk versus gain judgements – with the possibility of getting it wrong – and know that absent malfeasance or incompetence, the Directorate of Operations and the Agency will support their efforts when a compromise occurs.

Not long after the IG report was published (I was retired by now), I received a letter from the Director. In it he quoted from the report and then reprimanded me for 'poor management standards'. In response, I wrote a letter to him making clear that I did not accept the IG conclusions and believed the report to be hopelessly flawed. I could not, therefore, accept his reprimand. I returned his letter. Bravado perhaps, but I felt strongly about what I had experienced. It was unacceptable. My action, an unusual one I knew, apparently ruffled no feathers because three months later, in September 1996, I was called to Headquarters and awarded the Distinguished Intelligence Medal (DIM), the Agency's highest award.

The ceremony was emotionally draining. (I was particularly gratified to see in the audience Dr Tim Miller, who, in defiance of the odds, had saved my life after my Congo experience and allowed me to continue and ultimately complete my career.) To a packed audience, the Director spoke in laudatory terms about my career and my contributions over the years. He made only scant non-critical reference to the compromise that had caused me so much grief. Expressing my gratitude for the honour bestowed on me, I made some remarks but I fear they were affected by the emotions I was feeling. I was only able to convey portions of what I felt. Still the response was warm and strongly supportive. I was deeply moved. The whole tawdry affair was over. Was the fact that I had been awarded the DIM a vindication? In a way, I guess it was, but it doesn't matter much now, does it?

There were other hazards faced by Clandestine Service case officers during my career. Congress was certainly one of them. Decisions taken for political reasons or taken in response to a media furore are frequently bad decisions. If I thought about it for a while, or if I thought anybody cared, I could produce a long list of such decisions, but I won't. Without delving too deeply into history, a few examples should suffice.

When the Cold War ended, some in Congress actually called for the dismantling of the Agency. It's difficult for me to understand the logic they employed. Did they really think that the United States, the world's leader and sole superpower (whether we like it or not), should face the post-Cold War period blind and deaf? Ignorance can be excused and for some ignorance is bliss, but to take decisions based on ignorance is dangerous. Clearly we needed more intelligence not less. Fortunately, saner heads and reason prevailed. Such was not the case, however, when domestic political considerations prompted calls for the infamous 'peace dividend' in the early 1990s. Heedless of warnings they received and lacking an understanding of the dangers still extant in the world, Congress abruptly wielded its budget-cut axe. Recall the totally unexpected and capricious 50 per cent budget cut suffered by the Clandestine Service in late 1992. At the same time, we were implementing a plan mandated by Congress that severely cut the size of the Agency – Clandestine Service (the nation's most effective foreign intelligence collection capability) included. Those cuts persisted throughout the decade of the 1990s. So, at a time when our strength should have been stable or even greater, the Service experienced deep cuts.

In the mid-1990s, there was a dust-up over operational decisions taken in a Central American station. There was considerable ill-informed press coverage. Then, a hue and cry, posturing and some leaks from (where else?) Congress prompted an edict (by the Director) placing constraints on who the Clandestine Service could recruit – only nice guys was the bottom line. Recruiting boy scouts and choirboys would be fine, we were told, but not somebody with a poor human rights background. (The edict was certainly an inhibiting factor in the Directorate's efforts to recruit individuals with access to information we were tasked to collect.) And, inexplicably unforeseen was the obvious fact that boy scouts and choirboys don't have access to the plans and intentions of terrorists or drug dealers. Like it or not, in quest of the intelligence we are tasked to collect, we must sometimes deal with 'unsavoury' characters whose human rights records ain't all that great. The edict was a hazard too but following the devastating attack we suffered in September 2001, the edict has been rescinded.

The daily hazards involved in carrying out operational activities all over the world are infrequently mentioned but ever present – they will continue. The specific dangers are as difficult to predict as they are to guard against but I have no doubt that everything possible is being done to mitigate the risks our officers must face. But they cannot be denied. Witness the seventy-seven stars etched into the marble wall of honour in our Headquarters. They are stars for people who died in service to their country. At least a dozen of those stars are for men I knew and worked with. Two, Mike Deuel and Bill Buckley, were close friends. We all knew the perils were there, but we looked beyond them towards the tasks at hand. The only way to remain completely safe would have been to stay at home. None of us ever considered that option.

Officers who betray us, Aldrich Ames is an example, represent another hazard. Fortunately their number has been mercifully small and no effort should be spared to keep it that way. They are a problem that comes from within the ranks and that makes them all the more difficult to ferret out. It may well be that the best place to stop those individuals is at the front door and it is up to our screening and security process to do just that. There are no guarantees, but the vast pool of dedicated and talented young Americans we have to choose from gives us highly favourable odds.

The Clandestine Service experienced difficult periods during every decade of my career. The period since the end of the Cold War, however, may have been the hardest one to endure. The severe resource constraints (to which I have already alluded) that persisted throughout the decade of the 1990s and ultimately cut the Service's strength by, according to numerous press reports, 25 per cent, were a contributing factor. Not only was there a paucity of new blood in the Service, the image of a sinking ship caused experienced mid-level officers (some of our best) to leave. Risk aversion reared its ugly head and morale slumped. The Agency had five directors in the first seven years of the 1990s – which doesn't do much for stability or continuity. The Service languished under woefully inadequate leadership of both the Agency and the Service itself during the period from 1995 to 1997. That leadership exacerbated our problems by, among other things, placing unreasonable restraints on our ability to recruit agents. The administration failed to define a global role for the world's only superpower and pursued a foreign policy lacking either focus or purpose. During the Clinton years, contact and dialogue with a White House that was frequently enmeshed in domestic problems and scandals was infrequent. The President did not read our reporting and seemed uninterested. Consequently, support for the Service from within his administration (or in Congress) was limited. The resource crunch persisted.

The administration that came to power in November 2000, even before the disaster of September 2001, voiced its strong support for efforts to rebuild the Service's capabilities and took prompt steps to begin the process. President Bush has demonstrated a keen interest in foreign intelligence and maintains close contact with the Agency. Thus times have changed dramatically and despite the problems and the hazards I have listed, prospects are, in my view, bright for the future of the Clandestine Service. It will have a key role in the global war on terrorism in which it will function as the nation's first line of defence.

One could argue that the wounds were cauterised and efforts to stabilize and then rebuild the Agency began in July 1997 with the appointment of George Tenet as the new Director. (Few lamented the departure of John Deutch – Tenet had been Deutch's Deputy for two years.) Although a political appointee, Tenet's previous jobs in Washington had given him great knowledge about and familiarity with the intelligence community and the Agency. (I remember meeting him before testifying at the SSCI when he was the chief of staff for that committee.) He assumed command with a full working knowledge of the Agency's programmes and activities. And, as opposed to his predecessor, Tenet made it clear then, and has over the ensuing years, that he is proud and honoured to be the Director. He cares, I believe, about the Agency and its people. One of Tenet's first moves was to name Jack Downing, a talented and highly respected Clandestine Service officer, as the new DDO. Downing's return (he had retired two years previously) signalled the end of the 'dark age' that was so painful for the Service. He promptly initiated a no-nonsense 'back to basics' approach aimed at rebuilding capabilities that had atrophied. He argued strongly for increased resources. He placed a high priority on overseas activity, the Service's core business. And he took immediate steps to increase the cadre of operations officers. Downing was a godsend to a Service in dire need of trustworthy, experienced and professional leadership.

The Agency's, and in particular the Operations Directorate's, efforts in Afghanistan after the terrorist attack we suffered in September 2001 have been duly recorded in the open press – in greater detail than the Agency would have wanted, I suspect since various sources and methods were jeopardized in the process. The picture that emerges is one of a Service that responded splendidly to a national demand for action. Within, literally, days, a plan for the nation's response was on the President's desk. The plan was approved and almost immediately thereafter, dedicated professional officers were 'on the ground' in Afghanistan. Those officers conducted a series of bold operations and skilfully set the stage for subsequent actions. Joined within weeks by our military forces, they quickly attained one success after another. 'Humint' – what Washington calls human intelligence collection, the Clandestine Service's most important priority – played a major role. Selective application of experience gleaned during the 1980s when the Agency managed the United States' programme to support Afghan resistance to Soviet occupation was also important. It is true that we were surprised by the severity and the audacity of the attack we suffered; it is also true, however, that the Service was at the pointed end of the spear our country launched in response to al Qaeda's perfidy. The war is not over but the battle has been joined. Whatever Osama bin Laden and his followers expected, they know now that Americans will not be cowed by terrorism. They signalled their own demise.

Exactly why we were surprised by the attack is, of course, an important question. Inevitably, recriminations have begun. 'We need answers' is the cry echoing throughout Washington as bits and pieces of information surface and a joint investigation by the oversight committees of the House and Senate begins to examine why there was an 'intelligence failure'. 'We just want facts,' the committees have announced, 'we're not looking for scapegoats.' (Now where have I heard that before?) Hindsight analysis, second guessing and widespread use of the conditional tense (would have, could have, should have) is the order of the day in Washington's political circles. I welcome the scrutiny that the intelligence community will fall under and I'm hopeful that the committees' efforts will surface areas that can be improved. Those hoping or expecting, however, that any effort carried out by humans can be reorganized, restructured, or 'tinkered with' to the point of perfection will, again, be disappointed. If the investigation finds incompetence then, by all means, jump on it. If it finds, as seems likely, that greater intelligence sharing between the CIA and the FBI is needed, then that too should be mandated. Whatever the committees' efforts reveal that could usefully be changed (or created) should be done.

Playing the blame game, however, or seeking out a scapegoat (or goats) will be of little value to the country. For critics to suggest that analysts at either the Agency or the FBI could have pieced together the disparate bits of information that were available before the attack and subsequently thwarted the 11 September atrocity is simply unrealistic. The skilled and dedicated officers involved could only do their best and I'm confident they did. We are not dealing with a perfect world. Rather we are dealing with a world in which our terrorist enemies have absolutely every advantage. They can attack us anytime, anywhere and via any means they choose. And, as senior officials have underscored repeatedly in recent months, we will be hit again. To suppose otherwise is folly. We strive on the one hand to protect the freedoms we value so highly by unleashing the full capabilities of the intelligence, law enforcement, judicial and other arms of our government. On the other hand, we must accept that some of the newly proposed actions will be more intrusive than was the case prior to 11 September. Some find increased intrusiveness by the government difficult to accept. I see the new proposals as reasonable steps aimed at enhancing the capabilities of those tasked to protect the country. We must accept that striking a balance will be difficult but I am confident that middle ground will be found.

The threat of terrorism against our country's citizens and interests, or those of our allies, will be a major concern for many years to come. It is a new threat in the American homeland and I am pleased to see the initiative aimed at creating a Department of

Homeland Defense. We must take immediate steps (and in many areas we already have) to tighten our border controls, protect our nuclear plants and water supply, enhance inspection regimes for incoming cargo containers, assure greater safety in air travel and in general 'harden' the security of potential targets for terrorist attack. All should understand, however, that as we make targets harder to attack, the terrorists will veer away and select softer targets – a busy shopping mall, for example. Seen in light of the terrorist threat we face, attacks by terrorist organizations (some with global capabilities) that will not hesitate to employ weapons of mass destruction and to target civilian noncombatants, prospects for the nation's future are troubling. Once created (which will be no mean feat given the complexity of the issues involved) and functioning, the responsibilities of the Department of Homeland Defense will be great indeed. The new department may not solve all of our problems, but, as Dwight Eisenhower once said, a good organization won't guarantee success but a bad organization will guarantee failure. It is a step we must take.

The situation underscores the need for a strong and effective Clandestine Service. Its clear goal must be to penetrate the terrorist organizations (like al Qaeda, Hamas, Islamic Jihad and Hezbollah) that threaten us. Accurate intelligence about their personnel, plans and intentions will enable us to destroy – or at a minimum neutralize – those organizations. The administration has recently announced its intention to, in specific cases, pre-empt attacks against this country – to create and employ a first-strike capability. An applicable, in my view, sports adage avers that the best defence is a good offence. It's a decision that makes good sense. When we know, as we often do, that an organization is planning attacks against us, beating them to the punch should be an option that we not only consider but selectively employ. It places, however, an even greater premium on solid intelligence collection and analysis. To play its critical role effectively, the CIA's Directorate of Operations, the nation's Clandestine Service, must be ready. Changes mandated by the current congressional investigation, or by the President, must promptly be implemented. Efforts to increase the strength of the operations officer cadre must be accelerated. Requisite language skills for those officers, acquired either by high-level training programmes or as a native skill, remains a high priority. Politics and process have no place in the risk-laden arena of international terrorism and espionage. Rather, highly motivated and dedicated people who are well led will guarantee future successes. The Clandestine Service for which I laboured for three and a half decades, an élite (yes, I said, élite) organization staffed by talented men and women who were willing and able to meet any challenge they were given, would have met the test. I have every confidence that today's Service will do the same.

ACKNOWLEDGEMENTS

Writing this book was a lot more difficult than I had anticipated. Part of the effort required was to dredge up from my dimming memory the details I needed to write about specific events, people and places. To refresh and confirm my recollections, I called upon colleagues with whom I had served at various times in my career. A lunch, a phone call, or perhaps an e-mail all served to put a given subject into better perspective. They were all generous with their time and willingly responded to my questions aimed at making my manuscript as accurate as possible. As there were many, I won't attempt to list each name here, but you know who you are. Please know also that I very much appreciate the help you gave me.

Without naming them, I make special note of the three individuals who suffered with me the trials and tribulations of 'the Great Inspector General Investigation Débâcle'. I will not forget the wisdom, patience and support they gave during a period that was most trying.

I must also acknowledge the enormous help provided to me by my editors, Rachel Leyshon and Linda Osband. Rachel merits special thanks as she dealt with my manuscript in its earliest form. With a sensitive and judicious application of her excellent editorial and language skills, Rachel gently but persistently guided me through one chapter after another. Rachel and Linda are British and, thanks to their efforts, we also managed to clear the obstacle that is our 'common' language. For all of their help, I am most grateful.

Last, but certainly not least, I express my gratitude to Richard 'Dick' Helms. An icon in the US intelligence world, he was a respected leader throughout the period that encompassed my career. Our paths crossed many times, most notably perhaps at the beginning and at the end. In the mid-1960s, it was Dick Helms, then the Agency's Deputy Director for Plans (now Operations), who arranged to send a plane to rescue me from the Congo and he subsequently took time to visit me at Walter Reed Hospital. Three decades later, we had lunch at his club and he urged me to record my experiences, noting that, 'If we don't write about the Cold War period, it will be written about by journalists and academics and they will get it wrong.' His encouragement led me to a decision I had never anticipated making – to write this book. My thanks to Dick Helms for all he has been and done, for me and for our country's Clandestine Service.

INDEX